LATIN AMERICAN HISTORICAL DICTIONARIES SERIES
Edited by A. Curtis Wilgus

1. *Guatemala*, by Richard E. Moore, rev. ed. 1973.

2. *Panama*, by Basil C. & Anne K. Hedrick. 1970.

3. *Venezuela*, by Donna Keyse & G. A. Rudolph. 1971.

4. *Bolivia*, by Dwight B. Heath. 1972.

5. *El Salvador*, by Philip F. Flemion. 1972.

6. *Nicaragua*, by Harvey K. Meyer. 1972.

7. *Chile*, by Salvatore Bizzaro. 1972.

8. *Paraguay*, by Charles J. Kolinski. 1973.

9. *Puerto Rico and the U.S. Virgin Islands*, by Kenneth R. Farr. 1973.

10. *Ecuador*, by Albert W. Bork and Georg Maier. 1973.

11. *Uruguay*, by Jean L. Willis. 1974.

12. *British Caribbean*, by William Lux. 1975.

13. *Honduras*, by Harvey K. Meyer. 1976.

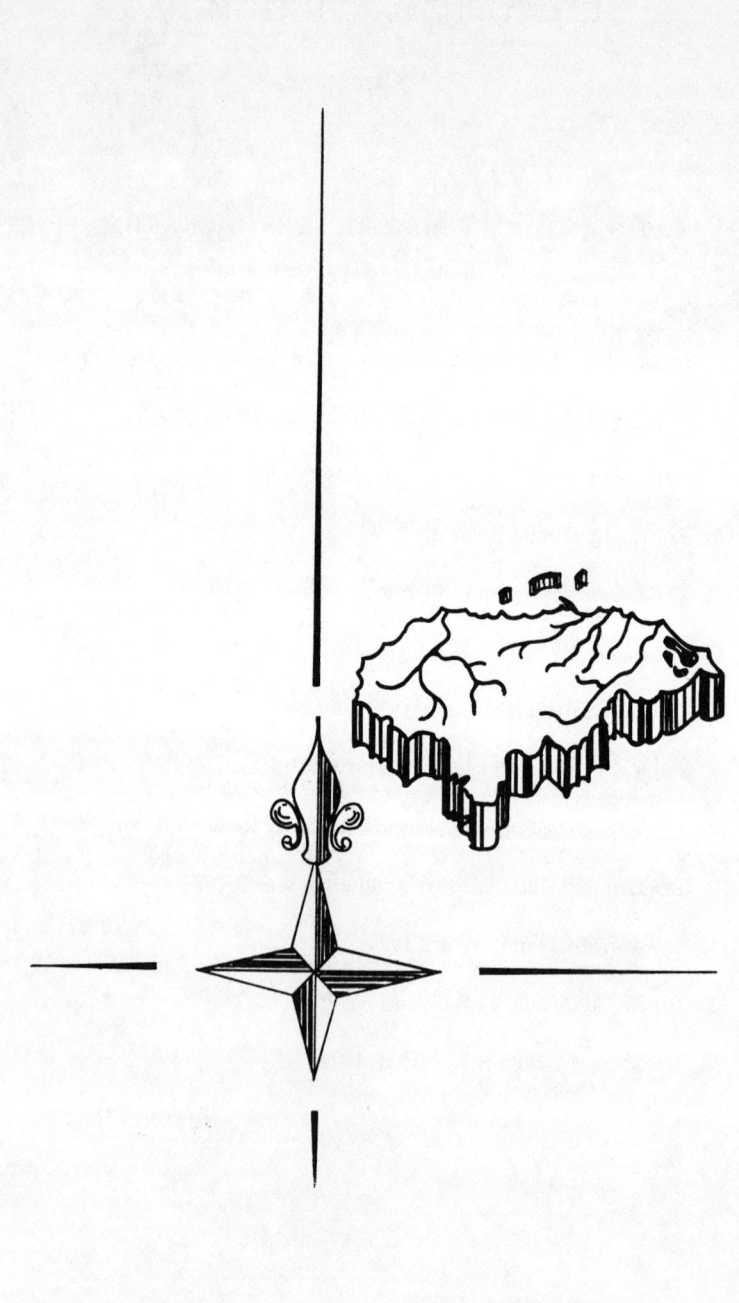

# Historical Dictionary of HONDURAS

by

HARVEY K. MEYER

*Latin American Historical Dictionaries, No. 13*

The Scarecrow Press, Inc.
Metuchen, N.J.     1976

All illustrations and maps are by the author. They are chosen to be particularly representative of Honduras: forts, Maya glyphs, dugout canoes, stirrups--these are the unique and different objects in their local form which express the individuality of the country, which differs markedly from its Central American sister republics.

Library of Congress Cataloging in Publication Data

Meyer, Harvey Kessler, 1914-
   Historical dictionary of Honduras.

   (Latin American historical dictionaries ; no. 13)
   Bibliography: p.
   1. Honduras--Dictionaries and encyclopedias.
I. Title.
F1502.M56        972.83'003        76-4539
ISBN 0-8108-0921-4

Copyright © 1976 by Harvey K. Meyer

Printed in the United States of America

EDITOR'S FOREWORD

Dr. Harvey Meyer, the author of this volume, is the only person who has compiled a second Dictionary in this Series. His previous book, No. 6 in the series, is the Historical Dictionary of Nicaragua. It seemed only natural to him, and to me also, that he should write about the neighboring state of Honduras. After all, the winds of history have often swept across these two countries, frequently bringing the same or similar problems to their governments and peoples. As the author has clearly shown in this volume, it is sometimes difficult to separate the five Central American countries (excluding Panama) in a clear-cut fashion economically, socially and intellectually, while politically, events overlap each other as much or more than in any other closely related nations anywhere. The history of one is in part the history of the others. Besides, their varied relations during nearly four centuries with Spain, Britain and the United States have given them common national objectives and international experiences.

As in the case of previous authors of these Dictionaries, Dr. Meyer was given the assignment of arbitrarily selecting the subject matter to be included--some of which was hard to find and even unreliable--keeping in mind that the resulting compilation should be reasonably comprehensive and balanced, but that the end product would be a dictionary and not an encyclopedia.

Since preparing his previous volume, Dr. Meyer has continued his many Central American interests, and he has added to his numerous personal accomplishments. Having retired as Professor from Florida Atlantic University at Boca Raton, he is now enjoying the opportunity to read and write in the fields of his vocation and avocations. And with his wife he travels in regions of Pre-Columbian culture in Middle America, an area which has interested him for some fifty years. In Central America he has traveled by most means of transportation: outboard motorboat, tugboat, pipante, dori and cayuca, and of course by train, automobile, mule, horse, helicopter, airplane and on his own feet. In all, he has visited Honduras, a country which he loves, ten times in the past twenty years, accumulating vivid impressions and useful experiences, many of which are recorded in this volume.

Besides his concern with military affairs because of his service in naval aviation, and his long-time interest in cartography and architecture, Dr. Meyer's chief interest over the years has been, of course, in education. He has served in all the professional ranks in colleges and universities, he has been a member of the faculty of three universities, holding professorships, deanships and directorships. He has supervised graduate research and has been a member of graduate committees. He has even served as a college trustee.

Writing style is a developed character attribute, and Dr. Meyer has found ways of expression, both philosophical and picturesque, which are uniquely his own. Since his interests are curriculum-wide, and his thinking is realistic and imaginative, he has prepared a work which should have wide appeal as a reference tool. Perhaps his emphasis may not suit everyone, but he offers a Dictionary, illustrated with his own drawings and maps, covering a wide spectrum of information about this interesting Central American country.

A. Curtis Wilgus,
Emeritus Director,
School of Inter American Studies,
University of Florida

MAPS AND ILLUSTRATIONS

MAPS
1. Honduras v
2. Islas de la Bahía 29
3. Lagunas--Yojoa and Caratasca 52
4. Copán (diagram) 97
5. Bay of Fonseca 139
6. Guanaja 159
7. Honduras--Political Divisions 174
8. Interoceanic Railroad 176

ILLUSTRATIONS
1. Bananas 23
2. Hieroglyphs of the Maya 45
3. Cayuca and Paddle 48
4. Dori 49
5. Comayagua--The Cathedral 61
6. Ceiba Tree 66
7. Stela and Altar--Copan 99
8. Estribo-Antiguo (also Cubeta) 108
9. Flint (eccentric--Copán) 137
10. Omoa Fortress 142
11. Omoa Fort (plan) 142
12. Cannon and Mercury Flasks 143
13. Mapache 220
14. Maya Numerical System 224
15. Pipante 276
16. Typical Country Homes 294
17. Corn God 308
18. Fort-Cuartel (in Ruinas de Copán) 309
19. San Antonio de Oriente 313
20. Cuartel Tower (and Plaza), San Pedro Sula 315
21. Seal and Flag 321
22. Presidential Palace 344
23. Tegucigalpa--The Cathedral 345

v

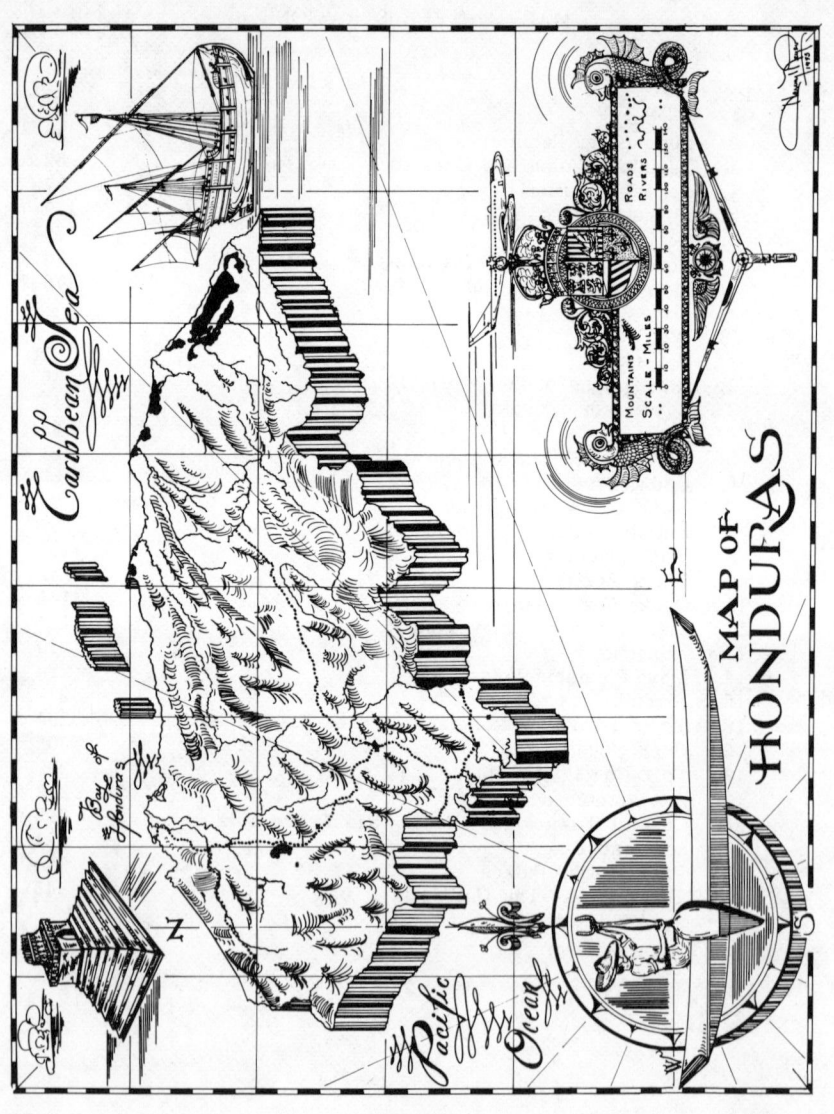

INTRODUCTION

One of the earliest reasons given us to focus an interest upon Honduras lay in the chance that brought Dr. Archie Carr of the University of Florida to our door in 1949. The Carrs were just returning from some years spent in Honduras. Archie, a world authority on sea turtles, wrote his first "turtle book" in our home. Later, his High Jungles and Low was not only an entrancing window into the other-world of Honduras, but also a unique entree to the rainforest side of Central America, in the Nicaraguan selva. The Carrs' antique Honduran furniture was cramped in our pseudo-early-American house which they had rented, for it was used to the spaciousness and the tile-roofed shade pools of a hacienda patio. But the interest sparked in Honduras added fuel to the Central American flame of fancy already burning bright.

We were hooked!

From then on, it seemed, both choice and chance propelled us to the great cordilleran spine stretching from Mexico to South America.

This Historical Dictionary of Honduras then, which originated in a life-long interest in Central America on the part of the compiler, was brought to fruition by a series of experiences in that part of the world over the past twenty years, including extensive travels with friends and family as well as a two-and-a-half-year period of residence.

We lived in Nicaragua, but were in and out of Honduras on numerous occasions. These ventures into the land of our present subject always turned out to be adventurous--something always happened!

For some examples: we were in Honduras during a "state of siege" in 1956, confined to our Tegucigalpa hotel. We were kept aboard our aircraft in May of 1957 while touching down at the airport in Tegucigalpa. That morning, flights of Nicaraguan P-51's had taken off for the "Dawn Patrol" on the Río Coco, when the "Territorio en Litigio" was in armed dispute. In a few days the little war was over. We had to fly around Honduras during the "soccer war" of 1969, for that conflict had caught us in what was then British Honduras, at Belize. And on December 3, 1972, we arrived in San Pedro Sula just in time for the December 4 "golpe de estado" next morning, which put Oswaldo López Arellano back in power for (as he announced) five years of military rule.

These events did not reach the front pages of the world in most cases, but they were of great import to the people of Honduras. Over the centuries, Honduras has had even more than a fair share of patriots, heroes, tyrants, villains, pirates and prelates, all of whom contribute to the weaving of an intricate and vastly colorful web of history.

There were some more personal adventures--simple, but memorable ones, ranging from the incredibly tasty roadside meal of an avocado fresh from a village market, cut in half and filled with tomato catsup and lime juice in the seed socket, to the deadly seriousness combined with abandoned exhilaration of armed countrymen moving in truckloads toward the capital to have a voice in a "golpe" of state.

There are the quietly awesome ruins of Copán, that sacred city of the Maya in its shady vale, punctuated by stelae and altars rich in baroque intricacies of sculpture, and crowned by majestic temple pyramids reached by stairways where each step is a cryptic message of myriad hieroglyphs.

There are the reminders of rulership as the ghosts of long-dead caciques look down upon the young officers of the Cuerpo Especial de Seguridad, going two-by-two like the Guardia Civil of Old Spain, but with jaunty western-style hats and with the poised air of a Gary Cooper ready for a fast draw.

There are the amusing memories, often combined with a spice of dangerous uncertainty, such as the time at one border crossing during a state of siege in one of the countries, when the "policía" were ready to hold us because an exhaustive search of our belongings turned up a road-map, undoubtedly there for some sinister political purpose!

There are the recurrent and startling contrasts, from stark cliffs to a riot of orchids, from simple dirt-floored thatched-roofed homes of the campesinos to tiled and iron-grilled marble palaces of the wealthy. There are the wry contrasts such as those of available facilities for travelers. In San Pedro Sula we had hotel accommodations of an excellent and modern character, with concert-quality piano music for happy hour each evening, and a first-rate cuisine in the quiet luxury of the dining room looking over a South Seas-styled pool-patio. But once near the Gulf of Fonseca, years ago, we stayed in "un buen hotel en el centro" which had pigs rooting in the patio under our unscreened window, no furniture whatever in the bare plastered room except tijeras ("scissors" cots like army issue), a pavement of human excrement in the public shower, and a sauce of buzzing flies on the breakfast beans and tortillas. The one bright note in this otherwise revolting picture consisted of one monogrammed and scrupulously clean linen sheet on each cot!

Introduction

If there is a certain "swashbuckling exuberance" to be detected in these otherwise staid and serried ranks of words thus alphabetically confined to covers, it must be laid to the nature of Central American history and the realities of life itself in the isthmian area.

Within one short week during a fact-finding expedition, one may encounter a coup d'etat, the lifting of mahogany logs by balloon, dugout canoes pushed by lawn-mower engines, a disastrous earthquake or hurricane, a rusty old tug-boat on a jungle river, pre-Christian era sculpture, a jungle-strangled cone-stacked steam locomotive, a hundred cannon scattered or piled like cordwood, a jicaro tree full of orchids, and cay-studded reefs around the turquoise bay in which float high jungle islands. These entirely literal descriptions become in themselves exotic. The various minor adventures need no embellishment whatever to lend an air of excitement to the most prosaic journey in search of facts.

When considering facts, however, one must recognize that they present a certain sterility when unaccompanied by a feel. And the inclusion of some emotional content produces a more accurate approach to truth than the dull recital of what is merely true.

Let us take an example:

FACT: In the 17th century the mining of silver became a significant enterprise in the area of Tegucigalpa, Honduras, and was a major economic factor during that portion of the colonial era, cherished by Honduras and recognized by Mother Spain.

FEEL: Drive a four-wheel-drive Japanese "jeep" in lowest gear over five kilometers of ladder-like rock-ledge road into high pine-clad hills. Look from the crest of a forbidding cliff across a gorge to the white colonial church and the barrel-tiled roofs of the little mining village of San Antonio de Oriente. Look to the left at the bare scarred cliffs where the old silver mines flourished more than three centuries ago. Pick out the black tunnel mouths like a hundred brooding eyes on the silver mountain. Stumble over the cobbles with the slender pigs and chubby children who now walk the steep streets of San Antonio. Talk to the storekeeper, stand by the door of the church looking far across the Zamorano Valley toward El Volcán. Ask about that Velásquez of San Antonio, who from being the village barber and popular mayor, went on to hemispheric renown as the primitive artist who carefully painted every roof-tile, one by one, in his many stylized portraits of his home village. Let the 17th century permeate your consciousness with these people as they now live, with the old mines, with the eyes of the artist for his beloved home town.

It is in this manner that stark economic facts can have an extended meaning and a human dimension. It is the difference between knowing about a country and knowing a country. No book, and certainly not such a proscribed effort as a historical dictionary, can convey the totality of needed knowledge about a subject, but it should be the effort and responsibility of even such a prosaic production as this one to light the spark of human interest somewhere buried in the dry tinder of statistics.

This volume was planned for travelers as well as scholars. It pulls together a great deal that is hard to find and widely scattered. It is also aimed at a mood of understanding, or as was said earlier, a feel to add form and perspective to mere facts.

There are historical byways to pursue, using the dictionary entry as a signpost. The history of the Swan Islands and United States involvement is a case in point. Even more sweeping are the seven attempts of Great Britain to capture and keep the Bay Islands. And there are historical highlights which in quick summary are:

1. Site of the first capital of Central America, Grácias.
2. First aerial bombardment of a city in Latin America (Carías, 1924).
3. Major Maya center, the southeasternmost (Copán).
4. Principal offshore islands on both coasts.
5. An anchor post of the Colonial Spanish Frontier (Omoa, Trujillo).
6. Nemesis of William Walker's "Manifest Destiny."
7. First discovery of the Central American mainland (Columbus, 1502).

There has been no effort in this dictionary to set up tight categories for the various classifications of materials. However, the wide variety of the entries does lend itself to a broad division. The choices of entries have been quite arbitrary and by no means exhaustive. Rather, there has been an effort to present representative material over an extended spectrum of people, places, and events. If completeness had been sought, twenty volumes of this size would be insufficient. The criteria of choice have been sixfold: significance, typicality, uniqueness, general interest, structure, eclecticism.

For example, it is significant that Honduras was once chosen as the site of an interoceanic rail line. In this case, geography affected both the original choice and the ultimate rejection. It is typical that from pre-conquest times the Indian inhabitants used a non-fermented drink made of corn and chocolate. It is unique that Honduras represented an area of cultural shear (in pre-Columbian times), between North and South America. It is of general interest that Honduras is a major source of the widely used fruit, bananas, and of a secondary general interest that as such, the country may be considered a "banana republic" with the politically unstable overtones which that term has come to suggest. It is structural to point out the nature of legal and constitutional bases of government, and to identify the designated political subdivisions. It is eclectic in that a wide variety of sources have been used and from them an even wider variety of choices have been made for inclusion in this work.

Four categories may be loosely defined as the end product of the application of the six criteria. They are:

1) <u>Geography</u>: The behavior of people and the development of their cultural characteristics are always affected by the geographical matrix in which they develop, whether it be jungle fastness or polar ice. Geography is, therefore, to some extent the mother of history, as history finds origin in a geographic womb and is nurtured by the environment. Therefore, a historical treatment, especially with the specificity of a dictionary, must concern itself with villages, towns, cities, farms, ranches, pastures, mines; streams, mountains, lakes, coasts and capes; railroads, highways, shipping lines, air lines, islands, isthmuses, canals and bays; provinces, territories, departments, and states.

2) <u>People</u>: The basic unit of society is the individual, and each person in his unique way provides not only a building block of the social structure but also an individual contribution which is not exactly matched by any other. Therefore, presidents, bishops, governors, artists, poets, writers, lawyers, doctors, merchants, chiefs, officials, conquerors, freebooters, missionaries, priests, and pirates, planters, miners, and herdsmen all become threads in the fabric and units in the design.

3) <u>Culture</u>: As the sum total of the human transmission through time vertically and through interchanges laterally, the cultural experience is not only the summation of the human performance, but also is the multiplied product of the human impact. Evidences of the cultural resultant are language, costumes and customs, education, ceremonies, dances, radio and television, newspapers and books, transportation, feast days, hymns and songs, legends and traditions, and the like.

4) <u>History</u>: In a sense, history is the resultant synthesis when people, places and events are placed in the hopper of time and milled out in scope, sequence, and significance. While history is primarily concerned with people and events, the residue gives us much of what we know of history in ruins, hieroglyphs, buildings, wars and battles, churches and temples, movements and organizations, conquest and piracy, settlement and occupation, rule and overthrow, legislation and decree.

Under this general umbrella of criteria and in the caldron wherein the four major categories are indiscriminately mixed, there is a necessary arrangement, which in this dictionary is not only alphabetical, but cross-referenced in many cases. There is provision of variants in spelling because so many may be found, even to the point of difficulty in recognizing widely differing forms of the same. There are multiple names for the same entry (most notable of all, the Río Coco, Wanks, etc.). Names of people include not only such obvious ones as presidents, but also a limited selection over a very wide range of people significant as examples of a unique category (e.g., missionary medical doctors), or as of special individual interest, (e.g., the soldier-of-fortune, Lee Christmas). While most are Hondurans, some are foreigners from the early Spaniards through the polyglot pirates to the modern entrepreneurs. Where there are names and phrases beginning with the definite articles la, el, las, and los, they are arranged under the word which follows the article, except in the case of surnames and the names of towns and other political entities and subdivisions.

There has been no effort to give complete biographies of all individuals mentioned. Rather, because of the reference aspect of a dictionary, the emphasis has been on the significance to Honduras of each person. There are several categories of chief executive of Honduras, each of which has bearing upon the history at a particular period. They fall under four periods:

I. Spanish Colonial (1522 to September 28, 1821)

   President of the Audiencia, Guatemala (when "Guatemala" represented all of Central America).
   Captain-General, Guatemala (usually but not always synonymous with the audiencia presidency).
   Visitador (interim appointments when colonial governors were being investigated or when offices were vacant).
   Governor (provincial official assigned to Honduras as a provincial entity. These were on occasion synonymous with presidents above, but in general were separately designated officials during the last colonial half-century, principally military men).
   Interim Officials for each category.
   Lieutenant-Governor, occasionally assigned.

II. Independence to Federation: (September 18, 1821 to July 28, 1825)

   Colonial Governor, still in office following independence.
   Interim official, named by the Colonial Governor.
   Interim Governor, named by the Constituent Assembly of Honduras.

III. Chiefs of State, Central American Confederation: (1825 to 1839)

   Chief of State.
   Interim Chief of State.
   Provisional Chief of State.
   Counsellor (during brief periods between elections, etc. Five counselors were incumbent during the last year of the federation).
   Vice-Chief of State.

IV. Presidents of the Republic: (August 20, 1839 to date.)

   President (Constitutional).
   Interim President.
   Council of Ministers (a frequent device between elections, following coups, etc.).
   Provisional President.

Vice President.
Senator (as a designated chief of state).
Deputy (as a designate).
President by Law (contrasted to a constitutional presidency, during constitutional hiatus).
President, First Designate.
President, Second Designate.
Junta Militar (committee rule).
Supreme Chief (for a period from Oct. 28, 1952 to May 9, 1853).

It is of interest that there are twelve forms of title used by the chief executive power during the 136 years of independence of Honduras as a sovereign nation.

Honduras has a unique location vis-à-vis the pre-Columbian inhabitants and the various Amerindian groups represented, for only in Honduras is there a clear collision point for three major cultural streams. One might almost say that Honduras, being the only one of the Middle-American countries with an east-west geographical axis and an essentially elliptical configuration, provided the site for a whirlpool of the ancient migration streams and a resultant maelstrom which has continued to the present time. Where Guatemala is predominantly Mayan, and El Salvador and Nicaragua more Mexican (Nahua) and Chibchan (the Sumus and the Lencas), Honduras in the northwest is dominated by the remnants of a major classical Maya center, Copán. Throughout there are residual Mexican influences, perhaps carried through by, and reminiscent of, the Pipiles. Then there is the strong strain of the northward-flowing easternmost stream on the east coast, which deposited the Sumu-related tribes who eventually became the warlike Miskitos and Payas, and the less belligerent Jicaques, as well as the strongly loyalist Lencas. To add to this swirling of Indian tribes and three major cultures, a fourth was introduced, probably pre-Columbian, but also by 18th century action of the British--the Carib-Arawakan. To further complicate matters, the African genes of early slaves in the Caribbean were laced through the east coast tribes to form the Sambo-Miskitos as well as the "Black Caribs." It is as if the purity of Maya Copán on the one frontier were balanced by the potpourri of bloods and cultures on the other, the Caribbean littoral.

In recognition of this situation there have been included here some Miskito (Sumu-Chibchan) entries in addition to references to the prevalent Maya (Chorti) and the still-pervasive north coast Carib.

Comparison of the major Maya sites leaves Copán one of five from Yucatán to El Salvador that are pre-eminent, each in its own way. Tikal's lofty temple pyramids are unmatched; the governor's palace at Uxmal is probably the most beautiful single Maya structure; the observatory at Chichén Itzá has no equal; the Palenque palace with its tower is unique in structure and beauty. At Copán every Maya idiom is expressed, in the great plaza of stelae and altars, and in the hieroglyphic stairway found in such elegance nowhere else. The serenity of Copán is achieved in a low wooded site by a stream, and with an architectural subtlety which is consistent and yet excitingly diverse.

The Maya ceremonial city of Copán and the great 18th century fort at Omoa create an aura of conquering colonial Spain submerging an ancient and superb architectural tradition.

Among the Amerindians of Honduras, due to the overlap of cultures, there are such fascinating speculations as the relationship of the Jicaque to the Choco of eastern Panama, or the Cuna Cuna of the San Blas Islands. It is the South American Chibchan origins which open the possibility.

Finally, it would be graceless indeed not to mention all those persons who helped in this enterprise. One would be obliged to list a number of Nicaraguan friends, and several Salvadoreans, in addition to the people of Honduras who welcomed us and assisted in the endeavour. The efforts of Moisés Toledo of Puerto Cortés deserve special mention as does the hospitality of Dr. Sam and Grace Marx. Throughout, the compiler has been either accompanied or encouraged by wife Jessie, daughter Carol, and sons Kessler and Matt. For all but Carol (who lives now in Panama), Tegucigalpa in 1955 was their first introduction to Central America and the subsequent years spent in the isthmian lands in the mid-1950's, a vital memory they cherish. Our family grieves with Honduras over the hurricane-flood tragedy of 1974.

No volume with as many sources and as diverse direct resources as this can be without error. For those inevitable "goofs" I take full responsibility.

To Charlotte Paton, Katharine Meier and Dorothy Weber, goes my special appreciation for their efforts in organizing and performing the major typing chores, some of which were done by Debbie Gray.

Overall, even though the method is piecemeal, the purpose is to present a land of beauty, a people of vitality, a tradition of excellence in antiquity and of promise in futurity. Honduras means "the depths." Where there are depths there are heights; high mountains marching between the seas, high human hopes unquenched by temporary disaster or despair.

- A -

ABAUNZA, ALVARO GOMEZ DE. This oidor served as interim governor until the arrival of Criado de Castilla (q.v.); that is, from 1596-1598. He had problems with the ayuntamiento of Santiago.

ACADEMIA DE LA LENGUA DE HONDURAS. The Honduran Academy of Language was founded by Rafael Heliodoro Valle (q.v.), as was the Ateneo de Honduras (q.v.).

ACATL. Thirteenth day of the Aztec month; meaning, "wool."

ACHIOTE see ANNATTO

ACOSTA, OSCAR. Poet and anthologist (see DEL VALLE, POMPEYO). Born in Tegucigalpa, 1933, has held posts as Secretary of the Honduran embassy in Peru and Chief of Public Relations of the Honduran government. He also headed the Editorial Department of the national University of Honduras. He has been secretary of the Honduran press association and the representative of the Honduras chapter of the Comunidad Latino América de Escritores. He has won prizes such as the Rubén Darío prize for poetry (Nicaraguan) and has a number of published works between 1955 and the present. The anthologies Exaltación de Honduras and Antología del Cuento Hondureño are in part his.

ACOSTA BONILLA, MANUEL. Lawyer Acosta Bonilla was made Minister of "Hacienda" and Public Credit (Treasury) in the López Arellano (q.v.) government following December 4, 1972.

ACT OF ANNEXATION TO MEXICO. On January 5, 1822, just a few months following the declaration of Independence of the Kingdom of Guatemala, including Honduras, the Sovereign Provisional Legislative Committee submitted an act annexing Central America to Mexico, under the "empire" established by Agustín Iturbide. The geographical divisions adhering to the act were Comayagua (as a province), Chiapas, Quetzaltenango, Sololá, the intendency of Nicaragua. This implies that while others did not specifically adhere, they were involved as part of Guatemala.

ACTA DE INDEPENDENCIA DE LA PROVINCIA DE COMAYAGUA.

Acuerdo Declarando 2

While the Kingdom of Guatemala declared independence on September 15, 1821, the province of Comayagua, representing what is now Honduras as the provincial capital, promulgated an Act of Independence on September 28, 1821, which was sustained by the city of Tegucigalpa on September 29, 1821, by Gracias on October 5, by Santa Barbara on October 23, by Trujillo on October 4, and by Omoa, October 2.

ACUERDO DECLARANDO OFFICIAL EL IDIOMA ESPAÑOL. On December 18, 1882, Spanish was declared the official language of Honduras, for use in all schools and colleges, all public pronouncements, all official documents.

ACUERDOS. Executive decrees, agreements and rulings which have the force of law, and which can be enacted as decree-laws by the President when congress is not in session or with the concurrence of his Council of Ministers in cases considered to be emergency or public necessity. While exceptional courts are prohibited, special courts for "military crimes" are allowed, and can be applied to civilians when charged with such crimes. It must be understood that the nature of acuerdos tends to vary from administration to administration.

ACUÑA, DIEGO DE. In contrast to the Conde de Gómera's turbulent preceding presidency, Acuña's term as President of Honduras from 1826-33 was a quiet one.

ADAMS, ALONSO. Claimant of the Swan Islands (q.v.) in 1893.

ADARME. A weight measure of 36 grams.

ADELANTADO. Prior to assumption of power by a Viceroy, this official was usually the highest one, being governor in newly acquired territory under the Spanish colonial system. See the various forms--A. DEL MAR, A. MENOR, A. FRONTERIZO, A. MAYOR.

ADELANTADO DEL MAR. When during conquest and early Spanish colonial days a commander of an exploring expedition was commissioned to become governor of a territory discovered or conquered, this was the title given. Once the conquest was complete, other and more elaborate administrative structures took over. The early development of Spanish colonial administrative techniques and accommodations was almost as much of a miracle as the discovery and conquest.

ADELANTADO FRONTERIZO see ADELANTADO MENOR

ADELANTADO MAYOR. A governor with military, judicial, and administrative power under the Spanish colonial system.

ADELANTADO MENOR. Also called a "fronterizo." Such a Spanish colonial official held power in frontier outposts essentially as

military chieftain administering under military law. Since the
frontier was frequently a war zone, this was for the times a
usual and practical approach to government. The colonial frontier crossed Honduras from Puerto Caballos (q.v.) through
Olancho (q.v.), and continued down to the Fort Inmaculada (El
Castillo Viejo) in Nacaragua.

ADMINISTRATION FOR INTERNATIONAL DEVELOPMENT. The
AID organization developed in the United States under the Alliance for Progress and as a succession to FOA, ICA, etc.
By 1971 it was under fire, and its future in doubt.

AEDES AEGYPTI. A mosquito, carrier of the violent disease called
Panama Fever, or Woodsman's, Chagres, or Yellow Fever.
The pest lives in tall forest trees. Yellow fever still occurs
occasionally in the isthmian area, and is carried by monkeys
as well as man. An epidemic occurred in the sparsely settled
Darien isthmus region of eastern Panama in 1974, and one
along the Central American Caribbean coast in 1956.

AEROVIAS NACIONALES DE HONDURAS. This airline operates internally and to the Bay Islands, and also provides charter service.

AGRARIAN LAWS FROM 1829 TO 1970. A tracing of the history of
agrarian legislation in Honduras shows that there were relatively
early efforts following independence to encourage a wider distribution of land ownership.
    The first land law of 1829 made possible the sale of
former royal holdings to private citizens, a mark of the shift
five years previously from being a colony of Spain to an independent federated republic. There were limits to the amount
of land for individual purchase.
    In 1837 the government was permitted by law to give
land in payment of loans to individuals and in payment of government salaries. Poor farmers could also get land more
easily, and municipalities could have land grants.
    By 1872 there was a law that anyone working national
land for three years could become the legal owner--in essence,
this was a homestead law.
    Beginning in 1888 (with 1898 and 1902 amendments), a
system of title grants and surveys was instituted to facilitate
selling government land to farmers.
    By 1924, the constitution incorporated a more comprehensive agrarian law which also made constitutional the previously legal methods of land acquisition. The 1924 Agrarian
Law also made possible grants of fifty acres each to rural
families.
    This was modified with liberalizing amendments, and
was in effect until 1962, when a new and very comprehensive
agrarian reform law was passed. The purpose of the 1962
law was to establish fair land tenure and use systems, and included creation of the Instituto Nacional Agrario (q.v.), the INA.

Agreement 4

This Agrarian Institute has a number of liberal provisions regarding those living on national land, expropriation, etc. The INA is also sponsoring new settlement on national land. The largest project is in the Aguan Valley, for 6,000 families on 175,000 acres. The law also provided for taxation on uncultivated land.

AGREEMENT OF INTEGRATED INDUSTRIES. This 1959 agreement was a step toward the economic integration of the Central American Common Market.

AGRICULTURAL EXTENSION SERVICE. This is a small service, numbering one agent for 5,000 farmers. In general it concentrates on corn, beans, cattle and hog production. The research work is done at Comayagua, in the National Agricultural Center.

AGRICULTURAL PRODUCTION. Between 1952 and 1966 there was an increase of food production at a rate of 3.1 per cent per annum. This was also the approximate population increase. A low of 2.5 per cent increase in 1967 was balanced by a high of 7.8 per cent in 1968, although there was a drop in several succeeding years. Per-acre production is low due to relatively primitive methods; mechanization is minimal.

AGUACATL. Original Nahuatl word for avocado, or, as used in Spanish-speaking Central America, aguacate. The small fruit grows wild.

AGUAN, RIVER. A river arising in Yoro department and flowing east, parallel to the north coast of Honduras, before it empties into the Caribbean near Santa Rosa de Aguan (q.v.), having crossed Colón department. Principal town along the river is Olanchita.

AGUERO, ROSENDO. Minister Agüero was "President by Law" from February 9, 1893 to April 18 of that year, following constitutional presidencies of Leiva (q.v.) and Bográn (q.v.). There was increasing trouble with the New Liberal Party under Policarpo Bonilla (q.v.).

AGUILAR, FRANCISCO. Senator Aguilar presided over the country briefly during the National War (q.v.) period from November 8, 1855 until February 17, 1856, when General Santos Guardiola became constitutional president. See BUESO, MONICO.

AGUILAR PAZ, ENRIQUE. Dr. Aguilar Paz was made Minister of Public Health in the cabinet of General López Arellano (q.v.) after the December 4, 1972 takeover.

AGUIRRE, JOSE MARIA. With Elías Cacho, Aguirre presided over the Honduran government from May to September 1869.

AGUIRRE, SALVADOR. Dr. Aguirre was one of a council of ministers who received the executive power of the state when it was necessary for Francisco Bertrand (q.v.) to flee from a revolt. The uprising had been caused by his obviously unconstitutional intent to retain the power in 1919. The council included Jesús Bendaña h., Héctor Valenzuela, Federico Smith, Dr. Antonio Bermúdez, and General Santiago Meza Cálix.

AHAU. The twentieth and final day of the Maya ritual month; meaning, "Sir." This title of address and the day itself bore a special meaning and importance in the religio-astronomical schema of the Maya calendar and the attendant ritual observances.

AHUAS. One of twin villages (the other being Paptalaya), on the lower reaches of the Patuca River (q.v.). There is a grass airfield at Ahuas, and twice-weekly airline service with DC-3 aircraft carrying passengers and freight. There is a clinic supported by the Moravian Church mission effort, the Clínica Moravo de Ahuas. See MARX, SAMUEL. There are two churches of that faith in the twin villages. The Patuca at this point runs through flat pine and scrub savannahs like those of coastal Georgia, South Carolina, and Florida, U.S.A. The Mission Aviation Fellowship (q.v.) also has a plane and pilot stationed here, in cooperation with the clinic, which provides medical, surgical, and other health services for a wide and remote area of the country.

AID   see ADMINISTRATION FOR INTERNATIONAL DEVELOPMENT

AIR FORCE, HONDURAS. The Military Aviation School (q.v.) and the command post of the single armed force unit which the air force comprises are located at Toncontín Airport near the capital. The major fighter category consists of F-4-U Corsairs, but the complement of planes (using U.S. designations) also includes Beechcraft, C-46, C-47, Convair PBY, several trainers such as NAA T-6, Lockheed T-33, Beech AT-11, PT-13, PT-17, PT-23, as well as Sikorsky S-52 helicopters. The air force maintains a high profile in political influence, as evidenced by its role in the coup of 1956 and the damage on El Salvador's oil installations in 1969. Communication, transport, and civic action work are major peace-time endeavors. There were 85 usable airfields and two seaplane stations by 1970.

AIR SERVICE OF HONDURAS. The largest of Honduran airlines, this one (SAHSA) was organized in 1944, and is a joint venture with Pan American Airways, the Honduran government, and some private stockholders. With 13 aircraft, SAHSA carries 150,000 passengers annually, providing international service to the rest of Central America, to Colombia, and to

New Orleans. It offers internal services on numerous routes, including the Bay Islands.

AJUTERIQUE. Less than ten miles from Comayagua, this municipal cabacera is a particularly picturesque Indian center, in the southern reaches of the Comayagua valley. There are Maya ruins in the hills nearby. There is an interesting colonial church of "earthquake baroque." Ajuterique is especially known for this parish church which is small and simple but remarkable in that the second tower was never constructed, a large square pier taking its place. Like most of the colonial churches, it went through several stages of construction and restoration.

AKBAL. Third day of the Maya month; meaning, "Night."

ALALC. The Asociación Latinoamericana de Libre Comercio, a free trade commission working in the development of regional agreements, and stemming from the Punta del Este presidential meetings of 1967 in Uruguay. Such organizations as the Mercado Común Centroamericano, of which Honduras was an original member, are involved in regional agreements, and the MCCA is a pattern which might well be extended under ALALC.

ALAMEDA, COLONIA. A southeastern suburb of Tegucigalpa.

ALAMINOS, ANTON DE. Pilot of the Caribbean area in the early 16th century. He had been with Columbus on the second voyage, and under Ponce de León gained fame in the discovery of Florida, when he piloted the caravel "Santiago." He also piloted Juan de Grijalva who was credited with the discovery of Yucatán in 1518, although de León had been there five years before, in 1513. Aluminos also piloted Córdoba in 1517 when Yucatán was revisited. These precursors of Cortés were the real discoverers of Mexico. In 1518 Alaminos, Spain's primary Caribbean pilot, again set out with Alonso Alvarez de Pineda and Francisco de Garay, winding up in the area of Tampico, Mexico. By this time Alaminos had great familiarity with the Gulf of Honduras.

ALAS PARA LA SALUD see WINGS FOR HEALTH

ALAUTUN. This is the hieroglyph which introduces the initial series in Maya dates, and is the foundation of the calendrical notation, "Day one of Year one," so to speak. It represents 23,040,000,000 days. These 23 billion days are the rough equivalent of 63,123,300 of our 365-day years! This is truly an astonishing base from which to figure elapsed time to the exact day!

ALBARAZADO. The cross of a Coyote (indigenous Lobo) male with an Indian female. See RACIAL MIXTURES.

ALBARDA. A saddle peculiar to Honduras and adjacent parts of
 central America. The "tree" consists of two cylindrical
 bundles of reeds tied tightly, and laid parallel to the steed's
 backbone, with a covering of a single large piece of leather
 which is often 30" or more from front to rear and the skirts
 of which may drop 30" on each side. Slender stirrup-straps
 carry small hooded stirrups (see illustration, p. 108).
 In colonial days these were often of brass. Such stirrups
 are now rare and valued antiques. The albarda's great
 single hide cover and skirts are usually elaborately carved.
 A single cinch is used. A new albarda is quite imposing.
 No albarda is very comfortable for either rider or animal.
 See also MONTURA.

ALBINO. A cross between a Morisco (q.v.) male and a Spanish
 female. See RACIAL MIXTURES.

ALBITEZ, DIEGO DE. Captain Albitez in 1527 was sent by
 Pedrarias Dávila with a scribe or notary and a magistrate to
 warn Hernan Cortés against incursions into the territories
 discovered by Gil González Dávila and populated (sparsely)
 under the "founder" Hernández de Córdoba in 1524. The
 conflict of interest converged in Honduras. Albitez could not
 take office as Honduran governor in 1532, as he died enroute;
 Andrés de Cereceda was named to succeed him.

ALCALDE. A local official at municipality level who served as
 both executive and judiciary, actually as mayor and judge.
 The position has been historically both appointive and elective.

ALCERRO OLIVA, JOSE NAPOLEON. Dr. Alcerro became minister of Public Education in the cabinet of General Oswaldo
 López Arellano (q.v.) following December 4, 1972.

ALDEA. A subdivision of a municipio (q.v.) which is essentially
 a village or hamlet. Since many municipios have under 1,000
 inhabitants, the aldea may be very small indeed.

ALFALIT. A Honduran group dedicated to alphabetization or literacy programs. They not only teach people to read, but follow up with the distribution of literature.

ALGUACIL. In the administration of Spanish colonial America, the
 alguacil was a sort of deputy, to assist in law enforcement
 or to perform related tasks.

ALGUACIL MAYOR. A Spanish colonial post equivalent to Constable, a position prized and frequently purchased.

ALLEGER, DANIEL E. From 1926 to 1931, an agricultural expert
 attached to the United Fruit Company in their Honduran and
 Guatemalan operations. Later, as Agricultural Economist,
 he served the University of Florida in Costa Rica. One of

the North Americans who is extremely knowledgeable about backland Honduras.

ALLIED STATES. A term applied to Costa Rica, Honduras, and Nicaragua, when in January, 1839, they signed offensive treaties against El Salvador. They were suspicious of the leadership of Francisco Morazán there. They invaded El Salvador under Francisco Ferrera in early 1839.

ALMIRANTA. The ship carrying the admiral in a "flota" (fleet), usually bringing up the rear while the "Capitana" led off. See also CAPITANA and NAO.

ALMIRANTA (Honduras fleet). In 1605 this vessel had about $200,000 in gold and silver aboard when lightning struck the mainmast and she sunk in 1000-foot-deep water near Santo Domingo. There were 11 survivors of 101 aboard.

ALMOHADILLADO. The "cushioned" form of engaged columns found in some colonial church architecture in Honduras. See CATHEDRAL, TEGUCIGALPA.

ALONSO TAMAYO, MELCHOR. Governor in 1644.

ALTAMIRANO, PEDRO see REMANZO

ALTAMIRANO Y VELASCO. Governor from 1654-57, this nobleman (Conde de Santiago y Calimaya) was engaged in factional disputes during his incumbency, and died during the residency. His replacement, the Conte de Priego, died en route in Panama, and the serious divisions in the Audiencia caused them to attempt collective government from 1657-59.

ALTO VIAJE. The "high voyage" of Columbus (his fourth and last), in 1502-1504, when he discovered Honduras, first on the shores of the Bay Island of Guanaja.

ALTSCHUL, FRANCISCO see ARIAS, JUAN ANGEL

ALVARADO, CASTO. With Julián Tercero and Juan Morales in 1844, and again in 1845, Alvarado served as part of presiding groups of the Council of Ministers during brief interims in the rule of Francisco Ferrera (q.v.). In 1847 the council of ministers ruling the country for six weeks consisted of Alvarado and two generals famed for their vigor, Francisco Ferrera and Santos Guardiola.

ALVARADO, F. ALFREDO. First Director of Public Instruction. See PUBLIC EDUCATION, DIRECTION OF.

ALVARADO, GONZALO DE. Founder of the first provincial capital, Gracias a Dios in Honduras, this brother of Pedro Alvarado (q.v.) was one of his captains and a fellow conquistador.

He became a regidor in 1535. He settled on Honduran land near Gracias, and was acting governor of Guatemala during the 1526 rebellion, which was caused when he ordered Indian children to dig placer gold.

ALVARADO, JORGE DE. One of that numerous family so important in Central American annals. He was governor in 1602.

ALVARADO, LEON. One of the commissioners acting for Honduras in the chartering of the "Honduras Interoceanic Railway Company" (q.v.) in 1853.

ALVARADO CONTRERAS, PEDRO DE. From 1525 to 1541 a Spanish Governor of the Kingdom (or Chancellorate) of Guatemala which included the present national territory of Honduras. In 1531 and following, he was able to open up transportation along the Río San Juan from Granada to the Caribbean, which provided a Caribbean trade outlet to Spain for all of Central America. One of the spectacular early conquistadores, Alvarado was significant to the history of Central America because of his conquest of Guatemala. The Audiencia of Guatemala later included Honduras. With Cortés in Mexico at the time of the "noche triste," Alvarado left for Guatemala in December 1523. He organized Spanish government there and became the first governor. His cruelty was legendary and was the source of rebellion and unrest. Nevertheless he ranks with Cortés and Pizarro as a general and explorer.
 While later he went to Peru, his restless nature led him to a plan for South Seas conquest. Before leaving, however, he was killed in 1541 while trying to put down an Indian revolt in Mexico. He was married to two noble sisters, nieces of the Duke of Albuquerque--first Doña Francisco de la Areva, in 1528, and at her early death, Doña Beatriz, in 1538. Alvarado was more than any other the Conquistador of Central America.

ALVARADO MANGANO, RAFAEL. Held ministerial powers of the executive on two occasions--May to November, 1883, and August 30 to November 17, 1884. Again from January 30, 1903 to February 18, 1903, as one of a council of ministers holding the executive power, he served during the conflict over the 1903 election, between Sierra (q.v.) and Manuel Bonilla (q.v.). See GUTIERREZ, ENRIQUE and ARIAS, JUAN ANGEL.

ALVAREZ, FRANCISCO. Spanish engineer who began construction of the main structure of Fort Omoa (q.v.) under the general direction of Díez Navarro (q.v.) who had been recalled to Guatemala. The clearing and leveling began in 1756. Alvarez could find no appropriate stone nearby. Stone was finally quarried as much as 90 miles from Omoa, over a 20-year period. Labor was also hard to come by.

ALVAREZ ALFONSO ROSICA DE CALDAS, SEBASTIAN. Governor from 1668 to 1672, when he died in office. He was unusual in that he traveled in the Audiencia as far as Nicaragua. The Bishop of Guatemala served out his last year in office. It was a period of English intrusion, both in terms of piracy and of the logwood cutters on the Honduran and Nicaraguan coasts.

ALVAREZ CASTRO, MIGUEL (1785-1856). Serving under Francisco Morazán as Minister of Foreign Affairs of the Central American Federation, Alvarez Castro was a forceful critic of Frederick Chatfield (q. v.) and the interference by Great Britain which Chatfield represented in the period following 1834, when the Bay Island and Tigre Island matters were part of the problem. He was also a major Salvadorean poet.

AMAPALA. Municipal cabacera and port on Tigre Island in the Bay of Fonseca. Site of an airport and the major Honduran seaport on the Pacific Coast. Historically the port was a pawn during the tussles between Squiers (q.v.) and Chatfield (q.v.) as they represented respectively the United States and Great Britain during the mid-nineteenth century, when each of these powers was attempting to gain a foothold for transisthmian canal or transportation rights. In the end the United States forged ahead, with the final result being the opening of the Panama Canal in 1914. In the 1850's a United States firm had built a saw mill and planing mill there to process timber from the interior. It was during this period that the incident developed between the British and United States representatives. Due to interior transportation problems, Amapala is not a significant seaport as is Puerto Cortés on the north coast.

AMAPALA, GOLFO DE. Mid-nineteenth century alternate name for the Gulf of Fonseca. Amapala is a port on Tigre Island.

AMAPALA, PACT OF see MILWAUKEE, U.S.S.

AMATINGNI, RIVER. On the northeast coastal area of Honduras, emptying into Brus Laguna, this stream is part of a system of coastal waterways, and may be considered an alternate "pass" in the delta of the Río Patuca; it is navigable by dory and pipante (q.v.).

AMERICA, ORIGIN OF NAME. Cristopher Columbus discovered the mainland of America on the Honduran coast in early August, 1502. A recent theory developed by Jorge Espinosa Estrada, in Nicaragua, Cuna [cradle] de America, suggests that the name of America may have originated in the name of the mountain range (Amerrique, Amerissque, or Americ) which lies northeast of Lake Nicaragua, rather than in the name of Amerigo Vespucci. Elements of this fascinating speculation (which was advanced first in 1888) are:

No major geographical place has been named for the given name rather than the surname of an individual. Locality names persist through many generations (as ancient Greek Gades, Spain's Cádiz). Place names in Central American Indian dialects end in ique or ic, meaning "great" or "prominent."
Following his 1502 discovery of Honduras, and a long beat against the wind along the north coast of Honduras, Columbus stopped at a place on the Nicaraguan Coast--Cariai or Cariay. Perhaps this was "Carcai," home of the Carcas Indians (area of Amerissque range). The Carcas had gold, and mines still are active in the western end of the range. These Indians were also called Cookras and that name still appeared on 19th century maps.
The name as a synonym for a golden country would hence have been known among illiterate seamen in European ports.
Columbus would have refrained from using the word in his letter "Rarissima" to Ferdinand the King, if he felt someone had been there before. Perhaps Cabot had preceded him on that coast, although Samuel Eliot Morison discounts this theory.
Parenthetic to this discussion of the name, there is some reason to believe that Amerigo Vespucci (q.v.) himself preceded Columbus to the Honduran coast by several years. No certain proof exists, however. The theory of a name is intricate, fragile, but ingenious and interesting to pursue.

AMERICAN FRUIT AND STEAMSHIP COMPANY. One of a number of banana companies shipping fruit from Honduras prior to the blights of the 1930's.

AMERICAN TREATY, 1670. Second of the treaties of Madrid (1667 and 1670) which gave England a "legal" and diplomatic foothold in the Caribbean throughout the following century. In this treaty Spain not only pledged peace, friendship, and the suppression of piracy, but also permitted trade and, far more significantly, abandoned her claim that only she and Portugal had occupation rights in the New World. To the King of Great Britain was granted title, in effect, to all lands he then occupied. This had later meaning to Mosquitia and Belize even though the signatory kings were probably not aware of them as entities at the time. It also affected the Caribbean coastal area of Honduras, northeast of the existing Spanish colonial frontier. The second Treaty of Madrid (q.v.) was termed the American Treaty because it became the essential basis for the English strength in the Caribbean for over 100 years following 1670, and in that sense was a major factor in the British hegemony which became, due to her sea power, a world-wide phenomenon.

AMESQUETA, BARTOLOME. Professor of Law in the University of the Kingdom of Guatemala in 1686, who was to sail in that year on the "mercury fleet" for Honduras to take up his post. This seems to have been the most direct route of access to Guatemala at that time of year (September-October). It still left a rough overland journey from Trujillo or Puerto Caballos to (present-day) Antigua, then the capital.

AMPARO. An order of restraint against administrative acts infringing on individual rights, or against imprisonment.

AMUNATEGUI, CAYETARIO DE. Interim governor of Honduras in 1787.

ANACH see ASSOCIACION NACIONAL DE CAMPESINOS DE HONDURAS

ANCIENT CITIES OF THE NEW WORLD, THE. Early definitive book on Maya archaeology by Desiré Charnay (q.v.).

ANCIENT MAYA, THE. Comprehensive and authoritative book by Sylvanus Morley (q.v.). A standard reference on the Maya, clear, simple, and complete.

ANDESITE. The fine-grained and very even-textured volcanic stone, principally feldspar and plagioclase, which is the material of the sculptures at Copán. Unlike the limestone of other Maya sites, the andesite is about the same hardness before quarrying as afterward, hence is more difficult to handle. It is excellent for carving except for the flint nodules which occur throughout. Stone chisels will not work these flints. The Mayas often chipped them out or worked them into the design.

ANDRES ZUÑIGA, LUIS. Honduran poet, author of Aguilas conquistadores, and one of the most influential of the nation's literary figures.

ANGLO-AMERICAN RIVALRY IN HONDURAS see RIVALRY, BRITAIN AND THE UNITED STATES

ANGLO-MISKITO COLONY. While it was indeed a series of disconnected settlements, from the 1600's through most of the 1700's the British had a colony which stretched from Belize on the north and west to Bluefields and Greytown on the south and east, with major holdings on the Honduran Bay Islands, at Black River, and at Brewers' Lagoon. The Mosquito Protectorate and kingdom was a semi-fiction of this enterprise.

ANGLO-MOSQUITIA. Term applied to the Mosquito Coast and the quasi-colony or loose protectorate there maintained by the British during the 18th and 19th centuries. See MOSQUITO SHORE. Notice that Miskito, Mosquito, and variations are used more or less interchangeably.

ANGUIANO, RAMON. Intendant of Honduras from 1793-1812, and listed as Governor in 1796, Anguiano advocated abandoning Omoa (q.v.) and Trujillo (q.v.) and returning to the Yoro-Sonaguera frontier. English ships shelled Trujillo for two days in 1799.

ANGULO, NICOLAS (1803-1879). Long-term military figure in the matter of Central American unification, this officer served with Francisco Morazán (q.v.) in the turbulent period from 1826-1840 which ended in the breakup of the Central American Federation. As a Salvadorean, he was a major opponent of Honduras in the war of 1845.

ANHSA   see   AEROVIAS NACIONALES DE HONDURAS

ANIL. Indigo, a major crop in Honduras in the 17th century. Honduras was closer to Spain in sailing time than Veracruz in Mexico, hence shipping indigo was advantageous.

ANILERO. A grower of indigo.

ANNATTO. This plant, bixa orellano, also called "achiote," has a fruit whose pulpy parts have been used by Indians since pre-conquest times to color chocolate drinks. It has a red color, and was added to chocolate, maize, and chile. Annatto is also a dye, but not a very reliable one. The Indians also used the pulp of the crushed fresh fruit to paint their bodies, for relief from insects. It is also used as a dye for coloring butter, cheese, oils, and varnish, and is exported for that purpose.

ANNEXATION TO UNITED STATES. There was a movement among Honduran leaders to annex their country to the United States in the 1850's, a move similar to that of El Salvador some years earlier. The impetus for the movement, which actually gained little force, was the Honduras Interoceanic Railroad Company (q.v.) initiated by the efforts of E. G. Squiers (q.v.). Santo Domingo was another Caribbean country which sought U.S. annexation.

ANOTTA. A variant of Annatto (q.v.).

ANTIGUA OCOTEPEQUE. Two or three miles from the Ocotepeque departmental cabacera of Nueva Ocotepeque, this "old" village was in colonial days the original site. It is on the Río Lempa a few miles from the Salvadorean border, and it was in this area that fighting was especially heavy during the 1969 war between Honduras and El Salvador. The valley here is flanked by rugged ranges. The word comes from Nahua "ocote" (pine), and "tepec" (hill). In English it might be "Pinecrest."

ANTILLAS, MAR DE LAS.  The sea of the Antilles, frequently
    used in Spanish-speaking Latin America to denote the Carib-
    bean sea, or "Mar Caribe."

ANTONELLI, JUAN BAUTISTA.  Engineer officer sent to the
    Caribbean in 1585 by Philip II of Spain to investigate the
    state of defense and recommend measures.  He advised forti-
    fications and coast guards at Havana, San Juan de Ulloa (Vera
    Cruz), San Juan de Puerto Rico, and Portobello.  It is sig-
    nificant to Honduras that he presumed that coast guard pa-
    trols from these fortified ports could defend the long Carib-
    bean coast of Central America.  This proved not to be feas-
    ible, and as a result, Honduras suffered repeated piratical
    depredations, in spite of the considerable coastal fortifica-
    tions at Omoa and Truxillo.
      Antonelli and Diego López de Quintanillo studied the
    Honduran transisthmian route at about the same time as
    Francisco de Valverde (1590) but while the latter was enthu-
    siastic about the possibilities, Antonelli came to an opposite
    conclusion.  The Puerto Caballos-Bay of Fonseca route was
    long, would be expensive, and there would be need for
    11,000 oxen, 2,000 Negro slaves, and 500 Spanish farmers
    to keep it going.  Such elaborate "reports" from four cen-
    turies ago are of interest.

ANTONIO DE CASTELLA, CARLOS  see  HERVIAS, GABRIEL DE

ANTROPOLOGIA Y HISTORIA, INSTITUTO NACIONAL DE  see
    NATIONAL INSTITUTE OF ANTHROPOLOGY AND HISTORY

AOBAIA.  A circle dance of folk character done in river commu-
    nities of Mosquitia.  There are hopping and running steps
    done to a continuing chant.  The derivation seems to be ori-
    ginally from Spanish creoles.

APH  see  ASOCIACION DE PRENSA HONDURENA

APLICANO MENDIETA, PEDRO.  Director of Mayan studies of the
    Cultural Center of the American Maya Movement, with acti-
    vities in San Pedro Sula, Tegucigalpa, and El Progreso.

ARADA, LA.  Site of an 1851 battle when the Honduran and Salva-
    dorean forces supporting union were beaten as they attempted
    an invasion of Guatemala.  This success of Guatemalan Rafael
    Carrera was the downfall of the union movement by Honduras,
    El Salvador, and Nicaragua known as the Representación Na-
    cional (q.v.).

ARAMACINA.  Silver mining area worked in colonial days.

ARANJO Y RIO, JOSE.  Captain General in Guatemala who directed
    the building of a road from Guatemala City (Antigua) to Omoa
    (q.v.).  The road was completed by 1756, and ran from the

capital to Chiquimula and down the valley of the Chamelicón, through the big Indian town of Quezailaca and through a narrow canyon in the Sierra de Omoa. The route was about 400 miles long. Díez Navarro (q.v.) altered the last part to go through San Pedro Sula.

ARBENZ REGIME. Honduras was involved in the Guatemalan developments of 1954 when the Jacopo Arbenz regime was considered to be enmeshed in the intrigues of "international communism." When arms were sought in Eastern Europe by Arbenz, and delivered in May 1954, the United States airlifted arms (on May 24, 1954) to Honduras and Nicaragua. The invasion of Guatemala which followed, under the leadership of exiled Guatemalan Colonel Castillo Armas' forces, was assisted by the United States' Central Intelligence Agency and was launched from Honduran soil. On June 20, 1954 Guatemala asked the Security Council of the United Nations to intervene and to have the invaders apprehended by the countries of Honduras and Nicaragua. The Inter-American Peace Committee of the Organization of American States voted unanimously to create a Commission of Enquiry to proceed to Guatemala, Honduras, and Nicaragua. Guatemala suddenly decided not to cooperate with the OAS in this matter. The fall of the Arbenz government to military threat by Armas precluded further Commission action. This Cold War activity in the Western Hemisphere was a profound shock to Latin Americans in general, and was a precursor of later events in Cuba.

ARCE, MANUEL JOSE. Elected President of Honduras under the First Federal Constitution of Central America, with José Cecilio del Valle (q.v.) as Vice President. The election was annulled.

ARCHAEOLOGICAL SURVEY, FIRST. The initial serious survey of the rich Central American archaeological remains was carried out by a Frenchman, Guillaume Dupaix, who was sent by Charles IV of Spain to report on Mexican ruins. Dupaix took with him a Spanish draughtsman, Casteñada. The turmoil of the Napoleonic wars during their 1805-07 period of work helped to keep its importance from being recognized. While their work was largely done in Mexico, they were indeed forerunners of such men as John Lloyd Stephens (q.v.), Lord Kingsborough (q.v.), Sir Alfred Maudsley (q.v.), and Sylvanus Morley (q.v.). This sequence of exploration was significant in the revelation of the great Honduran Maya site of Copán (q.v.), one of half a dozen of major import in the western hemisphere.

ARCHAEOLOGICAL ZONES. There are now designated and protected zones in Honduras. See ARCHAEOLOGY, HONDURAN.

ARCHAEOLOGY, HONDURAN. There is a sequential development of archaeology in the Middle American region from Mexico to Panama which includes such names as Dupaix (q.v.), Kingsborough (q.v.), Stephens (q.v.), Maudsley (q.v.), Charnay (q.v.), and Morley (q.v.). The crown of Honduran archaeological development is at Copán, and the unearthing and restoration there accomplished, as well as the museum in the nearby town, are among the best to be found in Middle America. There is, however, much archaeological exploration and consequent work remaining to be done. Squier (q.v.), in his work called Notes on Central America, shows on a comprehensive map and lists in his text ruins as follows: Tenampua, Chapuluca, Chapulistagua, Calamulla, Jamalteca, Maniani, Guasistagua; others near Flores in Gracias Department, south of Minas de Oro, near San José and Rosario in the northwest. While these references are 130 years old, there is little doubt that some of them are valid sites. Latest maps have the intriguing reference to ruins which have been sighted from the air in the remote southern corner of Colón Department, called "Ciudad Blanca." The large ruined area described by Squier as Tenampua is not now easily traceable.

ARCINIEGAS, GERMAN. Liberal educator who has spoken out loudly against Latin American dictators. He takes to task Tiburcio Carias, Tacho Someza, and Rafael Trujillo, calling them the "three T's."

ARCOS Y MORENO, ALONSO DE. Captain General in Guatemala 1754-1760 who called Díez Navarro back to the capital from Omoa (q.v.) in 1756, leaving the construction of the fort there to Francisco Alvarez (q.v.).

ARDILO GOMEZ, RUBEN. A young Colombian adherent of Sandino (q.v.) who, as courier to the American legation in Honduras in 1929, tried to deliver a Sandino missive addressed to the President of the United States.

AREA OF HONDURAS. Wilgus, in Latin America, 1492-1942, has published an unusual map which shows that Honduras is the size of New Hampshire, Vermont, Massachusetts, New Jersey, Connecticut, Delaware, Rhode Island, and the Panama Canal Zone combined. To use a European comparison, Honduras is equal to a combination of the Netherlands, Switzerland, and Denmark. The area in square miles was recorded by Squier in 1855 as 39,600 square miles. A U.S. government publication of 1971 lists the area as 43,277 square miles. A Rand McNally atlas of 1969 gives that same figure, as does the National Geographic Atlas of 1963 and the Worldmark Encyclopedia of Nations, 1960. This figure is sufficiently consistent to be accepted.

ARELLANO  see  LOPEZ ARELLANO, OSWALDO

AREVALO, JUAN JOSE. A president of Guatemala (1945-51) prior to the Arbenz regime of the 1950's, Arévalo, as an intellectual and an exile from his country, wrote a controversial but significant book, translated into English in 1961, The Shark and the Sardines. This volume is important to students of the Central American scene for two reasons: first, it presents a scathing point of view concerning the United States of America and interventions in Latin America; second, and specifically, it uses the recent history of Central America (from 1850 to date of publication) as an example of the theme of the book. In that sense it relates to Honduras as to the other countries. The language is passionate, even poetic, often extreme. But the message needs to be understood in order to understand some of the very basic problems in U.S.-Latin American relations.

ARIAS, CELEO. A temporarily liberal Guatemalan Government, with the help of El Salvador, toppled the Medina (q.v.) government in Honduras in 1872 and put in their liberal "puppet," Arias, as president. When a new Guatemalan chief executive wished to replace Arias with Leiva, Arias would not resign, sponsored a new constitution in 1873 to support his incumbency, and turned back Leiva's invasion. In 1874, however, he surrendered to Leiva at Comayagua, and under restoration of the 1865 Constitution, Leiva became Constitutional President. Arias was founder of the Liberal Party in Honduras in the late 1800's. See TWO-PARTY SYSTEM.

ARIAS, JUAN ANGEL. One of the council of ministers holding power during the Sierra (q.v.) and Bonilla (q.v.) disputed election in 1903. The others were Rafael Alvarado Mangano, Máximo B. Rosales, Daniel Fortín, h., Manuel Sabino López and Francisco Altschul. Arias was then acting as President from February 18 to April 13, 1903 when, after Bonilla's (q.v.) march on the capital, he took over.

ARID LOWER TROPICAL ZONE   see   LIFE ZONES

ARID UPPER TROPICAL ZONE   see   LIFE ZONES

ARID ZONES   see   LIFE ZONES

ARIEL. A fortnightly periodical published by Froylán Trucios (q.v.) in Tegucigalpa, in the late 1920's and early 1930's, essentially in support of Sandino (q.v.).

ARIZABALAGA, VINCENTE. One of the Lieutenant Colonels who were officers of Gálvez leading the cross-Honduran attack on the British at Black River in 1782. See TRUJILLO, BASE ... 1782.

ARMAS, CASTILLO   see   ARBENZ REGIME

ARMED ACTIONS. The Republic of Honduras has experienced armed action more than 280 times since independence, beginning in 1827. It is estimated that during these periods of conflict, over 20,000 Hondurans lost their lives from direct action, with those dying from causes related to the wars and revolutions doubtless numbering many more. Numbers of these "armed actions" represented full-scale war, the most recent being the war with El Salvador in 1969.

ARMED FORCES, REGULAR. The armed force for external security is separate from the police force assigned to internal security. (See CUERPO ESPECIAL DE SEGURIDAD.) The regular strength of the armed force is around 5,000 men, distributed in regional units (see MILITARY COMMANDS). There are also some special corps in the army, and a small air force. Combat-trained and -oriented forces are in special corps and few in number. Seldom do external situations confront the army, but this was true in the 1969 war with El Salvador. External response potential is limited. There is provision for rapid expansion in time of war.

During the 19th century, civil conflict frequently arose due to political splits, and the armed force would support one or another faction, often splitting itself. Loyalties were to "caudillos" or other individuals.

Under President Juan Manuel Gálvez from 1949-54 there was an effort to modernize the armed forces, the first such concerted effort in history, and this continued under the military junta which took power in 1956. The 1957 constitution gave the army considerable autonomy. While Ramón Villeda Morales built up a separate Civil Guard before 1963, modernization continued. The López Arellano regime, following a 1963 coup, replaced the Guard with the Security Corps, which was virtually a branch of the armed forces, though legally separate. The armed forces have become the essential arbiter of the national political scene, and the López Arellano regime which began December 4, 1972, has quite understandably continued this role.

ARMS, SANDINO. During the inception of the Sandino (q.v.) guerrilla war in Nicaragua, César Agusto Sandino was working at the San Albino mine in northern Nicaragua. With a savings of $300, he contacted Honduran gun-runners in October 1926, and began to arm some followers, the first band being twenty-nine men; on November 2 he led an attack on the garrison of Jicaro, near the mine. The attack failed. Seven years of conflict followed, one of history's most significant guerrilla enterprises, as guaged by its impact upon Latin America in general.

ARRECIFES DE LA MEDIA LUNA. Large offshore reefs northeast of Cabo Gracias a Dios about fifty miles. There is a series of cays, banks, and reefs extending nearly 100 miles to the north. The early maps showed this a shallow bank excluded to navigation, which was realistic.

ARRIERO. Muleteers of the 1800's in Honduras. Mule trains were still a major form of transport.

ARROBA. A measure of weight, 25 lbs or 11.5 kilograms.

ASOCIACION DE PRENSA HONDUREÑA. Honduran Press Association, similar in purpose and function to such associations elsewhere.

ASOCIACION NACIONAL DE CAMPESINOS DE HONDURAS. An association of countrymen and farmers, nationwide, with considerable political impact.

ASOCIACION NACIONAL DE INDUSTRIALES see NATIONAL MANUFACTURERS ASSOCIATION

ASSOCIATED PRODUCERS PROGRAM. Sponsored by the United Fruit Co. (q.v.), this plan enables independent growers to purchase or rent banana land from the company. The company thus supports the work of hundreds of independent operators, furnishes technical assistance and purchases the banana crop.

ATENEO DE HONDURAS. The Honduran Atheneum was founded by Rafael Heliodoro Valle (q.v.) in 1912.

ATILILLO. A drink made from dry corn.

ATL. A very fundamental root-word of the Nahuatl tongue. In this context a month, festival, day and god of the ancient Nahuas meaning water. It is the ninth day of the Aztec month. The many combined forms, even of the other named months, show the universal importance of water, from a pantheistic as well as a pragmatic standpoint. Often used with "Lan" (place) in the combined form "Atlán." (Resemblances to "Atlantic," "Atlantis," "Atlas," etc. are of interest even if coincidental.) While there is more Maya than Nahua influence in Honduras, the Mexican-Nahua cultural ripples permeate the whole isthmian area as far southeast as Costa Rica, and are paradoxically rather separate from the Maya culture although in such frequent geographical contiguity.

ATLANTIC AND PACIFIC STEAM NAVIGATION COMPANY. One of numerous 19th century projects for opening water (or other) transport across the American Isthmian area. The company was involved in the Clayton-Bulwer Treaty (q.v.) and was to be supported by both signatory nations, Britain and the United States.

ATLANTIDA, DEPARTMENT. Bounded on the North by the Caribbean Sea (Bay of Honduras); on the South by the Cordillera de Nombre de Dios which rises to near 8,000 feet on the border between Atlantida and Yoro department; on the East by Colón department, and on the West by the Río Ulua and Cortés Department. The cabacera is La Ceiba (q.v.), with Tela, El Porvenir, and Jutiapa as other population centers. The area is 1,660 square miles and the 1973 population was 71,653 in the cabaceras and 71,941 otherwise, for a total of 143,594. There are four hospitals. There is major banana culture in this coastal area.

ATLANTIDE BANK   see   BANCO ATLANTIDA

ATOL.   A drink made from green corn.

AUASTINGNI, CRIQUE.   Stream in the eastern Caribbean lowlands of Gracias a Dios department. See CRIQUE.

AUDIENCIA. In Spanish colonial administration the audiencia was a check and balance device, which as an advisory council served in both executive and judicial capacities. It was at once a final court of appeal (the viceroy being "chief justice"), and between terms of viceroys (who often were delayed many months before arrival) was the colonial executive. At any time it had direct access to the Spanish crown--a considerable power. Normally and day-to-day it served as a council of state or Cabinet. Needless to say the prestige was great. An audiencia remote from the viceregal seat was called a "presidencia." During the first Spanish century in America the audiencia was probably the most powerful governmental entity. To understand the modern government of Honduras it is useful to have some grounding in the colonial forms which were antecedent.

AUDIENCIA DE LOS CONFINES   see   PROVINCIAL ADMINISTRATION 1542

AUDIENCIA OF 1542   see   CENTRAL AMERICAN UNION, FIRST

AUGURTO Y ALAVA, JUAN MIGUEL DE. Overshadowed by previous presidents resident during his term, Augurto y Alava governed from 1682 to 1684.

AUTHENTIC FEDERATION OF HONDURAN UNIONS. The FASH was a federation begun in 1963 outside the large Confederation of Honduran Workers (q.v.). Affiliated with the International Federation of Christian Trade Unions, the Europe-based movement began with about 2,000 Honduran members. See ORGANIZED LABOR.

AUTONOMOUS MUNICIPAL BANK. A state bank created in 1961 and owned jointly by all the municipalities in Honduras. It

AVENDAÑO, DIEGO DE. Governor from 1642 to 1649, Avendaño died in office after long illness. He was notably modest, honest and pious.

AVILA Y LUGO, FRANCISCO DE. Governor, 1639.

AYALA, ANTONIO DE. Governor of Honduras, 1698.

AYCOOK, J. FELIX. Manager of the Tela Railroad Company during the 1954 general strike. He told the strikers there could be no negotiation until the strike ended, and appealed personally to 2,000 strikers camped in Tela on behalf of the Tela Hospital, managed by the United Fruit Co. (UFCO), which was running out of food.

AYUNTAMIENTO. At local municipal levels, a council of important citizens during Spanish colonial times, composed of heads of leading families and of property owners, resulting in considerable local autonomy. After the conquest period, central governmental appointment of local officials lessened the significance of the Ayuntamiento.

AZOGUE. Special ships used to freight mercury to the mines of New Spain for the reduction and refining of silver ores. The mercury cargoes of one ship could be worth $1,000,000, and 200 to 500 tons of mercury were sent annually from the old world to the new. At Fort Omoa are to be seen today many of the cast iron bottles used for shipping mercury to the Honduran mining areas.

AZULES. A term for the "blue" political party, conservatives, in the early part of this century.

- B -

BACCALOREAT. The baccalaureate, required as a preliminary to admission to university. See CICLO DIVERSIFICADO.

BADGER, BRIG see NELSON, HORATIO

BAG, COFFEE. A unit of coffee merchandising, the "bag" is slightly more than 132 pounds of unprocessed coffee beans. The world crop of 1974-75 was predicted to be 15,000,000 bags.

BAHAMONDE, JOSE SAENZ. Governor of Honduras in 1760.

BAHIA DE OMOA. The bay on the northwest corner of Honduras, part of the Gulf of Honduras and the Caribbean Sea, and crossing the border between Honduras and Guatemala, which border is at this point of the coast denoted by the Motagua River (q.v.) mouth. The Motagua is the principal river discharging in the bay.

BAHIA DE TRUJILLO. One of the four major bays on the Honduran Coast, and most sheltered of the three on the North Coast. The site of Trujillo (q.v.) and of Puerto Castilla, the bay is a crescent curving behind Cape Honduras, and is about six miles across. It was extensively fortified by the Spanish at several points, and was important in early colonial defense and commerce.

BAIXOS, ISLAS DEL. Alternative form of "Bay Islands," shown on a 1730 Ottens (q.v.) map.

BAKTUN. Twenty katun in Maya notation, or a period of 400 years of 360 days each, hence 144,000 days. See PICTUN, CALABTUN, KINCHILTUN and ALAUTUN.

BALANCE OF PAYMENTS, 1970. (Stated in United States Dollars.)
Imports                              $ 186,500,000
Exports                                165,400,000
Balance of trade                        21,100,000
Freight Insurance                       16,400,000
Balance on Current Accounts             50,600,000
Balance on Capital Accounts             41,200,000
Tourism                                  6,000,000
Foreign Investment Income               14,800,000

BALBOA, VASCO NUÑEZ DE. Discoverer of the Pacific Ocean, who nominally governed Honduras when it was part of Castilla de Oro (q.v.).

BANANA. This tropical fruit shares with coffee the distinction of being a major Honduran export. Since the total economy is based upon agriculture, the banana culture is a central factor. Geographically centered on the north coast, the greatest development was under the stimulus of firms from the United States in the final years of the 19th century. Honduras was typical among the so-called "Banana Republics." The economic impact of the foreign-owned banana firms had political implications, with accusations of undue influence, etc. The nation's first general labor strike occurred in 1954. Following the strike, increasing demands and added governmental restrictions affected operation of the companies. Labor unrest continued through the 1960's, and the 1969 war with El Salvador affected banana production.

    The north coast of Honduras produces almost 40 per cent of the Gross National Product, with bananas foremost in this figure. Fifty per cent of all exports by value are bananas. Two large foreign-owned companies dominate. Standard Fruit Company is centered around La Ceiba, United

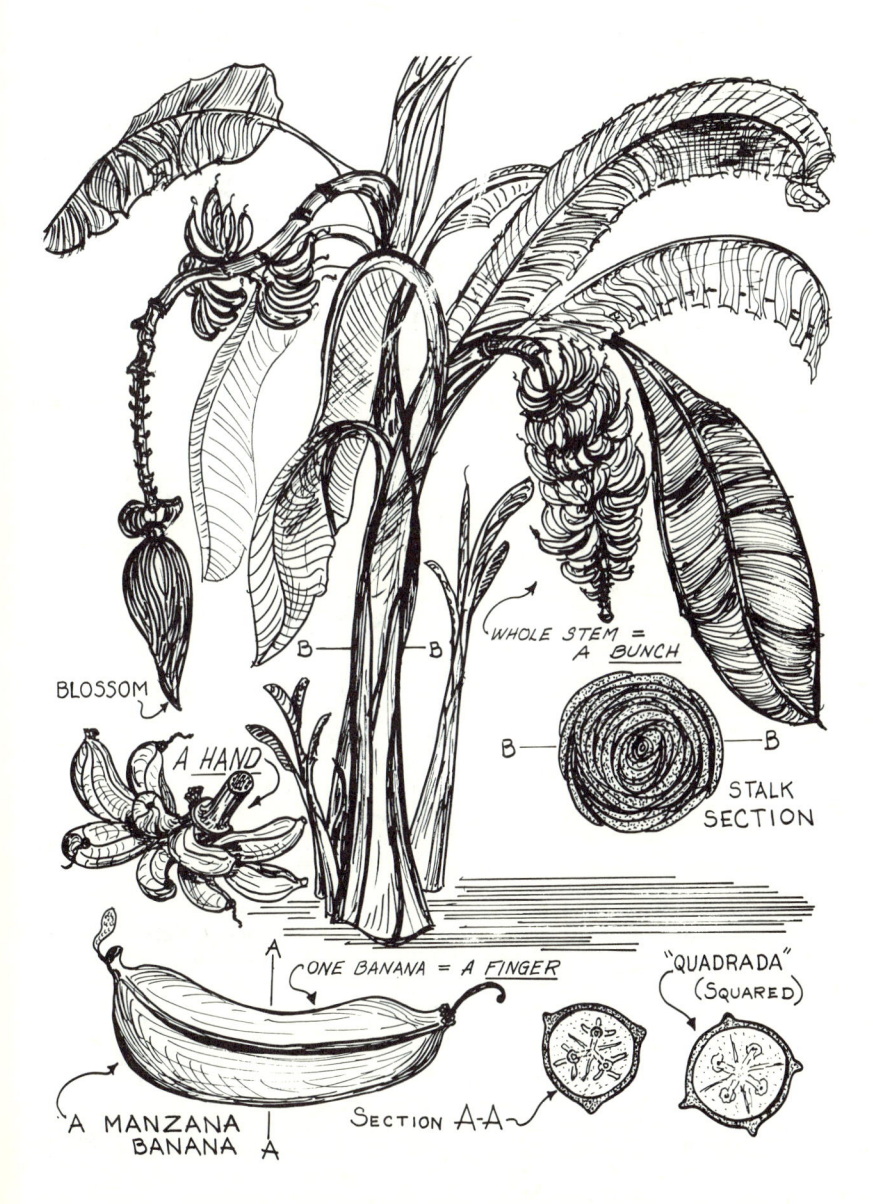

BANANAS: The stately broad-leaved plants provide a major export.

Fruit in the Puerto Cortés-Tela-La Lima triangle. Programs and development of disease-resistant varieties by these companies have been significant in the banana industry and, in consequence, within the whole Honduran economy.

In 1968, 1,250,000 metric tons of bananas were produced. A hurricane dropped production to 1,000,000 tons in 1969. The 1968 level was to be reached again in 1973. Honduras is one of the three largest banana exporters to the United States. West Germany gets as much as 24 per cent of all Honduran exports, bananas, lumber and coffee being the main items. It must be summarized that bananas are probably the single most significant item in the Honduran economy.

The disastrous hurricane "Fifi" (q.v.) of 1974 nearly destroyed the North Coast banana plantings, with two years being required to return the plantings to near normal production.

This fruit is so significant to the whole area that a word on its origins is appropriate. The banana was brought to the new world by a Spanish priest, Padre Tomás de Berlanga, who came to Santo Domingo in 1516. Known in India in the time of Alexander the Great, 4th century B.C., the fruit had come to Africa where the Portugese found it on the Guinea Coast in 1482. Father Tomás brought his plants from the Canary Islands. Bananas are rich in vitamins and minerals.

BANANA INDUSTRY, ORIGINATOR IN CENTRAL AMERICA see KEITH, MINER COOPER

BANANA PRODUCTION, HONDURAS AND CENTRAL AMERICA, 1974. The "Banana War" (q.v.) emphasizes the significance of this agricultural product in the Western Caribbean. Production levels in 1974 were as follows (in 40-pound crates):

| | |
|---|---|
| Honduras | 50 million crates |
| Costa Rica | 55 million crates |
| Guatemala | 15 million crates |
| Panama | 30 million crates |
| Nicaragua | 5 million crates |
| Ecuador | 73 million crates |

Note that only Ecuador and Costa Rica exceeded Honduras. The effects of hurricane "Fifi" are not included here.

"BANANA REPUBLICS" see BANANAS

BANANA WAR - 1974. The tax on bananas (q.v.) of early 1974 caused developing unrest, with the Standard Fruit Co. accused of plotting against three governments, and the countries themselves having dissension among themselves. The press began early to term the whole matter the "Great Banana War of 1974."

The Union of Banana Exporting Countries (q.v.) was formed by Honduras, Nicaragua, Panama, Costa Rica, Colombia, Ecuador and Guatemala to provide mutual protection for their important agricultural product, bananas. The tax imposed was levied by each country, but in June 1974, it had only been collected by Panama, Honduras and Costa Rica. Guatemala had passed the law, but at that date had not collected the tax. Ecuador meanwhile left the organization. Nicaragua and Colombia were hesitant about the tax. It was in Honduras that Standard Fruit deliberately destroyed 100,000 cases of pineapples, 25,000 of grapefruit and 10,000 of coconuts to apply pressure to the government to repeal the tax. They also threatened to remove their Honduran-Panama operation to Ecuador. Overshadowing the uncertainties of the "Banana War" for Honduras was the late September 1974 hurricane "Fifi" (q.v.) which destroyed most of the crop.

BANASSA. Name of the Island of "Guanaja" or "Bonacca" as shown on the sketch map by Bartholomew Columbus. He also has a note on the map, "aque [sic] cacao," or "here is cacao," for the chocolate (cacao beans) which was used as money by the Indians of the coast. As Samuel Eliot Morison says in following the voyages of Columbus, "Bonacca is a handsome island."

BANCAHSA see BANCO DE LA CAPITALIZADORA HONDUREÑA

BANCO ATLANTIDA. A principal commercial bank in Honduras, founded in La Ceiba in 1913. In 1970 there were foreign branches in Guatemala and Nicaragua, nine Honduran branches, five agencies and a rural mobile unit. The resources topped $30,000,000 and the deposits were almost half of the total commercial deposits in the country. A controlling share of this bank was bought in 1967 by the Chase Manhattan Bank of New York.

BANCO DE EL AHORRO HONDUREÑO. The third largest commercial bank and the largest domestically controlled savings bank in Honduras.

BANCO DE LA CAPITALIZADORA HONDUREÑA. A bank started in 1948 by Salvadorean interests as a savings bank; it became a full commercial bank in 1968.

BANCO DE LAS TRABAJADORES. A bank of mixed private and state ownership which began in 1967 to serve credit needs of small businessmen, peasants, and laborers.

BANCO DE OCCIDENTE. A small, regional bank located in Copán.

BANCO HIPOTECARIO. Mortgage bank formed in 1969 by a group of San Pedro Sula businessmen, with the purpose of financing middle class home construction.

BANCO MUNICIPAL AUTONOMO see AUTONOMOUS MUNICIPAL BANK

BANCO NACIONAL DE FOMENTO see NATIONAL DEVELOPMENT BANK

BANDERA DE LA RAZA, DIA DE. The "day of the flag of the race" was chosen by an agreement with a Uruguayan Commission as the third of August of each year. This is the anniversary of the day when Columbus sailed from Palos for America the first time. The "Flag of the Race" was designed by a Uruguayan Captain, Angel Camblor. The agreement was dated June 15, 1933.

BANK OF AMERICA. In 1966 this international banking corporation opened commercial banks in San Pedro Sula and Tegucigalpa.

BANK OF HONDURAS. The "Banco de Honduras" has six branches in the country, and is the second largest commercial bank. First National City Bank of New York holds a controlling share of the total stock, following a 1965 affiliation.

BANK OF LONDON AND MONTREAL. Commercial bank with two branches in San Pedro Sula, one in La Ceiba, and one in Tegucigalpa. It is Honduras' fourth largest commercial bank.

BARAHONA, JOSE MARIA. Native Honduran who became a general in the Salvadoran army in 1876, and who had to flee to Nicaragua when the Salvadoran President Rafael Zaldívar was overthrown. Later he was the leader of an unsuccessful coup against another Salvadoran President, Francisco Menéndez. Barahona was one of those leaders who in crossing the Central American National borders with partisan conflict contributed to a century of political instability.

BARAHONA, SOTERO. Dr. Barahona was Minister of Public Instruction under the Bonilla Government in 1906 when the Second Code of Public Instruction was promulgated. See CODES OF PUBLIC INSTRUCTION.

BARBA AMARILLA. The dangerous poisonous snake known as ferde-lance. This species is widely distributed in the mountain areas of Honduras.

BARBARATTE. Alternate spelling used in the early 19th century of the Bay Island now known as "Barbareta."

BARBARETA ISLAND. About three miles long, and also known as Barbaratte, this Bay Island lies between Roatán and Guanaja, along a line of reefs which extend at varying depths between the two islands. Only a mile or two off the northeasternmost tip of Roatán, the island relates to that largest of the

Bay islands rather than to the somewhat farther Guanaja or the far distant Utila.

BARD, SAMUEL A. Pen name of Ephraim George Squier (q.v.) when he wrote Waikna; or Adventures on the Mosquito Shore in 1855.

BARK BEETLE. A pest which threatened Honduran pine forests in the 1960's, and which was target of a campaign of Civic Action (q.v.) by the armed forces.

BARNICA, PAUL. Private secretary of President Ramón Cruz (q.v.) at the time of the coup d'etat which ousted Cruz, December 4, 1961. Barnica announced that Cruz was relatively undisturbed about the events and would resume the practice of law. He also announced the tranquillity of Tegucigalpa.

BARRA DE AGUAN. The bar, at the mouth of the Rio Aguán, which empties into the Caribbean just east of Trujillo.

BARRA DE BRUS LAGUNA. Bay at the opening from the Brus Laguna (q.v.) or Brewer's Lagoon to the sea, the lagoon being fed by three minor rivers, the Tuas (q.v.), Sigre (q.v.), and Amátingui (q.v.).

BARRA DE CARATASCA. 1) The entrance of the huge Laguna de Caratasca (q.v.), inland body of salt water on the northeast coast.
2) A small village at the bar where the Laguna de Caratasca (q.v.) enters the Caribbean. There is a shrimp fishing establishment now in this location, near Puerto Lempira.

BARRA PATUCA. The bar at the mouth of the Río Patuca (q.v.), and also the village at the same site. Also known as Butukamaya.

BARRAS. Miskito chieftain of the early 1800's on the northeast coast of Honduras.

BARRERA, CLAUDIO. Pen-name of Vicente Alemán (hijo), born in La Ceiba in 1912. He founded the literary magazines Surco and Letras de America in Tegucigalpa in 1949. In 1954 he won the Ramón Rosa prize for literature, and has published works in Honduras and El Salvador.

BARRIOS LEAL, JACERITO DE. A general who organized an expedition against the Lacandón Maya during his incumbency as governor, 1688-95. He was the center of dissension and strife, and after a three-year residency in 1691-94 was reinstated. Beside the expedition against the Lacandones, he led an early penetration into the country of the Itzaes, in the Petén area.

BARRIOS OF TEGUCIGALPA. The capital city has a number of suburban barrios: Buenos Aires, El Bosque, Las Colinas, Viera (site of the Viera hospital), El Eden, and Casamata, all to the northeast. In the southeast are the barrios San Rafael and El Guanacaste.

BARSINO. The cross of a Coyote (indigenous Lobo) male with a Mulata (q.v.) female. See RACIAL MIXTURES.

BARVA. Marine parasites which rapidly destroy ship timbers in tropical waters. They were especially bad in the northern Honduran ports.

BATRES, CESAR A. Lawyer Batres became Foreign Minister in the new cabinet of General López Arellano (q.v.) following the December 4, 1972 coup d'etat.

BAY ISLANDS. Long a subject of armed and diplomatic tugs of war, this island group north of the central Honduran mainland, about 30 to 40 miles offshore, is a place of great natural beauty with its wooded hills and cay-rimmed reefs. Occupied by the British "Baymen," by Dutch and French pirates, by Caribs exiled there by the British, the islands were a target for freebooters as late as William Walker's (q.v.) advent in 1860. In 1969 the island population was near 10,000, 80 per cent black. See also GUANAJA, SANTA ELENA, MURAT, BARBARETA, ROATAN, and COLONY OF THE BAY ISLANDS.

BAY ISLANDS COLONY see COLONY OF THE BAY ISLANDS

BAY ISLANDS DEPARTMENT. Three large islands (Roatán, Guanaja and Utila) and three smaller ones (Santa Elena, Morat, and Barbareta), plus numerous reefs and cays, comprise this unique waterborne department parallel to the North coast of Honduras and 30 to 40 miles out from the mainland in the Bay of Honduras in the Caribbean Sea. The total area of the islands is just over 100 square miles. There are four municipios, and the cabacera is Roatán, on the island of that name. The islands of the Bay of Fonseca are not departmentalized, but are simply offshore territories; thus only the Bay Islands among Honduras' major insular possessions comprise a separate department. Perhaps this is especially appropriate due to the colorful and varied political history and ownership during almost 500 years. The population of the cabaceras was 5,098 in 1973, and of the rest of the island area 5,285, for a total of 10,383. There are no hospitals. The Bay Island area is known for fishing, shrimping, and boatbuilding activities, and has a delightful climate. The offshore reefs are a special feature, crowned with many inhabited but tiny cays. These islands have been declared an urban area, thus permitting foreign ownership of property. Since they are Caribbean beauty spots, a growing group of

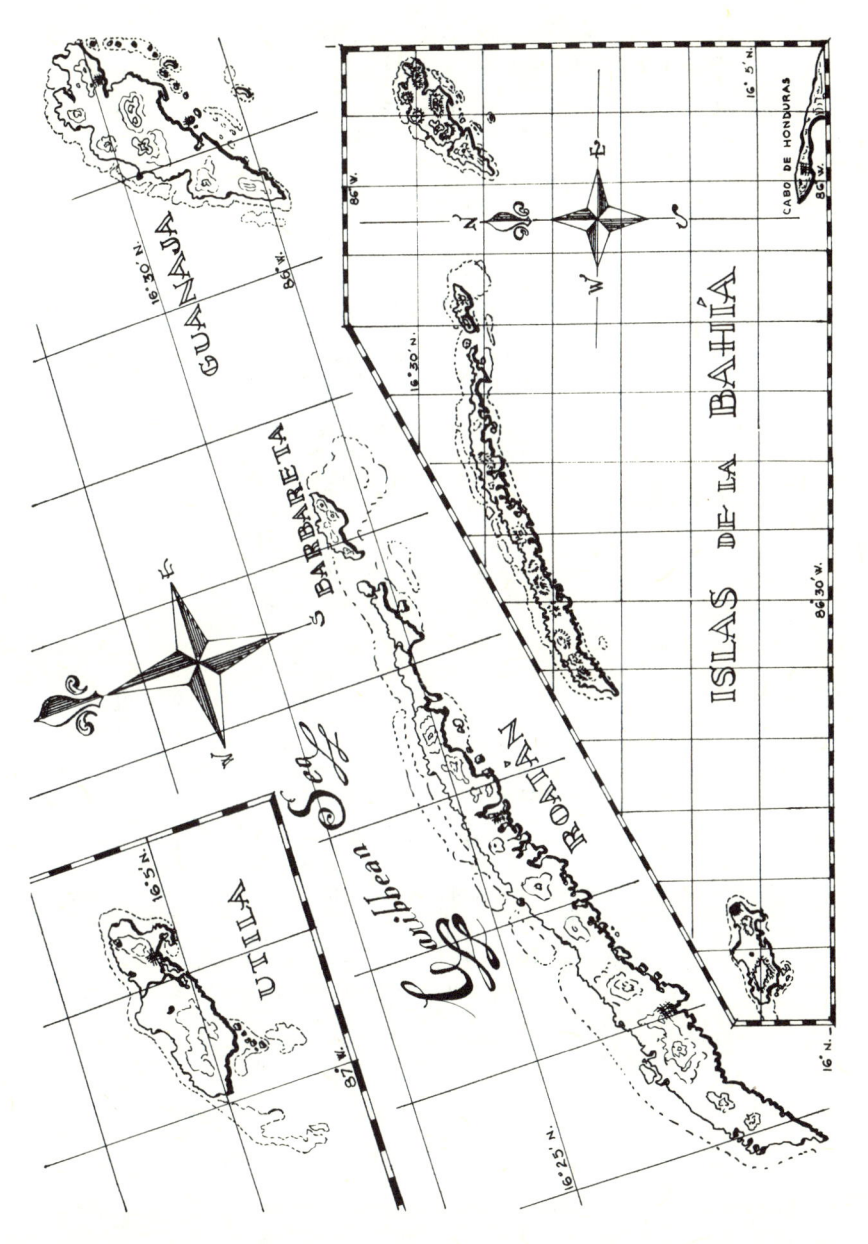

ISLAS DE LA BAHIA: The oft-disputed Bay Islands, off the north coast of Honduras.

yachtsmen and connoisseurs is taking advantage of the ownership provision. See also ROATAN, GUANAJA, UTILA, etc.

BAYMEN. British logwood cutters (and petty pirates) who occupied areas of the Bay of Honduras. Some of them retired to the Bay Islands following Rosado's (q.v.) 1779 attack.

BCIE. The Central American Bank for Economic Integration. This bank was approving credits of $40,000,000 for reconstruction programs in Honduras in late 1974.

BEALS, CARLETON. North American liberal journalist and exponent of causes who, through Froylán Turcios (q.v.), received escort from Honduras to reach Sandino (q.v.) for an interview. Beals wrote a good deal about Sandino, and in turn his writings influenced some North American opinion in favor of Sandino, a campaign to this purpose being waged by radicals and liberals. Beals understood Sandino's lasting impact on Latin America better than did other writers. See AREVALO.

BEANS. An important food crop, as beans and rice are staple fare; the 1970 crop was around 53,000 metric tons. Beans are often exported to nearby crowded El Salvador.

BELLS, LEGEND OF. In caves near the villages of Naco and Cofradia, about ten miles from San Pedro Sula, there are found from time to time little copper bells like sleigh-bells or little rattles, and they are often engraved with a solemn Indian face. The ancient legend was that a girl named Hope, or Xquina, was courted by a youth, Silvestre, who was very addicted to strong drink--the fermented "chicha" (q.v.) of the region. When Xquina asked Silvestre to bring her a copper bell, supposed to be miraculous, she agreed to marry him if he found one. He came back weeks later with two bells, and she made a wish then and there upon the bells that he would not return to drinking. Silvestre laughed at her, and went off to his "chicha." But lightning struck near him, and when he dived into the water to escape it, a great crocodile attacked him. This experience cured Silvestre and they lived happily ever after. However, they added to their Catholic ceremony of marriage a litany in the language of Xquina-- Chorti and Lenca languages are still spoken in the area.

BEN. Thirteenth day of the Maya month; meaning "wool."

BENDAÑA HIJO, JESUS see AGUIRRE, SALVADOR

BENK, EL. In Gracias a Dios Department, this village is on the northern edge of the Río Coco delta, and is named for the river by one of the numerous appellations of that stream; Benks, Wanks, or Wangke, one of the Sumo-Miskito words applied to the big river. There is an airport nearby at Raya, a close neighbor village.

BENNATON, JOSE ABRAHAM. Lawyer Bennaton was made Minister of Economy in the cabinet of General Oswaldo López Arellano (q.v.) following the coup of December 4, 1972. It was alleged that Bennaton received the bribe from United Brands which resulted in scandal and the ousting of López Arellano as President in May 1975. See also BLACK, ELI M.

BEQUIPE. A vine from which poisonous sap is used to stupefy fish and render them easy to catch.

BERGHAUS. Prussian geographer, compiler of a Physikalischen Atlas published in 1840, which E. G. Squier (q.v.) states was the best representation of Honduras (in the map of Central America) available up to that time--in fact, until his (Squier's) own production following 1853, published in his Notes on Central America.

BERMUDEZ, ANTONIO see AGUIRRE, SALVADOR

BERMUDEZ, JUAN. Owner of one of Columbus' four ships when in 1502 he discovered the coast of Honduras, Bermúdez later gave his name to the then uninhabited mid-Atlantic island group which he discovered in 1515. The ship "Santiago" was nicknamed "Bermuda" after her owner.

BERMUDEZ MILLA, HECTOR. Poet born in San Pedro Sula in 1927, student in the National University and press attaché in the Honduran embassy in Washington, D.C., in 1957. Active on such periodicals as Surco and Honduras Literaria.

BERMUDEZ, RUBEN. Poet and author of "Mi Poema al Río Ulúa," Bermúdez was born in Juticalpa in 1891, studied at the Massachusetts Institute of Technology in the United States, and was at one time superintendent of the National Railroad and deputy to Congress, as well as Mayor of San Pedro Sula.

BERROSPE, GABRIEL SANCHEZ DE. Governor from 1696 to 1701. The dispute which began under oidor and interim governor Escals (q.v.) continued and deepened during Berrospe's term. Civil War broke out between Berrospistas and Tequelies (the latter following Francisco Gómez de la Madrid, who was visitador). Berrospe had to flee, and Juan Jerómino Heduordo finished the term as oidor. Berrospe fortified the Petén Garrison in the remote jungle of the Itzá.

BERTRAND, FRANCISCO. Dr. Bertrand became President as a result of mediation by the United States (see TACOMA, U.S.S.) and took office March 28, 1971 after the long conflict between General Dávila (q.v.) and Manuel Bonilla (q.v.). In 1912 he was succeeded by Bonilla. As Vice President he served again following Bonilla's death, from March 20, 1913 to July 28, 1915. Again as Constitutional President, he served from February 1, 1916 to September 9, 1919, when a revolt chased him out of the country.

BETANCOURT, IVAN. A secular priest from Medellín, Colombia, who disappeared June 21, 1975, in Olancho department, during an alleged army crackdown on a peasant march from Olancho to the capital, Tegucigalpa. The march was to be for 310 miles and to be participated in by 12,000 peasants. Two landowners of Olancho were arrested in connection with the disappearance; Manuel Celaya and Carlos Bahr. Three military men were also in custody as a result of the affair. Betancourt had been removed from a bus along with two Honduran nuns. His body was found later in a well.

BIEN PATA. "Bean food," a special preparation which is often used in Mosquitia on festive occasions. It is used also as an exchange for extra labor, on the occasion of "pana-pana" (q.v.).

BIOTIC PROVINCES see LIFE ZONES

BIRDS. In brief listing of birds to be found in Central America the following birds may be identified; First, <u>American Types</u> of both continents:

| | | |
|---|---|---|
| grebes | dippers | cuckoos |
| cormorants | vireos | rails |
| pelicans | orioles | plovers |
| hawks | jays | gulls |
| falcons | blackbirds | terns |
| ospreys | | pigeons |
| vultures | | owls |
| herons | | kingfishers |
| ibises | | swifts |
| ducks | | hummingbirds |
| quail | | thrushes |
| swallows | | mockingbirds |
| flycatchers | | wrens |
| warblers | | |

Second, <u>South American types</u>:

| | |
|---|---|
| tinamons | trogons |
| storks | quetzal (a trogon) |
| flamingos | |
| guans | motmots |
| limpkins | puff-birds |
| sun bitterns | Jacamars |
| sun grebes | barbets |
| jacanas | toucans |
| parrots | tapa culos |
| macaws | ant birds |
| potoos | wood hewers |

Second, South American types (cont.):

manakins                                          honey creepers

Third, North American types:

turkeys             creepers           chickadees
wax wings           titmice

BLACK, ELI M. Chairman of United Brands Co. who fell to his death from the 44th floor of his Manhattan office. It was alleged that the 53-year-old executive's suicide was related to revelations concerning a $1,250,000 bribe paid by United Brands to Honduran officials (see LOPEZ ARELLANO, OSWALDO). The bribe was admitted by the company, but Lopez' part in the matter was never clearly defined. The scandal, however, caused him to lose the Presidency.

BLACK CARIBS. The Carib Indians brought to the Bay Islands from Dominica in the eighteenth century have mixed with blacks to form what is actually a fourth "mestizo" racial group to add to the Sambos (Indian-negro), Miskitos (Sumu-pirate) and Creoles (negro-Spanish-Indians) of the Mosquito Coast. Many "Black Caribs" are on the North Coast of Honduras.

BLACK RIVER. Most important of the British 18th century settlements in Honduras. On the present Río Tinto (Río Negro) the British site was selected by William Pitt, who came to the Mosquito Shore from Bermuda. Homes, plantations, and trading posts were established. Pine timber for masts and spars, wild bananas, sarsaparilla, cacao, logwood, and sugar planting provided occupations and trade. By 1759 the Black River settlement had 3,706 inhabitants. The main settlement was 16 miles up-river from the mouth. The shoremen lived on cattle and rum and casaba. Their trade amounted to $65,000 by 1759. They finally discovered that contraband trade was most profitable of all, and a considerable illegal trade on the northern Honduras coast increased during the first half of the 18th century, conducted by these shoremen.

BLACK RIVER CAMPAIGN, 1782 see TRUJILLO, BASE ... 1782

BLANCO Y ROJO. Political periodical headed by Guillermo Bustillo Reina (q.v.).

BOGRAN, FRANCISCO. Dr. Bográn served as chief executive under the title of President, Second Designate, from October 5, 1919 to February 1, 1920. His brief incumbency served to allow elections which placed General Rafael López Gutiérrez (q.v.) in power. Bográn succeeded the Council of Ministers, including Salvador Aguirre (q.v.), which had presided after Bertrand (q.v.) had to flee from the revolt which toppled him.

BOGRAN, LUIS. General Bográn held supreme power either as one of a designated council of ministers or as president six times between May 1883, and November 1891. (See GUTIERREZ, ENRIQUE.) He was one of the ministerial council with Gutiérrez and Dr. Alvarado Mangano from May 1883 to November 30, 1883. He then became Constitutional President from November 30, 1883 to August 30, 1884. Then another ministerial council ruled from August 1884 to November 1884 when Bográn was president again from November 17, 1884 to March 21, 1885. A short term of "Presidente por Ley," minister Poinciano Leiva (former president), intervened from March to June 1885, and Bográn once more held office until April 1886. Leiva once more served April 15, 1886 to August 28 of the same year, and then Bográn served out a term until November 1887, and succeeded himself by re-election. He died in office before his term ended in 1891, Leiva once more serving from November 30 until February 9, 1893. General Bográn managed to keep reasonable calm in Honduras for the seven years he was involved, and, as was important early in his term of office, kept on good terms with Barrios, the Guatemalan strong man.

BONACA. Alternate form of the name of the Bay Island, "Guanaja," as shown on Squier's Map of Honduras and San Salvador (1854) (q.v.).

BONILLA, MANUEL. Having received most votes in the 1903 election against Sierra (q.v.), Bonilla led a march on Tegucigalpa and in effect seized the government, upon which event in April he was declared president by Congress. He served until February 25, 1907. General Bonilla was again elected President in 1912 and served until his death on March 20, 1913. Manuel Bonilla, like Policarpo Bonilla (q.v.), was an active president who revised civil, military, and penal codes, made some moves toward developing roads, and negotiated reduction of European debts which had been incurred as loans for railroad building in the 1867-1870 period, under the Medina (q.v.) administration and others at that time.

Bonilla also stimulated a new constitution of 1906 by calling a constituent assembly. He fell, however, because of differences with the government of Guatemala and with the vigorous regime of strongman José Santos Zelaya, who ruled Nicaragua from 1893 to 1909. In 1906 Guatemala invaded Honduras, and later the same year a lop-sided treaty by Honduras with El Salvador and Guatemala offended Nicaragua, and the Nicaraguan army entered Honduras and helped local leaders to force Bonilla out.

BONILLA, POLICARPO. Dr. Bonilla became the candidate of a new liberal party in 1891. The party under his leadership protested the election of 1891 which placed former president Leiva (q.v.) in office. Leiva was forced to resign by 1893, and a year later a revolt aided by Nicaraguan forces put the government in Bonilla's hands. At once he called a constituent assembly, and was made Provisional President. The assembly drafted a new Constitution and under its provisions Bonilla became constitutional president on February 1, 1895, serving a four-year term until February 1, 1899. Bonilla managed to keep the peace and to institute some needed reforms. He did depend heavily on the external support of foreign powers, but his revision of civil, mining, penal, military, and commercial codes were monuments to the regime. A pact uniting Honduras, El Salvador, and Nicaragua was signed in 1895 but the union was destroyed by a Salvadorean revolt in 1898. Bonilla's term was considered one of the most productive of those during the 19th century.

BONITO PEAK. Pico Bonito is part of the Cerros de Cangrejal (q.v.) mountain complex just behind La Ceiba, and is around 8,000 feet altitude.

BONNET, STEDE. Major Bonnet of Barbados was known as a "gentleman pirate" who took up piracy in 1717. With his sloop, the Revenge, of 10 guns and a crew of 70, he cruised the Bay of Honduras in late 1717 until his meeting with Edward Teach (q.v.). Bonnet was hanged on December 10, 1718, for his piracies.

BORDER CULTURE, 1927-1934 (Sandino period). During these years of the Sandino (q.v.) War in Nicaragua, the southern border of Honduras in the area of the Cordillera de Depilto, and in the state of El Paraiso just south of the town of that name, became a major hide-out area for the considerable Sandino guerrilla forces. The border people had "little respect for boundaries or laws," as one scholar puts it. They had been tossed back and forth over centuries by governments of both Honduras and Nicaragua, and the area had become a haven for bandits and smugglers. The natives of the area often had marginal small farms. They were attracted to Sandino's flamboyancy, and served as a source of food and shelter for his forces. Besides, they comprised an intelligence system in giving him information about movements of the enemy. They were the "sea" in which, according to Mao Tse Tung's guerrilla doctrines, the warrior "fish" could swim. Sandino's famous stronghold, "El Chipote," was right up against the Honduran border. Arms smuggling was rife, with the Honduran side a major delivery point.

BORDER INCIDENT, 1961. The delicate Honduran-Nicaraguan border dispute, ostensibly settled first in 1906 by arbitration and then confirmed in 1960, broke out in minor form when two people were killed on the Nicaraguan side of the border. Honduras apologized, and Nicaragua expressed regret for the student demonstrations against Honduras which had taken place in downtown Managua. The conciliatory mood was in contrast to the events of 1957 and those on many earlier occasions.

BORDER REVOLTS, 1920-1921. Unrest along the Honduran-Nicaraguan border in these years caused the United States to send 10,000 rifles, some machine guns, and millions of rounds of ammunition to the Nicaraguan government. Honduran Liberals had been accused of participating in these uprisings. Years later many of these arms showed up among adherents of Agusto Sandino (q.v.). Representatives of Honduras, Nicaragua and El Salvador met to attempt to stop the uprisings, and each agreed to prevent political immigrants from fomenting invasions. The strongman of Nicaragua during this period was Emiliano Chamorro, the "Lion of Nicaragua."

BORDONE'S MAPS. In his Isolaris, published in Venice in 1528, Bordone shows the central American coast but in such ill-defined form that it only indicated existence, not any degree of surveying. Honduras was not recognizable.

BOSTA. Liberal weekly shut down by the Lozano regime in 1956. The editors were jailed for subversion.

BOTILTUK. In Gracias a Dios Department, a typical one of about a hundred tiny villages, usually located along streams for transportation by dugout canoe, since the rivers are the only roads.

BOUNDARY DISPUTE, GUATEMALA. Honduras had boundary questions from earliest times, partly because of the remoteness of her mountain fastnesses. Like the Nicaraguan boundary dispute, the "Territorio in Litigio" (q.v.), the Guatemalan boundary problem centered about the remoteness and general inaccessibility of the area. In the colonial period when the whole territory was under the audiencia of Guatemala, the boundary between Honduras and Guatemala was internal and provincial, and was considered to follow the crest of the Copán Mountain range. There was a diocesan boundary of 1786 which was confirmed by an 1845 agreement, but the lack of surveys left the exact geographical location still in question. Honduran companies in the early 1900's began to operate in the Motagua River Valley, causing a resurgence of boundary claims by both countries. U.S. mediation was offered and rejected in 1923, and armed conflict was imminent over the matter in 1928. In 1931 a tribunal of arbitration met in Washington, D.C. A survey resulted in the agreed boundary by April 1933. Maps state at the line, "Laudo de Washington de 23 de Enero de 1933."

BRASILIANO, ROCHE. A pirate of the Bay of Honduras and the Caribbean in the 17th century.

BREA. Pine pitch used for caulking ships and sealing wine casks, a favorite export to Peru in the 17th century. A quintal of pitch sold on the Gulf of Fonseca for 20 reales brought six times as much in the Peruvian vineyards. By 1647 the trade had reached 30,000 quintals annually.

BREWER'S LAGOON. Now known as Brus Laguna, this was the English name used for this Northeast coastal lagoon in the 1850's, when there were still major influences from the English settlers in the whole coastal area. The name was probably much older. The lagoon was also the site of Fort Dalling (q.v.). The Brus is simply a corruption.

BRICEÑO, FRANCISCO. During the period when the Audiencia was in Panama (see LANDACHO, JUAN) there was nevertheless necessity for a local governor and captain general on the spot in Guatemala, and Briceño was assigned from 1565 to 1569. When the designated successor, Juan Bustos de Villegas, died en route to Guatemala, Briceño continued ad interim for four more years, until 1573.

BRICIO, PEDRO. Colonel and Commandant of the garrison at Cabo Gracias a Dios where Gálvez (q.v.) hoped to settle some Galician-Asturian colonists in 1787.

BRITISH-AMERICAN RIVALRY IN CENTRAL AMERICA see RIVALRY, BRITAIN AND THE UNITED STATES

BRITISH CLAIMS - 1848. Great Britain claimed not only the Bay Islands but also about a third of the present Honduran territory as part of the extended Mosquito Protectorate (q.v.). The claim line extended south from just east of Cape Honduras near Trujillo to the point where the Río Coco becomes the border between Honduras and Nicaragua, in general a north-south line. By 1852, British claims affected no mainland territory of Honduras, only the long-disputed Bay Islands.

BRUS LAGUNA. 1) Originally called "Brewer's Lagoon" (q.v.) from the time of occupation of British dyewood cutters in the 17th century, this large coastal lagoon, about six by 12 miles in dimension, is located on the northeast coast in the center of the long Gracias a Dios Department's coastline, and from its location is a part of "La Mosquitia."

2) Cabacera of the municipio of the same name, and located on the namesake lagoon, it is one of only a half-dozen settlements of any size in the vast department of Gracias a Dios. There is an air service, but otherwise access is by water. Actually the village is on the northwest

corner of the delta of the Río Patuca, and there is internal access to the river by channels of the delta.

BUESO, FRANCISCO. One of the council of ministers who ruled from March 10 to April 30, 1924 following the Gutiérrez (q.v.) unrest. The others were Dr. José María Ochoa Velásquez, Dr. Rómulo E. Durón, Dr. José María Sandoval, General Roque J. López and Marcial Lagos.

BUESO, MONICO. With Francisco Aguilar, Bueso headed the Honduran state on behalf of the Council of Ministers from August 27, 1839 to September 21, 1839. This was the first month or so following breakup of the Central American Federation.

BUESO, SANTIAGO. Just after the turbulent Cabañas (q.v.) administration, Vice President Bueso took over from October 6, 1855 until November 8, 1855. This was during the period of the National War (q.v.) when Santos Guardiola (q.v.) was leading armies against Walker in Nicaragua. See also SCHOOL, FIRST OFFICIAL.

BURGOS, LAWS OF. As early as 1512, Spanish recognition of a necessity to have a code for the specialized purpose of governing native Americans resulted in the thirty-two laws promulgated by King Ferdinand II at Burgos, Spain. The cause of such a recognition was the treatment and enslavement of Indians. The Burgos code limited the number of workers in mining to one-third of a total encomienda, took steps to assure adequate food and shelter, limited working hours, and held the work-year to nine months. The laws were never adequately enforced in the far flung empire, and the maltreatment and exploitation of Indians continued. The laws provide a good example of the major problems faced by Spain in the colonial administration, of her valiant efforts to solve them, but likewise of the difficulties due to the vast geographical expanse involved and the glacial slowness of transport and communication.

BUSTILLO, FELIPE. As Vice-President, Bustillo was in brief power from September 21 to December 2, 1848, while the uprising against Lindo (q.v.) was in progress.

BUSTILLO, JOSE MARIA. President of Honduras immediately following the breakup of the Central American Federation, from August 20, 1839 to August 27 of the same year. This brief term was to be repeated all too frequently in subsequent Honduran annals.

BUSTILLO REINA, GUILLERMO. Born in Comayaguela May 5, 1898, and with a degree in law from the University of Honduras, was Director of the National Press, and of the political paper Blanco y Rojo. He was also Consul General of

Honduras in New York in 1920, and the Administrator of Customs in Puerto Castilla in 1923. Like many other educated Hondurans, he was a poet as well as diplomat and executive.

BUTLER, NATHANIEL. The British captain of the Providence Company (q.v.) who attacked Trujillo in 1639, destroying, killing and taking spoils.

BUTLER, SMEDLEY. Major General of the United States Marine Corps whose extended comments on U.S. interventions in Latin America included, "I helped make Honduras right for American Fruit Companies in 1903." This was expressive of U.S. "dollar diplomacy" during the first third of the 20th century. Butler won a dubious reputation in Latin America during the long occupation of Haiti. The policies upheld were not only dollar-oriented but racist and imperialistic.

BUTUKAMAYA. In Gracias a Dios Department, this is the Sumo-Miskito name for the Barra Patuca, and there is a village called that in Spanish. The location is just west of the Patuca Estuary on the Caribbean.

- C -

CABACERA. The capital of a department or a municipio (q.v.). A rough parallel to departmental cabaceras would be state capitals of the United States of America. Several departments of Honduras are as large as small states of the U.S.A. The cabaceras of municipios might be considered as parallel to county seats in U.S. usage. The municipio and its cabacera frequently bear the same name, and in general the cabacera is the principal population center of the municipio. Frequently, however, in Honduras the cabacera may have fewer than 1,000 people. The population is so concentrated in a few areas that there are many mountains and savannahs quite sparse in settlement.

CABALLERIA. A measure of land used in old Spanish grants and amounting to about 33-1/3 acres, English measure.

CABALLERO DE GONGORA, JUAN ANTONIO. An archbishop and viceroy of New Spain who attempted to work out a plan to win support of Caribs, Sambos, and Miskitos to assure Spanish control over the Mosquito Coast.

CABAN. The seventeenth day of the Maya month; meaning, "land."

CABAÑAS, JOSE TRINIDAD. Constitutional president from March 1, 1852 until October 28, 1852. Cabañas was not acceptable to the conservatives then holding the power balance in Guatemala, due to his liberal beliefs and support. He was defeated by Guatemalan forces in 1855, following a constitutional term once again from December 31, 1853 to October 6, 1855. Meanwhile there had been two provisional incumbencies. (See CASTELLON, FRANCISCO and GOMEZ, FRANCISCO.) Cabañas was followed by Santos Guardiola, arch-conservative. Cabañas was responsible for uprisings in El Salvador, such as the one of 1865, and was a unionist from the time of his service under Francisco Morazán (q.v.).

CABBAGES AND KINGS  see  O. HENRY

CABEI  see  CENTRAL AMERICA BANK FOR ECONOMIC INTEGRATION

CABILDO. The basic town government of Spanish America. The municipal building has come to bear the same name. Police work, taxation, public works, health, sanitation, property matters, wage and price regulation, and general control of the community situation were under the cabildo organization, with officials chosen each year by the ayuntamiento (q.v.). When the central government took over the function, it changed the character and quality of local government. This contributed to a lessening of significance in the later colonial period. The "cabildo abierto" was held as an open meeting, called by the provincial governor, when matters of great gravity were to be dealt with. In this sense the "open" cabildo was advisory to the governor. Cabildo officials were usually two alcaldes ordinarios (municipal judges); an alfares (or ensign); an alguacil (or constable), and from four to twelve regidores (a city commission).

CABINET. Under the 1965 Constitution there are twelve executive departments, each headed by a cabinet minister. The Cabinet sits as a Council of Ministers. The ministries are:
      Government and Justice
      National Defense and Public Security
      Communications and Public Works
      Labor and Social Security
      Natural Resources
      Public Education
      Social Welfare
      Public Health
      Economy
      Treasury
      Foreign Affairs
      Office of the President
These constitutional cabinet posts or departments may be modified by creating others, combining or deleting several. For example, in 1970, the López government operated with ten cabinet posts, with economy and treasury combined in one, and public health and social welfare in another. The cabinet appointees have the same requirements technically as the presidential candidates. They may not be the president's

close relatives, must not be engaged in carrying out government contracts, and must not be indebted to the public treasury. They are required to submit annual reports to congress concerning the activities of their respective departments. Congress cannot force the resignation of a cabinet member without declaring grounds for impeachment. The matter then goes to the Supreme Court.

The cabinet, in effect, is a longer arm of the presidency, and has little real autonomy. Constitutionally, any presidential decrees affecting the departments must be endorsed by the affected cabinet minister. Suspension of constitutional guarantees or the contracting of long-term loans, or such other matters as are held by the President to be of national import, must be approved by a majority vote of the Council of Ministers.

CABO CAMARON. The cape near the Río Tinto entrance in Gracias a Dios department; the point at which the north coast takes its first southeastward trend. It and the Barro Ulua (q.v.), the Cabo de Honduras (q.v.), the Punta Patuca (q.v.), Cabo Falso (q.v.), and Cape Gracias a Dios (q.v.) make up the six "corners" of the Honduran Caribbean coast.

CABO FALSO. A swelling in the coast, considered a "false cape" when seeking to make a land-fall on the much more prominent Cabo Gracias a Dios. The latter is the delta of the Río Coco (q.v.), largest in Central America, while the false cape is the delta of the Río Kruta (q.v.). See also FALSE CAPE.

CABRERA, ANASTASIO. First normal school director in 1891. See NORMAL SCHOOL, FIRST.

CABRERA, JUAN MARQUEZ DE. Governor following Suazo (q.v.) and in the 1650 period.

CABRERA, JUAN PEREZ DE. Named by the Audiencia of Santo Domingo, Cabrera had jurisdiction only on the north coast of Honduras in 1543, due to a royal decree of 1534, even though the Central American Audiencia of Guatemala was in effect under Alonso Maldonado. In 1552-55 he was again governor, under the captaincy-general of López de Cerrato (q.v.).

CACAO. While this important crop had been raised preconquest throughout central America, the 16th century efforts and the 17th and 18th century "booms" were more significant along the Pacific coast than in most of Honduras. The San Pedro Sula area was an early growing region, however, by 1535. Lower parts of river valleys were favored growing areas. Central American native cacao is held to be superior to other varieties, but fragile to handle.

CACAO DRINKS. The Indians of Central America mixed cacao with maize, chile, and achiote for a thin gruel-like drink. They continue to use corn meal or fresh corn paste called "massa" to make a cacao drink. Europeans early added sugar, vanilla, and cinnamon. Various of these drinks are called by such names as tiste or pinolillo.

CACAO PALASTE. A species of cacao.

CACAOTAL. A cacao grove for production.

CACERES, ALONSO. Lieutenant to Francisco Montejo (q.v.) and governor of Honduras in 1539.

CACERES LARA, VICTOR. Poet and editor born in Gracias, Lempira Department, in 1915. Educated in the National University, he was a deputy to the national congress, Honduran Ambassador to Venezuela, and Director General of the Honduran Postal Service. At one time President of the Honduran Press Association, he was editorialist of the daily El Dia of Tegucigalpa, and is known as a historian as well. There are numerous published works of biography, history, and poetry by Cáceres Lara.

CACHO, DON JOSE MARIA. Secretary of State of Honduras in 1838, constructor of a map of that country in 1838, available in manuscript form to Squier (q.v.) in 1853. He was also a writer and observer concerning the Department of Gracias in Honduras, who prepared materials useful to such researchers as Squier in the 19th century. As Commissioner of the Census of 1834 for Gracias Department, he gathered much more data than was developed in other parts of the country.

CACHO, ELIAS see AGUIRRE, JOSE MARIA

CACICAZGO. Chieftaincy, or tribes and territories under the rule of a chief or cacique. Since the word came from Haiti, the general use was probably spread throughout the Caribbean by Spanish conquerors, stemming from that island originally. See CACIQUE.

CACIQUE. A word used widely in Spanish America to denote headman or chief. Of Haitian origin, the word came into the Spanish early, and has come to represent through Latin-America the influential leaders in local politics. The system is called caciquismo (q.v.). (See also CACICAZGO.) The use has become very general. For example, it was used in Spain during the Spanish Civil War of the 1930's, and was essentially synonymous with caudillo.

CACIQUISMO. From the term cacique (q.v.) or chief, this noun represents the system of political bosses, from village, town, or provincial level on up in a hierarchy. While not as common as previously, it is still a familiar pattern in Latin America.

CACM see CENTRAL AMERICAN COMMON MARKET

CADIZ, SPAIN. Ancient Gades of the Greeks, adjacent to Biblical Tarshish (or the kingdom of Tartessus), tied in the work of some scholars to the lost continent of Atlantis, Cádiz from 1774 was the official Spanish port to which Honduran colonial commerce could be directed. The port was changed from Seville due to the far better harbor at Cádiz.

CAFES SUAVES CENTRALES, S. A. DE C. V. A multinational company formed in 1974 to demand higher prices for coffee from world markets, broadly following the example of the Arab oil sheikdoms. Besides Honduras the members are Mexico, Venezuela, Costa Rica, Guatemala, Nicaragua, and the Dominican Republic. Fuausto Cantu Pena, director of Mexico's Coffee Institute, and a major planner in the new organization, had stated that January 1975 would see the new organization in operative order from offices in Mexico City, prepared then to negotiate coffee prices. The 1974 price on the international market varied with coffee quality from $56 to $74 per bag. Colombia and Brazil, two other major coffee producers, will not join the company initially. Venezuela pledged $80 million to finance retention of coffee and thus to peg higher coffee prices to consuming countries.

CAHOON see MANACA

CAJAS DE COMUNIDADES INDIGENAS. Established by the Dominicans in Central America, these "community chests" were a kind of credit union for Indians, but they turned into a species of village cooperative to guard against Spanish and Creole seizures and taxes. They prevailed in sections which retained more of the Indian customs and culture, especially in highland Guatemala and such remote mountain regions as parts of central and western Honduras.

CALABTUN. A Maya calendrical unit, a multiple of 20 Pictún, hence 57,600,000 days. See KINCHILTUN; ALAUTUN.

CALAHUELA see COROSSO

CALDERA. A familiar geographical feature, especially in southern Honduras. A geological term for a crater, frequently the result of subsidence of the top of a volcanic mountain. Largest caldera in the world is in Aso, Japan (over 100 square miles), and best-known in the U.S. is Crater Lake, Oregon. There are probably many old calderas in volcanic mountain regions which have not been thus identified.

**CALDERA, AUGUSTO.** A Nicaraguan General, Commander of volunteers against Sandino (q.v.), who was accused of violating the Honduran border on March 17, 1928. Liberal President of Honduras Vicente Mejía Colindres had just taken office. That border violation and the Las Limas Incident (q.v.) caused strained relationships with Nicaragua and the United States.

**CALEL.** Name given to chiefs in the valley of the Río Chamelicón in the pre-conquest days. These were Maya-related tribesmen.

**CALENDAR, AZTEC.** The Aztec calendar bears a strong relationship to the Maya calendar (q.v.), but due to language differences (Nahuatl versus Maya) the day names differ. They appear in this work under the individual names, and in a list under "Days, Aztec names."

**CALENDAR, MAYA.** The calendar of the Mayas, as evidenced by myriad hieroglyphs at Copán, Honduras, is so accurate and intricate as to elicit wonder and almost to defy description (see illustration). There are references to the calendar in this dictionary. See DAYS, AZTEC NAMES; DAYS, MAYA NAMES; MONTHS, MAYA CALENDAR; TAN, TOZOLKIN, BEKTUN, HAAB, etc.

It is impossible here to go into all the ramifications, but the remarkable nature of the calendrical competence and achievements of Maya astronomer priests is indicated by the following:

    1 Katun equals a solar year multiplied by the 52 year cycle or 18,980 days
    936 Solar (civil) years of 365 days equal 341,640 days
    18 Katuns equal, then, 341,640 days
    1314 Ritual years of 260 days are 341,640 days
    949 Maya years of 360 days (tun) are 341,640 days
    585 Years of the Planet Venus of 584 days each are 341,640 days
    438 Years of the Planet Mars of 780 days each are 341,640 days

There are at least seven other combinations which result in this figure. To tie the sun, Venus, Mars and the ritual years together in such a fashion seems a stunning feat, and many centuries of observations must have passed before this calculation became possible.

**CALENDAR ROUND.** The Maya name for the 52-year cycle of the Maya calendar is lost. The 52 years originates in the manner in which the two Maya calendars interlock. The 360-day calendar (18 months of 20 days each--plus a 5-day month of unlucky days), is paralleled by the 260-day sacred calendar of 13 months of 20 days each. Every date recurs respectively 365 and 265 days apart, that is, on the annual interval, but since every day has two references, one for each calendar,

45 Calendar, Maya

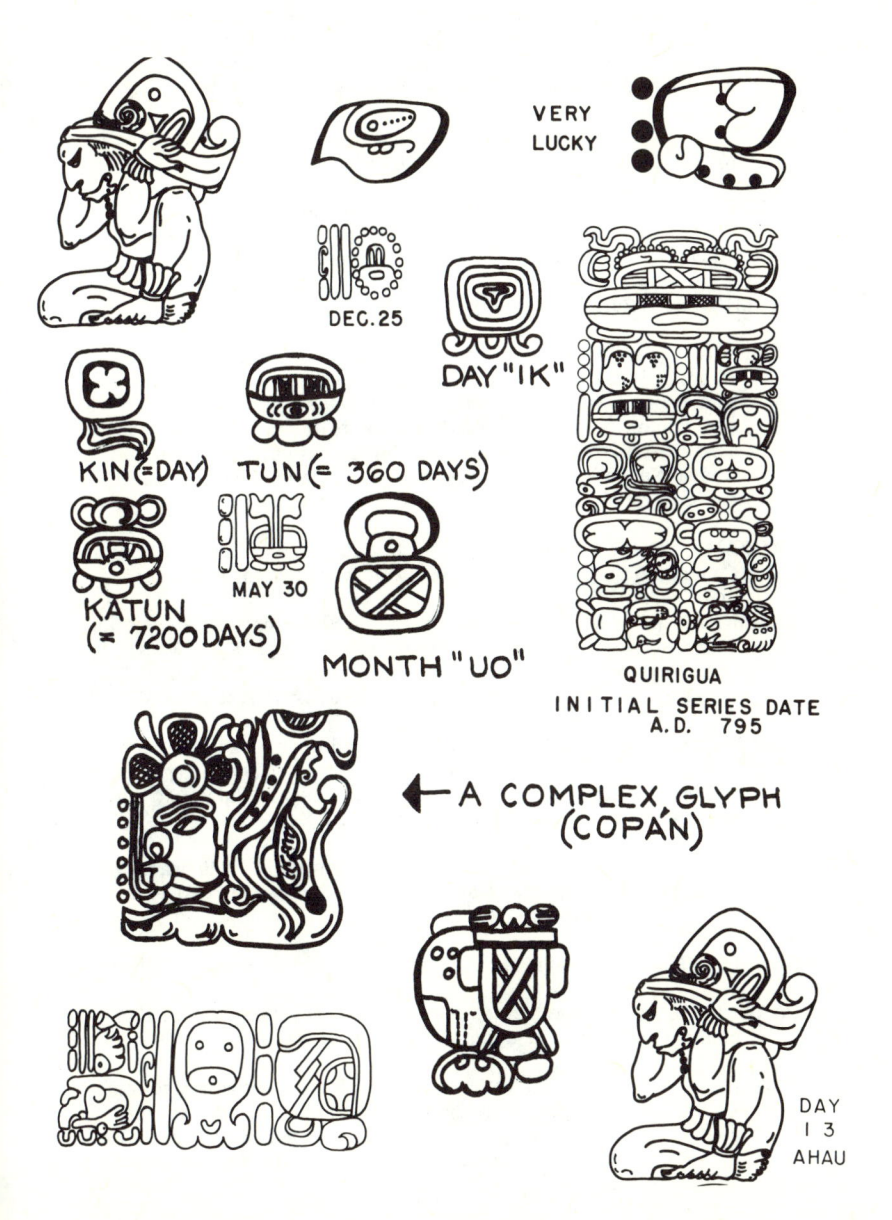

HIEROGLYPHS OF THE MAYA: Some examples of the many glyphs used by the advanced Maya in calendrical and other notation.

Calipash 46

the recurrence of the same double reference for any given day will occur only every 52 years. This is the Calendar Round, a very sacred period among the Maya, when stelae were erected, special ceremonies took place, etc.

CALIPASH. Made from the tender parts of the loggerhead turtle (q.v.), a soup (also called calipee).

CALLI. Third day of the Aztec month; meaning, "house." A "god-house" was "Teocalli." The phonetic resemblance to "theology," "Diós," etc., is of interest.

CALMULLA. Ruins, probably Mayan, near Guajiguero.

CALPULLI. An institution something like a town council which effected local government under the cacique in a cacicazgo. The council was concerned with defense, justice, commerce and trade, as well as related aspects of government. It was a basic unit of social organization in Middle America and was a Nahuatl word. This was the extended family, sometimes a whole clan, confined to a limited geographical area.

CALZADO, JUAN. Captain of the "Nuestra Señora de la Limpia Concepción" (q.v.), when she was wrecked in 1622.

CAMMOCK, SUSSEX. The British Captain, former officer of the Somers Island Company, who in 1633 occupied the Mosquito Coast around Cabo Gracias a Dios, and thereby initiated the turbulent history of that area. See PROVIDENCE COMPANY.

CAMPBELL, ARCHIBALD. British Brigadier who as governor of Jamaica in 1781-84 provided aid to the British Mosquito Shore Colony, sending an expedition under Despard (q.v.) to aid Lawrie (q.v.). See TRUJILLO, BASE ... 1782.

CAMPOY Y PEREZ. Made bishop of Honduras in 1840 when José Trinidad Reyes (q.v.) was reported dead. The political regime was opposed to Reyes.

CANAC. The nineteenth day of the Maya month; meaning "thunder."

CANAFISTULA. A product of the cassia tree, this was a 17th century cathartic in demand in Europe.

CANALES, ALVARO. Artistic director of the Mexican Magazine Variedades Artísticas de México, a Honduran who by the 1970's had lived and painted in Mexico over 30 years. He painted a large Tegucigalpa bank mural; his themes bear the character of a social commentary.

CANALIZATION, ULUA AND BLANCO RIVERS. An ambitious project proposed in 1882 and signed by representatives of the Honduran government, the plan was advanced by George W.

Shears and Dr. M. G. R. Fritz Gaertner (q.v.). They agreed to improve the channels of the two rivers, cleaning them out and "canalizing perfectly" to the greatest extent of navigability, and to place on the rivers a steamboat or steamboats as might be necessary to the commerce developed. They also agreed to bring in immigrants and to establish population centers in the zone of the two rivers; to maintain the steamers, etc. For their efforts, they were to receive about 1200 acres of state-owned lands. They would also get mineral rights, and could import necessary machinery duty-free. The contract was to be void if a steamboat did not appear within a year.

CANNON ISLAND. A small island in Brewer's Lagoon where Edward Trelawney (q.v.) built a fortification in 1742. It was at the same time that he strengthened Roatán (q.v.) as a military base, establishing New Port Royal with a fortified harbor. Belize, Bluefields, and Black River bar were fortified at the same time. Cannon Island was also the site of a stockade put up by Hodgson (q.v.) during the early 1700's.

CANOE. A word which seems to have derived from the eastern Caribbean Arawak tongue, and which from the time of Columbus has been given to lightweight indigenous craft--English: "canoe." The canoa of Honduras is now essentially extinct. Relatively small, it has not the shape or capacity of the other dugout types such as dori, pipante, or cayuca (see illustrations). Examples show a rounded bottom, interior ends rounded off, and a unique and characteristic deck-like projection at both ends, not extending over a graceful hull-continuation as in the pipante, but shelf-like, about 2" to 3" thick and quite squared-off at the outer extremities. Such vessels are shown in Egyptian wall-painting hunting scenes of 5,000 years ago. Such deck projections are found among some Pacific peoples and the Florida Seminoles. The canoa seems to have been planned as a one- or two-man boat, and was probably paddled, not rowed. It is generally characteristic of dugout canoe types of Asia, Africa, and the Americas.

CANTU PENA, FUAUSTO see CAFES SUAVES CENTRALES

CAOBA see MAHOGANY, HONDURAS

CAOUT-CHOUC. The gummy substance produced by the congealed milk of the rubber tree, castilloa.

CAPE HONDURAS. Prominent headland on the Honduran north coast, visible from the island of Guanaja, Columbus' first sight of the Central American mainland in August 1502. He called it Punta Caxinas (q.v.).

Canoe

CAYUCA AND PADDLE: Typical of smaller coastal dugout craft used on lagoons, rivers, and estuaries. This particular paddle is characteristic.

Canoe

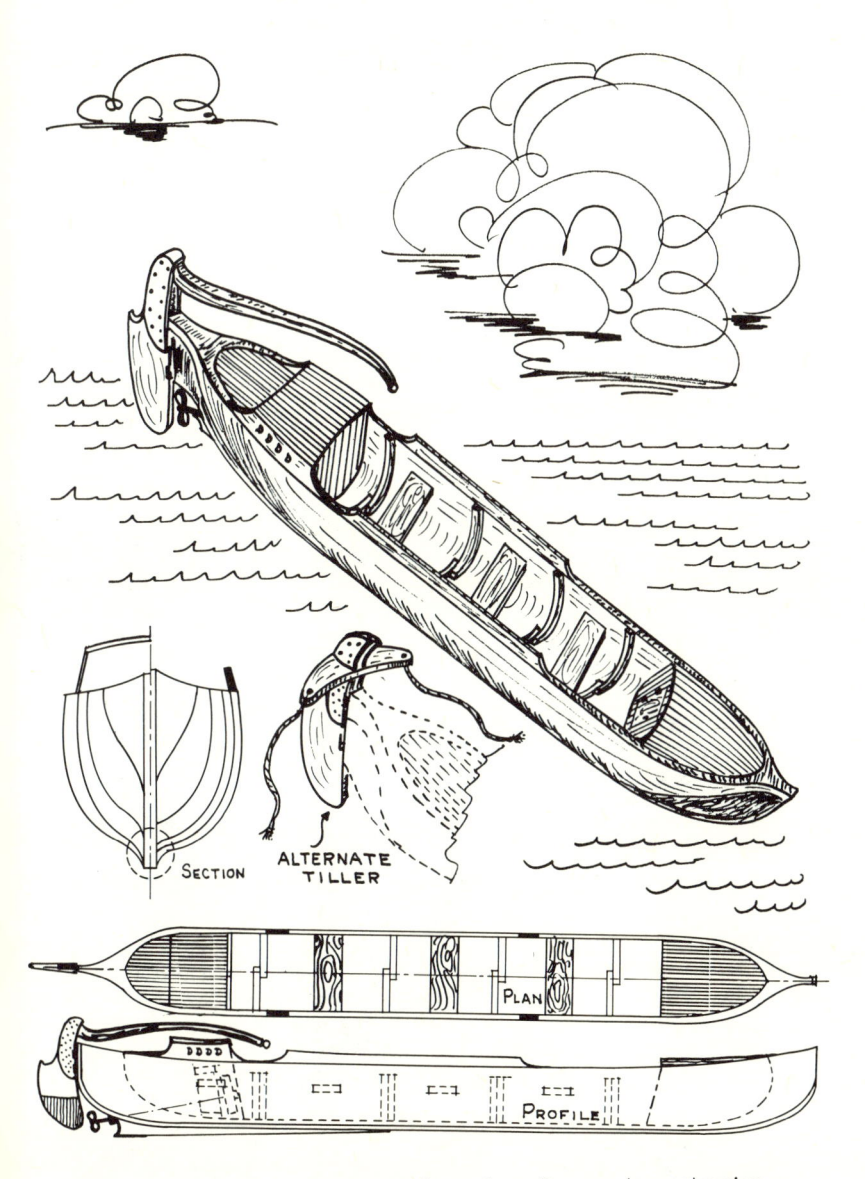

DORI: The dugout sea-going craft used on the coasts, estuaries, and especially in the Bay Islands. Round-bottomed, double-ended, now usually powered and with a rudder.

CAPES, PRINCIPAL. (Some of these may be referred to elsewhere, as "Cabo" or listed by proper names):
    Punta Caballos; near Puerto Cortés
    Cabo Salsipuedes or Punta Sol: near Tela, to the west
    Punta Hisopo or Obispo: east of Tela
    Punta Cangrejal: east of La Ceiba
    Punta Castilla or Caxinas, also Cape of Honduras: near Puerto Castilla
    Cabo Camerón: east of Iriona (and extending on eastward on the Mosquito Coast)
    Cabo Falso
    Cabo Gracias a Dios (at the border between Honduras and Nicaragua--Río Coco Delta).

CAPITANA. The leading ship of a fleet, usually the largest, carrying the fleet commander, typical of those used in the Honduran trade. In 1650 a 700-ton capitana was 140 feet long by 38 feet beam with 17 1/2 feet draft. By 1700 a 1,500-ton capitana was 165 feet long, 46 feet beam. The mainmast was 130 feet tall.

CAPITULACION. Whimsically defined as a "license to steal," this was a royal license of Spanish colonial days permitting a conquistador to appoint officers, exploit land and people, and recruit an army and colonists. In return he gave as tax to the crown the "royal fifth," or 20 per cent of the "take."

CAPTAIN GENERAL. The office of the nominal head of the Captaincy General of Guatemala, of which Honduras was a part, was very much that of provincial viceroy, other than in matters of very important policy decisions. In effect these Spanish Governors ruled with close ties to Spain, in many respects closer than to the vice-royalty. Often travel to Spain by sea was less trying than travel to Mexico by land, in spite of Cortés' outstanding feat of overland travel from Mexico to Honduras. After about 1700 the captains-general were usually military men rather than lawyers, due to the mounting troubles with England in the Caribbean.

CAPTAINCY GENERAL OF GUATEMALA. The political entity under the colonial Viceroyalty of New Spain which included Honduras. The capital was in Antigua (old Guatemala City) until 1773, when it was moved to the present site of Guatemala City following disastrous earthquakes. The Spanish rule under the Captaincy General was not as complete as might be supposed. In effect this political unit, which comprised in addition to Honduras the other Central American States, and Chiapas and Belize, was semi-independent of the viceroyalty centered in Mexico, and had close ties to the Council of the Indies and the king. It was also referred to as the "Kingdom of Goethemala."

CARACAS CONFERENCE. Held in March 1954, in Caracas, Venezuela, the conference was the tenth of an Inter-American series, and of the American republics only Costa Rica did not attend. The chief act of the conference was the passage of an anti-communist resolution, sponsored by the United States because of the Arbenz communist-influenced government in Guatemala, and opposed only by Guatemala, with abstention by Argentina and Mexico. There was more sympathy for the Guatemalan position than the 17-to-one vote expressed.

CARATASCA, LAGUNA. Largest of the Honduran coastal bodies of inland water, a true "lagoon" geologically, the Caratasca extends for over fifty miles along Honduras' eastern Caribbean coast. In colonial times sometimes called "Cartago," the big lagoon is part of a system of waterways which extend from the delta of the Río Coco to the Patuca delta (see BRUS LAGUNA), and which permit inland waterway travel through the low-lying northeastern littoral for a distance of over 100 miles. The departmental cabacera, Puerto Lempira, is located on the south side of the lagoon (see map), and along the outer bar are several settlements such as Cauquira (or Kaur Kira), Uhi, Pruminitari, and Yahurabila. The 20-mile-long island of Tansín lies along the inland shore of the lagoon, and separates the larger body of water from the Laguna de Tansín and the Laguna Warunta. The rivers Nakunta, Ibantara, Warunta and Ribra enter the lagoon from the almost uninhabited reaches of Gracias a Dios to the west.

CARBINES, CAVALRY, HONDURAN. A quantity of 10,000 United States Springfield Armory Rifles were sold in a clouded transaction to France during the Franco-Prussian War. These rifles, marked "USN Springfield 1870," were planned for the U.S. Navy, but Secretary of the Navy Robeson sold them on a pretext. A number of these were converted to cavalry carbines in one of the Honduran government arsenals where they were shortened, saddle rings added, etc. The type of arm was a Remington Rolling-Block 50 caliber.

CARCAMO, JACOBO. Poet, editor, and writer, born in Yoro in 1916, Carcamo was active on the daily paper El Cronista and the magazine Tegucigalpa. In Mexico from 1942 until his death in 1959, he was active on the Mexican dailies El Nacional and El Popular.

CA-REEB. Phonetic pronunciation of "Carib," also used to delineate the language spoken on the north coast of Honduras and in the Bay Islands which has many Carib words in it. The Carib mix with negroes has originated a group of "Black Caribs" (q.v.).

CARGOS, HONDURAS, MID-1600's. In addition to silver, recorded cargoes from Honduras included sugar, citronella, vanilla, lignum vitae, coconuts and tobacco.

Caratasca, Laguna

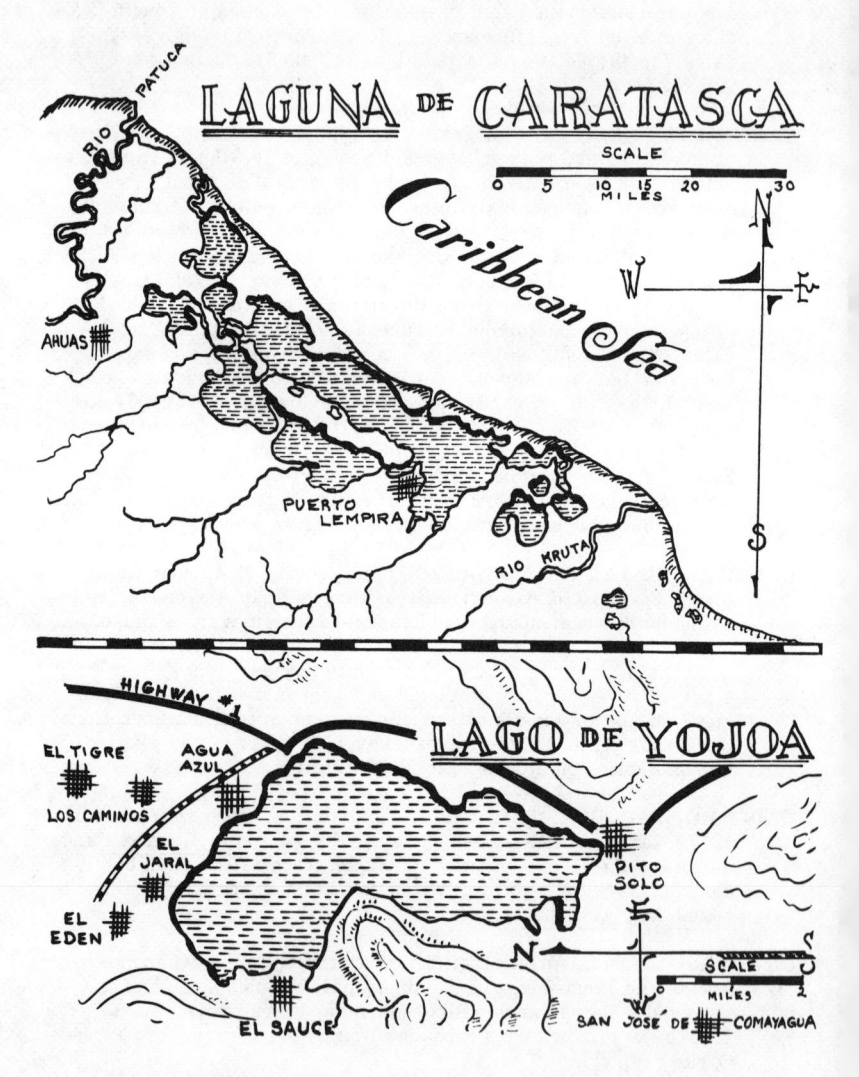

LAGUNAS - YOJOA AND CARATASCA: Inland freshwater lake and large coastal salt water lagoon.

CARIAS ANDINO, TIBURCIO. General and lawyer, Carias dominated the political scene in Honduras from 1923 through 1948. He was Constitutional President from February 1, 1933 to January 1949, a record unequaled in the country's history. He was a remarkable man in that he combined the strength of a dictator with a political sensitivity and sense of justice which kept him from accepting the Presidency for ten years after he might have seized it, and which made the long period which he dominated the only one in Honduran history not marred by revolution. There was economic progress, although world and internal conditions did not assure very substantial economic gains, as the problems of the economy in a worldwide depression were too great.

The Carias hold on the Presidency was assured by the drafting of a new constitution, which was completed in 1936. In 1943 an amendment permitted him one more term. Carias only gave up the presidency when a national party candidate, Gálvez (q.v.) was safely launched in the 1948 election. General Carias was a remarkable man in several respects. For a Honduran he was a giant, at 6 feet, 4 inches, weighing over 260 pounds. As an old man in retirement his full head of hair was still dark. Born in 1876, he was 47 when as a popular candidate he won a clear plurality but not 50 per cent of the total vote. By 1924 the resultant election confusion and chaos caused Carias to take military action. Miguel Paz Baraona was given office as President, and in 1928 Carias again backed Mejía Colindres, a Liberal, though he could easily have seized power. By 1932 his forbearance and popularity won him a decisive victory. While he is recorded as a dictator, he did not seize power by force. In 1936, however, the new constitution established the "continuismo" principle.

Typical, versatile Latin American leader, Carias was farmer, mathematics professor, military leader, and politician. He adopted a belt-tightening program in the economy and balanced the budget, and he maintained good international relations. He did not conspire with nearby countries, and thereby promoted regional stability. He did, however, stifle legislative initiative, and kept a tight rein on the press. He did engage in aerial bombardment in fighting during 1924, thus pioneering that activity in Latin America, predating the 1927 bombardment of Chinandega, Nicaragua, as an open city. He also ended municipal autonomy in the municipios. On woman suffrage and labor matters he was reactionary. His good will, honesty, and personal integrity, however, have never been questioned. It was a one-man government for most of two decades, and he was a major political figure for more than sixty years. He was the epitome of decisive, authoritarian leadership, which has in general been greatly admired in Latin America, though castigated in the press. Only in recent years has this pattern varied somewhat, although in the actions of Oswaldo López Arellana a resurgence of the respect for authoritarian regimes may be discerned.

Carias does not seem to have deserved such criticism as was directed to a Trujillo, a Somoza, or a Pérez Jiménez.

CARIB LANGUAGE. One of the curiosities of the Carib language, as brought from St. Vincent to Roatán (Bay Island) in 1796, is that there are different languages used by male and female. Some examples follow:

| Male Usage | Female Usage | Meaning |
| --- | --- | --- |
| ixanum | nucuxum | mother |
| yumaan | nucuxili | father |
| niananti | nirajö | daughter |
| macu (or) imulu | nirajö | son |
| ibuguia | (none) | brother |
| tubana | tujonoco | house |
| nonum | cati | earth |

(Obviously the female "nirajö" simply means "child" or "sibling.") Some other words used are:

| | |
| --- | --- |
| Paddle | Fagai |
| Let's go | Kimoi |
| Bring me water | Buraba duna nu |
| Let it alone | Igarybai |

CARIBAL. Name of the Carib or Caribee tribe which gave rise to the word "cannibal," because these fierce West Indian tribesmen were in the habit of eating captured prisoners of war (see BLACK CARIB). Such cannibalistic habits prevailed all along the eastern coast of South America during the 16th century.

CARIBBEAN COAST. The north and east coasts of Honduras greatly resemble the coastal areas of Florida or Louisiana. The coastal area is laced with inshore lagoons and is backed by a large swampy hinterland at many points. Mangrove islands, sluggish rivers, long wild beaches, and other characteristics are those of tropical or semi-tropical lowlands.

CARIBBEAN FEDERATION. As conceived by the filibuster William Walker in the 1850's, this federation would have consisted of the five Central American countries and the Island of Cuba, and would have developed as a significant power in the region, with the possibility of allying itself with the slave-holding states of the U.S. It was the scope of his ambitions and resistance to them which led to his execution by Honduran authorities in Trujillo in 1860.

CARIBBEAN INTRACOASTAL WATERWAY. Two-thirds of the roughly 300 miles of Honduran north coast are navigable for small shallow-draft craft (dugouts, etc.) in sheltered channels and lagoons, and since prehistoric times these waterways have been used for communication. There is no improvement of these passages, the only man-made additions being portage trails called "haulovers." However, a development similar to the U.S. Intracoastal Waterway would be quite feasible due to the similarity of terrain. The lagoons of Ibans (q.v.), Brus (q.v.), Tibalalkan (q.v.) and Caratasca are already a connected waterway with only minor haulovers.

CARIBBEAN LEGION. Significant to Honduras as a Central American phenomenon, a loose grouping of scattered armed bands of liberal and radical revolutionaries developed following World War II, avowedly dedicated to the overthrow of Latin American dictators. Hardly a formal organization, and more a "state of mind" as one writer characterized it, the Legion did take part in the Cayo Confites expedition in 1947, with which Fidel Castro and Alberto Bayo were connected. Bayo, a Spanish Loyalist colonel in the Civil War of the thirties, lived in Mexico after that war, studied Chinese guerrilla developments, and became an advisor to the Legion. In addition to Cayo Confites, members of this group also fought in Costa Rica in 1948. Bayo also trained Ernesto "Ché" Guevara--part of his written manual for the legion stated "always remember Sandino." Sandino (q.v.), the Nicaraguan bandit-patriot, received much support from Honduras. The Legion met during the 1950's in San José, Costa Rica, where the existing government was friendly to them. There was a "Sandino Brigade" of the Legion in the Cayo Confites operation. Guevara and Castro, following Bayo's legion tutelage, brought Sandino-style guerrilla warfare to Cuba. The legion was also involved in 1955 hostilities between Nicaragua and Costa Rica, as well as in several threats to Honduras. Events in 1974 in relation to the "Banana War" indicate shadowy possibilities that mercenaries, some of them Vietnam veterans, might again be employed. The Caribbean Legion was mentioned in rumors as the revived agency involved. While neither very credible nor accurately creditable, such rumors tend to highlight the persistence of a pattern, with a shadowland between legend and reality.

CARIBBEAN PINE. A significant commercial resource, growing in the eastern half of the country, perhaps stimulated by infertility of soil following "slash-and-burn" or milpah agriculture. See MILPAH. Pines and hills of the Río Patuca country were compared by one explorer to those of his native North Carolina.

CARIBBEAN SCHOOL, U.S. ARMY   see   SCHOOL OF THE AMERICAS, UNITED STATES ARMY

CARIBEES. Pronunciation often used by the coastal Caribs of Honduras in self-description.

**CARIBS.** In Honduras, these are represented by the Black Caribs (q.v.). In 1796 the British were having difficulties with these Indians (from whom the term "cannibal" was derived), and they deported a number of them to Roatán in the Bay Islands. By 1970 there were around 14,000 people on the north coast of Honduras and in the Bay Islands who had Carib blood, and by this time a major admixture of negro blood. Many of the men are boat- and ship-builders, especially expert in making the big dugouts (dorees) used throughout the islands and the coast.

**CARIBUJO.** Note the word "Carib," certainly relating to the "Black Caribs" (q.v.) in describing this cross between a Lobo (q.v.) or negro-Indian mix male with an Indian female. These Black Carib mixes began in the eastern islands of the Caribbean such as St. Vincent before the Caribs were transported to the Bay Islands of Honduras in 1796. See RACIAL MIXTURES.

**CARIMAN, ANDRES.** A Flemish officer in Spanish service who was named to the post of governor in Jicaro on the Nueva Segovia frontier, which was considered strategic in 1767. He was one of a cadre of 50 officers sent out by Charles III. The plan was to establish a standing colonial army. The problem of "criollos" (q.v.) versus "peninsulares" (q.v.) was hardly understood. This was an element in the frontier defenses between the Spanish and uncontrolled Indians, which included forts such as Omoa (q.v.).

**CARNE ASADA.** The time-honored form of preparation of beef in Honduras, El Salvador, and Nicaragua is to cut it in strips, salt it and sun-dry it. It is hung in the kitchen, and then, to cook it, is roasted on a spit or stick over the fire.

**CARR, ARCHIE FAIRLEY.** Dr. Carr has been indelibly identified with Honduras due to his years of service at El Zamorano (q.v.) and his book High Jungles and Low. The book, however, only serves to convey something more important, which is Carr's deep understanding of the Central American tropics, the country and the people. A native of Alabama, Carr spent several years in Honduras in the 1940's and has returned to Central America many times since; a world authority on sea turtles, he has written authoritatively concerning their migration, and has pursued them in research all over the world, in later years as graduate research professor at the University of Florida. Only a few writers have presented Central America with unmistakeable authenticity--John Lloyd Stephens, Ephraim Squier and Archie Carr are among these few.

**CARRACCIOLI, HECTOR.** Air force commander, age 34 and a Colonel when he and others engineered a coup on October 21, 1956, pushing Lozano out. See also RODRIGUEZ, ROQUE J.

CARRANZA, JERONIMO SANCHEZ DE. Governor in 1589. This was during the Mallín de Rueda period in the Audiencia.

CARRERA, RAFAEL (1814-1865). Continual victories over Honduran and Salvadorean armies helped to give this illiterate Guatemalan mestizo leader the prestige and power which made him the strong man of Central America following his defeat of Francisco Morazán in 1840. For 25 years, until his death, he dominated Guatemala and thereby the whole area, defeating unionist forces of Honduras and El Salvador at La Arada in 1851, at Coatepeque in 1863, etc.

CARRETA. The typical Honduran oxcart (now supplanted in part by the influx of trucks) is a heavy, rugged vehicle, capable of carrying two tons or more when drawn by a four-ox team; it is about the only form of workable transport in heavy axle-deep mud in wet seasons. It differs greatly from the Costa Rican lightweight, decorated "coffee cart." The cart resembles certain Egyptian carvings of carts used by the "Sea-Peoples" or Philistines, 1200 B.C. It has solid wooden wheels about 4', 6" in diameter, 4" and more thick, with iron 1/2"-thick segmented tires spiked on, and hubs 16" diameter and 16"-20" wide. The hubs run on wooden axles, held on by pins; the frame is simple and rugged, the yoke is attached by thongs to horns of the oxen, and is shaped for their necks.

CARRETERA DE OCCIDENTE. This highway goes through Seguatepeque with a branch to La Esperanza in Intabuca department and then another to Marcala. Through the town of Santa Bárbara the northern branch reaches Santa Rosa de Copán in Copán Department, and the southwestern branch then goes to the Salvadoran border near Nueva Ocotepeque.

CARRETERA DE OLANCHO. Under the Miguel Dávila administration this road was begun to extend from the Francisco Morazán Department as far as Juticalpa. The plan is to continue on into Gracias a Dios department. It has already reached Catacamas and Dulce Nombre de Culmí in Olancho Department.

CARRETERA DE ORIENTE. The Vicente Mejía Colindres administration initiated this road to Yuscarán and Danlí. A part of it is now being paved through El Paraiso department.

CARRETERA DEL NORTE. The highway to the north was a "king's road" or Camino Real in colonial days. During the Manuel Bonilla administration an improved road was begun from Tegucigalpa through Comayagua, Siguatepeque, San Pedro Sula, and ending at Puerto Cortés. In Potrerillo it connected with the National Railroad. Passing through mountain fastnesses and by Lake Yojoa, the road is a scenic one, recently paved under the López administration.  It is 152 miles long.

CARRETERA DEL SUR.  Under the administration of Marco Aurelio Soto, in 1881, a highway was undertaken from the city of Tegucigalpa to the port of San Lorenzo on the Gulf of Fonseca. This highway was improved during the administration of Generals Terencio Sierra and Manuel Bonilla; under the Manuel Gálvez administration it was further improved.  The road is now paved to the Interamerican Highway Junction at Jícaro Galán.

CARRETERA PAN-AMERICANA.  Honduras has the shortest segment of the Interamerican (Pan American) highway which runs from the United States-Mexican border through all the Central American countries and to eastern Panama.  Running along the Gulf of Fonseca between the Río Goascarán at the border of El Salvador, and El Espino on the Nicaraguan border, it passes through Nacaome in Valle department and Choluteca in Choluteca department, also through San Marcos de Colón (q. v.).

CARVAJAL, JUAN DE VARGAS.  Governor in 1566.

CASA DE CONTRATACION.  Known popularly and often referred to as the Casa de las Indias, this was the governmental agency established by the Spanish crown in 1503 to supervise and control for the crown the navigation, commerce, and emigration which was inevitable to the New World discoveries.  Due to the seaport characteristic of Seville on the Guadalquivir River, the Casa headquartered there.  The Torre de Oro, departure and arrival point for New World voyages, still stands.

For Honduras, technically all legal commerce and traffic had to come through Veracruz, Mexico, or through Panama, although the distances involved and the difficulties of enforcement made illegal and contraband activities almost mandatory, if any commerce at all were to be carried out. The policy of the Casa was somewhat liberalized by the 18th century, but the Casa remained an entity for 287 years until its dissolution in 1790.

CASA DE CULTURA.  Opened during the Gálvez regime in the early 1950's, the Casa sponsored plays, concerts, lectures, and other cultural activities in the hope that such efforts would advance the general level of cultural and educational attainment in light of the low literacy rate (30 per cent or less at that time).

CASA DE LEONES.  One of the first houses to be built in Gracias a Dios, Honduras, colonial capital early in the 16th century. The lintel of the main entrance is flanked by two heraldic lions.

CASAS, BARTOLOME DE LAS. Dominican priest who became a bishop and who was known worldwide in the sixteenth century as "Protector of the Indians," or a variant, "Apostle of the Indies." In 1532 he arrived in Central America as a missionary, and in the later 1530's he was in Guatemala and Honduras among tribes of Indians who were then warlike. It was Las Casas who courageously presented the case of the terribly mistreated natives of Caribbean America to the Spanish Court.

CASERA. Local name for a small poisonous snake of the Bothrops genus. So called because it crawls into houses.

CASERIO. A subdivision of the aldea (q.v.). Essentially these represent remote and widely scattered homes in the rural areas.

CASTAÑEDA BATRES, OSCAR. Poet born in Santa Rosa de Copán in 1925, author of Digo el amor (1960), La estrella vulnerada (1960), and Madre Honduras (1961), volumes of poetry published in Honduras and Mexico.

CASTAÑON, CARLOS. Governor of Honduras in 1810.

CASTAS. The 17th century groups of mestizos, mulattoes and negroes whose demographic increase alarmed the Spanish vecinos. With some Spanish blood, the castas nevertheless had few rights and privileges. Many were cowboys. They often terrorized Indian communities.

CASTELLANOS, VICTORIANO. As Vice-President, Castellanos served as chief of state from February 7, 1862 until December 4, 1862.

CASTILLA DE ORO. Name of the province assigned by King Ferdinand to one of his courtiers, Diego de Nicuesa, in 1508. This included everything from the Gulf of Darién to the Gulf of Honduras. At the time Vasco Nuñez de Balboa was governor of Castilla de Oro, it was considered to be a vast "island" extending to the Honduran shores as the northern limit; hence Balboa at that time was actually assigned the governing power over Honduras, although it is presumed that he never saw Honduran territory.

CASTILLA Y PORTUGAL, MANUEL. Governor of Honduras, 1827.

CASTILLO, MARIO M. Director of the Escuela Nacional de Bellas Artes in Tegucigalpa, and a native of San Pedro Sula. Sr. Castillo has been the recipient of prizes, diplomas, medals, and awards for his artistic accomplishments. He studied art in the Academia de Bellas Artes in Rome, and has participated in art exhibits such as the "Arte de America España" and the "Primer Certamen Centroamericana de Pintura," as well as in the Salón Anual de Pintura in Tegucigalpa. He also showed work at the San Antonio HemisFair '68 as well as at the New York World's Fair.

CASTILLOA ELASTICA. A tall-growing rubber tree, often reaching 50 feet, and as much as two feet in diameter. The tree is tapped after the fall rains, following ripening of the fruit. The flow of milk is from October to January. Cuts are made in a spiral around the trunk, or in a series of vee-shapes, such as turpentine tappers use in the southern United States.

CASTISO. A cross between a Spanish male and a Mestiza (q.v.). See RACIAL MIXTURES.

CASTLE AND COOKE. Parent company of Standard Fruit Co., Honduran banana giant. See TAX, BANANAS.

CASTRO, IGNACIO see JUNTA DE GOBIERNO, 1907.

CASTRO, PEDRO DE. Governor during 1602, same year as the incumbency of Jorge de Alvarado.

CASTRO AYALA, FRANCISCO DE. Governor of Honduras in 1676.

CASTRO AYALA, TOMAS DE. Interim governor in 1676.

CATACAMAS. Municipal cabacera in the very center of Olancho Department, where ranching and timber are the main commercial activities. Catacamas is near the tip of the great loop made by the Río Guayape as it moves to form, by joining another tributary, the major River Patuca less than 20 miles from Catacamas to the southwest. There is a gravel all-weather road leading to Tegucigalpa, and also an airfield.

CATEGORIAS DE MAESTROS see TEACHING CATEGORIES

CATHEDRAL, COMAYAGUA. Often styled the most outstanding of the colonial buildings in Honduras, the Comayagua cathedral is likewise ranked high among all the many extant examples of colonial architecture in Latin America. (The Franciscans alone had built 145 Honduran churches by the 18th century.) As the cathedral church in the old colonial capital, the Comayagua structure had a special status. Completed in the early 18th century, the cathedral replaced the La Merced (q.v.) church which had previously served in that capacity. The cathedral cupola is covered with two-toned tiles. The facade is characterized by three tiers of engaged columns, and is asymmetrical with one large, somewhat sturdy belfry tower and a columnar pier-tower on the opposite corner. The proportions are exquisite, the detailed workmanship of a high order, both inside and out. The interior is rich in carving, especially the pulpit. The cathedral was founded in

Cathedral, Comayagua

COMAYAGUA - THE CATHEDRAL: The asymmetrical facade marks this "earthquake baroque" structure as unusual. This was the central church in days when Comayagua was the colonial capital.

1537 and was the central church of Honduras during the days of the colonial seat of government in Comayagua. The town declined late in the 19th century, but the cathedral church has retained much of its early splendor and dignity. There is a religious museum at Comayagua.

CATHEDRAL, TEGUCIGALPA. Characterized by a unique type of engaged column or pilaster, the cathedral in the heart of Tegucigalpa is a superb rendition of colonial baroque architecture (often dubbed "earthquake baroque"), surpassed in Honduras, according to some art historians, only by the cathedral in Comayagua (q.v.). Such charming details as caryatids in the form of mermaids enliven the whole. The cathedral reached completion in about 1782, and is an imposing structure with the usual twin towers, but the facade is marked by two flanking structures under ogival arches, and by the unique cross-grooved engaged columns already mentioned. The columns are in two tiers of eight each, two pairs flanking the main entry on each side, and a similar group of eight superimposed and flanking a large octagon window on the second tier level. The horizontal grooving or moulding seems to be a developed form of this style, which is found in a limited way in the area of Cádiz and Jérez in Andalusia, Spain. The Comayagua structure is believed to be one of the very last completed with this feature, termed "cushioned." The Spanish word is derived from the Arabic, and is almohadillado. The first church on the site was replaced by the cathedral through the initial energies of the Cura Don Simeón de Zelaya. (See illustration, p. 345.)

"CATHEDRAL FOREST." Tall tropical rain forest where the high canopies of close-spaced large trees have shade-killed the undergrowth. They usually represent a great variety of species. Probably a fifth of Honduras is covered with such forest, especially on the Caribbean-facing north and east coasts.

CATHERWOOD, FREDERICK (1799-1854). While John Lloyd Stephens (q.v.) has been widely recognized as the father of Maya archaeology, there is little doubt that this illustrious parenthood would have had far less prominence without the illustrations of artist Catherwood. Stephens met the artist in London where he was displaying paintings of the ruins of Jerusalem done from Catherwood's drawings. Already interested in archaeology, the young Catherwood had been apprenticed to an architect, and in 1823 went to Greece to extend his understanding of classical architecture. Escaping from civil war in Greece, Catherwood was the first trained architect to draw Egyptian remains along the Nile, and later he sketched not only Thebes and Karnak, but Baalbek and the Mosque of Omar. From 1834 until Catherwood's death in 1854, he and Stephens had not only a firm friendship but a creative collaboration which was unique and vastly productive.

Catherwood's Maya drawings remain without peer after nearly a century and a half, and even today are often more revealing of the nuances of Maya art than are photographic essays. Especially good are those of Copán, Honduras, where the partners worked together early in their career. See COPAN - The Maya Ruins.

CATHOLIC CHURCH. Since the first priest came to Central America with Gil González d'Avila in 1522, and the first Franciscan church was founded in Granada two years later, the whole area has been predominantly Catholic. The church still has great local influence in rural and small-town parish settings. Many priests and other workers are from foreign groups, as there is a shortage of local clergy. There is, however, no official state religion, although the government assists in Catholic educational enterprises. There were Observant and Recollect missions during colonial days in Honduras, but they frequently operated under staggering hardships. Catholicism is also blended with earlier pagan observances.

CATTLE TRADE, COLONIAL. In the region of Comayagua and Gracias a Dios, a regular cattle trade developed as early as the 1570's in these Honduran highlands. Silver mining in the Tegucigalpa and Guascarán areas provided a nearby market for meat. Some exports went to the capital, Santiago in Guatemala. Exporting meat has been renewed in recent years as breeds and cattle raising techniques have improved.

CAUDILLISMO. The term applied to movements related to social and political upheaval which result in the emergence of a caudillo (q.v.). It represents a concentration of political authority in the hands of one leader, usually a man of military training and background. It once related only to provincial freedom movements, but now is used more generally (as "Francisco Franco, Caudillo de España").

CAUDILLO. A word meaning leader (Spanish, derived from the Arabic) and virtually synonymous with dictator. However, there are frequently caudillos other than single leaders of the country. Great political power in the hands of one person of this type is called caudillismo. Franco's regime in Spain places "Francisco Franco, Caudillo de España por gracias a Dios" on every coin. In the Caribbean area cacique (q.v.) is a virtual synonym for caudillo.

CAUQUIRA. (Also Kaurkira). Village with airport and anchorage on the other beach of the Caratasca Lagoon, just across the eastern end of that body of water from the departmental cabacera, Puerto Lémpira.

CAVALLAS, FELIPE DE. An agitator at the Corpus Mine (q.v.) in 1695. He fled to new Spain after the "visita" of Valenzuela Benegas (q.v.).

CAVENDISH. A blight-resistant strain of bananas currently being experimented with. The banana blights of a generation ago were devastating to the previous Caribbean coastal varieties. Often called "Giant" Cavendish.

CAXINAS. Arawak name for a tree common in the Honduran latitudes, and from which Columbus named Punta Caxinos (q.v.), now called Cape Honduras.

CAXONES CHANNEL. Seaway between Vivovilla Cay and Caoerorayne Reef off the east coast of Honduras.

CAYO. Spanish word for small island, from the Taino (Indian) word which is the same. Corrupted in English as "key." Also used in the form "cay."

CAYO BECERRO. Banks and cays located in the shallow area of the Caribbean Sea east of Honduras, about forty miles from the Barra de Caratasca (q.v.).

CAYO CINCO PALOS. On the same bank as Cayo Cocorocuma (q.v.), in the Caribbean.

CAYO COCOROCUMA. The tiny island of the melodious name is on a dangerous bank forty miles from False Cape (q.v.).

CAYOS CAJONES. Also known as Hobbies, these islands on a ten-mile bank are the northernmost of the great Caribbean shallows east of Honduras.

CAYOS COCHINOS. These "pig islands" are thirty miles east of the Bahía de Trujillo and are easily seen from the Bay Islands, as they are a group with a necklace of small islands on a reef. They are due north of Nueva América at the mouth of the Río Papaloteca.

CAYOS HOBBIES see CAYOS CAJONES

CAYOS MAJORES DEL CABO FALSO. About 25 miles offshore, this is a large group of tiny cays east of Cabo Falso.

CAYUCA see CANOE

CEBALLOS Y VILLAGUTIERRE, ALONSO. After the strife of the previous four terms, regular and interim, this governor from 1702-03 managed to quiet down the factions and restore a somewhat tenuous peace to the audiencia.

CECLA. Acronym for Comisión Especial de Coordinación Latina Americana.

CEDRO. The cedar, carapa nicaragüense, is a tropical aromatic hardwood--the Spanish cedar or "cigar-boxwood" which is light pink, light in weight, but stable and durable. It is used in Honduras as elsewhere for furniture, canoes, and building material throughout the areas of growth. Major stands are in the rain forest and north and east coastal areas. The appearance closely resembles that of mahogany, although the wood is much softer.

CEDRO REAL.  Royal Cedar.  See CEDRO.

CEH.  Twelfth month of the Maya calendar.

CEIBA. A natural-history journal published by the Pan American Agricultural School at Zamarano, founded in 1943 by the United Fruit Company.

CEIBA. The ceiba pentandra, majestic tree of the tropics. It produces the cotton-like kapok, and grows to tremendous heights and diameters. The trunk of ancient specimens may be ten feet in diameter just above buttress roots which spread sixty feet or more, and then may soar to 150 feet or more in height. It was considered a sacred tree in pre-Columbian times, and this belief persists among tribal descendants. Ceiba, probably an Arawak word, is very characteristic of Central American rain forest or cloud forest. Found frequently in Honduran forests, and in detached single trees.

CELIS, GARCIA DE. Joint governor of Honduras with López de Gamboa in 1541, under the direction of Maldonado (q.v.). Celís had only civil responsibilities.

CEMLA. Acronym for the Centro de Estudios Monetarios Latino-Americanos, a regional organization whose principal function is to effect and advance matters related to monetary and fiscal aspects of the region. A special committee worked on Central American regional credit mechanisms in 1968.

CENTRAL AMERICA - The Nations. Honduras is the second largest of the five Central American countries; the others are Guatemala, El Salvador, Nicaragua, and Costa Rica. In the Organization of American States (q.v.), these five small nations bear a weight due to their numbers (nearly one-fourth of the total membership), but somewhat disproportionate to their area (one-hundreth the total) or their population (one-fortieth the total).
        Geographically, Central America is the middle of the Americas, which stretch from 55 degrees south latitude to 85 degrees north. The five small nations occupy latitude bands between 8 and 18 degrees north. The longitude range is also 10 degrees from 82° 30' to 92° 30' west. The measure between extremities is 900 miles. The widest land between Pacific Ocean and Caribbean Sea is only 250 miles wide.
        Culturally, these small nations are part of Middle

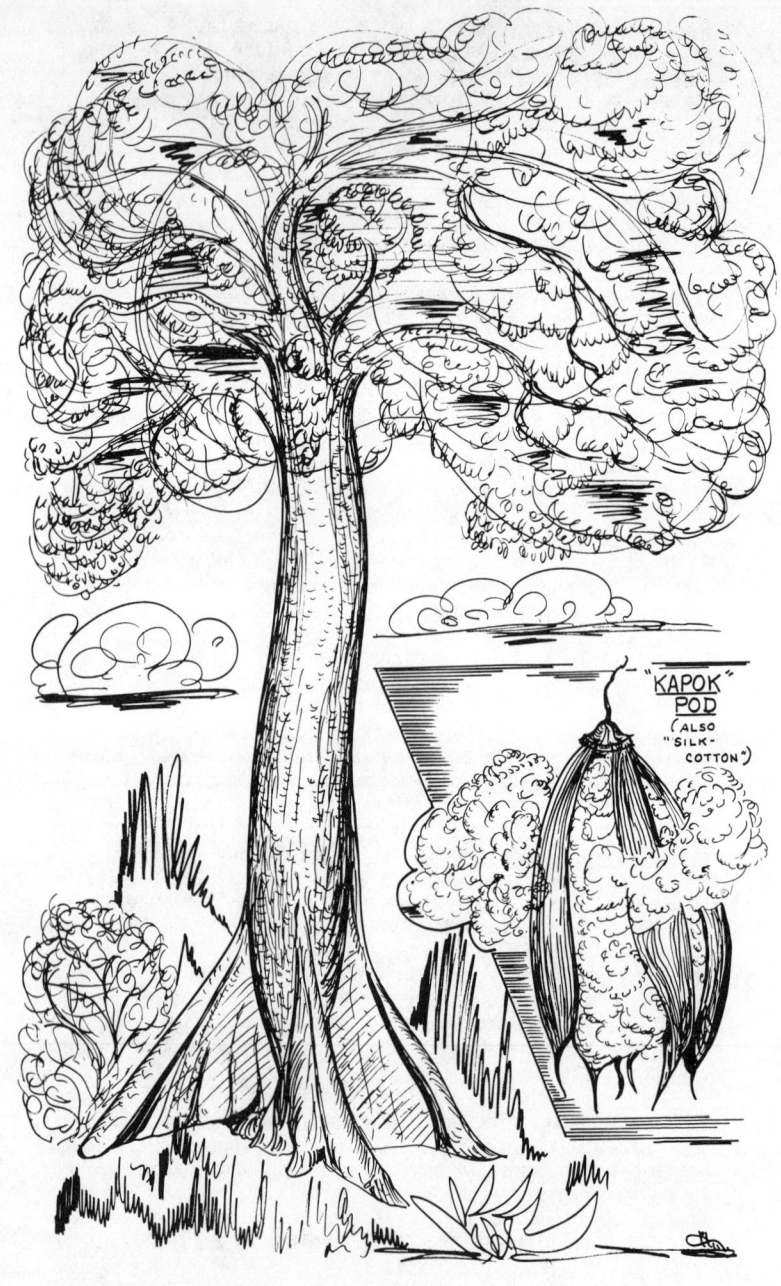

CEIBA TREE: The tree which in its majesty was considered sacred in Pre-Columbian Central America. Source of kapok.

America. Politically, each is sovereign. They are now associated in the Organización de los Estados Americanos and the Central American Common Market, as well as in the United Nations, although the war of 1969 between Honduras and El Salvador has seriously strained market and other relationships. Total population is about 11,000,000.

Geologically, during the Tertiary period a large part of Central America is believed to have been an island, although prior to that time (60,000,000 years ago) there seems to have been a land bridge. Then the link was broken and South America developed separately. The antedeluvian "island" probably included Mexico's Chiapas, Guatemala, Honduras, and most of Nicaragua, with other islands smaller and nearby. The land bridge may have been broken in accordance with the modern theory of "continental drift." Honduras has a flora and fauna partaking of both continents. It shares with El Salvador the highest percentage of mestizo population in the whole area, while nearby Guatemala has a majority of Maya Indian population.

CENTRAL AMERICAN ARCHAEOLOGY. First scientific work. See MAUDSLEY, ALFRED.

CENTRAL AMERICAN BANK FOR ECONOMIC INTEGRATION. The bank, created in 1961, was a final pragmatic step in the creation of a Common Market in Central America. The Common Market entered a period of strain following the El Salvador-Honduras five-day war of 1969. See BCIE.

CENTRAL AMERICAN CONFEDERATION. A league of three states created by delegates from El Salvador, Honduras, and Nicaragua under a constitution drafted at Chinandega, Nicaragua in 1845, when Honduras and El Salvador attacked Nicaragua. José León Sandoval took over the government, and two years later (1847) again, under an amended constitution, the three states united. This union was dissolved in 1853. The dream of eventual union persists in all the Central American countries.

CENTRAL AMERICAN COURT OF JUSTICE.
This body was created by conventions drawn up when a conference was held in Washington, D.C., convening November 14, 1907. The proximate cause was Nicaragua's Zelaya (q.v.) tampering with Honduran sovereignty. All five central American Republics had delegates, and one of the results of the conference was that Honduras should remain "forever neutral." At that time the country was considered as the usual trouble center of Central America. It was, of course, the only one of the countries with long land borders on three of the others. There were three especially important provisions in the setting up of the Court and the concurrent conference:
1) No government should be recognized which originated in a coup d'etat.

2) No other government should intervene in a civil war in any of the countries.
3) Presidential reelection should be prohibited and each country should attempt to effect this end, and to guarantee the principle of alternation in power.
The court was to sit in Cartago, Costa Rica, and each member state would pay a share of expenses. The "Lee Christmas (q.v.) Invasion" of Honduras happened soon after, in 1908, and while the Court did affect a compromise in the guerrilla war which ensued among Guatemala, El Salvador, Honduras, and Nicaragua, the tribunal lasted only until one country withdrew, and in 1918 it ceased to exist. It had some effect in decelerating the "habit" of war.

CENTRAL AMERICAN DEFENSE COUNCIL. Organization among the Central American countries which, among other unifying moves, has a standard for officer insignia. Adopted by Honduras, these are used for all but the general officer ranks.

CENTRAL AMERICAN MISSION HIGH SCHOOL. A secondary school of 150 students established by Protestant Missions in Minas de Oro.

CENTRAL AMERICAN MISSION HOSPITAL. A protestant missionary endeavor in Siguatepeque.

CENTRAL AMERICAN REGION. That portion of the isthmian area of Meso-America or Middle America between the two continents of the hemisphere and comprising from a political standpoint the five countries formerly included in the Federation of 1821-1839, just following their independence from Spain-- Guatemala, Honduras, El Salvador, Nicaragua, and Costa Rica. From a geographical standpoint, the area between the isthmus of Tehuantepec and the Darién area of Eastern Panama might be included. This would include British Honduras (or Belize); the states of Chiapas, Tabasco, Yucatán, Campeche, and the territory of Quintana Roo in Mexico; and Panama itself. Honduras is centrally located in this extended isthmian region, which is 1,100 miles long. British Honduras has no connection, geographically or politically, to Honduras. However, British Honduras or Belize has long been claimed by Guatemala.

CENTRAL AMERICAN TELEVISION NETWORK see TELEVISION

CENTRAL AMERICAN UNION, FIRST (Colonial). The first identification of Central America as a regional geographical unit came in 1542, under ordinances designated as "New Laws," promulgated in Barcelona, Spain, which placed an Audiencia in the "confines" of Guatemala and Nicaragua (then including Honduras). This governmental unit took the place of government by the early conquistadors, and created a political unit of these provinces. In 1543 Comayagua was designated as the seat of the Audiencia, hence was in effect the first capital. This location was at that time designated as Nueva Villa de Valladolid, but it was so far from the southern-most Spanish outposts in Chiapas and Soconusca that the presidente Maldonado decided to move to a more suitable location which was, however, also in Honduras. On May 16, 1544, the inaugural act was performed in Gracias a Dios (now Gracias), the departmental cabacera of the department of Lempira. The President was Licenciado Alonso de Maldonado. He was installed by Bishop Marroquín, who was also placed in office the oidores Pedro Ramírez de Quiñonez, Diego de Herrera and Juan Rogel. The Honduran site did not remain the regional capital for long. In 1548 it was removed to the city of Guatemala (now Antigua). In 1563 Nicaragua and Costa Rica were attached to the audiencia in Panama, while Honduras, Guatemala, Chiapas, Soconusco, and San Salvador came under the kingdom of Mexico. In 1568, however, the Guatemalan audiencia was established anew, and the fourteen provinces again comprised virtually the same area as present-day Central America. By the end of the 18th century there were four intendencies: León, Ciudad Real, Comayagua (Honduras), and San Salvador. There were also eight mayoralties or Maya principalities, most of them in present-day Guatemala, and two corregimientos (under corregidors). Costa Rica was a special case. These 15 entities comprised the Kingdom of Guatemala.

CENTRAL BANK OF HONDURAS. Created in 1950, this unit of the government controls monetary and fiscal policy and regulates credit, which enables commercial bank loans to be directed along government-approved channels. The president of the Central Bank is a member of the National Superior Planning Council.

CENTRAL DISTRICT. The seat of government, consisting of Tegucigalpa and the immediately adjacent Comayaguela.

CENTRAL HIGHLANDS. A geological as well as geographical subdivision which is part of the basic American cordillera that extends throughout Middle America; this particular portion is anchored in Mexico's State of Chiapas and continues through Honduras to Panama.

CENTRAL ZONE. The departments of Atlantida, Yoro, Francisco Morazán, El Paraiso, Valle and Choluteca comprise the Central Zone of Honduras, with one of the two major urban centers of the country, Tegucigalpa, its suburb of Comayagüela, and Choluteca, Tela, La Ceiba, El Progreso, Nacaome, and Yuscarán as towns of significance.

CENTRO DE EDUCACION FUNDAMENTAL. On May 29, 1952 centers of fundamental education, under the aegis of the UNESCO program based in Mexico at Pátzcuaro, were established.

**CENTURION, GASPAR.** One of the Genoese of Seville who helped back Columbus financially. He was associated with Juan Francisco Grimaldo. These men seemed to be particularly involved at the time of Columbus' fourth voyage when he discovered Honduras.

**CERAMIC TRAITS.** Characteristics of ceramic finds in archaeological sites in Central America as elsewhere are such as the following: polychrome paint, negative painting, pedestal bases, white-on-red pottery, tripod bases, zoned red paint, zoned hatching, rocker stamping, stirrup spots, etc. In Honduras combinations of low-relief sculpture and painted panels on the same pot are frequently found. This seems to be a mode of Maya derivation, and Honduras' Copán was one of the four or five major Maya ceremonial centers; others were Tikal, Palenque, Chichen Itzá and Uxmal. There are many private collections with an incredible variety of ceramics.

**CERECEDA, ANDRES DE.** Named governor of Honduras by López de Salcedo and Vasco de Herrera.

**CERIMOR.** One of the three caciques encountered by Olid (q.v.) during his abortive "conquest" of the north coast of Honduras in 1524. These coastal Indians were called sula zicaques.

**CERRATO, ALONSO LOPEZ.** Formerly President of the Audiencia in Santo Domingo, Cerrato was governor of Central America from 1548 to 1555, although technically relieved in 1553. In 1549 the seat of the audiencia was moved from Gracias a Dios to Santiago (Antigua) in Guatemala.

**CERRO ASANGBUSNA.** A portion of the Montañas de Colón (q.v.) to the north and adjacent to the Río Patuca at Pimienta.

**CERROS DE CANGREJAL.** The extinct or quiescent volcanic complex just southwest of La Ceiba, reaching an altitude of 8,100 feet and consisting of Cangrejal (or Congrehay) and Bonito Peaks. Brigham in 1887 reported an eruption of Cangrejal "several years" before, in which ashes fell on Belize, 150 miles away. The Bay Islands are part of this system of sierras. No volcanic eruptions have been reported in Honduras in the present century.

**CERVECERIA HONDUREÑA** see **HONDURAN BEER CO.**

**CES.** Known as "El Ces" (pronounced "Sayce"), this organization is the Cuerpo Especial de Seguridad (q.v.).

**CEYS.** The Economic and Social Council formed by the Honduran government to carry out relief, rescue, and aid efforts in the wake of calamitous hurricane "Fifi" (q.v.) in September 1974. CEYS is supposed to have created a "broad front of the masses," a populist combine of peasant leagues, labor unions, and similar groups. As such it was sometimes considered a threat to the essentially right-wing character of the government, although it was a governmental sub-function. Disasters such as earthquakes, volcanic eruptions, hurricanes and tornadoes almost always precipitate social unrest and movements with strong ideological overtones, as leftist leaders seize upon the occasion in the perpetually delicate equilibrium of underdeveloped countries.

CHACHALACA. A wild hen or pheasant.

CHALKER, AGNES GRANBERRY. Artist of Tegucigalpa who was born in Alabama in the United States, and who studied art in Mississippi and Florida. She has exhibited in Rome, Prague, and the United States, as well as in Tegucigalpa.

CHAMELICON, RIVER. Running southwest to northeast and entering the Caribbean just east of Puerto Cortés, this sizable stream has a deep valley, parallel to the Sierra de Espíritu Santo (q.v.) and the Sierra de Omoa (q.v.). It comes within about two miles of the Río Ulua near San Pedro Sula.

CHAMPA. Thatched-roofed, wattle-walled primitive dwellings prevalent in north-eastern Honduras and the Miskito coastal areas. Equivalent to the "ranchos de Pava" of other parts of Central America.

CHANCACA. Crude sugar made in two-pound cakes, as used in 19th century Honduras. Two or three crops of cane per year were grown at elevations between 3,000 and 4,000 feet.

CHANCELLORATE OF GUATEMALA. The English term frequently applied to the area of the Viceroyalty of New Spain which included the province of Honduras (following 1542). See KINGDOM OF GUATEMALA.

CHANISO. The cross of an Indian male with a Mestiza (q.v.) female. See RACIAL MIXTURES.

CHAPARRISTIQUE. Name of the Department of San Miguel when it was invaded by Alvarado. The ending "tique" is found frequently in the area of western Honduras.

CHAPULISTAGUA. Ruins in a valley near Comayagua, probably of Mayan origin.

CHAPULUCA. Ruins near Opoteca, probably of Mayan origin.

CHARNAY, DESIRE. French leader of a mission for the French Minister of Public Instruction who published a work that was translated into English as The Ancient Cities of the New World. Charnay worked from 1857 to 1882, and was a forerunner of Maudsley (q.v.), who did the first systematic work in Central American archaeology.

CHARTER OF SAN SALVADOR. A renewed effort for isthmian political organization and unity put forth on October 8-14, 1951, when the foreign ministers met in San Salvador. Part of the language of the charter follows:

> Considering that the Central American republics, disjoined parts of a single nation, remain united by indestructible ties which ought to be utilized and strengthened for the common advantage....

The Charter was the basis for the ADECA (q.v.), not a federation but a joint organization. In Honduras and in the other countries the emotional thrust toward unity has never been matched by practical and political reality. The many efforts toward union have usually been frustrated by the unilateral action of some caudillo.

CHATFIELD, FREDERICK. With the assistance of a British Naval force, this British agent and later consul-general in Central America occupied Tigre Island in the Gulf of Fonseca on October 16, 1849. It was he who was opposed by U.S. chargé d'affairs Ephraim Squier (q.v.), who had negotiated a treaty with Honduras, and to whom that country ceded Tigre Island temporarily in mid-1849, following insulting tactics by a British naval commander at Trujillo. The occupation of Tigre, Chatfield's answer to the cession, had the effect of finally forcing a crisis between the United States and Great Britain that resulted in the Clayton-Bulwer treaty (q.v.) of April 19, 1850. The occupation of Tigre Island did unite the central states and they planned, as a result, the Representación Nacional (q.v.), but that proposed union was shortlived.

Chatfield, as Great Britain's "Eternal Agent" in Central America, served there from 1834 to 1852, and was embroiled in a number of high-handed matters such as the Tigre episode. After the breakup of the union in 1839, he became a foe of renewed union, which he saw as against the interests of Great Britain. The British Mosquito protectorate and Bay Islands (q.v.) episodes were part of the problem. Chatfield maintained close alliance on a personal basis with Morazán (q.v.).

Chatfield was responsible for committing England to imperialistic activities in Central America when England did not know what she was doing, believing all the time that she was merely protecting her nationals. One of Chatfield's obsessions was that after the war with Mexico (1846-48) the United States would next pounce on Central America.

In 1850 Chatfield bribed the envoy Felipe Jaúregui to join with Santos Guardiola in a Honduran revolution to declare her independence of the temporary union then in force. He was also instrumental in the Bay Islands being declared a crown colony, and he helped the fall of Doroteo Vasconcelos in El Salvador. Chatfield was recalled and left in May, 1852. At that time he had three countries under his thumb due to his relationship with the serviles (the conservative parties) and his "divide and conquer tactics."

CHAVEZ, CORONADO. Constitutional president for the two years, January 8, 1845 to January 1847, Chávez survived longer than most early presidents of the republic.

CHAVEZ, HERNANDO DE. Spanish officer sent to subdue the Chiquimula (q.v.) province and Copán in 1530.

CHAVEZ, JUAN DE. Named governor of Honduras in 1544 at a time when the colonists called Francisco de Montejo to that office, resulting in divided loyalties and unrest.

CHEN. Ninth month of the Maya calendar.

CHICCHAN. Fifth day of the Maya month; meaning, "serpent."

CHICHA. A fermented liquor, made from corn, known widely in Central America and Northern South America, the name seeming to be also widely disseminated over regional and linguistic boundaries. The cry of "la chee-ee-chah!" is a familiar one at remote rail stations and similar spots throughout the area. Sometimes fruit is added to the drink. It varies from place to place and country to country. In the ancient manner of preparing it, the corn is chewed and spit into kettles by women, the saliva speeding fermentation. Modern "chicha" is of more variety, however (and perhaps of more sanitary origins). Columbus found chicha being used on the Honduran coast in 1502.

CHICLE. While this ingredient of chewing gum is derived more from Mexico, Belize, and Guatemala's Petén region than from Honduras, there are chicleros at work along the Río Coco, where a variety particularly used in bubble gum is found. The Sapodilla (q.v.) or Sapote tree (Achias Sapote), is the prime source of chicle, and usually the locations are in remote areas, where dugout canoes or muleback may be resorted to for transportation to shipping ports.

CHICLERO. A gatherer of chicle (q.v.).

CHIEFS OF STATE. Incumbents in charge of Honduras during the Central American Federation (1825-1839). See JEFES DE ESTADO.

CHIFLONES. A word, possibly Poya, used for rapids along the Río Patuca (q.v.).

CHILOTES. Little ears of green corn, often boiled when very immature and eaten cob and all. A Nahua word.

CHINACLA. One of the municipal cabaceras of La Paz department, near Marcala, and using a joint airfield with that town.

CHINAMIT. A basic unit of social organization in Middle America. This Quiché word is synonymous with Calpulli (q.v.).

CHIQUIMULA DE LA SIERRA. A province of New Spain which contained the magnificent Maya ruins of Copán (q.v.) and which was conquered by officers of Pedro de Alvarado. In 1530, Indians of the province revolted and were subdued by Hernando de Chávez. At that time Copán fielded 30,000 men in the defending army. The Copán then attacked was probably not the site of the ruins now so well known. Chieftain of the defenders was the Cacique Copán Calel. The cacique was a principal instigator of the revolt. Juarros' (q.v.) description of the battle shows that there was a spirited defense.

CHOLOMA. Honduran town in Cortés department ten miles north of San Pedro Sula, which was devastated in hurricane "Fifi" on September 19, 1974. A town of 7,000 inhabitants, and a municipal cabacera, Choloma was the victim of flooding of the Choloma River, when as much as 24 inches of hurricane rainfall flooded that stream, then dammed it with debris; the river finally broke the barrier and swept through the town. The exact death toll may never be known, as bodies were being cremated and buried in mass graves as they were found, in an attempt to prevent the spread of disease and consequent epidemics. But the number of dead apparently reached between 5,000 and 6,000, a greater toll than anywhere else in a similar sized area in the country, and probably more than half of the total deaths which resulted from the storm in all Honduras.

CHOLUTECA. Early in colonial days the full name of this southern Honduran town was Xérex de la Frontera de Choluteca, a name taken from the old Arabic spelling of the famous Andalusian town now called Jeréz de la Frontera, which has given its name in Anglicized form to that superb wine called "Sherry," which came originally from its nearby vineyards. There may have been illegal vineyards in the area in the early days of Choluteca, in spite of the prohibition against wine-making in the Spanish colonies. Located near the Bay of Fonseca, in the hot, rather desert valley of the Río Choluteca, the present-day town is the major Honduran center of the southern departments, and is the cabacera of the department of the same name, sharing commercial status and political title with the cabacera of Valle Department, Nacaome. Choluteca's 1973 population was over 23,000.

CHOLUTECA, DEPARTMENT. Southernmost of the Honduran departments, this one is bounded on the North by Francisco Morazán and El Paraiso departments, on the East and South by the international border with Nicaragua, on the West by Valle Department, and on the Southwest by the Bay of Fonseca. The Río Choluteca splits the department, and Choluteca (in early colonial times, Xérez de la Frontera de Choluteca) is the departmental cabacera. There are 16 municipios. The Pan American highway crosses Valle and Choluteca departments on its route from El Salvador to Nicaragua around the Bay of Fonseca. The area of the department is 1,625 square miles. The 1973 population was 44,914 in the cabaceras and 189,012 in villages and rural areas, for a total of 233,926, making it the most populous of the southern departments. There are two hospitals.

CHOLUTECA, RIVER. A considerable stream in flood stages, but a trickle in dry season, this river drains a large section of Honduran-Nicaraguan borderland in Morazán, Choluteca and El Paraiso departments, flowing past Tegucigalpa as well as its namesake city.

CHORTI. 1) Maya linguistic group of the area in western Honduras and eastern Guatemala around the Copán and Quirigua ruins. The group is related to the Chiapas--Tabasco linguistic area in Mexico. There seems to have been a three-fold division of the original Maya language: proto-Guatemala-Yucatan, Huastecan (farther north in Mexico), and the proto-Chiapas, from which Chorti seems to be derived.
    2) An Indian tribe of Honduras from preconquest days to the present, probably related to the Chol-tzeltal Maya groups in southern Mexico (see MAYA TRIBES); these were of the Maya language stock rather than the Ute-Aztecan. The Chorti used cacao as currency until the 1950's.

CHRISTENSEN, CHRISTINA FOURNIER. Contemporary artist of Tegucigalpa, a Costa Rican born in San José, and student at the Escuela de Bellas Arts of the University of Costa Rica, she holds a Master's degree in Fine Arts. Further studies were completed in Madrid, New York and Rome.

CHRISTMAS, LEE. One of the most colorful characters of a kaleidoscopic place and period, a former railway man, a locomotive engineer from Louisiana, "General" Christmas was a soldier of fortune with activities all over Central America. Reputed to have had four wives simultaneously, and embroiled in myriad revolutionary activities, Christmas was involved with the Zelaya-period disturbances, when in 1908 he led an invasion of Honduras from El Salvador which soon involved Nicaragua and Guatemala as well. This Honduran adventure gave the Central American court its first international case but war was finally prevented on this particular occasion.
    Christmas' exploits became legendary. On one occa-

sion, when running a locomotive on a Guatemalan railroad, he heard news of a revolt in Honduras, left the train right where it was, and hiked across jungles to join in the conflict. He once is supposed to have held off a whole "army" with a machine-gun, supported only by a Colonel Guy Malone, who in the 1920's was a superintendent of police in New Orleans. Christmas is said to have led troops varying from two men to 14,000. He was also at one time Chief of Police in Tegucigalpa. His military activities led to his citizenship being cancelled by the United States Government. Serving in the secret service in World War I, his citizenship was reinstated, but he died soon after the war in spite of a blood transfusion from his old compatriot Malone.

CHRYSOLALAMUS ICACO. Tree common along the Honduran sea-beaches; its common name is an Arawak word, Caxinas (q.v.).

CHUEN. Eleventh day of the Maya month; meaning "monkey."

CHURCHES, COMAYAGUA. Sixteenth to eighteenth century churches of this city are excellent examples of the squat-towered structures frequently known as "earthquake baroque." Among these are the Cathedral itself; also La Merced, which has very plain surfaces on the facade, a niche for a statue of the Virgin above the simple arched doorway, and a short but graceful bell-tower with a miniature tower-lantern on top. La Caridad has an unusual squat tower which was probably higher originally. The facade is simple, with an arched door, but bearing baroque scrolls at the parapet. La Merced has been somewhat restored. It was originally built in 1611. The cathedral has a squat but not ungraceful tower, and a magnificent altar within. The facade is decorated with eight niches containing statues, crowned with arches or broken pediments.

CIB. The sixteenth day of the Maya month; meaning, 'bird of prey."

CICARWS see WORLD COUNCIL OF CHURCHES

CICLO COMUN DE CULTURA GENERAL. The first cycle of secondary education, established as one of the two stages in 1970. The curriculum includes: Mathematics and Science, Language and Literature, Music and Handicrafts; optional are typing and foreign language (usually English).
    Secondary attendance is not compulsory. Only eight per cent of the secondary school age population was enrolled in 1968. Requirements are completion of primary school and age of 13 years. There were 28,000 secondary students in 100 schools in 1969, with 2,000 graduates. The 1970 enrollment was 35,909. Teaching at the secondary level tends to be academic and traditional, and there was hope of revision in the early 1970's.

CICLO DIVERSIFICADO. The second cycle of secondary education as established in 1970; the curriculum leads to diplomas in the following: Teacher training, Agricultural Arts, Commercial Arts, Industrial Arts, or to the baccaloreat, which is the examination prerequisite to university admission. There are specialized and secondary schools such as the National School of Fine Arts (q.v.) and the National School of Music (q.v.) which admit students directly from primary school.

CIES. Initials and acronym for the Consejo Interamericano Económico y Social. This economic and social council is a special organization of the CECLA (q.v.) and the objective is to present a unified Latin American policy on international commerce and economic development in relation to UNCTAD (q.v.).

CIMI. Sixth day of the Maya month; meaning, "death."

CIPACTLI. First day of the Aztec month; meaning, "lizard."

CIPE. Acronym for the Centro Interamericano de Promoción de Exportación, stemming from the 1968 Punta del Este meeting of presidents. The purpose is aid to Latin American countries in specialized information designed to promote development and diversification of exports.

CIRCUM-CARIBBEAN. A single cultural area which comprises the Indian peoples of Honduras, Costa Rica, Panama, Colombia, the islands of the West Indies and the northern part of Venezuela. This is particularly significant in that Honduras and the rest of Central America plus part of Colombia are considered an Intermediate Area which lay between the high civilizations of the Central Andes and of Meso-America, and which received cultural influences from both the areas--a meeting ground. Compared to Middle America and the Andean area, little is known of this Circum-Caribbean area. Definitive archaeological and ethnological research is yet to be accomplished. Honduras is, of course, on the southern fringe of the important Maya area, with the major Maya ceremonial center of Copán just inside its borders.

CIRCUM-CARIBBEAN INDIANS. An arbitrary grouping of indigenous peoples by geographical region which is used to include some Honduran tribal groups and all the Indians of Nicaragua, Panama, Colombia, Costa Rica, the West Indies, and northern Venezuela. Less is known of this group than of the Middle American (Mexican-Mayan) or the Ecuadorean-Andean groups. Whereas in Nicaragua immigrants from Middle America included Chorutegas of the Macro-Otomangean "superstock" and Nahuatl-speaking Nicaraos and Siguas, the southern-most of the Utaztecan language family, in Honduras there was a region of separations from the important Maya culture and its fore-runners. Earliest Circum-Caribbean peoples seem to have been hunters over 10,000 years ago, in the pre-projectile-point state of development. Manioc cultivation began 3,000 to 7,000 years ago, and pottery and organized agriculture possibly around 5,000 years ago. By A.D. 600 to 800 there was inter-regional trade through the Central American area, from the Mexican-Maya to the north possibly as far as Ecuador and Inca-dominated Peru to the south.

CISNE, LAS ISLAS DEL   see   SWAN ISLANDS

CISNEROS, FRANCISCO DE.   Interim governor of Honduras during part of 1526.

CIUDAD BLANCA. A presumably Mayan ruined city, visible from the air, on the slopes of Montaña Punta de Piedra, in the southern tip of Colón department, at an altitude of over 3,000 feet. It shows up in the jungle because the structures are white, hence the name. It must be recognized that, as in the Maya areas of Yucatan, there are as yet a considerable number of sites undiscovered.

CIVIC ACTION, ARMED FORCES. The 1965 Constitution provides that Honduran armed forces will work with the executive branch of the government in such fields as agriculture, literacy and education, transport and communications, health and conservation, and land settlement. The armed forces are conceived as a governmental agency for economic development and public well-being. See also "WINGS FOR HEALTH."
     There is a major assigned in charge of the civic action program, and while long-term projects have been avoided, many others have been carried out such as school construction, literacy projects, and cultural activities. In a three-year period up to 1965, 500 rural school classrooms were built. Vocational classes in mechanics, animal husbandry, and farm management have been held. The bark beetle pest in Honduran forests was attacked. The health programs of the nation have been aided. Major roads have been built, and aid given to street, sewer, bridge, and phone-line construction.

CLARK, H. C. Dr. Clark was engaged in the 1920's in research on poisonous snakes and the effect of their bites at the Tela Hospital of the United Fruit Co. in Honduras. He and associates were attempting to identify and classify specimens, and also to secure antivenes for specific species, and polyvalent antivenes when the species was unknown. The banana plantations had found that snake population increased as the jungle was cleared. The fer de lance is one of the several very dangerous species indigenous to Honduras.

CLAYTON-BULWER TREATY. An accord between the United States and Great Britain, of April 19, 1850, taking effect July 4, 1850, concerning their respective roles in Central

America, with particular reference to cross-Isthmian transportation. Neither nation was to seek exclusive control of a transit route anywhere in Middle America, nor would they colonize, settle, or fortify anywhere in the area. They would further support the efforts of the Atlantic and Pacific Steam Navigation Company (q.v.) in efforts to provide a transit route across Nicaragua. The treaty was named for the respective representatives, U.S. Secretary of State John M. Clayton and British Ambassador to the U.S., Sir Henry Upton Bulwer. Because the Mosquito Protectorate was essentially unimpaired and British influence in Belize (British Honduras) confirmed, the treaty was generally advantageous to England. She violated the agreement two years later by establishing the Colony of the Bay Islands (q.v.).

CLINICA MORAVA. This clinic at Ahuas, Honduras, in Gracias a Dios department is a missionary endeavor of the Moravian Church (the Unitas Fratrum). The clinic is in a remote place, served only by air or by dugout canoe on the Río Patuca. SAHSA (q.v.) aircraft make stops every other day. To give some idea of the volume of activities, it is reported that in a two-month period of 1970, 9,116 patients were served, 99 operations were performed, and 299 patients interned.

    The names of Dr. Sam Marx and his nurse-wife Grace are significant because of their long service in Ahuas at the clinic, a service which was terminated in 1974. They housed and dined 100 guests a year; Dr. Sam hand-cranked the Diesel generator every day; he also had radio contact with doctors in the United States for medical advice. Son of missionaries to India, he dedicated much of his life and his great medical skill to the Honduran backlands. Nurses Norvel Goff and Helen Hodgson were Central Americans who gave major assistance at the clinic, as did Canadian nurse Ethel Suetter. The clinic's new building, erected in 1971-72, contains 4,000 square feet. The materials had to be shipped from the United States in 52 crates. It was dedicated August 12, 1972. Dr. Oscar Vides, Honduran physician, is to follow Dr. Marx at the clinic.

CLOUD FOREST. Also called montaña in Honduras, the term covers the deep jungles of the highlands where the forested peaks seem always enveloped in clouds, and where the trees "weep" constantly because of the condensed moisture. (See La Llorona.) There are many cloud forest peaks in Honduras. As many as a dozen may be seen from one position in some of the southern and western valleys. The cloud forest lies above the pine woods or ocotal, and even above the pinabete, a pine growing at higher altitudes. The cloud forest is about ten degrees cooler than the lower slopes, the tree cover being solid with numbers of huge oaks and other species, tree ferns, some palms, and many big-leaved plants such as wigandias. There are also pteriodophytes, begonias, fuchsias, a variety of lichens, and many other species. The great tree trunks are buttressed and fluted, harboring many of the smaller plants of all types. Very characteristic are the epiphytes, the myriad air-plants which thrive in the water-vapor atmosphere which soaks the larger trees and constantly drips. The epiphytes are especially dominant above the 6,500-foot level, where frequently dwarfed and wind-twisted trees carry huge burdens of the air plants. One of the amazing features of the cloud forest is that so few animals live there. Among those that do is the royal quetzal bird.

COATEPEQUE. Salvadoran site of a battle in February 1863, which was the result of an alliance between Honduras and El Salvador that was used as a pretext by Rafael Carrera for a Guatemalan invading expedition.

COATL. Fifth day of the Aztec month; meaning, "serpent."

COBRE. Copper coins in Honduras following 1839. See MONEDA PROVISIONAL.

COCA (River) see RIO COCO.

COCABILA. Village in Gracias a Dios Department.

COCHINEAL see GRANA COCHINILLA

COCKBURN, JOHN. An Englishman who travelled in Central America in 1730, and who wrote about what he saw, especially describing the Indians.

COCO, RIVER see RIO COCO

COCOLIZTHI see PLAGUE

COCOMES see MAIAN

CODE OF COMMERCE. In 1950 a code was established which in general terms regulates foreign and domestic companies. There is a .05 per cent annual capital assets tax. The code regulates checks, letters of credit, bankruptcy, insurance, and related matters.

CODES OF PUBLIC INSTRUCTION. The first basic educational code governing Public Instruction was given under the government of Marco Aurelio Soto, taking effect on February 12, 1882. There followed a series of updates and revisions:
 Second: February 8, 1906, under the Manuel Bonilla government.
 Reformed: Congress decreed on February 14, 1910, that a four-year plan of studies should be instituted.
 Second reform: On April 10, 1912, Congress again reformed the law to require in normal schools that classes in

morality and manners should be taught.

Third reform: On April 2, 1914, schools were classified as urban and rural, as well as schools for small children (kindergartens).

Third Code: In 1923, on March 29, the national congress acted to confirm a new code of public instruction. Under this code a council of education, the Consejo Nacional de Educación was named, to advise the Director General of Primary Instruction. In 1924 new regulations were issued for primary education, under the general aegis of this code. A retirement law was enacted in 1928 (see LEY DE RETIRO).

Fourth Code: On March 13, 1947, another code for public education was enacted.

Regulation of "Educación Media" was enacted in 1953.

COELLO, AUGUSTO C. One of the most prolific of Honduran authors, born in Tegucigalpa in 1884 and died in San Salvador in 1941. Graduate in law of the Universidad Central de Tegucigalpa, he was early known as a poet. As early as 1904, he was elected a deputy, and became presidential secretary, and sub-secretary of the foreign ministry. Early in the century in Costa Rica he worked on the periodicals La República and La Prensa Libre, and later edited El Pabellón Rojo y Blanco and El Diario. In 1907 he was writing for the Diario de El Salvador. In 1904, at age 20, he wrote the national hymn, set to music by Carlos Hartling in 1915. He was a delegate to the Seventh International Conference of American States in Montevideo in 1933.

COFFEE EXPORTS, 1974. In July of 1974 Honduras and Guatemala joined El Salvador, Costa Rica, and Mexico in halting coffee exports. The World Coffee Organization reported that the export suspension was to be "indefinite." The countries in question produce coffees known as "central mild" which are premium blending coffees. Meanwhile the world coffee crop for the 1974-75 season was predicted to exceed demand by 3,000,000 bags.

COFRADIA. A religious organization which frequently was a cloak for pagan worship and for saturnalic orgies. The group was swept up in a recreation of the old Indian village societies. The seventeenth century depression had the effect of accelerating the return to pre-conquest formats of government and religions, with a thin overlay of hispanicization.

COHEP see HONDURAN COUNCIL OF PRIVATE ENTERPRISE

COINAGE, CURRENT see LEMPIRA SYSTEM

COINAGE, DECIMAL GOLD. Honduras issued only limited quantities of regular issue gold coins, in one, five, and ten peso denominations in 1879-80, and in one, and five peso coins from 1887-1922, with only a few 10- and 20-peso coins struck in 1888-1889. As few as 33 ten-peso and 39 twenty-peso pieces may have been struck.

COINAGE, PROVISIONAL, 1823-62. The first coins were struck at Tegucigalpa and Comayagua, under the aegis of the Mexican imperial government, and included one and two-real pieces. The coinage of the Central American Federation followed the old Spanish system of one silver peso, eight reales to the peso, and a gold onza, worth 16 pesos, and divided in eight escudos, each worth two pesos. Even after the federation dissolved, the same coinage was used until 1851. Typical was the obverse of five volcanoes and the sun, very similar to present-day Nicaraguan coinage in Córdobas, and on the reverse a ceiba tree (q.v.). Two-real pieces were minted in Tegucigalpa in 1831-32 and 1825. Half-reales were also minted in 1830-31. From 1832-1851 similar 1/2-real, 1-, and 2-real pieces were minted in Tegucigalpa. The same volcano and ceiba designs were used, but the money was minted as "Moneda Provisional del Estado de Honduras." In 1862 a copper series of 1, 2, 4, and 8 pesos was struck.

COINAGE, RARE. A fifty-centavo standing liberty coin of 1879 was struck in Honduras using dies from a private U.S. concern. Only a few were produced during a two-month period.

COINAGE, REGULAR ISSUE, 1869-70. Under the "Real System" of coinage from 1869-70, Honduras had coins struck in Paris of 1/8 real, 1/4 real, 1/2 real, and one real. The obverse had a modified national arms; the reverse, a wreath and the value. The small denominations and values of the coins speak eloquently of the poverty-stricken economy.

COINAGE, REGULAR ISSUE, 1871-1922. Under a Decimal System, Honduran coinage proceeded with dies from the Philadelphia mint in 1871, although except for a few trial coins struck early, the dies were not used until 1879. In 1881 a new series used dies designed by Freuer (q.v.). The denominations were one-half, one, two, five, ten, twenty-five, and fifty centavos, with as many as seven types of one-centavo piece, using a modified arms-wreath-value design. The coins from five centavos up were basically silver, and the fifty-centavo and one-peso pieces from 1883-1908 had an obverse design of a "standing liberty" figure, holding a book and flag.

COJUNE PALM. The attalea cohune, known for its huge clusters of edible nuts. See MANACA.

COLD WAR, 1954 see ARBENZ REGIME

COLEGIO DE JUTICALPA see SECONDARY EDUCATION, EARLY

COLEGIO TRIDENTINO DE COMAYAGUA. Eighteenth and nineteenth century secondary academy in the old capital city.

COLINDRES, MANUEL. One of two ministers who served for five August days in 1876 as chief executive of Honduras. See MEJIA, MARCELINO.

COLOJETE, PARISH CHURCH. Southeast of Copán and near Comotán, Guatemala, this "earthquake baroque" church is one in which the original statues of the facade have survived. The surface is decorated with a lacelike stucco effect. The interior has mudejar arches and an unusual roof structure.

COLON, MONTAÑAS DE. In these mountains between the Río Coco and the Río Patuca there are tributaries no more than two miles apart flowing respectively into each. This is a very remote section of the country.

COLON DEPARTMENT. Bounded on the North by the Caribbean Sea, cut by the Río Aguán (q.v.); bounded to the Southwest by the Sierra de la Esperanza, and on the whole Southern border by Olancho Department; on the East, by the Gracias a Dios Department; and on the West by Yoro and Atlántida Departments. The cabacera is the historic port of Trujillo, near Cape Honduras or Punta Caxinas where Columbus made his first Central American mainland landing in 1502. There are nine municipios. The cabaceras had a 1973 population of 20,346, and the villages and rural areas had 46,146, for a total of 66,592. The land area is 3,450 square miles.
　　　Trujillo is of great historical interest as a fortified port (involving the whole bay of the same name), and it is the place where the famous filibuster William Walker (q.v.) was shot in 1860.

"COLONIAL" FORMATIVE CULTURES. A period of Formative (q.v.) cultures which extends from about 3000 B.C. to about 1200 B.C.; a period of wide ceramic distribution in the Americas, probably by seaborne colonies. (This term "colonial" is not in any way related to the much later Spanish colonial era.) The geographical span is from Ohio to Ecuador and Peru. See THEOCRATIC FORMATIVE.

COLONIAL HONDURAS. In 1786 Honduras was made a separate political entity somewhat resembling her present territory, when at the same time as Nicaragua and San Salvador she was made an intendency. Formerly administered for two centuries as an ecclesiastical unit by the bishop of Comayagua, the advent of the intendency was a prelude to independence, and Honduras became a state of the federation in December 1825. There was continual violence and federal intervention during the ensuing period of fourteen years until January 1839, when Honduras was the second state of the Central American union to become a separate constitutional government.
　　　José del Valle (q.v.) of Choluteca and Francisco Morazán (q.v.) of Tegucigalpa had each played important parts in

the transition from a colonial to a federal status, but this fact did not seem to ease the travail of Honduras.

COLONIAS, TEGUCIGALPA. Several southern suburbs include the Colonias Humuya, Maradiaga, Miramonte, and Banco de Fomento.

COLONIZATION, NORTH COAST. The colonization of the late 1700's proved most successful at Trujillo. See GOYANECHE, MIGUEL DE.

COLONO. Term used for an agricultural worker who lives on a large farm owned by others and who is permitted to use part of the land for part of his income. About four per cent of farmers are in this category, which is different from sharecropping, where 1/4 to 1/2 of the crop goes to the owner. The colono is a laborer who is granted this subsistence concession.

COLONY OF THE BAY ISLANDS. On July 17, 1852, a proclamation issued by the superintendent of the British holdings in Belize, Col. P. E. Wodehouse, stated that "her most gracious majesty the Queen has been pleased to constitute and make the islands of Roatán, Bonacca, Utilla, Barbaretta, Helena, and Morat to be a colony, to be known and designated as the colony of the Bay Islands."

Since this proclamation was clearly contrary to the Clayton-Bulwer Treaty of July 4, 1850, between Great Britain and the United States, the Committee on Foreign Relations of the U.S. Senate countered with a resolution stating that the Bay Islands "constitute part of the territory of the Republic of Honduras," and that the British occupation which had been consummated by Wodehouse on August 10, 1852 was clearly in violation of the treaty. Wodehouse occupied Roatán when he landed from the British brig Persian. The Clayton-Bulwer Treaty provided that "neither ... shall ever occupy, fortify, or colonize ... any part of Central America." The Superintendent, Wodehouse, was a new appointee; this was the last of seven British attempts to take the Bay Islands.

COLORADOS. A term for the "red" political party, extreme left-wing liberals, used in the early part of this century. The conservative-liberal split has always been the fundamental one in Central America.

"COLOSSUS OF THE NORTH." For decades a most frequently used term applied to the United States of America by Central Americans to indicate the dominance of the North American giant as well as to express their displeasure at policies which were interventionist in nature. Such intervention took place in each of the countries, in Honduras particularly in relationship to railroad and banking concessions, the greatest activity being during the period just after mid-nineteenth century. As late as 1974 a great U.S. private corporation was being accused of intervention. See BANANA WAR.

COLUMBUS, BARTOLOME. Significant to Honduras because he showed an island of Honduras, "Banassa" (modern Bonacca or Guanaja), as well as the mainland of Honduras on a sketch map, and likewise identified cacao as a Honduran product. This brother of Christopher Columbus was aboard the Santiago de Palos (nicknamed Bermuda) on Columbus' fourth voyage to the Americas. The sketch map in question, done by Alessandro Zorzi (q.v.), was apparently based on information from Bartolomé Columbus, and is presently in the Biblioteca Nazionale of Florence, Italy. It shows the northern Honduran coast, mis-oriented by 90 degrees, with the Bay Islands clearly shown, the land identified as "Asia," and the note "aque Cacao," denoting the existence of that characteristic American product very early in the history of the area.

Bartolomé and Christopher were both chart-makers, the former having presented a world map to King Henry the VII. The Zorzi-Columbus map bears a strong resemblance to the famous Juan de la Cosa (q.v.) map of 1500.

COLUMBUS, CHRISTOPHER, 1435?-1506. Cristobal Colón, as he was called in Spanish, was the Genoese-born discoverer of the "New World," the Americas, the Western hemisphere. Columbus' first sight of the mainland between the American continents was in Central America, when he viewed the coast of Honduras near the Bay of Trujillo, at Cape Honduras, or, as he named it, Punta Caxinas. When he first saw the mainland coast he was at anchorage, probably on the southwest shore within the reefs of the island of Guanaja (q.v.). It was while at this anchorage that he was visited by a huge dugout canoe, perhaps 70 feet long, and apparently the royal barge of a Maya chieftain, judging by the description of clothes and artefacts worn by the men and women aboard. It was here that Columbus was introduced to cacao beans used as currency. The Indians on the island itself seem to have been Payas (q.v.) or Jicaques (q.v.).

Columbus left the island for the mainland at Cape Honduras, and anchored in Trujillo Bay for over a week. He then decided to sail east, and from early August until mid-September beat along the Honduran coast against headwinds, anchoring every night, and averaging no more than seven miles per day. He may actually have faced hurricane winds. Columbus said he had never seen a "tempest" that lasted so long.

The fact that Columbus was a Genoese had much to do with his voyaging. The considerable Genoese colony of Seville proved to be of major assistance to the Admiral. Francisco de Riberol was a financial backer of the fourth voyage, and Columbus felt him to be such a friend that Riberol held his personal papers while Columbus sailed on that voyage. Another of his financial backers was Gaspar Centurión. Columbus had worked for the Centurione in Lisbon in 1477. The role of the Portuguese and Spanish expatriates from Genoa was very considerable in the early discovery and opening of America. The discovery and conquest were in a major sense the result of private enterprise, and it was the Genoese in the main who furnished the necessary money.

COMAL. A clay ceramic griddle used for baking tortillas in colonial Honduras.

COMAYAGUA. Early capital of Honduras, where in the late sixteenth century a long rivalry began which lasted over 200 years, due to the rise of Tegucigalpa following silver discoveries of 1578. Comayagua is located in a magnificent valley of central Honduras, and has a population of about 50,000, with a total of over 100,000 in the whole department of the same name. It is at present the departmental cabacera but, like León and Granada in Nicaragua, is still conscious of its previous importance in the colonial era, and is still a center of political unrest due to that ancient rivalry with the present capital. In the 1880's Comayagua had about 10,000 inhabitants, and was therefore a sizable municipality for its time.

Originally named, when founded in 1537, Valladolid de Santa María de Comayagua, the city in 1578 was one of six colonial centers; others were Trujillo and San Juan de Puerto Caballos on the north coast; inland, San Pedro Sula and Gracias a Dios, and San Jorge de Olancho. This was at the time (1578) when Tegucigalpa was established. Neither Comayagua nor Tegucigalpa desired independence in 1823, again because of the old rivalry, for neither wanted the other to be the capital. In 1824 a plan was worked out to alternate the Honduran capital between the two contesting cities. Needless to say, this plan contained the seeds of controversy and ultimate failure.

Comayagua is a center of agricultural activity, but also a commercial center for the western part of the country. The new (1970) paved highway from San Pedro Sula to Tegucigalpa, passing through Comayagua, has replaced the old and rough "Camino Real" to give better access to the interior of the country. Cattle, sugar cane, and various staple food crops are raised in the area.

COMAYAGUA DEPARTMENT. One of the first seven departments of Honduras, established in 1825, and one of the 18 existing today. Bounded on the north by Yoro Department, on the east by Francisco Morazán, on the south by Valle and La Paz departments, on the northwest by Santa Bárbara and Cortéz departments, with the Lake Yojoa as a short part of the border between the latter pair. Comayagua (q.v.), for many years the colonial capital of the Honduran Spanish Colonial Province, is the departmental cabacera. There are 18 municipios. The area is 2,003 square miles. The 1973 population of the cabacera was 51,798, only sixth in the country in spite of Comayagua's status as a former capital. The large urban areas have grown up elsewhere. The rural and village population was 96,197, for a total of 148,195. There are three hospitals. Situated in a broad valley, from early Spanish days Comayagua was considered a choice agricultural area. Nearby pre-Columbian ruins, in the valley and on its highland perimeter, are quite extensive, indicating a similar agricultural excellence in pre-historic times. The Interoceanic Railroad was to be built with its central section bisecting the Comayagua valley. A new major paved highway now runs across Honduras from San Pedro Sula through Comayagua to Tegucigalpa.

COMAYAGUA PLAIN. In the geographical center of Honduras, and site of the colonial capital city, the plain is from 5 to 15 miles wide and about 40 miles long, running north and south. As early as the time of the historian Juarros it was recognized as significant in any plan for transport from Atlantic to Pacific through Honduras. The present highway runs through much of it, and 19th century rail projects depended upon it.

COMELENGUA. The "tongue-eater," a mythical animal with the body of a short snake, wings of a buzzard, face of a panther. When cattle die during the dry season, starving dogs and coyotes pull the tongues out and eat them. This seems to be the basis for the legendary Comelengua.

COMMANDANTE GENERAL DE ARMAS DE HONDURAS see VERA, JUAN DE

COMMERCE, 16th AND 17th CENTURIES. During the years 1550-1650, Honduran trade, measured as a percentage of port traffic through Vera Cruz, varied from a high of 19.4 per cent in 1556-60 to a low of 2.78 in 1641-45. In general, there was an upward trend from 1565 to 1630, averaging about 9 per cent. This does show, however, the extreme fluctuation and the "boom and bust" nature of an economy successively based on gold, cacao, and indigo.

COMMERCIAL COMPANIES. There are six commonly applied types:
Sociedad Anónima ("Anonymous Society"--incorporated);
Sociedad Cooperativa;
Sociedad en Comandita;
Sociedad en Comandita Por Acciones; and
Sociedad en Nombre Colectivo (Partnerships). See also
LIMITADA.

COMMISSION OF ENQUIRY, UNITED NATIONS--1954 see ARBENZ REGIME

COMMUNICATIONS AND PUBLIC WORKS  see  CABINET

COMMUNISM, INTERNATIONAL  see  ARBENZ REGIME

COMMUNIST ACTIVITIES. During the period of the Honduran General Strike (q.v.) Communists based in Guatemala are alleged to have poured $850,000 into Honduras to finance the strike. Four strike leaders were subsequently exiled as Communists. The particular focus of Communist activities was the group of companies owned by United States firms. The strike did accomplish the objective, which was the crippling of the Honduran economy.

COMMUNIST PARTY OF HONDURAS. Present name of the party which in the 1954 General Strike (q.v.) was the Partido Revolucionario Democrático Hondureño; the six-point program is: 1. Nationalization of forests, minerals and all land; 2. Liquidation of all large landholdings; 3. Nationalization of all public services, electricity power; 4. Revision of all concessions to both Hondurans or foreigners; 5. Nationalization of routes of communications; 6. Prohibition of new contracts to foreign companies.

COMMUNISTS. Allegedly active for a long period in Honduras before the Sandino (q.v.) conflicts of 1927-1934, the Honduran Communists organized cells in Nicaragua during the winter of 1931-32. There were ten persons so suspected, who were raided in Managua in February 1932, but twenty-one persons were arrested. Communists were active again in the General Strike of 1954 (q.v.).

COMMUNITY DEVELOPMENT PROJECTS. The Río Coco area, under the ministry of education, is conducting courses in health education, home economics, agricultural techniques, primary literacy, the Spanish language, and so forth. Basic to this effort was the earlier work (1950's) of the "Educación Fundamental" activities of CREFAL under UNESCO auspices, in the Río Coco Pilot Project. This work proceeds on both the Honduran and Nicaraguan sides of this boundary river, a boundary finally confirmed in 1960 after long dispute, conflict, and litigation.

COMPADRAZGO. Relationships between a child's parents and godparents. Where family ties are stronger than churches, clubs, and other organizations, this pattern has special significance. Padrino (godfather) and madrina (godmother) are both part of compadrazgo in the relationship of a child's parents and godparents. It is a ritual kinship, but important and a respected pattern in Honduras. Sometimes these friend-relatives are used to build loyalties toward furtherance of political or economic careers.

COMPAÑIA AZUCAREÑA HONDUREÑA, S.A. This Honduran Sugar

Company is the country's largest producer of sugar, most of which is grown for this one company in large irrigated plantings near San Pedro Sula. The central area of Francisco Morazán Department, western Olancho, as well as Copán, Yoro, Comayagua, and Santa Bárbara departments all grow cane. In 1967 Honduras exported sugar. In 1970 the crop was 65,000 short tons.

COMPAÑIA NAVIERA AGUILA, S.A. On July 2, 1973, this shipping company opened direct express shipping service between Miami and Central America. A Honduran company, the organization operates refrigerated and bulk cargo space in the motor vessel Morazán, with access to Central America via its terminus at Puerto Cortés, on the north coast of Honduras near San Pedro Sula.

COMPENDIA DE LA HISTORIA SOCIAL Y POLITICA DE HONDURAS see HISTORY, HONDURAS

COMPTROLLER GENERAL, OFFICE OF. This is an organ subordinate to the unicameral Congress (q.v.) which reviews government expenditures and informs the Congress of irregularities, a type of continuous audit.

CONASA LINE see COMPAÑIA NAVIERA AGUILA, S.A.

CONCHAGUA, GOLFO DE. Nineteenth century (and earlier) alternate name for the Gulf of Fonseca. Conchagua is also the name of a town and volcano in nearby El Salvador.

CONCORDIA. In Western Olancho Department, a municipal cabacera with an airfield in the shadows of the Montaña de Misoco. As in most of Olancho, cattle dominate the economy.

CONCORDIA PARK. A unique park in the northwestern part of downtown Tegucigalpa which, while small, is characterized by a great variety of tropical plants, and by pools, arbors, and a miniature replica of a Maya temple. The park is chiefly used by the lower-income inhabitants of the capital city.

CONDECA see CENTRAL AMERICAN DEFENSE COUNCIL

CONFEDERACION DE TRABAJADORES DE AMERICA LATINA see CONFEDERACION SINDICATO DE LATINA AMERICANA

CONFEDERACION DE TRABAJADORES DE HONDURAS see CONFEDERATION OF HONDURAN WORKERS

CONFEDERACION INTERNATIONAL DE SINDICATOS LIBRES. Anti-communist international labor organization which helped end the 1954 General Strike (q.v.).

CONFEDERACION SINDICATO DE AMERICA LATINA. An organization based in Mexico whose purpose is union development in Latin America. The name of Vicente Lombardo Toledano has been synonymous with the C.S.A.L. as its foremost voice. Name changed later to Confederación de Trabajadores de América Latina (C.T.A.L.) (q.v.).

CONFEDERATION OF HONDURAN WORKERS. The three national federations of Organized Labor (q.v.) are joined in this "super" federation, initiated in 1964. Only the Authentic Federation of Honduran Unions (q.v.) is outside this confederation. The three federations are: Federation of Workers of the North of Honduras (q.v.); Federation of Free Unions of Honduras (q.v.); National Federation of Workers and Peasants (q.v.).

CONGREGACIONES. Centralized villages achieved by a process of "reduction" carried out by Franciscan and Dominican friars and Spanish planters. Under the pretext of "spiritual conquest" it made the handling of Indians much easier for the Spanish entrepreneurs, especially in the matters of labor assignments and collection of tribute. The Indian lands freed by this resettlement and centralization policy gave more opportunity for Spanish crops and cattle. While it ended by 1550, the effects of "congregación" lingered on.

CONGREHOY see CERROS DE CANGREJAL

CONGRESS. The legislative branch of the Honduran government consists of a unicameral Congress that meets for six months or more each year. There is a permanent legislative committee which serves as a staff for the congress when it is not in session. The Comptroller General (q.v.) is an organ of the congress.

In theory, the Congress can prevent complete Presidential control and, as a separate branch, has an independent role and effect in national policies and politics. In actual practice, and historically, the powers of Congress as separate from the executive are very rarely used. The overall preeminence of the executive is almost never challenged. The net result is a "strong-man" form of government, based in essence on caudillismo (q.v.). The Constitution of 1965 established a six-year congressional term and a popular election for 1971. Each department is entitled to one deputy (member of Congress) for each 30,000 inhabitants and one additional for any fraction over another 15,000. If the department has under 30,000, it still gets one deputy.

There has been no bicameral legislature since 1865. Regular congressional sessions are held from May 26 through October 26 annually, but can be extended by special resolution. The president or a majority of deputies can call special sessions. A majority of deputies constitutes a quorum for purposes of installing Congress and for regular sessions. Congress not only enacts ordinary legislation, but also declares war, makes peace, initiates impeachment proceedings, confirms higher military ranks, controls the strength of the permanent army, and controls revenues by voting the budget, establishing taxes, approving national debt limits and loans.

CONGRESS, FIRST NATIONAL, OF CENTRAL AMERICA. In February, 1825, under the Constitution of 1824, the Congress met, the issue of representation being a burning one, as the outlying areas did not wish Guatemala City to have undue influence or to be the capital. One of the tactics was to create a new state from the area around Quetzaltenango, Guatemala, to be called Los Altos. With a delegates-at-large policy, this could help to minimize Guatemala City's influence. The return of Chiapas (a state of Mexico) was also expected. Deputies were distributed as follows:

| Guatemala | 18 | Nicaragua | 6 |
| El Salvador | 9 | Costa Rica | 2 |
| Honduras | 6 | | |

The optimism of the 1825 meeting was ended by the outbreak of a three-year civil war, 1826-29.

CONGRESS OF MEXICO. Including representatives from the rival Honduran factions in Comayagua and Tegucigalpa, this Congress met in mid-1822 to deal with the matter of recent independence and proposed union. José Cecilio del Valle (q.v.) of Honduras was elected vice-president of the assembly, as the Central American present who ranked in prestige. Before the Congress could complete a constitution, it was dissolved by Iturbide, who had meanwhile made himself Emperor of Mexico.

CONQUEST. Honduras, in the region of the Gulf of Fonseca, was not only the site of the "Cultural Divide" (q.v.) between Mexican and South American indigenous influences, but it became also the crucial point between thrusts of the Spanish Conquest from Panama and Mexico, culminating in 1523 and 1524 with thrusts by Córdoba and Alvarado from the south, and Dávila, Cortés, and Alvarado again from the north.

CONSEJO DE DEFENSA CENTROAMERICANO see CENTRAL AMERICAN DEFENSE COUNCIL

CONSEJO DE LAS INDIAS. For supreme control of the American adventure, the "Royal and Supreme Council of the Indies" was established in 1524 to succeed the temporary headship of colonial affairs by Juan Rodríguez de Fonseca. The Council controlled all aspects of New World government. Cases reached it through both the audiencias and the Casa de Contratación (q.v.). In effect it was an executive and a supreme court. Lacking the means and responsibility for enforcement of its regulations and judgments, however, the council lacked unity, and decisions were often delayed for years, with disastrous impact on governmental effectiveness. The Council was placed under the Ministry of Navy and Indies in 1714, was made purely advisory in 1790, abolished in 1812, revived in 1814, and finally ended in 1834 (after most of the American colonial possessions had won their freedom).

CONSEJO DE UNIDAD SINDICAL (C. U. S.). This "council of unity" is a prevalent labor organization throughout Central America, and in general has extra-territorial affiliations.

CONSEJO SUPERIOR UNIVERSITARIO CENTROAMERICANO. This Higher Council of Central American Universities, organized in 1948, comes under a Central American Agreement for the Basic Integration of Education, providing for collaborative effort by the five Central American Republics for textbook improvement and teacher exchange programs. There has been particular interest in improving university education, and in studying the educational systems. Special problems of university education in the region include: lack of laboratory experiences; paucity of discussion sessions; emphasis on traditional professions, such as law (there is a great surplus of lawyers); neglect of natural sciences, applied engineering, etc.; part-time professional staffs; inadequate libraries; inadequate or non-existent research laboratories; low professional salaries; antequated and inadequate plant facilities.

With a Secretary General and a small staff responsible to a joint policy council composed of representatives from each member university, the Consejo has developed as a consultative group which is involved in pooling resources, sharing ideas, doing joint and regional research. A major contribution has been the choice of certain regional institutions as centers of excellence for a particular specialty (somewhat resembling the Southern Regional Education Board of the United States). Pooled effort and elimination of unnecessary competition and duplication are a desirable result.

CONSTITUTION OF 1812. Produced by the Cortes de Cádiz, the 1812 Constitution was an astonishing document of imperial reorganization, and might have retained the Spanish colonial empire if other matters had not intervened. The Kingdom of Guatemala was to elect 12 deputies to the Spanish parliament. Further, there were to be two regional bodies; one at León, Nicaragua, the other in Guatemala City. These "diputaciones provinciales" were something like modern development corporations. The reforms failed, but Spain's willingness to give her subjects a more representative form of government is worth noting. This constitution was the basis for the national governments which came later in Central America. Both system and terminology were adopted. Honduras under this Constitution was to be attached to the regional body in León.

CONSTITUTION OF 1824. On November 22, 1824, a Central American constitution was promulgated which was a compromise that attempted to reconcile the sharply differing political desires of aristocrats, liberals, and others, especially the major conflict between Serviles and Radicals. Based on the Cádiz Constitution of 1812, and to some extent on the United States Constitution of 1789, there were also in use the Colombian, Portuguese, and French plans and codes. Major organ of sovereignty was a Chamber of Deputies, elected by proportional representation of the people. Executive and judicial branches were under legislative control. The Senate had both executive and advisory functions. The Executive was almost powerless. State level government was similar. The states were "free and independent" in their interior administration. This clause provided later difficulties. Whether this constitution established a unitary republic or "federation" on the one hand, or whether it was a league of states or "confederation" on the other, is hard to assess. It was "states-rights" controversy based on this point which led to the final breakup of the Republic. In a sense, it was somewhat parallel to the United States Civil War of the 1860's, if the Confederacy had won.

CONSTITUTION OF 1957 see CONSTITUTION OF 1965

CONSTITUTION OF 1965. In 1965 a new basic document for Honduras was sought following the impetus provided by the overthrow in 1963 of President Villeda Morales, and the consequent coming into power of Colonel Oswaldo López Arellano. (López from 1972-1975 Brigadier General and President once again.) The 1957 Constitution, in force at the time of Villeda Morales' overthrow, had made significant changes in the previous constitution (1936), principally in the areas of social reform such as family, labor, electoral procedures, and in such matters as the disposition, character, and control of the armed forces. The 1957 document included some social guarantees and many specific human rights provisions not dealt with in earlier constitutional formulations. These moves had arisen during the liberal and labor-dominated regime of Villeda Morales.

The new fundamental charter, then, the 1965 Constitution, was drawn up by a constituent assembly elected in 1965 and dominated by National Party members in support of the de facto head of State, López Arellano. The constituent assembly designated López as the first President under the new constitution, to serve for six years, and voted themselves into being as the first congress under the 1965 document. The effect was to eliminate presidential and congressional elections until 1971. (The elections which took place in that year, resulting in the presidential incumbency of Ramón Cruz, were in effect nullified in December of 1972 when López Arellano again seized office in a calm and bloodless coup. Following this event, the 1965 constitution was declared to remain in effect.)

The 1965 basic document divides government into the Executive, Legislative, and Judicial branches, with the President as commander of the armed forces. The Congress is unicameral under proportional representation. The Supreme Court consists of seven justices elected by Congress for six-year terms. There are fourteen "Titles" in the constitution, each being separated into chapters and articles.

Title One gives territorial limits, general governmental structure, and the fundamental philosophy behind the whole. It avers Honduras' place as part of the Federal Republic of Central America, and nods toward restoration of a union, the perennial dream of Central American leaders and intellectuals ever since the breakup 135 years ago.

Title II deals with elections, political parties, and citizenship. Reciprocal citizenship provisions are an unusual feature, applied to immigrants from other Central American countries, who may earn Honduran full citizenship in one year. (This did not prevent problems with Salvadoran squatters during the 1969 war.)

Titles III and IV are detailed social and individual guarantees of rights. These include such familiar ones as habeas corpus, free speech and press, free assembly, and political asylum. The suspension of guarantees is provided for, however, in the presidential power to declare martial law (or an "estado in sitio") under a declared state of emergency which may last 30 days, or longer with congressional approval, and which expires in 45 days in any event. Of course, it may be renewed. Title IV also deals with several guarantees in relation to labor and education.

Title V takes up the organization and functioning of the three branches of government, while VI and VII cover the Supreme Court in particular and delineate its powers of judicial review. Title VIII deals broadly with economics, the position being that the national economy is based upon a private enterprise system. Titles IX and X are civil service rules and policies.

Title XI deals with the armed forces. The constitution attempts by strong wording to discourage both presidential continuation in office and military coups, which are a familiar part of Honduran and all Central American history. Title XII gives the geographical and political division of the land into departments and municipalities, as well as outlining their operation and internal government. Title XIII gives the process of constitutional amendment, and Title XIV provided the transition pattern for putting the new document into effect upon its inception, on June 6, 1967.

The net result is a highly centralized form of government with most of the real power in the hands of the President. The provision of checks and balances is more nominal than real.

CONSULAR TAXES see IMPORT DUTIES

CONSUMER PRICE INDEX. With 1963 as a base year, the consumer price index was 110 for foods and 118 for all items in

1969. By 1974 it was around 150. Inflation in 1974 was over 25 per cent and the hurricane "Fifi" contributed to its acceleration.

CONTARINI, G. M. Author of a World Map which was engraved in 1506 by Roselli, and which showed Cuba and Haiti very recognizably, as well as the north coast of South America. However, in the Central American area only ocean was indicated, with a large island in the general position of Yucatan. There seem to have been no published maps of the Honduran mainland this early, though Columbus had been there four years previously.

A manuscript world map of 1508 shows a blob of land with the island of "Guaneca" (off the Honduras coast) indicated. Apparently Columbus' charts had reached the "press" by this time. This is the first clear indication of Honduran Territory.

CONTINUISMO. "Continuation," or the technique of staying in power through quasi-legal means but without any real referendum by the people, has been a recurrent theme in Central America, especially since 1930. Cuadillos ruled in Guatemala and El Salvador, 1931-1944; in Nicaragua, 1933-56. Honduras has had its share of the pattern akin to that of the Mexico of Porfirio Díaz, whose regime ended bloodily following 1910-11.

CONTRABAND TRADE, 18th CENTURY. This trade was facilitated in northern Honduras by the presence of the British at Black River and other coastal points, by the money available from the rich Opoteca mines opened about 1700 near Comayagua, and by the geographical circumstance that there were rivers for transport and trade--the Patuca, Black, Ullua, and León among them. Livestock trading was especially important. There was an anglicizing of the Spanish frontier and a hispanicizing of the English settlements.

The contraband prices offered for Central American products such as farm animals were much higher than could be paid in legitimate trade by Guatemalan merchants.

The most active contrabandistas were ladinos of the frontier towns. The contraband trade reached at least 300,000 pesos annually by 1745. From 1655 to 1755 the English Shore colony had no official connection with the British government, and was a contraband center unto itself.

CONTRERAS, ALVARO. Director of the Institute at Santa Rosa de Copán, Contreras was named Director General of Public Education in 1923 under the new code (see CODES OF PUBLIC INSTRUCTION).

CONVENTO DE NUESTRA SEÑORA DE LAS MERCEDES. 18th and 19th century ecclesiastical establishment in Tegucigalpa, to which José Trinidad Reyes (q.v.) returned in 1828.

COOLIDGE, CALVIN. United States President who authorized and justified U.S. intervention in the Sandino (q.v.) troubles of the 1920s. In 1923 the five Central American countries had entered into mutual treaties in Washington, D.C. Coolidge said in his January 10, 1927, message to Congress that Honduras and the other Central American countries had agreed to an arms embargo on shipments to Sandino, and that the "stability, prosperity, and independence of all Central American countries can never be a matter of indifference to us." This was widely interpreted to imply an intervention policy, which indeed it did, as the history of the next six years attests.

COOLIDGE COROLLARY TO THE MONROE DOCTRINE. In April of 1927 President Calvin Coolidge of the United States made a statement which in spite of its general irrelevance to the Monroe Doctrine and its original intent to discourage European intervention, was hailed as a corollary to that Doctrine. Coolidge's statement included the following: "United States recognized responsibility toward governments of the countries this side of the Panama Canal that did not attach to other nations." It further expressed U.S. determination to discourage revolutions and to encourage peaceful elections as a method of settling political differences. In the case of Honduras and her Central American neighbors, this amounted to a license to meddle.

COPAL. An aromatic resin from several tropical trees, usually dark amber in color. When dried it is very brittle. It is widely used by Indian (especially Maya-related) tribes of Central America as a ceremonial incense for religious observances and fiestas. It was apparently extensively so used in Pre-Columbian Central America. Copal gum is a principal ingredient of good spar (marine) varnishes.

COPALLI. Original Nahuatl name for "copal" (q.v.).

COPAN - THE MAYA RUINS. The Maya ceremonial center of Copán is located in the western part of Honduras, in the Department of Copán. The site is farthest southeast of the Maya cities, that of Tazumal in El Salvador being the only other one as far extended along the isthmian area of Meso-America. The nearest town is San José de Copán, 3,000 inhabitants, which is now more generally called "Ruinas de Copán." The distance from Tegucigalpa is just over 300 miles.

Copán was first discovered by a European in 1576, and it was on March 8 of that year that Diego García de Palacio, of the Royal audiencia in Guatemala, wrote to his monarch, Philip II of Spain, with details about the ruins. His language was extravagant in praise of the sculpture and edifices of Copán, but he was unable to get any information from the local Indians as to the origin of the ruins, except that they were built in ancient times by invaders from Yucatán.

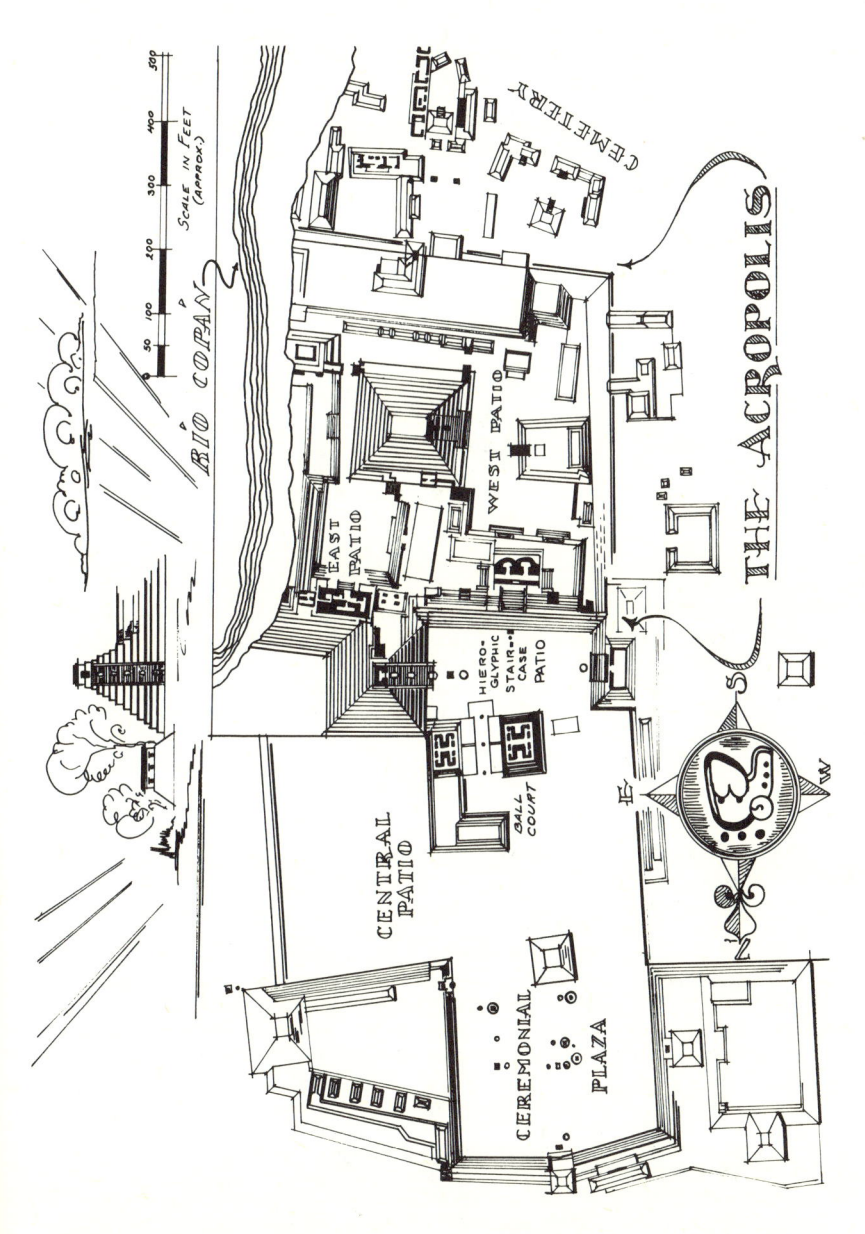

COPAN: Diagram of major features of Copán, one of the three or four major Maya ceremonial centers in existence.

Little further than García's visit seems to have happened for two and a half centuries. In 1833, Colonel Juan Galindo (q.v.), an Irishman in Central American service, visited the ruins. His articles helped to call attention to Copán in Europe and America.

It was five years later that John L. Stephens (q.v.) a diplomatic representative of the United States and a peripatetic amateur explorer who had already penetrated the Jordanian wilderness to the "rose-red" ruins of Petra, found his way to Copán. Fortunately he had with him an artist, an Englishman named Frederick Catherwood (q.v.).

It is of more than passing interest that, rare among the Maya sites, Copán bears the name that was being used four centuries ago. It may be that the Spanish named the place believing it to be the capital of the chief Copán-Calel, who fought the conquistadores in the 16th century. Maudsley (q.v.), Spinden (q.v.), Morley (q.v.), and Howard University all had a part in the unravelling of the Copán mysteries by excavation and archaeological research, from 1881 through 1942. Dr. Morley helped arrange with the Honduran government a contract whereby the Carnegie Institute would carry out excavations. This work went on from 1935-1942. One important phase of the work was redirecting the bed of the Copán River, the stream which had been cutting into the "acropolis" area of the ruins.

The site of the ruins, low in the Río Copán Valley, differs markedly from other Maya sites such as Tikal, Palenque, Uxmal, Tazumal, Chichén Itzá, or Tulúm, for most of these are on plateau or mountain spur platforms. The valley today is a major tobacco growing area. There is some reason to believe that early inhabitants reached the valley about 3000 B.C. It was a good food-producing region, where the Central American staples of beans, corn, and squash are still grown.

While there are as many as forty or fifty centuries of occupation of this valley, the site of the ruins flourished from the earliest date on one of the Stelae (q.v.), 465 A.D., until about 800 A.D. The height of the Copán cultural achievement, then, probably spanned three to five centuries. Copán was considered the scientific center of classic era Maya achievement.

There are throughout the valley 16 sites presently known, although it is only about eight or nine miles long and averaging less than a mile wide. At the major site is an involved complex of temples, stelae, courts, patios, stepped pyramids and the major upthrust of the acropolis itself. A major feature is the huge ceremonial court surrounded by low staircases, which if used as bleachers would seat over 50,000. In the great court are two forms of sculpture -- round carvings called altars, and vertical anthropomorphic "statues" called stelae, covered with hieroglyphs. There are nine in this court. The carvings and sculptures are done in andesite (q.v.). There is a ball court, with low sloping sides

STELA AND ALTAR - COPAN: The great Maya ceremonial site is characterized by many stelae and usually corresponding altars, intricately carved in full relief, bas-relief, and hieroglyphics.

vastly different from the vertical walls of a similar court at Chichén Itzá. The great Hieroglyphic Stairway (q.v.) leads up to the acropolis and a temple at its crest.

The acropolis itself has an east and a west court, with a beautiful sculptured Jaguar stairway on the East. Both courts are high above the general level. Where the river has washed away a portion of the acropolis, a vertical fence of masonry 118 feet high and 1,000 feet long is exposed, the longest such cross-section in the world, exhibiting the type of construction as well as the earlier plaza-floor levels.

To describe in detail the sculptures and the architectural nuances of Copán is far beyond the scope of the work undertaken here, but it should be said that this is one of the world's prime archeological sites, and compares in its own area with Tikal and Uxmal, and in the world at large with Machu Picchu, the Athenian acropolis, and that at Lindos, Rhodes, the castles on the Rhine and jungle-choked Angkor Thom. (See diagrams.)

COPAN DEPARTMENT. Named for the classic Maya ceremonial city which is near its central western border, Copán Department is bounded on the west and northwest by the international border with Guatemala; to the east and northeast is Santa Bárbara Department; to the southeast, Lempira Department, and on the south, that of Ocotepeque. The Cordillera de Merendón splits the department north to south. The cabacera is Santa Rosa de Copán; there are 23 municipios. The cabacera is over 50 miles by road from the famous ruins. The department had a 1973 population of 51,633 in the cabaceras while the village and rural population was 130,175, for a total of 181,808.

The area of the department is 1,208 square miles. There is one hospital. The whole area lends itself to tobacco culture, and there is also cattle-raising, as well as the usual subsistence farming of small plantings of staple crops. The ruins of Copán are a major tourist attraction, not so much for great numbers of tourists as for the quality of the site, appreciated by amateur or experienced Mayaphiles.

COPAN, FIRST SCIENTIFIC ARCHAEOLOGICAL WORK. Done between 1881-94 by Sir Alfred Maudsley (q.v.).

COPAN-CALEL. Semi-legendary cacique of the area about Copán, who fielded an army of 30,000 against the conquering Spaniards during the early 16th century. See CHIQUIMULA DE LA SIERRA.

COPANTL. Possible Nahuatl form of Copán, which has been translated as "pontoon" or "bridge." Others believe the meaning to be "capital of Co."

COPEN. The Permanent Committee of National Emergency. See HONDURAN COUNCIL OF PRIVATE ENTERPRISE.

COQUET, JOSEF. One of Gálvez' officers at Trujillo (q.v.) in 1782, who was sent with Colonel Domezaín (q.v.) with half the force of 1,500 soldiers, to attack the English establishments on Black River.

COQUIMBOS. The group of Central American unionists of the latter half of the 19th century, based in El Salvador, and adhered to by Honduran two-time president Trinidad Cabañas (q.v.). They first made plans in Costa Rica in 1842, and then took ship for El Salvador in the Coquimbo, hence their nickname. Morazán (q.v.) was the guiding light of their original plan, but his Costa Rican execution sent them back to the North.

CORDILLERA DE DEPILTO. High mountains on the Honduran-Nicaraguan border in the department of El Paraiso.

CORDILLERA ENTRO RIOS. The range of low mountains which crowns the narrow reaches between the large rivers Patuca (q.v.) and Coco (q.v.) along the Honduran southeastern borderland. The wildest part of the country, this between-rivers area rises to heights of 4,000 feet. The rivers are only about fifteen miles apart in several locations.

CORDILLERA NOMBRE DE DIOS. Spectacularly visible from the Bay Islands, just as Columbus must have seen them in 1502, these mountains are up to 4,000 feet altitude within three miles of the Caribbean, a veritable mountain wall, without the low littoral characteristic elsewhere on the north coast of Honduras.

CORDILLERAS. These major ranges may also be cited individually: Merendón, Celaque, Pucal, Opalaca, Montecillas, Agalta, Comayagua, Sulaco, Nombre de Dios, Misoco, Dipilto. See also MONTAÑAS.

CORDONAZO. A Pacific tropical cyclone; these tend not to have much effect upon Honduran weather, but are a regional weather manifestation.

CORDOVA, JOSE FRANCISCO. Author of the Second Act of Central American Independence, July 1, 1823. See SEGUNDA ACTA DE INDEPENDENCIA DE CENTRO AMERICA.

COREN. The National Reconstruction Committee. See HONDURAN COUNCIL OF PRIVATE ENTERPRISE.

CORINTO TREATY. In 1902, President Zelaya of Nicaragua called a session in Corinto which was attended by four Central American presidents including the Honduran President, in which they prepared a treaty accepting arbitration as a principle and establishing a regional tribunal. Rivalry between Zelaya and others doomed the plan.

**CORN CULTURE.** There were over 1,000,000 acres of corn in Honduras in 1969, with about 148,000 farms represented, indicating how small the average planting is. The 1968 crop was 390,000 metric tons.

**COROSSO.** A variety of palm which is grown commercially on the north coast of Honduras. With somewhat the appearance of a date palm in its upswept fronds and clusters of fruit, this oil palm produces on each tree thousands of oily nuts like miniature coconuts. The corosso has a parasite, Calahuala, which is thought to be good for treating cancer, and which is used by the ordinary Honduran for treating any internal upset.

**COROZO PALM** see **MONACA**

**CORPUS MINE.** One of the richest mines in the Tegucigalpa area in the late 1600s, site of disturbances characteristic of a raw mining camp. Food was sold at extortionate prices, and mining repartimentos (q.v.) of Indians were illegally assigned other tasks, etc. Profiteering in the resale of mercury was rife. The mine did not reform after the "visita" of Valenguela Banegas (q.v.), but officials and others were captured and prosecuted.

**CORREGIDOR.** A Spanish colonial official in charge of a district, having judicial as well as administrative power. Named by the viceroy until 1678, corregidors were designated by the Council of the Indies after that date. Because of the power to collect tribute and draft Indian labor, these officials were petty despots with great local power. Caudillismo and caciquismo may have their origins in this frequently abused office.

**CORSAIRS, 16th CENTURY HONDURAS.** English and French "pirates" sacked Trujillo three times between 1560 and 1576, and Puerto Caballos five times between 1589 and 1603. The Honduran governor put four cannon in Trujillo in 1575, but this was little help in such a spacious harbor.

**CORTES DEPARTMENT.** Bounded on the north by the Bahía de Omoa, part of the Gulf of Honduras of the Caribbean Sea; on the east by the Río Ulua; on the south and southeast by Comayagua Department and Lake Yojoa; and on the southwest by Santa Bárbara; on the northwest by the Sierra de Omoa and the international border with Guatemala. The cabacera is San Pedro Sula, the major industrial center of the whole nation. There are 11 cabaceras and municipios. The departmental area is 1,550 square miles. San Pedro Sula is the most rapidly growing population area in the country, and with 202,751 population in the cabaceras in 1973, the department was second only to Tegucigalpa, and climbing at an accelerated pace. The rural and small town population of Cortés is 117,551, for an overall total of 320,302, including the significant port of Puerto Cortés on the north coast. There is ample rail service, and the nation's only jetport with several national and international airlines serving it. Industrial development of Honduras is concentrated in this department. There is a relatively new university, and the greatest availability of hospitals in the country, with eleven.

CORTES DE CADIZ. Spanish government during the Napoleonic Wars. Enacted liberal Constitution of 1812, which was rejected by Ferdinand VII in 1814. In 1820 Colonel Rafael Riego rebelled and compelled Ferdinand to restore the 1812 document. These events were of significance to Hispanic America, including Honduras, because they helped to set the stage for independence. In Central America the tussle over Ferdinand strained relations between peninsulars (Iberian-born) and criollas (colonial-born). Note that Indians and mixed "mestizos" did not count politically.

CORTES, HERNAN. A conquistador who needs no introduction, but whose connection with Honduras lies in his epic overland trek in 1524, as far as Trujillo, Honduras (from whence he returned to Mexico in April 1525 to quell an uprising). The purpose of Cortés' incredible southeastward journey through the formidable Petén jungles of Guatemala was to secure Lake Nicaragua, the "Sweet Sea," from control by Pedrarias. He had also lost faith in his earlier emissary, Christóval Olid (q.v.). Cortés' 1524 march was incredible, but he did not succeed in preventing Pedrarias Dávila from securing the lake, nor did he reach the lake. Córdoba and Olid lost their lives for their treachery in the matter. Cortés established two major Honduran ports--Puerto Caballos (now Puerto Cortés) and Trujillo.

COSA, JUAN DE LA. With Columbus on his second voyage, 1493-94, Cosa is best known for his famous map which shows the first three voyages as well as the material which was provided after the voyage of John Cabot in 1497. A very early world chart, dated 1500, the Cosa map does not clearly delineate the Honduran coast, although other Caribbean features such as Cuba and Haiti and Maracaibo are unmistakable. However, some scholars see the Cabo Gracias a Dios area to the north of Cuba on the Cosa map, and comparison shows that the Zorzi (q.v.) map, made from data presumably provided by Bartolomé Columbus (q.v.), does show a similar coast, oriented 90 degrees off the known directions, with offshore islands identified on the Columbus map as the Bay islands, but unidentified on Cosa's. The mis-orientation could have arisen from an iron tool or weapon too close to the crude ship compass of the times. There is still reasonable doubt as to whether Cosa may have had more information than appeared on the map. The implication would be of an earlier voyage along the Central American Coast than that of Columbus.

COSEGÜINA, VOLCAN. 2820-foot volcano at the northwesternmost tip of Nicaragua, on the Coseguina Peninsula jutting into the Bay of Fonseca, a part of the volcanic complex surrounding that Honduran bay. An explosive eruption on January 20, 1835 ranks with the explosion of Krakatoa in the East Indies as one of the major volcanic events of recorded history. A lake presently occupies the large low crater. According to calculation the volcano was originally over 6,000 feet in altitude, and about half of that elevation was blown off in the eruption. Cinders reached Mexico and Colombia, and are believed to have covered 1,400,000 square miles as they fell. The sound was heard across the Caribbean in Jamaica.

COSIO Y CAMPO, TORIBIO JOSE. As governor and captain-general, 1706-16, he led an expedition against the Tzendals in Chiapas, and put down that Indian rebellion in 1712-13.

COSSU. Old miskito word for curassow, a large and edible bird, crested, about the size of a turkey.

COSTA DE LAS OREJAS, LA. Columbus named the north coast of Honduras the "coast of the ears" because he found the inhabitants with ear plugs as large as hen's eggs. These were probably Paya (q.v.) or Jicaque (q.v.) Indians.

COSTEÑOS. East-coast dwellers in Honduras, self-identified as distinguished from the ladinos.

COTO, AGUSTO. Secretary-general of the 1954 strikers (see GENERAL STRIKE 1954). He took the blame for failure of negotiations in June, and was arrested as a Communist.

COTTON. Introduced less than 25 years ago, cotton is grown in Olancho, Choluteca, and Valle departments, about 90 per cent of the crop being exported. In the mid-1960s the planting stayed around 31,000 acres for a yield of over 40,000 bales per year; by 1970 the planting was only half as much. 8,000 bales per annum are used domestically.

COUNCIL OF MINISTERS see CABINET

COYOL WINE see VINO DE COYOL

COYOLAL. A grove of coyol palm used in the making of Vino de coyol (q.v.).

COZCAQUAUHTLI. Sixteenth day of the Aztec month; meaning, "Buzzard." Throughout middle America the Nahuatl word "Zopilote" is used to name one kind of buzzard.

CRAME, AGUSTIN. Brigadier Crame was a fortifications specialist who in 1778 made an inspection of Fort Omoa (q.v.) for Matías de Gálvez who had been given supreme authority in military affairs for the Kingdom of Guatemala. Crame was a member of the Committee of Fortifications in New Spain, and his inspection of Omoa found the materiel in good shape, but there was a need for men, and he recommended transfer of 300 infantry at once from San Pedro Sula to the Fort.

CREER. A small boat used by the Black Caribs (q.v.).

CREFAL. Acronym representing Centro Regional de Educación Fundamental para la América Latina. A function of UNESCO with home office in Pátzcuaro, Mexico, and of particular interest to a special fundamental education project on the Río Coco. See also UNESCO.

CREOLES. A confusing term because of its multiplicity of uses and regional variations. In early colonial days it meant Spanish-American non-Indians born in the Americas. These American-born whites were usually relegated to secondary citizen status, Spanish-born "peninsulares" receiving the highest offices. Naturally antagonisms resulted. On the Mosquito coast of modern times, however, the English-speaking largely negroid population are often called "creoles," especially by whites of nationalities not indigenous. In this sense it is significant to review the different grades of blood mixture as identified late in the 19th century. See RACIAL MIXTURES.

CRIADO DE CASTILLA, ALONSO DE. From 1598 to 1611, President of the Audiencia of Guatemala, and author of the plan to change the Honduran gulf ports to Golfo Dulce and to retire Puerto Caballos and Trujillo. By 1604 he had moved some of the inhabitants of Puerto Caballos to the new location, Santo Tomás de Castilla. It was a poor place, and declined by 1617; Castilla's successor declared it a liability. By 1618 the trade returned to Puerto Caballos to a large extent. Criado de Castilla was a vigorous and controversial governor, and died during his residency.

CRIME. No comprehensive statistics on crime are available. In rural areas disputes tend to be settled locally, and in such areas there is little law enforcement. Major disturbances such as strikes and violence are usually in urban areas. Military and police forces tend to be concentrated in Tegucigalpa and San Pedro Sula. There has been no report of Communist guerrilla activity such as is found in several of the neighbor countries.

CRIOLLOS see CREOLES

CRIQUE. A fascinating example of adaptation of the English word "creek." On the east (Caribbean) coast of Honduras many of the small streams are called "criques." The appended names are usually Miskito, not Spanish--as "Crique Auastingni."

This is especially interesting since "Tingni" (q.v.) is Miskito for stream. The translation might be "Auas Creek-stream."

CRIQUE PALMA SUPA. A tributary of the Río Patuca near the Caribbean.

CRIQUE WAIWANTINGNI. A "creek" flowing into the Río Nakunta, and in turn into the Laguna de Caratasca (q.v.).

CRIQUE YAUNKRA. A tributary of the Río Patuca in the Delta area which enters a mile or two from the Patuca bar.

CRISTALES. A Black Carib village near Trujillo, very near where Columbus first landed on the Central American mainland.

CROP PRODUCTION. Agricultural production increased 150 per cent between 1952 and 1966.

Annual Production: (from 1968-70 period):

| | |
|---|---|
| Bananas | 1,250,000 metric tons |
| Coffee | 500,000 bags |
| Corn | 390,000 metric tons |
| Sugar | 80,000 short tons |
| Beans | 53,000 metric tons |
| Cotton | 20,000 bales |
| (down from mid 1960s period when it was 40,000 bales) | |
| Tobacco | ? |
| Rice | 24,000 metric tons |
| Sorghum | 69,000 metric tons |
| Soft wheat | 1,000 metric tons |
| Cattle (in 1970) | 1,800,000 head |

See also FARMS.

CROSS-ISTHMIAN ROUTE. When the disease-ridden Panamanian ports and poor harbors became seemingly insupportable, alternate transisthmian routes were sought. One of these was across Honduras, a road to be cut between the Honduran Gulf ports and the Gulf of Fonseca, via Comayagua. Land movement of goods, however, was slow, dangerous, and expensive compared to water transport in the 16th century. Nevertheless, in 1560, the Spanish crown decided on a route through Honduras, with Trujillo as a principal port of both Peru and New Spain. The idea, amazingly, was revived in the early 17th century.

CRUZ, BALTAZAR DE LA. Governor in 1647.

CRUZ, FRANCISCO. As designated deputy, Cruz served in the presidency from September 5, 1869 until January 14, 1870.

CRUZ, RAMON A.  Ramón Cruz was constitutional president from 1971 until the coup on December 4, 1972, which ousted him. It was the first military coup d'état in Central America since 1963 when governments in Guatemala and Honduras were overthrown. In Honduras the man who became President in October 1963 once again took power in December of 1972, General Oswaldo López Arellano (q.v.), Commander of the armed forces. Cruz was placed in house arrest, but there was little disturbance or disorder. Cruz had been serving, in effect, at the pleasure of the armed forces. When he took office June 7, 1971, it was as a bipartisan president. Threats of a coup had been heard a number of times during his term. His inability to reintegrate Honduras into the Common Market was considered a major problem. He also rejected the "Pactito" (q.v.) of 1971.

CRUZ, SALVADOR.  On August 30, 1876 Cruz became "Pseudo-President through Anarchy," one of the vicissitudes of the regime of Dr. Marco Aurelio Soto.

CSLA  see  CONFEDERACION SINDICATO DE LATINA AMERICANA

CSUCA  see  CONSEJO SUPERIOR UNIVERSITARIO CENTROAMERICANO; also, UNIVERSITY OF HONDURAS

CTAL  see  CONFEDERACION DE TRABAJADORES DE AMERICA LATINA

CTH  see  CONFEDERATION OF HONDURAN WORKERS

"CUARENTEÑO."  A quick-growing 40-day variety of both red and white beans, grown in the river valleys of Mosquitia.

CUBA, DIPLOMATIC RELATIONS.  Honduras in late 1974 was one of seven Latin American nations which did not have diplomatic relations with Cuba. The others were Colombia, Costa Rica, El Salvador, the Dominican Republic, Ecuador, and Venezuela. It was believed, however, that Honduras might soon ignore the OAS sanctions and establish relations with Cuba. The whole concept of inter-American cooperation and of the role of the OAS (q.v.) was admittedly at stake.

CUBERO DACOSTA, MIGUEL ALFONSO  see  RAMIREZ, ROBERTO

CUBETAS.  The elegant brass stirrups once widely distributed in Spain's colonial possessions, and still in use in the remote cattle country of Olancho around Juticalpa. They resemble a wooden shoe without a heel, and are part cast, part wrought. They are hung from saddles much like the familiar McClellan saddle of United States Civil War vintage.

Cubetas 108

ON SADDLE

PROFILE
(10½" LONG)

**ESTRIBO-ANTIGUO (also CUBETA):** The ancient brass stirrup as found to this day in Olancho department is a functional colonial relic.

CUERPO ESPECIAL DE SEGURIDAD. This force, known popularly as "El CES," replaced the Civil Guard in 1963. While it is a national police force somewhat like the Guardia Civil in Spain or the "Rurales" of Díaz' days in Mexico, it is accepted and carries out its duties much as a State Patrol would in the United States. The headquarters are in Tegucigalpa. While independent of the jurisdiction of military commands, the CES draws its membership from the armed forces and has a close cooperative relationship with the military services. The corps has a membership of 2,500 to 3,000. There have been some recent structural changes in the organization. Specialized police functions are also located in the capital. The corps has a jaunty and distinctive uniform with an "Australian"-type broadbrimmed hat. The members wear side-arms and are usually found in pairs.

CUETZPALLIN. Fourth day of the Aztec month; meaning, "letter."

CUEVA, FRANCISCO DE LA. Governor of Honduras in 1540.

CULTURAL DIVIDE. A line projected approximately from Trujillo, Honduras, on the north coast toward the Gulf of Fonseca on the south, then southeast to the Costa Rican Gulf of Nicoya, represented a real cultural dividing line between high pre-Columbian cultures of Mayan and Nahua derivation to the north and west, and widely differing cultures of South American origin to the south and east. In general these latter cultures were at a much earlier level of development. Honduras represents a real area of cultural overlap.

Honduras is to a very great extent the inter-continental "divide" of the hemisphere between North and South American pre-Colombian cultural influences. The Maya and Nahuatl pervasive cultures to the north have here not only overlapped with the Chibcha and Inca (Aymará, Quechua, etc.) influences to the south, but have been treated to the added fillip of the Carib-Arawakan cultures to the east, in the Caribbean islands. In this sense Honduras is a triple cultural divide. It is also a melting pot in which these original forces came together to provide a unique and in some cases a blended characteristic solely Honduran.

CURRENCY, ILLEGAL. By the mid-1600s coinage in the Audiencia of Guatemala was in such short supply that the miners around Tegucigalpa began shaving silver bars and using these silver parings as currency. This practice, though illegal, continued for more than a century. One of the solutions suggested was to bring in "peruleros" (q.v.).

CUSTOMS RECEIVERSHIP see FUNDING OF FOREIGN DEBT

CUYAMEL FRUIT COMPANY. In the 1920s and 1930s the Cuyamel Company was a banana concern which operated the National Railways and whose headquarters was at Puerto Cortéz. It had a large sugar operation also, with much of the product being shipped to Canada.

CYPHER, MICHAEL JEROME. A Franciscan priest who disappeared in Olancho department June 21, 1975, at the same time as Ivan Betancourt (q.v.). Known also as "Father Casimiro," the Medford, Wisconsin native had been doing social work in the province in cooperation with Betancourt when both disappeared. The same day five persons were killed and two wounded in a clash between peasant demonstrators and army patrols.

- D -

DALLING, JOHN. Governor of Jamaica, 1777-81, he was the moving force of a "Western Design" which was to cut the Spanish colonial empire at the Nicaraguan Lakes. This plan was related to events at Fort Omoa (q.v.), Honduras.

DALRYMPLE, WILLIAM. British Captain, commander of the Loyal Irish Corps in actions against Fort Omoa, 1779, in cooperation with Commodore Luttrell. See OMOA, 1779-- BATTLES.

DANLI. Municipal cabacera in El Paraiso Department, centrally located. A new paved highway is going through Danlí to the Nicaraguan border, where it will proceed on South through Ocotal. There is an airfield; Danlí is in the relatively level portion of El Paraiso, north of Cordillera de Depilto.

DANTE. Word used for the Tapir (q.v.).

DARIO, RUBEN. Pen-name of world-renowned Nicaraguan poet (see MODERNISMO). Leader of the school of modernism which arose around the turn of the century. In Honduras Darío was paralleled by Juan Ramón Molina (q.v.) and Troylán Turcios (q.v.). Darío's work proved to be definitive in modern Spanish literature.

DAVILA, MIGUEL R. General Dávila was installed as Provisional President, from April 18, 1907 until March 1, 1908, by the revolutionary "Junta de Gobierno, 1907" (q.v.) which had toppled Manuel Bonilla (q.v.) in that year. He became constitutional president when the constituent assembly called by the junta reinstated the Constitution of 1894. He then faced a series of revolts most of them led or managed by General Bonilla. Dávila's term was cut short by March 28, 1911, after Bonilla had taken over the Bay Islands and the north coastal port towns of La Ceiba and Trujillo. To avoid all-out war, both men accepted mediation by the United States, and on the cruiser Tacoma (q.v.) at Puerto Cortés an agreement was reached that Francisco Bertrand (q.v.) would become president.

**DAVIS, RICHARD HARDING.** The young man who became a celebrated war correspondent during the Spanish American War, and who wrote a book, The Cuban and Puerto Rican Campaigns, about that conflict, had two years before contributed to the literature on Honduras with his Three Gringos in Venezuela and Central America, a volume which was a clear-eyed and vivid, though somewhat superficial, presentation of the country 80 years ago.

**DAYS, AZTEC NAMES.**

| (Month of 20 days) | Meanings |
|---|---|
| 1. Cipactli | Lizard |
| 2. Elecatl | Wind |
| 3. Calli | House |
| 4. Cuetzpallin | Letter |
| 5. Coatl | Serpent |
| 6. Miquiztli | Death |
| 7. Mazatl | Deer |
| 8. Tochtli | Rabbit |
| 9. Atl | Water |
| 10. Itzcuintli | Dog |
| 11. Ozomatli | Monkey |
| 12. Malinalli | Grass |
| 13. Acatl | Wool |
| 14. Ocelotl | Tiger |
| 15. Quauhtli | Eagle |
| 16. Cozcaquauhtli | Buzzard |
| 17. Ollin | Earthquake |
| 18. Tecpatl | Flint |
| 19. Quiahiutl | Rain |
| 20. Xochitl | Flower |

This calendar of Mexican cultural derivation, yet so similar to the Maya calendar, was used by Nahuatl-speaking peoples. Since Honduras was a dividing point between Maya and Nahua influences, although to a lesser extent than between Maya and South American Chibcha influences, there was a good deal of multiple cross-cultural activity. The basic calendar of the two cultures was astronomically and mathematically quite similar, but the language differed.

**DAYS, MAYA NAMES.** Months are of 20 days.

| Name | Meaning |
|---|---|
| 1. Imix | Silk cotton tree (ceiba) |
| 2. IK | Wind |
| 3. Akbal | Night |
| 4. Kan | Precious (or beautiful) |
| 5. Chicchan | Serpent |
| 6. Cimi | Death |
| 7. Manik | Deer |
| 8. Lamat | Moon |

| Name | | Meaning |
|---|---|---|
| 9. | Muluc | Flood |
| 10. | Oc | Dog |
| 11. | Chuen | Monkey |
| 12. | Eb | Drought |
| 13. | Ben | Wool |
| 14. | Ix | Jaguar |
| 15. | Men | Bird of the Sun |
| 16. | Cib | Bird of prey |
| 17. | Caban | Land |
| 18. | Edznab | Flint |
| 19. | Canac | Thunder |
| 20. | Ahau | Sir |

One day is called a "kin."

DEATHS see LIFE EXPECTANCY

DEBROT, F. An Englishman who obtained a lease on the finished portion of the Honduras Interoceanic Railway in the 1870s. The lease was cancelled in 1875. Debrot had been British Consul in Puerto Cortés.

DECLARATION OF PANAMA (1939). A precursor to World War II, the declaration, following a meeting which had representation from all the American republics, stated that while the signatory nations maintained neutrality their waters would be kept free of hostile acts by non-American nations. Close on the heels of Hitler's invasion of Poland, the purpose and impact was obvious. In one sense this was an updating of the Monroe Doctrine.

DECLARATION OF PANAMA (1956). Held July 21-22, 1956, a meeting of all American presidents formulated a declaration, unanimously signed, which dealt with fiscal, political, and economic concerns of the American Nations. As a result there was some strengthening of the Organization of American States.

DECORATION FOR MERIT see MEDALS

DECRETO ABOLIENDO LA ESCLAVITUD EN CENTRO AMERICA, 1824 see SLAVERY, ABOLISHMENT

DECRETO DECLARANDO A HONDURAS. Estado Independiente. See INDEPENDENCE DECREE, HONDURAS.

DEJARRETAR. A colonial era practice of killing cattle for beef and hides by slashing the rear leg tendons from horseback. When the animal fell it was skinned and whatever was desired was taken. Often this was done only for the hides. The cruel and wasteful practice was outlawed in the mid-1600s, but the law was impossible to enforce.

DEL VALLE, GERTRUDIS DIAS. Mother of Honduran patriot and leader, José Cecilio del Valle (q.v.).

DEL VALLE, JOSE ANTONIO DIAZ. Cholutecan who was father of Honduran leader José Cecilio del Valle (q.v.).

DEL VALLE, JOSE CECILIO. Honduran leader during the stirring period of independence from Spain, del Valle was born in Choluteca, November 22, 1770, son of José Antonio Díaz del Valle and Gertrudis Díaz del Valle. They moved to Guatemala in 1779 for the better education of their son José Cecilio, who graduated from the Tridentino College, and was designated a lawyer at age 23, in the University of San Carlos Borromeo. During the independence movement, del Valle was head of the "Partido Evolucionista," and editor of the paper, El Amigo de la Patria.
    On September 15, 1821, in the Palace of the Captains General in Guatemala, del Valle was of the group who declared independence, and edited the Act of Independence itself.
    Del Valle was opposed to the annexation of Central America by Mexico under the short-lived "empire" of Iturbide. Named to the congress by Tegucigalpa and Chiquimala, he was an eloquent defender of Central American rights. Because of his outspokenness and courage, he was imprisoned in the Santo Domingo convent for six months by the order of Emperor Agustín I (Iturbide).
    When the empire fell, del Valle regained his post as Deputy, and continued to defend the rights of the people of his homeland. When the Provinces of Central America united, he occupied a high post in the executive power, and signed, in collaboration with Tomás O'Horan and José Manuel de la Cerda, the executive act of the first constitution of Central America, November 22, 1824. He was elected Vice President under Arce (q.v.) but rejected the post, alleging it was null and void, as was that of Arce. During the Arce regime, del Valle busied himself in writing and in editing a periodical. He was returned to Congress under Morazán (q.v.) and was a candidate for president, running against Morazán, who won. Del Valle continued his constructive work. Elected President in 1834, he died before taking office, at his hacienda "La Concepción" near Guatemala City. His public service and wisdom became legendary. In 1875 his collected works were published by the government.

DEL VALLE, POMPEYO. Poet, literary figure and anthologist who with Oscar Acosta produced the Exaltación de Honduras, an anthology of poetry with the unifying element of Honduran themes. Born in Tegucigalpa, 1929, del Valle is a director of the National University magazine. His poems have been translated into English, Russian, and Chinese.

DELEGATES, CENTRAL AMERICA, TO CORTES OF CADIZ. In 1810 six municipalities in the Captaincy-General of Guatemala were asked to provide delegates to help decide on the government to be created by the Cortes of Cádiz. All delegates were in accord with the Cádiz 1812 Constitution.

DELEGATIONS, MILITARY ZONES. In major ports and certain departmental capitals are Delegations of the Military Zones: They are in: Puerto Cortés, Tela, La Ceiba, Trujillo, Guanaja, Puerto Lempira, Amapala, Roatán and Utila. Subdelegations are in San Lorenzo. See also MILITARY ZONES.

DEMOCRATIC NATIONAL PARTY. Now the National Party, since 1923. See TWO-PARTY SYSTEM.

DEPARTMENTS IN 1825. The first constituent assembly of Honduras divided the territory of the nation into seven departments on June 28, 1825: Comayagua, Tegucigalpa (now Francisco Morazán), Gracias (now Lempira), Santa Bárbara, Yoro, Olancho, Choluteca.

DEPARTMENTS IN 1974.

| Name | Area (sq. mls.) | Population |
| --- | --- | --- |
| 1. Atlántida | 1641 | 143,594 |
| 2. Choluteca | 1626 | 233,926 |
| 3. Colón | 3427 | 66,492 |
| 4. Comayagua | 2006 | 147,995 |
| 5. Copán | 1237 | 181,808 |
| 6. Cortés | 1527 | 320,302 |
| 7. El Paraiso | 2787 | 153,747 |
| 8. Francisco Morazán | 3068 | 496,708 |
| 9. Gracias a Dios | 6421 | 18,298 |
| 10. Intibuca | 1186 | 97,956 |
| 11. Islas de la Bahia | 101 | 10,393 |
| 12. La Paz | 900 | 76,268 |
| 13. Lempira | 1656 | 148,927 |
| 14. Ocotepeque | 649 | 65,066 |
| 15. Olancho | 9402 | 156,019 |
| 16. Santa Bárbara | 1975 | 247,052 |
| 17. Valle | 604 | 109,769 |
| 18. Yoro | 3065 | 184,519 |

DERECHO DE ALMIRANTAZGO. A payment during colonial days to the descendants of Christopher Columbus, who as "Admiral of the Indies" received this admiral's tax of five silver reales on all vessels using the port of Seville.

DERECHO DE ALMOJARIFAZGO. This duty on imports and exports of colonial products was in effect during the Spanish colonial centuries and, in combination with the "avería," made a very heavy tax drain on the colonies. It was a 15 per cent to 20 per cent tax on all exports from the colonies to Spain, and 7 per cent to 10 per cent on Spanish goods for the colonies. Combined with the other taxes, colonial products could bear as much as 50 per cent taxation.

DERECHO DE AVERIA. This "average" was a tax imposed on all products exchanged between Honduras and other Spanish colonies and the mother country, the trade being either with Seville or Cádiz. The tax was 5 per cent on exports to the colonies and 21 per cent on imports from the colonies. The purpose of the tax was avowedly to maintain Naval fleets of galleons to protect the commerce.

DERRAMA. A system which allowed a local official during colonial days to become a merchant. He could buy goods in the cities and sell at high markups to the Indians, and buy their goods in turn at low prices and sell high in the population centers. The practice was immoral if not clearly illegal.

DESCELLIERS, PIERRE. French geographer and mapmaker who showed the "Islas Santa Ana" Swan Islands (q.v.)--for the first time in his World Geography of 1536. He apparently received his information from French pirates active in the area in 1529. A second edition of his world map appeared in 1540, and a third in 1550.

DESNAUX, SIMON. An Italian engineer who had served briefly at Fort Omoa (q.v.) in 1778, he was given command of the fort in August 1779, when war with England was already two months old. But he had yet to reach the fort, and did so in September. Commandant Desnaux had successfully defended Fort Boca Chica at Cartagena during the War of Jenkin's Ear. The action at the fort was spirited. See OMOA, 1779--BATTLES.

DESPARD, EDWARD MARCUS. An Irish visionary and Lieutenant of the 79th Regiment of British troops who invested "El Castillo" (q.v.), the "St. John's Fort" attacked in 1780; young Horatio Nelson, later the great British Naval hero, was also an active participant. Despard was chief engineer of the expedition, and was involved, as was Nelson, in the general plans of Jamaican governor John Dalling, who hoped to sever the Spanish colonial empire in Nicaragua. This involved attacks on Belize and the Honduran Coast as well.

Despard, later as Colonel Commandant of an eleven-ship force, was sent to Cabo Gracias a Dios, reaching it on August 17, 1782, where he organized a 400-man force to attack Fort Dalling, and followed the attack with the eleven ships of his fleet, advancing upon Black River with 1,000 men, including Sambo allies. On August 28 he appeared at Fort Inmaculada de Honduras, which was commanded by Tomás Julia, who surrendered August 31, 1782. This recapture of the Black River area by Despard for the British was a high spot of the largely unsuccessful British Central American campaign of the 1780s.

Much later, in 1803, Colonel Despard was involved in

a treasonous plot which led to his disgrace and execution, a sad end for the hero of the actions against two Forts, each named Inmaculada, one in Nicaragua and one in Honduras. Nelson appeared as a character witness at Despard's trial.

DEVELOPMENT PLANS. There have been four principal national goals in the development plans which have been prepared since 1955. They are: 1. Development of human resources; 2. Import substitution via industrial development; 3. Infrastructure development; 4. Agricultural development.

The first five-year plan came before 1955; it was amended in 1956 and again in 1957. 292,000,000 lempira were to be spent. The 1965-69 plan projected a 480,000,000 lempira expenditure, distributed as follows: 51% - Transport and energy; 21% - health housing, education; 17% - industry and agriculture. It was projected that private investment of the same period would be 634 million lempira. Neither plan was met. Even though external financing was available, people to implement the plan were not available.

The Program of Public Investment, 1970-74, was a supplementary plan which emphasized high priority but short-term projects. Costs were to be 566 million lempira. The Industrial Development Law of 1966 categorizes industry, and each of the three categories receives special tax exemptions. The law caused 200 enterprises to be either begun or expanded.

In 1969 the Central American Common Market came up with a fiscal incentives agreement which in effect superseded the Industrial Development Law, and due to its relative industrial weakness, gave Honduras a greater incentive reduction policy by 20 per cent.

DIA DE INDEPENDENCIA. The Central American (hence Honduran) Independence day is celebrated September 15. See INDEPENDENCE - 1821.

DIA DEL ESTUDIANTE. An annual "day of the student" set aside each year to give honor to Padre José Trinidad Reyes (q.v.), the date being his birthday, June 11.

DIA DEL SANTO DE DON PEDRO. A festival celebrated on 29 June in memory of Don Pedro Nufie, in recognition of his work in the Escuela Normal de Varones, which is the site of the celebration. He was called "Maestro Violeta" and was a popular educational leader. He died in Danlí in 1916.

DIAKONIA. A cooperative missionary endeavor which is a joint effort of the Mennonite Church, the United Church of Christ, and the Moravian Church. At Brus Laguna, Mr. and Mrs. Fred Worman in the early 1970s were detailed as agricultural missionaries. They help to distribute equipment for agriculture and community development in the area. Seeds, animal medicines, pumps, tools, and sewing machines were among the items distributed. They developed handcraft articles from the bark of the Tunu tree. They maintain contact with such agencies as the Peace Corps, Public Health, AID, etc. They also teach and demonstrate dietary improvement.

DIAZ DE PIMIENTA, FRANCISCO. The Spanish commander of the Windward squadron (q.v.) who attacked Providence Island in May, 1641, with 2,000 troops. He captured and attempted to hold the island. He then campaigned against Roatán, captured the colonists, and depopulated the island, even removing to the mainland the 700 Jicaque Indian inhabitants.

DIAZ DE SOLIS, JUAN see VESPUCCI, AMERIGO

DIAZ-ALVAREZ, EDELBERTO. Cuban consul in Puerto Cortés whose exequatur was cancelled by the Honduran government March 16, 1961. He was alleged to have intervened in the internal affairs of the country.

DICKINSON, ANDREW B. Abraham Lincoln's envoy to Central America in relation to transit projects. Author and negotiator of the Dickinson-Ayon treaty in June, 1868.

DIET, COLONIAL (1500s). Corn was almost 90 per cent of the diet and this has not changed too much in four centuries. Other items were beans, cacao, fruit, chile, squash. Meat was turkey and the edible dog so popular in Mexico. Nuts, roots, and grubs from the "monte" (q.v.) were a slender supplement.

DIET, MISKITO. Along the big rivers of Mosquitia, such as the Coco and Patuca, the diet consists of sweet manioc, yams, bananas, plantains and maize, sugarcane, and cacao. In some areas there is very heavy emphasis on the "siksa," or bananas. Where agriculture is practiced for cash as well as food, rice and beans are major crops.

DIEZ NAVARRO, LUIS. A lieutenant of engineers, 50 years old, who was ordered to Central America by the Spanish Crown on October 14, 1741, to use his skills as a military engineer in fortifying the frontier. Native of Málaga and experienced in many years of African campaigns, Díez Navarro had worked on the forts of Cádiz and had a part in the 1726 seige of Gibraltar. He had a major role in the reconstruction of the large fort of San Juan de Ulua at Vera Cruz, and had directed construction of a new mint in Mexico City.

As captain-general in Central America, Díez Navarro did most of what was accomplished during the next 25 years. He surveyed all Central American defenses in person, governed Costa Rica, commanded Fort Inmaculada on the San Juan River in Nicaragua, and was the officer who recommended the site and the original plan for Fort Omoa (q.v.). He also directed the early construction of that important bastion of empire.  He accepted Black River from the British in 1764, and as Brigadier-General and Master military engineer ended his days in Guatemala.

His specific activities in Honduras centered around selecting a new site for a north coastal fort, since the British reinforcement of Roatán had in turn made repair of the Trujillo fortifications a dangerous enterprise, especially with the nearby Black River and its Sambo-Miskito allied strength. He sounded the Gulf of Honduras and selected a small, deep bay called Omoa as the desirable site in March of 1743.

Díez continued through Honduras to Nicaragua where he studied the lake route defenses.  When he returned to Guatemala in mid-1744, his major recommendation was the building of a fort at Omoa (q.v.).  This would bring the Spanish power again to the Honduran coast, and would serve as a coast-guard base and a land base for offensive action against the British on the Bay Islands and farther west along the coast.

DIPUTACION PROVINCIAL.  A form of representative regional body planned by the Spanish Constitution of 1812, and upon which Honduras and other Central American governmental patterns were later based.  Under a jefe político, one of these regional groups was to be centered in León, Nicaragua, to deal with the areas now in modern Costa Rica and Nicaragua.  The other, in Guatemala, would be the senior one with a jefe político superior, and would attend to Honduras and El Salvador as well as to Guatemala.

DIQUIDUMBE  see  LIQUIDAMBAR

DIRECCION GENERAL DE INSTRUCCION  see  PUBLIC EDUCATION, DIRECTION OF

DISTINGUISHED SERVICE CROSS  see  MEDALS

DOLLAR DIPLOMACY.  A phrase used to denote the policy initiated by U.S. Secretary of State Philander C. Knox, under President William Howard Taft.  The basic plan was to force foreign interests inimical to the U.S. to withdraw from strategic areas by application of economic pressure on Latin American governments.  North American capital would fill the gap, backed by U.S. arms.  Defense was primary, economics secondary.  The boldness of the catch phrase elicited an understandably undesirable reaction throughout Latin America.  The bad effects of the terminology were somewhat dispelled when Franklin D. Roosevelt's slogan, "Good Neighbor Policy," supplanted it in 1933.

DOMAS Y VALLE, JOSE.  Governor of the Kingdom of Guatemala 1794-1801 succeeding Troncoso y Martínez (q.v.).  He was in his nineties when appointed, a further sign of Spanish weakness upon which the arrogant and recalcitrant denizens of the troublesome Mosquito coast capitalized. The Spanish colonial empire was two decades from its end at the termination of this governor's incumbency. The Mosquito insurgents along Honduras' northeast coast were a particular thorn in the flesh during this period.

DOMEZAIN, ILDEFONSO. Spanish officer under Gálvez at Trujillo (q.v.) in 1782. Colonel Domezaín was assigned to an attack on Black River, under Gálvez. He had half the total force of 1,500 soldiers.

DOMINGUEZ, FELIX. Commandant of Fort Omoa (q.v.) during 1780, when he organized an expedition to reoccupy Trujillo. The old port city was taken in March, after having been abandoned 150 years before. This gave the Spanish a base near the English settlement of Black River.

DUERKA-TAIRA. Miskito word for "doree" or dory, the indispensable seagoing dugout canoe used in coastal waters, bays, lagoons, and estuaries all along the Miskito littoral. Boats are very important to the people of the coast, for they represent both transport and livelihood.

DULCE DE AVISPA. Crystallized wasp honey, a rather exotic sweet found in big wasp nests called "panals."

DULCE NOMBRE DE CULMI. Farthest east of the municipal cabaceras of Olancho Department, this town of the elaborate "sweet name" is on the edge of a twenty-thousand-square-mile near-wilderness in southern Olancho and all of western Gracias a Dios departments. There is an airfield, and the town is a very old Spanish colonial settlement, an early outpost against the British on Black River. It is under the Malacate Range of mountains. The town is at the end of the graded gravel highway into eastern Honduras. The next graded road east is a spur running out from Puerto Lémpira over 100 miles to the east. The intervening country is the Patuca Valley and is quite remote, virtually inaccessible except by dugout canoe or helicopter.

DURON, JACINTO OCTAVIO. Ambassador from Honduras to Guatemala who was recalled during the 1954 general strike (q.v.) and the consequent deterioration of relations with Guatemala.

DURON, JORGE FIDEL. Rector of the University of Honduras in the 1950's and member of a distinguished Honduran family in the realm of arts, letters, law, and diplomacy. It is he who made a realistic appraisal of the Honduran political matrix when in a 1954 paper he said: "If it were well-governed, Honduras could easily be converted into a model. Nevertheless we have chosen to live in continual political agitation in which the best intentions are rendered helpless and where a cabal of professional politicians have taken advantages of the situation and have prospered. We have been prisoners ... of strong political, economic and commercial forces...."

DURON, ROMULO E. Born in Comayagua July 6, 1865, his parents were of a distinguished family; they were Francisco Durón and Casimira Gamero de Durón. He was graduated a Bachelor of Philosophy from the University in 1880. He was a teacher and later a professor of grammar and geography in secondary schools. In 1885 he became a lawyer, entitled to practice before the Supreme Court. He held many judicial posts from justice of the peace to magistrate of the appeals court, and was twice a member of the Supreme Court. Several times he was a deputy in the Congress, from 1910 to 1914 representing the department of Tegucigalpa, and from 1917 to 1920 that of La Paz. He was President of Congress in 1910. He worked with the Carnegie Institute in seeking international peace. He was in Washington, D. C. on many occasions as delegate and representative of his country. He was Foreign Minister in the Colindres administration from 1929 to 1932.

Durón married Fidelia Durón in 1894, and together they reared six sons, whose achievements carried on the family tradition. He published a number of works including poetry translations; a history of Honduran governors; Biographies; Honduras literaria, as well as History of Honduras and many related articles and works. Durón died August 13, 1942. See also BUESO, FRANCISCO.

DUTIES see IMPORT DUTIES

DYEWOOD. A major product of Mosquitia and the northern Honduran coast. The shoremen (q.v.) and the Baymen (q.v.) both provided dyewoods for the hungry English textile factories, as well as for the continent. The price was $150 a ton in 1670, and $500 a ton by 1700. Production increased greatly in the first half of the 18th century; 18,000 tons a year were shipped from Balize. Several species of tropical hardwood, such as logwood, make excellent dyes.

- E -

EARL OF WARWICK. Sailing under a letter of marque and reprisal, the Earl seized the island of Santa Catalina, called Old Providence by the British, just off the Central American coast. The old Providence company under the Earl established a trading station at Cape Gracias a Dios, thus helping to assure the British foothold on the Mosquito coast which was in effect for over two centuries. From here the English freebooters (with their comrades the Cutch) could prey on ocean traffic. The 1600s found the freebooters in their heyday, and the northeast coast of Honduras was a favorite "hangout," with the big bight of the Gulf of Honduras a favorite cruising ground for their depredations.

EASTERN ZONE. The three departments of Colón, Olancho, and Gracias a Dios comprise the eastern zone of Honduras. The principal towns are Trujillo, Juticalpa, Olancho, Puerto Lempira, Catacamas.

EB. Twelfth day of the Maya month; meaning "drought."

ECHEVERRI, JUAN DE. Captain of the Santiago (q.v.) when it was wrecked off the Honduran coast in 1660.

ECHEVERS Y SUVISA, ANTONIO PEDRO DE. Governor of Central America from 1724 to 1733.

ECONOMIC AND SOCIAL COUNCIL. Governmental Reconstruction Committee of 1974. See CEYS and HONDURAN COUNCIL OF PRIVATE ENTERPRISE.

ECONOMIC IMPACT, HURRICANE see RECOVERY, HURRICANE "Fifi"

ECONOMY, MINISTRY OF see CABINET

ECONOMY - 16th AND 17th CENTURIES. The economy of Central America was based on a series of "booms and busts" during the first two centuries following the conquest, significantly based on the following sequence--slaves, silver, cacao, cochineal, indigo. Honduras was concerned with all of these, particularly as to trans-shipment from its north coastal ports, but it was also the principal source of silver.

EDUCATION, FIRST LAW. On June 30, 1830, under General Francisco Morazán, came the first decree referring to primary schools, giving some support on a national basis to teaching.

EDUCATION, ROYAL DECREE. By a decree of 1770, and implementation of 1769, "public" schools were ordered. Colonial authorities did little to put the decree into effect.

EDZNAB. The eighteenth day of the Maya month; meaning, "flint."

EHECATL. Second day of the Aztec month; meaning "wind."

EJERCITO ALIADO PROTECTOR DE LA LEY. Formed of Honduran and Salvadoran troops, this allied army of the elaborate name was organized to "protect the law" by Francisco Morazán (q.v.) in 1828. The army captured Guatemala City on April 13, 1829.

EJERCITO PROTECTOR DE LA CONSTITUCION. A Salvadoran invading force under the command of Trinidad Cabañas (twice Honduran President), which invaded Honduras in the 1845 war.

They were defeated at Comayagua, and Sensenti, and had to return to El Salvador unsuccessful in "protecting the constitution."

EJERCITO PROTECTOR DE LA PAZ. Honduran and Salvadoran forces, frequently in alliance, joined to "protect the peace" in an invasion of Nicaragua which resulted in the capture of León on January 24, 1845. The army was led by Francisco Malaspín, but when he was deposed as Salvadoran President by Joaquín Eufrasio Guzmán, his particular defense of peace was permanently fractured.

EJIDATARIO. An agricultural worker under the ejido (q.v.) system.

EJIDO. A pre-Columbian form of land-holding in which the lands are held in common by a whole village. As in Mexico, the meaning in Honduras is this well-established one, whereas in some other countries the ejido refers to what is simply an agricultural cooperative.

EL ACEITUNO. Formerly a port, it is still used to evaporate salt. The salt pans are formed by damming shallow tidal water. When the water evaporates, brine is burned, and salt is the remainder. The little port is on a tidal estuary navigable by shallow-draft craft for 16 miles. It is on the Gulf of Fonseca.

EL ALTO VIAJE. This was Columbus' name for "the high voyage" which took him along the Central American coast from August 1, 1502, when he reached Honduras, until May 1, 1503, when he left Colombia for Jamaica. The Fourth Voyage was the "High Voyage" because of the adventures, vicissitudes, narrow escapes, and battles with the elements and the natives on shore. He considered it, quite evidently, the crowning event and enterprise of his life.

EL AMIGO DE LA PATRIA. The newspaper which was an organ of the Partido Revolucionista during the period of the Central American movement for independence from Spain. See JOSE CECELIO DEL VALLE.

EL CASTILLO VIEJO. The Spanish Colonial Frontier in middle America extended from Yucatán to Panama through the Central American states, and was remarkable in that the "untamed" sector was east rather than west of the Cordilleran spine of the isthmus. This condition arose because the Spanish had found the Pacific coast far more accessible than the Caribbean coast, and also much healthier, so in general the population centers arose to the southwest of the Mountains. The eastern littoral tended to be low, swampy, feverish, and occupied by scattered but often hostile and dangerous tribes. In the late 1600s there were still Itzá Mayas holding out in

Guatemala's Petén area. Anchoring the frontier were forts Omoa and Trujillo in Honduras, joined by the Castillo de la Concepción Inmaculada on the San Juan River of Nicaragua. This key fortification is now known in its partially ruined state simply as "El Castillo Viejo," the old castle. This anchor-bastion of the frontier was stormed by Horatio Nelson not long after his service along the Mosquito shore which was so popular with the scattered British there. The British attack was in 1780. William Walker's (q.v.) men used the fort a number of times during the National War (q.v.) of the 1850s. And here occurred the "incident," an execution of two Americans, which set off the long Marine occupation of Nicaragua in 1912. The ruins are still recognizable on their eminence 100 feet above a swift rapids of the San Juan River.

EL CHILE, BARRIO. A northern suburb of Comayaguela, just across the Río Choluteca from Concordia Park in Tegucigalpa.

EL CIUDADANO. Periodical in Tegucigalpa during the 1930s under the direction of Martínez Galindo (q.v.), who wrote under two pseudonyms.

EL CRONISTA. A Tegucigalpa daily paper. The editor, Alejandro Valladares, has allegedly been a guest of Fidel Castro in Cuba on numerous occasions.

EL EDEN   see   ESCUELA NORMAL RURAL DE VARONES

EL ESPINO. A customs and immigration point of entry on the Inter-American Highway, at the southern frontier of Honduras bordering on Nicaragua, approximately 200 miles from Tegucigalpa. Facilities are modern.

EL ESTADO LIBRE Y SOBERANO DE HONDURAS. The name of Honduras upon independence on November 15, 1838. See INDEPENDENCE DECREE, HONDURAS....

EL GALLEGO. One of Columbus' ships on the Fourth Voyage when Honduras was discovered. This was a nickname probably after the owner of the vessel. The "official" name we do not know--she was simply the "Galician" (see COLUMBUS, CHRISTOPHER). The little vessel was of 60 tons, under command of Pedro de Teireros (apparently a Portuguese name).

EL LIBRO DE ORO. National Party campaign book of 1923 in which were recorded 70,000 signatures, a number sufficient to win the election.

EL NISPERO. Municipal cabacera in the department of Santa Bárbara, about 15 miles south of the town of that name. Named for a hardwood species, the town is in the rugged country near the Lempira Department border.

EL PARAISO. 1) Municipal cabacera in the southern part of the department of the same name, deep in the Cordillera de Depilto, and within four miles of the Nicaraguan border. This was "Sandino country" from 1927 to 1933.

2) Municipal cabacera in the northern part of Copán Department, northwest of the famous ruins, and only six or eight miles from the Guatemalan border.

EL PARAISO DEPARTMENT. Bounded on the north and northeast by Olancho Department, and the south and southeast by the Cordillera de Depilto and the international border with Nicaragua; on the southwest by Choluteca Department, on the west by Francisco Morazán Department. The Choluteca River runs through western El Paraiso to the Pacific, and the Guayambre River through the eastern part to the Patuca River and the Caribbean. The cabacera Yuscarán is in the far western center of the department. There are 18 municipios. The area is 2,820 square miles. The 1973 population of the cabaceras was 32,748, the rural and village population 120,999, for a total of 153,747 in the whole department. Cattle ranching, timber, and mining are activities of the area. El Paraiso was the jumping-off spot for much guerrilla activity during the Nicaraguan war with Sandino (q.v.) in the 1927-33 period. The eastern portion of the department is wild and inaccessible. There is only one hospital.

EL PARAISO, MUNICIPIOS. The municipios and their cabaceras of this southern department of Honduras are Teupasenti, Moroceli, Potrerillos, Jacalapa, Danlí, San Matías, El Paraiso, Alauca, Oropoli, San Lucas, San Antonio de Flores, Texiguat, Vado Ancho, Liure, Yauyupe, and Soledad, a fascinating mixture of Nahua, Spanish, and several obscure Indian names.

EL PORVENIR. Lyceum in Danlí, from 1888-90, directed by Pedro Nufio (q.v.).

EL REPARTO, COLONIA. A north-eastern suburb of Tegucigalpa.

EL TACOMA. Periodical of the town of Juticalpa, edited by Alfonso Guillén Zelaya (q.v.).

EL VIZCAINO. "The Biscayan" was a nickname for one of Columbus' four small caravels which discovered the Honduran coast on his fourth voyage. She was the smallest, of only 50 tons, and was commanded by Bartolomé Fieschi.

EL VOLCAN. Local name for a mountain peak of about 7,000 feet altitude, looming over the Yaguere Valley of southern Honduras.

EL ZAMORANO. The valley of the Río Yeguare is the site of the Pan-American Agricultural College by this name. A pass

5,100 feet high is crossed between Tegucigalpa and the fertile valley at 2,400 feet. The school opened in 1942 under the presidency of Dr. Wilson Popenoe, whose "House in Antigua" (Guatemala) has been immortalized by the book of that name. Dr. Archie Carr (q.v.) was an early faculty member.
  Endowed by the United Fruit Company, the school is planned to train young men in agriculture from all over Central America. The graduates number 50 to 60 annually, and they are taught the latest techniques in agronomy and animal husbandry to take back to their home communities. The campus is beautiful, the buildings extensive and substantial, the fields and livestock are superior. In 1969 there were 905 applicants of whom only 77 were accepted. The school pays all costs for each student. The curriculum is as follows: first year--horticulture; second year--field crops (over eighteen varieties); third year--animal husbandry.

ELOTES. Large ears of green corn. A Nahua derivation.

EMPEROR OF MEXICO AND CENTRAL AMERICA see ITURBIDE, AGUSTIN

EMPRESA HONDUREÑA DE VAPORES, S.A. see HONDURAN STEAMSHIP CO.

EMPRESA NACIONAL DE ENERGIA ELECTRICA see NATIONAL ELECTRIC ENERGY COMPANY

EN MARCHA. A political periodical in Tegucigalpa, edited by the well-known Augusto C. Coello (q.v.).

ENAGUA. Also called "nagua," it is a long garment, the name meaning petticoat or skirt. Worn by country women in Central America, frequently with a line or two of ruffles at the hem.

ENCOMENDERO see ENCOMIENDA

ENCOMIENDA. One of the most significant institutions of the early days in colonial Spanish America, this was a system of forced labor, parading under the guise of "Christianizing" the native peoples. The encomenderos became very powerful, so that attempts at reform in the mid-1500s failed. Not until 1720 was progress made in ending the system which frequently encouraged cruelty and was in effect a feudal form of slavery, masquerading as religious conversion, improbable as that may seem.

ENEE see NATIONAL ELECTRIC ENERGY COMPANY

ENERGY. Honduras has no known fossil fuels within its borders. However, power plants and electrical usage increase. Sixty-three per cent of electric power is used by industry. Only

15 per cent of homes in the country are lighted by electricity. Over 90 per cent of homes use charcoal or wood for cooking; four per cent use kerosene. Home lighting is 37 per cent by pine torches and 45 per cent by kerosene lamps. Per capita electric power is about one-half that of the whole of Central America. There are 90 electric plants. (See NATIONAL ELECTRIC ENERGY COMPANY.)

Over half of installed electrical plants are hydroelectric, the remainder being thermal. Known capacity in 1970 was one million kilowatts. The Río Lindo plant was being enlarged from 30,000 kilowatts toward a potential of 160,000 kilowatts. The Tela railroad plant supplies electricity to Puerto Cortés, Tela, and La Lima. The Standard Fruit Co. plant serves La Ceiba.

ENRIQUEÑA, LA. Mine at Guascarán, a particularly rich silver lode; 17th century.

EPIPHYTES. The mosses, ferns, orchids, and bromeliads which crowd the tropical rainforests and are even more profuse in the cloud-forest.

EROSION. This first became a problem in the mountainous areas of Honduras in the 17th century. Farming techniques, grazing of animals, various "booms" such as raising indigo, all damaged the soil beyond repair.

ESCALS, JOSE DE. As Oidor, Governor pro tem for a year following the death of General Barrios Leal, 1695-96. He was the center of dispute concerning his rights to the position.

ESCOBEDO, FERNANDO FRANCISCO DE. As governor from 1672-78, Escobedo traveled even more than his predecessor. He was concerned about the slender Caribbean defenses, and went as far as Nicaragua to inspect and plan fortifications. He also attempted to exclude Spaniards and "Castas" from the Indian Villages, but had little success. He revised the audiencia constitution, and upon return to Spain attempted to get revision of Central American trade regulations. When he left Central America it was to become Great Prior of Castile of the Order of Malta.

ESCOTO, BARTOLOME DE. One of the proprietors of Olancho, Escoto led an expedition into Paya Indian country in the later 1600s.

ESCOTO, RAUL EDGARDO. An agricultural engineer, Escoto became Minister of Natural Resources in the López Arellano (q.v.) cabinet following December 4, 1972.

ESCUELA AGRICOLA PANAMERICANA see EL ZAMORANO

ESCUELA DE ARTES Y OFFICIOS see TRADE SCHOOL

ESCUELA DE ENSEÑANZA ESPECIAL see SPECIAL EDUCATION, SCHOOL

ESCUELA NORMAL RURAL DE VARONES. On April 5, 1944, the rural normal school was established, and was moved from the capital to the Río Calguapa, near Comayagua, under the name of "El Eden." It is presently called the Centro América.

ESCUELA NORMAL RURAL DE VILLA AHUMADA see RURAL NORMAL SCHOOLS

ESCUELA SUPERIOR DEL PROFESORADO FRANCISCO MORAZAN. This teachers college was established by decree of the military ruling junta in December 1956, with the purpose of: preparing secondary teachers, technical directors and administrators for education at all levels; professionalizing teaching personnel, both degree-holders and those rural teachers lacking such titles.

ESCUELA TECNICO TEXTIL. A special technical school in textiles was established in 1949 in Comayaguela, with the object of preparation of teachers and technical workers specialized in spinning and weaving in order to enhance the cotton industry of the country.

ESPAÑOLO. A cross between a Castiso (q.v.) male and a Spanish female. See RACIAL MIXTURES.

ESPARTA. In coastal Atlántida Department along the railroad, Esparta is a town of the banana-growing area, in the valley of the short Río San Juan.

ESPINO PLAIN. This broad and level valley north of the similar valley of Comayagua is along the Humuya River extending as far as Ojas de Agua. It is approximately 8 x 12 miles in extent, and 900 feet above sea level.

ESPINOSA DE LOS MONTEROS, JOSE OSORIO. Another peacemaker like his predecessor, Ceballos y Villaguiterre (q.v.), he continued to pacify the factional divisions of the Tequeli uprising; served 1703-1706.

ESQUIVEL, JUAN FRANCISCO. Oidor of the Audiencia of Guatemala, Esquivel was sent to handle the unloading of the Nuestra Senora de la Victoria (q.v.) in the Bay of Fonseca in 1657. The Bay of Fonseca was a smuggling depot for Chinese goods.

ESTACHERIA, JOSE DE. The Colonel who had been governor of Nicaragua and Commandant of Fort San Carlos, second in command to Gálvez at Trujillo in 1782 (q.v.). He was also destined to succeed Gálvez as Captain General in 1783.

ESTADO EN SITIO  see  STATE OF SIEGE

ESTADOUNIDENSE. A very convenient Spanish word, an adjective which has no English counterpart. If it had one, it would be "United-statesian," which would be an adjective of broad utility. "American" is obviously generic, and is inconsiderate when used quite patently to mean "of the United States." "Northamerican," while not precise for this use, is preferable to "American." Estadounidense is both accurate and melodious.

ESTANCA. A government monopoly, such as the sale of rum or "aguardiente" in mid-19th century.

ESTATUTO. A unionist constitution for Central America drawn up in Tegucigalpa in October 1852, following the departure of the disturbing Britisher, Frederick Chatfield (q.v.). Cabañas (q.v.), president of Honduras, begged his neighbors to retain the goal of union. But when defeated in Guatemala in 1853, Cabañas lost power, and by 1854 Rafael Carrera was the strongman of both Guatemala and Central America for the next 11 years.

ESTRADA, FRANCISCO  see  REMANZO and GONZALEZ, SIMON

ESTRADO, RAUL EDGARDO. Official of the reorganized strike committee in June 1954, during the general strike. He hinted at possible bloodshed.

ETHNIC GROUPS. The major ethnic group is mestizo, of mixed Indian and European blood, the major element in the latter being Spanish. The ladino (q.v.) culture designation is principally inclusive of the mestizos, and is considered to be 91 per cent of the total population. Indians comprise about three per cent of the total population, about 70 per cent of these being of the Lenca group (q.v.). Two minor but interesting groups are, first, the Black Caribs, descended from Carib Indian islanders from St. Vincent in the Caribbean, and negroes originally brought to the area in slavery; secondly, English-speaking blacks and whites on the offshore northcoast Bay Islands, called the Bay Islanders.

EXIM BANK. The United States Export-Import Bank, which over a long period of time has furnished credits to Honduras. As reconstruction following the fall 1974 hurricane was being planned, the ExIm organization took a dim view of long-term progress, partly due to serious balance-of-payment deficits prior to the hurricane. Expansion of the telephone system was an immediate issue. The acronym denotes the Bank which was established in 1934 and modified in 1945 to provide and promote the financing of United States exports.

EXPORT DUTIES. Coffee is the principal export on which duties are levied. It is $5.00 per bag, although there was a temporary reduction following 1969. Export duties also affect wood, bananas, and silver, and bring in about four per cent of government income.

EXPORTS. Before the mid-1960s bananas represented 50 to 60 per cent of all exports by value, but this figure dropped to under 47 per cent by 1969, and by 1974, the tax on bananas (q.v.) was having a wide effect. Meanwhile coffee, the second export, was also falling, with wood and lumber in third place. Bananas are produced by two large companies which are foreign-owned; coffee by 40,000 native producers on small farms. Lumber represents only eight per cent of exports, but Honduras is the second largest exporter of lumber in Latin America, due in part to the excellent mahogany still available.
 Live cattle and beef exports had increased during the decade, surpassing minerals as the fourth largest export. Meat exports rose from 200 tons to 10,000 tons over the ten-year period. Exports of silver at four per cent and all other minerals at three per cent were much less than in the colonial mining heyday. Other products were cotton, beans, corn, cement, tobacco, soap, shoes, clothing, canned fruit, chemicals, sugar, and margarine.
 Exports go to 50 countries, but 98 per cent of all to 18 countries. In 1968 the United States took 44 per cent of the total. West Germany is the second biggest customer.

EXPORTS, 1850. Estimates made by E. G. Squier (q.v.) were as follows:

| | |
|---|---:|
| Bullion (gold and silver) | $ 400,000 |
| Mahogany and Dyewoods | 200,000 |
| Cattle | 125,000 |
| Hides, sarsaparilla, tobacco, etc. | 400,000 |
| | $1,125,000 |

- F -

FAJA DE MONTAÑA. Local term in Southern Honduras for a long and narrow strip of cloud forest, which is narrow because it is residual from clearing and cultivation of the slopes nearly up to the crests.

FALANGES ESPAÑOLES. Groups founded to promote sympathy for and cooperation with the Franco regime in Spain. In some countries of Latin America they have met with repression.

FALANGISMO. Falangismo is hispanicism with a heavy stress on political objectives. See HISPANISMO.

FALSE CAPE. The "Cabo Falso" of colonial days, significant because often mistaken for Cape Gracias a Dios. About thirty miles northeast of that cape, named by Columbus in gratitude for the change of weather and a southward trending coast, False Cape is thus near the Honduras-Nicaragua border and in a particularly inaccessible part of Honduran Mosquitia (q.v.). See CABO FALSO.

FANCOURT, COLONEL. British officer appointed to take the place of Superintendent Alexander Macdonald (q.v.) at Belize. Fancourt referred a Honduran protest concerning the Bay Islands to Great Britain in 1838, and the result was that the British government backed Macdonald's high-handed actions. (See ROATAN.) In 1849 the islanders applied to Fancourt to establish a government on Roatán. He then recommended to the islanders that they form a Legislative Assembly of 12 members. By 1850 it was clear that neither the inhabitants of the Bay Islands nor the British government considered Roatán as under British authority.

FANDANGO. A Spanish dance which became popular in the Spanish colonies about 1765.

FANEGA. A measure of volume for grains, consisting of 24 medios (q.v.) of about 46 liters each, hence 1,100 liters.

FARM ANIMALS, COLONIAL. Pigs, sheep and cattle were introduced into Honduras via Gulf ports prior to 1530. They increased rapidly until the latter part of the century.

FARM DEMONSTRATION SCHOOL. Located at Catacamas, this school, like that at El Zamorano (q.v.) takes Honduran students, has a three-year program and is open to students with a sixth grade education. It is operated by the Honduran Ministry of Agriculture.

FARMING. Farms in Honduras are often small; a tenant, 13 acres; a sharecropper or colono (q.v.), 5 acres. Most such staples as rice, beans, plantains, and sorghum are raised on farms under 25 acres. Techniques tend to be primitive. Erosion is rife, and many crops grow on steep, easily eroded slopes. Crop rotation is little practiced. Hand tools are the rule, machetes (q.v.) being the principal tool. Fertilizer is little used (20,000 tons a year) and of 2,000,000 cultivated acres in the 1960s, less than ten per cent were irrigated. See COLONO and LAND TENANCY.

FASH see AUTHENTIC FEDERATION OF HONDURAN UNIONS

FATHOM EXPEDITIONS. Led by Dennis Standefer, a treasure-hunting and diving group which recently used 6" and 8" gold dredges to clear the wreck of the Leviathan (q.v.) in 54 feet of water, four miles south of the Fort Omoa (q.v.). They salvaged 1000 coins, some from Potosí.

FAUNA. Honduras has, in addition to a variety of birds (see

BIRDS), a large variety of reptiles, some amphibians, relatively few fishes.

Reptiles:
Turtles (3 families)
Lizards (iguanas, skinks, geckos, etc.)
Snakes, 7 (boas, worm snakes, coral snakes; pit vipers, such as the bushmaster and rattle-snake, and the fer-de-lance.
Crocodiles
Caymans

Amphibians:
Caecilians
Salamandars
Frogs and Toads (6 families)

Mammals
Include the unique weasel-related "mapache" (q.v.) (also see illustration) and five types of cat--the basic American lion or cougar (here called león); the jaguar (called tigre), the tigrillo or ocelot, and a brace of smaller cats, one of them a short-legged one called jacaranda. There is a variety of small mammals--squirrels, etc.

Fishes:
Characins
Gymnotid eels
Catfishes
Minnows
Kill fishes
Cichlids
Gar-pikes
Mud-eels
Sea catfish
Shark (off the coast)

FAYSSOUX, CALLENDAR. Commander of William Walker's (q.v.) "Navy," this talented officer was in charge of the armed schooner Granada. Fayssoux had been a member of the ill-fated Narciso López expeditions to Cuba a few years earlier. Favorite among Walker's officers, Fayssoux defied a British Naval Captain and in 1856 sunk a well-armed brig from Costa Rica. Fayssoux stuck with Walker through thick and thin, arranging Walker's last trip on the schooner Taylor, which ended in Honduras. Fayssoux later had a distinguished career in the U.S. Civil War as a Confederate officer.

FECESITLIH. Probably deserving an award as an awkward acronym, this one represents the Federation of Free Unions of Honduras (q.v.).

FEDERACION AUTENTICA SINDICAL HONDUREÑA see AUTHENTIC FEDERATION OF HONDURAN UNIONS

FEDERACION CENTRAL DE SINDICATOS DE TRABAJADORES

Federación 132

LIBRES DE HONDURAS see FEDERATION OF FREE UNIONS OF HONDURAS

FEDERACION DE ASOCIACIONES FEMENINAS HONDUREÑAS. This federation of women's clubs was instrumental in seeking and effecting women's suffrage in Honduras, and the decree issued in 1955 was a direct result of their efforts. See SUFFRAGE FOR WOMEN.

FEDERACION DE CENTRO AMERICA. One of numerous attempts to re-federate the Central American countries, this effort was made on September 9, 1921, six days before the 100th anniversary of independence. It had special significance for Honduras since Tegucigalpa was to be chosen as the capital. Since Nicaragua and Costa Rica had not had a part in the hurried constitutional assembly, they were not enthusiastic, and a new revolution breaking out in Guatemala brought the project to a "natural" death in 1922.

FEDERACION HONDUREÑA DE MAESTROS. Teachers' federation, not unlike such professional associations as the National Education Association in the United States.

FEDERACION NACIONAL DE TRABAJADORES Y CAMPESINOS DE HONDURAS see NATIONAL FEDERATION OF WORKERS AND PEASANTS OF HONDURAS

FEDERACION SINDICAL DE TRABAJADORES NORTEÑOS DE HONDURAS see FEDERATION OF WORKERS OF NORTHERN HONDURAS

FEDERATION OF CENTRAL AMERICA see PROVINCIAS UNIDAS DEL CENTRO DE AMERICA

FEDERATION OF FREE UNIONS OF HONDURAS. In 1959 over 30 small unions in the Tegucigalpa region banded together in this federation, which as yet has just over 3,000 members, while the Federation of Workers of Northern Honduras has over 14,000.

FEDERATION OF WORKERS OF NORTHERN HONDURAS. This federation of labor unions had its inception in 1957 with 25 separate unions and a total membership over 14,000. There are two large unions which make up about three-fourths of the total membership--the Tela Railroad Union (or SITRATERCO) and the Standard Fruit Company Workers Unified Union.

FENACH see NATIONAL FEDERATION OF WORKERS AND PEASANTS OF HONDURAS

FERNANDEZ, JOSE. Missionary priest of the Observant Order, who served for 25 years as a missionary to the Jicaques, with no military or financial aid. He died in the Ulua valley in 1712 at the age of 98. In spite of his lone success, the coastal Sumo-Sambo-Miskitos made slave raids upon the mission Jicaques.

FERNANDEZ DE HEREDIA, ALONSO. One of the two military commanders who took over the Central America Coast in 1745, Fernández first commanded Nicaragua and Costa Rica, but on the death of Vera (q.v.) he had to take over the Honduran coast also, and include among his herculean tasks the building of Fort Omoa. From Lieutenant Colonel he was promoted to Brigadier by the Marquis of Enseñada (q.v.). While Fernández remained in León (the Nicaraguan capital), he gave orders for galleons to be built to join the little corsair fleet of López de la Flor (q.v.). Two attacks on Belize in 1748 were basically unsuccessful. Díaz Navarro still could not be spared to work on Fort Omoa until 1750. The years of peace which followed were a favorable political climate for getting the fort built. Fernández was governor of Honduras in 1747 and again in 1761 and following.

FERRANDIS, ANTONIO. Colonel Ferrandis was governor in 1770 and following. From 1750 on, there was more of a tendency to appoint military officers in the governing posts.

FERRARA, FRANCISCO. General Ferrara served as the first constitutional president of the Republic of Honduras from January 1, 1841 to January 1, 1843, and after an interim of control by the council of Ministers (see TERCERO, JULIAN) he, in effect, succeeded himself from February 23, 1843 to October of 1844. Once again the Council of Ministers (see ALVARADO, CASTO) took over from October to November, and then General Ferrera served again from November 1844 to January 1, 1845. Ferrara had to put down several localized rebellions, and while he was indeed the first constitutional president, following his incumbencies he continued to rule the country as strongman from the posts of Minister of War and Armed Forces Chief, until 1848.

The Ferrara presidency represented the further breakup of the Central American Federation. Morazán, the great Honduran leader and first president of the Federation, was by the time of the elevation of Ferrara (1840 and following) the president of El Salvador. General Ferrara led Nicaraguan and Honduran forces against Francisco Morazán (q.v.), invading Salvadoran territory. As Morazán advanced to meet the invaders, disloyal Salvadorans staged a revolt in the capital at his back. Ferrara was wounded and defeated in the Battle of San Pedro Perulapán (q.v.) on September 25, 1839.

FERROBUS. Diesel car running on the tracks of the Ferrocarril Nacional de Honduras (q.v.).

FERROCARRIL NACIONAL DE HONDURAS. The government-owned railroad in the San Pedro Sula area. Potrerillos is the southernmost point inland, about 75 miles. There are 112 miles of track, 400 freight cars, 17 passenger cars. It services Puerto Cortés on the north coast. The rail guage is the same as that of the Tela railroad, so the two interchange cars and services.

FESITRANH see FEDERATION OF WORKERS OF NORTHERN HONDURAS

FIESCHI, BARTOLOMEO. Captain of the Caravel Viscayno (q.v.) on Columbus' 4th voyage. He was, like the admiral, a Genoese.

FIFI. The designation of a hurricane, sixth of the 1974 season, which struck the Honduran Bay Islands and the north coastal area of the country on September 18 and 19. Greatest devastation was along the coast. Extensive damage was done in Trujillo, which was reported at one time to be 90 per cent destroyed. There was lesser effect in the islands, but La Ceiba, Puerto Castilla, Puerto Cortés, Tela, and San Pedro Sula were all heavily damaged. Floods as a result of the heavy rainfall caused further damage and loss of life, with a major tragedy taking place at Choloma (q.v.). Some reports put loss of life as high as 12,000 in the whole country, with about half of that number meeting death in Choloma alone. This Cortés Department town is on a river of the same name, and the stream changed course and carried crests originating from 24 inches of rainfall, with cascades of the floodwaters and mud slides from the nearby hills doing the major damage.

A week following the storm there were 100,000 Hondurans homeless and perhaps 50,000 still isolated by the storm, some clinging to rooftops and trees, others subjected to the deadly fer-de-lance snakes which were also trying to escape the floodwaters. Banana crops, a means of livelihood for many workers as well as a major factor in the national economy, were reported 90 per cent destroyed. Damage estimates ranged up to as much as 1.8 billion dollars in the aftermath of the 130-mile-per-hour winds of the storm and the 24 inches of rainfall in a 24-hour period. Emergency supplies were sent in from Cuba, former enemy El Salvador, Costa Rica, Guatemala, the United States, and Mexico. Food was a central and immediate problem, with medical supplies running a close second. It was evident that it might be two or three years before things would get back to economic normality after the storm. There was, however, a courageous and hopeful attitude among the people at large, and the government mobilized to meet the emergency with massive effort.

FILIBUSTER. The word filibuster is anglicized from several sources, but originates in Holland Dutch as "vrybruiter"-- from "vry," free, and "bruiter," booty or spoils taken in battle. "Freebooter" is the English form of the original.

The Spanish filibusteros is applied in Central America to the pirates of the colonial centuries, whose depredations on the Caribbean coastal lowland areas were carried out using lagoons as bases for their shallow-draft craft. Many descendants of Dutch and English pirates are among the present Bay Island population of Honduras.

FILISOLA, VICENTE. The Mexican general who was involved in attempting to get Central American adherence to the shortlived empire of Iturbide (q.v.). He headed troops in Central America from June 12, 1822 to June 24, 1823, and after he had called an assembly to set up local government, in July of that year the emancipation act was published. Filisola died in 1850, aged 70.

FINANCIERA HONDUREÑA, S.A. In 1964 this concern opened to provide investment banking service to developing industrial projects and to underwrite securities for corporations trying to raise capital.

FINCAS DE CAFE. Coffee plantations.

FIORI, ALMA. Pen name of Victoria Bertrand, poet and editor born in Juticalpa, Olancho, in 1907; from 1917 until her death in 1952 she lived in New York where she directed the magazine Norte. Her father, Dr. Francisco Bertrand, was President of Honduras.

FIRST NATIONAL CONGRESS OF THE COMMUNIST PARTY. A secret meeting held in 1958. By 1962 there was reason to believe that most labor leadership had been purged of communists.

FISHERIES. In 1971 the Central American countries reported 11,500 metric tons of fish caught, as compared to a total of 500,000 metric tons from the Caribbean Sea as a whole. A major source of protein, the fish resources of Honduras are hardly tapped, although there are commercial shrimp operations on the Bay Islands and at the Caratasca bar.

FITZGIBBON. A U.S. citizen who was elected magistrate on the Island of Roatán (q.v.) in the 1840s, in defiance of British meddling.

FLAG, HONDURAN. The Honduran national flag developed from the flag of the Central American Union, which was approved by the first National Constituent Assembly in 1823. This consisted of three horizontal broad stripes, blue above and below, white through the center. An escutcheon was to be placed in the center of the white stripe. Honduras' flag today has the same description, except that there are five blue stars on the center white stripe (rather than an escutcheon), representing the five original united provinces. The first line of the chorus of the national anthem (see HYMNO NACIONAL), is "Tu bandera es un lampo de cielo," thus honoring the flag.

FLAGS OF CONVENIENCE see MERCHANT MARINE REGISTRATION

FLEET, COLUMBUS'. On his fourth voyage, Columbus had four caravels when he reached the Honduran coast and discovered mainland Central America. They were La Capitana (q.v.), Santiago de Palso, El Gallego, and El Vizcaino.

FLEET SYSTEM, SPANISH. In 1543 the depredations of French corsairs in the South Atlantic and Caribbean areas caused Spain to adopt a Venetian convoy system of shipping to and from America. Ships to Honduras sailed along the fifteenth parallel, stopping at Puerto Caballos, and later going to rendezvous at Havana for the homeward journey. Puerto Caballos was at this time the port for Guatemala.

In the latter half of the century the corsairs had become a menace of major proportions. No port was safe. Phillip II then ordered Honduran ships to stay with the fleet headed for New Spain (Vera Cruz) until they reached the western tip of Cuba, then to sail south. Criado de Castila (q.v.) founded Santo Tomás de Castilla to deal with this new situation.

FLINTS, ECCENTRIC. This term is applied to a class of archaeological finds which are chipped flints, as much as 12 to 18 inches long, shaped in the form of warriors with head-dresses, or of ceremonial axes and knives. The intricacies of these "eccentric flints" are incredible (see illustration). One found at Copán is 6 inches wide and was made about 750 A.D.

FLOR, MONTAÑAS DE LA. A mountain complex, sometimes called the Mountains of Sulaco (a town just to the west) and centering a number of river systems. Altitudes run to 7,500 feet. The complex is about 20 miles across. Tributary streams run from its heights into the Río Guayape, and hence the Río Patuca eastward; into the Sulaco and then the Ulua northward; into the Yaguala and hence the Aguán northeastward; and into foothill ranges to the South, into tributaries of the Choluteca.

FLORA. Honduras has the isthmian plant families as found through Central America. They are derived from both continents, North and South. Among them are:

| tree fern | oxalis | pineapple |
| podocarp (conifer) | malphighia | lily |
| pine | soapberry | canna |
| Pondweed | dillenia | orchids (a great variety) |
| sedge | cacti | custard-apple |

# MAYA FLINTS, etc.

COPÁN
(750 A.D.)
(MAN WITH HEADDRESS & BLADE)

BLADE — From Quiriguá Guatemala (NEAR COPÁN)

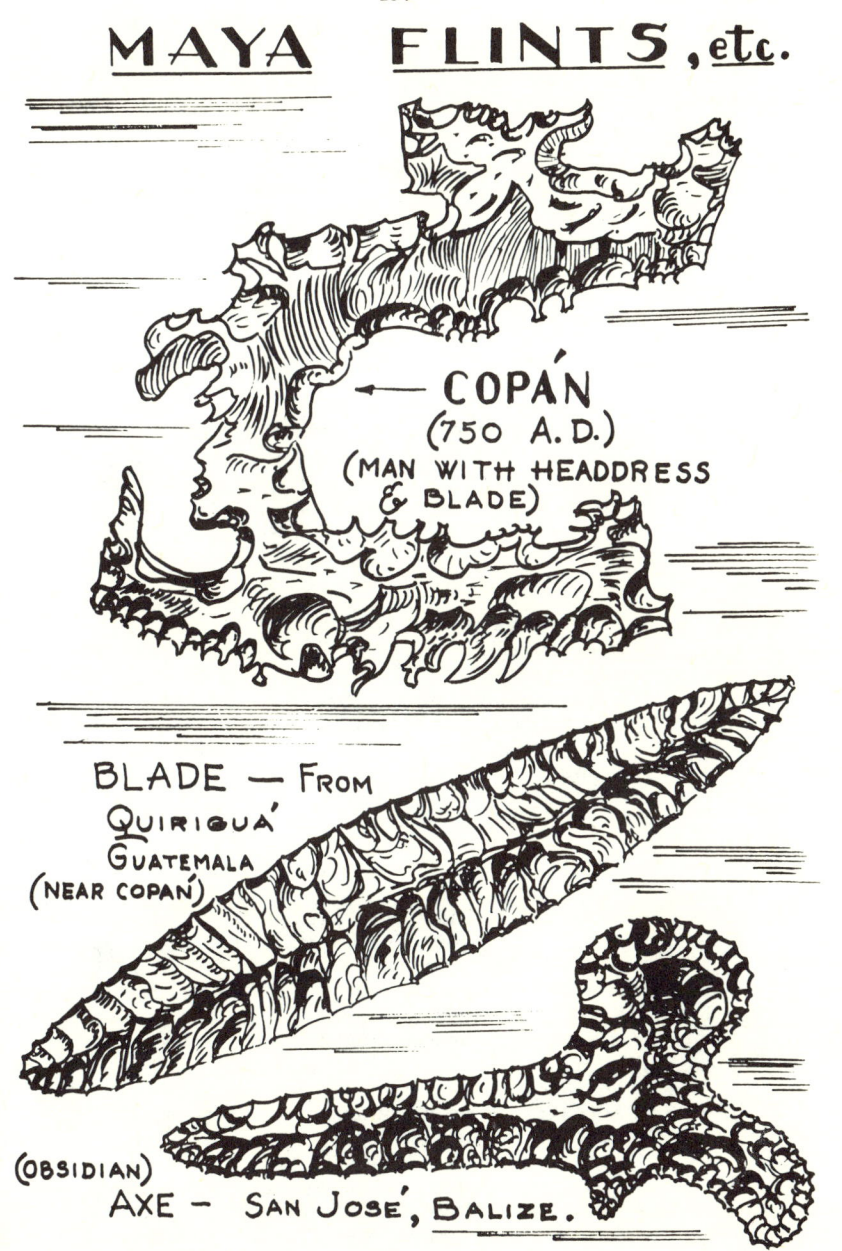

(OBSIDIAN) AXE — SAN JOSÉ, BALIZE.

FLINT: This "eccentric flint" found at Copán is an example of the incredible work in stone done by the Maya.

Flores, Oscar

| | | |
|---|---|---|
| palms | mallows | poppy |
| aroids | sterculia | saxifrage |
| pipewort | myrtle | witch-hazel |
| spiderwort | | rose |
| amaryllis | | legumes |
| iris | | spurges |
| primrose | | sapodilla |
| melastoma | | logania |
| heaths | | borages |
| dogbane | | vervain |
| morning-glory | | mint |
| figwort | | potato |
| bignonia | | gesnaria |
| madder | | acanthus |
| gourds | | |

FLORES, OSCAR. Minister of Labor, 1960s. He has been instrumental in getting communists removed from the various labor federations in Honduras. Flores was editor of the Liberal party organ El Pueblo during the Lozano period of the 1950s. He was exiled by Lozano on July 9, 1956.

FLOTA DE NAOS see NAO

FLOTA MERCANTE GRAN CENTROAMERICANA. A joint Guatemalan-Honduran merchant fleet which serves both countries.

FLOWER, NATIONAL. The national flower of Honduras was changed on January 12, 1946 from the rose to the Orchidea Brassavola Digbiana, an indigenous orchid considered to represent Honduras better than an import such as the rose.

FLYING CROSS see MEDALS

FOA see FOREIGN OPERATIONS ADMINISTRATION

FONDUEROS. Alternate spelling of "Honduras" as found on some old maps as early as 1600. This spelling is based on Spanish "fondo" as the "bottom of a hollow thing, the bottom of a hill or valley." The usual and presently accepted spelling is based on "Hondo," meaning deep, profound, or "low with respect to neighboring places." Obviously the general meaning is similar.

FONDURAS, CABO DE. Form of the name of Cape Honduras as found on Totten's map (q.v.).

FONSECA, BAY OF. Large bay with several estuaries, which includes all the Pacific Coast of Honduras as well as coastal waters of Nicaragua and El Salvador. It is in the line of the major volcanoes and also of the two Nicaraguan lakes. There is a belief that the three bodies of water are of similar origin, although the Bay of Fonseca is the only one open to the

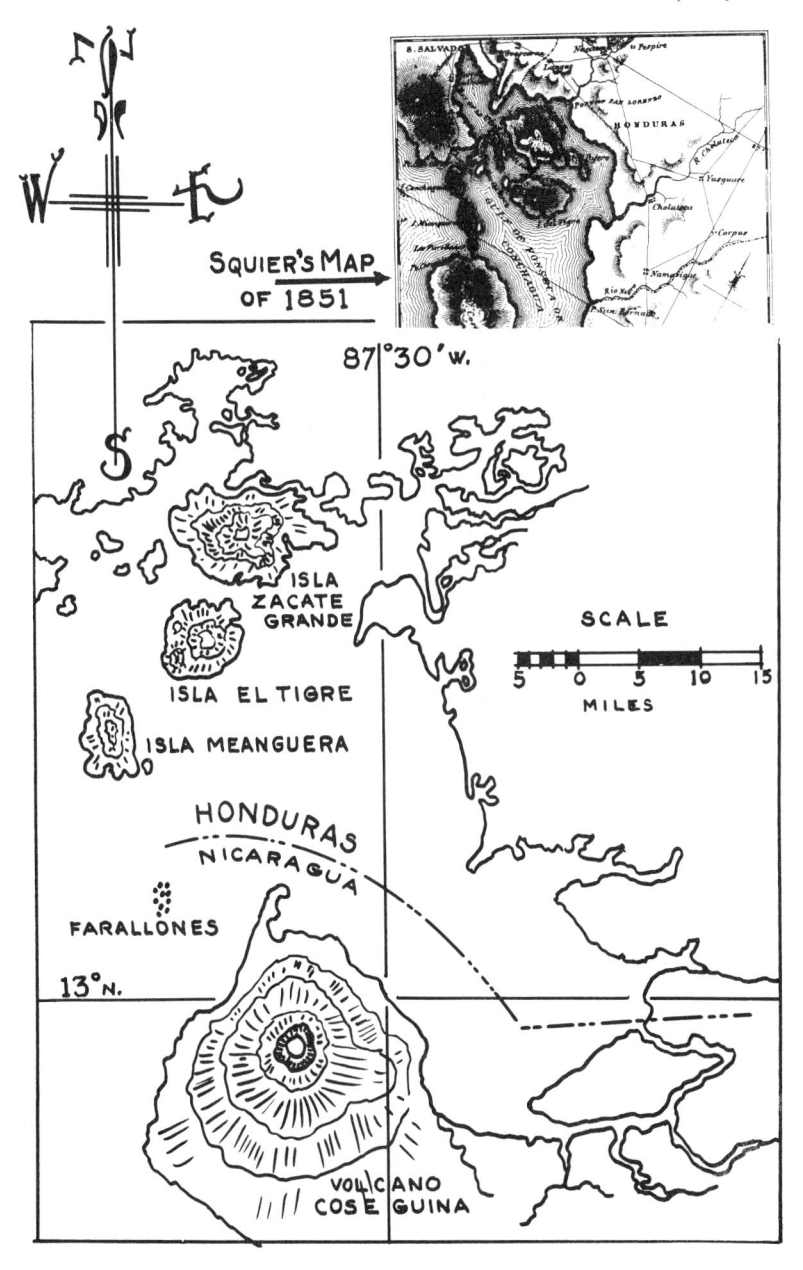

BAY OF FONSECA: Major Pacific coastal harbor with its volcanic islands, and ports of three countries--Honduras, El Salvador, and Nicaragua.

sea (see illustration).  See also FONSECA, JUAN RODRI-
GUEZ DE; SQUIER, EPHRAIM GEORGE; CHATFIELD,
FREDERICK.

FONSECA, GAUTAMA.  Lawyer Fonseca became the Minister of
Labor in the López Arellano (q.v.) cabinet following December 4, 1972.

FONSECA, JUAN RODRIGUEZ DE.  The counsellor to Queen Isabella for whom the Bay of Fonseca was named, and who had control of American affairs by her appointment from 1493 to his death in 1524.

FONTANA, JAIME.  Pen name of Victor Eugenio Castañeda, born in Tutule, La Paz, in 1922.  Law student, with degree from the National University, Fontana has published poems; Color naval was a 1951 prize winner in Buenos Aires.  He was cultural attaché in the Honduran embassy in Argentina, business attaché in Mexico, and Ambassador to Ecuador and later to Peru.

FOREIGN AFFAIRS, MINISTRY OF   see   CABINET

FOREIGN DEBT   see   FUNDING OF FOREIGN DEBT

FOREIGN INVESTMENT.  At the outset of the 1970s the United States had $265,000,000 of foreign investment in Honduras.  There is more such investment in Honduras than in any other Central American country, and the increase per annum is about eight per cent.

FOREIGN OPERATIONS ADMINISTRATION.  The U.S. international assistance agency, post-World War II.  The name was changed to International Cooperation Administration in 1956.  The succession of agencies had agricultural, military, educational, and other enterprises in Honduras as well as in other Latin American nations.  Among other projects in this country was a vocational school.  The Alliance for Progress is the latest title and manifestation.

FOREST PRODUCTS.  Although Honduras is the home of a fine mahogany generally known as "Honduran," the most important forest export is still pine, due to the vast quantities.  From 1963 to 1965 the Southern Pine beetle killed about 20 per cent of Honduras' quality pine timber, on 6,000,000 acres, with a loss potential estimated at $300,000,000.
 There are many sawmills, but transportation of logs is difficult due to the terrain.  Mahogany grows as isolated trees, and some mahogany logs were being lifted out of jungles by balloon in 1972.  Sawmills are a fifth of the total number of industrial plants in the country.  A paper and wood-processing enterprise, jointly funded by goverment and foreign interests, is scheduled to open in mid-1970s, with a $92,000,000

investment. There are actually more fine tropical hardwoods than pine, both in species and quantity, but the difficulties of logging and the building market still keep pine number one in demand.

FORMATIVE. A term applied by archaeologists to the earliest appearance of sedentary village life based on agriculture. Throughout Central America evidential information has been assembled including such ceramic studies as those of Lothrop and others.

FORT DALLING. Name for the English garrison and establishment at Brewer's Lagoon in the 18th Century. Named after the Jamaican governor who helped to initiate the abortive invasion of Central America in 1780.

FORT INMACULADA CONCEPCION DE HONDURAS. The fort at the Mouth of Black River (Río Tinto) which was thus renamed after the British defeat there in 1782 by Gálvez forces. See TRUJILLO, BASE ... 1782.

Named for the storied fort on the San Juan River in Nicaragua, the name was considered lucky in that it was a symbol of Spanish success and valor. The first commandant was the same Tomás de Julia who had reoccupied the Nicaraguan fort, and he doubtless was responsible for naming the Río Tinto redoubt. It was temporary, and in no way comparable to the San Juan River fortress, still extant.

FORT OMOA. In a bight of the Bay of Omoa, at the deepest Honduran penetration of the Caribbean Gulf of Honduras, there stands a colonial Spanish fortification of the first order, in excellent repair, and with many of the cannon assigned to it still stacked in the courtyard or scattered about the walls. It is a triangular structure, with three major bastions, one pointing landward, and between the sea-side bastions a great crescent of wall, battery-mounted, almost a quarter-circle arc. The sides are approximately 200 feet each, and the major battery arc is about 180 feet. The walls are 18 feet high and 12 feet thick; the fort carried as many as 150 pieces of artillery. Most of these iron cannon are still there.

The site was picked by Díez Navarro (q.v.), the construction authorized by the Marquis of Enseñada (q.v.). Charged with the execution was Juan de Vera (q.v.), and later Fernández de Heredia (q.v.).

The purpose of the fort was to help hold the Spanish frontier against English incursions based at Belize, the Bay Islands, and Black River, and when peace between England and Spain came after the War of Jenkin's Ear, and conciliatory policies followed, the main purpose of Omoa came to be the control of contraband. The Baymen and Shoremen (q.v.) were adept in the contraband trade, and the Spanish needed a major coastguard base, customs station, and military post of respected strength. Omoa seemed an obvious location for

**OMOA FORTRESS:** Major bastion of the Spanish colonial frontier, the 18th century fort remains in excellent repair on its strategic north coastal site.

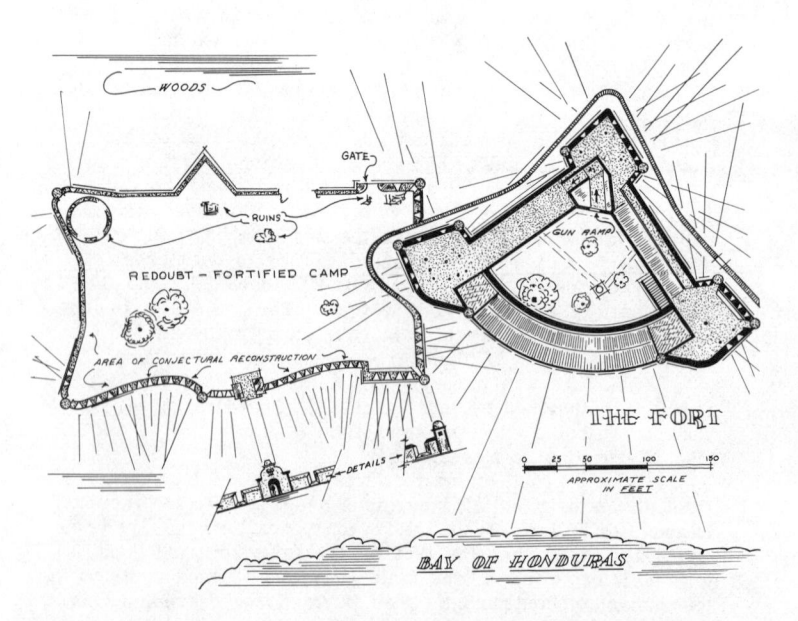

**OMOA FORT - PLAN:** The early barricade erected for protection during the construction of the fort is seen, overlapped by the triangular stronghold itself.

**CANNON AND MERCURY FLASKS:** Fort Omoa still has many examples of both these colonial necessities. The mercury was used in silver amalgamation.

these multiple and mutually supportive purposes. Omoa had
deepwater access, and was thus better than Santa Tomás nearby, Fort San Felipe on Lake Izabel, or Trujillo to the east.
The two former were on shallow waters; the latter, with its
open bay, was hard to defend. It was expected that trade
would flow through Omoa, with silver and indigo from the interior going there rather than to the Golfo Dulce (just over
the Guatemalan border). As a coast guard station, Omoa
would be the major strong point between Panama's Chagres
River (with its Fort San Lorenzo) and the major fortified
city of Campeche on Yucatan's west coast, a coastal span of
1,000 miles as the crow flies, and much farther along the
coast. The fertile Ulua valley and its available livestock,
just inland from Omoa, was considered a source of food supplies.

Díez Navarro's plan had been for a fort to house 2,000
soldiers, but the fort finally authorized was to hold a maximum of only 200 men. By 1752 the military engineer was at
work at Omoa. The actual building of the fort took 25 years,
millions of pesos, and some thousands of lives. Security was
a major early problem. For four years Díez Navarro spent
time erecting a small redoubt with low walls and embrasures
for cannon, a fortified camp within which workers and soldiers
could shelter while the adjacent fort was built. The redoubt
still exists in partly ruined form (see illustration of Omoa).
Thirty-two cannon were placed on the seaward wall of the redoubt.

Meanwhile a road was built and completed in 1756,
from Guatemala (Antigua) to Omoa. (See ARANJO Y RIO,
JOSE.) In that same year, construction began on the main
structure. Stone was only to be found at a distance, and labor had to be conscripted. So many Indians died in the labor
of fort-building that it became known as the "Graveyard of
Honduras." Smallpox seems to have been a major scourge--
most of the soldiers stationed at Omoa in 1771 were pock-
marked. It was finally deemed necessary to use Negro
slaves, and these were purchased from Jaspar Hall (q.v.) in
Jamaica. The town of Omoa to this day reflects the influx
of several hundred negro slaves.

In 1766 a tax collector was established in Omoa, with
tobacco, indigo, and silver being pertinent products. In the
year 1779 a major effort at conquest was made by the British
(see OMOA, 1779--BATTLES). While Omoa was regained,
the fort was in danger of defeat by diplomacy, for Spain
would have given up Oran in Africa, the whole island of
Puerto Rico, and Omoa itself in order to get its hands on
Gibraltar. The British, however, did not wish to trade.

During the 1780's the Spanish opened up and occupied
the north coast of Honduras on a more permanent basis.
They now held, from west to east, Omoa, Roatán, Trujillo,
Black River, and Brewer's Lagoon. Beyond Cabo Gracias a
Dios, however, the Sambo-Miskitos still held sway. Omoa
was finally completed in the late years of the century; Ramón

Anguiano (q.v.) actually proposed abandoning the fort about 1798, with an eye to returning to the old frontier of 1643.

By 1817 Omoa was a tax-free port. In spite of this fact, contraband trade continued. The history of Omoa, while quieter in the 19th and 20th centuries, yet has accent points. In 1950 the fort was occupied by 200 professional men who were political prisoners, and who were there as much as two years. They built a water system and the latrines, and lived as well as they could in the old fort.

Fort Omoa has had high significance. It was a major bastion of the Spanish colonial frontier. If it had not existed, the whole north coast of Honduras might well have been another British Honduras. As it was, it held the coast for Spain and later for the independent republic of Honduras, and is today preserved by the nation as a monument to the stirring era of conquest and colony.

FORTIN LIJO, DANIEL see ARIAS, JUAN ANGEL

"FOUR SEVENTIES." A phrase which arose during the administration of Villeda Morales (q.v.) and which referred to 70 per cent illiteracy, 70 per cent illegitimacy, 70 per cent rural population, 70 per cent avoidable death. It is a reminder of perpetual tragedy, being slowly dispelled in the modern era.

FOURTH VOYAGE, COLUMBUS. The voyage on which Columbus first sighted the American mainland, on what is now the north Honduran coast, was projected in a letter to the Spanish Monarchs on February 26, 1502. He wanted to sail to Hispaniola (Haiti) first, and then follow the continent beyond Cuba until he reached India. This was on the basis of a long extension of the Malay penninsula as drawn in Ptolemy's charts, and which Columbus believed was not far west of Cuba. Columbus did not know that he would be just west of Cuba and still half a world away from India. He even took Arab-speaking interpreters! The four caravels left Seville on April 3rd, and took departure from Cadíz on May 9. There were in the fleet 55 ship's boys and only 41 seamen. The former were paid 666 maravedis per month, the seamen 1,000. Captains were paid 4,000, masters 2,000.

When off the coast of Hispaniola on June 29, Captain Terreros (q.v.) predicted the coming of a hurricane; Columbus' ships took shelter, but a large fleet under Torres was lost. Columbus' navigational powers combined science and instinct. On July 14-18 they sailed past Jamaica, and they stayed for several days near the Isle of Pines off the south coast of Cuba. But then they sailed south by west three days, and reached the Island of Bonacca (Guanaja, q.v.) from which to the south they could see a long coast backed by blue mountains. After leaving the Honduran coast following 38 days of beating against storm winds, Columbus skirted the Nicaraguan and Panamanian coasts, then turned north to the Cayman islands and Cuba.

The coasting voyage had suffered from sharks and waterspouts, fever and Indian attack.  Columbus was ill much of the time.  With two ships left of the original fleet, and the 130 men aboard stranded on Jamaica, Columbus needed to get word of his plight to Hispaniola.  The sinking caravels were worm-eaten and rotten beyond repair, and they were beached together and used as a camp in Santa Gloria Bay, on the Jamaican north coast.  The Porras brothers (see PORRAS, FRANCISCO) led a meeting and finally went ashore.  Only 20 men stayed with Columbus.  He used an eclipse to convince the reluctant Indians of his supernatural powers so that the little band could continue to get food.  Two men had been sent to Hispaniola for help.  After a second meeting, a small caravel finally came and left, but then in June 1504, the survivors were rescued, sailing for Hispaniola June 29, after a year and five days on Jamaica.  On September 12, 1504, they departed for Spain, and finally landed at Sanlúcar de Barrameda on November 7.

Columbus, the admiral, was 53.  His son, Ferdinand, was 16, and his brother Bartolomé, was hale and hearty.  There was no profit to the admiral on the voyage, for his important patroness Isabella died November 26, 1504.  The fourth voyage had skirted the mainland of a New World, but the discoverer did not know it.  See COLUMBUS, CHRISTOPHER and FLEET, COLUMBUS.

FRANCISCO MORAZAN DEPARTMENT.  Named for the Central American hero, a Honduran native, this Department is the seat of the capital city, Tegucigalpa.  Bounded on the north by the Montañas de la Flor and Yoro Department, and on the northeast by Olancho; to the southeast by El Paraiso; on the south by Choluteca and Valle Departments; on the west by La Paz.  In touching seven departments it is similar to one other, Yoro department (q.v.).  The Choluteca River runs through the capital city and across the department; the Montañas Yerba Buena stretch across the southern end.  There are 27 municipios, and the cabacera is also the national capital, Tegucigalpa.  The cabaceras in 1973 had a population of 318,887, while the rural and small town departmental population was 177,821, for a total of 496,708, the most populous of the 18 departments.  The government, the principal educational institutions, ten hospitals, and much business and industrial activity are characteristic.  The presidential palace, the penitentiary, the national cathedral, and major hotels are located here.  There are many modern buildings and suburbs superimposed on the old Spanish colonial city.  The silver mining of colonial days was a major feature in establishing the capital here.  There is no rail transport to the city, nor is there a jet-port, because of the restricted valley location.  New paved highways have greatly eased transportation, however.

FRANCISCO MORAZAN TECHNICAL INSTITUTE.  This vocational-technical school in Tegucigalpa prepares students at above secondary level for advanced semi-professional positions. It is open to graduates of the industrial secondary course who are specially recommended for an advanced program. The name is that of the great Honduran figure of the independence movement.

FRANCO, GABRIEL. Governor of Honduras in 1759.

FRENER, JEAN BAPTISTE. Superintendent of the Guatemala mint in 1881, who designed the dies used for Honduran coinage following that time. See COINAGE, REGULAR ISSUE, 1871-1922.

FRITZ GAERTNER, M. G. REINHOLD. Dr. Fritz Gaertner (also spelled Fritzgärtner) was a Prussian who emigrated first to the United States and then to Honduras in the 1880s. He was an entrepreneur and was interested in mines, his interest carrying him to part ownership of the La Plomosa mine and to positions as Government Geologist and Inspector-General of Mines for Honduras. He also founded the first English language newspaper in Central America, the Honduras Progress. He was also involved in a contract providing for canalization of the Ulua and Blanco rivers, with George W. Shears, a citizen of the United States. They contemplated steamboat navigation and promised a steamer on the rivers in 1883. The project fell through.

FRONTIER OF NEW SPAIN, COLONIAL. The Spanish frontier in New Spain was, oddly enough, held by Spain on the western "South Sea," or Pacific side of the Central American isthmian area, rather than on the eastern or Caribbean side from which the Spanish came. There were geographical and historical reasons. Transportation up and down the mountainous isthmus between early-settled Mexico was easier on the rugged Pacific side than in the nearly impenetrable rain forests of the Caribbean littoral. The frontier itself extended from Chiapas at the root of the Yucatán peninsula all the way through Costa Rica. It was a crooked line, but a very real one, more than 1,000 miles long. Broken by the deep San Juan valley in Nicaragua and by the Ulua River basin in Honduras, it nevertheless was a major wall which in Honduras parallels the north coast, almost touching it at Trujillo, and then trends southeast into central Nicaragua. Central America is divided almost in half by this frontier. Only in Honduras do the frontier and north coast essentially coincide. The positions of major fortifications at Omoa (q.v.) and Trujillo (q.v.) were essentially quite vulnerable. The thin line of forts was anchored at Lake Petén in the Guatemalan jungle to the north, and at Fort Inmaculada in Nicaragua to the south, where the San Juan penetrated the frontier. Only there and at Omoa was the formidable geographic wall really penetrated.

South and west of the 1,000-mile line were fertile soils

and populous centers; north of the line, neither soil nor climate is inviting. Only along the Honduran north coast from Omoa to Trujillo was the climate bearable. Agriculture on the north side of the frontier was risky and difficult. The people lived as hunters and fishermen in a hostile, wild environment, which in turn conditioned their behavior. The Sambo-Miskitos (q.v.), descended from Sumus (q.v.) of South American Chibcha (q.v.) origin, became dominant in the area around Cabo Gracias a Dios. Even today this is a wild and sparsely settled area.

FUNDAMENTAL CHARTER OF LABOR GUARANTEES. A 1955 basic labor law with 875 articles covering in comprehensive fashion such matters as social security, collective bargaining, minimum wages and maximum hours. The Labor Code of 1970 incorporated this and other previous legislation. There had been no minimum wage law until 1967.

FUNDING OF FOREIGN DEBT. In 1909 Secretary of State of the United States Philander Knox attempted to conclude a treaty between the U.S. and Honduras that would have involved American bankers in the refunding and consolidation of Honduran debt. Such an arrangement had been developed in Haiti. Fundamental to the pact would have been the setting up of a customs receivership, since the duties collected in customs were the major source of national revenue. Such a receivership was set up in Nicaragua in 1911 only after the landing of U.S. Marines.

- G -

GACETA DEL GOBIERNO, LA. The first public periodical to be published in Honduras, on May 25, 1830.

GALEANO, ALBERTO H. Galeano was given a new charge as President of the Bank of Honduras under the government of López Arellano following December 4, 1972.

GALICIAN-ASTURIAN COLONISTS see GOYONECHE, MIGUEL DE

GALINDO, JUAN. Spanish name of John Gallagher, the Irish soldier of fortune who entered the service of the Central American confederation in 1827. He became colonel in the army, then governor of Petén department in Guatemala, and was finally killed in an Indian settlement inside Honduras. He headed the first expedition to Copán in 1834 and was the first European to call attention to the Copán ruins, by an article dated June 19, 1835, in the Transactions of the American Antiquarian Society. This remarkable Irishman also wrote generally on Central America, produced maps, and gave an 1833 account of the Caribs on the Honduran north coast through the Royal Geographic Society of London.

GALLAGHER, JOHN see GALINDO, JUAN

GALLINAS DE COSTILLA. Hens imported from Europe in colonial times.

GALLINAS DEL PAIS. Colonial term for tame ducks used for food.

GALO SOTO, RAUL. Colonel Galo Soto became the Minister of Defense and Public Security in the cabinet of General López Arellano (q.v.) following his takeover of the government on December 4, 1972.

GALVEZ, JUAN MANUEL. Dr. Gálvez was constitutional President from January 1, 1949 to January 15, 1954. After the long Carias "reign," Gálvez was a pro-National party choice, and the long period of internal stability under Carias continued as if by momentum. Only at the end of Gálvez' presidency was there a break in the tranquillity.

GALVEZ, MATIAS DE. A lieutenant general (highest ranking commission ever granted in Central America), he was Captain-General of Guatemala. This officer later became viceroy of New Spain following his initial posting to Central America in 1778. Brother of José Gálvez, Minister of the Indies, he was an experienced and thorough man who toured his new command through Honduras and Nicaragua, an unusual move for the times, and one difficult to effect. He had heard rumors of an impending British expedition to seize the San Juan River and Lake Nicaragua. He toured León and Granada and presumably all the defenses, and named Ignacio Maestre sergeant-major of the navy at Granada, charged with the building of a fleet on Lake Nicaragua. (It is of interest to reflect that it was at about this same time that similar naval and fortification activities were being carried out on a similarly strategic lake-river complex in North America--Lake Champlain. The parallel of the two frontier endeavors makes a fascinating historical comparison.)

Gálvez was the officer responsible for developing the defense of Fort Omoa (q.v.) in Honduras during the ensuing war with England, and recaptured the fort in 1779. Gálvez seems to have been at Granada in 1780 when the British attacked El Castillo in an effort to cut in two the viceroyalty and may have given the orders which caused hasty erection of Fort San Carlos and the ultimate "wearing out" of the British in their fever-ridden conquest, El Castillo. See EL CASTILLO and FORT SAN CARLOS.

GALVEZ BARNES, ROBERTO. A 31-year old major of the Honduran army who was one of three officers heading a coup ending the Julio Lozano regime October 21, 1954. Gálvez was the son of an ex-President. See also RODRIGUEZ, ROQUE J.

GAMBO. The buttress-root found on many tropical trees such as ceiba, mahogany, and guanacaste.

GANACA. Alternate form of "Guanaja" (island) as shown on the Sánchez Plainsphere (q.v.).

GARAIRTO DE LEON, GARCIA. Governor in 1612, during the time of the Conde de Gómera (q.v.) in the audiencia.

GARAY, CARLOS GUILLERMO. An artist of Tegucigalpa, born in that city, and graduate of the Escuela Nacional de Bellas Artes, Garay has exhibited in San Pedro Sula, Berlin, Hemisfair '68 in San Antonio, Texas, and in other places, and is a recipient of prizes and awards.

GARCIA-BULNES, ALBERTO. Alleged Communist who left with Matute-Gutierrez (q.v.) and others in 1961 for orientation and training in Moscow.

GARCIA CONDE, ALEJO. A Spaniard from Mexico, García was Honduran governor in 1789.

GARCIA DE PALACIO, DIEGO. As oidor of the Audiencia Real of Guatemala, it was García who first described the Mayo ceremonial center ruins of Copán in 1576. This means that he was the first European to take note of the Maya culture. Palenque was the second major site to come to the notice of early explorers. It was 120 years after García that the first Spanish saw the great Guatemala center of Tikál.

GARCIA DE SOLIS, FULGENCIO. Lieutenant Colonel García was governor of Honduras in 1755.

GARCIA GUTIERREZ, MIGUEL ANGEL see MILITARY ZONE COMMANDS, 1972

GARCIA TURCIOS, ABRAHAM see MILITARY ZONE COMMANDS, 1972

GARIF. A term used sometimes to apply to the Black Caribs (q.v.).

GARRIDO, ALFONSO. Pen-name of Celeo Murillo Soto (q.v.).

GARRIGO, MARIANO. An interim president of Honduras in August 1839 when the Central American federation was disintegrating. No term is shown for Garrigo, and dates indicate he was serving simultaneously during the week when Bustillo (q.v.) served.

GASCOIGNE, JOEL. In 1678 a "Thames school" cartographer by this name prepared a West Indies chart which shows the whole area from Trinidad to Nova Scotia with completeness and amazing fidelity. The Honduran Bay Islands, Utila and Guanaca, are named, but surprisingly, not Roatán. Honduras is spelled as today, but "Nicorago" is a bit different, as is "Iucata" for Yucatán.

GENERAL STRIKE, 1954. The first general labor strike in Honduran history erupted in May 1954. On April 10 of that year United Fruit Company (q.v.) dock workers at Tela refused to unload a ship, demanding double-time pay for Sunday work. Brought before a labor court, the judge ruled there was no provision for such pay.
    By the end of April the situation had degenerated so that President Gálvez (q.v.) sent troops to the major Caribbean Port, Puerto Cortés, and by May 4 the four north coast ports were on strike, about 20,000 men. La Epoca (q.v.), the "Carias" paper, blamed communists. UFCO North American families were threatened. Communications were cut. TWBA broadcast from Guatemala inciting strikers to seek a 50 per cent wage increase. Interior Minister Inestroza (q.v.) tried to mediate but made little progress. The strike began to spread to other parts of the country. So far there had been complete order in Tegucigalpa. On May 13, workers other than those in the banana industry struck, including the New York Rosario Mining Company, the Honduran Brewery and the British-American Tobacco Company as well as some smaller industries. By May 18, 50,000 workers were on strike. Mediators were sent to La Ceiba by the government, to no avail.
    Diplomatically, matters became so tense between communist Guatemala (under Arbenz) and Honduras that war was predicted. The United States sent arms to Honduras under a new treaty. Matters were coming to a head in Guatemala, meanwhile, as the government there was soon to be overthrown by Castillo Armas.
    The strikers began to feud with each other in June, some of them accusing certain of their leaders of bad faith. Four leaders were arrested by the government as known communists on June 2. They were Agusto Coto, Manuel A. Sierra, Rubén Portillo, and Modesto Rubio. Coto, as secretary general, was considered to have broken his word on UFCO negotiations. He was then blamed by other leaders for the failure of the negotiations. Professor Manuel Palencia (q.v.) disclaimed the communists and called a conference of strike leaders. This led to reopening of the Tela railroad and eventually toward agreements and the end of the strike. A blunder by UFCO in attempting to divide strike leaders led to a hint of bloodshed by Raúl Egardo Estrado, a high official of the strikers. The strike became more and more bitter. Anti-"Yankee" feeling was building (against United Fruit officials). But in mid-July, after eleven weeks, the two sides suddenly reached agreement, with workers getting most of what they sought.
    The strike was a terrible blow to the economy of Hon-

duras, never very strong at best. The two big fruit companies lost $15,000,000. Workers lost wages of over $2,000,000 and the Honduran government lost $1,000,000 in duties, a significant source of governmental revenue. The longest-lasting result was a new posture of Honduran labor, which presaged a real labor movement; Arthur Juáregui (q.v.) helped work on future union organization. After the strike the labor picture was never quite the same again.

GENERAL TREATY OF PEACE AND UNITY. Signed by all the Central American States in 1907, the treaty provided for compulsory adjudication of disputes between signatories and prohibited political intervention by any state in the internal affairs of another. A corresponding act of 1907 was the creation of the Central American Court of Justice, which was to decide disputes.
    In 1918, Nicaragua was first to abrogate this treaty due to dissatisfaction over disputes and rulings in connection with Costa Rica and El Salvador. The long-standing border dispute between Honduras and Nicaragua had not been settled under aegis of the court, and was not to be settled until the 1960s.

GENERAL TREATY ON CENTRAL AMERICAN ECONOMIC INTEGRATION. This 1960 agreement finally established a Common Market among the five Central American countries, and the benefits have persisted in spite of the war between Honduras and El Salvador in 1969, which shut off a great deal of commercial traffic across the Pacific shores of Honduras. A Salvador to Nicaragua ferry has taken up some of the slack. Signed in Managua on December 13, 1960, the treaty provided for a Central American Bank of Economic Integration and a quadripartite common market to be set up within five years. Only Costa Rica seemed reluctant.

GE-PANO-CARIB. A linguistic superstock, basic to the language spoken by Black Caribs (q.v.). See MARCO-CHIBCHAN.

GIANT CAVENDISH. This banana variety was developed by the Standard Fruit Co. (q.v.) and is significant because of its resistance to the Panama disease. It does, however, bruise easily, and must be shipped in cartons.

GOASCORAN RIVER. A part of Squier's (q.v.) ambitious plan for a cross-Honduran trans-isthmian railroad was the Valley of the Río Goascarán, a river which comprises the border with El Salvador for about 30 miles, and whose tributary valleys run roughly north and south to the south of Comayagua's great valley.

GOBIERNO OF COMAYAGUA. Early colonial government, which was limited after 1578 when silver was discovered near Tegucigalpa. That area became the Alcalde Mayor of Tegucigalpa, covering what comprises today the departments of Francisco Morazán, Valle, Choluteca, El Paraiso, Gracias a Dios, plus parts of some other areas. Comayagua then was limited to its own central area, as it was also crowded to the west by the Alcaldia Major de San Andrés de Nueva Zaragosa controlling modern-day Copán and Ocotepeque. This pattern of early restriction helps to account for the longstanding rivalry between Tegucigalpa and Comayagua.

GOLD (RIVER) see RIO COCO

GOLD-COPPER ALLOY, COPAN. Two small fragments of such an alloy were found at Copán under a stela, the only Maya classic period metal findings; Copán was the nearest classic Maya center to the metalworking cultures of Panama and Costa Rica.

"GOLD-WASHING." Placer mining activities for gold were carried on soon after conquest in a central Honduran belt which runs through southern Honduras to the Nicaraguan Segovias. Pedro de Alvarado was a principle placer entrepreneur around 1530 and later, and established the town of Gracias a Dios with that in mind. In 1540 there were 5,000 pesos refined in that town; in San Pedro there were 9,000 and in Trujillo 10,000 in the same year.

GOLFO DE CHOROTEGA. Aboriginal name given by the Nahuatl-speaking Chorotegans to the Gulf of Fonseca, bordered by Honduras, El Salvador and Nicaragua.

GOLFO DE HONDURAS. The large gulf, also called the "Bay" of Honduras--hence Baymen (q.v.)--which extends from the Quintana Roo coast of Yucatán past former British Honduras (now Belize) to the area of Cape Honduras. Its extent is indicated (while not geographically precise) by the fact that Honduras' large offshore islands have been called from earliest times the "Bay Islands" (q.v.); earliest charts tended to show the bay or gulf as narrower than it is actually. The bay has one of the world's largest barrier reefs, and coral formations are prevalent.

GOLPE DE ESTADO. In English, the "stroke of state" is more familiar as "coup d'état." The latest prior to publication of this work occurred on December 3, 1972. The event is a familiar one in Honduras as in all of Central America.

GOMERA, CONDE DE see PERAZA-AYALA CASTILLA Y ROJAS

GOMEZ, CRESCENCIO. Designated under a new constitution, this lawyer headed the state after the provisional presidency of Medina (q.v.) until Medina took office as constitutional president in February 1866. He served again in May to July 1871. As Senator he had acted previously from May 1, 1865 to

September 1, 1865. Gómez became President for five days in August of 1876, during one of the Medina (q.v.) hiatuses.

GOMEZ, FRANCISCO. Senator Gómez took temporary office from February 1, 1852 to March 1, 1852, following Lindo's (q.v.) refusal to run again; Cabañas (q.v.) followed with a brief constitutional term. Gómez served again in the same manner during Cabañas term, from May 9, 1853 to December 31, 1853.

GOMEZ, GERONIMO. Oidor sent from Santiago de Guatemala in 1672 to Tegucigalpa for a "vista" looking into fraud and related problems in the silver mining industry there. Legal matters tightened up briefly after his visit, but by the end of the century had deteriorated again.

GOMEZ, VICENTE. Honduran native who served as Salvadoran Senator, and later as acting President of El Salvador for 12 February days of 1854.

GOMEZ DE LA MADRID, FRANCISCO see BERROSPE, GABRIEL SANCHEZ DE

GOMEZ LOPEZ, BENITO. A Honduran artist, born in Horanjito, and a student of art in Italy as well as in Tegucigalpa's Escuela Nacional de Bellas Artes. Has exhibited at Hemisfair '68 in San Antonio, Texas, and in Rome, Milan, Miami, San Salvador, Mexico, and Havana, Cuba; as well as in Tegucigalpa and San Pedro Sula.

GONZALEZ, DIEGO. Alcalde of San Antonio de Texaquat in 1708, who furnished Indians to the Corpus mines (q.v.) in violation of the repartimento (q.v.).

GONZALEZ, JUAN ANTONIO. Lieutenant governor, 1769.

GONZALEZ, SANTIAGO. As President of El Salvador, González personally led a victorious army in the 1872 war with Honduras. Under his leadership civil liberties were preserved and education advanced.

GONZALEZ, SIMON. One of two Sandino (q.v.) lieutenants who tried to stir up trouble in Honduras by charging that the "Yankees" (United States) were dispatching troops to Honduras to protect the property of the United Fruit Company there. They had already engaged in raiding Standard Fruit Plantations. The other troublemaker with González was Francisco Estrada, who was later interned in Honduras.

GONZALEZ DAVILA, GIL. Explorer who in 1522, without jurisdiction, nevertheless may be considered as the first "governor" of Honduras by such rights as conquest and discovery afforded. It was, of course, Christopher Columbus (q.v.) who dis-

"Good Neighbor Policy"

covered the Honduran Bay Islands and mainland in 1502.

"GOOD NEIGHBOR POLICY." Probably one of the most effective diplomatic approaches to Latin American and United States accommodation, this policy advanced by Franklin Delano Roosevelt as U.S. President in 1933 was an outgrowth of good will moves by the long-previous Wilson administration, which had been submerged in interventionism through three successive incumbencies. Roosevelt acted to recall marines from the Greater Antilles and Central America. By his call for action as a good neighbor, he established a formal policy. Cordell Hull, U.S. Secretary of State, presented the policy as "official" to the 1933 Pan-American Congress in Montevideo. Troop withdrawals and non-intervention promises and pacts followed. Honduras had not been subject to armed intervention, except in the unfortunate event of Las Limas (q.v.), but she had certainly suffered economic penetration, a major element in the whole problem.

GOVERNMENT AND JUSTICE, MINISTRY OF see CABINET

GOVERNMENTS OF HONDURAS, NUMBER OF. Over the years of independence, Honduras has experienced 134 changes of government, nearly one per year.

GOVERNORS, HONDURAS. As distinguished from the Presidents (q.v.) and Captains-General of the Audiencia of Guatemala, who indeed "rulled" Honduras for the Spanish king, there was a sequence of individuals who were more intimately connected with Honduras, and who have been listed as "governors" of Honduras, although the term may not have been a title or correct in the full sense of the usual meaning. But the significance of these governors is such that they have been included, from Gil González Dávila in 1522 through José Gregorio Tiroco de Contreras in 1821.

GOYENECHE, MIGUEL DE. A contractor who agreed to send 210 families from Asturias and Galicia and the Canary Islands to help populate the newly-won north coast of Honduras in 1787. That spring these peasant farmers gathered, and the first ship reached Trujillo on July 15. Three other shiploads followed, and by 1788 a total of 1,298 had come. As it turned out, while the colonists were to be distributed along the coast of Mosquitia, most of them had been driven back to Trujillo by the end of the century, largely due to Sambo-Miskito depredations and hostility. Trujillo became the spot in which colonization was successful. On other parts of the north coast it failed.

GRACIAS. Town, known in colonial days as Gracias a Dios, not to be confused with the big eastern department of that name. Founded by Gonzalo de Alvarado of the famous conquistador family in 1536, this Honduran town became the seat of the

Audiencia de los Confines, and later of the Audiencia of Guatemala which made it the first Central American capital. The capital was moved from Gracias to Santiago de Guatemala (now called Antigua) in 1549. Located in western Honduras near the borders of both Guatemala and El Salvador, modern Gracias is the cabacera of Lempira Department. The surrounding area is very mountainous, with the Montañas de Celaque and the Cordillera Opalaca nearby. Gracias is on the Río Jicatayo, a tributary of the Ulua.

GRACIAS A DIOS, DEPARTMENT. Also called "La Mosquitia," this is the second largest and the least settled of the 18 Honduran departments, with a population density of less than one per square kilometer. It is bounded on the north and east by the Caribbean Sea (which portion of the Honduran littoral is also called the Mosquito Coast), extending from Cape Camarón to Cape Gracias a Dios. On the south it is bounded by the Río Coco (q.v.) and the international boundary with Nicaragua (subject at this point to years of controversy); on the west by the departments of Colón and Olancho. The area is low in altitude, and the great coastal lagoons are formed by the three deltas of the Río Tinto, Río Patuca, and the Río Coco.

Puerto Lémpira on the Caratasca Lagoon is the cabacera. There are only two municipios. The cabaceras have a population (in 1970) of 1812, while the remaining far-flung population is 16,486, for a total of 18,298, over an area of 6,500 square miles. There is very little agriculture, although the inhabitants raise the universally used "siksa" (bananas) as well as plaintains. Shrimp fisheries are established in the coastal inlets, and there is oil exploration being carried out on the shallow underwater banks offshore. There is one private clinic, the Clínica Moravo de Ahuas. The navigable Río Patuca cuts the department in half, and is the major transportation artery, other than airlines. The navigable border Río Coco also serves for transport, although on both rivers the dugout canoe and the raft are the major form of craft. A minimal number of dugouts, pipantes and doris, have outboard motors or small one-cylinder air-cooled "lawnmower" engines. Settlements other than Puerto Lémpira include Ahuas, Brus Laguna, and Wampusirpi.

GRANA COCHINILLA. Cochineal, usually called simply "grana," a dye product, bright scarlet, produced by coccus cacti, an insect, raised on the leaves of the nopal cactus, called "tuna." It takes 70,000 dried insects to make one pound of dye. Puerto Caballos was a principal exporter of "grana" in colonial times.

GRANA SILVESTRE. Wild Cochineal. See GRANA COCHINILLA.

GRANDE RIVER. The Río Grande is a major tributary of the Tinto (q.v.) in Olancho department.

GRANT, ULYSSES S. As U.S. post-Civil War President, Grant wished to pursue a vigorous isthmian canal policy. He used the strong phraseology: "I commend an American canal, on American soil, to the American people."

Grant appointed an Interoceanic Canal Commission (q.v.). He did his utmost during two terms to put the canal project on a sound basis. The diplomatic and political situation, partly due to the spectre of the Clayton-Bulwer treaty, was worse than ever. Grant agreed to lead the roster of American canal promoters, on the formation of the Provisional Interoceanic Canal Society (q.v.). While Honduras was not viewed as a canal site, it figured in the various negotiations as a viable cross-isthmian railroad site and, nationally speaking, as one of the concerned parties.

"GRAVEYARD OF HONDURAS." Term applied in the 18th century to the lonely Spanish colonial Fort Omoa, wedged between high mountains and hostile Indians to the south, and the Bay of Honduras with swarming pirates and the hostile British to the north. Fever, dysentery, and loneliness augmented its horrors.

GREAT CAPE RIVER see RIO COCO; also CABO GRACIAS A DIOS

GRECEDA, ANDRES DE. Named governor pro tem by Albitez in 1532.

GRIFO. The cross of a Lobo (q.v.) male with a Negro female. See RACIAL MIXTURES.

GRINGO. A nickname given to North Americans in much of Latin America. Used more to the north of Honduras than in that country.

GROSS NATIONAL PRODUCT. In 1968 Honduras' GNP grew by eight per cent, a record high, but the war with El Salvador (q.v.) in 1969 cut this rate to some extent, with the September 1969 hurricane adding to the problems. The annual rate of growth averaged 4.9 per cent between 1961 and 1968, and the total GNP in 1969 was the equivalent of $650,000,000 U.S. A five per cent growth was estimated for 1970. The gross national product is based heavily upon agriculture (38 per cent), with bananas the chief product, followed by cereals, grains and livestock. Manufacturing has about 16 per cent, but is the most rapidly growing sector. Commerce adds 13.5 per cent, transportation and communication, six per cent. The most important region vis-a-vis GNP is the north coast, producing around 40 per cent of the total.

GUAJIQUERO. An Indian dialect from the town of that name. It was one of the Lenca languages.

GUALCINCE. A small Honduran town where Vicente Filísola, commander of Mexican forces, took the February 21, 1823 surrender of a Salvadoran army which had opposed Central American annexation to Mexico.

GUALLAMBRE RIVER. Alternate rendering of Guayambre. Gold washings on this river were recorded in the 18th and 19th centuries.

GUANACOS. Nickname ("apodo") given to natives of the Republic of El Salvador.

GUANAJA ISLAND. The Honduran island from which Christopher Columbus (q.v.) first saw the Central American mainland, with the mountain wall behind the Bay of Trujillo. On July 30, 1502, the "Admiral of the Ocean Sea" reached the island after a three-day voyage from the area of western Cuba. Morison (q.v.) says "Bonacca (Guanaja) is a handsome island about 8 miles long and rising to 1200 feet, surrounded by a line of coral reefs.... The Spaniards found nothing profitable except tall pine trees."

The island's original name must have resembled its present designation, although it is variously denominated Bonacca, Banassa, and other phonetic variants of the name.

The latest marine chart of the island is based on a British survey of 1840. The present major settlement on the island is located on "Sheen Cays." There are also Cays (small islands) numbered from I through IX along the northeast portion of the south coast, and also Pond Cay, Southwest Cay, and Halfmoon Cay. There are several inland heights, and several bays, including Northeast, Savannah, and Mangrove "bights." There is a shallow canoe canal right across the island at a narrow neck about 1/2-mile across. The principal airport is immediately adjacent.

A shrimp processing plant and the town are on offshore keys, and transfer from two airlines which serve the island is by a one-mile boat trip to the inhabited cays. There are coming to be resort hotels of a modest sort about the island, and there is increasing absentee ownership. The reef-sheltered waters inside the numbered keys were an important emergency seaplane anchorage before the airport was built.

The history of the island following discovery has been varied and turbulent. Columbus found Paya and Jicaque Indians on the island. The latter were skilled in making gold jewelry. A Maya canoe "large as a galley" came by with 25 paddlers; the voyagers were people with elaborate clothing. From 1631 on, the Providence Company occupied the Bay Islands, particularly Roatán. This English company occupied islands from Yucatán to Hispaniola. In 1642 the Bay Islands were depopulated when the Spanish swept the English away.

By 1700 the English quietly reoccupied the Bay Islands. They were a sort of link of colonization between British Hon-

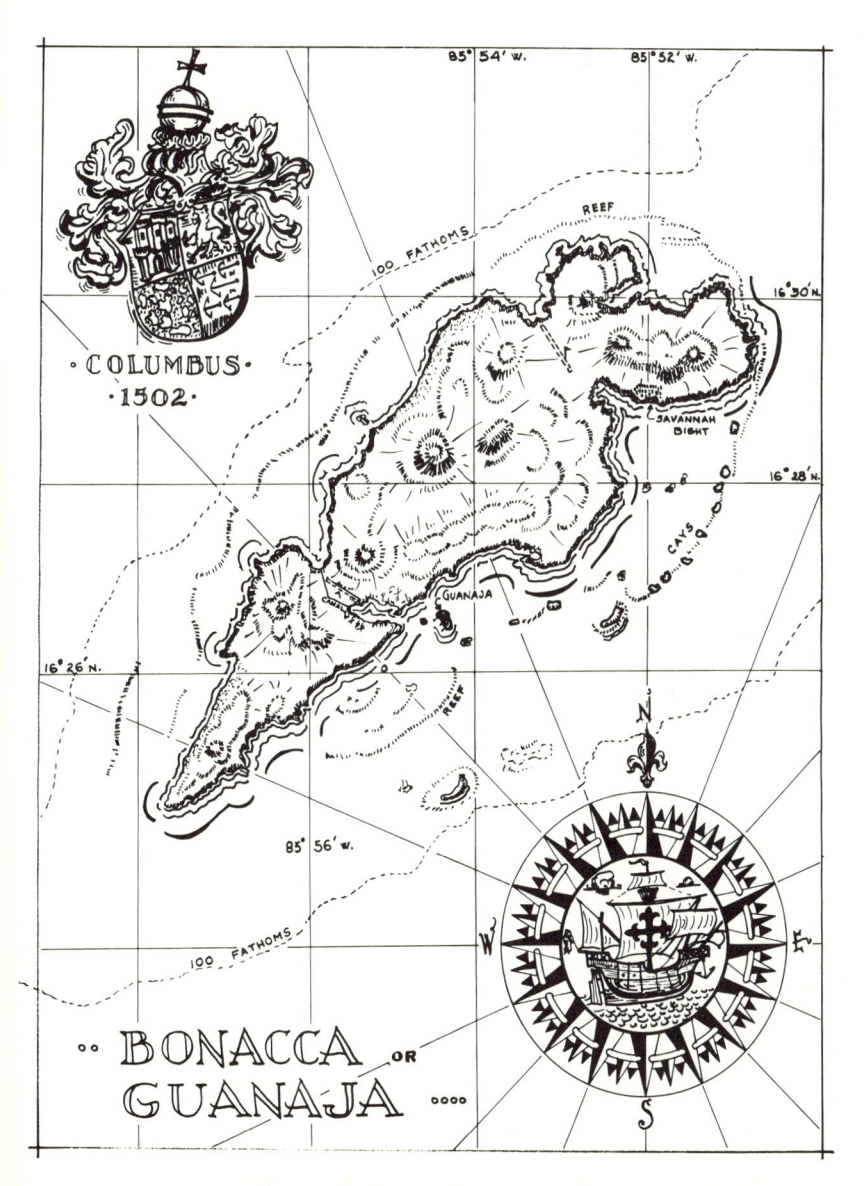

GUANAJA: Columbus' 1502 landfall from which he first sighted the Central American mainland--one of the three largest Bay Islands.

duras and the Black River colony of logwood cutters and
planters. The Baymen were allied with Sambo-Miskitos and
maintained a precarious security. Also by 1700, contraband
trade between the Spanish of the mainland and the English of
the Bay Islands was considerable. Meanwhile the islands had
been populated with a motley group of Indians, negroes,
Caribs, Dutch, Portuguese, Spanish, English, French, and
every possible combination thereof. Various pirate groups
had lent their genes to this polyglot population through the
past century and more.

The English settlements were strengthened under Hodgson (q.v.) during the 18th century. In 1742 Trelawney (q.v.)
fortified the Bay Islands (particularly Roatán). Great Britain
ordered the evacuation of the Bay Islands in 1748, under
William Pitt, and the Baymen were greatly incensed. Pitt,
however, was playing for bigger stakes than the tiny Paradise of the Baymen. By 1781 Gálvez (q.v.) planned to attack
the islands and then the mainland. He did attack Roatán,
and took it. Under an Anglo-Spanish Convention of 1786, the
area was joined to colonial New Spain. This agreement
brought a partial diplomatic solution to the problem of the
Honduran coast. The area was to be evacuated by the British
logwood cutters, settlers, and hangers-on, and by 1787 the
evacuation was being carried out. However, Catholics among
the evacuees were allowed to take an oath of allegiance to
Spain, which left British descendants in residence. By 1852
the Islands became a British colony, but they were turned
over to the Republic of Honduras in 1859.

The Island of Guanaja has more Spanish-speaking inhabitants than do the other Bay Islands, but there are also
many English-speaking Protestants. It is the most sparsely
settled of the three islands. There is a strong resemblance
to the "high islands" of the South Pacific, due to the surrounding reefs and cays.

GUANAJAS. A name applied in this plural form to the whole Bay
Island group. It comes from the name of Guanaja (q.v.).

GUANARI. Presumably the name used by Columbus for the island
of Guanaja, Bonassa, Bonacca, etc. One of the Honduran
Bay Islands from which he first saw the American mainland
on the Honduran north coast.

GUANASA. The spelling of the name of Guanaja (q.v.) or Bonacca
as shown on a Peter Martyr (q.v.) map of 1511.

GUANAXA. An alternate (Arabic-style) spelling of Guanaja (q.v.),
found in early publications and manuscripts (16th century).

GUANCASCO. The mutual exchange of patron saints by two towns
or villages. See VIRGEN DE LA CANDELERIA.

GUAPOTE see QUAPOT

GUARAJAMBALA RIVER. This major tributary of the Río Lempa is the borderline between Intibuca and Lémpira departments, heading in the Opalaca range of mountains.

GUARDA-COSTAS. These "coast guards" of the 18th century were ships fitted out in Spanish colonial ports and carrying commissions which were actually "letters of marque" from the local governors. They were manned by a rough element which had learned sea warfare in the rough school of the buccaneers. They were privateers, receiving their only return from the sale of prizes they captured. Indigo, cocoa, logwood, and Spanish money were all considered evidence of unlawful trade.

GUARDIOLA, SANTOS. Constitutional president of Honduras from 1856 to 1862, Guardiola's name is perpetuated in the cabacera of a municipio on Roatán Island. As a Honduran general Guardiola was noted in Central American annals for his cruelty. He was in command of a Legitimist army in Rivas on the occasion of William Walker's first battle in Rivas on June 29, 1855, at the beginning of the "National War." Walker's Nicaraguan allies fled, leaving his 55 Americans opposed by over 500 of the enemy under Guardiola, who had earned his appellation of "the butcher." Guardiola ruled the country until he was assassinated in 1862; he was followed by a series of conservative presidents. He was placed in the presidency by influential Guatemalan conservatives, and served from February 17, 1856 to February 7, 1860, and then by re-election until his death, January 11, 1862.

GUASCARAN. Site of the first major silver strike in the Honduran highlands in 1569, followed by similar strikes to the south and east. Earlier silver mining had been relatively sparse, principally in the Comayagua area.

GUASH. Also guass. Lenca Indian word for water. See HUAS.

GUASISTAGUA. Ruins, probably Mayan, near the village of that name.

GUATEMALA, 1853 WAR. A short conflict of border skirmishes, there was one pitched battle at Atulapa in July 1853. With Salvadoran mediation, a peace treaty was signed between Guatemala and Honduras in 1856. There was more politics than actual fighting in the whole affair. Between the fighting and the peace treaty came the "National War" (q.v.) which had meantime united all the countries in a common cause.

GUATEMALA, 1872 see SALVADOR and GUATEMALA, WAR OF 1872

GUATEMALA, WAR OF 1850 see SALVADOR, 1850 WAR

**GUATEMALA, WAR OF 1863** see **NICARAGUAN, GUATEMALA-SALVADOR WAR OF 1863**

**GUATULCO.** A southern Mexican port for departures to Honduras and Peru in Spanish colonial days; it is located just east of the Gulf of Tehuantepec. In spite of its early importance, it has disappeared from modern maps.

**GUAYAPE RIVER.** This stream joins the Guazambre (q.v.) to form the Patuca. It makes a remarkable bend in southern Olancho department, its major tributary, the Jalán, actually being closer to the Guajambre upstream from the Guazape junction than at the point of juncture. The Guazape may be said to be the "main" upper Patuca, one of the few large streams in Central America, the others being the Río Coco on the Honduras-Nicaragua border, and the Usumacinta in Guatemala.

**GUAYMURA.** Name of an original Honduran tribe, which designation was applied to the country by the first explorers. Then the floating gourds called hibueras were observed and the country was named for them. Later the depths (of waters offshore and valleys of the mountains) became the basis for the name Honduras.

**GUAZAMBRE RIVER.** A large stream tributary to the Río Patuca and joining the Río Guazam (q.v.) to form that stream near Azacualpa in southern Olancho department. The Guazambre flows from El Paraiso department in a north-northeasterly direction.

**GUAZUCARAN.** Best of the Tegucigalpa silver mines of the late 1500s, with the Enriqueña Pit being especially productive.

**GUCUMATZ.** A Guatemalan term for plague (q.v.). Also used to represent an important god.

**GUEGUENSI.** Name of an island in the Gulf of Fonseca.

**GUERRA DE AVALA, JUAN.** Governor in 1608 and following, the vigorous period of Criado de Castilla (q.v.), when the port changes were made.

**"GUERRA NACIONAL."** National War. Since the National War of Nicaragua in mid-nineteenth century turned out to be a Central American enterprise involving for one brief era of cooperation all the countries formerly confederated, a list of the Presidents at the outset, followed by a list of those at the centenary, is given:

12 September 1856

Nicaragua                Don Patricio Rivas

| | |
|---|---|
| Guatemala | General Rafael Carrera |
| El Salvador | Don Rafael Campos |
| Honduras | General Santos Guardiola |
| Costa Rica | Don Juan Rafael Mora |

Presidents at the centenary, 1956

| | |
|---|---|
| Nicaragua | General de División Don Anastasio Somoza |
| Guatemala | Coronel Carlos Castillo Armas |
| El Salvador | Coronel Oscar Osorio |
| Honduras | Don Julio Lozano |
| Costa Rica | Don José Figueres |

GUIABA. Alternate form of name early used for Roatán Island, as shown on the Sánchez Planisphere (q. v.).

GUILLEN ZELAYA, ALFONSO. Poet and author of the Carito a Honduras. Born in Juticalpa, Olancho, in 1888; died in Mexico in 1947. He had lived in both Mexico and the United States and traveled extensively in Europe. He had been Chancellor of the Honduran Consulate in New York. The last stanza of this song to his country is typical of the ardor and music of Honduran poetry:

> El pino es horizonte. El pino es un ejemplo.
> En nuestra vida tiene la majestad de un templo
> Pinares hondureños, pinares ancestrales,
> Enhiestos, eminentes, serenos, inmortales.
> Bandera de victoria contra las Tiranías;
> Vendran los días de oro; Vendran los nuevos días!

> The pine is the horizon, and the pine is an example.
> In our life it has the majesty of a temple
> Groves of Honduran pines, ancestral groves of pine,
> Erect and lofty, serene, immortal;
> Victory's banner against all tyrranies;
> The days of gold are coming; they're coming, the new days!

GUIMBE see IUMBE

GUIRISES. Honduran folk miners, usually Indians or members of poorer castes, who worked alone or in small teams. They opened tiny mines of their own. Many of these strikes were made in the 17th century, but the guirises were usually abysmally poor. Few of them paid tax. They knew little of safety. They were frequently mere scavengers of ore. Such miners exist in the Tegucigalpa region to this day. Their life is marginal in the extreme.

GUTIERREZ, ENRIQUE. General Gutiérrez with Luis Bográn and Dr. Rafael Alvarado Mangano held the executive post as a council of ministers from May 9, 1883 to November 30, 1883. See also ROSE, RAMON. Gutiérrez was one of a council in 1880.

GUTIERREZ, RAFAEL ANTONIA. Salvadoran president, 1894-98, who led El Salvador to join Honduras and Nicaragua in the Pact of Amapala on June 20, 1895, which established a union, the Republica Mayor de Centro América. This union caused Guitérrez' removal from office in 1898.

GUTIERREZ DE ARGÜELLOS, DIEGO. Governor of Honduras, 1717.

GUZMAN, ALBERTO. Dr. Guzmán was director of the tuberculosis division of the Honduran Public Health Service in 1970.

GUZMAN, ENRIQUEZ DE. The governor from 1684-88, he was instrumental in quelling civic and ecclesiastical disputes. He also ordered hospital construction in Santiago de Guatemala (Antigua) following an epidemic. He followed Serbellón (q.v.).

GUZMAN, JUAN JOSE. President of El Salvador during a unionization effort, culminating in the Pact of Chinandega of July 27, 1824, which joined Honduras, Nicaragua and El Salvador in the Confederación Centroamericana.

- H -

HAAB. The solar year of 365 days, which the Maya divided into 18 months of 20 days each (see TUN and TZOLKIN), but added the "bad luck" days of five each year.

HABILITADORES. Labor contractors of the nineteenth century era, who held Indian workers in virtual slavery.

HACIENDA SYSTEM. Based on the plantation or "hacienda," the hacienda system was essentially feudal in character, although as has been pointed out by Mario Rodríguez, it was also partly capitalistic. It is the blend which has enabled it to persist, for there are modified haciendas to this day. It was self-sustaining. In bad times this meant it would persist; in good times, it was a source of exports and profits. Monoculture was the pattern. Thus there were cacao, indigo, coffee, cattle, and other one-crop haciendas. Food often had to be imported. Productivity from a national standpoint was not great but the "hacendado" benefited greatly. Haciendas were part of the colonial pattern in Honduras as well as in the rest of Central America. The hacienda frequently manufactured everything it used, and raised everything it ate.

HACKE. Mapmaker in England who in 1710 published a map with inaccuracies far greater than those on some maps over a century earlier. Tegucigalpa was misspelled two different ways and shown far south of the Río Coco, and in the area shown as Nicaragua. This fact tends to illustrate both the spotty knowledge and errors which persisted two centuries and more after conquest, as well as the remarkable accuracy of some maps of the early 1500s.

HAGUE ATLAS, MAP. An anonymous atlas kept now in the Hague, Holland, in the Koninklijke Bibliothek, has a map of the Gulf of Mexico and the Caribbean which is in the style of the Portuguese portolan charts, and shows the north coast of Honduras in some detail, including a "Puerto de Cavallo," a cape "de Cameron" and "Cartago" (the latter referring to the Caratasca Lagoon).

HALF-MOON CAY. One of the major islets on the reef just to the east of Guanaja (q.v.), less than a mile offshore.

HALL, JASPER. Slave agent in Jamaica, representing the South Sea Company, who in answer to a request for slaves to be used by the Spanish in building Fort Omoa, quoted prices in lots of 100 (50 men, 30 women, 10 boys, 10 girls) at 140 pesos apiece. Men alone would bring 164 pesos each, all F.O.B. Kingston. Gold coast males, prime, were 204 pesos apiece. He charged 20 pesos for delivery. The Guatemala treasury junta decided to buy 100 men. Hall could sell rejected or ill slaves, upon delivery and examination by the surgeon at Omoa. In 1760 Hall once again furnished 100 males and 100 females. The present population of the town of Omoa adjacent to the fort includes many descendants of these Jamaican black slaves.

HANCE, JOSEPH L. see WATERBURY, JOHN J.

HARTLING, CARLOS. Composer in 1915 of the music for the National Hymn (q.v.), Hartling was of German extraction. The words were written by Agusto C. Coello (q.v.).

HARVARD COPAN EXCAVATIONS. Harvard University, specifically the Peabody Museum, carried out excavations and explorations at Copán (q.v.) from 1891 to 1894. They unearthed the Hieroglyphic Stairway (q.v.), some burials, and many sculptures.

HAYDON, R. H. A North American to whom the Honduras Interoceanic Railway was leased in 1881.

HEALTH SERVICES. The latest figures of the Pan American Health Organization indicates between 4,000 and 5,000 hospital beds, two per 1,000 persons. Most were in largest cities and towns, where the rate was 18 per 100, but the rate was only 9/10 per thousand in rural areas. Most beds were in government-operated facilities. There were around

40 hospitals. There is a shortage of medical personnel, with only about 350 graduate nurses of 1,300 total, and about 500 physicians and dentists.

HEDUARDO, JUAN JERONIMO. Following the Civil War in the term of Berrospe, Oidor Heduardo served as governor in 1701-1702.

HELENA ISLAND see SANTA ELENA ISLAND

HELIODORO VALLE, RAFAEL, 1891-1959. Ambassador to the United States of America in mid-20th Century, this distinguished Honduran was not only diplomat, but also a historian, noted bibliographer, and poet. He lived for some time in Mexico.

HENDERSON, CAPTAIN. A British officer who avowed in 1814 that the island of Roatán (q.v.), "as has been previously remarked, belongs to Spain, and a military station is retained on it." This recognition was to prove somewhat short-lived.

HENRY, THOMAS. Colonel Henry was one of the legendary original "Immortals" who landed with filibuster William Walker in Nicaragua in 1855. He returned to Nicaragua with Walker on the Fashion in late 1857, and again in the final abortive descent on Trujillo, Honduras in the schooner Taylor in early 1860. Henry met a particularly horrible death. Setting out from the fort at Trujillo with a Honduran guide, he scouted several days, and on his return, fortified with a few drinks and somewhat pugnacious, got into an argument with a lieutenant over Henry's lighted cigar in the fort's powder magazine. The resulting altercation caused the young man to shoot Henry in the jaw at close range with a pistol. The lower part of his face was shot away, and he could not speak to give the news of his scouting venture, although he attempted to write a message on a slate. Henry's suffering with his gangrenous wound was ended when Walker left a cup of morphine near him. Henry was able to swallow it for release. This is an example of the strong, strange loyalties men had for Walker.

HERBIAS RIVER see RIO COCO

HERMENEGILDO DE ARANA, TOMAS. Governor of Honduras, 1741.

HEROIC VALOR DECORATION see MEDALS

HERRERA, DIEGO DE. Governor and alcalde mayor in 1573, under the Villalobos (q.v.) regime.

HERRERA, DIONISIO. Honduran president of the Central American federation, 1830-34, a period of relative calm during which the Central American countries assumed the liberal look and attitude then prevalent on the isthmus. This was only a prelude however, to the secession of Nicaragua in 1838, first of the five to secede from the Provincias Unidas. Major impetus for the federation had come through Honduran leaders such as Francisco Morazán (q.v.). Herrera was also Chief of State from July 28, 1823 to May 9, 1827.

HERRERA, JUAN DE BUSTAMENTE. Governor in 1643.

HERVIAS, GABRIEL DE. A Lieutenant Colonel who was a veteran of the coastal campaigns in Honduras and Mosquitia, and who was named chief Spanish Commissioner in 1787. Hervias tried to work out arrangements with the Caribs, Sambos, and Miskitos, at first using Hodgson the Younger (q.v.), but results were not forthcoming. The Spanish finally baptized and renamed the Sumu chieftain known as Colville Breton. Breton became Carlos Antonio de Castilla, and his son was sent to Spain for an education. The British Miskito "King George" refused baptism. The Spanish plan to influence the coastal peoples came to naught by 1790. The British were continually more successful in this risky endeavor.

HEYN, PIET. Dutch freebooter who seized much of the treasure of New Spain near Havana in 1628, thus losing a whole year's export of indigo to Central America. Other losses came in 1656 and 1657.

HIBUERAS. A variant on "Honduras," of obscure origin, found in a Mexican publication of 1888. There seems to be no Spanish basis, unless it would be Jíbaro, an adjective meaning wild, rustic--or from Jiba, a hump (referring to hills). More likely it is an Indian aberration of pronunciation. Apparently it was used at the time of Cortés, and may be of totally Indian derivation, with only coincidental resemblance. See GUAYMURA.

HIEROGLYPHIC STAIRWAY. This feature of the Copán (q.v.) ruins, unique among known Maya sites, leads up from the Court of the Hieroglyphic Stairway, on its east side, to the small temple "No. 26." There are 62 steps, each carved with a row of hieroglyphics on the risers. It is 32 feet wide and 68 feet high and the number of glyphs there carved totals nearly 2,000--the longest Maya inscription known. There are statues every twelve steps in the center.

HIGHWAYS, COLONIAL. The first Honduran Highway was built by the conquistador Pedro de Alvarado, from Puerto Caballos (now Puerto Cortés) to San Pedro Sula.

HIGHWAYS, MODERN   see the various CARRETERAS

HIGÜERAS. An alternate form of the word "Hibieras" (q.v.) as a name for Honduras.

HISPANICISMO see HISPANISMO

HISPANIDAD see HISPANISMO

HISPANISMO.  Hispanicism in Latin America, fostered in Spain following the formation of the Unión Ibero-Americana in Spain and the 1941 formation of a Consejo de Hispanidad (Council of Hispanicism), which was formed by government decree in Madrid.

HISTORY, HONDURAN.  A historical work by Antonio R. Vallejo was published in Tegucigalpa in 1882-83. The title was Compendio Honduras.  It was planned as a college and secondary school text.

HODGSON, ROBERT THE YOUNGER.  Son of the first Robert Hodgson who had been sent to Mosquitia by Trelawney (q.v.) in 1739, Hodgson the Younger was also Superintendent of the Mosquito Shore for the British, but became a turncoat and was involved in a Spanish plan to control the Caribs, Sambos, and Miskitos, and to replace British influence.  The wily Hodgson, captured and taken to Cartagena, had convinced the Spanish that he would work with them in gaining influence over the Sambo-Miskitos.  He owned 200 negro slaves, several plantations, and a number of small ships, used in the Jamaica trade.  The Spanish under Caballero de Góngoro decided to give him a try, but he did not get results.  The Spanish were never able satisfactorily to eject the British and their influence from the Mosquito coast.

HOLIDAYS.  The public holidays include:

January 1           New Year's Day
April 14            Day of the Americas
5 days ending Easter Sunday - Holy Week
May 1               Labor Day
September 15        Independence Day
October 3           Francisco Morazán Birthday
October 12          Discovery of America ("Día de La Raza")
October 21          Army Day
December 24-25      Christmas Holidays
(also December 31)

In addition, the feast days of Roman Catholicism are observed.

HOLLINGSWORTH, IAN see MISSIONARY AVIATION FELLOWSHIP

HOMEN, DIEGO.  Mapmaker of the well-known Portuguese family of cartographers who in 1558 produced a map which is the first to show California as a peninsula--not to be so "discovered" again until Fray Eusebio Kino's maps of 150 years later. In this map the great San Juan River and Lake system of Nicaragua are clearly shown, except that while the general outlines are correct, lakes Managua and Nicaragua are shown as one. It is interesting that the slightly earlier map by relative Lopo Homen is more accurate on this count. The Bay Islands of Honduras are clearly shown, although the Bay of Honduras in its relation to Yucatán is somewhat distorted.

HOMEN, LOPO. A Portuguese mapmaker whose world map of 1554 shows a very recognizable Central America. The Honduran Coast and other features are very clear. (Present location of map, Bibliothèque Nationale, Paris.) It is believed he lived from 1497-1572. It is worth remarking that many later maps were not as geographically accurate about the isthmian area as was this one.

HONDURAN BEER COMPANY. Near San Pedro Sula, this modern plant bottles soft drinks as well as beer, and has exemplary living quarters for workers who live on the grounds.

HONDURAN BORDER AND SANDINO (q.v.). The Honduran border area in the Cordillera de Depilto was a recurring sanctuary for Sandino's forces, as well as a source of supplies and especially of arms. A great deal of the Sandino era action and intrigue centered about the remote and nearly inaccessible border area, and its existence made the prolonged guerrilla war possible. See REMANYO; ARMS, SANDINO; ARDILO GOMEZ; BEALS, CARLETON; CALDERA, AGUSTO; etc.

HONDURAN CAPITALIZING BANK see BANCO DE LA CAPITALIZODORA HONDUREÑA

HONDURAN COLONIAL PRODUCTS. Products of trade included suet, hides, cacao, arnatto, jalap, indigo, sarsaparilla, silver, placer gold, cochineal.

HONDURAN COUNCIL OF PRIVATE ENTERPRISE. This organization (COHEP) formed a National Reconstruction Committee (acronym, COREN) following the disastrous hurricane of 1974. There is some confusion in planning and some duplication of effort, as might be expected. The COHEP is essentially rightist, and is in opposition to some populist ministers of the government, in spite of the government's comparatively right-wing character. The permanent committee of the National Emergency, (COPEN) devoted to immediate tasks in aid and rescue, is under the extreme right wing of the military government. The COHEP refused to join in the government-sponsored reconstruction committee, CEYS (q.v.). Various international agencies are approving credits for reconstruction work (see BCIE, IDB, ExIm BANK). The World Bank and the Central American Monetary Stabilization Fund were asked for $50,000,000.

HONDURAN FINANCIAL COMPANY   see   FINANCIERA HONDUREÑA, S. A.

HONDURAN ROUTE.  A canal route proposed as early as the 17th century to run from the Bay of Fonseca up the valley of the Río Guascarán, thence down the Río Humuya to the Río Ulua, and on into the Bay of Honduras. Much later this route was perceived, in the 19th century, as desirable for an interoceanic rail line.

HONDURAN SAVINGS BANKS   see   BANCO DE EL AHORRO HONDUREÑO

HONDURAN STEAMSHIP CO.  This firm operates about 25 seagoing vessels between 2,000 and 8,000 tons registry each. There are also about 80 small craft in coastal shipping, only ten of which in 1970 could carry over 50 tons. Some of these craft also operate on the Patuca, Coco, and Ulua rivers.

HONDURAN SUGAR COMPANY   see   COMPAÑIA AZUCAREÑA HONDUREÑA, S. A.

HONDURAS ALMIRANTA.  A large ship wrecked in 1618 near Malabar, Florida, carrying silver, hides, indigo, and cochineal.

HONDURAS, CAPSULE CHRONOLOGY.

| | |
|---|---|
| Old Mayan Empire | 4th Century A. D. |
| Discovery by Columbus | 1502 |
| Spanish Occupation begins | 1522 |
| Gil Gonzalez Dávila explores the Bay of Fonseca | 1522 |
| Dávila heads expedition from Spain with royal commission | 1524 |
| Pedro Arías de Avila, governor of Panama, sets out for Honduras from Nicaragua | 1524 |
| Hernan Cortés dispatches two expeditions from Mexico | 1524 |
| Cortés goes to Honduras himself, in an incredible overland trek | 1525 |
| Extent of Cortés personal expedition | 1525-26 |
| Diego López de Salcedo, first territorial governor in | 1526 |
| Indian-Spanish War in Western Honduran Highlands (30,000 Indians led by Chief Lémpira) | 1537-39 |
| Audiencia de los Confines (including Honduras) | 1542 |
| Control of Honduras given to Captaincy-General of Guatemala | 1570 |
| Discovery of Silver near Tegucigalpa | 1578 |
| Establishment of Alcaldía Mayor de Tegucigalpa | 1578 |

| | |
|---|---|
| Pirate capture of Puerto Caballos | 1602 & 1639 |
| Fall of Trujillo to pirates | 1639 |
| Fall of San Pedro Sula to pirates | 1660 |
| Puerto Caballos burned by pirates | 1660 |
| During 18th century, war between Spain and England much of the period | |
| Siege of Omoa | 1779 |
| Fall of Fort Inmaculada and capture of Black River | 1782 |
| Consolidation of Comayagua and Tegucigalpa | 1788 |
| Uprisings as a prelude to independence, in Nicaragua and El Salvador | 1811 |
| Tegucigalpa again in separate alcaldía mayor | 1812 |
| Act of Central American Independence, September 15 | 1821 |
| Union with Mexican Empire of Iturbide | 1822, 1823 |
| United Provinces of Central America | 1824-38 |
| Constituent Assembly elects liberal Dionisio de Herrera as provisional President | 1824 |
| Central American Civil War | 1826-28 |
| Capture of Comayagua (the capital) | 1827 |
| Seizure of Honduran coastal towns in rebel plot | 1831 |
| Francisco Morazán moves Central American capital to San Salvador | 1834 |
| Major civil strife | 1837-38 |
| Honduras declared Independence as a Republic, October 26 | 1838 |
| Constituent assembly adopts first constitution of Republic of Honduras (January) | 1839 |
| Francisco Ferrera, first President | 1840 |
| A new federation agreed between Honduras, Nicaragua, and El Salvador | 1842 |
| Juan Lindo as President | 1847 |
| Trinidad Cabañas, Lindo's successor | 1852 |
| Guatemala invades and installs Santos Guardiola as President | 1855 |
| "National War" against Walker in Nicaragua | 1855-56 |
| Walker executed at Trujillo | 1860 |
| New Constitution | 1865 |
| Track laid for Interoceanic Railroad, near San Pedro Sula | 1871 |
| Celeo Arias as President by Guatemalan coup d'etat | 1872 |
| Marco Aurelio Soto--strong President | 1876-83 |
| New Constitution | 1880 |
| Liberal Party rise with Policarpo Bonilla | 1894-99 |
| Manuel Bonilla administration, debt reduction and road-building | 1903 |
| New Constitution | 1906 |
| Invasion of Honduras by Guatemala | 1906 |
| Invasion of Honduras by Nicaragua (Bonilla forced out) | 1907 |
| Revolts by Bonilla, who with followers took Bay | |

Honduras (General)

| | |
|---|---|
| Islands, Trujillo, La Ceiba | 1911 |
| Tiburcio Carias Andiño, Honduran long-term caudillo | 1923- |
| Carias elected president--absence of revolts, internal and external security (control!), and some economic progress | 1932 |
| New Constitution | 1957 |
| Nicaraguan and Guatemalan border disputes | 1957-62 |
| Coup under Osvaldo López Arellano | 1963 |
| López made President, and new Constitution | 1965 |
| López coup regains presidency (December) | 1972 |
| Devastating Hurricane "Fifi" (September) | 1974 |
| Melgar Castro succeeds López in bloodless coup (April) | 1975 |

HONDURAS (General). Called the "pivotal area of the landbridge between Mexico and South America," Honduras is also the meeting point, the cultural watershed or great divide between North American and South American Amerindian cultures. It is the contact point of Nahua and Maya thrusts from the north and Chibcha and Quechua probings from the south. It is this relationship which gives Honduras a particular significance and a persistent impact.

Modern Honduras is a constitutional republic with a rather highly centralized form of government, and in 1974 was under the rule of a former president and chief of the armed forces following a 1972 coup d'état. The constitution provides for social guarantees, and has been in effect since 1965.

Physical Data:

Honduras is a Central American country, one of the original five republics which became separately independent in 1839. It lies between 13 and 16 degrees north latitude, and 83 degrees 10 minutes and 89 degrees 20 min. west longitude. The area is 43,277 square miles, roughly an elongated "diamond" shape, bounded on the north by the Bay or Gulf of Honduras, a part of the Caribbean Sea, and on the southeast and south by Nicaragua; on the southwest by El Salvador; and on the West by Guatemala. At the southernmost point it has a short border on the Bay or Gulf of Fonseca, an arm of the Pacific (see PERIMETER). There are 40 miles of Pacific coast and 400 miles of Caribbean coast.

Honduras is second in size to Nicaragua among the Central American countries, and in the middle of the five in population, exceeded by Guatemala and El Salvador. The 1975 population is well over 2,500,000. Honduras is named for the "depths" of valleys between the high and tumbled mountain ranges. Eighty per cent of the land is mountainous, which isolates population pockets from each other. There are hot and generally humid lowlands which extend on the east to 75 miles inland. In higher elevations the climate is temperate, with daytime temperatures in the 70s (F.). Coastal lowlands average 88 degrees Fahrenheit. Mountains reach over 8,000 feet. Intermontane valleys are often at 3,000 and 4,000 feet. There are two seasons; the rainy one from May through October; the dry, November through April. Average rainfall varies from 20 to 200 inches annually.

Political Divisions:

There are eighteen departments and the Central District which is the governmental center and includes Comayaguela and Tegucigalpa, the latter being the capital. The president's palace, a Moorish style fortified mansion on the banks of the Choluteca River, is complemented by new government offices such as the skyscraper Social Security building. Departments are further divided into 281 municipalities which are governed by elected councils. Only 63 per cent of these are urban centers.

People:

Of the 2.5 million Hondurans, the greatest number, over 90 per cent, are mixed Spanish and Indian; six per cent are pure Indian, two per cent Negro, one per cent Spanish. The largest foreign groups living in the country in 1970 were Salvadoreans and Guatemalans.
    There are four significant pre-Colombian cultural influences: the Maya, whose major ceremonial center Copán is in Western Honduras; the Nahuatl, the Mexican influence so prevalent as far south as Costa Rica; the Chibcha, of whom the Honduran-Nicaraguan Sumu tribe are an offshoot, their roots being on the north coast of South America; and the Carib-Arawak, an influence on Honduras' eastward-projecting coast which came from the islands of the eastern Caribbean, and was reinforced by Carib islanders exiled to Honduras by the British. Indian languages are spoken, and words of several used, but the language of Honduras is Spanish, with a few English-speaking Islanders on the Bay Islands.

Investment, Trade:

There have been foreign influences throughout Honduras' 4 1/2 centuries of post-conquest history. At present the great banana concern, the Standard Fruit Company, has major plantation and railroad investments; the New York and Honduras Rosario Mining Company has revived mineral extraction; the British American Tobacco Company is active. Direct United States investments in 1959 were $130,000,000, and have since that time practically doubled. There are small merchant fleets, and Honduran participation in the Central American Common Market is of significance, although hampered recently by the 1969 War with El Salvador. Foreign enterprise of a capital nature has been welcome in Honduras. There is a

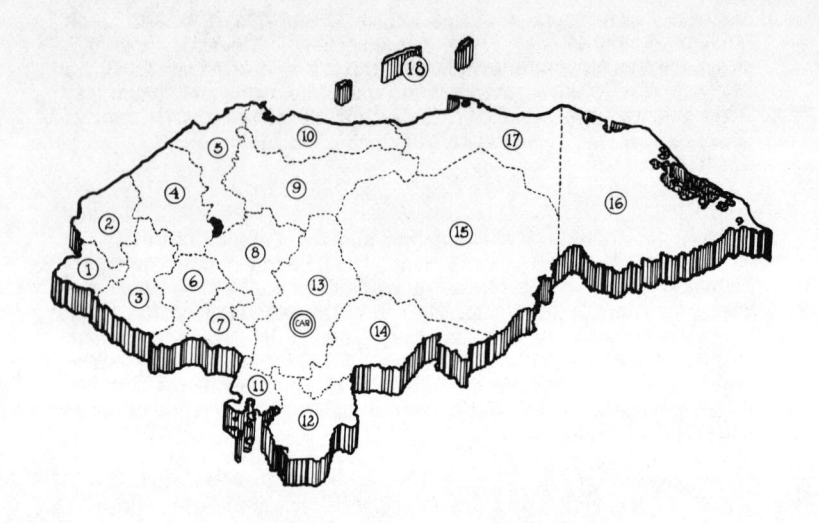

HONDURAS: POLITICAL DIVISIONS

### Departments of Honduras

1. Ocotepeque
2. Copán
3. Lempira
4. Santa Barbara
5. Cortés
6. Intibuca
7. La Paz
8. Comayagua
9. Yoro
10. Atlantida
11. Valle
12. Choluteca
13. Francisco Morazán
14. El Paraiso
15. Olancho
16. Grácias a Diós
17. Colón
18. Islas de la Bahia

National Development Bank (q.v.) as well as the Central Bank of Honduras (q.v.); 15 per cent of income tax proceeds go to the Development Bank Activities. A 1950 Code of Commerce regulates foreign and domestic firms and trade. Honduras has had relatively few foreign loans in recent years.

The General Culture:

Education is compulsory for children from seven to 15 years of age, but there are insufficient school facilities for strict enforcement. Urban illiteracy is about 43 per cent--rural illiteracy near 75 per cent; the general rate about 65 per cent. There are special schools for the handicapped and retarded; also trade and craft schools. The National University is in Comayaguela, granting degrees in physics, mathematics, law, social sciences, medicine and dentistry, chemistry and pharmacy, and economics. The famous Pan American Agricultural School is at El Zamorano (q.v.). There are libraries and museums, a National Archives, and in Comayaguela, a Palace of Fine Arts. A major cultural resource is the ruined Maya center of Copán (q.v.), and other lesser archaeological sites exist. There is nominal freedom of the press, with around two dozen daily newspapers, most of them in the two major centers, Tegucigalpa and San Pedro Sula. Social Welfare legislation was first enacted in 1954, and a fundamental labor charter lays down basic guarantees. Housing has been pursued by the government and a number of projects carried out.

Transportation:

The Pan-American Highway circles the Bay of Fonseca to cross Honduras from the Salvadoran border to the Nicaraguan frontier. A cross-country paved highway runs from a junction with the Pan-American highway at Jicaro Galán to Puerto Cortés on the north coast, passing through Tegucigalpa and San Pedro Sula. This road was completed in the 1960s. There are about 2,500 miles of road, most of it unpaved. There are several railroads, but none that cross the nation either from north to south or east to west (see TELA RAILROAD, and FERROCARRIL NACIONAL DE HONDURAS). The Honduran Steamship Company provides freight service, and several national and international airlines provide service internally and to other Central American capitals, as well as to New Orleans, Mexico, Panama, and Miami. There are 130 airfields, 100 of which are grass strips.

HONDURAS INTEROCEANIC RAILROAD COMPANY. Chartered in 1853, this company had ambitious plans, largely advanced by the erstwhile diplomatic representative of the United States, E. G. Squier, who signed the charter for the company and was joined by Léon Alvarado and Justo S. Rodas for Honduras when the document was completed on June 23, 1853. The

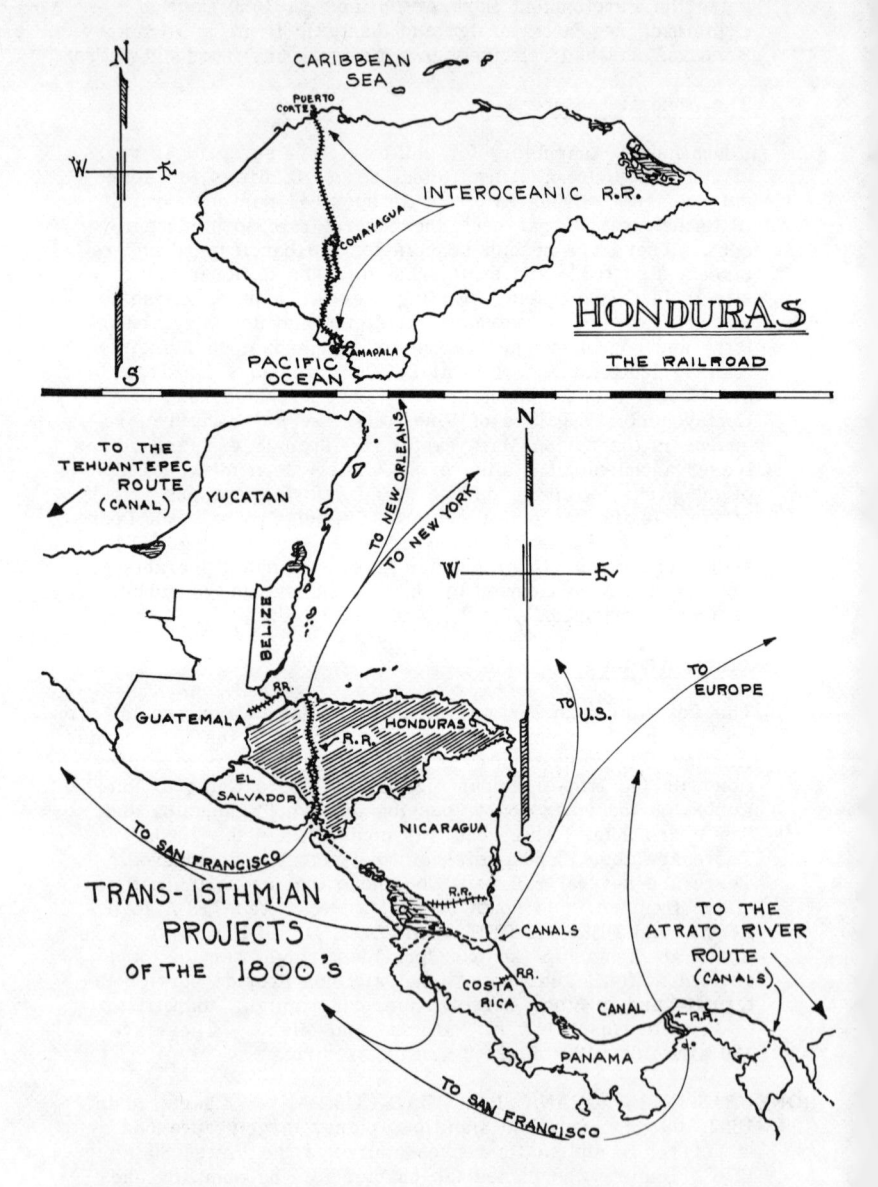

INTEROCEANIC RAILROAD: The 19th century project to link Atlantic and Pacific shores by rail, never realized.

charter was ratified on April 28, 1854.
  An exclusive right to interoceanic communication was granted, whether by rail or water, the right to last 70 years, but allowing eight years for completion of a viable route. Free passage, exemption of laborers from military service, and organization of a tax-exempt stock company were provided for. Convict labor was planned, also payment to Honduras of $1.00 for every adult through rail passenger carried. U.S. citizens would pass the route tax- and duty-free, and without passports. 1,000 square miles of land (4,000 caballerías) were granted to the company. Aliens settling on company lands would have rights and privileges of native-born citizens. The route would be declared internationally neutral, the terminal ports designated free ports.
  Costs of construction of a cross-Honduran railway were estimated at under $14,000,000, perhaps as little as $7,000,000. Revenues were estimated at $2,000,000 annually. Loans of $40,000 were extended to Honduras, which were diverted to arms purchase for fighting Guatemalan invaders. (Some Honduran leaders wished to annex the country to the United States.) Squier's company failed, however, before any track was laid. No adequate cross-Honduran surface transit route was available until completion of the San Pedro Sula-to-Tegucigalpa paved highway in 1963, 110 years after the Squiers project.
  The Honduran government tried to resurrect the railroad project by negotiating major loans from France and Britain. The resulting debt was a national burden well past 1900. A total of 57 miles of track were laid as far as San Pedro Sula from the Atlantic coast, but this swiftly fell into disuse.
  Modern rail lines in existence were largely built by the large banana concerns (see HONDURAN NATIONAL RAILWAY, TELA RAILROAD, etc.). The Honduras Interoceanic Railway Company figured in a British rapprochment with Honduras following Britain's conclusion of the Crimean War, and led to the concession by Honduras of necessary rights to the British-owned Honduras Interoceanic Railway Company on April 28, 1854. In August of 1856 two treaties were signed. According to the first, the Bay Islands (q.v.) were to become a free territory, following long dispute. While the Bay Island treaty actually defeated the purpose of Honduras to gain sovereignty over the islands (as it gave Great Britain treaty rights for their subjects who were previously simply squatters on the islands), it affected the transit route in that for the supposed concessions Hondurans in turn agreed that the neutrality of the cross-Honduras transit route was to be protected by Britain, although in neither case did Britain claim exclusive control. By the second treaty Britain agreed to abandon her Mosquito protectorate (q.v.) in Honduran territory, provided there would be a Mosquito reservation granted along the shore.
  In order to assure her rights to a trans-Isthmian cross-

ing (namely, the Honduras Interoceanic Railway plans), Britain then entered negotiations with the United States. Seeing through the British design, the U.S. Senate would not recognize the British convention of 1856 with Honduras, and this in turn influenced the Honduran government so that it would not ratify the two treaties. By 1859 the Honduras railway scheme had collapsed, as by this time the Panamanian cross-isthmian railway had been operating for several years. Only by the 1970s have cross-isthmian transit routes been available in all the Central American Countries (except El Salvador).

HONDURAS, JEFFERY'S MAP OF. A 1775 publication of Robert Sayer (q.v.) in London, showing interior, coastal and insular features in great detail for the period.

HONDURAS LITERARIA. A literary magazine of the University of Honduras, published in Tegucigalpa.

HONDURAS LOTTERY COMPANY see LOUISIANA STATE LOTTERY

HONDURAS MINING AND TRADING COMPANY. Significant in that in mid-nineteenth century Byron Cole (q.v.) owned a share. Events of the Legitimist and Democratic struggles in Nicaragua led him to attempt to protect his interests in Honduras by working out an agreement with rebel Democratic leader Francisco de Castellón to assist the rebel forces in León, Nicaragua. Cole agreed to send a 300-man army. Under a trumped-up "colonization" agreement to circumvent U.S. neutrality laws, it was Cole who finally sent Walker and his "Immortals" to Nicaragua, thus precipitating events which are still having repercussions over a century later. It is somehow fitting that the Honduran activities of adventurers like Cole and Walker (q.v.) should end with the violent death of both in the enterprise they launched--Walker at Trujillo before a firing squad, Cole in the Batalla de San Jacinto during the "National War."

HONDURAS NATIONAL LOTTERY (19th Century) see LOUISIANA STATE LOTTERY

HONDURAS PROGRESS. A bi-weekly newspaper, the first English-language newspaper in all of Central America, established before 1890. See FRITZ GAERTNER.

HONDURAS ROUTE. A term applied in the 1800s to a proposed canal route, later viewed also as a railroad route, from the Bay of Fonseca on the Pacific to the Bay of Honduras on the Atlantic side. Running almost due north and south, the route follows the bed of the Río Goascorán to its headwaters in the central plain of Comayagua, and down the valley of the ríos Hamuya and Ulua from the northern reaches of the same plain

to the Caribbean near Puerto Caballos.
The Honduras Route adherents pointed out that there were magnificent harbors at the termini of this route and that the ascent to the divide was considerably more gradual than along several other routes. (Among such considered were the Tehuantepec, Chiriquí, Atrato, Panamanian, and Nicaraguan.) A railroad would have to climb to more than 2,000 feet to cross the plain of Comayagua, but few serious grades would be encountered.
The railroad was never built, and the enthusiasm for it which reached a height in the nineteenth century has disappeared, especially because of the excellent paved road, recently completed across Honduras, and the prospect that such roads will continue to serve all expected traffic. The Panama Canal has successfully handled interoceanic commerce.

HONDURAS STEAMSHIP AND NAVIGATION COMPANY. A company established in 1853, auxiliary to the planned Honduras International Railroad Company (q.v.). Sea distance from New York to San Francisco via the Honduras route was estimated at 4,200 miles, versus 4,700 for the Nicaragua route and 5,200 for the Panama route. The Honduras land route would add 160 miles for a 4,360 mile total. This was, of course, of prime concern due to the California Gold Rush of the early 1850s.

HONDURIAS. Alternate form of "Honduras" found on an anonymous atlas map presently in the Koninklijke Bibliotheek in the Hague, Holland.

HOSPITAL AND DOCTOR AVAILABILITY   see   MEDICAL CARE

HOUSING INSTITUTE   see   INSTITUTE DE LA VIVIENDA

HUAMPUSIRPI   see   WAMPUSIRPI

HUANCS   see   RIO COCO

HUAS. Lenca Indian word meaning water, used as a combining form as in Ahuas, Amachuas, etc. There is some feeling that the word is a particularly Paya form. It is found as Wass, guass, wash, and guash. One wonders if German "wasser" (from some early pirate) was the origin!

HULE. The rubber tree species found in Honduras along the Río Coco.

HULERO. A rubber-cutter, one who taps the sap from a hule tree.

HUMID ZONES   see   LIFE ZONES

HUMUYA RIVER. A part of Squier's (q.v.) ambitious scheme for a trans-Honduran railroad in the mid-1900s was the generally north-south valley of this river which joins with the Yure and the Salaco near Santa Cruz de Yojoa to become the Río Ulua (q.v.).

HURRICANE "EDITH." A 1971 storm which did great damage along the Honduran-Nicaraguan border land of the Río Coco valley. Areas near Cape Gracias a Dios were nearly wiped out.

HURRICANE "FIFI." The terribly destructive storm of September 1974, which became a Honduran national disaster of major proportions. See FIFI; also RELIEF EFFORTS; PARTNERS OF THE AMERICAS; RECOVERY, HURRICANE FIFI; and CHOLOMA.

HURRICANE "IRENE." One of the two serious hurricanes of 1971 which damaged Honduran coastal areas. The other was Hurricane "Edith."

HURTADO, BENITO. A "Lagarteniente" or officer attached to Captain Francisco Hernández de Córdoba, Captain Hurtado was sent in pursuit of Gil Gonzales Dávila who had gone on to Honduras from Nicaragua in search of the elusive strait between Atlantic and Pacific. On this expedition he founded in early 1525 a settlement on the waters of the Río Jicaro, now known as "Cuidad Vieja," but then the first of several locations of "Nueva Segovia," named for the famed Castilian city. The "city" had to be moved to escape piratical depredations.

HUYTLATO. Alternate name of the Reyno de Payaqui (q.v.), the original Precolombian capital of Honduras being at Copán.

HYDROGRAPHIC SITUATION. There are two major watersheds in Honduras--one on the Caribbean Sea slopes, the other on the Pacific side, the first draining principally into the Bay of Honduras on the north (since Honduras has the only major east-west trending coast in Central America), and the other into the Bay of Fonseca. The principal rivers of the two sides are as follows: Caribbean: Chamelicón, Ulua, Leon, Aguán (or Román), Tinto (or Negro), de la Posessión, Patuca, Coco (Segovia or Wanks). Pacific: Negro, Choluteca, Nacaome, Goascorán. Most of these rivers are navigable for shallow-draft craft through their lower reaches, the Patuca and the border river Coco being the longest navigable waterways. "Pipantes," doris and bateaux, as well as rafts, ply these streams.

HYMNO NACIONAL. The national anthem begins, "Thy banner is a floating heavenly light." The anthem is popularly called "Tu Bandera." The words are by Augusto C. Coello, the music by Carlos Hartling, and it was authorized and adopted by Congress and the President in 1910. There are seven

verses of eight lines each, and an eight-line chorus. A
very free translation of the chorus follows:

> Your flag is a lamp of the sky;
> Crossed by a drift of snow
> And there on the sacred field
> Five stars of the palest blue;
> In your emblem a murmuring sea,
> With your savage waves en-shielded;
> Behind a volcano's naked peak
> There shines a star's clear light.

- I -

IA - ECOSOC. Interamerican Economic and Social Council.

IACHR. Interamerican Commission on Human Rights.

IACI. Interamerican Children's Institute.

IACW. Interamerican Commission of Women.

IADB. Interamerican Defense Board.

IAGS. Initials for the Servicio Geodésico Interamericano (q.v.).

IAIAS. Interamerican Institute of Agricultural Sciences.

IAII. Interamerican Indian Institute.

IAPC. Interamerican Peace Committee.

IARO RIVER. Another form of the "Yare" or Río Coco, found on a 1710 British map by Hacke.

IBAÑEZ CUEVAS, PANTALEON. Governor of Honduras in 1748.

IBANS LAGUNA. A small round north coastal lagoon about five miles in diameter, just west of Brus Laguna (q.v.). It lies between the mouths of the rivers Platano and Tinto (or Río Negro). The nearest settlement, to the west, is the village of Plaplaya, at the Tinto estuary.

ICA   see INTERNATIONAL COOPERATION ADMINISTRATION

ICARUS. Ship, involved in the final chapter of William Walker's (q.v.) incredible career. See also SALMON, NORWELL.

IDB. The Interamerican Development Bank, which approved loans to Honduras in late 1974 for livestock purchase, education, and water supply, all for $15,000,000. Another $89,000,000 is being considered for health, sanitation, infrastructure, and agricultural projects. In general these credits relate to the aftermath of Hurricane "Fifi" in September 1974.

IDEAS DE TEGUCIGALPA. An organization of women in literature, adhered to by such writers as Angela Valle (q.v.).

IIAA. Institute of Interamerican Affairs.

IK. Second day of the Maya month; meaning, "wind."

ILLISHLE. A species of iguana found on Guanaja Island in the nineteenth century as noted by travellers.

ILO see ORGANIZED LABOR

IMIX. First day of the Maya month; meaning, silk cotton (kapok) tree, or ceiba tree. This tree was especially sacred to the Maya.

IMMORTALS, THE. The filibuster William Walker (q.v.) was able to gather about him, for his venture into fame and ultimate death in Honduras, a remarkable group of men. Dr. Jones, officers Kewen, Hornsby, Anderson and Crocker, and others made up the adventurous band of 58 men who came to be called the "Immortals." Walker represented an extreme extension of the concept of "Manifest Destiny" prevalent in the United States in the mid-1850s. To such a man small countries were fair game--or pawns, as the case might be.

IMPERIO, ARMANDO. Pseudonym of Honduran writer Arturo Martínez Galindo (q.v.).

IMPORT DUTIES. Traditionally the single most important source of governmental revenue, the vital import duties fell behind sales taxes (q.v.) in 1968, and presently they account for only 21 per cent of total governmental revenue, whereas in 1961 they were near 50 per cent. By 1968, 70 per cent of imports were not dutiable, and of items produced by the Central American Common Market 98 per cent are duty-free. Consular taxes bring in around seven per cent of income; since 1906 all imports have had to be accompanied by an invoice signed by a Honduran consul in the country of origin.

IMPORTS. More than doubled during the 1960-70 decade; consumer goods are about 40 per cent of total imports, raw materials 27 per cent, capital goods 26 per cent. Machinery and transport equipment are 30 per cent of imports, other manufactured items 30 per cent, chemicals 14 per cent, food ten per cent. Honduras imports from 90 countries but 98 per cent of this is from 23 countries; the United States, the rest of Central America, West Germany, Japan and England supply 85 per cent.

INA. The Instituto Nacional Agrario (q.v.).

INCAE see INSTITUTO CENTROAMERICANO DE ADMINISTRACION DE EMPRESAS

INCAP. The Instituto Nutricional de Centro América y Panamá (q.v.).

INCOME TAX. Honduras had no income tax until 1949, and it was modified in 1963. By 1968 it was 26 per cent of total government revenue. There is a progressive structure from three to 40 per cent in highest income brackets. Tax statements are required annually from businesses and individuals with gross income of over $1,000. Eighty-five per cent of total income tax is paid by businesses, since only one per cent of the population is affected as individuals. Nonresidents pay income tax only on that portion of their income earned in Honduras. The 40 per cent rate applies only to net income over $1,000,000 annually.

INDEPENDENCE, 1821-1823. The independence of Honduras was strongly tied, as with all of Central America, to independence movements in Mexico, the culmination coming under Agustín Iturbide. The February 24, 1821, Plan of Iguala (q.v.) declared Mexico's independence, and while the future emperor did not enter Mexico City to occupy it until September 27, an act of Independence was declared in Guatemala City on September 15, 1821. The signed Act of Independence, when it reached the rival capitals of Comayagua (q.v.) and Tegucigalpa (q.v.), was received without great enthusiasm.

There was no strong popular movement for independence at this time, and it was the forceful initiative of the Mexican movement that carried Honduras and the other Central American states along. The two capitals differed in their reactions. Tegucigalpa sought Guatemala as a Central American capital, whereas Comayagua favored union with Mexico under Iturbide. The issue almost precipitated civil war right at the outset, but when the Guatemalan government opted for annexation to Mexico early in 1822, the conflict abated. Represented at the Congress of Mexico (q.v.), the Mexican-Central American union merged in the Empire established by fiat under Iturbide, and likewise was dissolved when that fell in March 1823. In February 1823 Vicente Filísola, a lieutenant of Iturbide, convened a constituent assembly in Guatemala City. He had been sent with troops to subdue El Salvador, which objected to the union. Filísola's assembly on July 1, 1823, finally confirmed Central American (thus Honduran) independence, when the five countries (former provinces) agreed to declare themselves sovereign as the United Provinces of Central America (q.v.). Mexico recognized this independence on August 20, 1823, signaling the end of the imperial interlude under Iturbide.

INDEPENDENCE DECREE, HONDURAS, NOVEMBER 15, 1838.
Having gained independence from Spain and then from the ill-fated Mexican Empire, the breakup of the United Provinces of Central America was the cue for a third act of independence. The Constituent Assembly of the State of Honduras had been in existence since the act of installation on August 29, 1824. Taking action for independence on November 15, 1838, the assembly decreed that the Sovereign and Free State of Honduras was independent of the "old" federal government and of all other governments or foreign powers. The stated objective was to constitute in the internal affairs of the country a disposition unique to their circumstances, and to assure external security. Ports and territories were to be the property of the state, including taxation rights, etc.

INDEPENDENCE, SPANISH COLONIAL. The sequence of the final moves for independence of the Spanish colonial empire from Mother Spain is summarized here so far as it is a part of the matrix of Honduran history:

| | |
|---|---|
| New Granada (Colombia) revolt in (under Miranda and Bolíver) | 1811 |
| (Note--Nicaragua had an abortive move toward independence in Rivas in 1811.) | |
| Colombia established as a republic (comprising New Granada, Venezuela, Ecuador) | 1821 |
| Guatemala (all Central America)--September 15 | 1821 |
| Mexican intervention under Iturbide--January 5 | 1822 |
| Mexican power established in Guatemala--November 4 | 1822 |
| Santa Anna and insurgents toppled Iturbide (and ended the empire)--April 23 | 1823 |

Central America then formed the Federal Republic of United Provinces, of five states including Honduras. A charter in April 1826; Chiapas adheres to Mexico. Nicaragua was first to secede from this federation as an independent entity on April 30, 1838, and first to write a constitution providing for separate governments in November 1838.

Honduras decreed independence on November 15, 1838. Other Spanish colonies reached independence after 1898--Cuba, Puerto Rico, the Philippines.

INDIAS, CASA DE LAS see CASA DE CONTRATACION

INDICADOR. A publication of the Oficina de Información y Publicidad de la Ciudad de San Pedro Sula, containing commercial information concerning the city, and also social, cultural, and professional data.

INDIGO. Seventeenth and 18th century Central American cash crop, important in Honduras. Used as dyestuff; the textile revolution of the 1700s created the demand. There were four types of plants as identified by Linnaeus, but apparently it was principally indigofera suffructiosa, and then a later introduction of indigofera tinctoria. See ANIL.

INDIOS LABORIOS. Indians who were free during Spanish colonial days, but who were nevertheless in service, virtually serfs if not slaves.

INDUSTRIAL DEVELOPMENT LAW, 1966 see DEVELOPMENT PLANS

INDUSTRY AND MANUFACTURE. Honduras is generally considered to be industrially underdeveloped, but changes are coming rapidly, especially in the San Pedro Sula area. In 1967 there were 634 plants employing more than five persons, and 1,400 artisan shops employing fewer than five (see FOREST PRODUCTS). Sawmills rank first, then clothing manufactories. The greatest number of small businesses were in shoemaking, with tailors and dressmakers next. Furniture shops were 12 per cent of the whole; brick and tile, nine per cent; and vehicle repair, nine per cent. Three-fourths of the factories are family-owned. Ninety per cent of all are located in Atlántida, Cortés, and Morazán departments; that is, near San Pedro Sula and Tegucigalpa.
Soap, vegetable oil, and margarine industries use palm and cottonseed oils, by-products of agricultural efforts. A large banana chip industry (20,000 tons a year) and a fine brewery are in the San Pedro Sula area. Housing has the most rapid growth of any industry, growing at 15 per cent per annum. A cement plant produces 300 metric tons a day, and also makes pipe, tanks, and roofing. A Puerto Cortés oil refinery is capable of 3/4 of domestic needs for petroleum products. Near San Pedro Sula is a plastic plant with a 300-ton per month capacity for polyethelene. The pulp and paper enterprise near Olancho, a barbed wire plant, and a steel plant at Agalteca are in process of development.

INESTROZA, FRANCISCO. Senator Inestroza headed the state from January 1 until February 15, 1864, and was followed by a constitutional president, for the first time in two years.

INESTROZA, JUAN ANTONIO. Minister of Interior of Honduras during the crucial 1954 general strike (q.v.), it was he who made a personal visit to the strike zone, but was rebuffed when he attempted to sit down and talk with strike leaders.

INFORPRESS CENTROAMERICANA. A press agency, similar in function to the Associated Press, with regional coverage as indicated in the title.

INHERITANCE AND GIFT TAX. This tax has been in effect since 1938. Rates are progressive from one to 20 per cent and vary with the closeness of beneficiary relationship.

INSIGNIA, MILITARY. Company Grade--Sublieutenant (one gold bar); Lieutenant (two gold bars); Captain (three gold bars). Field Grade--Major (one gold star); Lieutenant Colonel (two gold stars); Colonel (three gold stars). General--(row of four silver stars). Epaulets are used for dress uniform, either white or blue blouse. See also CENTRAL AMERICAN DEFENSE COUNCIL.

INSPECTOR-GENERAL OF MINES FOR HONDURAS see FRITZ GAERTNER

INSTITUTO CENTROAMERICANO DE ADMINISTRACION DE EMPRESAS. The Central American Institute of Business Administration conducts management seminars, as there is as yet a general lack of trained business personnel. Such training is industrially as well as commercially oriented.

INSTITUTO CIENTIFICO DE SAN CARLOS see SECONDARY EDUCATION, EARLY

INSTITUTO DE LA VIVIENDA. Housing institute established in 1957. This succeeded housing efforts handled by the Office of Public Works from 1955 to 1957. Most activities are in the Tegucigalpa and San Pedro Sula areas. Low-income housing does not attract private investors. The Instituto Nacional Agraria is also involved in housing. A major effort of the housing institute has been construction of the Colonia 21 de Octubre near Tegucigalpa, comprising 511 units with community center facilities, and another 1,000-unit project for the Federation of Workers of the North of Honduras union members.
    The Housing Institute was created to take care of the special problems in housing which were both historic and increasing. While in rural areas construction is handled by the National Agrarian Institute (q.v.), the Housing Institute had a 1965-69 plan for low income units, some of which has been accomplished in the areas of the capital, Puerto Cortés, La Ceiba, Olanchito, and in a few other places. A 500-unit project was carried out in the Sula valley. Before 1961, an estimated 4.3 houses per 1,000 people were built annually.

INSTITUTO GEOGRAPHICO NACIONAL. Agency of the Ministry of Communications and Public Works which produces maps and collects cartographical and geographical data. Located in Tegucigalpa.

INSTITUTO HONDUREÑO DE CULTURA INTERAMERICANA. The Institute, which was established by a group of United States citizens and Hondurans, provides small halls for such special programs as art exhibits, motion pictures, plays, concerts, and lectures. Its activities center in Tegucigalpa.

INSTITUTO NACIONAL AGRARIO. In 1962 a major law was passed creating the Instituto Nacional Agrario as an autonomous quasi-governmental agency responsible for land use, tenure, and ownership reforms. While agrarian reform was by no means a new concept, there was an increasing number of rural workers who owned no land. Under advisory policies initiated by a National Agrarian Council (q.v.), the INA is charged with carrying out provisions of the law, which includes expropriation and redistribution of private lands. In a five-year period (to 1958) 48,000 acres had been expropriated, 200,000 purchased, and plots up to 50 acres in size had been distributed to more than 5,000 families.

The INA also promotes new settlement on national lands, the Aguán Valley settlement being one of these, designed for up to 6,000 families. Rural marketing cooperatives, community development, and self-help projects such as wells or schools are encouraged. Hampered by lack of funds and trained personnel, the INA received a boost in 1969 with a 30 million lempira ($15,000,000 U.S.) bond issue. By 1970 the INA was involved in 14 resettlement colonies, the largest being the Río Aguán Valley project, with seven others near San Pedro Sula.

INSTITUTO NUTRICIONAL DE CENTRO AMERICA Y PANAMA. The Nutrition Institute of Central America and Panama deals with dietary problems of the region. In Honduras the Institute found that 50 per cent of families studied had available only 20 per cent of needed Vitamin A. This is typical of nutritional problems. Children under ten and rural families have greatest deficiencies. Riboflavin in rural areas is low in consumption. Other vitamins were insufficient.

INSURANCE. There is one domestic Honduran insurance company, and there are sixteen foreign concerns.

INTERAMERICAN DEVELOPMENT BANK see IDB and HONDURAN COUNCIL OF PRIVATE ENTERPRISE

INTERAMERICAN PEACE COMMITTEE. Empowered to act in case of any dispute between American nations, this group was activated in 1959, following certain portions of the Rio de Janeiro Treaty of 1947. At any given time the group has a membership from several American nations.

INTER-AMERICAN PEACE FORCE. A force created in May of 1965 as a result of the Dominican Republic landings by United States Marines. The OAS took over the force from the U.S. military command, and Latin American troops, admittedly in token number, became part of the force. Honduras furnished 250 army troops; Costa Rica, 20 policemen; El Salvador, three officers; Nicaragua, 164 army troops; Brazil, 1,115 soldiers, marines and officers. The principle invoked was similar to that which prompted United Nations forces to enter

Korea in the 1950s.

INTERMEDIATE AREA. From the Maya frontier just east of Copán in Honduras to the northern borders of South America's Inca empire, the Central American and South American regions involved have been termed by archaeologists the Intermediate Area. The major characteristic is disunity. There were no great ceremonial centers, or at least none have yet been discovered. But there were items of great beauty produced (see ULUA MARBLE). This sub-region of the Circum-Caribbean Indian peoples comprises those in Colombia, western Venezuela, and Central America. This intermediate area seems to have been a meeting place of the Andean and later Inca cultures from the south, and of the Maya and Nahuatl from the north. Honduras is central in the meeting area. Aztecan, Mayan, Pipil, and Chibchan influences exist.

INTERNATIONAL COFFEE ORGANIZATION. A group established among fifteen coffee-producing nations to standardize policies in coffee merchandising by the member nations, essentially centered on price stabilization and attendant control of production. In 1974 there was some expectation of monopolistic practice similar to that of oil producing nations.

INTERNATIONAL COOPERATION ADMINISTRATION. The U.S. aid agency which was a successor to the Foreign Operations Administration in 1956.

INTERNATIONAL RAILWAYS OF CENTRAL AMERICA. In 1912 Minor C. Keith (q.v.) incorporated the IRCA with an eye toward realizing his great dream of an international rail line from the United States to Panama. The financing was handled in London with bonds worth $5,000,000. The company purchased all Guatemalan and Salvadoran railroads. The first construction was from Zacapa, Guatemala, to the Salvador frontier, with two further stretches in El Salvador extending from the capital and Santa Ana. By the late 1920s the plan was still to go on to the Canal Zone, by building around the Gulf of Fonseca in Honduras, and on down to Panama. The total amount of new road was to be about 500 miles. The coming of the great depression and the subsequent development of automobile trucking dashed the hopes of a rail line throughout the isthmian area. The Pan-American highway has been constructed instead. The International Railway route had been surveyed by U.S. Army engineers around the turn of the century. This railway plan had a vastly different purpose than that of the Interoceanic (Atlantic-Pacific) projects of the mid-1800s.

INTER-OCEANIC RAILWAY, HONDURAS see HONDURAS INTEROCEANIC RAILROAD COMPANY

INTIBUCA, DEPARTMENT. Bounded on the north by Santa Bárbara

department, on the northeast by the Cordillera de Montecillos and Comayagua department, on the east by La Paz, on the west by Lempira departments, and on the south by the Río Torola on the El Salvador international border. The cabacera is La Esperanza, and there are 16 municipios. The area is 1,202 square miles. The population of the cabaceras in 1973 was 13,910, and of the outlying areas, 84,046, for a total of 97,956. Intibuca is one of the departments affected by Salvadoran immigration. It has a rugged terrain, and is halved by the Cordillera Opalaca. San Isidro, Jesús de Oto, Concepción, San Miguelito, Dolores, San Marcos de la Sierra, Camasca, San Antonio, Magdalena, Santa Lucia, Masaguara, and Colomoncagua are other towns.

INVESTMENT. Honduras is making a massive effort to improve its economic situation, which has lagged somewhat behind that of other Central American countries. Investment possibilities are such as this partial list indicates:
   MANUFACTURING: Glass, hand tools, screws, bolts, plated and enamelled metal products; auto and machinery assembly; ceramics, both industrial and domestic; furniture, flooring, and other wood items; bicycle assembly, small ship building; plastics; textiles in cotton, nylon, dacron.
   FOODS: Fish, lobster, shrimp, and related seafoods; meat-packing; fruit and vegetable canning; soups, jellies, dressing, juices; vegetables, honey.
   AGRICULTURE: Cattle, fruit, vegetable, flower, seed, chicle, rubber, poultry, leather, dairy, and related products.
   CHEMICAL: Oil, refineries, byproducts, fertilizers, phosphates, acids, polyesters, pharmaceuticals, salt.
   MISCELLANY: Building construction, paper, coffee, resins; mineral products, such as lead, gold, silver, marble, lime, quartz.
   Reasons for investment are cited as strategic central location in the Central American Market; ample low-cost labor; respect for foreign property and capital; stable currency; Atlantic and Pacific ports; good banking system. Two factors may have considerable effect on Honduran plans--the devastation wrought by hurricane "Fifi," and the world economic crises of 1974 and following.

INVIERNO. The winter season, although since Honduras is in the northern hemisphere it is actually summer time. This "winter" is so called because of the lowered temperature due to the frequent rains which fall for a six-month period. Rains in the area start around May 15.

IRCA   see   INTERNATIONAL RAILWAYS OF CENTRAL AMERICA

IRIAS, PEDRO   see   REMANZO

ISLAS DE LA BAHIA, DEPARTMENT   see   BAY ISLANDS DE-

PARTMENT

ISLA LOS PINOS. A name sometimes applied to the island of Guanaja (q.v.).

ISLAND AMERICA. In the early 1500s the new discoveries in America were still thought to be an island. Vasco Núñez de Balboa's discovery of the Pacific Ocean on September 25, 1513 was not fully grasped because of this island theory. The north coast of Honduras, with its extent of several hundred miles east and west, was considered to be the northern limit of this supposed island. The peninsula of Yucatan, sighted in 1503 by Pinzón and Solís, was considered to be another island. This view was dispelled by an expedition sent out by Francisco de Garay, Spanish governor of Jamaica. Under command of Alvarez de Piñeda, the expedition was charged to find a strait between Mexico and the "island" America. In 1518 Pineda discovered that land was continuous from Honduras to Florida. This elevated Balboa's South Sea to the status of a mystery, for Columbus had already demonstrated the lack of a strait from Honduras to the eastern end of the Panamanian isthmus. The island idea died hard--lower California was another "island" which persisted for centuries.

ISLANDS, HONDURAN. Honduras has two groups of islands, one on the north and east, or the Caribbean Coastal area, and one to the south, on the Pacific Coastal area, the latter being in the gulf or bay of Fonseca, the former partly in the Gulf of Honduras.

Bay Islands (north): Roatán, Guanaja, Utila, Barbareta, Elena, Morat.

Other Caribbean (north and east): Cayos Cochinos, Gorda, Zepotillos, Cajones, Vivorillo, Pichones, Becerro, Caratasca, and Islas de Cisne (the disputed Swan Islands).

Bay of Fonseca: Zacate Grande, El Tigre, Gueguensi, Violín, Pajaros, Sirena, La Vaca, Ratón, Coyote, Garrobo, Matate, Garza, Verde, Coneja, Tortuga, Guitarra, El Jícaro, Perejil, Almejas, El Comandante, Exposición, Mianguera.

The naming, it will be noted, relies heavily upon animals and birds, with "violin" and "guitar" as musical variants.

ITURBIDE, AGUSTIN. Iturbide was for a period the monarch of all Meso-America. Central America, following the Plan of Iguala (q.v.), was annexed to the Mexican empire briefly, soon after the Day of Independence, September 15, 1821, until June 24, 1823. The geographical and social fragmentation of Central America, as well as the colonial heritage, helped to make any union short-lived; the date of annexation was January 5, 1822. Thus Iturbide was emperor of Mexico and Central America 1822-1823 (see INDEPENDENCE, 1821). Iturbide was "elected" by a part of the Mexican Congress

May 19, 1822, crowned Agustin I on July 21 of that year. By March 19, 1823, Agustín was forced from his throne, due to financial problems and political unrest. The revolution which unseated him was led by Antonio López de Santa Anna, destined to make a long and deep mark in Middle American history, among other things as the Conqueror of the Alamo in San Antonio, Texas.

ITZCUINTLI. Tenth day of the Aztec month; meaning, "dog."

IUMBE. The old man, presumably a Maya, who was detained by Columbus as an interpreter from the crew of a huge canoe which approached the Spanish fleet while it was anchored in a harbor off the Honduran Island of Guanaja (q.v.). Iumbe was renamed Juan Pérez, and proved to be both intelligent and useful.

IVES, MABEL IRENE. A native of Juticalpa, Honduras, this Honduran artist has also studied in California, as well as in the Escuela Nacional de Bellas Artes.

IX. Fourteenth day of the Maya month; meaning, "jaguar." Similar to the 14th Aztec month, Ocelot (q.v.), meaning "tiger" (Tigre or Tigrillo). The jaguar was an extremely important creature from the mystical and ceremonial standpoint.

IXTLE see PITA

IZALCO. Vessel in which Honduran hero Francisco Morazán (q.v.) left his native region to go to Costa Rica on April 8, 1840, following defeat in El Salvador. The ship was named for the famous Salvadoran volcano also known as "Lighthouse of the Pacific."

- J -

JACKSON, WILLIAM. An officer of the Providence Company who made a retaliatory attack (for the Díaz de Pimientas [q.v.] raid) in 1643. His forces almost destroyed Trujillo, then over 100 years old. Even 150 years later the captain-general of Guatemala marvelled at the damage which had been done, and which at that late date was still evident.

JAGUAR. The big spotted American cat, widely distributed from Mexico through much of South America; "Felisonca" comes in a black color phase, loves to swim, has paws the size of a saucer, weighs up to 250 lbs., and trophy skins measure eight feet from nose to tail tip. A beautiful animal, dangerous when crossed. Called "Tigre" in Honduras. (The ocelot is "Tigrillo.") The jaguar also had great religious significance among the advanced Pre-Columbian tribes, such as the Maya, Toltecs, Aztecs, Zapotecs, etc.

JALAN RIVER.  A major tributary of the Guayán (q.v.).

JAMALTECA.  Ruins, probably Maya, in this area near the Comayaguan plain.

JAUREGUI, FELIPE.  Envoy to Leonese pact meetings in 1849-50, and participant in an abortive coup with Guardiola (q.v.), at the instigation of Frederick Chatfield (q.v.).

JEFE DE ESTADO.  Title, "chief of state," applied not only to Presidents but often to counselors or deputies who carried responsibility for as little as a month, a week, or even a day.  During the Central American Federation Honduras had 22 different men as chiefs of state from July 28, 1825 through April 27, 1839, less than 14 years.

JEFFERS, W. N.  U.S. Naval Lieutenant who accompanied E. G. Squiers (q.v.) to Honduras in 1853 to assist in a preliminary survey for the planning of a railroad from the Bay of Fonseca to Puerto Caballos.  He took a line across the continent with barometrical and other observations, and got the basic data for pertinent cartography on the ports, etc.  Jeffers was a former assistant Professor of Mathematics in the U.S. Naval Academy.

JEFFREYS, THOMAS.  Mapmaker and geographer to the King of England in 1775, and author of a map published by Robert Sayer (q.v.).

JEJENE.  A sandfly, terrible, biting, blood-drawing pest in the lowlands of the Gulf of Fonseca.

JEREMY.  Son of "King" Oldman, Jeremy was sent to Jamaica in 1687 to beg that Mosquitia be taken under the protection of the King of England.  Referring to the Earl of Warwick's Old Providence Island enterprise and "King" Oldman's fealty to Charles I, a group of the coastal settlers accompanied Jeremy to make his plea.  While the confirmation of his royal status was proceeding, Jeremy climbed a nearby tree in the British Major's uniform which had been given him by his sponsors.  The Earl of Albemarle, governor of Jamaica, is supposed to have granted the request, in spite of the Simian antics of the candidate.  By 1701 a regular English factory for trade was established on the coast.  A second trip by Jeremy further confirmed the arrangement on June 25, 1720, by Act of the Assembly of Jamaica, and Jeremy was sent back in a British sloop with a generous supply of rum, no doubt more to his taste than diplomacy.

JESUS.  Mountain a mile north of Honduran-Nicaraguan border, five miles northwest of Jalapa.  The altitude of the mountain's Nicaraguan portions is 5,857 feet, which makes it Nicaragua's third highest mountain even though the crest is in Honduras.

The border country is very rugged in this area.

JICAQUE INDIANS. There has been no completely satisfactory tracing of the Jicaque Indians, who when the Spanish arrived in Honduras were living between the Río Tinto, or Black River, and the Río Ulua. They were a relatively peaceful group, unlike the more belligerent Payas who lived to the eastward. They were also unlike the warlike Sumus, who later were part of the stock that formed the Sambo-Miskitos (q.v.). The Jicaques spoke a language which has been identified as related to the Chibchan of northern South America. Some scholars insist it belongs to the Hokan-Siouan language group, from Mexico and the United States.

The Jicaque had Spanish Christian missions established among them in the 1700s; Father Manuel Jesús de Subirana was a Catholic missionary to them in the 19th century.

By 1960 the Jicaque around Yoro in Yoro Department had been almost entirely absorbed in the ladino culture, but in Olancho there was a highland group of several hundred Jicaque holed up in the fastnesses of Montaña de Flor. This group of roughly 300 retained distinctive features of their original culture, and were descendents of two major family heads. Their houses were of planks, tied with vines, and palm thatched. Their food was yuca (q.v.), potatoes, taro, and yams. They hunted small game with blowguns and clay pellets, but they also used traps and bows and arrows. The blow-gun would seem to be of South American origin. They shared group labor, grew corn and coffee for cash. They worship the sun, but fear an evil goddess named TSII (q.v.).

JICARA. A calabash cup usually decorated with simple carving, used for chocolate drinking in particular. Made from the prolific fruit of the jicaro tree.

JICARAL, EL (El Salvador). A battle of March 19, 1839, which was the site of the opening of conflict between Honduras and Nicaragua (which had seceded from the Central American Federation) and El Salvador, in the War of 1839.

JICATAYO RIVER. This stream parallels the Río Chamelecón (q.v.) at a distance of about 25 miles, and with the tributary Río Otoro enters the Ulua near Pimienta, upriver from San Pedro Sula.

JILGUERO. Bird, the nightingale thrush (local name).

JIMINEZ BARRERA, GELASIO. Artist, a native of Cienfuegos, Cuba, and a naturalized Honduran, he is a graduate of the Academia San Alejandro in Havana. Has exhibited throughout Central America, at Hemisfair '68 in San Antonio, Texas, and has received prizes and awards.

JOINT OPERATIONS AGAINST SANDINO. On April 6, 1928, a

plan for such operations was worked out, among United States Marines, the Honduran Army, and Nicaraguan volunteers. But when President Mejía Colindres of Honduras declared martial law along the border, the congress of Honduras then sitting reduced the size of the army. See also CALDERA, AUGUSTO, and LAS LIMAS INCIDENT.

JUACOS see THUACOS

JUANA LAINEZ, CERRO. An eminence in the southern part of Tegucigalpa, near the stadium.

JUAREGUI, ARTHUR. Representative of the Confederación Internacional de Sindicatos Libres (q.v.), an anti-communist federation of labor, during June of the 1954 Honduran General strike (q.v.).

JUDICIAL BRANCH OF GOVERNMENT. This is composed of the Supreme Court and of Lower Courts, which include Appeals Courts (q.v.), Departmental and District Courts, and Labor Courts. At the lowest level are justices of the peace, appointed by regional judges. The appellate judges are appointed by the Supreme Court, as are the regional justices. The regional courts have one judge sitting; each appellate court has three. There is a special Labor Appeals Court. There are also special Rent Courts (q.v.). Through appointment power the Supreme Court has presumably great influence. The Public Ministry is the Office of the Attorney General. In actual fact the Court does not exercise much independence, rather deferring to the executive branch for review and decision. For over 50 years there has been no jury system. Judges render all decisions.

JUGUJUGU. A Black Carib (q.v.) celebration, held on Christmas Eve and New Year's Eve. Men and women dance separately all night.

JUITEMAL. The Kingdom of Guatemala (also "Goethemal" in colonial times), which received its name, according to tradition, from an Indian chieftain (probably Maya), named Juitemal. This "kingdom" included colonial Honduras.

JULIO, TOMAS DE. One of Gálvez' officers at Trujillo (q.v.) in 1782. He had formerly carried out the reoccupation of Fort San Carlos in Nicaragua, and was responsible for chasing Despard and the British out of the great frontier bastion of Fort Inmaculada on the San Juan River of Nicaragua. In 1782 Despard returned the favor by capturing Julio at Black River, Honduras. But while Julio lost this battle, at Inmaculada he had won the war.

JUNTA DE GOBIERNO, 1907. From February 23, 1907 to April 18, 1907, the ruling junta consisted of three Generals, Miguel

Oqueli Bustillo, Máximo B. Rosales, and J. Ignacio Castro.
This committee formed itself after the Nicaraguan invasion
and the fall of Manuel Bonilla, and soon installed General
Miguel R. Dávila as Provisional President.

JUNTA DE INDEMNIZACION, 1824 see SLAVERY, ABOLISH-
MENT

JUNTA MILITAR DE GOBIERNO, 1956-57 see RODRIGUEZ,
ROQUE J.

JUSTICES OF THE PEACE. Part of the Judicial system, the justices of the peace are appointed by regional judges, and often have broad authority because of the geographical isolation of their jurisdictions. They handle civil disputes over small monetary sums (in effect a small-claims court) and they have jurisdiction over criminal offenses of a minor nature; they occasionally hear major criminal cases, but only by permission of the regional judge. They are very low-salaried, and it is hard to retain qualified incumbents.

JUTICALPA. Cabacera of the largest department, Olancho; located about 75 miles northeast of Tegucigalpa. The area is cattle-ranching and timber-cutting country. There is a good graded gravel highway, and an airport. The Río Guayape flows nearby, and the setting is mountainous, with peaks up to 4,000 feet.

JUZGADOS DE LETRAS DE INQUILINATO see RENT COURTS

- K -

KALEL see CALEL

KAMINALJUYU. Important for the cultural influences of Teotihuacán (q.v.) which were transmitted from this Guatemala City site to Copán (q.v.), and which influenced that Classic Maya center in western Honduras.

KAN. Fourth day of the Maya month; meaning, "precious" or "beautiful."

KANKIN. Fourteenth month of the Maya calendar.

KATUN. Twenty Maya years of 360 days (TUN). This period of 7,200 days was a relatively small unit in Maya calendrical notation. See BAKTUN, PICTUN, CALABTUN, KINCHILTUN, and ALAUTUN.

KAUR KIRA see CAUQUIRA

KAZAB. Seventeenth month of Maya calendar.

KEARSARGE, U.S.S. In 1894, this famous ship of the United States Navy was dispatched to deal with a dispute which had arisen between Honduras and Nicaragua concerning a proposed "Republic of Central America," a merger plan. Honduran forces crossed the Nicaraguan border in January. The Kearsarge was wrecked on Roncador reef in the Caribbean when hurrying to the scene of action. This delay in the arrival of U.S. Forces allowed British Naval and consular officers to institute martial law in the name of the Mosquito reserve, backed up by the landing of British marines. The failure of the old Kearsarge to arrive thus changed the diplomatic situation with a conclusion less satisfactory to the U.S. and, presumably, to Nicaragua and Honduras than the ship's decisive U.S. Civil War victory over C.S.S. Alabama had been. The 32-year-old vessel was a total loss.

KEITH, MINER COOPER. In 1871 this Central American empire builder and entrepreneur landed in Costa Rica. He was later to build most of the railways in Central America, beginning at a time when the only rail line between the Rio Grande River and the Panamanian Isthmus was a short stretch in Honduras (the first Honduran rail venture had been planned by E. Q. Squier [q.v.]). Keith became not only the wealthy developer of a rail, banana, and coffee empire, but also the guarantor of foreign credit for more than one of the Central American countries. It was the bananas he brought to Costa Rica from Panama that began the Central American banana industry. Shipment began in 1873, but full cargo shipments began in 1881 to New Orleans. His tropical trading and transport company took over some of the banana interests, and the Atlas Steamship Line of England carried the fruit. He began a chain of stores on the Mosquito Coast, and extended it across Honduras, since the chain began in Bluefields, Nicaragua, and went as far as Belize, Honduras. In these "trading posts" Keith bought rubber, sarsaparilla, vanilla, and turtle shell. It was the Keith properties in Honduras, Panama, Costa Rica and Colombia that were the basis of the United Fruit Company, which absorbed the Keith interests just before 1900.

KEITH, MINER HUBBELL. Lumberman in Brooklyn and father of Minor Cooper Keith (q.v.) and Henry Meiggs Keith. He had married Emily Meiggs, whose brother was a lumberman and later the builder of Andean railroads. This was the heritage which helped Minor Keith to become a Central American empire builder.

KEKCHI. One of the lesser Mayan tribal groups which following the conquest spread northward from the land of their origins to the Honduran Gulf lowlands. In general the area of Honduras in pre-Columbian times was divided into many petty chieftaincies. A Kekchi dialect is still one of the identifiable Maya linguistic variants.

KHARIBEES. An alternate name used in the early 1800s to designate the Caribs who had been removed by the British from The Island of St. Vincent and conveyed to the Island Roatán in the Bay Islands of Honduras. Some had later settled on the north coast of Honduras in the area of Black River.

KIDDER, ALFRED V. As Head of the Department of Historical Investigation of the Carnegie Institute of Washington, Dr. Kidder served as consultant to the delicate and difficult restoration work at Copán (q. v.), proceeding under the direction of Dr. Stromiris (q. v.).

KINCHILTUN. Twenty Calabtún (q. v.) in Maya calendrical notation, hence 1,152,000,000. See TUN, KATUN, ALANTUM.

KINGSBOROUGH, EDWARD VISCOUNT. Lord Kingsborough, son of the Irish Earl of Kingston, was so taken with Mexican manuscripts in Oxford's Bodleian Library that he decided to devote his life to studies in New Spain, which he did. In 1831 he published seven volumes in the magnificent format of imperial folio. The price of the set was $1,470. The whole publishing venture and its cost of $660,000 impoverished him so that he was thrown in a Dublin prison, and died at 42 of typhus. Kingsborough was in direct line of archaeological investigators which extended from Charnay (q. v.) through Kingsborough, Dupaix (q. v.), Stephens (q. v.), Maudslay (q. v.), and the Harvard investigations, the last three of whom were particularly concerned with Copán.

KIRCHOFF, D. J. President of Castle and Cooke, San Francisco parent company of Standard Fruit Co., in 1974. See TAX, BANANAS.

KIRKPATRICK, SIR THOMAS. Representative of the British Crown sent to Comayagua in the late 1800s to supervise the English railway investment and its contractual arrangements. See LA VICTORINA.

KRUTA RIVER. A short but large stream entering the Caribbean at False Cape (q. v.); the river is wedged between the Río Coco (q. v.) and the huge Laguna Caratasca (q. v.) and rises in the eastern Honduran flatlands, the Llanos de Auka (q. v.). The Río Kruta's considerable volume drains the low swampy areas of easternmost Honduras just about 15 miles from the Río Coco bar on the border at Cape Gracias a Dios, in the department of the same name.

- L -

LA CAMPAÑA. An eastern suburb of Tegucigalpa.

LA CAPITANA. The flagship of Columbus on his fourth voyage,

when he reached the Honduran coast. It was a small vessel, of only 70 tons, even smaller than the Niña of his first voyage. La Capitana's real name was, like an earlier caravel, Santa María. The Captain of La Capitana (under Admiral Columbus) was Diego Tristán. Don Fernando Colón was also among the officers. See FLEET, COLUMBUS.

LA CARIDAD. A Honduras Nao (q.v.) of 350 tons, which sank in 1616 off Chipiona near Sanlúcar (the bar of the Guadalquivir river). The Captain was Francisco Monte. $50,000 in silver was aboard.

LA CEIBA. Important north coastal town midway between Puerto Cortés and Trujillo, with rail connections both east and west, an airport and seaport. La Ceiba has around 50,000 inhabitants. It is the cabacera of La Atlántida Department, and there is a good hospital. The major enterprise is banana culture. Behind La Ceiba rises Pico Bonito at about 6,500 feet and flanked by a dramatic mountain wall five miles or so from the coast.
    There are four suburban areas in La Ceiba: Barrios La Julio, Sierra Pina, and Bella Vista; also Colonia El Sauce.

LA CONDAMINE. A famous French astronomer who was sent to Central and South America by his government on an international scientific expedition, with the immediate purpose of measuring an arc of the meridian on the plain of Quito, Ecuador. La Condamine made instrumental surveys along the isthmus, and his conclusions included strong support for a trans-isthmian canal to join Atlantic and Pacific waters. He presented a brilliant paper on this subject to the Academy of Sciences in Paris in 1740. Spanish companions of La Condamine, Antonio de Ulloa, a renowned Spanish scientist, and Jorge Juan, a naval officer, were on the same expedition, and added much knowledge concerning the topography of the Pacific coastal portions of Central America. This was during a period of war with the English; no practical results could be carried out.

LA COSTA DE LAS OREJAS. Columbus' name for the northern Honduran coast, because of the heavy ear ornaments worn by the Jicaque Indians of the coast. They seem to have been skilled metallurgists. The "Coast of the Ears" was followed by the fleet for a month due to headwinds. See COLUMBUS, CHRISTOPHER.

LA CRONICA. Honduran newspaper, moderate during the 1954 general strike (q.v.).

LA EPOCA. Tegucigalpa daily paper which operated with the approval of the Carias (q.v.) government, at a time when criticism of the regime was not permitted. It was in effect a Carias paper, a quasi-official government organ, edited and

199                La Esperanza

directed by a political ally of General Carias, Fernando Zepeda Durón.

LA ESPERANZA. A literary group formed in 1890 by Jerónimo Reina (q. v. ) and others.

LA ESPERANZA, SIERRA. Row of mountain peaks extending from northeastern Olancho Department across the eastern end of Colón Department, parallel to and west of the Río Tinto (Sico or Negro), the Black River of the English "Baymen."

LA ESTRELLA SOLITARIA. A periodical founded in 1896 by Rómulo Durón (q. v. ), Manuel Sabino López, and Jerónimo Reina (q. v. ).

LA FEDERACION DE CENTRO AMERICA. One hundred years after the original union, in July 1921 a constituted assembly met once again to prepare a constitution for Central American Union. Four states including Honduras had signed the pact on January 19, 1921. Nicaragua walked out because the others would not accept the Bryan-Chamorro treaty. The plan of union began to fall apart when Costa Rica voted against joining and when a revolutionary government took over Guatemala. Many Central Americans consider that the U. S. sabotaged this movement toward union, the open act being recognition of the revolutionary government in Guatemala. The Federation ended February 7, 1922. Central American union remains a dream, paradoxically, in each of the five countries.

LA JUTOSA. A town in Cortés department heavily damaged by hurricane "Fifi" (q. v. ) on September 19, 1974. Residents there took refuge in a church, but were drowned when floodwaters roared through the building.

LA LIBERTAD. A small municipal cabacera about 20 miles north of Comayagua, in the department of the same name, and near the Río Humuya.

LA LLORONA. A popular term in back-country Honduras applied to the cloud-forests (q. v. ) in the highland areas. Actually the term is La Montaña Llorona, or the "Weeping Woods." In the cloud forest the water condenses on the dense jungle trees and falls like "tears" almost constantly.

LA MERCED. A Comayagua church which is one of the earliest extant buildings of the old colonial capital, known to have been under sonstruction in 1611, and added to later in that century. It served as the cathedral as well as an early parish church. It is a simple barn-like structure with one tower, but on the interior there is unusually delicate wood carving in relief on a side altar. In 1644 this church received from Philip IV a retable for the main altar, some ornaments, a crucifix, missals, and statues. Apparently these gifts from the king were decimated and lost long ago.

LA MESA AIRPORT. San Pedro Sula's airport, modern, capable of taking standard jet airliner traffic. Such traffic has to change here for Tegucigalpa which does not have a jet-port (see TONCONTIN AIRPORT). There are daily flights to the Bay Islands from La Mesa.

LA MONTAÑA LLORONA. In the many mountainous areas of Honduras, when the rural folk are asked the names of highest mountains, this phrase is the frequent answer. It means, in effect, the weeping woods. Often the answer is simply "La Llorona." This refers to the cloud forest, where the dense woods "weep" continually due to the condensation on their leaves and branches.

LA NATIVIDAD. Other form of the first name borne by Puerto Caballos. See LA NAVIDAD.

LA NAVIDAD. Original name given by Cortés in 1525 to Puerto Caballos, by which it was known through most of the colonial period. It is now Puerto Cortés. Formal name was La Navidad de Nuestra Señora. There were three attempts to establish a settlement; first by Francisco de las Casas in honor of Cortés in 1525, then by Cortés who named it, then in 1539 by Francisco de Montejo. By 1542, however, the port was established.

LA NUEVA EPOCA. Comayagua periodical of 1900 founded by Jerónimo Reina (q.v.).

LA PAZ, DEPARTMENT. Bounded on the north by Comayagua, on the east by Francisco Morazán, and on the west by Intibuca Departments, La Paz' southern border is the international boundary with El Salvador. The area is very mountainous, between the Cordillera de Montecillos on the north, and the Montañas Yerba Buena on the east. The cabacera is La Paz, in the far northeastern corner of the department. There are 19 municipios. The area is 915 square miles. The 1973 population of the cabaceras was 16,169, and the remaining population 60,099, for a total of 76,268. Other towns are Cabañas, Santa Elena, Yarula, and Chinacle.

LA PLOMOSA. A silver mine near Santa Lucia. See FRITZ GAERTNER.

LA PRENSA. This newspaper is a San Pedro Sula daily, an independent newspaper, member of the Sociedad Interamericana de Prensa. Founded in 1964, it represents a relatively moderate point of view, and essentially supported the 1972 coup as good for the country.

LA PRIMAVERA, COLONIA. A southern suburb of Comayaguela.

LA VICTORINA. The popular name for Victorine Berlioz, who came from France to Central America in the days of Guardiola. Her cousins were involved in early railroad surveys. She became very wealthy, owning among other things El Sitio, now the source of Comayagua's water supply. Her well furnished mansion was open to distinguished visitors in Comayagua, and was called the "posada Victorine" by María Soltera (q.v.). La Victorina owned a cane mill, a cacao plantation, and was founder of a store with mercantile endeavors throughout the Comayagua Valley and nearby mountains. La Victorina married Sir Thomas Kirkpatrick who was sent by Britain to handle the railway investments in Honduras. They had two sons whose descendants live today in Honduras; the sons were Elisse Berlioz Kirkpatrick and Edward Berlioz Kirkpatrick. A descendant is the historian José Reina Valenzuela.

LA VOZ CONVOCADA. An active literary group in La Ceiba. See MERREN, NELSON E.

LA VOZ DE MUJER. Club organized by the National Party in the 1920s, with one object of working for the election of General Carias.

LA VOZ LIBERAL. Liberal journal whose editors were jailed by the Lozano regime in July 1956.

LABOR. The labor force is counted at 1.2 million, and includes all persons over ten years old. Actual economically active persons were about 480,000 in 1970; 60 per cent were in agriculture, 12 per cent in services, eight per cent in manufacture, 4.5 per cent in commerce, the rest in mines, transport, construction, utilities, etc. In 1950 the agricultural percentage had been 80 per cent; 40 per cent are active wage earners, 38 per cent self-employed, the others unpaid as in family agriculture. The coffee harvest uses as many as 150,000 for seasonal work. When listed by occupation, two-thirds of the total are loggers, hunters, fishermen or farmers.

Some 10,000 people work for the central government. They receive substandard wages according to the Labor Code (q.v.), which does not cover them. Basic work week is 48 hours. Overtime pay runs from 25 per cent to 75 per cent of base. From 1959-1964 there was only one legal strike, but there were in the same period 2,000 disputes, most settled by a labor solicitor from the Ministry of Labor and Social Security (q.v.).

LABOR AND SOCIAL SECURITY, MINISTRY OF  see  CABINET

LABOR, GENERAL STRIKE 1954  see  BANANAS

LABOR CODE OF 1970. Incorporating and superseding the significant Fundamental Charter of Labor Guarantees (q.v.) of 1955, the new code is a progressive one, but is at this point more honored in breach than observance by both workers and employers. The code relies on legal approaches rather than collective bargaining. Government employees do not come under the Labor Code.

LADINO. A term used in Honduras, as elsewhere, to denote hispanicized people of mixed Indo-European blood. The term is basically non-ethnic, rather referring to assimilation of Spanish culture. It also has bearing upon social stratification. In Honduras the cultural and non-racial nature of the term has caused it to be used to include mestizos, Negroes, and whites, and even some pure-blooded Indians who have become acculturated. Silver mining in particular caused highland Honduras to "Ladinoize" rapidly in the 16th and 17th centuries.

LAGOS, MARCIAL see BUESO, FRANCISCO

LAGUAIABA. Alternate form of the name of the island of Roatán as shown on Totten's map (q.v.) published in 1600. This was undoubtedly the original Indian name.

LAGUANAIA. Alternate form of the name of Guanaja as shown on Totten's Map (q.v.), from the year 1600. This original Indian name has persisted to the present day.

LAGUNA MUKURO. The small lagoon near Ratlaya and just north of the Caratasca Lagoon.

LAGUNTARA. A coastal lagoon six miles in diameter north of the Laguna Caratasc⁻, joined to the complex of lagoons in the area, and with an outlet to the sea.

LAMAT. Eighth day of the Maya month; meaning, "moon."

LANCETILLA. A research and experiment station maintained for the study and development of tropical plants, and of plants from other climes which can be adapted to grow in the tropics. A function of the United Fruit Co., the laboratory was established near Tela, and includes a livestock and dairy farms.

LAND TENANCY. Honduras has nearly 20,000 small farms, three-fourths of them under 25 acres. It is probable that there are 27,000 farms under three acres, with only four per cent over 100 acres. Big holdings are in the hands of banana concerns like the Standard Fruit Co. which has 250,000 acres, out of a total arable land area of about 4,000,000 acres. Land distribution is, nevertheless, more equitable than in other parts of Central America. Twenty-one per cent of farms are owner-operated and these tend to average 90 acres. The ancient ejidal land ownership pattern is discernable in the municipally owned lands, with each village of 100 or more population having rights to 4,000 acres, and each municipality to 8,750 acres of national land.

In 1970, 2,000,000 acres were cultivated
4,000,000 acres were arable
9,000,000 acres were suitable for pasture only
13,000,000 acres were forested (note overlap)
Total area
27,000,000 acres
Owned by municipalities
4,500,000 acres.

Squatters occupy 11 per cent of the farms with no legal status, usually on national land; nine per cent of farmers are renters, and four per cent are sharecroppers. Around 64,000 agricultural workers have no land. Crops are coffee, corn, cotton, sugar, tobacco, bananas, plantains, sorghum, rice and beans. Diet would be rice, beans, corn and plantains.

LANDECHO, JUAN NUÑEZ DE. Governor, 1559-1563. He was charged with corruption in the manipulation of the cacao trade, and in arrangements with the cacao encomenderos. He was imprisoned, but escaped. The general scandal was such that the Central American audiencia was moved, the area being divided between Mexico and Panama. This plan was so unwieldy that the audiencia was returned to Guatemala in 1570, due to the influence of Bishop Bartolomé de las Casas (q.v.).

LANDSTROM, BJORN. Born in Finland in 1917, this artist-author is painter, lithographer, stage designer, playwright, novelist, and critic. He won international notice with The Ship in 1961. He has evoked the Caribbean in both prose and painting in his book Columbus, where the discovery of Honduras is one of the features; his analysis of maps is significant.

LANSA see LINEAS AEREAS NACIONALES, S.A.

LANZA. A dance, the Honduran modification of the Lancer Quadrilles; still danced in Comayagua in mid-twentieth century.

LARAY MOGROVEJO, ANTONIO DE. This oidor acted as interim governor upon the death of Avendano (q.v.) in 1649, for a six-year period to 1654.

LAS CASAS, BARTOLOME DE. Born in Seville in 1474, a graduate of the famous university at Salamanca, he first came to America in 1502. Ordained in Spain in 1510, he soon returned to the Americas. Known later as Protector of the Indians, he fought the cruel encomienda system of semi-slavery

for Indians. He made frequent trips back and forth to Spain in those difficult times, in behalf of the Indians. The introduction of Negro slaves in place of Indian slavery was not a long-range solution. He was Bishop of Cuzco, Peru; he became Bishop of Chiapas later, and died in Spain in 1566 at 92 years of age.
 Las Casas is also known for his major historical work, Historia General de Las Indias. He was one of the great figures of the dramatic century, with such giants as da Vinci, Macchiavelli, Cellini, Cervantes, Michelangelo and a host of others; his life and work were worthy to stand with theirs.

LAS LIMAS INCIDENT. A village claimed by Honduras on the ill-defined border between Honduras and Nicaragua in 1928. The village had been bombed when U.S. Marine Aircraft attacked a Sandinista (q.v.) band, March 23, 1928. By April, President Mejía Colindres asked the United States to "retire from our territory." U.S. Marine and Nicaraguan volunteer officers met a Honduran general on the border and worked out plans for joint operations against Sandino. When the president declared martial law in the border area, he was thwarted by his own Congress, which reduced the size of the Honduran Army.

LAS LOMAS DEL GUIJARRO, COLONIA. An eastern suburb of Tegucigalpa.

LAS PIEDRAS. Silver mining area in the Comayagua region in colonial days.

LATIFUNDIO. A land holding classification representing over 1,000 manzanas (or 1,750 acres). These huge landholdings are still extant in many parts of Latin America under the hacienda system. A small minority of individuals control a major part of the arable land. The system was a proximate cause of the Mexican peasant revolution of 1910 and following.

LAW AND JUSTICE. The basic penal code dates from 1906, and that in turn leaned heavily upon previous codes of 1866 and 1880. These in turn were derived from mid-nineteenth century penal codes in Chile and Spain. Another 1906 law is that of Court Organization and Attributes. The basis of the system resembles that of other Latin American countries in that it is based on Roman and Spanish antecedents. The constitution itself has many detailed legal and law enforcement guarantees. Provisions of the 1965 Constitution include prohibition of illegal search, arrest without warrant, military court handling of civilian matters, and capital punishment. Rights of free speech, free press, assembly, and political asylum are constitutional guarantees. Firearms require permits.
 There are in the court system four levels: justice of

the peace, trial, appeals, and a Supreme Court of Justice. Special military, labor and rent courts also function. The nation has over 1,000 practicing lawyers.

LAWRIE, JAMES. The British Colonel who followed Hodgson in 1776 as governor, or "superintendent" of the Mosquito Shore. See TRUJILLO BASE ... 1782.

LAZZARONI ANDINO, DANTE. Artist born in Río Lindo, Honduras; he has studied in the University of Mexico's Escuela Nacional de Artes Plásticas and in the Escuela Nacional de Bellas Artes in Tegucigalpa, where he is an instructor. He has exhibited in Hemisfair '68, San Antonio, Texas, as well as in Mexico, Boston, Tegucigalpa, San Pedro Sula, and Guatemala.

LEAD MINES. In the 17th century lead mines to provide lead and litharge as reagents for the silver mining industry were opened in Agalteca, Honduras and Chiquimula, Guatemala.

LEAF TOBACCO. The tobacco grown in the Copán and upper Chamelicón valleys, used for cigars (called "puros" locally).

LEAN RIVER. A short north coast stream carrying a good deal of water across Atlántida department, entering the Gulf of Honduras midway between Tela and Esparta.

LEGEND OF THE BELLS. A charming tale from the villages of Naco and Cofradia. See BELLS, LEGEND.

LEGUA. A measure of distance, 5,000 varas (q.v.) or 4,175 meters--over four kilometers, about 2-2/3 miles. One of many "leagues" in use since ancient times.

LEIVA, PONCIANO. Becoming President by revolutionary action, Leiva nevertheless restored a constitution, while he served from November 23, 1873 to April 29, 1874 as a conquering revolutionary, and from April 29, 1874 to February 2, 1873 as Provisional President during constitutional maneuverings. He became president under the restored 1865 constitution from February 2 to December 16, 1875, and then was overthrown by a Medina (q.v.) revolution. See also ARIAS, CELEO.
    Leiva was restored February 3, 1876 and served until June 8, 1876, when he was chased out again by Medina and a third Guatemalan-backed candidate, Marco Aurelio Soto (q.v.). Leiva twice served briefly as chief executive from 1885 until 1891, during and after the constitutional terms of General Luis Bográn (q.v.). In each case he was "President by Law," a designated term. Then, elected once again as constitutional president, he was challenged by Policarpo Bonilla, founder of a new Liberal Party. Leiva's repression of the Liberals was so harsh that various uprisings were

sparked, and finally conditions were so chaotic that Leiva was essentially forced to resign the presidency. The successors, Agüero and Vásquez, anti-liberals, were not able to quell the increasing revolts.

LEMPA RIVER. In the southwestern part of Honduras, the Río Lempa crosses Ocotopeque Department, and in El Salvador becomes large enough to support a major hydro-electric powerplant. The river becomes a part of the Honduran-Salvadoran border on the southeastern portion of Lempira department and then turns south and slightly west to enter the Pacific after having crossed El Salvador.

LEMPIRA, CACIQUE. Known as "Lord of the Mountain," Lempira was chieftain, "Cacique," among western Honduran tribesmen during the time of the first major colonial war between the Indians of Honduras and the Spaniards, in the years 1537 to 1539. Lempira was the ruler over 200 towns, and had at his command 30,000 warriors. His followers attributed to him some of the qualities of deity--he was believed to be invincible. The original Central American colonial capital, Gracias a Dios (the cabacera of present-day Lempira Department), was in the territory of the almost legendary leader. The Spanish established a military post in the valley of San Antonio, and in the mountains and tablelands known as El Barrancón, El Pinal, and Coyocutena are to be found ruins called "The Houses of Lempira." In the surrounding area is found also the Stone of the Sacrifices of Quelapa, and a fort thought to be Lempira's near Guacalapa, called "Stone of the Tiger." The war with Lempira was caused, according to Bishop Pedraya who wrote of the matter, by the cannibalism practiced by those Indians of Mexican derivation who accompanied Pedro de Alvarado on his Honduran expedition. The Mexican tribesmen killed and ate Lempira's people without regard to age or sex. Those Indians of the province of Cerquín (Lempira's people), were very near to the town Gracias which had been so recently founded by the Spanish. The Cacique Lempira gathered his army of 30,000 and occupied the heights of Congolón, Guacalapa, etc., fortifying a number of special strongpoints. Governor of Honduras Francisco de Montejo sent out the Captain Alonso de Cáceres to deal with the Indian army. Cáceres started with an army of 800 Spaniards and Indian allies. He established an armed camp in the San Antonio Valley; but it was through an act of treachery that Cáceres achieved the death of Lempira, who was at that time only 38 or 40 years old. His followers were so demoralized that this ended the war. Lempira is revered as an indigenous and authentic hero. He was described as of medium stature, but very strongly built, a brave and valiant man. In battle he was known to have killed 120 men personally. Lempira seems to have been a member of one of the Maya subgroups, as the ancient Maya Capital Copán was not far to the north.

**LEMPIRA DEPARTMENT.** Bounded on the north and northeast by Santa Bárbara Department, on the east by Intibuca Department, on the northwest by Copán Department, and on the southwest by Ocotepeque Department, it is further bounded on the south by the international border with El Salvador, marked by the Río Sumpul and the Río Lempa. The cabacera is Gracias, which was the first colonial capital of all of Central America, and whose full name was Gracias a Dios, not to be confused with the Cape and Department of the same name today, at the opposite end of the country. There are 27 municipios, and the area is 1,680 square miles. The cabaceras have a population of 18,169 and the remaining population is 130,758, for a total population of 148,927. No other department has such a high percentage of rural residents. Lempira has a long border on El Salvador and has had problems with illegal migration, which helped to create conditions causing the 1969 war between Honduras and El Salvador. The area is mountainous. Towns include San Juan Guarita, Guarita, Tomalá, Tambla, San Sebastián, San Manuel de Colohete, Santa Cruz, San Andrés, Gualcince, San Francisco, Candelaria, La Virtud, Mapulaca, Piraera, and Virginia.

**LEMPIRA SYSTEM, COINAGE.** The present Honduran system of coinage based on the Lempira came into being by authorization of a law dated April 3, 1926, but the first coins under the system were struck in 1931. The lempira has retained a consistent valuation equal to one-half dollar U.S. The dies were varied slightly in 1954. Most have been struck in mints in Philadelphia, Pennsylvania.

Coins used are copper (one and two centavos); copper-nickel (five and ten centavos); silver (twenty and fifty centavos and one lempira). The copper and copper-nickel coins have the national arms in the obverse, the value in a wreath on the reverse. The silver coins have the arms on obverse, a portrait profile bust of Lempira (the Indian Chieftain) on the reverse. Fineness (.900) is minted on the silver coins.

**LENCA.** The Lenca Indians were apparently among those Sumu tribes, originally of the South American Chibchan culture, who had pushed north from South America, probably around the year 1000, during the period when the Maya civilization was collapsing. These tribesmen who came from the southeast made contact with the peaceful Maya and the Pipil tribesmen from Mexico on the central plateau area, and by the time of the Spanish conquest the Lencas had already absorbed some of the previously indigenous culture.

The Lencas resisted the Spanish onslaught, begun really when in 1525 Cortés established Puerto de Caballos and 1526 when he founded Trujillo. Under their chief, Lempira (q.v.), the Lencas northeast of Comayagua maintained a strong resistance, although as time went on the Spanish established a frontier line through San Pedro Sula in Cortés department, and Catacamas in Olancho.

By the 1960s the Lenca remnant comprised 70 per cent of all the Indians in Honduras. They were principally dwelling in the high mountains of Intibuca department where the population had an Indian majority in that decade, and also in La Paz and Lempira departments. The Lenca have essentially been absorbed in the Ladino culture, as they were earlier in the Maya.

LEON, JUAN PONCE DE. Best known as the discoverer of Florida, León was claimed as discoverer of Honduras, New Spain and Guatemala by a descendant nearly a century following his voyages. See RIVERA, PERAFAN DE.

LEON, PACT OF. As the basis of the Representación Nacional (q.v.), the pact of León was a confederation agreement signed November 6, 1849, between Honduras, El Salvador, and Nicaragua, in the old Nicaraguan capital.

LEPATERIQUE MOUNTAINS. Mountain range, a southern extension of the Comayagua range, rising to around 7,000 feet altitude.

LESTER, MARY see SOLTERA, MARIA

LETRAS DE AMERICA see CLAUDIO DE BARRERA

LEVIATHAN, H.M.S. The British ship which took aboard booty valued at a million pesos following the British attack on San Fernando de Omoa (q.v.) in 1799. She sank near the coast, with $200,000 in gems and precious metal aboard. She was recently found by magnetometer, and material raised from the wreck near Omoa. See FATHOM EXPEDITIONS.

LEY DE RETIRO Y JUBILACION. A retirement law for teachers and a fund for retirement were created in 1928, to be directed by the national congress and administered by the Treasurer of Public Instruction. The law was rescinded on March 17, 1932. There were no funds.

LEY ORGANICA DEL INSTITUTO NACIONAL DE ANTROPOLOGIA see NATIONAL INSTITUTE OF ANTHROPOLOGY AND HISTORY

LIBERAL PARTY. The liberal party organization was established in 1891 around the person and public personality of Policarpo Bonilla (q.v.). Split several times, it revived in 1920, but only temporarily, coming to the fore again in 1954, during the Villeda Morales period, and lasting until the military coup of 1963. By 1970 there was a serious rift. Most of the power of the party had been stripped under President López.

LIFE EXPECTANCY. Honduran life expectancy at birth is 47, compared to the lowest in the hemisphere, Haiti, at 29, and the highest, in Canada and the United States at 66. Deaths per 1,000 in Honduras are 74 for one-year olds, 186 for all ages. In Guatemala, among the Indian population it is 100 for one-year olds, 175 for all, and in Haiti, 222 for all ages. In the United States the comparable figure is 31.

LIFE ZONES. Also called "biotic provinces." They may be divided thus:
    I. Humid Lower Tropical - The Caribbean lowland. Rainfall from 80 to 200 inches annually. Jungles and monsoon forests. Huge trees with many epiphytes (q.v.). Animals such as the big cats, wari (q.v.), tapir, etc. This is the coastal selva.
    II. Arid Lower Tropical - Between Humid Lower Tropical and the Upper Zones on the high mountains lies the arid area of pine woods--the ocotal (q.v.). Rainfall is 20 to 40 inches. Cactus, thorn plants, acacia, mimosa, and similar dry area plants. Animals, such as deer, armadillo, fox, skunk, porcupine, anteater, rattlesnake.
    III. Arid Upper Tropical - The ocotal is more pronounced. There are rock outcroppings, thin soil; quail, jays, road runners, bluebirds; animal life is more northern than tropical. The sweet-gum trees grow in the upper reaches (see LIQUIDAMBAR), there are many epiphytes (q.v.) and there are lizards, snakes, tree frogs, squirrels.
    IV. Humid Upper Tropical - The real cloud forest, usually over 6,000 feet in altitude; called the "montaña Llorana" in Honduras (weeping woods). Cloud-forest has many fewer species than typical lowland rain-forest. The trees are huge--up to 200 feet in height. Many Honduran cloud-forest trees, perhaps a majority, are oaks of several species, or aguacates (avocado). The cloud forest is the major haunt of epiphytes (q.v.).

LIGNUM VITA. Two tropical American trees bear this name, the quaiacum officinale and the quaiacum sanctum. They are evergreen trees and the wood is very heavy, resinous, tough and durable. It has often been used for bearings with metal shafts, as in the propeller-shafts of ships. It is widely available in Honduras.

LINDO, JUAN. Constitutional President from February 12, 1847 to July 16, 1848, and again from July 16, 1848 to September 21, 1848, Lindo had these two terms but an unbroken incumbency due to adoption of a new constitution in 1848. He had to contend with a nearly successful revolt stemming from a dispute with England over loans and from opposition originating in Guatemala. He had to flee in 1850 from Tegucigalpa, and he refused a third term in office in 1852, although with help from both Nicaragua and El Salvador the uprising had been quelled and he had been in office from December 2, 1848 to February 7, 1852. On Lindo's refusal to run, disorder erupted once more.

While he was also the last to serve in governing Honduras under the Spanish colonial aegis, from 1821 to 1824, he was not, properly speaking, the last colonial governor, for that post was really held by Tinoco de Contreras, who appointed Lindo to an interim term. Lindo was then succeeded by another interim governor, who was appointed by the Constituent Assembly of Honduras, Juan José Díaz. Lindo served technically from November 21, 1821 to February 11, 1824. Lindo was a Comayagua native who studied in Mexico. His life (1790-1857) paralleled that of José Trinidad Reyes (q.v.), and included the presidency of neighboring El Salvador for one year, 1841, where he was instrumental in establishing that country's Colegio de la Asunción. When this became the University of El Salvador in 1847, Lindo, who remarkably had become President of Honduras, raised the Academia Literaria established by Reyes to the status of a University, renamed the University of Honduras, where civil and canon law, Latin and philosophy were the principal advanced studies. Lindo is remarkable as having been the President of two countries and founder of two universities.

LINEAS AEREAS NACIONALES, S.A. A recent company which is following many internal routes similar to those of SAHSA (q.v.) for example the Bay Islands route. Acronym, LANSA.

LIQUIDAMBAR. The sweet gum tree which grows in wetter portions of the arid upper tropical zone and near the edge of the cloud forests. In Honduras the trees reach great heights, 100 feet or more and up to five feet in diameter. Local names are liquidumbe, liquidambe, or diquidumbe.

LITERATURE. While the cultural traditions of Honduras in pre-Columbian days are dominated by the Maya masterpiece of Copán, from Spanish colonial times to the present there are two cultural influences to which Hondurans point with justifiable pride--the colonial ecclesiastical architecture as exemplified in the Comayagua cathedral (q.v.), and the literary heritage and tradition, as well as current literary effort and production. José Cecélio del Valle (q.v.), 1780-1834, was a writer and philosopher as well as a prominent political figure, and as such was the outstanding intellectual figure of the colonial era. Father José Trinidad Reyes, poet and intellectual, was the founder of the Society of the Spirit of the Enterprise and Good Taste in 1845, which later evolved into the National University of Honduras. Juan Ramón Molina, 1875-1909, became a modernist poet, one of the new type exemplified by the internationally recognized Rubén Darío of Nicaragua. Molina's contemporary, Froylán Turcios (q.v.), was poet, novelist, and short story writer as well as a colorful and controversial politician and supporter of Sandino (q.v.). Favorite Honduran literary subjects were legend, the beauties of nature, and pre-Columbian and colonial folklore. Lacking much public support due to the limited literacy (hence limited market) and the scarcity of money, the literary Honduran has usually published in periodicals rather than in books. The successful ones have usually lived as expatriates in some more receptive foreign locale, such as Mexico, the United States or Europe. Typical contemporary writers include Rafael Heliodoro Valle, (historian); Clemintina Suárez (poet); Oscar Acosta (poet); and Orlando Henríquez.

LLANOS DE AUKA. Plains in the upper reaches of the Río Kruta (q.v.) valley in Gracias a Dios department. A geographical feature of far southeastern Honduras, these piney flatlands are between the Río Coco (the border) and the rivers emptying into the Caratasca lagoon just to the north. A remote part of Mosquitia, the plains are part of a flatland area approximately 50 by 100 miles in extent, reaching as far as Brus Laguna (q.v.).

LLANOS DE ILTARA. Flatlands just north of the Río Coco in southeastern Gracias a Dios Department.

LOBATO, JUAN. Governor of Honduras in 1617.

LOBO. The "wolf" cross (a commentary on racial attitudes) between a Negro male and an Indian female; this general mix was often called Sambo in the idiom of the British squatters during colonial centuries in Mosquitia. See RACIAL MIXTURES.

LOCUSTS. Recurrent plagues of locusts caused difficulties in colonial times; the 1680s were particularly bad. But the worst years were in 1616 and 1618. The Cochineal (q.v.) industry was seriously damaged.

LOGGERHEAD TURTLE. Frequently caught for food and shell in Mosquitia, the Testudo Caretta is large, with variegated shell colors. In the 18th century some were found weighing over 1,000 pounds, but the turtle fisheries are now greatly depleted.

LOGMAN, ENRIQUE. Governor, 1711.

LOGWOOD. The cutting of logwood and other dyewoods along the Caribbean Coast of Honduras went on from the earliest accession of English freebooters in the area, in the first decades of the 17th century. Sir T. Modyford, governor of Jamaica, reported this activity as taking place at Cape Gracias a Dios and "Mosquito," as well as in other places. He said a dozen vessels were engaged in the trade in 1670. The logwood cutters helped to maintain a tenuous British foothold on the Honduran coast, and were the basis upon which later claims and conflicts were based, first between England and Spain, and then after independence, between England and

Honduras. These claims also were a basis of United States and British conflicts and rivalries in the area. While once a bone of contention between the Spanish colonial administration and the "illegal" logwood cutters of the shores of the Bay of Honduras, the dye-wood was highly prized. It is Haemotoxylon campechianum, and is widely distributed in coastal Mexico and Central America. The dye derived from the heartwood of logwood is dark brown to black.

LOGWOOD SETTLEMENTS. The squatters who cut this important dye-wood on the Honduran coast in the 16th to 18th centuries received some recognition in 1762, when Spain had to tolerate their presence and leave the settlements alone. England in turn (in the Peace of Paris) agreed not to fortify the camps. Settlement boundaries and cutter's rights were not defined, so the English colonies in Honduras remained in dispute.

LONSTRELET, JUAN BATISTA. This commandant of the Bay Islands was stationed at Port Royal on Roatán (q.v.) with a sergeant's guard and some convicts. When some Grand Cayman islanders wished to settle on Roatán in 1838, Lonstrelet informed them they must get Honduran government permission. Some of the emigrants did, but others appealed to Superintendent Alexander Macdonald at Belize for his support, and Macdonald then appeared in the British sloop-of-war Rover, and taking down the Central American flag, hoisted the British colors. When the commandant objected, he and his detachment were seized by Macdonald and forcibly transported to the mainland. Macdonald's removal in 1843 did not solve the matter.

LOPEZ ARELLANO, OSWALDO. Air Force Colonel López Arellano became provisional president on October 3, 1963, serving until June 6, 1965, when he became constitutional President. In 1963 the disarming of the Civil Guard and the antimilitary position taken by Modeste Rodas Alvarado, leading candidate, seemed to be factors in the coup under General Roque J. Rodríguez (q.v.) and the fellow members of the Junta Militar de Gobierno. The liberal economic policies introduced in the previous administration by Villeda Morales were revoked, and order was restored in the political arena, as well as a measure of stability in the financial realm. Elections were held in 1965 for a new constituent assembly, which drafted a new constitution and provided for López Arellano to be elected constitutional president for a term running until June 1971. Ramón E. Cruz (q.v.) served from that time until he was overthrown by a coup of December 4, 1972, when General López Arellano, this time as Commander of the armed forces, took over the government. The official statement by López and supporters in a communique averred that the 1972 act had been due to "the incapacity of the deposed government to resolve the serious problems that Honduras suffers and the

chaotic state reigning in Honduras." Cruz had been placed in house arrest and given guarantees. There was little or no disorder.
Following the "golpe" there was relative calm in the country. Within two days a new cabinet was appointed. Until 1975 the regime had been a tranquil one, apparently accepted by a large majority of the Honduran citizenry.
First elected President by the 1965 Constituent Assembly, López had ruled Honduras through the military organization from October 1963 forward, even during his successor's brief term. In 1963 he had been involved in the coup against the existing government ten days before scheduled elections were to be held. The term of Ramón Villeda Morales, president just prior to López, had been turbulent. There were frequent insurrections, border disputes with Nicaragua and Guatemala, and a rise of Communist anti-government activity. In 1959 Villeda Morales established an independent Civil Guard, but disarmed the 2,500 men just prior to the 1963 elections, and the coup followed at once. López, then an Air Force Colonel, took over the government, reversed many Villeda Morales policies, restored political order and some measure of financial stability. Under the new 1965 Constitution (q.v.) and the elections of the same year, López was slated to serve until June 1971. The new constitution was largely the work of the Nationalist Party.
By 1970 the López government was operating with ten departments of the executive, and while minor unrest existed among student, teacher, and labor groups, the government supported moderately conservative policies and maintained internal calm by comparison with the previous very disturbed regime. Influence of the Liberal Party had been decimated, while the National Party became a personal political vehicle for López. The general strike of 1968 caused a declaration of martial law for 13 days, and in 1969 there was a national teacher's strike. By 1970 the President was a Brigadier General.
Under a "Political Plan of National Unity," and contrary to rumors that López would perpetuate himself in office, Ramón E. Cruz had been elected President in 1971. But by December of 1972, there was economic chaos, countrymen were marching on the capital to demonstrate, and López once again took over, with the announcement that his military regime would stay in power at least five years.
A tremendous challenge to the government developed two years later in the disastrous hurricane "Fifi." The López Arellano government, however, on the whole proceeded smoothly under the personable and energetic López, whose achievements in highways and other public works are remembered from his 1965-71 term in office. An interesting sidelight on the peaceful nature of the 1972 coup is indicated by López' presence at the world amateur baseball championships the night before, held in Nicaragua. Cruz had been serving, in effect, at the pleasure of the armed forces and their leader

López.
    López was succeeded by Juan Alberto Melgar Castro
    in late April 1975. Melgar (q.v.) was one of the leaders in
    the bloodless military takeover. López, it was alleged, had
    taken a bribe of $1,250,000 from United Brands Co.,
    which admitted in early April 1975 that such a bribe had been paid,
    with the intent to gain a lowering of banana-export taxes
    (see BANANA WAR, 1974). The bribery allegations were
    further connected with the suicide of Eli M. Black (q.v.),
    United Brands executive, in February 1975. Reports circulated
    in May 1975 that López and his family would go by air
    to exile in Madrid. There seemed to be no mood or movement
    to try or to punish him. It was said of López by Hondurans,
    "He wasn't the best President in the world, but
    he is the best any of us can remember!" By June 1975 it
    was alleged that Minister of Economics Abraham Bennaton
    had actually received the bribe.

LOPEZ DE GAMBOA, JUAN. Joint governor with Celis (q.v.) in
    1541, under the direction of Maldonado (q.v.). López de
    Gamboa, however, had solely military responsibilities.

LOPEZ DE LA FLOR, FELIPE. A corsair captain who was
    charged by Juan de la Vera (q.v.) with bringing a pirogue
    force along the northern Honduran shore. López' patrols
    were essentially unsuccessful. He attacked Belize twice in
    1748.

LOPEZ DE SALCEDO, DIEGO. One of the three who briefly
    governed Honduras in 1526. He was under the authority of
    the Audiencia of Santo Domingo.

LOPEZ GRIJALVA, JUAN see MILITARY ZONE COMMANDS,
    1972

LOPEZ GUTIERREZ, RAFAEL. General López Gutiérrez was
    elected after the Bertrand (q.v.) debacle in 1919, and for a
    term from February 1, 1920 until February 1, 1924. But
    there was much unrest, with four uprisings in 1920 alone.
    By the elections of 1923 there was so much strife that no
    candidate received a majority. Tiburcio Carias Andino obtained
    most votes, ushering in a period when he dominated
    Honduras for almost 25 years.

LOPEZ, JUAN. General López was first designate for the presidency
    between two terms of General José María Medina, from
    April 27, 1867 to November 21, 1867.

LOPEZ, ROQUE J. see BUESO, FRANCISCO

LOPEZ RODEZNO, ARTURO. Artist and founder of the Escuela
    Nacional de Bellas Artes in Tegucigalpa, López Rodezno was
    also Director of Cultural Services and Artistic Education in

the Honduran Ministry of Education. Born in Copán department, an engineering graduate of the University of Havana in Cuba, he also studied art at the Academia San Alejandro in Cuba, and in the Academie Julian in Paris, where he worked on mural painting. An exhibitor in many places, and recipient of numerous awards, López Rodezno has continued to provide leadership in art circles as well as in the Escuela de Bellas Artes, and through the Instituto Hondureño de Cultura Interamericana.

LOS DOLORES. A church in Tegucigalpa, founded in 1732 and finished in 1815; restored in 1910. The pilasters of the facade are decorated with rosettes, each studded with a ball. This is considered the most original of the special types of pilaster found in "earthquake baroque" throughout Central America. The symmetrical tower twins are unusually slender. The star windows are crowned by angel heads, and have fruit swags beneath. A blind balustrade goes across the whole facade including both towers. Much of the decoration is brilliant ceramic, including large statues.

LOS ESTADOS UNIDOS DE CENTRO AMERICA see REPUBLICA MAYOR DE CENTRO AMERICA

LOUISIANA PARTNERS see RELIEF EFFORTS, PARTNERS OF THE AMERICAS

LOUISIANA STATE LOTTERY. A lottery enterprise which was "exiled" from Louisiana in a celebrated U.S. Supreme Court decision which held that the United States mails could not be used to send or receive matter pertaining to any lottery. Mexico, Colombia, and Nicaragua each declined to accept the lottery as an enterprise, and it finally settled in Puerto Cortés, Honduras. The country was paid $20,000 per year and 20 per cent of the gross earnings of the lottery. The first drawings in Honduras were held in about 1893. A large frame mansion was built to house the lottery operation, which operated under the name of "Honduras Lottery Company." Prizes were as high as $75,000 per drawing, with a total of 3,434 prizes and 100,000 tickets per drawing. The lottery was further restricted in 1895.

LOZANO DIAZ, JULIO. During the deadlock which arose in the the elections at the end of Gálvez' (q.v.) term, the vice president at the time, Lozano Díaz, took control, from January 15, 1954 to December 6, 1954. Then, as de facto leader of the government from that date until October 21, 1956, he faced removal by a military coup and was succeeded by a military junta. This series of events initiated a return to older patterns in the Honduran government.

LUNA MEJIA, MANUEL. Writer, born in Santa Rosa de Copán in 1911, Luna Mejía studied in Guatemala and graduated from the Universidad Nacional Autónoma de Honduras. He was a deputy to the National Congress, member of the Council of State, ambassador of Honduras to El Salvador, and had other governmental responsibilities. Several works of poetry and prose affirm his literary ability.

LUTTRELL, COMMODORE JOHN. British Commander in 1779 who was involved in relieving the Baymen at Balize and in the attack on Fort Omoa in late September. See OMOA, 1779--BATTLES.

LYNCH, SIR THOMAS. Governor of Jamaica, 1681-84, who is best-known for his suspension of some-time pirate chieftain Henry Morgan from his official duties and who enforced laws against piracy, thereby stopping the depradations, many of which had been aimed at the north Coast of Honduras and the Bay Islands with the last of these efforts taking place anti-climatically post-Lynch in 1689, when some mining towns were raided.

LYTTELTON, WILLIAM HENRY. Governor in Jamaica, 1762-66, when Joseph Otway (q.v.) was planning attacks on the Spanish frontier, which crossed Honduras from west to east. He presumably gave authorization for the attack on Fort Inmaculada which came in 1762.

- M -

MAC. Thirteenth month of the Maya calendar.

MACACO. The cut money of the old Kingdom of Guatemala, replaced by the cobres or moneda provisional (q.v.) in 1839.

MACDONALD, ALEXANDER. The English superintendent at Belize, British Honduras, appointed on February 25, 1826, as regent over the Mosquito Coast by the nominal "King" of Mosquitia, Robert Charles Frederick. The king was a virtual prisoner in Belize. Macdonald was determined to constitute Belize a regular British colony, and 300 white settlers of the place declared themselves independent from Central America (then a struggling federation) on March 14, 1835. In 1830 Macdonald seized Roatán (q.v.) and again in 1841 occupied it for the British crown. Recalled in 1845 for his high-handedness with Honduras and Nicaragua, he nevertheless left a legacy in that the British Mosquito protectorate persisted 50 years, and Belize remained a crown colony until independence in 1972. The efforts on the Bay Islands were not resolved until the Wyke-Cruz (q.v.) treaty in 1859.

This remarkable British officer who was responsible for several stirring episodes in relation to the Bay Islands, and who was superintendent and virtual founder of the crown colony at Belize, was a veteran of the Napoleonic wars, having entered Spain as an ensign, and later commanded a regiment at Waterloo. Decorated by his own king with the Order of the Bath and by Russia as well, he was brother to the adjutant general of England, Sir John MacDonald, and cousin to Marshal MacDonald of France. His connections were so important that his high-handed actions were overlooked for years. He achieved crown-colony status for Belize, and nearly did so for the Bay Islands. He did manage to keep that Honduran territory in limbo for a number of years.

MACHADO, LUIS. Interim governor in 1745, followed by Colonel Juan de Vera.

MACHADO, MANUEL. This citizen of Gracias was Honduran governor in 1778.

MACHETE. The long knife (see MOSCHEATE) used for a variety of purposes throughout Central America. Similar to the short broad naval swords called "cutlasses," the machete has a flat blade around thirty inches long, usually somewhat curved on the cutting edge. The "Collins" brand of machete has been sold throughout the area for over a century, and the price has not fluctuated much--from about $1.00 to $3.00 U.S. The name derives from Spanish "macho," meaning ax, which probably comes from Mozarabic "maza" or mace. The present-day machete is the most ubiquitous tool in isthmian America, seconded only by the large hoe. It is used to mow grass, cut cane, and is a formidable weapon in the hands of irregular troops.

MACHISMO. Masculinity is much valued in Honduras and the rest of the isthmian area, especially since the male and female roles are sharply differentiated. The man represents dominance, assertiveness, drive; the female, submissiveness, devotion, dependence. Man is free, woman is homebound. Sexual prowess is a major factor in machismo. Women's liberation is antithetical to this element of the culture, yet women are not mistreated.

MACRO-CHIBCHAN. One of the three linguistic superstocks of the Caribbean area and northern South America. The others were Andean-Equatorial and Ge-Pano-Carib. The Lencas (q.v.) of Honduras were in the Macro-Chibchan grouping. Black Caribs (q.v.), transplanted to the Honduran north coast, are linguistically of the Ge-Pano-Carib family.

MACUELIZO. A town founded in 1788 by colonists from Galicia and Asturias. It is west of San Pedro Sula, in the valley of the Chamelicón. Cabacera of one of the northern municipios of Santa Bárbara Department, the town has an airport and is quite near the Guatemalan border, which at this point is the summit of the Sierra Espíritu Santo range. See GOYONECHE, MIGUEL DE.

MADRE, DIA DE LA. Mother's day was established as the second Sunday in May annually, the decree being dated January 25, 1927.

MAESTRO JUAN. A ship which was wrecked on the reefs of Honduras' Serrana Island (itself named for a wreck) in the years of earliest exploration. Survivors drank turtle blood to stave off thirst until rescued.

MAESTRO VIOLETA. Name given affectionately to Don Pedro Nufio (q.v.), longtime master of the Escuela Normal de Varones.

MAF   see   MISSIONARY AVIATION FELLOWSHIP

MAFIA. The devil in the Carib language (q.v.).

MAHOGANY. A color, of "moderate reddish brown," which derives from one of the Honduran Indian Languages. The name of the wood derives in turn from this color, and has been applied to several species, not only Honduran mahogany, but also Santo Domingan, as well as to species such as luuan, or "Philippine Mahogany," which like "African mahogany" is botanically not mahogany at all.

MAHOGANY, HONDURAS. The fine furniture woods called Honduran Mahogany are swietenia macrophylla and swietenia swietenia. They are lighter in color and weight than the old San Domingan mahogany used by such cabinet makers as Duncan Phyfe. That wood is swietenia mahogani. The Honduran wood is found throughout Central America, and is usually called "caoba" locally. It is not found in groves but in separate trees, often widely separated in otherwise dense jungle. This makes it expensive to log and to transport.

MAIA. Jicaque Indian name for the northern Honduran coastal area. "Maya" is obviously close, and probably related.

MAIAN. In 1506 Bartolomé Columbus (q.v.) wrote of the area in northern Honduras and called it "a certain province called 'Maian'." Later it transpired that the area opposite Bonacca Island (q.v.) was indeed called Maia by the Jicaque Indians. It was part of the Mayan empire of the Cocomes, which fell in 1485.

MAIZE CULTURE. The development of corn cultivation in the Middle American area seems to have begun about 8000 B.C. with the domestication occurring possibly 5000 B.C., as indicated by studies by MacNeish in the Valley of Tehuacán, in Pueblo, Mexico. It is a staple crop and diet item in Honduras as in the rest of Central America.

MAIZE GOD. This Mayan diety, Yum Kax, the God of corn, was

frequently portrayed in full sculpture, often with high quality stone portraiture presenting a handsome young man. One of the finest examples is found in the Museum in Ruinas de Copán (see illustration p. 308).

MALAZAHUATL  see  PLAGUE

MALDONADO, ALONSO DE. First sent to Central America as visitador from Mexico in 1536 to look into Pedro Alvarado's venture in Quito, Maldonado became governor, or President of the Audiencia of Guatemala, and served from 1542 to 1548. The seat of government was first in Comayagua, Honduras, then in Gracias a Dios. During this period the New Laws were announced, but Maldonado was slow to enforce them.

MALESPIN, FRANCISCO  see  EJERCITO PROTECTOR DE LA PAZ

MALINALLI. Twelfth day of the Aztec month; meaning, "grass."

MALONE, GUY. Onetime revolutionary, Colonel Malone was an associate of Lee Christmas (q.v.).

MANACA. The corozo palm, cohune palm, attalea cohune, also called cahoon. Manaca is also a term used to denote the palm-leaf thatch of the corozo palm used as roofing in rural Honduras, for as many as 95 per cent of all buildings in Gracias a Dios department. Such structures are called champas.

MANIANI. An alternate name for the plain of Espino (q.v.) along the Humuya River between Comayagua and Ojos de Agua. In Spanish colonial days there was boat transport from this point to Puerto Caballos, probably large dugout canoe types.

MANIANI, ARCHAEOLOGICAL SITE. Ruins, probably Mayan, in the Espino valley.

MANIK. Seventh day of the Maya month; meaning, "deer."

MANZANA. A land measurement equal to ten thousand square varas (one hundred varas [q.v.] on a side) or 1.72 acres. One square mile equals 372.09 manzanas. The word is also used in the sense of "city block" in giving directions and expressing ownership.

MAP OF HONDURAS  see  REYNO DE GUATEMALA, MAPA DE

MAP OF HONDURAS AND EL SALVADOR. In his 1855 volume called Notes on Central America, E. G. Squier (q.v.) published a map of Honduras and El Salvador which was in part a result of his own work, and which probably is the most complete map of the interior of Honduras up until that date.

Mapache 220

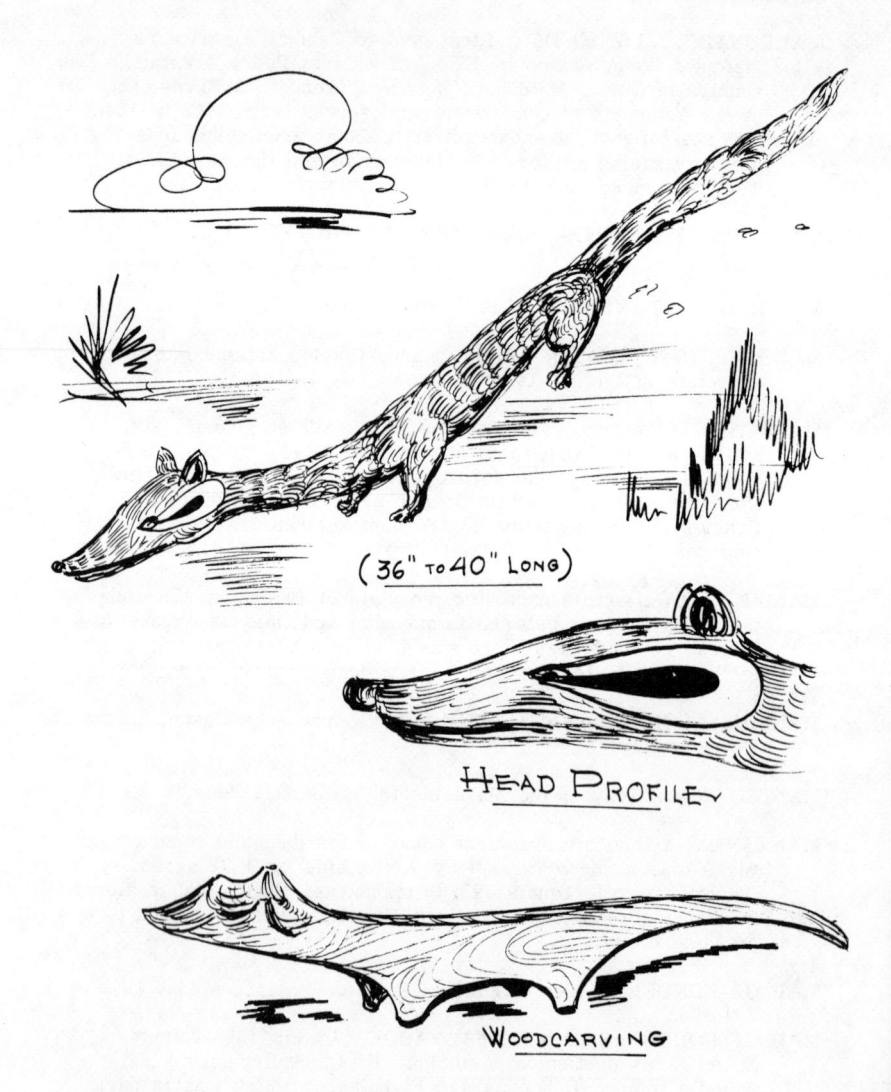

(36" to 40" Long)

HEAD PROFILE

WOODCARVING

MAPACHE: A small indigenous animal shown here in natural form as well as in carved replica.

221                     Mapache

Jeffers (q.v.) and Woodhouse (q.v.) had helped with the observations. Lithographed by Sarony and Co. in New York in 1854, the map shows detailed hachured topography in the settled western portion, and goes into such detail as listing an obscure village like Ajuyapysni (modern Ahuas), in the unknown eastern plains. Across the country he shows a proposed rail line, the Honduras Interoceanic Railway (q.v.) which was a dream project of the author's. The mines at San Antonio de Oriente (q.v.) and the ruins at Copán (q.v.) are accurately marked. Considering the general inaccessibility of the country, the map is a remarkable achievement.

MAPACHE. A small and rarely seen Central American animal, apparently related to the weasel (see illustration). The animal, 30 to 36 inches long, is divided in thirds with the narrow head and long neck making up the first third to the front legs, the slender cylindrical body the second third to the hind legs, and the tail the remainder. It has the coloring and fur of a gray squirrel, with a large tear-drop shaped white spot behind the eye and a black tear-drop shaped spot inside the white one. The animal is quick and alert. The legs are very short, so it appears low and long. The species is not illustrated in ordinary animal reference works.

MAPS, PRE-CONQUEST (Honduras and Central America). Bagrow's great work on the History of Cartography recounts that in 1520 Hernán Cortés described to his Emperor (Charles V) how Montezuma sent him "a chart of the whole coast," painted on cloth. Drawn and painted on a material woven from agave fibre, or on fig-bark paper or prepared skins, these maps were systematically destroyed with other native documents by Spanish churchmen. In 1525 envoys of Tabasco and Xicalango drew for Cortés "a figure of the whole land, whereby I calculated that I could very well go over the great part of it." This map extended almost to Panama, and guided him in his overland journey to Honduras. This is the first recorded map of the area. Its loss to archaeology is inestimable. Cortés undoubtedly used it in his epic march from Mexico to Honduras.

MAPS see PTOLEMY, HOMEN, MUNSTER, BORDONE, COSA, PIRI REIS, WALDSEEMULLER, RIBEIRO, VERREZANO, GASCOIGNE, TOTTEN, SANCHES PLANISPHERE, HAGUE MAP, MARTINEZ MAP

MARCHA DEL HAMBRE, LA, OF 1972. This "march of hunger" took place in the early days of December 1972, when the ANACH (q.v.) called through its board of directors for a march to protest Honduran economic conditions. The coup d'état of December 4 occurred on the very day when truckloads of rural people were converging on the capital, and since the coup was considered as a response to their wishes, they dispersed rather quietly.

MARIA. This wood, often called "Santa María," is a handsome striped open-grained tropical hardwood, claphyllum Baasiliense. It is used in panelling and construction.

MARINE DESERTERS. In the 1927-1934 Sandino (q.v.) War, United States Marines who deserted and crossed the Honduran border were arrested by Honduran forces and turned over to U.S. Authorities, but the prevalent arms traffic was hard to stop, due to the ruggedness of the border terrain.

MARQUIS OF ENSEÑADA see SOMODEVILLA, ZENON DE

MARTINEZ, MANLIO. Made Executive Secretary of the Superior Council of Economic Planning following the December 4, 1972 coup of López Arellano (q.v.), Martínez was particularly charged with planning for improvement of the total economic situation of the country and for moves toward reintegration in the Central American Common Market.

MARTINEZ DE LA RIVA, FRANCISCO. Governor in 1632.

MARTINEZ GALINDO, ARTURO. Born in Tegucigalpa in 1900 and assassinated in Trujillo in 1940, he was a poet and reporter in both Honduras and the United States. When editing the periodical El Ciudadano, he used two pen-names--Armando Imperio and Julio Sol.

MARTINEZ MAP, 1578. One of the astonishing matters concerning 16th and 17th century map-making was the frequency of lapses and reversions, such as that following Homen's (q.v.) definitive showing of the Gulf of California which was not equalled for over a century. The Martínez hemisphere map of 1578 is extremely rudimentary in the area of Guatemala and Honduras, even though very detailed maps were extant as long as thirty years previously.

MARTYR, PETER. In the Decades of the New World of 1511, Martyr included a map of the Caribbean which showed and named "Guanasa" (one of the Bay Islands). The map was in the general style and idiom of the Portolan charts.

MATAFALO. The strangler vine which kills tall trees and often stands alone while its victim rots and falls, due to the many buttress roots it has projected.

MATUTE-GUTIERREZ, DIONISTO. Alleged Honduran Communist who went to Moscow for orientation and training in 1961. See MEJIA, MEDARDO.

MAUDSLEY, ALFRED P. Probably the first explorer-archaeologist to make an intensive study of the ruins of Copán (q.v.). He first visited the area in 1881, and in 1885 began to carry out the investigations which resulted in a topographic map and the initial nomenclature of the ruins, monuments, and sculptures found there in abundance. Photographs, plaster casts, and drawings of the sculpture were a part of his legacy. Sir Alfred and wife Anne were at Copán in the period between 1881 and 1894 when Maudsley's fourteen years of systematic archaeological work resulted in what must be called the first substantial professionalized work in Mayan archaeology. Five volumes which resulted have been termed the "first scientific account of Central American Archaeology."

MAYA CALENDAR, DATE OF ORIGIN. While it is possible to go back 63,000,000 years and more in Maya notation, the date of beginning of the Maya calendar as recorded by carvings on Stelae at Copán is 3113 B.C.

MAYA CIVILIZATION, CENTERS. Copán (q.v.) was one of four major Maya centers in terms of importance in ancient times. The others were Tikál in Guatemala, and Uxmál and Chichén Itzá in Yucatan. In Sylvanus Morley's classification of 116 sites, he placed Copán preeminently. Such important ruins as those of Palenque, Kabáh, Sayíl, and Labná he places second or third in significance.

MAYA NUMERICAL SYSTEM. The remarkable vigesimal (to the base 20) numerical system of the Mayas seems to have been a standard for the Mexican and Central American area as early as 1500 B.C. Monte Alban in Oaxaca has evidence of the system. Numbers are usually noted vertically, with the unity level at the base. Dots represent unity, bars mean five. Hence one dot above one bar reads "six." The increasing levels above unity compare to a decimal system as follows (the simplest Maya form--there are in some of the notations discrepancies at the higher levels):

| Decimal | Maya Vigesimal |
| --- | --- |
| 1000 | 8000 (etc.) |
| 100 | 400 (20 x 20) |
| 10 | 20 |
| 1 | 1 |

The Maya used the concept of "zero" long before its adoption in the Western World. The zero sign is a shell symbol (see illustration of Maya numbers). The Maya system is vigesimal, probably because with toes and fingers each human has 20 digits! Numbers were written vertically. See COPAN, CALENDAR, etc.

MAYA ORIGINS. Possibly coming from Asia, the Mayan people were inhabiting the central highlands in Central America from at least 1000 B.C. They were agriculturists, practicing an intensive cultivation. By the first century A.D. the first great city was founded at Uaxactún, Guatemala. By the fifth

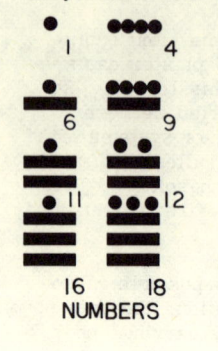

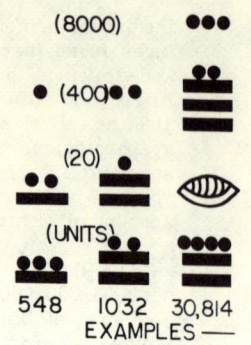

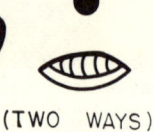

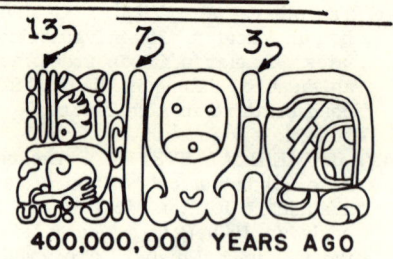

MAYA NUMERICAL SYSTEM: The vigesimal system which included the use of zero before its discovery by "western" culture.

century A. D. the significant classic period at Copán, Honduras, was in existence.

MAYANGLE, COLONIA. A suburb of Comayaguela, part of greater Tegucigalpa, including the Instituto San Francisco and the Country Club.

"MAYPOLE." In Honduras on the Mosquito coast, as throughout Mosquitia, a species of Saturnalia was held for a month (usually in early April) on the northeast coast area as late as the 1930s. The festivities were characterized by erotic dances held around certain chosen big trees, after a pattern established by pagan Britons in ancient times. The Mosquito peoples with various shades of blood mix were the chief participants, and the custom seems to have been introduced (or modified) by British logwood and mahogany cutters and traders in the 17th and 18th centuries. Vestiges of the practice persist.

MAZATL. Seventh day of the Aztec month; meaning, "deer."

MECHINO. The cross of a Coyote (Lobo) (q. v. ) with a Lobo (q. v. ). See RACIAL MIXTURES.

MEDALS. There are two national awards for military distinction: the Decoration for Merit is the highest military award and may be given to foreigners as well as Hondurans; the Heroic Valor Decoration is for exceptional heroism. Other awards are as follows: Distinguished Service Cross (meritorious service); Flying Cross; Soldier's Medal (enlisted, outstanding); Medal for Technical Merit; and Conduct Medal.

MEDIATIONS. An effort to mediate the five-year old hostility between Honduras and El Salvador failed in early 1974. General Anastasio Somoza of Nicaragua had attempted to get a summit meeting of all Central American Presidents. His visits to the two capitals concerned proved fruitless, although Somoza was the courier for various formulae, hoping to stem the arms race which the two countries had initiated. See PRESIDENTS' MEETING, CENTRAL AMERICA, 1974.

MEDICAL CARE. Hospital beds per 1000 inhabitants are 2.0 in Honduras, versus 11.2 in Canada (the hemisphere's highest), and 0.6 in the Republic of Haiti (the worst). Costa Rica is best in Central America with 5.1. Inhabitants per doctor in Honduras are 4,800, in Costa Rica 2,700, in Guatemala 6,300, in Haiti 9,800, in the U.S. 780.

MEDICAL EDUCATION. Medical training for Hondurans takes place at the National University in the capital district. There is a seven-year course in medicine, five years in dentistry and three years in pharmacy. Graduates are as few as a dozen a year. Practical nursing as well as registered nursing programs are offered in the same place.

MEDIDA. A measure of volume, for grains, of 2.872 liters. See MEDIO and FANEGA.

MEDINA, JOSE MARIA. Senator Medina served as chief executive twice during the post-Guardiola (q.v.) period, first for two days from February 5, 1862, and then from June 21, 1863 until January 1, 1864. As General, Medina then became constitutional president on February 15, 1864, and served from that day until May 15, 1865; then again from September 1, 1865 to September 28, 1865, and after that date under a new Constitution until October 2 of the same year as Provisional President. He was again Constitutional President from February 1, 1866 to April 27, 1867 and from November 21, 1867 until May of 1868. Reelected by the Constituent Assembly, he took over again on January 14, 1870 until February 2, 1871, and then once more from May 17, 1871 to July 2, 1871 following the Xatruch (q.v.) revolution. His next stint was October 1871 to April 5, 1872.
There followed another revolution and brief presidency by Céleo Arias (q.v.) and, through rebellion, another Medina (Juan Antonio) became "semi-President." José María was in again by revolutionary takeover from December 16, 1875 to January 13, 1876, and once again as "Presidente General" from August 16, 1876 to August 27, 1876 (a notably short term). At this point, after 14 years of in and out presidencies, Medina lacked the needed Guatemalan support (even though he had led a revolt against Leiva [q.v.] at Guatemalan instigation), and so, although he had defeated Leiva as planned, he resigned. His successor, Soto (q.v.), became a strong and popular president during an eight year period. The incumbencies of José María Medina tend to highlight the perennial problem of Honduran politics--coup and counter-coup.

MEDINA, JUAN ANTONIO. Another General Medina (not José María), was "semi-President" in July of 1872, during the Arias (q.v.) rebellion.

MEDINA SANTOS, GUILLERMO see RENDON, MARIO

MEDIO. A measure of volume (such as a bushel) for grains, consisting of 46 liters. It is also 16 medidas (q.v.). See FANEGA.

MEJIA, MARCELINO. General Mejía served as President for one week in June 1876. He then served again as part of a Council of Ministers who took charge in August 1876 for five days from the 12th to the 16th, cojointly with Colindres (q.v.).

MEJIA, MEDARDO. Widely published Honduran author, born in Manto, Olancho, in 1907. Founder of the magazine Ariel in 1964, in Tegucigalpa, devoted to humanistic studies. His book Cuentos de camino won the prize in the 1930 scientificliterary competition of the Ministry of Public Instruction. He wrote biography, drama, and history, as well as poetry. Among many publications are his History of Honduras (Vol. II, 1970) and the drama Cinchonero. Mejía was also known as a Communist activist in Guatemala during the Jacopo Arbenz regime. In the late 1950s he served as Professor of Social Sciences in the University of Honduras. In 1961 he went to Moscow for orientation and training.

MEJIA COLINDRES, VICENTE. Dr. Mejía Colindres served as Constitutional President February 1, 1929 to February 1, 1933. His election was a surprise, as in the prevailing National Party atmosphere under Carias it would be expected that their candidate would win, but the United Liberal Party candidate, Mejía, was the winner, and after a pact of conciliation between him and Carias, Mejía remained through his term. It was in this period that there were border incidents on the Nicaraguan frontier, since it was the period of the Sandino (q.v.) War and the heavy involvement of the United States marines in that prototype action.

MEJIA NIETO, ARTURO. One of Honduras' important writers, as novelist and critic. Born in 1900.

MELGAR CASTRO, JUAN ALBERTO. Colonel Melgar became Chief of State of Honduras following a bloodless coup ("golpe de estado") at the end of April 1975. Oswaldo Lopez Arellano (q.v.) was ousted in the action which was not unlike the one by which he last took power in December 4, 1972. López was overthrown finally by a group of young military officers, reported to have left wing leanings, who had caused him under pressure to resign in March 1975 from his military position as Commander in Chief of Honduran armed forces. Melgar had taken López' place in that post. Colonel Melgar became Ministro de Gobernación y Justicia in the cabinet of General López Arellano (q.v.) following the coup of December 4, 1972. Colonel Melgar in 1974 was the leader of the extreme right wing of the military government then in power, and had been mentioned (in the fashion of such rumors) as the leader of a possible coup against Oswaldo López Arellano, the president.

Melgar had been Minister of Interior and following the March change in command, as head of the military forces, gained the prestige and power often accruing to that job. He is considered to be more conservative than the twenty-five young officers of the Supreme Council of the Armed Forces who were instrumental in giving him the presidency or chieftaincy of state outside the constitutional process. López had achieved the same position in the same manner.

Programs which are expected from the change are: some measure of nationalization of industry; land reform; and ultimately, a return to civilian government. In 1972 López had promised military rule for at least five years. It was generally conceded that now the Armed Forces group would rule the country, rather than Melgar as an individual.

In June 1975, the two Honduran political parties issued a joint statement calling for a take-over of the Tela Railroad Co. (q.v.), a subsidiary of United Brands, which is reputed to have holdings valued at $100,000,000 in Honduras. The party statement called for unused banana lands to be given to landless Honduran peasant workers. A similar move had been made by the López government when timberlands and timber exports were taken over by the government in March 1974. Moves like these are to be expected under the Melgar regime.

MEMBREÑO, ALBERTO. Dr. Membreño served as First Designate and held the executive power from July 28, 1915 to February 1, 1916, when Bertrand (q.v.) became Constitutional President.

MEN. The fifteenth day of the Maya month; meaning, "bird of the sun."

MENCOS, MARTIN CARLOS DE. Following the division and dissension under Altamirano and Velasco, Mencos was a very popular governor from 1659 to 1668, and was instrumental in improving Caribbean coastal defenses, especially the Honduran gulf port of Río Dulce and its fort San Felipe. He was, however, involved in illegal commerce, which was true of most Spanish colonial officials in this period (see SMUGGLING). During his incumbency, Mencos was the first of a new breed of military officers, rather than lawyers, who would be captains-general of Guatemala. He was formerly General of the Armada. It was he also who had built Fort Inmaculada on the frontier in Nicaragua.

MENDOZA, ESTEBAN. Foreign Minister under the Junta Regime of Roque Rodríguez, Héctor Carraccioli, and Roberto Gálvez (q.v. all), who resigned in 1957, causing a governmental flurry.

MERCEDARIANS. This great monastic order became a major landholder near La Choluteca in 1607, with a grant of 16 caballerías (about 600 acres).

MERCEDES DE ORIENTE. Very near the border with El Salvador, this municipal cabacera is in the tumbled terrain along the Guayiniquil River, in La Paz Department.

MERCHANT MARINE REGISTRATION. The registry of merchant vessels, particularly large oil tankers owned by the maritime nations, has in recent years been transferred to Honduran, Panamanian, or Liberian registers in order to evade high union wages and guarantees for both seamen and longshoremen.

Most of such vessels never come near to the Honduran coasts or to the other "flag of convenience" nations. This practice has contributed very significantly to the decline of the merchant marine of the United States of America.

MERCURY AMALGAMATION. A real advance in silver extraction which developed in the late sixteenth century was the mercury amalgamation process of extracting silver concentrates. The provision of mercury for this so-called "patio-process" was a royal monopoly, the mercury coming either from Almadén in Spain or Huancavélica in Peru. The royal mercury was, however, too expensive for some miners. Cast-iron mercury bottles in great numbers still exist in the old Fort Omoa on the north coast of Honduras. (See illustration, p. 143.)

MERCURY FLEET. The ships carrying mercury to Honduras (and other points in New Spain) for the reduction of silver ore to bullion in the 17th century.

MERREN, NELSON E. Born in La Ceiba in 1931, and graduate of the University of El Salvador as a Doctor of Odontology, he practiced in La Ceiba. In 1963 his first poems were published in the Honduras Literaria, and in 1969 he won the Juan Ramón Molina poetry prize. He has published poetry and other work, his Calendario negro appearing in 1970.

MESO-AMERICA. A geographical area between the continents of North and South America encompassing central and southern Mexico, the peninsula of Yucatán, Belize or British Honduras, Honduras, El Salvador, and Nicaragua. Costa Rica and Panama might also be considered as part of the area. The sub-regions are the Valley of Mexico, the area of Oaxaca, the Gulf Coast Huastec region, the southern part of the Gulf Coast, western Mexico, the Mayan highlands, the southern and western lowlands, the Guatamalan Pacific Coast and Chiapas, the flat northern area of Yucatán, the Honduran and Nicaraguan highlands, etc.

MESTIZO. Also Ladino. A cross between a Spanish male and an Indian female; meaning, "mixed." See RACIAL MIXTURES.

METALLURGY, PRE-CONQUEST. There is much evidence of inter-regional trade in metal work, principally jewelry, in the area of Honduras, Nicaragua, El Salvador, Panama, and Costa Rica around A.D. 600-800. Work was also done in semi-precious stones, such as jade.

METATE. The word, found in several variants, derives from Nahua sources and denotes a milling stone, with a concave surface, usually three legs, and a double-tapered stone roller. Such mills are sold in Honduran markets to this day, although of simpler and cruder form than the works of art frequently found in ancient times and now preserved in museums. Often in Nahua form, metatl.

METRIC SYSTEM. The metric system of measurement is official in Honduras, by law of February 22, 1897. However, there are some units in use which stem from ancient Spanish or other sources; the legua, medida, medio, fanega, manzana, caballería, arroba, adarme and quintal, as well as the familiar English ounce, pound, gallon, inch and foot. Any of these measures may be found somewhere in the country.

MEXICAN TRIP, SANDINO. In 1929 the irrepressible guerrilla chieftain, César Agusto Sandino, (q. v.) made a journey to Mexico to see the Mexican President, Portes Gil. He expected to receive substantial military aid after three years of guerrilla warfare, in order to return and continue. Dwight Morrow, U. S. ambassador to Mexico, agreed with Gil to grant political asylum to Sandino, and arranged for his passage across Honduras, El Salvador, and Guatemala. Sandino was escorted across Honduras by Honduran troops and, as stated by the U. S. military attache to Honduras, during the transit was treated "strictly as a criminal." Later, several of Sandino's chief lieutenants were interned in Honduras. See REMANZO; ESTRADA, FRANCISCO; IRIAS, PEDRO.

MEXIQUE BAY. Term applied to the Gulf of Mexico by some of the early 16th century explorers.

MEXIQUE SEA. Term applied on some old maps to the western Caribbean area along northern Honduran shores, east of Yucatán and west of Jamaica.

MEZA CALIX, SANTIAGO. General who was elected Provisional President of Congress by the Honduran Liberal Party on December 1, 1954, in anticipation of a victory for Liberals. See also AGUIRRE, SALVADOR.

MIDDLE AMERICA see MESO-AMERICA

MIEL DE PALO. Honey from a small stingless bee, it tends to be dark and strong. It is sometimes used to sweeten Coyol wine. See VINO DE COYOL.

MILIA BERMUDEZ, FRANCISCO. Liberal party chairman in 1956 when exiled to Guatemala on July 9 by President Lozano, along with Flores (q. v.) and Villeda (q. v.).

MILITARY AID AGREEMENTS. Bilateral military assistance agreements between the U. S. and Latin American countries all have somewhat similar characteristics. The one of May 20, 1954, between the U. S. and Honduras, provides that military equipment is to be returned to the assisting government (that is, the United States) if no longer used. The U. S.

parts and replacements must be purchased continually to keep the arms "in use." In exchange, the Government of Honduras is to "cooperate with the Government of the United States of America in measures designed to control trade with nations which threaten the security of the Western hemisphere." The U.S. is also to have access on demand to raw materials available in Honduran territory. U.S. operations will be tax-free in Honduras. The agreements have been interpreted as largely for profit-motive on the part of the U.S.

MILITARY ASSISTANCE AND MILITARISM. Some observers such as Edwin Lieuwen and U.S. Senators Morse and Fulbright have seen a causal relationship between such assistance and Latin American militarism in particular. Other observers see such assistance as a part of the modernization process in developing countries--among them are Kalman Silvert, Theodore Wyckoff, and Charles Wolf. The issue is by no means a passive one. See RESPONSE TO "GOLPES."

MILITARY AVIATION SCHOOL. Located adjacent to Toncontín Airport in Tegucigalpa this school provides training for Air Force cadets, technicians, and pilots, sometimes supplemented by training in the United States.

MILITARY COMMAND STRUCTURE. Nominally the President of Honduras is at the apex of the military command pyramid. He may declare war and make peace if Congress is not in session, but must call a special session in either event, and Congress in session has exclusive jurisdiction in defense matters. The President with prior congressional authorization can send Honduran troops into foreign countries, and Congress can admit foreign troops to Honduras.
The superior Council of National Defense has an advisory function and is composed of the President, the Secretary of Defense, the armed forces commander and his chief of staff, and the top military commanders. When the armed forces' top position is vacant, the council chooses a replacement from native-born senior officers; Congress appoints, for a six-year term. The armed forces chief handles all military assignments, such as zone and unit commanders (see MILITARY ZONES). He is assisted by a General Staff.
There are special units such as the First Engineer Battalion and the Presidential Honor Guard. The latter has a special significance. Defense spending is down from 25 per cent in 1940 to about ten per cent currently.

MILITARY ORGANIZATION. There is a cabinet post, Secretary of Defense, a Department of Defense, and a Superior Council of National Defense. The Secretary of Defense is a member of the cabinet or Council of Ministers, and the Department handles administrative and logistical concerns of the armed forces. The secretary does not exercise a command function. Armed force military commanders can deal directly with the

President.  See MILITARY COMMAND STRUCTURE; CUERPO ESPECIAL DE SEGURIDAD and ARMED FORCES, REGULAR.

MILITARY RULE, HONDURAS--1972 AND FOLLOWING.  When General de Brigada Oswaldo López Arellana took over the Honduran government on December 4, 1972, the pattern of military government throughout the American hemisphere was as follows:

| | |
|---|---|
| Argentina | General Alejandro Lanusse |
| Cuba | Commandante Fidel Castro |
| Brazil | General Emilio Garrastazu Médici |
| Ecuador | General Antonio Rodríguez Lara |
| El Salvador | Colonel Fidel Sánchez |
| Guatemala | Colonel Carlos Arana Osorio |
| Honduras | General de Brigada Oswaldo López Arellano |
| Nicaragua | General Anastasio Somoza DeBayle |
| Panama | General Omar Torrijos |
| Paraguay | General Alfredo Stroessner |
| Peru | General Juan Velasco Alvarado |

Since that time Chile has been added to the ranks of military rule, ex-Colonel Perón has returned in Argentina (only to be succeeded by his widow), etc.  More than half the nations of the Western hemisphere remain under military regimes.

MILITARY SCHOOL, FRANCISCO MORAZAN.  The "West Point" of Honduras, this school began to train enlisted men for promotion in 1952, and in 1957 began to accept military cadets direct from civilian life.  A preponderance of Honduran junior officers are now graduates of the school.

The United States Military Mission to Honduras conducted the only military training course available in Honduras just after World War II.  The opening of the Morazán school tended to take over this function, but the mission has had a considerable part in providing commissioned officer training, both at the capital and in the Canal Zone, at the School of the Americas (q.v.).

Admission to the Morazán school maintains a high standard, taking as few as six per cent of applicants.  Curriculum includes both secondary subjects and military courses.  All room, board, tuition, uniforms, etc. are free.  The course is five years, leading to a diploma and a commission as sub-lieutenant.  Graduation is followed by a scholarship for one year of study abroad.

MILITARY SERVICE.  Military service is compulsory for all by the 1965 constitution.  Conscription, however, is rare, as in peacetime the armed forces are a volunteer service.  Male citizens from 18 to 32 years of age are subject to peacetime military service up to 18 months, and in wartime all citizens are subject to being called.

About 1970 there were 4,500 in the regular armed force, 3,000 in the Special Security Corps, and a reserve of all able-bodied men from 18 to 55. Training is handled by Honduran officers, but the United States Army's School of the Americas in the Panama Canal Zone still provides extensive training for both enlisted men and officers. Officers are trained in the Francisco Morazán Military School (q.v.).

MILITARY ZONE COMMANDS, 1972. Following the coup d'état of December 4, 1972, since it represented a takeover by military authorities, the command of the nine military zones (q.v.) was of special import. The Commanders were by zones:
1. Central District--Infantry Colonel Policardo Paz García
2. Comayagua--Infantry Major Isidro Tapia Martínez
3. First Zone--Commander, Fermín Ramírez Landa
4. Second Zone--Infantry Colonel Miguel Angel García Gutiérrez
5. Third Zone--Infantry Lieutenant Colonel Abraham García Turcios
6. Fourth Zone--Lieutenant Colonel J. Jorge Solórzano Moncada
7. Fifth Zone--Infantry Captain Alonzo Tercero Bertrand
8. Sixth Zone--Infantry Captain Juan López Grijalva
9. Seventh Zone--Infantry Colonel Ernesto A. Zepeda Rodríguez.

These appointments were set out by a decree of December 4, 1972 and were disseminated by the Department of Public relations of the Armed Forces in the interests of "security and tranquility of the Honduran family."

MILITARY ZONES (prior to 1970 Geographical Divisions). There were six military zones or divisions of Honduras, as follows (by departments):
First Zone: Francisco Morazán, Choluteca, Valle, and El Paraiso
Second Zone: Cortés, Yoro, Colón, Atlántida, Bay Islands
Third Zone: Copán, Ocotepeque, Lempira, and Santa Bárbara
Fourth Zone: Comayagua, La Paz, Intibuca
Fifth Zone: Olancho
Sixth Zone: Gracias a Dios.

MILUT, JUAN TOMAS. Governor of Honduras in 1688, he was involved in what seems to be a plot. Two ships of the Spanish flotilla that year entered harbor at Trujillo loaded with oil, wine, etc. The governor allowed only a little to be unloaded, on the pretext of poverty of his people. He took the ships to Vera Cruz and sold the cargo on the higher market there. Two Dutchmen aboard seem to have been involved.

MILWAUKEE, U.S.S. This naval vessel of the United States was the site of a meeting in 1923 when Carias (q.v.) forces and others were fighting in a disputed election. The U.S. arbitration effort resulted in the installation of a provisional president, Tosta (q.v.), and elections were held soon after. The Pact of Amapala was the pertinent agreement. It was the beginning of the quarter century-long "Carias Era."

MINA MORAMULCA. A newly developed gold and silver mine in the northwestern borderland of Choluteca Department.

MINAS DE ORO. The name, "gold mines," indicates early industry in this municipal cabacera in northwestern Comayagua Department. There is an airfield. There are also Maya ruins in the nearby area. The terrain is very rugged.

MINERALS. Commercially produced minerals are zinc, lead, gold, silver, iron, cadmium, and antimony. In 1970 the Department of Mineral Resources was undertaking mineral surveys of a 4000-square-mile area of northwestern Honduras. In 1970, 1,500 persons were employed in mining. Sixty-five per cent of mining production is in the minerals above, with the other 35 per cent in non-minerals such as sand and building stones. Only traces of petroleum have been discovered.

MINIFUNDIO. At the opposite end of the scale from latifundio (q.v.), this word represents very small land holdings, generally under five acres. It is a basis for subsistence farming at a very low productive level, and is still the basis of the agrarian society persisting in much of Latin America, including Honduras.

MINING, HONDURAN COLONIAL. Due to a series of economic circumstances coupled to geographic remoteness, the Honduran mining enterprise in colonial days became subject to much fraud and was semi-autonomous. The 17th century depression helped to stimulate this result. Among the frauds were not only "claim-jumping" by officials, but circumvention of the use of mercury in the so-called "patio process" (q.v.). Gold and silver were not declared for taxes. In Tegucigalpa crude silver was often used as currency to buy food and such necessities. Many mines were dangerous due to flooding. Labor shortage was a major problem at Corpus (q.v.) and other Tegucigalpa-area mines. Brawling, riotous miners were a continual problem of government. The center of Honduran economic life tended to move from the Caribbean littoral into the mountainous central area because of the silver strikes. Mining also encouraged stock raising for food supplies. Lead mines were opened to provide smelting reagents. Salt was evaporated out on the Fonseca shores.

MINISTERIOS. The various cabinet ministries, by the 1965 constitution twelve in number, which comprise the executive departments of the government. See CABINET.

MINISTRY OF NAVY AND INDIES. This combined entity of the Spanish Government took over for a time the administration of the vast American colonial holdings (such as Honduras) in 1714, rather late in the era of the colonies. In one more century came the independence of most of the colonial holdings. To combine the direction of the far-flung empire overseas with naval affairs was more logical than at first appears, because of the great distances involved and the dependence upon maritime shipping, convoys, naval defense, and in the general sense, the naval nature of the administration and defense of the whole Caribbean area, the heart of the empire.
    This ministry was appointed in Spain in 1714 to take over the affairs formerly handled by the Consejo de las Indias, with that council subordinate to the ministry. By 1790 the council was purely advisory and the ministry was in charge. It is significant that the problems of the 18th century were considered predominantly military.

MINOR TAXES. Very unimportant as to total government revenue are taxes on telegrams, merchant marine registration, sawmills, incorporation of new companies, on insurance policies, and on aircraft passengers. Public "spectacles" are taxed, unless they are benefit performances.

MIQUIZTLI. Sixth day of the Aztec month; meaning, "death."

MIRANDA, JUAN DE. Governor of Honduras during 1619 and following.

MISKITO (Language). Spoken all along the northeast Honduran coast and in the Río Coco Valley and up several of the eastern jungle rivers such as the Patuca and the Tinto, this Indian-derived tongue has a sound all its own--a whining singsong.
    "Nakh-sahn" (a greeting)
    "Mairen Kampura" (a beautiful woman)
    "Ay-sa-veh" (good-bye)
Signs on the east coast are often in three languages, such as in this example
    --In Case of Fire
    --En Caso de Incendio
    --Pauta Ambia Kaka (Miskito)
Origins probably are with Quiribies and Sumus (q.v.). The early tongue may even have come north from the South American mainland, and as such would be of Chibcha origins. The Miskito tongue has suffered corruption over the centuries but it still has an unusual sound. A few examples follow:
    "Close your mouth"    Bilam praka
    "Give me a knife"    Kishura kum alik

"Take care of him"           Witin ramaind kaiks
"Did a snake bite you?"      Piuta mai Saman
"I lost all my money"        Lalaki sut tikri
"Divide it in half"          Bakriki kat baiks
"My stomach hurts"           Biara klauhisa
"Where's my gun?"            Roksi anira sa?
"Banana"                     Siksa
"Mean man"                   Waina saura

MISSIONARY AVIATION FELLOWSHIP. A Protestant missionary air service for remote posts. There is a plane stationed at Ahuas. Rescue and medical missions are performed, and transportation to remote sites for mission workers is provided. In 1970 missionary aviation pilot John Watson flew 1,888 flights totalling 594 hours and covering 70,285 miles. The plane used is a Cessna 180. Half the flights are ambulance calls, which terminate at the Clínica Morava near where the plane is based; 3365 passengers were transported in 1970, and 104,395 pounds of cargo.

Ian Hollingsworth is another MAF pilot doing duty in Honduras, as is Steven Marx, son of a mission doctor and nurse, and recent volunteer in the program.

MOBILITY, SOCIAL. Generally difficult though not impossible. There is little mobility from laboring or farm worker classes to the middle class. It is, however, possible, and depends on educational opportunities. The leap from middle to upper classes has the same dependency but is even harder. Usually marriage is an entrée, but the decision is made by the elite. Land possession is still an important criterion for social position--hence "family."

MOCAL, RIO. A tributary of the Río Lempa in southern Lempira department.

MOCLONES see PERULERO

MOCORON. A village and airstrip in Gracias a Dios department at the junction of the small rivers Mocorón and Dursana.

MOCOTON. Mountain on the Honduras-Nicaragua border eleven miles northeast of Ocotal. According to best survey information, the mountain is 6,913 feet in altitude.

MODERNISMO. A literary movement which received principal impetus at the beginning of the twentieth century. The leader was a Central American, the poet-diplomat Rubén Darío of Nicaragua, and his influence was felt throughout the Spanish-speaking literary world. The movement from a technical standpoint sponsored free verse, internal sub-rhythms, and individualism; subjectivity, and a free creativity were evident both on banners and in the results. The modernism movement was an overdue rebellion against the academic literary

standards of the day, against conformity and a pervasive naturalism. It was paralleled ultimately in the realm of the plastic arts.
Perhaps the first leader of the modernists in Honduras (see POETRY) was Juan Ramón Molina (q.v.), and a contemporary of Molina's was the poet-politician Froylán Turcios (q.v.). The Honduran writer has always been enamored of legend, folklore, and the exuberant natural beauties of his homeland.

MOE. Eighth month of the Maya Calendar.

MOLENDEROS. The "mills" used with metates (q.v.) (metlates or metatls) to prepare the corn for tortillas, with channels for the escape of the water used in preparation. Archeological pieces of this nature, often found, are elaborately and beautifully carved, even though made of hard and rather coarse stone.

MONASTERIO, JUAN DE. Commander of the Honduras fleet from Spain in the year 1607, who managed to drive off the Dutch corsairs who attacked him. This was about the worst period of the corsair depredations.

MONEDA PROVISIONAL DEL ESTADO DE HONDURAS. Honduran money during the first years of independence, consisting of copper coins slightly alloyed with silver, in quarter and half pesos. The ratio to silver in value of these "cobres" was 12 to 1. See COINAGE, PROVISIONAL, 1823-62.

MONROE DOCTRINE. Honored almost as much in the breach as in the observance, and subject to errors in both citation and interpretation, this "doctrine" was a part of U.S. President Monroe's message to Congress on December 2, 1823. Threats of the Holy Alliance to reconquer rebellious Spanish colonies, as well as North American incursions by Russia and a general distrust of Great Britain, were among the causes for the pronouncement. The crux was that European intervention in either of the continents could not be viewed "in any other light than as the manifestation of an unfriendly disposition toward the United States." The doctrine also disavowed intention to interfere in European wars and excursions, so in that sense was reciprocal. Though it was aimed at Europe, the mistaken notion has frequently been rife in Latin America that the Doctrine was a blueprint for hemispheric intervention. Several "corollaries" have been added.

MONSEÑOR FIALLOS, COLONIA. A suburb of Comayaguela, part of greater Tegucigalpa.

MONTAÑA PUNTA DE PIEDRA. A huge mountain complex, over 4,000 feet in altitude, northeast of Dulce Numbre de Culmí (q.v.) and on the border between Olancho and Colón departments.

MONTAÑAS. These mountain ranges may also be cited individually elsewhere: San Juanillo, Guajiquiro, Opatoro, Pacaya, Similatón, Yarula, Cacauterique, El Trige, Curarén, Azacualpa, Cinegua, Santa Elena, Las Mores, La Flor, Moropocay, Valle de Angeles, Santa Cruz de Cacaloteca, Danlí, San Marcos, San Martín. Other ranges are cited as Cordilleras (q.v.), and there are yet other minor ones in this extremely mountainous land. "Montes" is a term also used.

MONTAÑAS DE CELAQUE. These mountains rise to over 9,000 feet in altitude in the northwestern part of Lempira department, south of Santa Rosa de Copán and just west of Gracias. They are among the highest in Honduras, where none top 10,000 feet.

MONTAÑAS DEL MALACATE. A continuation of the Sierra de Agalta (q.v.) mountain range, between those heights and the Sierra Río Tinto (q.v.).

MONTAÑAS DEL TIBURON. These "shark mountains" back up the Bahía de Tela on the north coast halfway between Puerto Cortés (q.v.) and La Ceiba (q.v.). They rise to lesser heights (2,000 feet) than many of the other coastal ranges, and are a spur of the Cordillera Nombre de Dios (q.v.) in Atlántida department.

MONTAÑERO. A woodsman, skilled in the high forest, the "montaña."

MONTE. In Honduras, the uncultivated land assigned to each Indian village. Here could be gathered roots and grubs for food, and hunting produced deer, turkeys, other birds and jaguars, for meat and decorative skins and feathers. Timber and fibers for construction were also a product of the monte. It was culturally significant as nearby hill-tops were often places of worship (like the Canaanite "hill-shrines" in the Old Testament). The word also means "mountain."

MONTE, FRANCISCO. Captain of the La Caridad, a vessel of the Honduras fleet, when she sank in 1616 near Sanlúcar, Spain.

MONTEJO, FRANCISCO. Governor of Honduras in 1536, under Maldonado (q.v.) and Ortiz (q.v.). On April 9, 1544, Montejo was called to the governorship by the Honduran colonists. Juan de Chávez, however, was named for the post by the captain general of Guatemala.

MONTERO. A mahogany hunter, often a Carib. In the past century the hunter marked trees which would square out at no less than 18 inches.

MONTES, FRANCISCO. First and fourth of six interim terms of chiefs of state following Guardiola, Senator Montes held office from January 11, 1862 to February 5, 1862, and again from December 4, 1862 to June 21, 1863. He was a conservative. During the decade the presidency changed hands more than a score of times.

MONTFORT, ANTONIO DE. Governor of Honduras, 1702.

MONTHS, MAYA CALENDAR. In western Honduras, the influence of the great ceremonial center of Copán and other Maya imprints upon the culture assures that there is even today a considerable body of Maya lore pertinent to the area. The months of the Maya calendar are as follows:

| | | | | | | | |
|---|---|---|---|---|---|---|---|
| 1. | Pop | 6. | Xul | 11. | Zac | 16. | Pax |
| 2. | Uo | 7. | Yaxkin | 12. | Ceh | 17. | Kayab |
| 3. | Zip | 8. | Mol | 13. | Mac | 18. | Cumhu |
| 4. | Zotz | 9. | Chen | 14. | Kankin | 19. | Uayeb |
| 5. | Tzec | 10. | Yax | 15. | Muan | | |

The determination of months was also related to religious meanings, as each month had its particular deity. For example, in the "year 13 kan," the month Pop had the Jaguar as the "deity of the month," with an appropriate hieroglyph. It must be remembered that the Maya number system is vigesimal (to the base 20). While the year had 18 months of 20 days each, the closing month, Uayeb, had only five days.

MONTURA. A saddle which, in contrast to the more prevalent albarda, resembles the "Western saddle" of the United States except that there is no prominent saddle horn, as the use of the lariat (la reata) is generally by "tail-dally," meaning it is tied to the horse's tail. Horses are trained to set their feet in relation to the strain on the tail-dallied lariat rather than to pull back as with the saddle-horn-dallied lariat. The origin of such a saddle was in the "war-saddle" of the Spanish conquistadors, and it has been modified in one form or another throughout the Americas. See ALBARDA.

MORAN, JUAN. Alcalde mayor, Honduras, 1562. See ALONZO ARTEZ DE ELGUETA.

MORAT ISLAND. One of the smallest Bay Islands, less than a mile in diameter, Morat lies at the northwest tip of Roatán Island.

MORATTE. Alternate spelling used in 1800 for present-day Isla Morat.

MORAVIAN MISSIONS. The Moravian Mission work in Honduras is relatively new (dating from 1930), compared to the more than a century of activity by this church (known also as the

"Unitas Fratrum") in Nicaragua. There are a number of mission churches along the Río Coco Valley, and the other endeavors are in La Mosquitia, with churches at Brus Laguna, Ahuas, Paptalaya, Kauquira, and in other places. Significant are the efforts in agricultural assistance at Brus, and the clinic and medical services at Ahuas.

MORAZAN. Motor vessel of the Compania Naviera Aguila, S. A. (q. v.).

MORAZAN, FRANCISCO. The great Central American hero and leader of the nineteenth century was a native Honduran, born in Tegucigalpa, October 3, 1792, to Don Eusebio Morazán and Doña Guadelupe Quezada de Morazán. His childhood and youth was that of an upper class colonial, guided by fond parents, and he developed as a handsome lad soon to be irresistible to the girls of his acquaintance. He was favored with physical beauty, an excellent mind, and a superior character. He learned rapidly under tutelage, was attracted to the arts and sciences, and developed the self-discipline to which his later leadership attested. The young Morazán entered business with his father and early showed concern with judicial and administrative posts, where he gained experience so essential to his later life. While not a student of any military academy, nor a soldier attached to any fort or barracks, he had an innate ability, such as that of Xenophon, Wellington, or Robert E. Lee, to handle the exigencies of military tactics within the larger framework of a strategic concept. As with so many leaders of his region, his talents were of a blended politico-military nature. At the age of 29 he entered public life when the Captain-general of the Kingdom of Guatemala was Gabino Gainza, and when a manifesto declared Guatemala (hence the Honduran Province also) separate from Mother Spain and attached to newly independent Mexico. Morazán took the rank of Lieutenant in the defense of Tegucigalpa during the conflict which arose. When Dionisio de Herrera was Chief of State, Francisco Morazán was named Secretary-general. From April 7 to May 9, 1827 the defense of Comayagua, old colonial capital, was the young officer's concern, and then on November 11, 1827 the battle of La Trinidad was a triumph against forces under Colonel Justo Milla. In 1828 Morazán marched to El Salvador, where a Guatemalan siege was in progress, and when the Guatemalans under Lieutenant Colonel Mariano Aycinena capitulated on October 9, 1828, Morazán humanely allowed the soldiers of the opposing army to return home.

Morazán returned to Honduras as Chief of State, and with the object of pacification, organized the "Allied Army for Protection of the Law" and marched to Guatemala, which he entered on April 13, 1829. In elections which followed he became President of the Central American Federation. As the American and French revolutions greatly influenced events in Central and South America, Morazán was sometimes called the "George Washington of Central America." As President, he attempted to make democratic principles effective in Central America and to establish education in the form of public instruction, the Academy of Studies, the University of San Carlos, and Colleges of Law and Medicine. He promoted industry, organized the diplomatic service, developed commerce and immigration, and genrally provided and projected an enlightened leadership in the highest democratic traditions, based upon regard for law.

Morazán was faced with almost continual conflict, however, either in the form of invasion from neighboring countries, or subversion and insurrection from within. There was armed action in El Salvador against Chiefs of State José María Cornejo and Joaquín San Martín, between 1832 and 1834. A new election gave Morazán a second term as Federal President, after losing to José Cecilio del Valle, who died March 2, 1834; the resultant election in June confirmed Morazán in the Presidency. He entered office again February 14, 1835. Morazán now faced growing problems, dissent and disorder. There was argument about the location of a Federal District, and in 1833 the capital was moved to San Salvador. Some of the nobility and the clerics favored the rebellions fomented by Anastasio Aquino and Rafael Carrera. The economy was in turmoil; the native "criollos" and the mestizos were in process of taking control from the "peninsulares" who were dominant during colonial days. A cholera epidemic tended to create a focal point for further opposition. In Guatemala, the Carrera rebellion led to a proposal that Morazán be made a dictator, which he angrily rejected. A second, third, and fourth such offer followed, and upon his continued rejection of the proposals, the clergy and nobility of Guatemala, convinced that only the trappings of monarchy or dictatorship could control the situation, threw their support to the rebel Carrera. Assassinations and further unrest followed. Morazán's term, begun in 1835, ended on May 30, 1838 by decree of the Federal Congress, and on January 18, 1839 the governments of Honduras and Nicaragua allied against El Salvador, as the final act in the breakup of the 18-year-old federation. Morazán, wounded at the battle of Espíritu Santo, was proposed by the legislative Congress of El Salvador as their President, Chief of State. Soon after, General Francisco Ferrera of Honduras invaded El Salvador and at the battle of San Pedro Perulapán (q.v.), Morazán with 500 Salvadorians attacked Ferrera at the head of 2,000 troops, winning the fight and wounding General Ferrera. Morazán then invaded Guatemala in March of 1840 with 1,400 soldiers, and occupied Guatemala City on March 18, 1840. Carrera counterattacked, and Morazán was driven back to El Salvador. Hoping to stop the bloodshed, the popular but defeated Morazán decided to leave Central America, and went to Peru, where the President, Marshal Gamarra, offered him the Ministry of War or the command of 5,000 troops to march against Chile. Morazán declined both offers, for his heart was in his homeland, torn now more than ever by conflict and division. He returned to Central America on a call from the Supreme Director of Nicaragua, seeking help for a threat to sovereignty of that state. On February 12, 1842, he arrived in the Gulf of Fonseca at the Salvadoran port La Unión, and a bit later organized troops on the beaches of Costa Rica, where he was found in April. When Central American invading troops arrived, the Chief of State of Costa Rica, Braulio Carillo, sent General Vicente Villaseñor with 2,000 men. At El Jocote the opponents met April 11, 1840, and concluded a peace treaty which led eventually to Morazán's entry into the capital. He then became Chief of State of Costa Rica on July 10, 1842, and was known as the "Liberator of Costa Rica." His troops were known as the "División Libertadora." But the Assembly sought to require Morazán to repel troops from Nicaragua who were trying to recover the northern Costa Rican territory of Guanacaste. Meanwhile, Morazán was attempting to organize the public life of Costa Rica for progress. The presidents of the other four Central American countries cut relations with Costa Rica. The Costa Rican Assembly then authorized an army, not only to retake Guanacaste but to initiate a crusade toward ultimate union in all Central America. A complex series of events led to real civil war. A Portuguese, José Antonio Pinto, emerged as a bitter enemy of Morazán. Pinto's rebels attacked the Morazán "Guardia" or stronghold on September 12, 1842, with the result that the government house was abandoned. Morazán was offered his life, but would not accept it without gaining the lives of his "little army" as well. After 88 hours of fighting, the end finally came. Going to Cartago, Morazán went to the house of his friend Pedro Mayorga, and was there taken prisoner on September 14, 1842 with two of his generals. Morazán was sent to San José. Before a firing squad, the condemned hero Morazán was given permission to command his own execution, which he did. As he said, "Ahora, bien ... Fuego!" the loud discharge followed, and Morazán was seen to lift his head and was heard to say, "Estoy vivo!"--"I am alive." A second discharge ended his life. This execution took place on September 15, 1842, just as the Central American freedom from Spain "came of age"-- twenty-one years to the day. The bodies of Morazán and his general Villaseñor were left until 9:00 p.m. when Juan Mora Fernández appeared to cover the bodies; he later arranged their burial. The greatest Central American of his time was thus the victim of assassination under the command of the Portuguese, Pinto.

Few men in history have achieved or suffered as did Morazán. President of several sovereign states, brilliant strategist and able tactician, supporter of the highest principles of democracy, freedom, and political virtue, as well as of the highest tenets of art, science, and education, Morazán was a true patriot, a superb soldier, a faultless leader, a Renaissance man and, at the end, a martyr to the ideals he espoused. The causes of Central American union and progress which he fostered and advanced have been taken up by none other to match him, and yet the ideal of Central American union is an attractive but ephemeral dream in the minds of patriots and intellectuals.

MORENOS. An alternate name sometimes applied to the "Black Caribs" (q.v.) of the north coastal areas. The term is also applied to certain villagers near Nandaime in Nicaragua, supposed to have been descended from "Moors" in southern Spain, and there may be similar vestigial usage in Honduras. These widely divergent uses of the term indicate the lack of precision and the strictly local application of the word throughout Central America. The appellation has in common, however, its application to people of very dark skin, not necessarily or obviously negroid. The term was not applied to the negroes brought in to build forts or to work banana and other plantations.

MORGAN, HENRY. Well-known in the annals of piracy, this freebooter who rose to high office in Jamaica was the scourge of the western Caribbean in the late 17th century. One author terms the years 1660-85 the "great years of English piracy." Henry Morgan's raid on Trujillo, Honduras came during this time, and a similar descent upon Puerto Caballos was added to his better known exploits in Panama and Nicaragua.

MORISCO. A cross between a Spanish male and a Mulata (q.v.) female. See RACIAL MIXTURES.

MORISON, SAMUEL ELIOT. Distinguished American historian who is best known for his studies of Columbus, Morison has long been identified with Harvard University. His Admiral of the Ocean Sea (a definitive work on Columbus), The Caribbean as Columbus Saw It (with Obregón), and the recent European Discovery of America--The Southern Voyages (published in 1974 when Morison was 87 years old) all have numerous references to Honduras, especially in relation to the Fourth Voyage of Columbus. In the last-mentioned volume, Morison records that Columbus crossed 360 miles of the Caribbean in three days, from Cayo Largo off Cuba, to sight the "first of the lofty, highly colored and spectacular Bay Islands." It was here that the Spaniards found a 70-foot canoe with a Maya (or Jicaque) chieftain and his retinue. The canoe was loaded with beer, cacao, metal and other craft objects. Columbus' fleet later anchored at Puerta Castilla near Trujillo on the Honduran mainland.

MORLEY, SYLVANUS GRISWOLD. Great authority on the Maya culture, who lived and worked in Middle America (principally in Yucatán) for forty years. His work The Ancient Maya has been cited as the most complete and most authoritative statement on the unique Maya culture and civilization. Morley died in 1948, and at that time was Director of the School of American Research and the Museum of New Mexico in Santa Fe. His principal work was done as an associate of the Carnegie Institution.

MORTALITY RATE AND FACTORS. Death rate reported for Honduras by the Pan American Health Organization in 1964 was 9.5 per 1,000 population. The United Nations, however, estimated 17 per 1,000, based on a high mortality rate for children, approximately 45 per cent under five years old. All death rates have decreased, however, during recent years.

Principle causes of death are unsanitary conditions and contaminated water supply, deaths from such causes being 7.3 per cent of the 1964 total. Enteritis, gastritis, and related diseases are increasing while those from infections and parasitic causes are decreasing. Accidental death and chronic disease are on the increase. Homicide, suicide, and accidents made up seven per cent of 1967 deaths, with those from respiratory disease at six per cent. Half of recorded deaths were vague as to cause. Medical facilities and health resources are in short supply, as are finances to increase them.

MOSCHEATE. An early 19th century spelling of "machete," the long knife so generally used as an agricultural tool and on occasion as a weapon in Central America. British traders also sometimes called it a "cutlass."

MOSCOES. A variant term for the Caribbean coastal tribe found from Cabo Gracias north and west along the Honduran littoral.

MOSKITIA. A variant spelling of the word designating the Miskito coast, or "Mosquito" Kingdom.

MOSQUITO PROTECTORATE. To a large extent a semi-fiction of one of the backwash episodes of British imperial days, the protectorate over the Mosquito Shore, or Miskito Coast, or "La Mosquitia" as it is now called, was exercised by Great Britain in the hope not only of supporting their semi-piratical logging enterprises of the 16th and 17th centuries, but also of retaining some rights toward an Atlantic to Pacific transit, either in Honduras or Nicaragua, by canal, or later by rail. That transit represented to the English the only ocean to ocean entry they did not control during the 200-year "Pax Britannica," and they fought with Spain and nearly did so with the United States a number of times over the disputed isthmian area, in the interests of the geopolitical plum. The Protectorate ended late in the nineteenth century.

MOSQUITO SHORE. Loosely, the geographical area between Belize (now British Honduras) and Bocas de Toro (in Western Panama), which was occupied by the British following 1700, when the Spanish power in Yucatán had forced the British to abandon the coast in the Campeche area as well as the Panamanian coast near and west of Porto Bello. They settled for the wild littoral between. The Mosquito coast proper extends from the region of Cape Gracias a Dios to the Río Maiz, just north of the San Juan River. It is likely that all the coastal settlements during this period contained fewer than 1,500 Englishmen.

These outposts on the English-Miskito side of the Spanish frontier accounted for, at best, a few thousand population compared to over a million in the Spanish parts of Central America by the end of the 1700s. However, the Mosquito Coast was a continual thorn in the flesh of Spain and later of Honduras and Nicaragua, for it was an area of conflict which included not only Spain and the two Central American countries but also Great Britain and the United States.

MOTAGUA, BARRA DE. The bar at the mouth of the Motagua river, which for ten miles or so is the border between Guatemala and Honduras, just before the river empties into the Bahía de Omoa.

MOTAGUA RIVER. For a few miles before it empties into the Bay of Omoa (q.v.), the Motagua is the border between Guatemala and Honduras. The valley is deep and rugged. Longest and most significant of Guatemala's rivers, the Motagua has its source in the Quiché highlands, and along its 250-mile course are gold placers, as well as considerable small craft trade in such staples as fruit, hides, coffee, and the ever-present plantains and bananas.

MOUNT PICACHO. As a backdrop to Tegucigalpa, and looming 1,200 feet above the city center, this eminence is crowned with United Nations Park. As in Concordia Park (q.v.), there is a Maya temple replica and there are formal gardens, roses, hedges, playgrounds. Natural rock formations provide a rugged setting and the view over the Río Choluteca, Tegucigalpa, and Camayaguela is sweeping and spectacular.

MOUNT UYUCA. Eminence in south central Honduras, high enough for cloud forest.

MOVIMIENTO MAYA AMERICANO. There is a considerable intellectual movement toward the revival of the ancient Maya culture. Pedro Aplicano Mendieta (q.v.) is in the forefront as editor of materials on the Maya.

MOYA POSAS, DAVID. Born in Comayaguela in 1929, and dying in Tegucigalpa in 1970, poet Moya Posas left Imanaforas and Metafora del angel among his poetic works. He worked on El Nacional in Mexico and La Prensa Gráfica in San Salvador.

MUAN. Fifteenth month of the Maya calendar.

MULATO. A cross between a Negro male and a Spanish female. See RACIAL MIXTURES.

MULES. The trade in these essential animals was widespread in colonial central America, the Honduran area of Gracias a Dios being a principal source, sending mules as far as Panama. Around La Choluteca the alluvial plain was a favorite place for raising mules. Great numbers of mules were needed for transshipping China goods from Acapulco to Puerto Caballos and Granada, and for handling Honduras' silver production around Tegucigalpa.

MULETEER'S DANCE. The rhonda of the muleteers, done in the 1800s with the mules decked out in gay harnesses and trappings surrounding the dancers and the dancers weaving in and out between them.

MULTILATERAL TREATY OF 1958. A treaty basic to the establishment of the Central American Common Market. Nicaragua has been a major exponent of the concept of economic integration among the five states.

MULUC. Ninth day of the Maya month; meaning, "flood."

MUNICIPALITIES see MUNICIPIOS

MUNICIPIOS. Major subdivisions of the Honduran departments. There are 281 such entities, but fewer than 100 are urban centers. Two-thirds have populations under 1,000. As to the nature of the entity, if the department is considered equivalent to a "state" (as in Mexico, Brazil, or the United States), then the municipio might be paralleled to a county, although it also partakes of the idea of township. However, the municipio always has a principal town, or cabacera, which is like a U.S. county seat in central location and local governmental function. Municipios vary widely in size depending upon the degree to which the country or region is settled, which also varies very widely in Honduras, especially in the sparsely settled eastern Caribbean coastal areas.

MÜNSTER, SEBASTIAN. From the Orbis Novus of Basle, 1532, Munster's World map shows the Central American Coast and the projection of Honduras clearly. Thus between 1511 (see PTOLEMY) and 1532 the Honduran coast had reached map publication. See BORDONE and WALDSEEMÜLLER.

MURGA, ANTONIO. As Lieutenant Colonel, he was one of two officers sent to work on Fort Omoa (q.v.) after a plea from Salazar (q.v.) in 1767. He was accompanied by Sub-Lieutenant Joaquín Peramas, and the two officers were able to speed up the work, although the supplies of stone were limited.

Indians were trained as masons. Ladinos were sent to Omoa in two-month shifts.

MURILLO SOTO, CELEO. Poet, writer, and public official born in Olanchito, Yoro Department in 1911. Graduate in law of the national university, he was secretary of the general staff of the Honduran army during General Carias Andino's incumbency, and was a deputy to the congress elected in 1954. He was Honduran Consul in New Orleans, United States, in 1956, and in 1965 was named president of the National Elections Council. He had also been President of the Honduran Press Association on more than one occasion. He worked on the dailies La Epoca, Prensa Libre, El Nacional and El Día, and on the weeklies La Nación, Nuestro Criterio and Avance, in reportorial and/or editorial capacities. He used two pennames; Gerardo Serena and Alfonso Garrido.

MUSICAL INSTRUMENTS, COLONIAL. The Spanish introduced guitars, mandolins, and violins. It is possible that the marimba was also introduced at this time, and that farther north it was an aboriginal instrument, for it has had long use in Guatemala. The pre-conquest existence of the marimba in Honduras is, however, problematical. Some few aboriginal instruments were also used in colonial times, such as drums, whistles of ceramic and wood, bamboo and wood trumpets, clay and wood flutes.

MUTUAL SECURITY APPROPRIATIONS BY THE U.S. United States appropriations for security in several of the Latin American countries from 1945 to 1965 are instructive concerning the disparities in such aid. The following are shown to present comparisons between the amount given to Honduras and to some of her near neighbors. For example, Honduras received almost twice what El Salvador received for the period, but Guatemala received nearly four times as much as Honduras. This was during the Castillo Armas takeover in Guatemala, when U.S. commitments there were heavy. Note that Honduras' share of total U.S. aid for Latin America was just over two per cent.

| | |
|---|---:|
| Honduras | $ 18,400,000 |
| Nicaragua | 10,000,000 |
| Panama | 18,400,000 |
| El Salvador | 9,600,000 |
| Guatemala | 74,000,000 |
| Costa Rica | 10,000,000 |
| Venezuela | 32,500,000 |
| Haiti | 43,600,000 |
| Latin American total for the period | $889,900,000 |

See RESPONSE TO "GOLPES" and MILITARY ASSISTANCE AND MILITARISM.

- N -

NACAOME. Departmental cabacera of Valle Department, along the Pan-American Highway not far from the border with El Salvador. Nacaome is in the semi-arid "hot lands" of the Bay of Fonseca, and is on the usually dry bed of the Río Nacaome. The population is around 12,000.

NACAOME RIVER. A stream in Valle and Choluteca departments which empties into the Bay of Fonseca, with headwaters near Jiojona.

NACO. A cacique encountered by Olid (q.v.) during his incursions on the north coast of Honduras in 1524. The site of this chieftain's area and capital was 20 miles southeast of San Pedro Sula.

NACOME, PACT OF. An agreement signed by Honduras, El Salvador and Nicaragua in the small town of Nacome, Nicaragua, on October 7, 1847. It was a pact leading to formation of a federal government. Little progress was made on the union plans due to the absence of Costa Rican and Guatemalan representation.

NAGUA  see  ENAGUA

NAMASIGUE, BATTLE OF. Nicaraguan troops invaded Honduras as a result of Honduran troops allegedly violating Nicaraguan soil in a revolutionary gambit in 1906. On March 18, 1907, the Battle of Namasigue was distinguished by being the first occasion of the use of machine-guns in Central American warfare. The battle in the Portillo de Namasigue lasted for five days following March 18th of that year, and toppled the Manuel Bonilla government. Namasigue is a municipal cabacera of Choluteca department, and is near enough the Bay of Fonseca and the Nicaraguan border so that it was a point of defense against the invading Nicaraguans under General Juan Estrada. This is another of the Central American "firsts" in warfare, in addition to those during the 1927-33 Sandino insurrection, especially in aviation matters. During this period many European governments were unloading Gatling-type repeating guns in Latin America, prior to getting gas-operated machine guns for their own armies.

NAME, HONDURAS  see  REPUBLICA DE HONDURAS

NANCE. A fruit-producing tree found in conjunction with pine trees on the Mosquito coast.

NAO. A transport ship, carrying personnel and freight in the 16th to 18th centuries. Similar to a galleon, but not heavily armed. A flota de naos was usually a fleet of these transports accompanied by two to four large armed galleons. The typical size in the late 1500s was 300 to 600 tons, about 100 feet long, 32 feet beam, and 20 feet deep. By 1650 the tonnage averaged 700, at 140 feet length, 38 feet beam, but less draft (17-1/2 feet). Capitanas and Almirantas might be of 1,200 to 2,000 tons with 90 bronze cannon on three decks. By 1700 the size was reduced to 450 to 900 tons. These fleets were critical to maintaining Honduran north coastal ports and forts.

NATERA Y MENDOZE, HERRERA. Governor of Honduras in 1765, following Pedro de Salazar.

NATIONAL AGRARIAN COUNCIL. A five-member body created by a comprehensive agrarian reform law of 1962, and charged with advising and policy-making for the Instituto Nacional Agrario (q.v.).

NATIONAL AGRARIAN INSTITUTE see INSTITUTE NACIONAL AGRARIO

NATIONAL AGRICULTURE CENTER. Located in Comayagua, the center works on cattle breeding and corn variety improvement. See also EL ZAMORANO, and FARM DEMONSTRATION SCHOOL.

NATIONAL AIR TRANSPORT see TRANSPORTES AEREOS NACIONALES, S.A.

NATIONAL AIRLINES OF HONDURAS see AEROVIAS NACIONALES DE HONDURAS

NATIONAL DEFENSE AND PUBLIC SECURITY see CABINET

NATIONAL DEVELOPMENT BANK. An autonomous institution which not only does planning and research, but invests in specific projects of a developmental nature. Prior to the establishment of this entity and the Central Bank (q.v.) in 1950, practically all economic development had been left to private enterprise. The president of the Development Bank is part of the National Superior Planning Council (q.v.).

NATIONAL ECONOMIC COUNCIL. Original title of the coordinating entity now known as the National Superior Planning Council.

NATIONAL ELECTIONS COUNCIL. This is the key organization in the electoral process, as it has charge of all election proceedings. It registers political parties and candidates, appoints departmental electoral boards, administers an electoral census, and supervises local election boards to assure compliance with the law. The council is composed of one member and one alternate from each political party registered, from merchant, farmer, and industrial organizations, from the professional associations and labor federations, and from the Federation of University Students and the Honduran Women's Association. If the council fails to declare a winner in presidential or congressional election, the national congress then accepts the responsibility. The system is well planned, but has been subject to frequent abuses. Force has been traditional in settling disputes.

NATIONAL ELECTRIC ENERGY COMPANY. The Empresa Nacional de Energía Eléctrica is an autonomous entity of the Honduran government administered by a directorate of five members. Created in 1957, the ENEE succeeded a company then operating under the Development Ministry. This enterprise now operates about half of the Honduran electric plants. The Río Lindo expansion (see ENERGY) is one of the ENEE developments. The ENEE generates nearly two-thirds of the total of over 1,000,000 kilowatts in the country.

NATIONAL FEDERATION OF WORKERS AND PEASANTS OF HONDURAS. A number of local farm labor committees seeking an improved bargaining position on large farms and plantations formed this federation in 1962. There are now over 6,000 members.

NATIONAL FOLKLORE DANCE GROUP. A group of 23 dancers perpetuating Indian and colonial folk-dances and folklore, composed of Honduran high school and university graduates, young professionals, and peasant or campesino artists. In November 1974 their group performed in the United States, sponsored by the Vermont-Honduras Partners of the Alliance, raising funds for Honduran relief needed as a result of the September 1974 hurricane along the north coast. A number of the concerts were presented in Vermont cities. See PARTNERS OF THE AMERICAS.

NATIONAL GUARD OFFENSIVE, HONDURAN BORDER, 1929-1931. The United States Marine-trained National Guard of Nicaragua carried out a strong campaign following 1928 elections to clear Sandinistas (q.v.) out of the Honduran border area, and to cut the supply routes in and out of Honduras. The Honduran towns of Choluteca (the Bay of Fonseca) and Danlí (in El Paraiso department) had become collection points for supplies and weapons for the tenacious Sandino (q.v.). Local citizens in those towns carried out a profitable trade exchanging war material for the gold, cattle, and other goods which had been "confiscated" by Sandino and brought across the border for trade. Munitions came up the trails of Choluteca and El Paraiso departments from the ports on the Fonseca gulf. From the Caribbean side, goods came up the Río Coco and the Río Patuca to reach the border exchange points. The Honduran government attempted to curb this lucrative traffic, but was nearly powerless to stop it. The 500-mile border was almost impossible to patrol. Much of the border area was impenetrable, a mountainous jungle.

NATIONAL INSTITUTE OF ANTHROPOLOGY AND HISTORY. On July 22, 1952 there was established in Tegucigalpa, by a governmental accord and executive act, an institute which was to have the following sections; Archaeology, Ethnography, Music, Colonial Art, History, and Tourism. On February 1, 1956 an organic law to regulate such matters as archaeological exploration was established. When created in 1952, the Institute took at once as a major responsibility the Archaeological Zone at Copán (q.v.) and continues to administer it with maintenance and conservation personnel and activities.

NATIONAL INVESTIGATION CORPS. A branch of the Cuerpo Especial de Seguridad (q.v.), this investigative group has four departments: Immigration, Identification, Intelligence, and Criminal. It handles police investigations in the two major urban areas, and in some other areas of particular unrest or criminal activity. The immigration section occupies frontier posts. The frontier and rural units are particularly concerned with illegal entry of foreigners and with contraband goods.

NATIONAL MANUFACTURERS ASSOCIATION. With Tegucigalpa headquarters, an association which is a type of industrial national chamber of commerce.

NATIONAL PARTY. One of the only two significant long-term political parties in Honduras. Philosophically it stems from the 1840-60 era, but formal organization took place only in 1916. The Carias Andino (q.v.) faction soon dominated party councils, as well as the nation at large. Following 1920 the party was strong and close-knit, with a definite and clear program putting emphasis on strict constitutional observance, financial and monetary reform, freedom in elections, improved administration, removal of some politics from government, and protective moves for the labor force and the capital entrepreneurs. By the 1930s the party was a major influence in the peaceful incumbency of Carias, who held power longer than any other chief of state in Honduran history. Following Carias' departure in 1948, the party still dominated politics, although by 1954 factionalism arose and the reunited Liberal Party won an election. With López in 1963 the National Party again became a political force majeure. It was essentially a personal political movement for López. By 1970 there was a three-faction split. Under López again after 1972, reimposed unity was in effect.

NATIONAL RAILROAD OF HONDURAS see FERROCARRIL NACIONAL DE HONDURAS

NATIONAL RECONSTRUCTION COMMITTEE see HONDURAN COUNCIL OF PRIVATE ENTERPRISE

NATIONAL REFORMIST PARTY.  A short-lived political movement under the leadership of Abraham Williams in mid-20th century.

NATIONAL REPRESENTATION  see  REPRESENTACION NACIONAL

NATURAL RESOURCES, MINISTRY OF  see  CABINET

NATIONAL SCHOOL OF FINE ARTS.  The school provides leadership in the support of artists and their work, as well as instruction.  A number of currently popular Honduran artists have been prepared in the Tegucigalpa institution, and some have taught in it.

NATIONAL SCHOOL OF MUSIC.  Located in Tegucigalpa, a conservatory.

NATIONAL SUPERIOR PLANNING COUNCIL.  Created in 1955 under the title National Economic Council, this group is headed by the Minister of Economy, and includes two other cabinet members, the Ministers of Natural Resources and of Communications and Public Works.  There are two representatives of industry, and the presidents respectively of the Central Bank and the National Development Bank.  Functions include development plans, proposed economics legislation, proposed tax revisions, budget reviews, and the approval of foreign loans.

NATIONAL UNITY PARTY.  Under Lozano (q.v.) this was essentially a political vehicle for the leader himself, and it disappeared with the leader.

NATIONAL UNIVERSITY.  Founded in 1847 in Tegucigalpa, the National University is now in Comayaguela, just across the Choluteca river from the capital.  Degrees are granted in law, social sciences, medicine and surgery, chemistry and pharmacy, physics and mathematics, economics, nursing, and dentistry.

NATIONAL WAR (Central America).  The Walker filibuster war of 1854-57 was the only major conflict to unite the five countries between the 1839 breakup of Central America and the economic cooperation now current.  The action was centered in southern Nicaragua and a little in northern Costa Rica.  Troops from all five republics, totaling an estimated 17,000, gathered to repel Walker.  Many Honduran officers and men were included (see GUARDIOLA).  Costa Rica furnished most of these men, doubtless due to poor overland communications from the other countries.  While the five small countries are very nationalistically minded as individuals, this unity against the invading Walker was Central American in character, and it is interesting that as such it has been dubbed the "national war."  There is still much feeling for union in spite of the separatist events of the past century and a half--a strange ambivalence.

NAVA, JOSE JUAQUIN DE. Former governor of Costa Rica, commandant of Fort San Carlos and one of Gálvez' officers at Trujillo (q.v.) in 1782.

NAVAL FORCE. There is no Honduran navy. One small coastal patrol boat is manned by army personnel.

NAVIDAD DE NUESTRA SEÑORA see LA NAVIDAD

NAVIGABLE RIVERS. Only the Ulua, Coco, and Patuca are navigable for any distance, and then only by small shallow-draft vessels. The Patuca is navigable for 60 miles upstream; the Coco farther, but only for very shallow draft. Steamers have plied the Ulua and Coco.

NEGOTIATIONS, EL SALVADOR, 1974. In July of 1974 military officers from Honduras and El Salvador met at the border to negotiate concerning armed clashes which had been occurring in the several months just previous. They were hoping to "avoid future confrontations which might unleash a new armed conflict between the Central American states." High Honduran army officers had charged that regular Salvadoran troops as well as private citizens had fired on Honduran border police. The charge was denied by El Salvador. Both sides were anxious to prevent repetition of the bitter border conflict of 1969, the "soccer war."

NEGRO RIVER. An alternate name for the large north coastal stream. See TINTO RIVER.

NELSON, HORATIO. A little-known passage of the victor of Trafalgar's early life involves his service on the ship Bristol under Sir Peter Parker in 1779 as third lieutenant, which led to his subsequent promotion later in the same year to command of the sloop of war Badger. Nelson's first command was not as post captain; that position was awarded him on June 11, 1779, when he was given command of the 20-gun Hinchinbrooke. It was while captain of the Hinchinbrooke, and in continuation of his Central American experience, that Nelson participated in the ill-fated expedition to capture "Fort St. John" (Castillo de la Concepción Inmaculada) up the San Juan river in Nicaragua.

But it was in the Badger, a brig-rigged vessel, that Nelson served on the Mosquito shore in early 1779. Lasting for only a few months, this service nevertheless won Nelson the plaudits of the Baymen. A book published in 1806 gives a comment on the service and its result: 'Being ordered out to the Musquito shore for the better protection of the Baymen from the depredations of the American privateers, he [Nelson] there shewed himself no less attentive to the moral duties of private life than he had before proved he was to those of his profession. By his care, his gentleness of manner, and conciliating conduct, he gained the entire love of all the settlers, who, when his time of service on that station expired, voted him their unanimous thanks for his conduct, and expressed their regret at his departure in the most affectionate terms." This tribute to the 20-year-old Nelson is found in John Charnock's Biographical Memoirs of Lord Viscount Nelson.

Nelson's orders read that he was "sent to protect the Mosquito shore and the Bay of Honduras...." It was recognized that the area was technically within the Spanish Captain-Generalship of Guatemala. The protectorate was informal, but Nelson's orders gave him operations along the coasts of southern Mexico (Yucatán), Guatemala, Honduras, Nicaragua, and Costa Rica. The settlers were apprehensive that Spain might join France to aid the American Revolution then in progress in the northern colonies.

The brig Badger is of interest in her own right. It was customary for the British Royal Navy to purchase American-built vessels for naval use, as the American Revolution approached. One such was the Badger, drawn at Portsmouth dockyard as a naval vessel in June 1877. Several vessels of the name were purchased or taken as prizes in quick succession. Which one, exactly, was Nelson's first command, is not certain. However, one of these, a 130-ton brig, was commissioned at Port Royal, Jamaica in June 1776, and was considered unusable by November 1777. In her place to take the name Badger was a "rebel privateer" (meaning from one of the Thirteen Colonies), and this may have been Nelson's command; she was probably similar to the 130-tonner, of Chesapeake Bay or Bermuda construction. Such tiny warships would be around 70 feet long, 22 feet beam, 11 foot draft and carry about 12 carriage guns plus as many swivels on the bulwarks.

NEOTROPICAL SPECIES. Honduran animals belong to this South American group of species. There are a few, however, belonging to the North American or Nearctic group which have followed the highlands south. Such are the white-tailed deer, the raccoon, the turkey, and the puma. The northward-moving neotropical animals are such as the opossum, parrots, armadillos, peccaries, and termites.

NEPOMUCENO DE QUESADA, JUAN. Served as governor 1782; named gobernador intendente in 1786.

NEUTRALITY, HONDURAN see CENTRAL AMERICAN COURT OF JUSTICE

NEW LAWS. Promulgated during the 1540s, these laws were intended by Mother Spain to counteract the worst abuses of the American Indians under the Spanish colonial encomienda system. This new legislation against Indian slavery and near-slavery was pressed by Bartolomé de las Casas (q.v.), and, in the Guatemalan area of which Honduras was a part, by Alfonso López de Cerrato. It was the latter who began to free Indian slaves. Unfortunately, it seems he often applied the "New Laws" to those least powerful in the colonial community, and he did not break up the great encomiendas as he was charged to do.

NICA. Nickname or apodo for Nicaraguans, used throughout the Central American area.

NICARAGUA-GUATEMALA-SALVADOR WAR OF 1863. Carrera of Guatemala was the Indian strongman of the area during this period, and he disapproved of an alliance treaty signed in 1862 by El Salvador and Honduras. Border incidents arose again, as in the Guatemala War of 1853, and in this case Guatemala and Nicaragua joined against the treaty allies of 1862. Carrera was beaten in El Salvador at Coatepeque, but later, with Nicaraguan help, won at Santa Ana. There was a four-month siege of the Salvadoran capital of San Salvador before the city was taken in October 1863.

NICUESA, DIEGO DE. Conquistador who with Ojeda made an expeditionary attempt to explore the Central American coast in 1509, and who was named by Bishop Fonseca as governor of the western part of "Castilla de Oro" (Panama) (q.v.), covering the coasts of Nicaragua and Honduras. This looked good on paper. Nicuesa reached Cartegena with 700 men late in 1509, but he soon gave up. This award under King Ferdinand in 1508 was later to become Honduras and most of the rest of Central America, and was known as the province "Castilla de Oro" (q.v.). For a time the governor was Balboa (q.v.).

NIÑERA. A trained teen-aged girl, particularly those given special work in child-care, to help handle preschool children in day nurseries located over the Los Dolores market in Tegucigalpa and the San Isidro market in Comayaguela.

NOPAL CACTUS. This Mexican plant is a base for raising insects to produce cochineal (q.v.). It is also called tuna.

NORMAL SCHOOL, FIRST. In Camasca there was established in 1891 the first normal school in Honduras, directed by Anastasio Cabrera, a native of the place. Actually the school operated from 1891 to 1893 and from 1901 to 1904.

NORTH. A term used by English settlers on the Honduran coast, to indicate the winds which begin in October and last till February. They identified "wet norths" and "dry norths." Wind records indicated most winds came from east northeast or northeast.

NUESTRA SEÑORA DE LA LIMPIA CONCEPCION. A small nao (q.v.) with a long name, this Honduras ship of only 100 tons was wrecked in Bermuda in 1622 while on an Atlantic crossing. It is possible that her wreck was discovered in 1964 by Donald Canton. The captain of the vessel was Juan Calzado.

NUESTRA SEÑORA DE LA VICTORIA. The almiranta, smaller of two "Manila galleons" which sailed from the Philippine Islands, July 20, 1656. After an eight-month voyage it reached the American coast, but, considerably off course for the usual port, Acapulco, it anchored in the Bay of Fonseca. One hundred and fifty of the crew were dead, the others emaciated from lack of food and water. Trading began at once. The demand for the Chinese goods it carried was tremendous. Honduras and the Kingdom of Guatemala in general seldom got all they wanted.

NUEVO PACTO. The "new pact" or agreement was a statement in the first article of the Federation of Central America of April 30, 1838. The pact was one of "true federalism."

NUFIO, PEDRO. Born in Guatemala in 1863, Nufio came to Danlí to direct the Escuela Superior until 1887, and then directed the lyceum El Porvenir in Danlí until 1890. In 1897 a secondary Colegio was formed, and Nufio directed it until 1902. He then went to Tegucigalpa and directed the trade school, under the Ministry of Development. In 1906 he helped found and direct the Escuela Normal de Varones, and in 1907 resigned because of political conditions. By action of the students, he was returned to the school in 1908 (see DIA DEL SANTO DE DON PEDRO). Honored and revered, Don Pedro died in Danlí in 1916.

NUMISMATICS see COINAGE, LEMPIRA SYSTEM

NUTRITION. Diseases caused by malnutrition are anemia and goiter. Iodine deficiency and the resultant endemic goiter prevalence is a major health problem. Malnutrition causes arrested and improper bodily development, height and weight being markedly affected by age five. It seems, however, that a higher consumption of nutritive foods after reaching adulthood tends to compensate to some extent for deficient childhood diets. The Instituto Nutricional de Centro América (q.v.) found, however, that overall physical health of the population of Honduras was good, especially in rural areas.

NUTRITION INSTITUTE OF CENTRAL AMERICA see INSTITUTO NUTRICIONAL DE CENTRO AMERICA; also NUTRITION

- O -

OACI see ORGANIZACION DE AVIACION CIVIL INTERNACIONAL

O.A.S. see ORGANIZATION OF AMERICAN STATES

OBROJE. A plant for the treatment of indigo, characterized by broad vats or "pilas." Here the indigo plants were steeped, then beaten, in later years by water-wheel-powered paddles or poles. The puntero (q.v.) gauged the mess to see when it was ready to settle. The water was drained off, a thick sediment remaining in the vats. After drying, the indigo was cut in solid bars and shipped. It was said that a wagonload of leaves produced only one pound of dye. Quality depended upon the freshness and age of the plant, and the skill of the puntero. La Choluteca was a principal Honduran base of the industry.

OBSERVANTS. Missionary order who were given support for a missionary effort in Honduras. They went to serve the Jicaques in 1686-7. They moved into mountains around the Yoro Valley in 1688. See FERNANDEZ, JOSE.

OC. Tenth day of the Maya month; meaning, "dog."

OCELOT. Leopardus pardalis, one of the several big cats indigenous to Honduras. Attaining weights of up to 40 pounds, but usually around 25 pounds, the animal is nocturnal and a swift-killing predator. A delightful pet when a kitten, it is very dangerous when full-grown.

OCELOTL. Fourteenth day of the Aztec month; meaning "tiger." The name "ocelot" obviously stems from this word. In the isthmian area the ocelot is called "tigrillo" or little tiger in Spanish.

OCHOA, MATEO. A colonial vecino of Trujillo in the 1600s, owner of 30 leagues of savannahs and large herds of cattle. Wishing to return to Spain, he could not dispose of his riches in land and cattle since there were no buyers. This was typical of Central America during the 17th century depression.

OCHOA VELASQUEZ, JOSE MARIA   see   BUESO, FRANCISCO

OCHRES. Colored earths found in the vicinity of Guajiquero in La Paz Department, used by the aborigines for painting, bodies and otherwise.

OCOTAL. A pine woods of ocote (q.v.) pines. Also in the form Ocotlán, although in Central America final consonants are frequently lost or modified as in this case. The typical ocotal is usually rather arid and on a mountain slope.

OCOTE. A word of Nahuatl derivation, meaning "pine." This is the Pinus Oocarpa. It is widespread in the arid upper tropical zone. See LIFE ZONES.

OCOTEPEQUE, DEPARTMENT. Westernmost of the political subdivisions of Honduras, Ocotepeque is bounded on the west by

Guatemala and on the south by El Salvador, on the east by Lempira Department, and on the north by Copán Department. The Cordillera del Merendón extends north and south across the department, and the Río Lempa's upper reaches are in the western portion. The cabacera is Nueva Ocotepeque, and there are 16 municipios. The area is 653 square miles. It is the southwesternmost corner of the land, and borders on both Guatemala and El Salvador. It was here that some of the sharpest conflicts took place during the 1969 war with El Salvador, and this was largely due to the influx of illegal entrants from that country. The population is dense, with 17,242 in the cabaceras, and 47,824 in the rural areas, for a total of 65,066. The Cordillera del Merendón, running across the department, contributes to a very rugged terrain. Towns include San Fernando, La Encarnación, San Jorge, Dolores, Fraternidad, Santa Concepción, Sihuape, San Francisco del Valle, San Marcos, and Plan del Rosario.

ODECA see ORGANIZACION DE LOS ESTADOS CENTRO AMERICANOS

OFFICE OF THE PRESIDENT see CABINET

OFFSHORE TERRITORIES. Honduras is unique among the Central American countries in having a number of offshore island possessions. (See BAY ISLANDS, GUANAJA, ROATAN, etc.) The Island group in the Bay of Honduras is the separate Bay Island Department (q.v.), but the large islands of the Pacific Bay of Fonseca such as Tigre and Zacate Grande are simply designated as offshore territories.

O. HENRY. Pseudonym of William Sidney Porter, 1862-1910, the well-known short story writer in the United States, popular in the early part of this century in particular, whose stay in Trujillo, Honduras, gave him the material for his perceptive Central American tales, best known among them being Cabbages and Kings. Somehow Porter captured the special charm, magic, and flavor of the land and the people, the comedy as well as the pathos and the tragedy.

O'HORAN, TOMAS. The first federal constitution was signed by this Irish expatriate, whose activities in Honduran politics were later matched by a relative (probably a daughter), who was a principal companion and political advisor to William Walker (q.v.) in Nicaragua. She was a "mystery woman," variously called "La Niña" or "Mariena." Her name was Irena.

OIL AGREEMENTS, VENEZUELA. On December 14, 1974, Carlos Andrés Pérez, President of Venezuela, joined with rulers of Honduras, the other Central American countries and Panama in signing agreements for $2 billion worth of development aid during the period up to 1980. The seven presidents sat

259 Ojo de Agua River

in meetings planned to revolutionize the international coffee market and to make closer the relationships of the poorer countries to the oil-rich states such as Venezuela. The development project monies will be left in banks in the Central American countries to the extent of over 50 per cent of all sales transactions. Six dollars a barrel will go to Venezuela and about $7 will be held in the development funds. Venezuela will also support Cafés Suaves Centrales (q.v.) to the tune of $80 million.

OJO DE AGUA RIVER. This "eye of water" is a short swift tributary flowing from the Sierra Río Tinto into the Río Tinto itself, almost due north from Olancho into Colón department.

OLANCHITO. In the far eastern part of Yoro Department, this municipal cabacera has a railroad connecting with both Sonaguera and La Ceiba; also an airfield. It is in rugged mountains which rise over 5,000 feet nearby, and is near the upper reaches of the Río Aguán.

OLANCHO DEPARTMENT. Largest of the Honduran political subdivisions at approximately 9,400 square miles, Olancho is bounded on the north by Yoro and Colón departments, on the east by Gracias a Dios Department; and on the southeast by the international border with Nicaragua, entirely defined in this section by the course of the Río Coco (or Río Wangki as the Honduran maps show it); on the south is El Paraiso Department and on the west, Francisco Morazán Department. The cabacera is Juticalpa. There are 22 municipios. Major rivers drain the vast and largely uninhabited area into the Caribbean; the Ríos Tinto, Patuca, and Wangki. The mountains rise to over 8,000 feet in the Sierra de Agalta. Other ranges are the Montañas de Malacate, La Mora, and Azacualpa. The cabaceras had a population of 39,941 in 1973, with other areas having 116,078, for a total of 156,019. Olancho is a cattle and timber country, its vast reaches harboring old haciendas from colonial times. Other towns are Magulile, La Unión, Jano, La Guata, Manto, Saloma, Guarizama, Gualaco, San Esteban, Dulce Nombre de Culmí, San Francisco de Becerra, Campamento, Santa María del Real, and Esquipulas del Norte.

OLANCHO, GOLD. The Guayape River was an important gold producer in the 1540s. Some estimates indicate that a total of 1,750,000 gold pesos was the value of Guayape gold. The field dropped in importance by 1560 for lack of labor.

OLANO, MARGARITA. In the 1870s and 80s, the Hotel de Comayagua was owned by Sra. Olano, and was situated on the Plazuela de San Francisco in that city.

OLD MAYAN EMPIRE. Honduras was a principal location for the Old Mayan Empire, the site of Copán (q.v.) being outstanding in this regard. Flourishing especially between the fourth and ninth centuries A. D., this civilization was so advanced that it devised a literacy based on elaborate hieroglyphics, traced and recorded the recurrent movements of planets, moon, and sun, evidenced high artistic ability in sculpture and architectural expertise in elaborate construction, and carried on trade over a far-flung commercial network. By about three centuries before the Spanish discovery, the Maya centers had moved to Yucatán.

OLDMAN, CHIEF. A chief of the Mosquitoes whose son had been taken to England, and who was later crowned and purportedly commissioned as King Oldman of Mosquitia by Charles the II. The settlers had arranged this travesty of rulership in 1685 to effect their control over the land.

OLID, CRISTOBAL DE. Native of Andalucia, the town of Baeza, Olid is considered as the conqueror of Honduras. One of the major captains under the order of Hernán Cortés, he was more or less co-equal with the somewhat better-known Alvarado (q.v.). He was sent by Cortés to Havana in 1524 to assemble the horses and other necessary means for the conquest of Honduras. He left Havana with 370 Spanish men-at-arms, 100 archers and 22 horses, in five small ships. On the 3rd of May, 1524 he landed this force on the coast of Honduras, near Puerto Caballos, which is the present Puerto Cortés. Having been influenced before departure from Havana to rebel against Cortés, Olid took possession of the country in the name of the King of Spain and of Cortés (apparently wanting to keep some tie to Cortés). Cortés sent a small army to punish the rebel Olid, under Francisco de las Casas, but due to a disastrous bout with an offshore wind, Casas was captured.

Meanwhile, Gil González Dávila was marching northward, under the King's commission from Spain to take possession of countries he had partially explored two years before. Olid, progressing eastward, encountered Dávila and ordered Juan Ruano to capture Dávila. Olid held enmity for Dávila because the latter would not aid him against Casas.

Olid treated his prisoners as guests, and they conspired against him, attacking him with table knives. Meanwhile, Casas and Dávila proclaimed themselves legitimate governors of the region, while the badly wounded Olid hid in the woods. The chaplain, Brother Juan Pérez de Velásquez, sought to save the life of the wounded Olid, but when by this means Casas and González Dávila discovered Olid they held a summary travesty of a trial and beheaded him.

The conquest of Honduras, begun peacefully by Olid, thus turned into a bloody endeavor further aggravated by his assassination. These events, and conflicts with another expedition setting out from Nicaragua, caused Cortés (q.v.) to make his epic trek across Guatemala and into Honduras in 1525.

It may be added that Olid was sent by Hernan Cortés to oust Gil Gonzáles Dávila following the latter's discovery of the "Sweet Sea" (Lake Nicaragua), and that Olid was charged to take over for Cortés the whole isthmian area as far south as Panama, to be annexed to Cortés' Mexican possessions, now assuming almost the character of an empire. A further note is that Olid met Hernando de Soto, who was sent from Córdoba's mistaken landing on the Honduran coast, to go south and secure the big lake in Nicaragua for Córdoba, by preventing Gil Gonzáles Dávila's party from pushing on south. A great confusion reigned, with the result that each man schemed to shake off control of his master and grab a part of the land and riches for himself, as in the case of Olid. Having, understandably, lost faith in Olid, Cortés finally tried to straighten things out himself, and personally to become Master of the Sweet Sea. Thus, it was Lake Nicaragua as a prize that stimulated Cortés' incomparable march. Cortés had trusted the Gulf of Honduras to Olid, but Olid's conflict with Dávila and Francisco de las Casas proved fatal.

OLLIN. Seventeenth day of the Aztec month; meaning, "earthquake."

OLMEC CULTURE. The Olmecs built the first large-scale ceremonial centers on the Mexican gulf-coast, 12th to 15th centuries B. C. From Olmec beginnings the religion, calendar, and hieroglyphic system spread until it attained such sophistication as is evidenced in Maya Copán (q. v. ).

OMOA. Small town located on the Bahía de Omoa, ten miles from Puerto Cortés. Location of the 18th century fortification, Fort Omoa (q. v.), still in an excellent state of repair. It is also a municipal cabacera. Many of the inhabitants are descendants of negro slaves who were brought there from Jamaica in the 1700s to work on the great fortress.

OMOA, BAHIA DE. A bay on the northwestern Honduran coast near the Guatemalan border, whose fortification was a major concern of Spain during the 18th century. See FORT OMOA.

OMOA, 1779--BATTLES. As war with England came in June of 1779, Spain was better prepared for such a conflict than she had been for nearly 200 years. The English governor of Jamaica, John Dalling, hoped to cut the Spanish colonial empire by seizing the San Juan River and the Nicaraguan lakes. He had adequate naval support and a sizable detachment of infantry. When the Spanish ally, France, failed to sustain the siege of Savannah, Georgia by Admiral d'Estaing, and when Gibraltar kept Spanish forces pinned, the Caribbean forces at Dalling's disposal were ample to initiate his plan. It was this almost worldwide consideration which had bearing on Honduran events. When Dalling learned that Belize was to be attacked, he sent naval forces to defend the Baymen (q.v.). Commodore John Luttrell had a force of three frigates and a schooner, sailing via Black River to pick up reinforcements, with a second squadron of three ships sailing direct. Both were too late.

By late September Luttrell was ready to attack Fort Omoa. When three ships approached the fort, Desnaux (q.v.), the defending commandant, was prepared but apprehensive. On September 25 the ships sailed in sight but veered off. Luttrell having examined the ground, prepared to assault the fort by land and sea. He got help from the Roatán Baymen (q.v.). There were also Shoremen (q.v.) from Mosquitia, and some Sambo-Miskitos and Caribs.

On October 16 a force was put ashore at Puerto Caballos, ten miles from the fort. Desnaux found the situation ominous; he sent 45,000 pesos of royal money back to New Guatemala. Some of the soldiers began to desert. Desnaux brought the citizens of the town of Omoa into the fort. Late in the day Luttrell opened a cannonade from his ships. Dalrymple, on land, had burned the town to drive out snipers. An artillery duel went on for four hours. By the night of the eighteenth, Dalrymple planned a dawn assault next day. Desnaux' messages to Gálvez (q.v.) for help had borne no fruit. When the assault came, the British gained the walls by scaling ladders. One hundred Spanish soldiers deserted, 30 were killed, and the weary Desnaux surrendered. Dalrymple refused a ransom of 300,000 pesos for British withdrawal; 365 prisoners were taken and two Spanish ships with cargo worth 3,000,000 pesos were captured. Meanwhile Gálvez had left Guatemala with a 1,000-man force of regulars and militia. When en route he heard of the fall of Omoa, Gálvez knew that if Fort Inmaculada (El Castillo Viejo [q.v.] in Nicaragua) fell, this might end Spanish rule in Central America. The 69-year old general did not falter He called for reinforcements to gather at San Pedro Sula for a counterattack. By November 23, 1779, he had moved from San Pedro for the coast, and on November 26 began a siege of the fort, using Vauban's system of trenches. On November 28 Dalrymple quietly boarded his fleet and left for Jamaica, apparently under British orders not to resist a strong investment by a Spanish force. Actually, Omoa could do the British little good except as a pawn in bargaining at the treaty tables. Gálvez entered the fort the same day. He was promoted to brigadier, and he went on to Nicaragua to face a greater crisis. Desnaux suffered disgrace in a long trial, seemingly with little justice.

Omoa was once considered by Spain as a joint sacrifice, with Puerto Rico and Oran, to help Spain regain Gibraltar. The British, however, were not interested in such a trade, and they retain the Mediterranean bastion to this day.

ONDURAS. Alternate form of the name "Honduras" as shown in the use of "Cape Onduras" on the Sánches Planisphere (q.v.).

OPALACA, CORDILLERA. A mountain area crossing Intibuca Department, with altitudes to 6,000 feet.

OPOTECA MINES. Near Comayagua, these mines opened in about 1700, and were a boon to English contrabandists who received a flow of silver and gold from them. There were 14 other mining districts similarly opened during the next four decades.

OPOTERO. An Indian dialect used in Intibucat during the 19th century and later.

OQUELI BUSTILLO, MIGUEL see JUNTA DE GOBIERNO, 1907

OREGON PARTNERS see RELIEF EFFORTS; PARTNERS OF THE AMERICAS

ORGANIZACION DE AVIACION CIVIL INTERNACIONAL. The civil aviation branch of the United Nations, involved in central Europe and Latin America.

ORGANIZACION DE LOS ESTADOS CENTRO AMERICANOS. Since 1955, the five small states (see CENTRAL AMERICA) have been united in this organization, which is a voluntary grouping of sovereign states rather than a federation, the last of such affecting Central America being the Provincias Unidas del Centro América (q.v.), in 1823-38.

ORGANIZACION REGIONAL INTERAMERICANO DE TRABAJO. An anti-communist international labor federation which helped to negotiate and mediate during the Honduran General Strike (q.v.) of 1954.

ORGANIZATION OF AMERICAN STATES. Honduras is an active member of the OAS, which is the world's oldest international organization. It has united the 21 western hemisphere republics in a community of nations dedicated to peace, security, and prosperity for all citizens. The idea was first conceived by the South American liberator, Simón Bolívar, in 1826, but the present agreement originated on April 14, 1890, when a union of American Republics became a reality. Then, in 1948, a charter was adopted giving the OAS its present name with the Pan American Union as its permanent secretariat. The OAS has successfully handled a number of international conflicts, such as the Honduras-El Salvador War of 1969.

ORGANIZATION OF PETROLEUM EXPORTING COUNTRIES (OPEC) see PEREZ, CARLOS ANDRES, and OIL AGREEMENTS, VENEZUELA

ORGANIZED LABOR. The movement to unionize labor in Honduras is the latest to organize in Latin America, beginning in March 1950. It is a small but responsible movement, with a total 1970 membership of about 30,000 in 80 unions of service, industrial, and agricultural workers. The movement originated in Cortés department around San Pedro Sula. Three unions have over 1,000 members each, and there are five federations of labor on a national basis: the Federation of Workers of Northern Honduras (q.v.); the Federation of Free Unions of Honduras; the National Federation of Workers and Peasants of Honduras; the Confederation of Honduran Workers; the Authentic Federation of Honduran Unions. Ninety per cent of the labor force has not completed primary schooling.

    The Institute of Central American Trade Union Studies is located in Honduras, a regional labor training organization, and Honduras is a member of the International Labor Organization, the ILO.

O.R.I.T. see ORGANIZACION REGIONAL INTERAMERICANA DE TRABAJO

ORLINGO. Honduran name for the Mycetes stentor, mycetes palliatus, the howler monkey, also called congo and mono colorado.

ORO RIVER see RIO COCO

ORTEGA, MIGUEL R. Writer born in San Marcos, Santa Bárbara, in 1922. Graduate in law of the national university, he was secretary to the Honduran embassy and later Consul General of Honduras in Guatemala.

ORTEGA, RAMON. Poet born in Comayagua in 1885, he lived both in Guatemala and his native Honduras, where he died in Tegucigalpa in 1932. His works include El amor errante and Flores de peregrinación.

ORTELIUS, ABRAHAM. Mapmaker of Antwerp, whose Atlas of 1581 showed a map entitled "Peruviae Auriferae Regionis Typus," which extended to the southern border of Honduras. Significant because it showed fairly detailed knowledge of the area. In Ortelius' Theatrum of 1587 there is a printed map which shows in distorted but clear fashion the Gulf of Fonseca as well as a fair representation of the general shape of both coasts of Central America.

ORTEZ, MIGUEL ANGEL. Sandinista general who in May 1931 commanded a crack guerrilla outfit of over 100 men. Most of these were Hondurans. This force attacked the National Guard barracks at Palacaguina, Nicaragua, on the night of May 14-15. There was a battle and Ortez was killed. He was considered by his enemies as one of Sandino's best officers, valiant and disciplined. As a guerrilla, he was less successful than illiterates like Pedrón, who would not expose themselves, and hence lived to "fight another day." This

self-preservation has become classic guerrilla tactics. See
SANDINO.

ORTIZ, ALONSO DE. Lieutenant Governor to Alonso Maldonado
(q.v.), who was named by the Viceroy of Mexico to the
Audiencia of Guatemala, 1536.

ORTIZ, ELQUETA DE. Governor for a period when Juan Morán
was alcalde mayor in 1562. Ortiz also served in an interim
capacity in 1576.

OTTENS, JOSIA and REINERO. Amsterdam mapmakers who
showed the Honduran northwest coast on a 1730 atlas map.
However, the Caratasca Lagoon area was rather imperfectly
shown, and the Bay Islands were misplaced.

OTWAY, JOSEPH. Captain Otway succeeded Hodgson (q.v.) as
Mosquito Superintendent in 1759, and was unable to control
the trigger-happy Sambo-Miskitos who wished to raid the
Spanish frontier and coastal area. They did not bother Omoa
(q.v.), fearing its strength, but they did raid deep into Nicaragua, under Carib Chief Carlos Antonio Yarrince (q.v.).
Otway may have been involved in the Inmaculada attack of
1762.

OVIEDO Y VALDEZ, FRANCISCO GONZALO FERNANDEZ. Historian of the Spanish New World, author of the Historia general y natural de las indias, Oviedo records the discovery of
Honduras as part of the "Kingdom of Goethemala," and many
events contributing and subsequent thereto. He is a substantial and contemporary chronicler and authority, and a
base of information for both pre- and post-conquest data on
indigenous inhabitants as well as their customs, numbers,
etc.

OZOMATLI. Eleventh day of the Aztec month; meaning, "monkey."

- P -

PACAYA. A palm variety with edible pods or buds (Euterpe edulis).

PACIFICATION ZONE, VIOLATION OF. In May of 1974 it was reported by Honduras to the Organization of American States
that the pacification zone established between Honduras and
El Salvador following the 1969 war had been violated, with
Honduran border patrols attacked and Honduran air space invaded by El Salvador. The government of El Salvador denied
the charges, attributing the charges to "Honduran politics."

PACT OF CHINANDEGA. An instrument of international unity
signed by Nicaragua, Guatemala, El Salvador, and Honduras
in 1842. This was to establish the Confederación de Centro-

américa. A reaction against the "George Washington of Central America," Francisco Morazán, the agreement ceased to be in effect in 1845. The original agreement resulted from the move of Superintendent Macdonald of Belize in action at San Juan de Nicaragua (del Norte).

PACTITO, 1971. The "little pact" just following the 1971 elections in Honduras was between the Liberal Party and the Nationalist Party of Osvaldo López Arellano. The pact was to divide up government appointments and to prescribe the bipartisan nature of the Ramón Cruz (q.v.) government. Cruz rejected the pact in late summer, 1971, and a Nationalist Convention made no public statement concerning it. Rumors of a coup then increased.

PADRE, DIA DEL. Father's Day was established to fall annually on March 19th, by legislation passed on December 8, 1959.

PAHO. Pan American Health Organization.

PAIGH. Pan American Institute of Geography and History.

PAKWI. In Gracias a Dios Department, this village is between Cabo Falso and Cabo Gracias a Dios, on the Mosquito Coast.

PALMA, JOSE DE. Captain of veteran soldiers and coast guard who went to Fort Omoa (q.v.) in 1752 to guard the construction of that stronghold. Palma was made engineer in charge when Arcos (q.v.) became dissatisfied with Alvarez (q.v.) in 1759.
Palma tried to stop the contraband trade as coast guard commander. His efforts and those of two Costa Rican governors brought a near-war situation, but Spain and England were conciliatory at that time. Palma himself bought several contraband slaves, but died before charges were brought.

PAN AMERICAN CONFERENCE, 1928 see QUILALI

PAN AMERICAN SCHOOL OF AGRICULTURE see EL ZAMARANO

PANADERO. The village baker, a significant figure in rural areas of Honduras.

PANAMA CONFERENCE. An 1826 meeting called by the South American liberator, Simón Bolívar, who saw the desirability of Pan Americanism, and who hoped to bring the Western Hemisphere nations into an accord against external (European) attack, as well as to promote collaboration. A practical failure, the Conference had representation from only a few nations; and even among those, national pride and attendant jealousies precluded agreement or any persisting joint action. Almost a century passed before relatively stable and effective Pan Americanism became a reality, with such approaches as the Pan American Union and the Organization of American States.

PANA-PANA. An exchange of labor. The Miskito word implies a return of extra labor when there is some special endeavor like crop planting. The exchange somewhat resembles "barnraising" in early rural America.

PANELA. Brown crude sugar produced for home consumption, usually by small farmers. The annual production of this rural product may be as much as 20,000 tons.

PAPAGALLOS. Very cold northerly winds (in the singular, "papagayo") destructive to cacao plantings and other coastal agriculture. These sudden storms occur when cold polar air pours into Central America, usually flowing around a "low" to the east and north.

PAPALOTECA RIVER. Entering the Caribbean at Nueva Armenia, the lower reaches of this stream are banana country, at the eastern edge of Atlántida Department. It is a short stream running down from the high Cordillera Nombre de Dios behind Jutiapa and Balfate.

PAPEL SELLADO. While not unique to any one of the countries, the policy of selling "sealed paper" to record transactions such as sales is a simple form of taxing widely practiced in Latin America. For example, a "papel sellado" for the sale of a horse might cost approximately a U.S. dime. See STAMP TAX.

PAPTALAYA see AHUAS

PARGA, FRANCISCO DE. Was probably governor of Honduras in 1740.

PARQUE CONCORDIA. In the midst of this tiny block-square city park in Tegucigalpa is a model replica of a Maya temple to about one-half scale. This is only one of the surprises of a unique park, unlike any other in the world with its carved pillars, surprise pools, arbors, walks, statues, carvings, little bridges, and exotic plantings.

"PARROT STORMS" see PAPAGALLOS

PARTIDO DEMOCRATICA REVOLUCIONARIO HONDUREÑO. The Honduran Communist party which became active during the 1954 general strike (q.v.).

PARTIDO UNION NACIONAL. This party was formed in October 1955 with a view to supporting the policies and the personality of Julio Lozano Díaz, who had assumed dictatorial powers in

Honduras as a result of the flawed election of 1954. The PUN won all 56 assembly seats in 1956, but a military junta turned Lozano out of the national palace on October 21, 1856. He died a year later in Florida exile.

PARTIDO UNIONISTA CENTROAMERICANO. A new party of union for the five countries, set up at the turn of the 20th century as a party of revolution to make a fundamental change in the social, political, and economic structure, not alone to simply change the ruling oligarchies. It was founded by a Nicaraguan native, Dr. Salvador Mendieta. In 1904, it had support in Honduras as well as the other Central American countries. It originated in the failure of union efforts in 1898. The movement helped to shape leaders in each of the small nations.

PARTIES, POLITICAL. Through Honduran history, a number of parties have developed, although the Liberal and Nationalist parties have always been the principal ones. Some of the others are as follows (all prefaced by Partido):

Federal
Servile
Anexionista
Separatista
Moderado
Popular
Aristocrático
Colonial (or Gacista)
Guardiolista (or Cotorro)
de los Rojos (or Fiebres, or Anarquistas)
Polocarpista
Nacionalista
Liberal

PARTNERS OF THE AMERICAS. A voluntary organization, partially government-sponsored, whereby cities and states of the United States take "partners" of countries and cities in Latin America and carry out cooperative and beneficial endeavors in health, agriculture, education, art, etc. See RELIEF EFFORTS....

PASAQUINA. A battle in this Salvadoran place on March 16, 1871, resulted in the repulse of an invading Honduran army. The Salvadoran forces under Francisco Xatruch then entered Honduras, but were soon recalled.

PATENTES DE CORSO. Letters of Marque, the special commissions given by governments as late as the nineteenth century to permit ships bearing them to attack vessels of a declared enemy. The patentes were granted to merchant vessels in cargo service, but their activities often resulted in outright privateering.

PATINO, JOSE. Named Minister of the Indies in 1726 by King Philip V of Spain, this young and capable naval officer had rebuilt Spanish naval power as intendent of the navy, so that by 1718 there were squadrons manned by 25,000 men. By

1725 he had already begun to attend to American defenses; he established in that year a naval base and dockyards in Havana. He realized the weakness of Spanish naval power in the Caribbean, and the concomitant lack of defensive capabilities in such areas as the Honduran frontier. Patino appointed an experienced officer, Rivera y Villalón, to deal with the Anglo-Miskito problem of the northern Honduran Coast.

PATIO PROCESS see MERCURY AMALGAMATION

PATOOK RIVER. Alternate name for the Río Patuca as shown on an 1854 map published by E. G. Squier.

PATUCA RIVER. Longest river in Honduras and exceeded in Central America only by the Río Coco of the southern Honduras border with Nicaragua, and by the Río Usumacintla of Guatemala and southern Mexico. The Patuca rises (via a major tributary) in the eastern part of Francisco Morazán Department. By its major tributaries of the Río Guayape, the Río Jalan, the Río Telica, and the Río Juticalpa, it drains more than half of Olancho Department, and the large tributary Río Guayambre drains half of El Paraiso Department. The Guayape, which is the main tributary stream and may be considered the "upper Patuca," makes a 35-mile loop, doubling back on itself in central Olancho, to fork with the Guayambe and to become the Patuca near Azacualpa, with the Azacualpa Range as the mountain spine between the arms of the loop. The lower Patuca is large, very meandering, and varies in depth through twenty feet or more in flood stages. At Wangkibila it crosses into big Gracias a Dios Department after having been within ten miles of the Río Coco near Sicsayeri on that stream. From Juticalpa and Catacamas in central Olancho, where there are airfields, there is no regular access to the river banks except at Wampusirpi, nearly 200 miles downstream, and then 40 miles farther down at Ahuas. The lower river meanders through the huge delta, and then enters the Caribbean at Barra Patuca, called Butukamaya in Miskito.

PAULAYA RIVER. A major tributary in Gracias a Dios Department. See TINTO RIVER.

PAX. Sixteenth month of the Maya calendar.

PAZ, ALONSO DE. Lieutenant to the governor of Guatemala in 1548 (Cerrato, q.v.) and assigned to Honduras.

PAZ BARAONA, MIGUEL. Dr. Paz Baraona was Constitutional President from February 1, 1925 to February 1, 1929. Carias Andino (q.v.), who had emerged as the strong man of Honduras in the 1923 elections, with the new National Party strength which developed in that election, was an element in the fighting which broke out after the congress failed to select a new president. Carias renounced force, even though he could have taken power. The United States entered the situation as arbiter and aboard the U. S. S. Milwaukee (q. v.) at the port of Amapala, the Pact of Amapala was signed by the contending parties, an agreement which called for the installing of a provincial president and an election called soon thereafter. Carias entered Tegucigalpa with his troops soon after, and Paz Baraona, his former running mate, won the elections. Carias was "behind the throne."

Paz attempted immediately upon assuming the presidency to carry out the reforms which were being proposed by Carias and his National Party. Roads, schools, an agricultural vocational school, better credit standing, and eased immigration restrictions were among the reforms. Carias seemed genuinely to wish to minimize the partisan dissensions which had so often led to insurrection. Paz declared amnesty for all those who had recently engaged in revolutionary activity. The old British Interoceanic Railway loans were liquidated under an agreed plan. In 1926 there was minor insurrectionary activity, but in general the administration of Paz was consonant with his name, and the material gains and essential harmony of the period were a welcome relief from the turbulence of the century since independence.

PAZ GARCIA, POLICARDO see MILITARY ZONE COMMANDS, 1972

PAZ PAREDES, RAFAEL. Born in Colinas, Santa Bárbara, in 1911, he studied in the United States and received a law degree in Mexico in 1936. In 1947 he was named Chief of the Department of International Civil Aviation of the Secretary of Communications in Mexico and in 1953 was named to a juridical post in the United Nations Civil Aviation branch, the OACI. He is author of several books of a professional nature regarding international law in relation to specific matters, such as The Commercial Flights in International Transport and The Border Question Between Honduras and Nicaragua. He is also a poet, having published El egoista, a drama, Humedad adentio (poetry) and other works.

PEABODY MUSEUM. The Harvard University research function which led in systematized study of such Maya sites as Copán and which began such studies with a first expedition in 1888.

PEACE CORPS. This enterprise of the United States of America had activities in Honduras during 1970 and following, in the areas of university education, teacher training, community development, agriculture, home economics, nursing, cooperatives, credit unions, and small business development. The major emphasis was on basic needs in rural areas. A typical team was dealing with basic agriculture and cooperatives in Ahuas and Paptalaya on the Río Patuca in 1972-73.

PEACE FORCE, DOMINICAN REPUBLIC. In 1965 the armed

intervention of the United States in Dominican affairs was turned as rapidly as possible into an "Interamerican Peace Force" by means of an OAS resolution in May. Honduras gave 250 army troops to this endeavor; by comparison, the U. S. had 10,900 troops; El Salvador, three officers; Nicaragua, 164 troops; and Brazil, 1,115 soldiers, marines, and officers.

PEAKS, MOUNTAIN. Highest and best-known mountain peaks are Sumpal, Uyuca, Cerro de Hule, Erapuca, Cayagüanca, Congolón, Canguacota, Pico Bonito, Congregoy, Guajiquiro. Some have alternative names.

PECCARY. Dycoliles libiatus, an animal smaller than the waree (q. v. ).

PEDRARIAS. In his ninety years of life (1441 to 1531), Pedro Arias Dávila (d'Avila) was a major figure in early Central American history as provincial governor under the Kingdom of Guatemala in the viceroyalty of New Spain. Scion of an old family of St. Teresa's Roman-walled city of Avila, Pedrarias (as he was usually called) early distinguished himself as a General in wars against the Moors of Granada, and on an African military expedition. Brother of a Count (de Puño en Rostro) and married to a countess (de Moya), Pedrarias had an "in" at the court of Queen Isabella. A man of his time in political connection, military prowess, and noble lineage, he was destined for notice, which he received when appointed Governor of Darién. He arrived in Panama in 1514, followed by a group of ruined nobles seeking new fortunes. He was the murderer of Balboa in 1519, and in a cruel age among ruthless men developed an especial reputation for cruelty and unscrupulousness. He sent Gil Gonzales of his home city on explorations of Nicaragua and Honduras, was instrumental in the conquest of Nicaragua and Costa Rica, and was Governor of Nicaragua from 1526 until his death, having been credited with the death of 2,000,000 Indians as well as of a number of his compatriots.

PEDRAZA, CRISTOBAL DE. Bishop and royal official in Honduras in the mid-1500s, he was a friend of the Indians, and began to aid in enforcing the laws against Indian exploitation and persecution. He spoke out freely in condemning the cruelty and greed of early conquistadors and their followers. He was very much like the better known Bartolomé de las Casas (q. v. ).

PEDRO SERRANO. A ship, for which the Serranilla shoals (q. v. ) were named. The survivors of the Serrano wreck saved themselves by eating turtles and drinking their blood.

PENINSULARES. Used to denote Spanish-born whites (from the Iberian peninsula) during Spanish colonial days. Contrasted with white "Creoles" (q.v.), these Spanish-born colonials always held the highest offices, taking precedence over Creoles in every case.

PEQUEÑA PROPRIEDAD. A land holding classification used to indicate twenty to fifty manzanas (approximately 35 to 88 acres).

PEQUEÑAS INDUSTRIAS, ESCUELA NACIONAL DE. The school for small industries was established in Santa Bárbara on May 10, 1956, as another link in vocational education.

PERAMAS, JOAQUIN see MURGA, ANTONIO

PERAZA AYALA CASTILLA Y ROJAS, ANTONIO. This nobleman, Conde de Gómera, had a long incumbency as the chief royal officer in Central America, 1611 to 1626. From one of the high noble families of Spain, the count was the first military person appointed governor. His incumbency was an unsettled one, including his suspension and reinstatement on charges of corruption. He was noted for efforts to revive the sagging and precarious economy of the area. It was he who revised his predecessors' port policy in the Bay of Honduras. See CRIADO DE CASTILLA, ALONSO.

PER CAPITA INCOME. In 1969, per capita income was the equivalent of $242 (U.S.), which placed Honduras 15th among the Latin American Nations. This compares with $89 in 1945, $104 in 1949, and $114 in 1952.

PERE, DAVID. Panamanian Ambassador to Costa Rica in 1974 who reported a threat to the Honduran government. See TAX, BANANAS.

PEREZ, CARLOS ANDRES. President of Venezuela, taking office in March 1974, who became a critic of the industrialized nations as Arab-inspired oil price rises began late in that year to have impact upon the world economy. Early pacts with Honduras and other Central American countries were among his foreign policy moves in an expression of Venezuela's active role in the Organization of Petroleum Exporting Countries. One of his gambits was to support the Cafés Suaves Centrales (q.v.) with an eye to pegging the world prices of coffee at much higher levels. See OIL AGREEMENTS, VENEZUELA.

PEREZ QUIJANO, AGUSTIN. Governor in 1775.

PEREZ QUIJANO, BARTOLOME. Lieutenant Colonel Pérez was governor in 1769, following González.

PERIMETER, HONDURAN BORDERS.
        The Atlantic Coast                      545 miles
        The Guatemalan Frontier           211 miles

|  |  |
|---|---|
| The El Salvador Frontier | 212 miles |
| The Pacific Coast | 95 miles |
| The Nicaraguan Frontier | 545 miles |
| Total | 1,608 miles |

PERIODISTA, DIA DEL. On May 20, 1930, a "day of journalists" was established to be celebrated on May 25 of that year as the 100th anniversary of the appearance of La Gaceta del Gobierno, the first public periodical in Honduras.

PERMANENT COMMITTEE OF NATIONAL EMERGENCY. Known best by the acronym COPEN. See HONDURAN COUNCIL OF PRIVATE ENTERPRISE.

PERSIAN. His Majesty's British brig-of-war which was used by Wodehouse when he occupied Roatán and the adjacent Bay Islands on August 10, 1852, in violation of the July 4, 1850, Clayton-Bulwer (q.v.) treaty. This represented the establishment of the "Colony of the Bay Islands" (q.v.).

PERSONALISMO (Spiritual Value). Part of the Catholic and Hispanic heritage is the intense individualism which is expressed as personalismo. As a consequence, leading Central Americans are not too interested in the everyday routines of commerce and government. Scholarship and artistic or literary creativity, rather than business powers, are traditional marks of the ideal or "upper-class" man. The individual soul is more important than pragmatic or technical achievements. This becomes a fundamental point to help illumine differences in cultural, social, business, and governmental relationships as compared to countries with Anglo-Saxon antecedents.

PERULERO. The perulero (Peruvian) peso, worth 8 reales in 1650, was devalued to 6 at that time. This act tended to keep this inferior coinage in circulation. It was significant that the audiencia proposed to send all perulero money to Tegucigalpa, where it could be refined into silver bars of specified purity. In effect, however, many merchants refused the debased Peruvian money, which caused a Central American money crisis, its height coming in 1670.

PETACA. A Carib basket hamper. The word is Spanish, but the Caribs are especially skilled at this sort of basketry.

PETEN, FORT. Frontier fortress in the formidable Petén jungle of northern Guatemala, established somewhat anticlimatically between 1699-1714; related to Honduras in that it was the northwestern bastion of a frontier line loosely held by Spain and anchored in the southeast by the great Fort Inmaculada (El Castillo) on the San Juan River of Nicaragua; it was maintained in the center by Fort San Felipe near the Guatemalan coast, and by Forts Omoa and Trujillo in Honduras. The line was incredibly far-spaced, but had nevertheless an effect disproportionate to its scanty strength, as the British discovered to their sorrow just after 1780. Half or more of Honduras was east of the frontier, in the untamed hinterland.

PETROLEUM EXPLORATION. Offshore oil exploration is being carried out on the north coast from Puerto Cortés to Cabo Gracias a Dios. Helicopters for international companies work out of Puerto Lempira on the Laguna Caratasca.

PIALERAS. A rawhide lariat or lasso ("la reata") which is used in Olancho department by the unique method of "Tail-dallying" --that is, the pialera (or lariat) strands are braided into the cow-horse's tail, and when the lasso loop settles over a steer's head, the pony faces away from the steer and sets his feet.

PICADAS. A term used by rubber-hunters to describe the lines laboriously cut with machetes to check a timber stand--the trails along which "timber-cruising" is accomplished.

PICADILLO. A vegetable dish made in Honduras with "vegetable pear" (or avocado) and potato, chopped fine with onion and a little garlic, and boiled.

PICHE, GUILLERMO. Spanish name for the Black River British entrepreneur, William Pitt (q.v.).

PICO BONITO see BONITO, PEAK

PICO DE NAVAJA. A 6,500-foot peak in southern Honduras in the San Juancito Mountains.

PICTUN. A Maya calendrical unit, multiple of 20 Baktún (q.v.), or a total of 2,880,000 days. See CALABTUN; KINCHILTUN; ALAUTUN.

PIERRE LE GRAND. French freebooter who operated in the Bay of Honduras in the 17th century.

PIET HEYN. Dutch admiral who operated with 28 ships mounting 600 cannon near Havana in 1628. The silver bearing naos from Honduras were threatened. He sunk the Santiago Nao (q.v.). Dutch, English, French, and Spanish were in frequent contest (often piratical) for two centuries in the Caribbean Sea.

PIJEVALLE. Palm nuts, like miniature coconuts but in very large clusters of up to several hundred, similar in taste to chestnuts.

PILA. A vat or water tank; a term used broadly to cover everything from obrajes (q.v.) for the preparation of indigo, to simple laundering tubs or storage tank facilities.

PIÑA DE AZUCAR. Sugar-pine or pineapple, fruit weighing as much as six pounds. Wild pineapples grow in mountain valleys.

PINABETAL. A place where the pinobete (q.v.) pine grows. The "-tal" is a Nahuatl ending, probably originally "-tlan." The Nahua word for pine is "ocote"--hence "ocotal" or "ocotlán."

PINABETE. Local name for a species of pine different from the usual "ocote" pine (q.v.). The pinabete is Pinus pseudostrobus, and the wood is similar to white pine.

PINE FOREST. In colonial times one of the great pine forests of the Americas stretched between Tegucigalpa and the Nicaraguan northern region of Nueva Segovia. Pines in remote tiny virgin stands of that area to this day are over four feet in diameter and 60 to 80 feet to the first limb.

PINEDA, ALVAREZ DE. In about 1515, Pineda was sent by Francisco de Garay, Spanish governor of Jamaica, to find the mythical "strait" between the Atlantic and Pacific oceans. As a result of his voyage, the land was found to be continuous from Honduras to Florida; hence from Panama to Florida since the Panama-Honduras link had been previously established.

PINEDA, RICARDO. Second director of Public Instruction. See PUBLIC EDUCATION, DIRECTION OF.

PINEDA GOMEZ, JOSE. Secretary general of the Honduran Communist Party, the Partido Democrática Revolucionario Hondureño, during the 1954 General Strike period.

PIÑOL MUÑOZ, JOSE MARIA. Governor of Honduras in 1812.

PINUELA. Also called pinquin, this tree produces a fruit not unlike pineapple.

PINUS CARIBEA see CARIBBEAN PINE

PINUS OOCARPA. North American pines which grow down into and through Honduras from the countries to the north, but which are found no farther south than about the Central Atlantic Coastal area of Nicaragua.

PINZON, YANEZ see SOLIS, JUAN DIAZ DE

PINZON-SOLIS. An expedition of 1508-09 which took the explorers south to Yucatán and Honduras, all the way to Brazil in search of a passage to Asia.

PIPANTE. A dugout canoe found only in this part of Central America, one of four or more distinct types. The pipante

PIPANTE: Also called pitpán, the flat-bottomed dugout especially characteristic of the Río Coco. Usually poled rather than paddled.

(see drawing) is a narrow, flat-bottomed, shallow, very graceful dugout usually made from cedro real, or royal cedar ("Spanish" cedar, aromatic, often called in the U.S. cigar-box wood). This strong, light, mahogany-like wood is very durable. A twenty-foot dugout is often under 150 pounds in weight, the thickness being under an inch at the gunwales. The bow usually has a 3"-square mortise cut through it to enable the pipante to be moored by thrusting a pole through the opening into the stream-bed. The size averages 20" beam, 25' length. It is estimated there are 20,000 or more pipantes used on the border Río Coco and other rivers of Nicaragua and Honduras, such as the Río Patuca, emptying into the Caribbean.

PIPILES. The Pipiles were Nahua who, following the fall of the Nahua-influenced Teotihuacán north of Mexico City in around 650 A.D., began a major migration to the southeast. The Pipiles were "nobles" or "princes" who established themselves on the north side of the Isthmus of Tehuantepec and then continued on in the same direction to settle in southern Guatemala, all of El Salvador, and in limited numbers in and beyond the Gulf of Fonseca in Honduras and Nicaragua. A few Pipiles reached Colombia (on the Pacific side) and down as far as northern Peru. The settling of this group in the Central American area was a result of pursuit by the Olmecs of the Tehuantepec Isthmus.

 Torquemada wrote in 1590-1616 of the Pipil-Nicaraos. Words ending in "galpa" are of Pipil derivation (such as Tegucigalpa).

 It is remarkable that an early location of the Pipiles was in Xolotán on the northern Tehuantepec coast, and that Xolotlán was the name (still often used) of Lake Managua in Nicaragua. The Pipiles represented a major influence in culture, although not in numbers. They were aristocrats, noblemen, and leaders, something like those similar refugees who settled Venice after the fall of Rome.

PIROQUE. A Spanish vessel developed by the navy in 1670 to fight pirates. They were as much as 90 feet long, 18 feet beam, with an armament of five guns. They were light, fast, and maneuverable. The word is very like pirogue, a term applied widely in the Gulf of Mexico and Western Caribbean to a type of canoe, usually a dugout.

PITA. A form of agave, also called by the Nahua word "Ixtle," giving fibres of all degrees of coarseness and used in the manufacture of thread, hammocks, and paper.

PITCH see BREA

PITPAN see PIPANTE

PITT, WILLIAM. Not to be confused with the statesman, Pitt was a lumberman and trader, banana and sugar planter at Black River (q.v.) following 1699. He chose the site. Pitt had a sumptuous mansion up the Black River 40 miles, and became personally wealthy. Black River was called "Guellermo Piche's Town" by the Spanish. Piche is used as a given name in Central America in modern times.

PITT, WILLIAM. British statesman and Prime Minister who in a conciliatory policy toward Spain, ordered British evacuation of the Bay Islands in 1748. The Baymen and the Shoremen were furious. Pitt was anxious to improve Anglo-Spanish relations in order to meet the real enemy, which he considered to be France.

PLACER DE LA VIVORA. Also called the Pedro Bank, the main route north and around Cuba past Honduras (in colonial times) was between this bank and the Serranilla shoals (q.v.).

PLAGUE. In the 16th century Central American and Mexican highlands, those of Honduras in particular, were swept by plague, probably the flea-carried pulmonary or bubonic plague familiar in its terror to 14th century Europe. These related diseases were called variously cocolizthi, malazahuatl, or gucumatz, all Indian names.

PLAN DE IGUALA. The basic plan of a Mexican empire by which the Mexican venture of Agustín Iturbide was established. Dated February 24, 1821, it came prior to the September 15 Act of Independence of Central America. The plan provided for an independent New Spain, the Roman Catholic religion, a Spanish emperor, a governing junta and a provisional government; a Constitution and Cortes for imperial Mexico, an army to protect the "three Guarantees," which were Catholicism, Independence, and Union of Americans and Europeans. The junta and the army, clearly, were to rule, with elections promised. The plan was signed simply, "Iturbide."

This project proposed not only the establishment of a Mexican empire, but that it be headed by one of the Bourbon dynasty in Spain. This appealed to Central America. Provincianos hoped to shake off the control of Guatemala City. Chiapas joined; it is now part of Mexico. The alternative was a Central American republic. Honduras adhered to the plan. If the plan had gone through, the isthmus area from Tehuantepec to Colombia might have been part of a single empire extending from California to the southern continent. Georgraphy was a major deterrent to union. The ruggedness of the terrain made transport and coordinated effort difficult if not impossible.

The Plan of Iguala was actually the basis for Mexican and (by the "domino effect") Central American Independence (q.v.) in 1821. Independence ultimately brought separation rather than union.

279  Plan Político

PLAN POLITICO DE UNIDAD NACIONAL. A plan for party unity between the National and Liberal parties, whereby patronage was to be distributed by previous agreements, and under which Ramón E. Cruz was elected President in 1971, only to fall in December of 1972, after 18 months in office, when a coup led by Brigadier General Oswaldo López Arellana (q.v.) toppled the government of Cruz.

PLANO AGUATAL. A high and level glen or cove in the San Juancito Mountains, characteristic of high valleys in the Honduran mountains. Trees grow to immense sizes in the cloud forest at altitudes of 5,000 to 8,000 feet.

PLATA, GENERAL. Honduran commander of a border patrol in the Danlí-Ocotal border region in 1932 during the Sandino (q.v.) troubles. Plata's task was to prevent illegal arms from crossing into Nicaragua, in accordance with the General Treaty of Peace and Amity of 1923. But even before Plata arrived on the scene, a large arms shipment reached Sandino, part of it reputedly from Honduran arsenals.

PLATANO, MONTES DEL RIO. Just west of the Río Plátano (q.v.) these sizable mountains rise to altitudes of 4,000 feet. The Río Paulaya is just north of them, a major tributary of the Río Tinto.

PLATANO RIVER. The "Plantain River" flows into the Caribbean with no intervening lagoon, just to the west of the Brus Lagoon (q.v.) bar.

PLAYA DE LOS MUERTOS. An archaeological site in the Ulua river area of northwestern Honduras, probably dating to a period between 1000 B.C. and 1000 A.D. (hence similar to Copán).

POETRY. Poets make up the major component among Honduran authors. Local difficulties of publication make the production of books, especially novels, almost prohibitive, whereas poetry can reach an audience through the press and periodicals. Froylán Turcios (q.v.), Oscar Acosta (q.v.), Clementina Suárez, Rafael Heliodoro Valle (q.v.) and numerous others are or were distinguished Honduran poets. See LITERATURE.

POLICARPISTAS. Adherents of Policarpo Bonilla (q.v.) in the 1923 election.

POLICE. Where police forces are part of the military organization in some countries, these functions are assigned to the Security Corps in Honduras, and the regular armed forces (q.v.) are separate. See CUERPO ESPECIAL DE SEGURIDAD.

POLITICAL DIVISIONS, MID-18th CENTURY. Around 1850 there

were seven organized political divisions, with names and approximate sizes as follows:

| Name | Square Miles |
| --- | --- |
| Choloteca | 2,000 |
| Comayagua | 4,800 |
| Gracias | 4,050 |
| Olancho | 11,300 |
| Santa Bárbara | 3,250 |
| Tegucigalpa | 1,500 |
| Yoro | 15,100 |

Tegucigalpa Department had in 1850 about 60,000 inhabitants, and Comayagua had 70,000.

POLITICAL PARTIES. The bases of most political organizations which have emerged since independence were the individual concerns of a particular leader, and during most of the 19th century such parties were actually armed political bands or, in effect, private guerrilla armies. There is a guarantee in the 1965 Constitution that political parties may legally register and function, provided they are not divided on sex, class, or racial bases. There is a provision aimed against Communist movements, or any others which "threaten the sovereignty of the state." The net result is that political parties in Honduras have had less real effect than in some of the other Central American countries, and unlike some others, Honduras has just two major parties, Liberal and National.

PONCE DE LEON, PEDRO DE GODEY. Governor in 1672.

PONCE DE LEON, RODRIGO. Governor in 1582 and again in 1594.

POND CAY see GUANAJA ISLAND

POP. First month of the Maya Calendar.

POPE, WILLIAM L. A British subject and a priest who was the founder of a proposed colony on the north Coast of Honduras. Pope's scheme was deceptive. He had contracted for 250 Irishmen rather than the British and French colonists advertised, and had advertised the site as San Pedro Sula, when the charter showed the site to be 130 miles east near Trujillo. The resolution concerning the colony was passed in Tegucigalpa on May 3, 1879.

POPENOE, WILSON. Dr. Popenoe's career of service to Central America is unparalleled. He was the founder and Director of the Escuela Agrícola Panamericana at El Zamarano (q.v.) in Honduras from 1942 until 1957, and following that time was Director Emeritus. From 1913 until 1925 he was with the United States Department of Agriculture, and from 1925 to 1957 with the United Fruit Company, which sponsored the internationally known Escuela Panamericana. Dr. Popenoe has been decorated with medals and orders of merit from many Latin American governments from Honduras and Guatemala to Peru and Chile, and has been awarded several honorary doctoral degrees. His favorite title, however, was "Mr. Avocado" because of his role in introducing that tropical fruit into Spain and the rest of Latin America. Dr. Popenoe's son, Hugh, has followed in his father's footsteps. The Popenoe colonial home in old Antigua, Guatemala, is internationally famous.

POPULATION. At the end of the colonial period, Honduras was fourth in population among the Central American countries, with fewer than 200,000 people. By the 1930s the population was around a million, and Honduras was in third place, with about 42 persons per square mile. The 1970 population was 2.6 million.

Recent census data indicate a racially mixed population, with 90 per cent mestizo, 7 per cent Indian, two per cent Negro, and one per cent white. Most of the original native Indian groups have lost cultural identity. The British influence in the Bay Islands has had a numerically small but culturally significant effect on the population. In the 1950s there were about 33,000 foreign-born living in the republic, 90 per cent of these being from other Central American countries. Present growth rate is 3.7 per cent per annum, but present density is still just over 60 per square mile. Ninety-two per cent of the population are settled on 56 per cent of the land, with the eastern third of the country very low in population. The western departments adjacent to Guatemala and El Salvador, are most densely populated. The average in this area is 80-90 per square mile. City areas are growing rapidly, particularly Tegucigalpa and San Pedro Sula.

The population, typical of developing countries, is young. In 1969 half the total was under 17 years. A special problem, which led to war in 1969, is the number of Salvadorans, many of them illegally living in Honduran territory. (This is in spite of the fact that constitutional citizenship is easily attained.) The estimate at the time of the conflict was 300,000, and after 1969 about 60,000 of them were returned to El Salvador.

Population, with present trends, will be, by publication date of this volume, approximately three million. Family planning is occurring in some areas, with established clinics, although the practice is opposed by the Catholic Church.

POPULATION CHANGE. Honduran population growth over two decades, rural and urban, is as follows:

Population Data

|       | 1950      | 1960      | 1970      |
|-------|-----------|-----------|-----------|
| Rural | 955,000   | 1,165,000 | 1,500,000 |
| Urban | 430,000   | 590,000   | 900,000   |
| Total | 1,385,000 | 1,755,000 | 2,400,000 |

|                  | (1950-1960) | (1960-1970) |
|------------------|-------------|-------------|
| Per cent increase | 27%        | 37%         |

POPULATION DATA, 1971, 1973. The total population of Honduras has increased at a rate of about 3.7 per cent in recent years:

| Year | Urban Population | Rural Population | Total Population |
|------|------------------|------------------|------------------|
| 1971 | 731,100          | 1,926,600        | 2,657,700        |
| 1972 | 769,000          | 1,986,600        | 2,755,600        |
| 1973 | 809,300          | 2,049,500        | 2,858,800        |
| 1980 (est.) | 1,130,000 | 2,533,000        | 3,663,000        |

Distribution by Economic Activity:

| Activity | 1971 | 1972 | 1973 |
|----------|------|------|------|
| Agriculture, Forestry, Fishing | 538,200 | 555,200 | 573,600 |
| Mining | 2,500 | 2,500 | 2,600 |
| Manufacturing | 69,300 | 74,200 | 76,700 |
| Construction | 18,200 | 19,600 | 20,300 |
| Transportation | 14,900 | 15,400 | 15,900 |
| Services (electricity, etc.) | 4,100 | 5,100 | 5,300 |
| Commercial | 44,600 | 46,900 | 48,500 |
| Administration, Defense, etc. | 33,800 | 29,900 | 30,800 |
| Banks, other services | 99,900 | 104,000 | 107,500 |

Work Force Totals

(included are some others than those above)   759,500   784,000   810,700

The percentage of unemployed has remained at eight per cent; the average real income per capita from $509 to $515 per annum. In 1972 the labor unions had 67,956 members.

POPULATION IN 1492. According to modern demographic scholarship, the population of the Americas at the time of European discovery may have been as great as 80,000,000, or considerably more than the European population of about 60,000,000 in the 16th century. Estimates vary downward to a tenth of that number. There is strong indication that Honduras and the rest of Meso-America supported a very heavy population in the 15th century, quite probably much greater than at present. Great epidemics diminished these concentrations of populations, with attrition as much as 90 per cent during the first two post-conquest centuries.

POPULATION, 16th CENTURY. The Honduran population in 1524 was listed as 400,000, probably an under-estimate. Sixty years later the official count was under 5,000, (probably a low figure). This terrible attrition was due to war, slavery, and disease.

PORCUPINE. British war-sloop under Captain Dalrymple (q.v.) in the action against Fort Omoa (q.v.) in 1779.

PORRAS, FRANCISCO DE. Captain of the Santiago de Palos on Columbus' (q.v.) fourth voyage, the one of Honduran discovery. Porras had been forced on Columbus by Alonso de Morales, Treasurer of Castile. Diego de Porras also went along. These two were brothers of Morales' mistress, and Francisco was charged with care of all valuables obtained on the voyage. The Porras brothers were later to mutiny and to make much trouble for Columbus.

PORTAL DEL INFIERNO. Narrow canyon where the Río Patuca debouches in a gorge and rapids from the mountains into its lower reaches at an altitude of 400 feet above sea level in southern Olancho department. However, mountains follow the river on both sides of its valley, as high as 2,500 feet, until the line is crossed into Gracias a Dios Department. The "Gates of Hell" can be navigated in small craft, dugouts and rafts.

PORTILLO, RUBEN see GENERAL STRIKE, 1954

PORTS. On the Caribbean side, Puerto Cortés, La Ceiba, Trujillo, Tela, Roatán, El Porvenir, Caratasca, Puerto Lempira, Castilla. On the Pacific side (Bay of Fonseca), Amapala, San Lorenzo, Las Conchas, Patria, El Aceituno, La Brea.

PORTUGUES, BARTHOLOMEW. A pirate of Portuguese ancestry who operated in the Bay of Honduras in the 17th century.

POSTAL SERVICE. Honduras has 20 first-class post-offices and about 430 others. As in most Central American countries, stamps are colorful and rates are generally comparable to United States postal rates.

POYAIS, REPUBLIC OF. A mythical republic purportedly on the Mosquito Coast, proposed by a joking stock-broker in London when the post-Waterloo era in Britain saw great financial support given to the emerging free nations of Spanish America. Hoax though it was, the "Republic of Poyais on the Mosquito Coast" had its stock over-subscribed!

POYAS (or PAYAS). An Indian tribal group of northeastern Honduras, the Poyas remained isolated for much of the colonial period, thus maintaining their basic culture and traditions. Like the Sumos and Miskitos, their language and culture were related to those of the forest Indians of northern South America. They practiced "milpah" slash-and-burn agriculture, food crops being manioc (or yuca [q.v.]) and plantains. There were divisions of labor between the sexes, the men being primarily hunters; South American-type blowguns were used as well as bows and arrows. There were still a few hundred tribal Poya (or Paya) left in the mid-twentieth century, living near Santa María del Carbón and Dulce Nombre de Culmí in Olancho Department. Unlike the Miskito, the Poya did not intermarry. Their language has been uncertainly identified as belonging to the Macro-Chibchan group.

POYER. Alternate name for the Paya or Poya Indians.

PRAYER, CARIB. When Carib boatmen are becalmed, they will say a Spanish prayer as follows:
"Sopla, San Antonio, Barba de oro cachimba de plata."
"Blow, St. Anthony, with golden beard and pipe of silver!"

P.R.D.H. see PARTIDO REVOLUCIONARIO DEMOCRATICO HONDUREÑO; also COMMUNIST PARTY OF HONDURAS

PREGO, VASQUEZ. Captain General who in 1753 asked for permission to get slaves from Jamaica for the building of Fort Omoa (q.v.). This was approved in 1755. See HALL, JASPER.

PRESENTE. A periodical of arts and letters, Central American in focus, in the 1970s. See SOSA, ROBERTO.

PRESIDENTIAL HONOR GUARD. This guard is unusual in that it is not under immediate jurisdiction of the chief of the armed forces, but reports directly to the President. Under Brigadier General Osvaldo López Arellano up to 1970, and since his accession to power following the 1970 coup, the guard consists of about 1,000 men, the largest single military command unit; it includes a band and a drum and bugle corps. The headquarters is near the capital at Las Tapias. See ARMED FORCES; MILITARY COMMAND STRUCTURE.

PRESIDENTS, AUDIENCIA OF GUATEMALA. Throughout this volume the Presidents of the Audiencia of Guatemala, acting as Captains-General, have been considered as governors of Honduras because of their large responsibilities, dealing with all of Central America. They are, however, not synonymous with those who were essentially responsible for Honduras on a provincial basis, and a number of conquistadors who in a loose sense governed from 1522 until 1542 when the capital of Central America was established in Comayagua. If there is confusion concerning these overlapping "governors" it is because the situation was in itself confused.

PRESIDENT'S MEETING, CENTRAL AMERICA, 1974. In May of 1974 a meeting of all Central American Presidents was planned to take place in northern Nicaragua. Strongman General Anastasio Somoza DeBayle had invited presidents of the other four countries to a meeting at Jalapa, on one of his properties. The meeting would have been the first such to take place in 67 years.
On May 30 it was announced that the President of El Salvador, Col. Arturo Armando Molina, had requested a postponement. A major subject of the session was to further peace between Honduras and El Salvador. President of Honduras General Oswaldo López Arellano replied to the postponement by stating that El Salvador was not interested in peace. The two countries have had broken relations since the three-day War in 1969. Most serious of the factors in the five-year feud was the arms race developing between the two countries. See WAR, EL SALVADOR, 1969.

PRESIDENTS OF CENTRAL AMERICA. (Dates indicate terms of office)

| | |
|---|---|
| Gainza, Gabino | 1821-1822 |
| Filísola, Vicente | 1822-1823 |
| Arce, Manuel José | 1823-1828 |
| Beltranena, Mariano | 1828-1829 |
| Barrundia, José Francisco | 1829-1830 |
| *Morazán, Francisco | 1830-1839 |

*(Honduras was one of the Confederated states under this aegis, and Honduran F. Morazán (q.v.) was a significant leader in independence and confederation.)

PRIEGO, CONTE DE PRIEGO see ALTAMIRANO Y VELASCO, FERNANDO DE

PRIMARY SCHOOLS. The first official creation of a school "system" was under the administration of Juan Lindo on October 30, 1822. The curriculum was reading, writing, singing, and Christian doctrine.
There are now four levels or categories of primary schools in Honduras:
Primera clase: Over 350 students
Segunda clase: 150 to 350 students
Tercera clase: 60 to 150 students
Cuarta clase: 60 or less.

PRO PATRIA. A Tegucigalpa-based political periodical edited by the widely known author, Augusto C. Coello (q.v.).

PROCLAMATION OF THE ARMED FORCES OF HONDURAS. The proclamation made by Colonel Carracioli and Major Gálvez when they ended the Julio Lozano regime on October 21, 1956, by a bloodless coup.

PROGRAM OF PUBLIC INVESTMENT, 1970-74 see DEVELOPMENT PLANS

PROPERTY TRANSFER TAX. This tax is imposed on all real estate and building transfers, and is two per cent for urban, 1.5 per cent for rural property.

PROTESTANT DENOMINATIONS. In the late 1960s, the following denominations were represented in Honduras, with approximate numbers given:

| | |
|---|---|
| Methodist (predominant in the Bay Islands) | 14,000 |
| Church of God | 9,600 |
| Seventh Day Adventist | 6,000 |
| Assemblies of God | 5,000 |
| Central American Mission | 4,800 |
| Friends Board of Missions (California) | 3,000 |
| Evangelican and Reformed | 2,000 |
| Jewish | 250 |
| Bahai and Moravian | (No numbers known) |

PROTOCOL OF 1960. A step beyond the Multilateral Treaty of 1958 and the Agreement of Integrated Industries, toward the economic integration of Central America.

PROTOCOL OF 1964. A protocol of further agreement subsequent to the General Treaty of Economic Integration of Central America.

PROVIDENCE COMPANY. Formed in 1630 for the purpose of occupying Providence and Henrietta islands in the western Caribbean, this British company was trying to get a foothold in that area at the expense of Spain. The Earl of Warwick and the Puritan John Pym were leading figures. James II of England issued a charter for trade all the way along the coast as far up as Yucatán, and authorized the company to occupy any land not actually held by Spain. By 1635 the company had occupied islands all the way from Tortuga off the north coast of Haiti (later the notorious haven of the buccaneers), to Roatán, the largest Bay Island, some 50 miles off the Honduran coast. The Bay Islands were to be a pawn of empire for nearly three centuries. Balize in British Honduras was occupied by other Englishmen in 1638. The mainland coast was occupied around Cabo Gracias a Dios. It was under Captain Sussex Cammock that the Mosquito Coast was occupied in 1633.

PROVINCES OF CENTRAL AMERICA. The first colonial grouping (following 1568) was as follows:

Chiapas (and Soconusco)
Chimaltenango
Chiquimula
Comayagua (Honduras)
Costa Rica
Escuintla
León (Nicaragua)

Quezaltenango
Sacatepequez
San Salvador
Sololá
Sonsonate
Suchitepequez
Totonicapán

Chiapas became a Mexican state; Costa Rica and San Salvador, separate countries. The others are now towns.

PROVINCIAL ADMINISTRATION, 1542. On November 20, 1542 the Spanish King assigned by decree the government of much of Central America to the Audiencia de los Confines, with the seat established as Valladolid, later called Comayagua (q.v.). The decree included--in addition to Honduras--Tabasco, Chiapas, Soconusco, Yucatán, Cozumel, Guatemala, Nicaragua, Costa Rica, Veragua, and Panamá. The "capitol" was transferred to Gracias a Dios on May 16, 1544, and to Guatemala in June of 1550.

PROVINCIAS UNIDAS DEL CENTRO DE AMERICA. A federation established after secession from Mexico, proclaimed by a constituent assembly in Guatemala on July 1, 1823. It included the states of Honduras, Nicaragua, Guatemala, El Salvador, and Costa Rica. Civil War came soon afterward, with the result that Francisco Morazán was made president in 1830. His liberal followers proposed a liberal program.

The Confederation known as the United Provinces of Central America persisted for a period of sixteen years, 1823-1839. A league of confederated states rather than a federal republic with strong central government, the period of the union was riddled by civil war and the union itself was made tenuous by inherited social ills, a strong residual caste system, the hacienda pattern, agricultural monoculture, the fact of civil war, and factional strife of several sorts. Under the "George Washington of Central America," Francisco Morazán, and while he was president (1830-1839), the administration, in spite of conflict and vicissitudes, was able to promote public education, reorganize the administrative aspects of government, and within the limits of time and geography, develop industry and commerce. Morazán was instrumental in getting Central America to adopt the criminal code originally drafted by Edward Livingston for Louisiana. The capital of the United Republic was moved to San Salvador in 1835.

Guatemalan forces under the strong leadership of Rafael Carrera were responsible for the collapse of the Confederation on May 18, 1838, when civil war broke out again. Morazán met defeat at the hands of Carrera, and the Confederation ended in 1839, when Morazán resigned. Honduras and the four other states have since then been independent nations. Central American unity is a dream widely praised but little pursued in all five of the countries.

PTOLEMY - MAPS. The editions of Ptolemy's Geographia which appeared in Rome in 1507 and 1508 did not show the Honduran coast, although it had been discovered five years previously (see COLUMBUS). The north coast of South America and parts of the Greater Antilles were shown, however, with surprising fidelity. By the 1511 edition the Antilles were better shown in Bernardus Sylvanus' world map, but still no Central American Coast. Meanwhile, Waldseemuller's (q.v.) 12-part map of 1507 did seem to indicate that coast with the Honduran projection.

PUBLIC EDUCATION, DIRECTION OF. Following the Code for Public Education (q.v.) in 1882, on January 4, 1895 there was established a Dirección General de Instrucción Primaria, and the first director appointed was F. Alfredo Alvarado, who was soon followed on June 30, 1896 by Ricardo Pineda.

PUBLIC EDUCATION, FREE AND COMPULSORY. A decree by the national Congress on February 21, 1866 established primary education for both sexes to be supported by the municipal authority, to be free and available. The law of September 15, 1875 implemented this concept more specifically.

PUBLIC EDUCATION, MINISTRY OF see CABINET

PUBLIC HEALTH, MINISTRY OF see CABINET

PUBLIC SECURITY, MINISTRY OF see CABINET

PUERTO CABALLOS. This northern Honduran sea port was the principal outlet and European port of the Audiencia of Guatemala from the 1570s until 1604. The import traffic included wine, oil, hard goods, and furnishings; exports were indigo, hides, silver, cacao, cochineal and indigo. Pirate raids in 1591 and 1596 greatly discouraged the use of the port. Illegal exporting of such items as indigo often took place, directed to other colonial ports such as Havana and Cartagena. Wine, oil, and silver were frequently illegal trade items.
    This port of entry, located on the east side of the Bay of Omoa, was so called because in 1524 Gil González Dávila had to throw some horses overboard when caught in a storm. In 1525 it became La Navidad (q.v.) and the name was changed in 1870 to Puerto Cortés (q.v.) in memory of the famed Mexican Conquistador.

PUERTO CASTILLA. One of the two seaports on the north coastal Bay of Trujillo (the other being Trujillo itself), Puerto Castilla is near the tip of the Cape Honduras (Punta Caxinas). The port is actually an island surrounded to the north, east, and west by a canal. Ruined Spanish fortifications lie near the sea.

PUERTO CORTES. North coastal port on the Bay of Omoa, Puerto

Cortés is the major seaport on the Caribbean side of Honduras, served by the rail line to San Pedro Sula. This fact partially accounts for the considerable industrial development of that latter city. The port is also the site of major dock installations, most complete in the country. The bay is sheltered from prevailing winds, and while the terrain is low, it is an effective harbor site and has been so since earliest conquest times. Puerto Cortés is on a multiple delta formed by the Chamelicón and Ulua rivers. It is also a municipal cabacera. The name in colonial times was Puerto Caballos (q. v.).

PUERTO LEMPIRA. Cabacera of big Gracias a Dios Department, this is the largest settlement in that vast area. Located on the Caratasca Lagoon, it is not far from the bar of the lagoon, and from consequent access there to the Caribbean. A shrimp-packing industry has developed. There is no port for large shipping, however, and no accessible hinterland to support in any event. Oil company explorations are being carried out in the Caribbean shallows just to the east. There is an airfield and biweekly air service.

PUN see PARTIDO UNION NACIONAL

PUNTA CAXINAS. Columbus' name for the Cape Honduras (see CABO DE HONDURAS), north of Trujillo, which juts prominently toward the Bay Island of Guanaja where he first landed. He named it after the Arawak name of a tree found there in abundance, the Chrysobalanus icaco; common name, caxinas. Now called Punta Castilla, the point is long and low, sheltering the bay of Trujillo. Columbus made his first Central American mainland landing here on August 14, 1502.

PUNTA PATUCA. One of the six major points or capes on the northern Caribbean Coast, at the point of the Río Patuca delta. See CABO CAMARON.

PUNTERO. A "point watcher," a professional who checked the readiness of indigo in the pilas for allowing the liquid to settle. His skill had a lot to do with the final quality of the dye.

PURO. Native cigar made from the excellent "leaf tobacco" grown in western Honduras.

- Q -

QUAPOT. A freshwater fish caught in the rivers. Same species of cichlid as the "quapote" in Nicaragua. (Pronounced wah-poh-tee.)

QUAUHTLI. Fifteenth day of the Aztec month; meaning, "eagle."

QUEEN ANNE'S REVENGE. A pirate ship in the Bay of Honduras in 1717-1718, commanded by the privateer-turned-pirate called "Blackbeard," Edward Teach (q.v.).

QUEPRIVA, FORT. New name of Fort Dalling in 1782. See TRUJILLO, BASE ... 1782.

QUEQUISQUE. A purplish root plant, edible and nutritious, which is known in English as "dasheen." Used in soups and stews, it is a delicious tropical vegetable.

QUESADA, ANTONIO RODRIQUEZ DE. Governor of Central America from 1555 until his death in 1558, Quesada was a reformer of the judicial system of the audiencia and its treatment of Indians. He established the system of municipios.

QUETZAL. A trogon (trogon resplendens) of magnificent plumage which is the sacred bird that in combination with a sacred snake gives the term "Quetzal-coatl," Nahua word for a godman of prehistory.
 The bird's green plumage has caused it to be hunted in many parts of Central America, but in the cloud-forests of Honduras quetzals still flourish in limited numbers, especially in such remote ranges as the Merendón. Royal bird of the Mayas also, it is the national bird of Guatemala.
 Another classification is Pharomacrus mocino, of the family Trogonidae. The bronze-green and red plumage has an almost metallic quality, and the long flowing tail-feathers of the male were used traditionally in royal and priestly head-dresses of the pre-Columbian Aztec and Maya rulers.

QUIAHUITL. Nineteenth day of the Aztec month; meaning "rain."

QUILALI. Following a daring exploit of medical evacuation by air, the marines fighting Sandino (q.v.) forces withdrew from Quilalí in Nicaragua. This was more or less simultaneous with a National Guard revolt in Somotillo. Nine guardsmen had attacked the Marine portion of the garrison at Somotillo and while four were killed, the other five fled into Honduran sanctuary across the border. This became a very visible international incident because delegates of the hemispheric nations were gathering at the time for a conference in Havana, Cuba. One of the results of the mutiny and Honduran flight was stepped-up U.S. Marine activity in Nicaragua.
 Soon after, an attack on the nearby Sandino stronghold, El Chipote, was made more ruthless because Honduran and Mexican newspapers had published a picture of an aviator who had been captured, hung, and photographed by the guerillas.

QUIÑONES, PEDRO RAMIREZ DE. Interim governor upon the death of Antonio Quesada (q.v.), Quiñones led an expedition into the country of the Lacandón Maya, during 1558-59.

QUIÑONES Y OSORIO, ALVARO DE. As governor, 1634-42, Dr. Quiñones y Osorio made efforts to better the social conditions of rural Spaniards and Castas by settling them in towns. He was lost at sea on a trip to Peru.

QUINTAL. A measure of weight, four arrobas (q.v.) or 46 kilograms.

QUINTANILLA, DIEGO LOPEZ DE. An aide to Juan Batista Antonelli (q.v.) in his report on the cross-Honduran transisthmian route about 1590.

QUITO CONFERENCE, OAS. The November 1974 meeting in Quito, Ecuador, called to consider lifting economic and diplomatic boycotts of Cuba, failed to get the necessary two-thirds vote to lift the sanctions. Honduras and six other of the 21 nations were believed to be ready to reopen relations with Cuba's Castro government on a unilateral basis. See CUBA, DIPLOMATIC RELATIONS.

QUITO SUEÑO SHOALS see SERANILLA SHOALS

- R -

RACIAL MIXTURES. In the late 19th century as many as fifteen terms were used to indicate as many racial mixtures in Central America. With some local variations, and not including the late use of "creole" or of "sambo," these delineations were similar to those in use in the United States of America, which included mulatto, quadroon, octaroon, and mustee.
The table which follows was prepared by William T. Brigham in 1887 in his classic Guatemala, The Land of the Quetzal.

|     | Cross | Male | Female |
| --- | --- | --- | --- |
| 1.  | Mestizo | Spaniard | Indian |
| 2.  | Castiso | Spaniard | Mestiza |
| 3.  | Espanolo | Castiso | Spanish |
| 4.  | Mulato | Negro | Spanish |
| 5.  | Morisco | Spaniard | Mulata |
| 6.  | Albino | Morisco | Spanish |
| 7.  | Tornatras | Albino | Spanish |
| 8.  | Tente en el Aire | Tornatras | Spanish |
| 9.  | Lobo | Negro | Indian |
| 10. | Caribujo | Lobo | Indian |
| 11. | Barsino | Coyote (lobo?) | Mulata |
| 12. | Grifo | Lobo | Negro |
| 13. | Albarazado | Coyote | Indian |
| 14. | Chaniso | Indian | Mestiza |
| 15. | Mechino | Coyote | Loba |

While many of these terms tend to die out, others persist.

The table (reissued in 1965 in facsimile by the University of Florida Press), is notable in some respects for what it leaves out--for example, the cross of an Indian man with a Spanish woman, or of a Spanish man with a negro woman. Presumably such crosses were not admitted? Undoubtedly other terms were current to the extent of the number of mixes. The "Coyote" may have been the "Lobo," as is indicated in the table.

RADIO. Radio is a major means of communication in Honduras, more significant than newspapers and certainly more widespread. The reasons are: considerable illiteracy, which makes speech a better medium than the written word; rugged terrain, and few other communication media in some areas; and the recent prevalence and availability of inexpensive transistor radios from Oriental manufacturing sources.

RAILROAD, STANDARD FRUIT COMPANY. A narrow-guage line, not interchangeable with the Tela RR (q.v.) and the Ferrocarril Nacional (q.v.). Owned by the Standard Fruit Company, this is the longest rail line in the country, with 300 miles of track, 1,000 freight cars and 31 passenger cars. The line extends inland to Olanchito up the Aguán Valley.

RAIN SHADOW. A phenomenon of rainfall which occurs in high mountains athwart trade winds. The heights cause the wet winds to "dump" their rain to windward, and on the opposite slopes to leeward the result is a desert. This condition of micro-climate is found frequently in Honduras, with resultant desert areas and semi-barren steppes.

RAINFOREST. The rainforest in Central America usually develops on the windward side of the mountains thrust up into the easterly trades. The wet winds from the tropical Caribbean release their moisture as they rise, and the easterly-facing slopes gather it, with a resulting riotous wealth of vegetation. Rainforest in terms of types of growth resembles cloud-forest (q.v.), which, however, depends more upon altitude for its peculiar phenomenon. Honduras, due to its east-west orientation, does not have a great expanse of rainforest. Most of it is in Olancho and Gracias a Dios departments.

RAMIREZ, ROBERTO. Lawyer Ramírez was named president of the Supreme Court of Justice under the López Arellano government following December 4, 1972. He replaced Miguel Alfonso Cubero Dacosta.

RAMIREZ DE GUZMAN, LORENZO. Governor of Honduras in 1679.

RAMIREZ LANDA, FERMIN see MILITARY ZONE COMMANDS, 1972

RAMON MOLINA, JUAN. Honduran writer and editor, born in

Comayaguela in 1875, died in 1908 in San Salvador. He was the editor of El Bien Público in Quelzeltenango, Guatemala, and later (1898) was Sub-Secretary of Development for Honduras. In 1899 he edited the Diario de Honduras, and later El Cronista. In 1906 he was named secretary of the Honduran delegation to the Panamerican Congress in Rio de Janiero; the other secretary was the well-known poet, Froylán Turcios (q.v.). Ramón Molina's work in poetry was perhaps enhanced by friendship with Rubén Darío in Guatemala in 1890; this began his literary career at the age of 15. He traveled widely to New York, Paris, Lisbon, Madrid. His career was indeed remarkable for a young man who died at the age of 33. It was said that when he died, Honduras lost its highest poetic expression. His published works are many, among them Tierras, Mares, y Cielos. In 1970 there was a movement afoot to erect a monument to the memory of Ramón Molina as an outstanding Honduran intellectual. He was in many respects to his native Honduras what Rubén Darío was to Nicaragua.

RANCHO. A one-roomed house, combining cooking, sleeping, and living functions. Over 90 per cent of such buildings have earthen floors, are of wattle or adobe construction, and are frequently thatch-roofed. Manaca (q.v.) is the palm covering used. The exterior walls are called bajareque. The most primitive are basically similar to aboriginal dwellings of an equivalent nature. Twenty-four per cent of Honduran homes answer this description. Ninety-seven per cent of such rural homes lack sanitation facilities. Champa is the term used for rancho in eastern part of the country.

RAPIDO PISTAL KITAN. A rapid with a typical Miskito name on the Río Coco.

RAPIDO TILBA. A major rapid on the light-draft navigable portion of the Río Coco, above Carrizal.

RAPPROACHEMENT, EL SALVADOR. The first sign of serious rapprochement following the 1969 "Soccer War" (q.v.) between Honduras and El Salvador occurred in July 1974, when Presidents Osvaldo López Arellana (q.v.) of Honduras and President Arturo Molina of El Salvador gave indications of moving toward friendship. López stated that he "trusted in the good will and understanding of the peoples" of the two countries. He also spoke of El Salvador as a "sister republic," which augured well for future relationships. One of the reasons for the move to resume relationships was the so-called "Banana War" (q.v.) in which banana-producing countries were imposing taxes upon major banana concerns such as the Standard Fruit Co. of San Francisco. Normal relations with El Salvador would help Honduras and Central America in assuring unity on the banana tax issue.

TYPICAL COUNTRY HOMES: Simple materials of local stone, earth, and timber are used in most rural home construction.

RATTAN. Alternate spelling of name for the Bay Island, Roatán (q. v. )--from the period about 1775.

RAUDALES SOTO, JULIO. Lieutenant Raudales Soto was chief of information for the Melgar (q. v.) regime in mid-July 1975 when he announced that a special commission had recommended immediate takeover of the banana industry under a new policy. He also predicted a suit against United Brands as a result of the bribery scandal earlier in the year. See BLACK, ELI M., and LOPEZ ARELLANO, OSWALDO.

RAYA. A Río Coco delta village, with an airfield, near the mouth of the river, and ten miles from Cape Gracias a Dios, which is to the southeast. See BENK, EL.

READING, ACT OF INDEPENDENCE. On September 7, 1877, an act of the Secretary General of the Constitutional government provided that the Act of Independence of July 1823 should be read on each anniversary of National Independence, by public readers in each municipality.

RECOPILACION DE LEYES DE INDIES. The Spanish colonial experience was a remarkable burgeoning of administrative technique, with obvious imperfections and stifling bureaucratic overtones, but nevertheless unequalled both in challenge and response by any similar event or condition since. The first publication of laws and regulations pertinent to the Indies was in 1567, with several versions during the next century. In 1680 a "final" and definitive edition was published, and lasted until 1805, almost the remainder of the colonial period; it covered all aspects of the colonial government and life --property, ecclesiastical matters, servitude and slavery, fiscal and related policy, all were treated. Not lacking in humanitarian emphasis, it was nevertheless a compilation so complex that enforcement proved to be, if not impossible, at least highly improbable and ineffective. Honduras, as a part of the colonial "Kingdom of Guatemala," was affected by the Leyes.

RECOVERY--HURRICANE "FIFI." This worst Central American storm in 25 years left devastation and death in its wake. Recovery time was estimated as two or more years. With the nation having an annual per capita income of $270, and a 1973-74 inflation rate of 20 per cent, the blow dealt by this storm was especially heavy. With deaths between 5,000 and 10,000, homeless more than 30,000, and damage of $500,000,000 on a gross national product of $900,000,000, the terrible impact was compounded by the fact that governmental tax income and foreign exchange earnings would drop to near-catastrophic levels. Staple crops such as corn, beans, and rice were affected and famine loomed. The dual problem of recovery stemmed not only from the direct results of the hurricane disaster, but also from the long-term poverty and underdevelopment which have been prevalent.

REGIDOR see ADMINISTRATION, LOCAL

REGLAMENTO DE CENSURA CINEMATOGRAFICA. The regulation of motion pictures by a censoring process was established by a decree of the Secretaria de Gobernación y Justicia on November 17, 1955.

REINA, JERONIMO J. Poet and dramatist as well as government official and founder of periodicals, Reina was born in Tegucigalpa in 1876. With Augusto Coello (q.v.) and Luis Andrés Zúñiga (q.v.) he formed a literary group called "La Esperanza." He became Director of the National Library in 1896. In 1898 he was instrumental in founding the periodical La Estrella Solitaria. Made a judge in 1900, he became Commandant and Political Governor of Comayagua, where he founded the periodical La Nueva Epoca. As a result of political reverses he went to live in Guatemala and El Salvador. But in 1915 he returned as Commandant and Governor to Santa Rosa de Copán. In 1916 he became Minister of War and Marine, and was the founder of the Military Academy in 1917, as well as principal author of the Military Law of 1918, in which year he died in Tegucigalpa. A book of poetry, Copos de humo, and a comedy drama, La vision del opresor, are among his published works.

REINA VALENZUELA, JOSE. Historian descended from La Victorina (q.v.).

REINEL, PEDRO. Mapmaker who in 1519 made a "New World" Map which shows much of the Caribbean area with remarkably accurate detail, including the Honduran north coast and the Bay Islands. The Map is in the Miller Atlas in the Bibliotèque Nationale, Paris.

REIS, PIRI. A Turkish hydrographer and mapmaker whose fragment kept in the Topkapu Soray of Istanbul shows the Atlantic and the new world, with coastal outlines which might be considered to represent Central America. Reis stated that he copied it from a chart obtained from an Italian seaman who had been on three voyages with Columbus and was captured by the Turks in 1497. Of course, if this were true, there was at this time supposedly no knowledge on Columbus' part of the Central American coast. The possibilities are intriguing--among them that either the "sailor" or Reis lied. However, by 1513 the knowledge of that coast did exist. In the meantime, there have been theories of other pre-1502 visits, among them the remote possibility that one of the Cabots (Venetians sailing for England), was an early Central American explorer. Columbus' first Honduran contact was on the Bay Islands. Amerigo Vespucci (q.v.) may have seen the Honduran coast first. The famous world map fragment of

1513 by Reis discovered in the Topkapi palace shows the Atlantic and Islands of the New World, as well as the South American Coast, as if viewed from a satellite! Yucatán is shown as an island, and the Honduran Coast is well-detailed, including what might be considered as the Caratasca Lagoon. Some observers have averred that Reis could not have given the view he did from sea and ground surveys. This seeming anomaly is fascinating in itself.

RELIEF EFFORTS, PARTNERS OF THE AMERICAS. In the cause of relief needed as the aftermath of the 1974 Hurricane "Fifi" (q.v.), the Partners came to help Honduras promptly. Vermont, the state which is a partner of Honduras, sent a survey team to assess emergency needs shortly after the disaster. Louisiana Partners sent Cecil Warren with three planeloads of relief supplies which later included a complete field hospital. Oregon Partners, under Dr. Forrest Rieke, collected a considerable relief fund. Tennessee Partners coordinated relief efforts from a full-time Memphis office. Other hurricane relief partner efforts were mounted by Florida-Colombia, Massachusetts-Antioquia, and Wisconsin-Nicaragua.

RELIGION. Honduras is still a Catholic country as in colonial times, with 89 per cent of the population professing Catholicism. Church and State are legally separate, there is complete religious freedom, and there are at least 20 Protestant sects making up the remaining 11 per cent.

REMANYO. A town near the Honduran border where the Sandinista (q.v.) chiefs met in June 1929. Designated leader during a Sandino absence, Francisco Estrada did not wish the honor, and he and Pedro Irías wanted to cross into Honduras. Pedrón Altemirano was wanted for brigandage in both Honduras and Nicaragua, and decided to take his chances in the latter country. The others disbanded, hid their arms, and their soldiers were ordered to disperse into Honduras in twos and threes. Estrada and Irías were interned in Honduras.

RENDON, MARIO. Rendón replaced Guillermo Medina Santos as president of the National Development bank at the time of the governmental takeover by López Arellano after December 4, 1972.

RENT COURTS. These are special courts which deal only with landlord-tenant disputes.

REPARTIMIENTO. The encomienda system of forced labor was used to provide workers for mining and plantation activities in the Spanish colonial era. The repartimiento was either a distribution or assignment of Indian laborers for similar purposes, and was also used as a means of forced sale of goods to the Indian natives. This distribution or assignment system was also used to carry out public enterprises, drafting artisans or farmers accordingly. After epidemics of the 1570s this became a major source of labor, to some extent superseding the encomienda system. The repartimiento was planned by the Spanish Crown to assure a fixed wage, sufficient diet and housing. It often did not work that way.

REPRESENTACION NACIONAL. The "National Representation" was a government envisioned as the third general government of Central America. It was conceived in January 1851, and was short-lived, although E. G. Squier (q.v.) attempted to promote the union. He was an early protagonist of the "Western Hemisphere Idea" (q.v.). Honduras was the only state remaining faithful to this union by 1852, when the Representación moved to Tegucigalpa. The advent of Carrera and William Walker ended the union.

REPUBLIC OF CENTRAL AMERICA. A project for the elusive Central American Union of 1893, which resulted in war between Honduras and Nicaragua in 1894, when Honduran troops crossed the border at Cape Gracias a Dios. Nicaragua occupied Bluefields (Mosquitia) on February 11, hauling down the Mosquito Flag. Chief Clarence of the Mosquitoes protested.

REPUBLICA DE HONDURAS. On May 8, 1862, a decree was ratified confirming the name of the country as a republic. The decree further provided that this appellation should appear on the money, before governmental offices, on the flags of militia, on the coat of arms, and on official seals.

REPUBLICA MAYOR DE CENTRO AMERICA. Under this title, an attempted Confederation of Honduras, El Salvador and Nicaragua was the fruit of the Pact of Amapala (q.v.), on June 20, 1895. A provisional Triumvirate was organized on Independence Day, September 15, 1896, and the Constitution of the new union was declared in effect November 1, 1898. The name of the new republic was chosen as Los Estados Unidos de Centro América.
    This long-term dream of Central American intellectuals and far-sighted leaders (still extant in 1975) was shattered on November 13, 1898 when El Salvador withdrew, under the aegis of a coup engineered by Tomás Regalado, who seized and kept power there for over four years. The dream of union had only outlived its official inception by 12 days. As the "U.S." of Central America, this "Greater Republic" was to be a loose confederation of the three states, and under the British blockade of Corinto in 1895, added to the strong leadership of Nicaraguan President José Santos Zelaya (who was the strongest of Central American presidents in this period), there was impetus toward union. Essentially aimed to represent the three governments in external and diplomatic relations, rather than in internal affairs, the union was short-lived, dying when El Salvador withdrew in 1898. The union

was, however, unusual in that only three of the five original states were involved.

REQUERIMIENTO. A bit of legalization used in Spanish colonial times to justify war upon or conquest of native peoples, this document, which was read to the colonial victims, contained a description of the Papacy and Christian history, and the word of the Pope in assigning the helpless victims and their territories to the Spanish crown. Hence, since the natives were on crown lands they owed not only allegiance but taxes and labor to the crown!

RESERVADO. An Indian exempt from tribute in 16th century Central America. These people tended to be able to rise both socially and economically from positions such as sacristan and chorister in the new churches being built.

RESIDENCIA. Frequently resorted to by the crown during the Spanish colonial period in America, the residencia was a detailed investigation of all officials, even to the viceroys, upon their leaving office. Often the investigating official, who sat in effect as a judge, became the successor to the official investigated. Complaints, scandals, injustices, all came to light, and the witnesses were immune from retaliatory action. The general effect was to emasculate politically the colonial officials who, in fear of exceeding their authority by acting, frequently did nothing but the most routine and obvious specific duties. Since the empire was so far-flung, the problem of inaction was compounded by slow transportation and almost non-existent communication.

RESINS. A product of Honduran woodlands much in demand during the late 16th century was the variety of gums and resins, including balsam, liquid amber, beeswax, copal, and some perfumed resins. Brea (q.v.) was a major product of this category.

RESPONSE TO "GOLPES." Official reaction of the administrations of the United States to coup d'états has had for over a century considerable effect on the history of Central America and the whole Caribbean area. As an example, President John F. Kennedy had a special response to military takeovers in 1963 which was in line with the point of view that military assistance is a contributor to the modernization process in developing countries, rather than the cause of militarism. Kennedy responded to seven coups in 1962-63, by official censure in the cases of Honduras, Guatemala, Peru, and Argentina. Aid was suspended, diplomatic relations severed, and since such policies did not seem effective, the modified response of 1963 was exemplified by Ecuador, where the military junta was very soon recognized. This was viewed as a realistic policy. Honduran history since 1963 bears out the changed approach.

REVENGE. Pirate ship in the Bay of Honduras in 1717, under the command of Stede Bonnet (q. v. ).

REVISTA MILITAR DE HONDURAS. The official armed forces magazine.

REYES, JOSE TRINIDAD. Early scholar and leader born in Tegucigalpa in 1797, who due to humble origins was not admitted to the Colegio Tridentino de Comayagua, and so went to León, Nicaragua where he was helped by Bishop García Jérez and received a degree in Philosophy, Theology, and Canon Law. He became a priest in 1822, left Nicaragua in 1825 for Guatemala, and in 1828 returned to his native Honduras.
   In 1840 he was named Bishop of Honduras, but the president reported to Rome that he had died, and in 1844-45, because he was considered in opposition to the regime, Padre Reyes was in prison. By December of 1845 he was instrumental in founding an academy which two years later became the University of Honduras. The school was the Academia Literaria de Tegucigalpa. In 1852 he was a deputy to a Central American Congress. In 1846 he was named the Poeta Nacional, or poet laureate of Honduras. He brought the first piano to Tegucigalpa! Reyes' published works include a text in physics which was a Honduran standard for years, and the Pastorelas which is well-known. Reyes, as poet, priest, politician, and educator, was the father of Honduran higher education.

REYNO DE GUATEMALA, MAPA DE. A map mentioned by E. G. Squier (q.v.) in his notes on Central America. The map was in manuscript form, dated 1818, and was drawn by the royal engineer, Col. Lacierra. It was distinguished by the fact that the states of Honduras and San Salvador were left blank, showing to some extent the then current state of knowledge. The rest of Central America was fully shown. It was Squier's feeling that there was no extant map of Honduras, this only 120 years ago!

REYNO DE PAYAQUI. The first kingdom known in the area of Honduras, ruled from Copantl (Copán--q. v. ).

REYNOSO, JUAN CISNEROS DE. Alcalde mayor of Tegucigalpa in 1581, Reynoso reported 30 silver mines in the area, but only two of consequence. He complained about shortages of slaves.

RIBEIRO, DIOGO. A Portuguese cartographer in the service of Spain whose world map of 1527 is probably the earliest to show clearly both coasts of Central America. This early effort of a well-known mapmaker shows with beauty and clarity Yucatán, Honduras, the Isthmian area, and the Antilles. At this early date the Caribbean is well-defined. There are tantalizing indications on other maps, but none as clear as on this Mercator-type projection. It is an extremely competent world chart considering the extent of knowledge at that time, especially in its accurate proportioning of the vast extent of the Pacific Ocean.

RICE. One of the two or three diet staples along with beans and corn, rice is planted on small acreages, with 45,000 acres distributed among 15,000 farms. The yield is around 140 pounds per acre; the 1969 production was about 25,000 metric tons.

RIEKE, FORREST. Dr. Rieke, as Chairman of Oregon Partners of the Americas, was involved in hurricane relief efforts in 1974. See RELIEF EFFORTS, PARTNERS....

RIO COCO. So universally used as to be almost one word, this is currently the principal designation for that major stream which is the border between Honduras and Nicaragua in its lower reaches. Longest river in Central America, and more, the longest between the North and South American continents, it rises near San Marcos de Colón near the Pacific Coast of Honduras and enters the Caribbean at Cape Gracias a Dios, thus crossing the widest part of the isthmian area between Guatemala and Colombia. For many years the Honduran-Nicaraguan borderland on the lower Coco was in dispute-- Territorio in Litigio--but this disagreement was finally settled by decision of the International Court of Justice on November 18, 1960, thus ratifying an arbitration of December 23, 1906 which had never been really accepted or wholly honored by Nicaragua. As late as 1957 there was brief war over the matter between the two neighbor countries. The border now seems clear. The Coco has served as an artery of transport, as it is navigable for several hundred kilometers by shallow-draft steamers and launches, which plied on the river in the early 1900s, and much farther up its rapid-strewn higher reaches by the pipantes and 'bateaux" which are the characteristic craft--there must be today over 20,000 of these flat-bottomed river-style dugouts along the hundreds of miles of the Coco. Rafts are also widely used to float produce to infrequent markets. Rubber and chicle, as well as placer gold, come down from the upper Coco and such major tributaries as the Bocay and the Huaspook (Waspuk). Throughout history it has been a highroad by water across the rugged Central American highlands, for priests, pirates, conquistadors and colonists. The upper third of the river is strewn with cascades, rapids, and falls. There are at least 24 known names for the river, several of them from some form of "Gold River" (such as Río de Oro, Yoro, Then Yare and Yari); others stem from the original Indian name, the Sumo word "Huancs" (phoneticized in both English and Spanish as Benks, Wanks, Vankes, Wanx, Wonks, and even Río Huanqui, which sounds amusingly like "Yankee"). It is also called Encuentro, Wallis, Great Cape River, and Pantasma and Telpaneca. The last two are tributaries, and the application of their names to the whole stream is probably simple error.

RIO DEL CABO see RIO COCO

RIO DEL ENCUENTRAS see RIO COCO

RIO HUANQUI see RIO COCO

RIPERDA, BARON DE. This appointee as governor did not take up his post in 1779.

RIVALRY, BRITAIN AND THE UNITED STATES. The geopolitically inspired rivalries between Great Britain and the United States in the whole isthmian area were based on trade and territorial uncertainties stemming back to colonial days. In mid-nineteenth century both countries were trying to gain or maintain rights to an isthmian crossing for commerce, by either canal or railroad. The Mosquito and Honduran Bay territories loosely claimed or held by Great Britain were further sources of friction. American filibusters in the area--e.g., William Walker (q.v.)--and Honduran "invasions" in 1860, helped to bring matters to a head, when in that year Great Britain finally released her hold on Honduran and Nicaraguan territory. She did not release, however, the Honduran Bay territory adjacent to "Spanish" Honduras, that coastal portion now known as Belize, and for many years called British Honduras. Belize is still claimed by Guatemala as her own territory.

RIVAS, ANTONIO JOSE. Born in Comayagua in 1924, poet Rivas has been an instructor in the University of Honduras and Chief of a Section of the Foreign Relations Ministry. A book of poems is Mitad de mi silencio.

RIVAS, RODRIQUEZ DE. Governor, 1716-1724, he was responsible for retaining the capital in its original location after the disastrous earthquakes of 1717. The move did not take place until nearly 60 years later.

RIVERA, MIGUEL ANGEL. Engineer Rivera was made Minister of Communications, Transport, and Public Works in the Cabinet of General López Arellano (q.v.) after the December 4, 1972 takeover.

RIVERA, PERAFAN DE. Descendant of Ponce de León (q.v.) who insisted his ancestor had been the "discoverer" of Nueva España, Guatemala, and Honduras; Rivera's plea was before the audiencia of Guatemala in 1608. The claim was probably a mistake based upon voyages of Córdoba and Grijalba in 1517-18.

RIVERA-RODIL, RODIL. Alleged Communist who left with Medardo Mejía (q.v.) and others in 1961 for orientation and training in

Moscow.

RIVERA Y SANTA CRUZ, TOMAS DE. Governor from 1742 to 1748.

RIVERA Y VILLALON, PEDRO. In 1733 this Spanish officer of 30 years service became Captain General for Central America, charged with developing and carrying out a military plan to deal with the Anglo-Miskito (q.v.) problem. He had been commandant at Campeche; in 1723 had commanded the Windward Squadron (q.v.), and had inspected New Spain forts and governed Vera Cruz twice. Rivera grasped the problem of the Mosquito Coast, although he still underestimated the strength of the English establishment of Black River (q.v.). His plan was late, coming a year after his patron Patino's (q.v.) death. He thought one frigate could reduce Black River and its fortification. He established two coast-guard stations at Trujillo, Honduras, and on the Matina Coast of Costa Rica. He recognized that the coast must be occupied to be held. The War of Jenkins' Ear of 1739 spoiled Rivera's plan. As Governor from 1733 to 1742, he had a background advantage in having been on an extended trip through the American colonies of Spain from 1724 to 1728. This was unusual for colonial officials of the era.

ROAD, GUATEMALA TO OMOA see ARAUJO Y RIO, JOSE

ROADS (Recent). In June 1973 announcement was made that Honduras had received a World Bank loan of $18.8 million toward the cost of a road program of $26 million. It is planned to pave over 100 miles of roads and to build necessary bridges for access to remote areas of the country and to enable commercial development to take place.

ROATAN CAMPAIGN, 1642 see DIAZ DE PIMIENTA, FRANCISCO

ROATAN, CAPTURE 1782 see TRUJILLO, BASE ... 1782

ROATAN ISLAND. Largest of the Honduran Bay Island chain, Roatán is over 20 miles long and averages two or three miles in width. There are several good small-craft harbors. Roatán, the departmental cabacera of Bay Islands department, is located near the southwest end of the island. Apparently occupied by Paya and Jicaque tribesmen in pre-Columbian times, as were all the Bay Islands, Roatán as the largest by far. With its safe havens for ships, its fine climate, and the security of an island position, it was soon an object desired by the rovers of the Caribbean as well as their governments at home. A group of British freebooters descended on the island in 1642. So near to Spanish territory, the island base was a pirate's nest from which the buccaneers could attack the nearby coasts. By 1650 the Spanish expedition of four warships under Francisco Villalva y Toledo (q.v.) had driven the English out, but the islands were wasted and depopulated as the natives left through fear of slavery.

By 1742 the English entered the picture again, fortifying Roatán with materials and arms carried off from their attacks on Trujillo and other Honduran mainland points. When war with Spain was ended in 1763, the treaty included the proviso that "his Britannic Majesty shall cause to be demolished all fortification which his subjects have erected in the Bay of Honduras...." In spite of the treaty, the English retained Roatán. By 1780 England and Spain were again at war. The Guatemalan authorities once more expelled the English from Roatán, and the peace treaty of 1783 provided for English abandonment of "all islands whatever dependent upon it"; that is, upon the continent.

The islands were abandoned by the British in 1786, but when war again arose in 1796 the tenacious Britons once more occupied the islands, and they were made penal settlements to which Caribs of the Leeward Islands, particularly St. Vincent, were sent. About 2,000 of these were placed on Roatán. By 1970, around 14,000 Hondurans had Carib blood.

An expedition under José Rossi y Rubia (q.v.) was sent to Roatán and expelled the British once more in May of 1797, and the British evacuated, leaving, however, their Carib prisoners. By August 1814, at the end of the Napoleonic wars, Britain and Spain concluded a treaty which was again to repeat the 1786 provisions regarding the Bay Islands; this treaty obtained until the Spanish colonies gained their independence in 1821.

To this point England had tried to seize the Bay Islands by force four times, and each time had been expelled. Henderson (q.v.) recognized Spanish ownership. When Central America became independent, Roatán and the other islands were dependent upon the province of Honduras. In May 1830, the British Superintendent of Belize descended on Roatán and seized it on behalf of the British crown, as a result of pique over Honduran treatment of runaway slaves. The Central American states remonstrated, the British government disavowed the act, and the invaders left. In 1838, when a party of freed slaves from the Cayman Islands came to settle, the Superintendent of Belize tried once again (see LONSTRELET). This time, with the Central American states just breaking up, the British government backed the action of their agent Macdonald when his successor Fancourt (q.v.) referred the matter to them. Weakened Honduras could not assert her authority. The Roatán population was increased by 1,000 Cayman Islanders. Fancourt tried to get them to elect a Legislative Assembly, but they preferred their own magistrates. By 1850 it was clear that the British government did not claim the islands as under their authority, and the islanders did not consider themselves British. But there was to be one more attempt, the 7th and last, when P. E. Wodehouse (q.v.), newly appointed Superintendent at Belize, annexed the islands to Great Britain in violation of the Clayton-Bulwer Treaty of 1850. This act on August 10, 1852 was Britain's swansong in the area, for in 1859, by the Wyke-Cruz (q.v.) treaty, the islands were finally returned to Honduras, and have been under that Republic ever since.

ROBERTS, ORLANDO W. Known for his only literary work, Narrative of Voyages and Excursions on the East Coast and in the Interior of Central America (1827). Roberts was a trader on the Mosquito Coast for many years, and his career began with command of a brig in Kingston, Jamaica in 1816. He had many trading adventures from Panama to Honduras, but in 1822 was "captured" by Spanish authorities and taken to León the basis for his highly informative book and the excellent map accompanying it. Roberts is an interesting example of the broadly educated "practical" man of the 19th century. His book has a considerable number of references to the Honduran Bay Islands, the Caribs, and the Miskito tribesmen.

ROBLETO, JUAN DE DIOS. A Carib, nephew of Carlos Matías Yarrince, who was involved in the British-Spanish conflict of 1779 and after on the Miskito shore; his uncle had been imprisoned by Spanish treachery.

RODAS, JUSTO S. One of the commissioners acting for Honduras in the chartering of the Honduras Interoceanic Railway Company (q.v.) in 1853.

RODAS ALVARADO, MODESTO. Leading candidate for the presidency in the October 1963 elections. The coup, resulting in the Junta Militar under General Roque J. Rodríguez, cut short Rodas Alvarado's expectations, and he, having taken an anti-military stance, certainly contributed to the expected coup which occurred ten days prior to elections. He had been elected Provisional Secretary of Congress by the Honduran Liberal Party in 1954, in anticipation of a victory for Liberals.

RODEZNO, JOSE. Governor in 1715.

RODRIGUEZ, INOCENTE. As designated deputy, Rodríguez occupied the presidency from February 2 to March 26, 1871.

RODRIGUEZ, ROQUE J. Commander of the Honduran Military Academy, General Rodríguez was the leader of a military triumvirate, a junta that seized power from Lozano Díaz and ruled from October 21, 1956 to December 21, 1957. The other officers were Colonel Héctor Caraccioli and Major Roberto Gálvez Barnes. A constituent assembly was elected and chose Ramón Villeda Morales (q.v.) as president.

RONDA DE LAS MULATEROS see MULETEERS DANCE

ROSA, RAMON. One of a council of ministers who exercised executive power from June 10 to July 30, 1880. The others were Enrique Gutiérrez and A. Zelaya.

ROSA ROJA. National flower of Honduras.

ROSADO, JOSE. Lieutenant Colonel Rosado was the Spanish Commandant at Fort Bacalar who attacked British forces north of Balize in September 1779, and it was his attack which caused the Baymen to retire to the Bay Island Roatán. They went to New Port Royal on Roatán, and at the same time Commodore John Luttrell arrived there. See OMOA, 1779-- BATTLES.

ROSAL, JERONIMO DEL. Adjutant to Díaz Navarro (q.v.) in 1743, when decisions were being made about fortifications on the north coast of Honduras. Rosal surveyed the situation at Trujillo, confirming his commander's belief that the project of refortifying that harbor would be both hazardous and inordinately expensive.

ROSAL, PEDRO DEL. Governor following 1625.

ROSALES, MAXIMO B. see ARIAS, JUAN ANGEL; also JUNTA DE GOBIERNO, 1907

ROSARIO MINE. In the 1920s the Rosario Mining Company had the largest silver mine in Central America, 25 miles from Tegucigalpa. The United States-owned mine was in San Juancito, and could only be reached by mule train. At that time, however, 800 men were employed in the mine, directed by 30 North Americans. The mine had 70 miles of tunnel, and in 1923 shipped 2,000,000 ounces of silver. Now owned jointly in New York and Honduras, the Rosario Company still leads mining enterprises in Honduras, and is one of the major foreign investment concerns, along with the large banana combines.

ROSEWOOD. Also called grenadilla, this lovely tropical hardwood is found in eastern Honduras. The name applies to several species of the genus Dalbergia. The wood has a very prominent grain, is dark reddish or dark brown in color, and is prized as cabinet and veneer wood. It is extremely dense, stable, and durable.

ROSSI Y RUBIA, JOSE. On orders from the Guatemalan capital, and by action of the Intendant of Honduras, this officer was sent with a force of officers and men to the island of Roatán, to expel the British there. The island surrendered in May 1797. This was the end of the last 18th century attempts by the British to take the Bay Islands, but not the last ever. Four times she attempted that seizure, and was to try again in 1838. See LONSTRELET; also ROATAN.

RUANO, JUAN. A subordinate captain under Cristóbal de Olid (q.v.) during the Honduran expedition of 1524.

RUBIO, MODESTO see GENERAL STRIKE, 1954

RUEDA, PEDRO MALLEN DE. President of the Guatemalan Audiencia from 1589 to 1592, his short incumbency was a time of contention, litigation, and unrest, even though he built some new buildings and bridged the Río de los Esclavos. Under a visita by Francisco de Sande, he was deposed and, shortly after, died insane.

RUINAS DE COPAN. This town about six miles from the Guatemalan border is shown simply as Copan on the maps. It has taken its present name from the great Maya archaeological site nearby in the same valley, that of the Río Copán. The cabacera of a municipio, it is a pleasant and typical Central American small town. There is a church on a spacious plaza, a hotel with bougainvillea-shaded patios, a fine small museum with authentic treasures from the Copán ruins including the famous "Corn-God" bust. On a nearby hill is the cuartel, a post of the armed forces built as a nineteenth-century fort, whitewashed and prominent on its eminence above the town. Narrow streets are varied by school playing fields in the valley nearby. (See Corn God and Fort illustrations.)

RUIZ MATUTE, MIGUEL ANGEL. Honduran artist and student of Diego Rivera, great Mexican muralist. Having already established himself as a muralist, Ruiz Matute in the late 1960s was experimenting with a variety of styles. He has won numerous prizes and has studied abroad under fellowships.

RURAL NORMAL SCHOOLS. A rural normal school for men was established in 1944, and on February 24, 1950 a similar establishment was set up for young women, near Danlí, in El Paraiso Department, the Escuela Normal Rural de Villa Ahumada.

RUS RUS. In the most remote portion of the Republic, Rus Rus is located in southern Gracias a Dios Department on the Río Coco tributary which is also named Rus Rus. It is one (and quite typical) of fewer than sixty tiny villages in the vast reaches of La Mosquitia.

- S -

SAAVEDRA, HERNANDO DE. A lieutenant of Cortés, it was he among others who governed Honduras in 1526.

SABINO LOPEZ, MANUEL see ARIAS, JUAN ANGEL

CORN-GOD: Maya sculpture from Copán, characteristic of the best period in such art.

FORT - CUARTEL: Modern (late 19th century) fort in the town "Ruinas de Copán"--a Guatemalan border garrison.

SAENZ DE MAÑOSCA Y MURRILLO, JUAN DE SANTO MATIA.
Bishop of Guatemala during the presidency of Sebastián Alvarez Alfonso Rosica de Caldas, he served as governor in the capacity of visitador, 1670-72.

SAHSA   see   AIR SERVICE OF HONDURAS

SAJINO.   Local name for the collared peccary, a wild pig smaller than the wari (q.v.).

SALAZAR, PEDRO DE.   Governor of Honduras, 1765.

SALCEDO, DIEGO LOPEZ DE.   Captain Salcedo was named by the Governor of Honduras in 1527 to proceed to Nicaragua and take possession of the country as far as the lakes. There is reason to believe that Salcedo killed many inhabitants of the country along the route. Imprisoned in the recently established fortification of León (now León Viejo, an archaeological site), Salcedo finally returned to Honduras in 1529 with a soldier escort, but took with him 381 Indian slaves from Nicaragua. This was the first and last such campaign of Indian enslavement in the history of the country, although under Pedrarias and within the encomienda system there was a decimation of the Indian population, in what was virtually slavery. The event of 1529 represents the introduction of slavery into Honduras.

SALES TAXES. By 1968 consumption and sales taxes were producing about 29 per cent of governmental income, the most important single source. Most foods, drugs, and clothing are exempt. Services are taxed as well as commodities. Retail establishments with monthly sales over $1,500 must maintain records. A three per cent general sales tax has been in effect since 1963. Some non-essential consumer products have been taxed at ten or 20 per cent since 1968.

SALMERON, PEDRO. Interim governor, 1623-1625.

SALMON, NORVELL. Captain Salmon of the British warship Icarus delivered filibuster William Walker (q. v.) to the Hondurans at Trujillo in September 1860. Walker was then executed by a firing squad. He had believed he was surrendering to Great Britain (in the person of Salmon) rather than to the Honduran authorities, who by due but expeditious process then shot Walker, ending his incredible career as doctor, lawyer, editor, filibuster, general and president.

SALVADOR, 1850 WAR. Guatemala was invaded by El Salvador and Honduras in 1839 as a culmination of border incidents and skirmishing which had involved all three of the states. It was the period of unrest which had followed the breakup of the Central American Confederation in 1839. Carrera of Guatemala defeated the combined armies at Arada, Guatemala, in February 1851, and captured and controlled several key border towns of both opponents. Again it was a case, as so often in nineteenth century Central American conflicts, of Conservatives versus Liberals. In this instance Carrera installed conservative regimes in the defeated countries. Francisco Dueñas was made President of El Salvador and Santos Guardiola (later known as the "Butcher" during the National War), President of Honduras.

SALVADOR, WAR OF 1863 see NICARAGUA-GUATEMALA-SALVADOR WAR OF 1863

SALVADOR, WAR OF 1839. During the effective breakup of the Central American Confederation, of import for Honduras as for the other four countries, the federal army led by Morazán (q.v.), Honduran patriot and "George Washington of Central America," invaded Guatemala, capturing the capital March 18, hoping to rescue the faltering Union. But Carrera's forces were spurred on by conservative aristocratic elements in the capital, and Morazán and his forces were driven out. Returning to El Salvador, Morazán attempted to raise another army, but was driven out and left the country in April. John Lloyd Stephens (q. v.) was in the midst of some of this fighting, and has left a spirited account of it in his writings (see Bibliography).

SALVADOR AND GUATEMALA WAR OF 1872. Due to the harboring of Conservative Party exiles from both countries in Honduras, El Salvador and Guatemala formed an alliance aimed at Honduras, whereupon Honduras severed diplomatic relations with El Salvador. The split in each of the countries was more between Conservative and Liberal Parties than on a national basis. The allies invaded Honduras and captured Comayagua, also inflicting Honduran losses at battles near Potrerillos and Santa Bárbara. The war lasted two months, and the peace treaty, while ending the fighting, had little significance otherwise.

SALVADOR AND HONDURAS VERSUS GUATEMALA, WAR OF 1876. The perennially durable Justo Rufino Barrios was a vigorous successor to Carrera in Guatemala. Strong feeling against Barrios in Honduras and El Salvador lit the spark of war among the three countries. Following the severing of diplomatic relations, Barrios led an army of about 9,000 into El Salvador and sent nearly 2,000 men into Honduras under General Gregorio Solares. Barrios won at Apaneca, El Salvador, in April 1876, and in the same month Solares won control of San Miguel and La Unión departments. Peace was made April 25, 1876, and the hostile President of El Salvador was replaced. Honduras did not fare so badly.

SALVATIERRA, PEDRO DE. Governor from 1555 to 1562, during the Quesada (q.v.), Ramírez de Quiñones (q.v.), and Núñez de Landecho regimes in the Audiencia.

SAMBO see SAMBO-MISKITOS

SAMBO ATTACKS, 18th CENTURY. In 1702 the Sambos attacked San Pedro Sula by ascending the Ulua River. In 1704 they took 40 captives from a coastal Ulua village; they also attacked deep into Nicaragua and as far east as Bocas de Toro in Panama. The English tried to control their Sambo quasi-allies, but were unable to. In 1720, a large force of Sambos defeated Spanish corsairs off the Honduran Coast. In 1723, again in Honduran waters, they attacked a Spanish flotilla carrying 180 Spaniards, all but nine of whom were killed.

SAMBO-MISKITOS. The mixed-blood inhabitants of the Miskito Coast who emerged as early as the mid-1600s as a blend of white, Negro, and Sumu Indian. The Sumus were indigenous, the whites were early traders, and the blacks were brought in as slaves to work plantations and to cut timber. Their number was further augmented by the wreck of a Cartagena-bound Portuguese slaver in 1641, on the mid-point of the Miskito coast. The Sambo-Miskitos allied themselves with the buccaneers who appeared in numbers in the late 1600s, and who led raids on the Spanish frontier to the westward in the Segovias of Nicaragua and up the Río Patuca of Honduras. In the 18th century, they proved warlike at every opportunity. The Sambo-Miskitos were particularly enamored of rum and firearms, to add to their existing arsenals of poison arrows and their prevalent drink of fermented corn-juice, la chicha (q.v.).

SAMPEDRANO CENTRO CULTURAL. This adjectival form of San Pedro Sula is the name of the Bi-national North American-Honduran Center established in that city. In the late 1960s it was under the direction of Mr. James F. Channing; classes were offered in English, cultural events were scheduled, and there is a library.

SAN ANDRES BAY. Original name of the Bay of Omoa. See PUERTO CABALLOS and LA NAVIDAD.

SAN ANTONIO. Municipal cabacera in northern Copán Department, on the Río Chamelicon and in the Sierra Espíritu Santo foothills.

SAN ANTONIO DE CORTES. A favorite name (there are nearly a dozen San Antonios in Honduras). This town is a municipal cabacera a few miles north of Lake Yojoa, and in the southern end of Cortés Department.

SAN ANTONIO DE FLORES. On the Río Nacaome, this town is a municipal cabacera on the northern border of Choluteca Department, and on the main road from the Pan American Highway to Tegucigalpa.

SAN ANTONIO DE ORIENTE. The ancient mining village near El Zamorano in eastern Francisco Morazán Department. A municipal cabacera, it has been made famous by its former mayor and town barber, José Antonio Velásquez, whose primitive paintings depict his village in meticulous and charming detail. Part of the Tegucigalpa silver mining area which revolutionized the colonial economy in 1578, San Antonio is a living museum of the colonial era. Above the town broods the great bare tunnel-pocked cliff which once produced the rich silver ores. No significant mining activity goes on now. The site is spectacular, with a sweeping view over the nearby fertile valley.

SAN FERNANDO DE OMOA, CASTILLO DE see FORT OMOA

SAN FRANCISCO DE YOJOA. A municipal cabacera in Cortés Department just to the north of Honduras' largest inland lake, this town is just off the main road from San Pedro Sula to Tegucigalpa. The sister village of Santa Cruz de Yojoa, seven miles distant, is on a less travelled track.

SAN JORGE DE OLANCHO. Sixteenth century original name given

SAN ANTONIO DE ORIENTE: The famed mining village near Tegucigalpa--home of the primitive artist Velásquez.

    to the town now known simply as Olancho.

SAN JUAN DE PUERTO CABALLOS. Early name (1578) of the northern Honduran seaport on the Bay of Honduras, commonly called Puerto Caballos, and now Puerto Cortés.

SAN JUAN GARITA. Border town in Lempira Department near El Salvador, and just off the Río Sumpul.

SAN MANUEL DE COLOHETE. Central in Lempira Department, this town is a municipal cabacera, in the foothills of the high Celaque range of mountains, and 15 miles southwest of Gracias, the departmental cabacera and first colonial capital.

SAN MARCOS ARCHEOLOGICAL SITE see TENAMPUA

SAN MARCOS DE COLON. High and cool above the steaming Choluteca valley, in the department of that name, this municipal cabacera is the last town before the Pan American Highway border-crossing into Nicaragua at El Espino. It is located on the Río Comali, an early tributary of the Río Coco, which goes from here, near the Pacific, all the way to the Caribbean, to become the longest river in Central

America.

SAN MARCOS DE LA SIERRA. High in the tumbled hills of southern Intibuca Department, this municipal cabacera rides a ridge between the Río Chinacla and the Río Guarajambala. The nearest airfields are to the south and at Magdalene and near Concepción.

SAN MILLAN ISLAS. A mistaken designation of the Swan Islands (q.v.) on older navigation charts, as early as 1596.

SAN PEDRO PERULAPAN. Critical battle on the 25th of September, 1839 during the breakup of the Central American Federation. See MORAZAN, FRANCISCO.

SAN PEDRO SULA. Major industrial city of Honduras, San Pedro Sula is the departmental cabacera of Cortés Department, located near the Río Chamelicón about thirty miles south of the major seaport, Puerto Cortés. The city is divided into four zones by the Primera Avenida into east and west, and by the Boulevard Morazán (Primera Calle) into north and south. There is an avenue of "Circumvalación" which surrounds the city with a perimetral traffic artery. There are barrios or colonias (suburbs and areas), as follows: Northeast: Barandillas, La Granja, Las Flores, Morazán, El Progreso. Northwest: Guamilta, Las Acacias, Los Andes, La Ciudad Cervecera, La Zona Militar, Colonia Bella Vista, Juan Lindo, Colonia Colombia, Parte del Boulevard Morazán. Southeast: Medina, Concepción, Colonia Sucery, San Francisco, Colonias Cabañas and La Navidad. Southwest: El Centro Lempira, El Benque, Paz Baraona, Suyapa, Río de Piedras, Colonia Trejo, Colonia Figueroa, Santa Anita, El Altiplano, La Guardia.

The city covers 10.3 square miles, and the population went from 75,000 in 1965 to approximately 150,000 ten years later. Only the Tegucigalpa area has a larger urban population. The rate of growth has been phenomenal. There are ten banks, five cinemas, sixteen consulates, and thirteen cooperatives in the city. There are thirty public and private schools and five kindergartens, as well as the campus of the Universidad del Norte. The industries are of a great number and diversity, including sugar refineries, dairies, breweries, distilleries, metal fabrication, coffee beneficios, laboratories, printing plants, furniture factories, plastic plants, hat and clothing factories, battery plants, etc. Five airlines serve the nearby jet airport, La Mesa. There are fifteen radio stations. Many professional offices of architects, lawyers and doctors are maintained here.

Founded by Don Pedro de Alvarado on June 27, 1536, the city was destroyed by the pirate François de L'Ollonais in 1660. For a while, the population was decimated. By 1825, San Pedro Sula was part of the Department of Santa Bárbara, and on August 4, 1893 the Department of Cortés

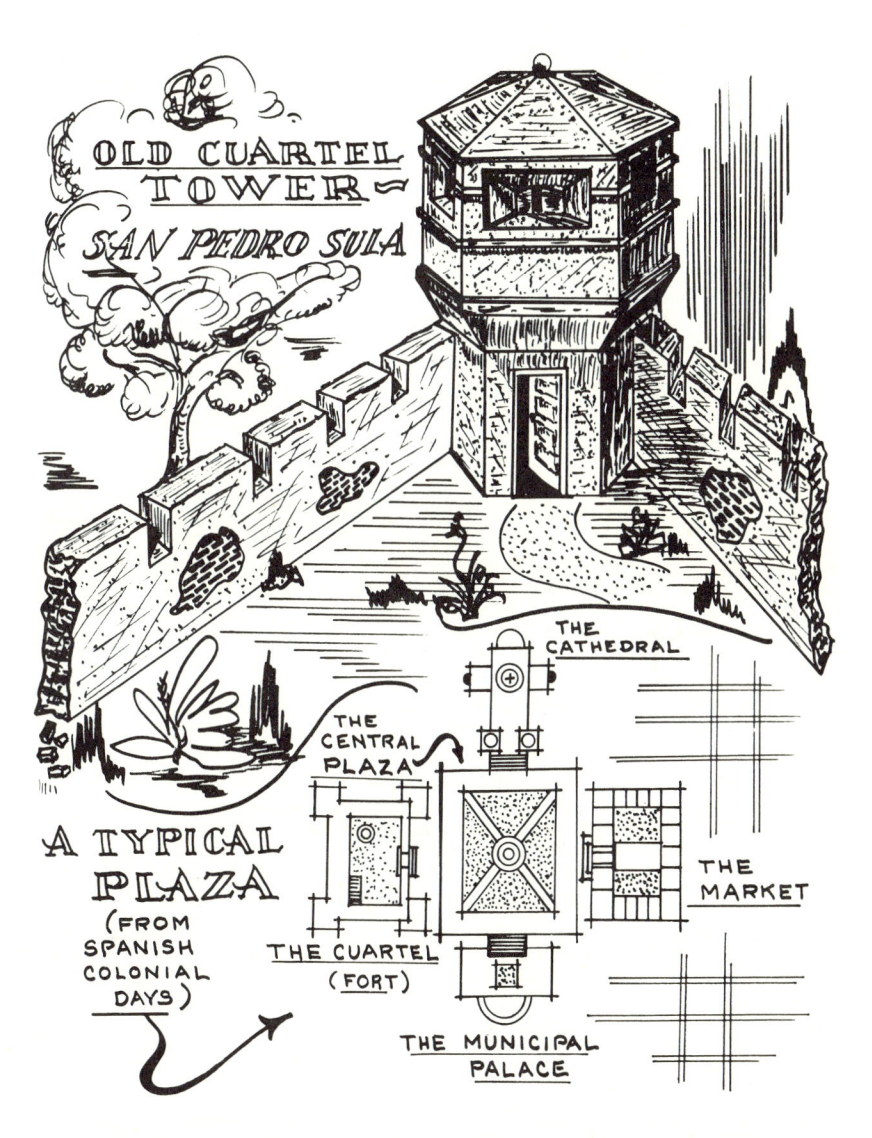

CUARTEL TOWER (AND PLAZA): In San Pedro Sula, the corner tower of the town's fortified barracks is now in the environs of a modern hotel. Cuartel, municipal palace, market, and cathedral faced four sides of the central plaza.

was formed, with the city as its cabacera. In 1888 the city still had only 1,714 inhabitants. Yellow fever took a terrible toll, causing the city to be virtually abandoned in 1892. Electric lighting came in 1912. The first automobile was driven by Carlos Pagán from San Pedro Sula to Santa Rosa de Copán in 1918. The trip took 33 days! The first airplane came in 1928.

SAN PIO. A corvette used by Hervias (q.v.) in entertaining the Sambo king in 1787, and in activities along the Miskito shore.

SANCHES, ROBERT M. Tegucigalpa native, contemporary artist and graduate of the Escuela Nacional de Bellas Artes. Student of sculpture in Rome, where he served as Cultural Attache in the Honduran embassy. Held post as Assistant Director and Professor of Sculpture in the Escuela de Bellas Artes.

SANCHEZ, PHILLIP V. United States Ambassador to Honduras in the 1970s, who coordinated many aid activities during disastrous hurricane "Fifi" (q.v.).

SANCHEZ PLANISPHERE. In London's British Museum is a beautiful map of 1623 which gives North and South America, with the Bay of Honduras and its islands clearly delineated, as well as the coastal areas of Honduras. The Bay Islands' names are given as Utila, Guiaba, and Ganaca.

SANDE, FRANCISCO DE. A visitador to the Audiencia of Guatemala in 1592 (see RUEDA, PEDRO). He deposed Rueda and then became governor from 1593 to 1596. He was deeply involved in the illegal trade with China, and in 1596 was appointed to New Granada.

SANDINISTA. Term applied to an adherent of César Agusto Sandino (q.v.), whose operations near the Honduran border, 1927-34, caused many a border incident and difficulties in relationships between the two countries. There was a self-styled "Sandinista" group operating in Nicaragua in 1975, of an urban guerrilla nature.

SANDINO, CESAR AGUSTO. Central American guerrilla leader in the 1927-1933 period. Operating in the northern Nicaraguan area near the Honduran border, Sandino and his guerrilleros depended on gun-running based in Honduras to keep his military activities alive and his forces in action. Other supplies also came in across the rugged border of El Paraiso Department, defined by the Cordillera de Depilto. The significance of Sandino extended far beyond Honduras and Nicaragua, however, in that he is considered by some scholars to be the first of the modern organizers of a "people's army," and was, in fact, a contemporary of Mao Tse Tung in his guerrilla days. Further, Sandino has remained a symbol of Latin

American liberation, with a group calling themselves "Sandinistas" still active in Nicaragua in 1975. Born May 18, 1895, the "natural" son of Gregorio Sandino. His mother was a servant girl, Margarita Calderón. He early went by the name of Agusto Calderón, changing his name later to the more imposing "César Agusto" as a result of reading in his father's considerable library of the classics. He studied in Granada, worked in his home town of Niquinohomo, Nicaragua, and later worked in Honduras for Vaccaro Brothers and Company (later known as Standard Fruit). Sandino worked in La Ceiba, and later in Guatemala and in Tampico, Mexico. It was in Mexico that he became (under the influence of Mexican Nationalism with the Revolution still in progress) possessed of a mystic sense of mission and a messianic vision concerning Latin American liberation. It was at the San Albino mine in northern Nicaragua that in 1926 he purchased arms from Honduran gun-runners to arm a band of 29 men. He then joined a group of Constitutionalist rebels under Moncada. When a peace was signed in Tipitapa, Nicaragua, Sandino did not lay down his arms. There followed years of fighting U.S. Marines in the rugged Segovias. In classic guerrilla patterns, his men fought and ran. Terror was their tactic, their strategy evasion. Battles such as that at Ocotal in 1927 and the attacks by air on his fortress El Chipote, became legendary. The David and Goliath exploits attributed to Sandino have become the theme of songs and ballads. Articles, biographies, and novels have celebrated his struggle. U.S. Marines dubbed his men bandits; many Central American countryfolk considered him a hero, and in the intervening half century the legend has grown. Although Sandino was killed treacherously while attending a peace conference in 1934, his ghost continues to haunt Pan-American reunions and good will emissaries from the United States. His fame has reached beyond the hemisphere, and it was in Sandino's tactics and strategy that Ché Guevara was trained in Mexico before the Cuban coups of the 1950s.

SANDOVAL, JOSE MARIA   see   BUESO, FRANCISCO

SANI.   Flexible bark strips found in Mosquitia in five species, and used for cords, rope, etc.

SANTA ANAS ISLAS.   An early and alternate name for the Swan Islands (q.v.).

SANTA BARBARA, DEPARTMENT.   Bounded on the northwest by the Sierra Espíritu Santo lying on the international border with Guatemala; on the north and northeast by Cortés Department.   To the east is Honduras' only large inland lake, Yojoa (q.v.), and the lake is a part of the border where it corners with Cortés and Comayagua departments.   To the south is Intibuca Department; to the southwest, Lempira Department, and on the West, Copán Department.   Santa Bárbara, the town, is the departmental cabacera; there are 26 municipios. The area is 2,005 square miles. Population of the cabaceras was 65,963 in 1973, plus 181,089 for villages and rural areas, totalling 247,052, making Santa Bárbara the fourth most populous department, after Francisco Morazán, Cortés, and Choluteca. Tobacco, cattle, and other agricultural products come from the fertile valleys of the Chamelicón and Jicatayo rivers. On the Guatemalan border are the mountain ranges of the Espíritu Santo and Omoa. Other towns are Azacualpa, Macuelizo, Quimistán, San Marcos, Protección, San José de Colinas, San Vicente Centenario, Arada, Santa Rita, El Nispero, San Francisco de Ojuera, San Pedro Zacapa, San Francisco de Yojoa, Petoa, Trinidad, Chinda, and Gualala.

SANTA CRUZ DE YOJOA. Municipal cabacera near Lake Yojoa in Cortés Department. See SAN FRANCISCO DE YOJOA.

SANTA ELENA ISLAND. Known also by the English-speaking islanders as Helena Island, this is the smallest of the Bay Islands other than tiny cays on the reefs. It is a couple of miles from the other small island, Morat, and near the northeastern tip of Roatán.

SANTA LUCIA. Rich 17th century colonial mine, Guascarán area.

SANTA MARIA. A beautiful figured tropical hardwood, Calophyllum Calaba, with more pronounced grain than mahogany, but similarly open grained. Used for general construction.

SANTA MARIA DEL CARBON. River town in the Department of Olancho, where in the 1950s there were still several hundred Paya Indians living.

SANTA ROSA DE AGUAN. Located at the Bar of the Río Aguán, just east of Trujillo some 20 miles, this municipal cabacera is on the Caribbean shore, in Colón Department.

SANTA ROSA DE COPAN. Departmental cabacera of Copán Department, this large and old town has a population of over 20,000. It is the tobacco raising area of the upper Chamelicón valley region. The famous Copán ruins are not, however, nearby.

SANTANDER, MONTAN. Governor in the 1632 period, under audiencia presidencies of Acieña and Quiñones de Osorio (q. v.).

SANTIAGO. In 1660, this vessel laden with gold and silver worth $500,000 was wrecked in a storm on one of the deserted islets on the shallow banks off the northeastern Honduran coast. The survivors worked for 52 days building a small schooner from the remnants of their wrecked ship; 276 men boarded their creation and sailed to the mainland. The treasure is still there (wherever the islet is!).

SANTIAGO, NAO. A Honduras ship attacked by Piet Heyn (q.v.) in 1629 as she approached Havana. She sunk there in 75 feet of water.

SANTIAGO BALAN Y COMPAÑIA. A Cuban firm in Honduras in 1954 (pre-Castro), involved in the strike of that year. See GENERAL STRIKE, 1954.

SANTIAGO DE CALIMAYA, CONDE DE see ALTAMIRANO Y VELASCO

SANTIAGO DE PALOS. One of Columbus' four small caravels on his fourth voyage, when he discovered Honduras. The nickname of this vessel was "Bermuda," after her owner Juan Bermúdez (q.v.). She displaced only 60 tons, and was commanded by Francisco de Porras. Bartolomé Colón (q.v.) also sailed aboard her.

SANTIAGO PURINGLA. Municipal cabacera in the Cordillera de Montecillos in the northern-most part of La Paz Department. There is an airfield.

SANTO TOMAS DE CASTILLA see CRIADO DE CASTILLA

SAPODILLA. This is a heavy, dense wood, often used by the ancient Maya for lintels and other carved members (Achias Sapota). Fresh wood is red. The wood is very tough.

SARSAPARILLA. Medicinal plant, Aralia Nudicaulis, in great demand in 16th and 17th centuries. It was considered more efficacious than has been proven since, and Spain and the rest of Europe consumed great quantities. From Trujillo, Honduras to the Guatemalan highlands was a principle producing area. From Trujillo as many as 125,000 pounds annually were sent to Spain. The trade died out in about 1650.

SAVA. At the border of Yoro Department, this town in Colón Department has an airfield and is the cabacera of a municipio. It is near the rail line which crosses Colón and is located on the navigable Río Aguán. The railroad is several miles away across the river. Savá is significant as an interior gateway to Colón.

SAVANNA, HONDURAN. During the 18th century, the savannas of northern Honduras supported vast herds of cattle, horses, and mules. This helped the contraband trade up and down the rivers. The existence of these natural pasturelands has been very little recognized or exploited in recent times.

SAVANNAH BIGHT CAY. Old name for one of the cays or islets

off the Coast of Guanaja (q.v.). There is a village located in the "bight."

SAYER, ROBERT. Name of a firm of map printers in London's Fleet Street, 1775, which published a Map of the Bay of Honduras, the Island of Jamaica and Cape Gracias a Dios in 1775, the map ascribed to Thomas Jeffreys, geographer to the King. This map is very complete, showing Indian tribal regions, trends of mountain ranges, towns, rivers, off-shore soundings, islands, reefs, shipping tracks, etc. It exhibits the extensive geographical knowledge of even remote areas 200 years ago, largely due to the activities of seamen, traders, and explorers.

SCCS. Special Consultative Committee on Security.

SCHOOL, FIRST? In the year 1683, there was record of an established school in Goascorán.

SCHOOL, FIRST OFFICIAL. In Comayaguala, in 1820, a school was organized under the Master Santiago Bueso, being the first officially sponsored and recognized school in the country, although other schools had preceded it.

SCHOOL ATTENDANCE. In Honduras, 31.2 per cent of the population attended school in 1961; 1/10 of one per cent attended university, 3/10 of one per cent secondary or technical school. These last two figures are about one-tenth of the Latin American average. The figures had not changed materially by 1974.

SCHOOL OF THE AMERICAS, UNITED STATES ARMY. The military school located in the Canal Zone which trains cadres of Honduran military officers and men. See MILITARY SERVICE.

SCIEP see SERVICIO COOPERATIVO INTERAMERICANO DE EDUCACION PUBLICA

SEAFARERS (Middle American). Seagoing tribes seem to have reached the Colombian coast from Middle America about 500 B.C. It is also probable that Florida and the Bahamas were reached, accidentally or otherwise, by these seafaring peoples of 25 centuries ago. Columbus saw a 70-foot vessel on his fourth voyage in the Caribbean area (1502) off the coast of Honduras. The occupants spoke of the Maía (or Maya) hinterland. Central American stones and artifacts have been found in the easternmost Bahamas, indicating a limited commerce.

SEAL OF HONDURAS (COAT OF ARMS). The design of the official escutcheon of the Republic of Honduras consists of a pyramid, with towers and a volcano centered, under a sun

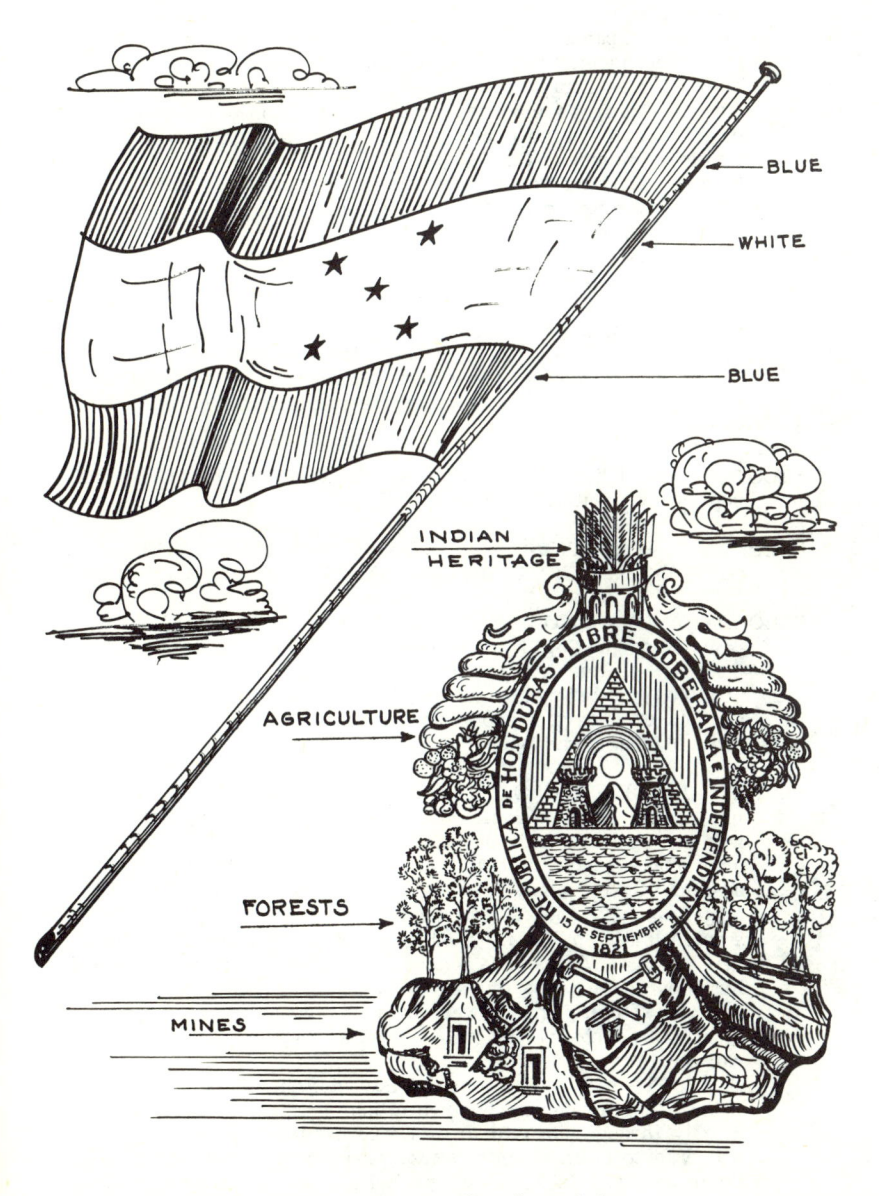

SEAL AND FLAG: The Honduran national symbols.

and rainbow, backed by cornucopias and a quiver of arrows, and supported by a mining and forest landscape with miner's and woodsman's tools. Around the oval central seal are the words, in Spanish: "Republic of Honduras--free, sovereign, and independent," and the date 1821 (see illustration). In 1544 Charles I gave a coat-of-arms to the province of Honduras. This was modified under Philip IV in 1684. In 1823 the first arms were decreed for the United Provinces of Central America. On October 3, 1825 the present form in its general characteristics was adopted, with the motto or legend being added in 1866. The recognized and deliberate elements of the escutcheon are:
> The range of mountains (volcanoes)
> The mines
> The tools
> The pines and oaks (three of each)
> The cornucopias showing native products
> The arrows in their quiver (symbolizing Indian arms)

The great seals of the republic are identical to the coat of arms.

SECO. An Indian tribe of northeastern Honduras in the 1850s, still separately identifiable then.

SECONDARY EDUCATION see CICLO COMUN DE CULTURA GENERAL and CICLO DIVERSIFICADO

SECONDARY EDUCATION, EARLY. On October 29, 1874, in Santa Rosa de Copán, was opened the Instituto Científico de San Carlos, the first established secondary instruction in the country. In 1875 was founded the Colegio de Juticalpa as another secondary school. In the same year the Colegio de Santa Bárbara was opened.

SECRETO DEL ESTRECHO. The "secret of a strait" was the object of search by conquistadors and others for decades, and was not realized until the technical achievement of the Panama Canal, opened in 1914, as there was no natural strait to be found by the many seekers, from Alaska to the Strait of Magellan. By 1551 it was fairly established that the route from Atlantic to Pacific would have to be built or cut, rather than found. While three routes held attention (those through the Nicaraguan lakes or the Panamanian or Tehauntepec isthmuses) these routes were basically considered for canals. Much later Tehauntepec was viewed as the site for a ship railway.

The rail route from the Bay of Fonseca to Puerto Caballos in Honduras received attention in the mid-1800s largely through the efforts of E. G. Squiers (q.v.) whose plan was to build an interoceanic railway (q.v.) along the Humuya and Goascarán valleys. The plan was never carried out, entirely, in spite of repeated revivals. There exists now no interocean rail route in Honduras, and only in 1970 was a satisfactory highway opened across the country.

SEGOVIA RIVER. The Río Coco on the Honduran border is often called the Río Segovia, as the northern departments of Nicaragua are called Las Segovias, after the ancient town of Segovia in Spain.

SEGUNDA ACTA DE INDEPENDENCIA DE CENTRO AMERICA, 1823. The second act of independence became necessary when the collapse of the Mexican empire and its essential ineffectuality caused a new move, which asserted by a decree of the National Constituent Assembly of the Provinces of Central America that the September 15, 1821 Independence Act was renewed as of the later date, July 1, 1823. This freed the Central American provinces from the imperial Mexican venture, and made them not only free from old Spain, but also from Mexico and any other power. The act constituted within itself the formation of a sovereign nation, and the former Kingdom of Guatemala, as a provincial entity of old Spain, became the Provincias Unidas del Centro América. The author of the act was José Francisco Córdova. The ultimate result was the division into the five present Central American republics.

SELVA. The Spanish word signifying forest or jungle, used in the eastern part of Central America in a particular sense in relation to the wild forested regions of such areas as Olancho and Gracias a Dios departments in Honduras. The term not only distinguishes from plains and mountains, but is often applied to rainforest or cloudforest environments.

SENSENTI, TREATY OF. A treaty ending the 1845 War between Honduras and El Salvador, signed November 27, 1845.

SERBELLAN DE SANTA CRUZ. Lieutenant Governor, 1863.

SERENA, GERARDO. Pen-name of Celeo Murillo Soto (q.v.).

SERRANILLA SHOALS. The dangerous coral banks off the northeast Honduran coast were a graveyard for many ships. Part of these banks were also called the "Stop Dreaming" (Quito Sueño) shoals. They were named after a ship, the Pedro Serrano, which wrecked not far away.

SERRANO POLO, NORBERTO. Interim governor of Honduras in 1815.

SERVICIO AEREO DE HONDURAS see AIR SERVICE OF HONDURAS

SERVICIO GEODESICO INTERAMERICANO. The Interamerican Survey, carried out in cooperation with the countries concerned and with the assistance of U.S. Army engineers, consisted of triangulation and accurate astronomical establishment of position, as well as 30,000-foot-altitude air-photography (with other supplemental data), and accurate ground classification of detail. The survey operations were effected in the Central American area during the 1950s and 1960s, with the result that accurate topographical maps are now available for the western third of the country. Some east coastal areas have not been accurately mapped as yet.

SERVILES. Conservative party favoring a strong centralized government at the time of the establishment of the United Provinces of Central America (1822). Serviles were opposed by the Radicales. The center of the Servile group, which hoped to continue the aristocratic, conservative domination of colonial days, was Guatemala City. By and large this liberal-conservative split is the major political fact of all Central America to this day.

SEUTTER, ETHEL. Registered nurse, native of Canada, who gave years of service up until 1973 at the Clínica Morava (q.v.) in Ahuas.

SEVILLA, SPAIN. Port on the Guadalquivir River which from the settlement of New Spain until 1774 was the only authorized Spanish port to receive the commerce of Central America. Until 1663, when an earthquake changed the bed of the San Juan River, the traffic was direct from Granada (on Lake Nicaragua) to Sevilla, or from the north coast of Honduras points to the same port. Early colonial Honduras had little direct traffic from its own coast, since the ports were remote and east of the frontier. Pack trains would be dispatched to Granada in Nicaragua.

"SHARK AND THE SARDINES, THE" see AREVALO, JUAN JOSE

SHEARS, GEORGE W. see FRITZ GAERTNER

SHEEN CAYS see GUANAJA ISLAND

SHEGELLA FLEXNERI. A virulent form of bacillary dysentery, with deaths resulting. In 1970, Brus Laguna reported 13 deaths in three months from this disease. The medical services at the Clínica Morava (q.v.) in Ahuas saved many lives during epidemics of this and similar diseases.

SHIP-RAILWAY, TEHAUNTEPEC. Significant to the Central American region in that this plan, to carry fully-loaded seagoing ships across the Mexican isthmus on multi-track railroad, was one of three rival plans considered viable about 1880: 1) The de Lesseps sea-level canal plan for Panama, never realized in that form; 2) The Tehauntepec Railway, never started; and 3) The Nicaragua lock-canal and lake-river route, often surveyed.

Famed engineer Eads had lent his approval to the railway plan which had been first proposed by Dr. William F. Channing of Providence, Rhode Island, 30 years before, and patented in 1865. It was to have been effected originally across Honduras by the British-Honduras Interoceanic Railway Company. E. G. Squiers' (q.v.) book, Notes on Central America, devoted much of its text and a detailed map to the original cross-Honduran Railway project, of which this was a further development. The early antecedents of this plan were more than 25 centuries before when the ancient Greeks had a similar ship transit over the Isthmus of Corinth.

SHOREMEN (MOSQUITIA). Designation of the 17th, 18th, and 19th century English squatters on the "Mosquito Shore" who were interested principally in dealing in contraband in the Spanish colonies. Generally thought by the Spanish to be encouraging the Sambo-Miskito (q.v.) raids, they probably were not doing so, for to them the contraband trade was more profitable than booty. However, the Sambo-Miskitos served almost as a standing army for the shoremen, as they kept the Spanish on the defensive. The area included the north and east coastal area of Honduras. The shoremen were engaged in logwood and mahogany cutting, as well as agriculture, especially in the Black River area of the northern Honduran Coast.

These English settlers squatted on the Mosquito and other Caribbean coastal areas from Trujillo, Honduras to western Panama. Black River, Honduras, and Bluefields, Nicaragua were major centers. Typical of the settlers was William Pitt (q.v.), who had a mansion on Black River. London insisted that due to her relationship with the Sambo-Miskitos (q.v.), the coast was not Spanish soil. The protection of the Shoremen was considered to lie in the establishment of the "Kingdom of Mosquitia," which began about 1687. The Shoremen ultimately curbed Sambo-Miskito raids to keep the contraband trade with Spanish colonists active. After 1710 the Shoremen had peaceful relations with the warlike Sambo-Miskitos.

The War of Jenkins' Ear in 1739 further reinforced the Shoremen. It was at this time that Robert Hodgson (q.v.) was sent to the Shore as Superintendent. The evacuation of the Bay Islands (q.v.) in 1748 infuriated not only the Baymen but the Shoremen as well. By 1752 Fort Omoa (q.v.) was conceived as a base for Spanish action against both Baymen and Shoremen. By 1763 there were forts at Black River and on the Bay Islands, and when war with Spain ended in 1764, the British-supported Shoremen were in firm possession of the Honduran Coast. They actually got George III of England to change governors in 1776, as a direct result of his alarm over the rebellion of the North American colonies. In 1780 some of the shoremen were driven from their plantations by a Spanish offensive, but were ultimately to win out by default as the Spanish left. A Black River Spanish Fort was named

"Inmaculada Concepción," but it soon fell. In 1786 a treaty implicitly unfavorable to the Shoremen was signed, and the colonists left Black River as the Spanish under Hervias and Vallejo occupied the area. The evacuation was complete except for some very few who took the oath of loyalty to Spain. After a hundred years, the smuggler-planters-lumbermen of the Shore were officially gone. But the Shoremen in Belize, 3,500 of them, caused that place to become a main base for contraband trade with Honduras. The Spanish did manage to prevent the long Honduran north coast from becoming another British Honduras, however.

SHRIMP PRODUCTION. Little is done on the Pacific side, although a small quantity is shipped from San Lorenzo to Tegucigalpa. On the Caribbean coast, especially in the Caratasca Lagoon area, there is a shrimp packing enterprise near Puerto Lempira, and there is a shrimp cannery on the Isla de Guanaja.

SICO RIVER see TINTO RIVER

SIERRA, MANUEL H. One of the 1954 strike leaders. See GENERAL STRIKE, 1954.

SIERRA, TERENCIO. Constitutional President from February 1, 1899 until January 30, 1903, Sierra wished to succeed himself, but in the 1903 election Manuel Bonilla was the largest vote-getter, and with his supporters marched against the capital. Bonilla was declared president by Congress in April, his official term running from February 1, 1903 to February 26, 1907.

SIERRA DE AGALTA. A major mountain range up to 7,500 feet altitude in Olancho Department, between the upper reaches of the Río Grande and the Río Patuca.

SIERRA ESPIRITU SANTO. Mountain range paralleling the Guatemalan-Honduran border in the department of Santa Bárbara, just west of Macuelizo, and above the Valley of the Río Chamelecón.

SIERRA OSORIO, LOPE DE. As visitador to Escabedo, when the latter was ordered back to Spain, he governed pro tem from 1678-82.

SIERRA RIO TINTO. Between the Río Paulaya and the Río Tinto lie mountains which are up to 6,000 feet altitude, but lower toward the Caribbean. In the western part of Gracias a Dios Department, they are one of several parallel ranges running southwest to northeast.

SIGNATORIES OF THE ACT OF INDEPENDENCE, 1821. The Province of Comayagua actually spoke for what is now the country of Honduras in the Act of Independence of September 28, 1821, thirteen days after the primary act in the Kingdom of Guatemala. Those who signed were as follows: José Tinoco, José Francisco Zelaya, José Nicolás Irías, Pedro Nolasco Arriaga, Francisco Gómez, Liberato Valdez, Juan Miguel Fiallos, José Joaquín Lino Avilez, Fray José Antonio Murga, Francisco Javier Bulnez, Santos Bardales, Juan José Montes, Santiago Bueso, Juan Nepomuceno, Cacho Gómez, Jacinto Rubi, Ciriaco Velásquez, Juan Garrigo, José de la Cruz Pascua, Esteban Travieso, José María Rodríguez, José Calixto Valenzuela, José Antonio Bueso, Raimundo Boquín, Nicolás Folofo, Cayetano Bosque, Joaquín Lindo (Secretario).

SIGRE, RIO. This stream in the department of Gracias a Dios empties into the Brus Laguna, flowing north to do so.

SIKSA. Miskito word for "banana"--hence used a great deal, as this is a very basic east-coast food.

SIKSA, LAGUNA. This "banana lake" is a small one, northernmost of the Caratasca complex of lagoons which parallels Honduras' northeast coast for 60 to 70 miles.

SIKSATINGNI, RIO. This river flowing into the Río Warunta and then into the Laguna de Warunta is noted by the redundant name "River Banana-Stream," Río in Spanish, Banana-Stream in Miskito.

SILAK. A lance with a removable and retrievable head, used by the natives of Mosquitia in the 19th Century when hunting such animals as Manatee.

SILVA MUÑOZ, EUSEBIO. Interim governor in 1812.

SILVA SALAZAR, ALONSO DE. Governor, 1639 period.

SILVER. In 1569 the first major silver strike was made in Guascarán, and not long after, similar "hard-rock" strikes were made in the wild area south and east of the colonial capital Comayagua, the area now known to surround Tegucigalpa. There were 30 silver mines in that area by 1580 (see SAN ANTONIO DE ORIENTE). The Guascarán strikes changed the whole Honduran economy. Honduras became a mountain mining province. In the 17th and 18th centuries, silver was the most important industry of central Honduras. One problem, however, was that the primitive technology of the era found it hard to deal with the exceptionally hard rocks of the Tegucigalpa mining field, and underground water was another prevalent hazard. Reduction processes were also primitive until mercury amalgamation (q.v.) was developed.

SILVER PRODUCTION. Honduras is tenth in the world in silver production. The old Rosario (q.v.) mine was reopened in 1970 after a 16-year dormant period, and a pair of New York

Sindicato de Tela

and Honduran companies were getting out not only silver, but gold, copper, lead, and zinc. The Honduran silver mines in colonial days were a proximate cause of the development of the Tegucigalpa area.

SINDICATO DE TELA RAILROAD COMPANY. Also known by the acronym, SITRATERCO, the Tela Railroad Union. See FEDERATION OF WORKERS OF NORTHERN HONDURAS.

SINDICATO UNIFICADO DE TRABAJADORES DE LA STANDARD FRUIT COMPANY see FEDERATION OF WORKERS OF NORTHERN HONDURAS

SINZONTLE. The black robin. This name is of local Indian derivation, and is used in southern Honduras.

SIRSIRTARA. In Gracias a Dios Department, this village on the Río Ibantara is connected by road to Puerto Lempira, which is about 32 miles away.

SITCA see TOURISM COUNCIL OF THE CENTRAL AMERICAN STATES

"SLASH AND BURN." The basic agricultural form in Meso-America. In the Honduran gulf area, this form of agriculture can support up to 200 persons per square mile, even though in the accepted cycle about ten acres should lie fallow for one in cultivation. In some of the Tierra Templada, the use-cycle of rotation could be as little as two or three years, with consequently higher productivity. It is thought that the wastefulness of this agricultural mode doomed the classic Maya, as long as ten centuries ago.

SLAVERY. There were slave raids in the Bay Islands and on the north coast of the Honduran mainland, possibly as early as 1510, and surely by about 1515. The Indian captives were taken to Cuba to replace already-depleted Indian slave populations there. Following the conquest a slave trade continued from Yucatán and northern Honduras. Nicaragua, however, was the major center of the Indian slave trade. By 1550 the source of slaves in Honduras was depleted and the trade essentially ended then. For awhile--about 1520-1550--Indian slaves were the principal Central American export.

SLAVERY, ABOLISHMENT. The decree abolishing slavery in Central America was early in relation to some of the "civilized" powers of the world, among them the United States of America. Slavery persisted in Brazil until late in the 19th century.
    The decree by the National Constituent Assembly of the Provinces of Central America, dated April 17, 1824, provided complete freedom for all slaves of both sexes, prohibited entry of any foreigner employed in slave traffic, provided

for treaties between nations on the matter of escaped slaves, and provided indemnities for slave owners. A Committee for Indemnities was established, and penalties were set up for infractions of the act. The executive of Honduras at the time stated, in enthusiastic accord with the act, that it "merited tables of bronze ... to the honor of the human race." Slavery persisted in Spanish Puerto Rico until 1872, and in Cuba until 1880.

SMART PULAIA. Miskito for "playing it smart"; this is an example of an English combined form. Spanish forms and words in combination also exist. "Smart pulaia" actually means taking advantage of someone else.

SMITH, FEDERICO see AGUIRRE, SALVADOR

SMITH, DR. GEOFFREY. Public Health specialist on a several-week tour of duty in 1974 at the Hospital Atlántida in La Ceiba, sponsored by the Vermont Partners of the Americas (q.v.), and under the direction of the Honduran Ministry of Health. Reconstruction projects are being developed on a long-range basis.

SMITH, JOHN. "General" Smith was a Sambo who considered himself the ruler of the Black River Area, and who assisted in the attack on Fort Dalling (q.v.) in August of 1782. He was involved in the massacre which took place there. See TRUJILLO, BASE ... 1782.

SMUGGLING. From the earliest times of trade between Honduran ports and Seville, Spain, there was illegal trade going on. The height of smuggling operations occurred when trade was carried on with the ships of Spain's enemies in American ports. The 17th Century depression encouraged deliberate Central American clandestine commerce. Near Fort Omoa in 1675 a cargo of woolen goods was purchased from an enemy ship and transported clear across Honduras by muleback into Nicaragua before authorities could catch up. It was two years before the case was closed. Contraband was good business. The seizure of Curaçao by the Dutch in 1634 and Jamaica by the English in 1655 provided active bases for smuggling operations. Jamaica became the greatest receiving point for Central American goods due to its contiguity to the Bay of Honduras. Old Providence Island, just off the Nicaraguan coast, was a curse to Spanish coastal traffic out of the Bay of Honduras. In fact, the Providence Islanders seized Trujillo in 1639 for a large ransom. Elaborate and extensive smuggling was carried out in the early 18th century, with Jamaica and Curaçao more than ever involved. Finally, massive smuggling became the only way by which Central America could carry on sufficient trade to satisfy, even partially, its growing needs. By 1715, contraband trade was the principal activity of commerce in Central America. The

Bay of Honduras ports and the Bay islands were particularly involved.

SNAKES, POISONOUS see CLARK, H. C.

SOBERANA JUNTA LEGISLATIVA PROVISIONAL, 1822. The body which passed an act of annexation to the short-lived Mexican "Empire" under Agustín Iturbide, on January 5, 1822. The entities subscribing to this annexation comprised all of Central America, called the Kingdom of Guatemala within the empire. See ACT OF ANNEXATION TO MEXICO.

SOBERANIA DE HONDURAS, DECLARACION see SOVEREIGNTY, HONDURAS

SOCCER WAR see WAR, EL SALVADOR, 1969

SOCIAL SECURITY see MINISTRY OF LABOR AND SOCIAL SECURITY

SOCIAL SECURITY TAX. Only judicial, military, and telegraph employees pay a social security tax.

SOCIAL WELFARE, MINISTRY OF see CABINET

SOCIEDAD AMIGOS DEL CAMPO. A planting and conservation society to control fruit trees; actually a quasi-governmental organization administered through local municipal authority, and established by decree-law in May 1956.

SOCIEDAD DEL GENIO EMPRENDEDOR Y DEL BUEN GUSTO. An academy founded by José Trinidad Reyes (q.v.) on December 14, 1845, which became under president Juan Lindo (q.v.) the University of Honduras (q.v.) on September 19, 1847. See LITERATURE.

SOL, JULIO. Pen-name or pseudonym of Honduran writer Arturo Martínez Galindo (q.v.).

SOLIS, JUAN DIAZ DE. Early explorer of the Gulf of Honduras and Yucatán, in 1506, who claimed with his partner Yáñez Pinzón to have been the first on these coasts, attempting to preempt the just claims of Columbus.

SOLORZANO MONCADA, J. JORGE see MILITARY ZONE COMMANDS, 1972

SOLTERA, MARIA. Pen-name of Mary Lester, a lady of English descent who had been born in the Pyrenees Mountains and had lived in such diverse locales as the Fiji Islands and Australia. Her story of a journey by sidesaddle across Honduras in 1881 is one of color and adventure which was not shared by the typical woman of her class and period. She was an early free spirit among her sex, and her book, A Lady's Ride Across Spanish Honduras, is both entertaining and informative.

SOMODEVILLA, ZENON DE. The Marquis of Ensenada, who became Minister of the Indies in 1743. As a confirmed Anglophobe he was anxious to drive the British off Spanish soil. His plan was first to attack and take Belize, then the Bay Islands and Black River. The effect of his policy was to delay the building of Fort Omoa (q.v.). He issued orders along these lines in 1745.

SOMOTILLO see QUILALI

SONAGUERA. A tiny village southwest of Trujillo which became the frontier post after the destruction of Trujillo by Jackson (q.v.) in 1643. See FRONTIER OF NEW SPAIN, COLONIAL.

SORGHUM. In 1970 almost 70,000 tons of sorghum were produced, on as many as 44,000 farms, principally in the southern part of the country. Production has been as high as this only once, but the crop is well-established.

SOSA, ROBERTO. Prolific writer and anthologist, born in Yoro in 1930. Directs publication of Presente. In 1968 he won the Spanish Adonais prize for poetry. Member of the "vida nueva" literary group. Publications: poetry, Caligiamos, Muros, and Mar interior, all in Tegucigalpa, and Los pobres, Madrid, 1969.

SOTO, MARCO AURELIO. Dr. Soto was provisional president from August 27, 1876 to May 30, 1877. He became Constitutional President on the latter date, and served until June 1880, then again from July 30, 1880 until May 9, 1883. Soto may have been the most popular nineteenth century president. He had support both in Honduras itself and in Guatemala, which seemed to be a key factor at the time. He was conspicuously lenient to former enemies and was tolerant of all shades of political grouping. This liberal policy gave him freedom to organize a postal and telegraph service, open a national library and a mint, establish a budgetary policy and department, and set up free primary schooling. He tried to curb the armed forces by institutionalization. A new constitution was approved in 1880. Soto only left in 1883 under pressure from Guatemalan President Barrios.

SOVEREIGNTY, HONDURAS. Honduran sovereignty was formalized by a decree of the national Congress on January 28, 1950, and placed in effect January 17, 1951. It provides for sovereignty over the undersea shelves of both the continent and islands, to the distance of two hundred nautical miles. The right of navigation by other sovereign nations is not impaired.

SOUTHWEST CAY see GUANAJA ISLAND

SPANISH COLONIAL OFFICERS GOVERNING GUATEMALA. (Captains general and others--includes acting governors, with the inclusive dates giving approximate terms of office.)
Alvarado Contreras, Pedro de, 1525-1541
Cueva de Alvarado, Dona Beatriz de la, 1541
Marroquín, Francisco, 1541-1542, jointly with
Cueva, Francisco de la, 1541-1542
Maldonado, Alonso de, 1542-1548
Cerrato, Alonso López, 1548-1555
Quesada, Antonio Rodríguez de, 1555-1558
Ramírez de Quiñones, Pedro, 1558-1559
Landecho, Juan Núñez de, 1559-1563
Briceno, Francisco, 1564-1569
González, Antonio, 1570-1572
Villalobos, Pedro de, 1573-1578
Valverde, García de, 1579-1589
Rueda, Pedro Mallén de, 1589-1592
Sande, Francisco de, 1593-1596
Abaunza, Alvaro Gómez de, 1596-1598
Criado de Castilla, Alonso, 1598-1611
Peraza Ayala Castilla y Rojas, Antonio, 1611-1626
Acuna, Diego de, 1626-1633
Quiñones y Osorio, Alvaro de, 1634-1642
Avendaño, Diego de, 1642-1649
Lara y Mogrobejo, Antonio de, 1649-1654
Altamirano y Velasco, Fernando de, 1654-1657
Carrillo de Mendoza, Jeronimo Garcés, 1657-1659
Mencos, Martín Carlos de, 1659-1667
Alvarez Alfonso Rosica de Caldas, Sebastián, 1668-1670
Sáenz de Manosca y Murillo, Juan de Santo Matía, 1670-1672
Escobedo, Fernando Francisco de, 1672-1682
Augurto y Alava, Juan Miguel de, 1682-1684
Enríquez de Guzmán, Enrique, 1684-1688
Barrios y Leal, Jacinto de, 1688-1695
Escals, José de, 1695-1696
Berrospe, Gabriel Sánchez de, 1696-1700
Heduardo, Juan Jerónimo, 1701-1702
Ceballos y Villagutierre, Alonso, 1702-1703
Espinosa de los Monteros, José Osorio, 1704-1706
Cosio y Campa, Toribio José de, 1706-1716
Rivas, Francisco Rodríguez de, 1716-1724
Echevers y Suvisa, Antonio Pedro de, 1724-1733
Rivera y Villalón, Pedro de, 1733-1742
Rivera y Santa Cruz, Tomás de, 1742-1748
Araujo y Río, Juan de, 1748-1751
Montaos y Sotomayor, José Vásquez Prego, 1752-1753
Velarde y Cienfuegos, Juan, 1753-1754
Arcos y Moreno, Alonso de, 1754-1760
Heredia, José Fernández de, 1761-1765
Salazár y Herrera Nájera y Mendoza, Pedro de, 1765-1771
Gonzales Bustillo y Villaseñor, Juan, 1771-1773

Mayorga, Martín de, 1773-1779
Gálvez, Matías de, 1779-1783
Estachería, José de, 1783-1789
Troncoso, Martínez del Rincón, Bernardo, 1789-1794
Domas y Valle, José, 1794-1801
González Mollinedo y Saravia, Antonio, 1801-1811
Bustamente y Guerra, José, 1811-1818
Urrutia, Carlos, 1818-1821
Gainza, Gabino, 1821.

SPANISH HONDURAS. Term sometimes applied to the Republic of Honduras to differentiate it from the longtime British Crown Colony of British Honduras, now becoming independent. There is little relationship, other than contiguity to the Gulf of Honduras, between the two countries.

SPANISH POPULATION, 17th CENTURY. The number of Spaniards was incredibly small. In about 1620-1660 the populations of Spanish vecinos were as follows in Honduran towns:
  Comayagua          100
  Gracias a Dios      50
  Trujillo and
  Puerto Caballos     30
  La Choluteca        60
  Olancho             20
Remarkably, this small number ruled the land for over a century following the conquest.

SPECIAL EDUCATION, SCHOOL. An Escuela de Enseñanza Especial was created by Congress on February 18, 1950, for children with physical and mental disabilities and abnormalities. There were three sections: one for the blind, another for the mentally retarded, and another for the deaf and dumb.

SPECIAL SECURITY CORPS see CUERPO ESPECIAL DE SEGURIDAD

SPINDEN, HERBERT J. Author of the "Spinden Correlation" for placement of Maya dates, and of the book, A Study of Maya Art. Dr. Spinden did a great deal of work at Copán in 1913.

SQUIER, EPHRAIM GEORGE. Born in 1821 in Bethlehem, New York, Squier was an example of the many-faceted 19th century man. Squier was a civil engineer, but also an accomplished dilettante in archaeology, ethnology, linguistics, diplomacy, railroad entrepreneurship, editing, and writing. He resembles in many respects the ubiquitous John Lloyd Stephens, an early contemporary, the father of modern Maya archaeology and a major official of the cross-Panama isthmian railroad.

Squier was assigned by President Zachary Taylor as U.S. Chargé d'Affaires to the governments of Central America in 1849 (a decade after Stephens), and sailed in May for his post in the brig Francis. His diplomatic ventures included a near-war between Britain and the United States over territorial concessions disputed in the Bay of Fonseca. His significance to Honduras is tied to his efforts to create a rail link across Honduras between Atlantic and Pacific, a technically feasible route of 160 miles. The Honduras Interoceanic Railroad Company (q.v.) failed, but it was the inspiration for a Squier volume of great general interest concerning mid-nineteenth century Honduras, the Notes on Central America, Particularly the States of Honduras and San Salvador, published in 1855. This was added to his near-classic two-volume Nicaragua, Its People, Scenery, Monuments, and the Proposed Interoceanic Canal of 1852, and the only novel he ever wrote, Waikna, or Adventures on the Mosquito Shore, under the pen-name Samuel A. Bard. The latter also has Honduran references of value for comparisons, especially in the regions of eastern Honduras where information is sparse and cultural change glacial in speed. Before his death in 1888, Squier was editor of Frank Leslie's Illustrated Weekly. He was somewhat of an authority on the American Indian, and as a result of his self-taught ethnological competence became a member of a number of scholarly societies in Europe and America. Squier manages to evoke Honduras on a perceptive emotional basis as well as a voluminously factual one, and his books could well be useful guides even today.

STAMP TAX. The oldest national tax, in effect since 1897. "Papel sellado," prestamped paper, is used for official acts, and documents such as invoices and contracts.

STANDARD FRUIT COMPANY. This banana-raising concern is the largest single landholder in Honduras, its holdings reaching a total of over 250,000 acres. Most of the land is devoted to banana culture. Beginning early in the 20th century as Vaccaro Brothers and Co., Standard Fruit had first purchased fruit from small growers, but early began to produce its own fruit on controlled plantations. Standard Fruit operates around La Ceiba, which is virtually a "company town." It developed the Giant Cavendish banana, resistent to the destructive Panama disease. Standard Fruit also has 500 acres in citrus planting, and maintains commercial stands of coconuts. It also raises livestock, with large ranches near Papaloteca and San Juan del Norte. The company's electric plant provides service to La Ceiba, and its telephone system has 50 lines radiating out from La Ceiba. It also has the longest railroad in the country, with 300 miles of track and 1,000 freight cars, 31 passenger cars, all near La Ceiba. Standard Fruit administers the seaport of that city. All in all, Standard Fruit is a major socio-economic force in the republic, as becomes apparent at such times as those of the 1974 "banana war" (q.v.).

STANDEFER, DENNIS see FATHOM EXPEDITIONS

STATE CONTROL OF EDUCATION. The nation assumed control
of the administration of education by a decree-law of the
Military Junta on October 16, 1957. The annual budget was
to provide for primary education, although private or local
schools could be established under other auspices; in any
event they must conform to the national requirements. Fair
classifications of schools, according to school population,
were established, as were two classes of teachers, those
without and those with a teaching credential, "Titulo Docente."

STATE OF SIEGE. In times of crisis or emergency as judged by
the President, all constitutional guarantees are suspended;
curfew and other restrictions are imposed. This power is
less frequently used than a generation ago, but can still be
experienced in any of the Central American republics. In
older days, the state of siege was used as a technique for an
administration to stay in power beyond its normal time.

STATES OF CENTRAL AMERICA (from independence to present).
    Chiapas        (Now part of Mexico since the Iturbide empire)
    Costa Rica    (Independent)
    El Salvador   (Independent)
    Guatemala     (Independent)
    Honduras      (Independent)
    Los Altos     (In existence as a "maneuver" from 1825-1840)
    Nicaragua     (Independent)
Panama, formerly part of Colombia, is not considered part
of Central America, although geographically it is most certainly isthmian America.

STEEL. Large iron ore deposits are found near Agalteca, north
of Tegucigalpa. From 1568 until 1863 they were mined and
the ore turned into iron with crude charcoal-fired smelters.
A Mexican company has joined the Honduran government in a
venture to manufacture steelbars, hoping to reach an annual
100,000 metric tons by the mid-1970s.

STEPHENS, JOHN LLOYD. As an agent of the U.S. government,
Stephens was sent to Central America by President Van Buren
in 1839. Stephens in his official capacity was to investigate
cross-isthmian transit, and he recommended the Nicaraguan
canal route in strongest terms, advising that surveys made
by engineer Bailey should be continued. He estimated the
canal cost at $25,000,000. However, the revolutionary activities current in the several countries concerned caused
him to recommend that capitalists should be cautious in investing. Stephens arrived in Central America just as the republics were breaking up, and he was personally exposed to
open warfare in El Salvador, as Morazán fought some of his
final battles.
    Stephens was best known for his incidental activities,
for his considerable travels through Central America led to
two published works of two volumes each, which have become

classics. He is considered the father of Maya archaeology, and his accompanying artist, Catherwood (q.v.), did a great deal to assure the opening up of Mayaland. The drawings of the magnificent ruins at Copán in Honduras were particularly effective in representing stelae. Copán was the first major site they visited.
  Stephens was later active in the building of the cross-Panama railroad.
  In his Incidents of Travel in Central America, Chiapas, and Yucatan Stephens gave detailed distances and elevations on the proposed canal route across Central America, and added much interesting information on each of the countries. An earlier travel saga, to Petra and through Russia, had already established the remarkable Stephens in the literary world. His adventure in Central America, including Honduras, recorded contacts with the Honduran hero, Morazán (q.v.). His descriptions of Copán are particularly spirited, and especially interesting for comparison with the ruined city in its present condition. See COPAN, THE MAYA RUINS.

STEPPES. Grass-covered semi-arid plains such as are found in east-central Europe. Southern Honduras has many steppe areas. See LIFE ZONES.

STIRRUPS see ESTRIBO (illustration, p. 108)

STONE, DORIS ZEMURRAY. This author, daughter of United Fruit Company's dynamic Samuel Zemurray, produced a history of Honduras based on her own intimate knowledge of the country, the Estampas de Honduras, published in Mexico City in 1954. The period covered ranges from the conquest to the latter 1800s.

STROMIRK, GUSTAV. Archaeologist who was in charge of excavations at Copán (q.v.) from 1935 to 1942, under auspices of the Carnegie Institute. The work was delayed by World War II. Dr. Stromirk has previously carried out stela restoration at Quiriguá, Guatemala. Returning to Copán after the war, Stromirk left in 1947.

SUAREZ, CLEMENTINA. Editor of the magazine Mujer. Born in Juticalpa, Olancho, in 1906, she has lived in Havana, New York, San Salvador, and Mexico, where she developed a Gallery of Central American Art. Publications of poetry include Corazón sangrante, 1930; Templos de fuego, 1931; Veleros, 1937; Engranajes, 1935.

SUASNAVAR, COUSTANTINO. Born in León, Nicaragua, of Honduran parentage in 1912. Has worked with Surco and Honduras Literaria (q.v.); poetry published includes Perfil al erente, 1959; Sonetos de Honduras, 1965; Cuarto a espodas, 1967.

SUAZO, JUAN DE. Governor in 1650 and following; Juan Márquez de Cabrera during same period.

SUBIRANA, MANUEL JESUS. A priest who went as a missionary to the Jicaque (q.v.) Indians in the 19th century. It was he who introduced them to corn agriculture, and who assembled them into villages. The demand for forced labor, however, caused them to retreat into the Montaña de la Flor.

SUBURBS, TEGUCIGALPA. Other than various barrios and colonias (q.v.) there are several suburban areas; La Granja, Lotificación Quesada, La Guadelupe, La Reforma, El Manchén, La Bolsa.

SUFFRAGE FOR WOMEN. A decree of January 24, 1955, under the Lozano Díaz administration, gave suffrage to women in Honduras. There were specifications as to foreign birth and naturalized citizenship, and then suffrage was extended to all men and women over 21 years of age, to married men and women over 18, and to literate men and women over 18.

SUKIA. Title of priests of the Coco-Bocay region in pre-conquest times. They presided over a religion which had among other divinities the Wulasha and the Lewire. The Sukia was soothsayer, doctor, wizard, and intermediary with the gods.

SUKYA. Sambo name for a shaman or medicine man among the Miskitos and Sambos who was consulted about such matters as making raids on the Spanish settlements.

SULA XICAQUES. Name of the Indian tribe contacted by Olid (q.v.) in 1524 when he landed on the north coast. They were in the area of present-day San Pedro Sula. See XICAQUE.

SULACO, MOUNTAINS OF see FLOR, MONTES DE LA

SULACO RIVER. Tributary of the Ulua (q.v.) on the line between Yoro and Comayagua departments.

"SUMMIT" MEETING, CENTRAL AMERICA, 1974 see PRESIDENTS' MEETING, CENTRAL AMERICA, 1974

SUMPUL RIVER. This large tributary of the Río Lempa comprises about half of the border between Honduras and El Salvador, and is in the area of dispute which caused the outbreak of the 1969 war (q.v.). The line is the southern edge of Ocotopeque department and part of the Lempira department's southern border.

SUMUS. Indians who live as a tribal remnant along the upper Río Coco--probably of South American origin, possibly Chibcha. The Sumus are related to the early Miskitos of the Caribbean coast, before they were mixed with Carib and Negro blood infusions. The present tribesmen pan some gold as a cash basis on the tributaries of the upper river. The original Miskito language was based on Sumu.

SUPERIOR COUNCIL OF NATIONAL DEFENSE see MILITARY ORGANIZATION AND MILITARY COMMAND STRUCTURE

SUPREME COUNCIL OF THE ARMED FORCES see MELGAR CASTRO, JUAN ALBERTO

SUPREME COURT. Constitutionally, there is a Supreme Court of seven justices and five alternates. All are appointed by the National Congress (q.v.). The subordinate judicial officials are appointed by the Supreme Court; they are appellate justices or magistrates, lower court justices, (regional-departmental) labor judges, registrars of property, and the offices of the Attorney General. Powers also include impeachment of high officials if Congress declares grounds; nullification of unconstitutional laws (as judged so by the court); and petitions of amparo (q.v.). The Court, which has its seat in the capital, requires appointees to be qualified as are cabinet ministers. Members must be citizens by birth, aged over thirty, and each must be a lawyer who has been a judge at a lower level a minimum of five years. Terms are for six years, subject to reappointment. The President of the Court is chosen for the full six-year term by the Justices at their first session. It is worthy of remark that the jury system was discarded in 1924. The Supreme Court has tended to be somewhat subordinate to the executive. This is in line with the ambient realities of "caudillismo." Since the bloodless military coup of December 1972, the strong executive system has been in the ascendancy once again.

SURCO. A magazine of literary review published in Tegucigalpa in 1949. See CLAUDIO BARRERA.

SWAN ISLANDS. The islands were discovered, according to Francisco José Durón (q.v.), on July 26, 1502 by Columbus, four days before he landed on Guanaja, one of the major Bay Islands, from whence he first caught sight of the Central American mainland (Cape Honduras north of Trujillo). The discovery and ownership of these tiny islands 100 miles north of eastern Honduras has been in dispute during most of the nearly five centuries since they were first sighted. Significant in that they were, as cited on one 18th century map, points of departure for ships sailing from Jamaica to either the Miskito Shore or the Bay of Honduras, the tiny keys were originally called the Islas Santa Ana, because they were discovered on the day assigned to that Saint. Fresh water was obtainable there, which was, of course, highly significant to early sailors. Because of their capacity for refreshment and their navigational position, the Swan Islands were established early in the 16th century as a part of the route Jamaica-Swan

Island-Guanaja and Cape Camerón, a promontary of the Honduran mainland southeast of the Bay Island Guanaja. In 1524 by royal order the government of the whole area from Chiapas to Costa Rica was assigned to González Dávila, including the Islas Santa Ana (Swan). French corsairs appeared as early as 1529 and were responsible for data appearing on subsequent maps, such as those of Descelliers (q.v.). By 1600, maps by Gabriel Totten (q.v.) were available, and in 1700 Guillermo d'Lisle, French royal geographer, published a map showing the "Islas Santanilla," a diminutive form of Santa Ana. By 1775 the Jefferys (q.v.) map showed the islands as "Santanilla or Swan Islands."

The matter of maps is significant in the development of the Swan Islands case because it is central to the tracing of ownership claims by Honduras. Through the days of independence and confederation, the titles were often confused by the action of British subjects and a miscellany of freebooters who occupied or used the Honduran offshore islands. During the 1830 through 1850s period, British claims to the Bay Islands (and attacks thereupon) affected Honduranian sovereignty; they also disturbed the United States because of treaty violations and the Monroe Doctrine position.

Bizarre events continued on both the Bay and Swan Islands. William Walker (q.v.) landed and occupied the Swan Islands in his final and abortive attempt once more to seize power in Nicaragua. His execution by Honduran authorities in 1860 cut short that design. On April 22, 1861, the government of Honduras declared all the islands (including Swan) and the Miskito coast under its sovereign dominion, tracing the rights back to the Spanish discoveries. Maps of the West Indies from 1800 through 1877 continued to show the Swan Islands. But in 1934 and 1961, maps of the U.S. National Geographic Society showed the tiny islands as owned by the United States. What was the basis of the change indicated on these maps?

In 1893 an adventurer from the United States, a sailor with an old schooner, landed on the islands, and apparently ignorant of their existence and long, nautically significant history, planted the U.S. flag and "took possession" by right of discovery. The fact that he was 391 years late did not deter him, since he didn't know it. This "discovery" came to light in a New Orleans newspaper as late as 1922. Author Durón characterizes it as "absurd and ridiculous." Nevertheless, in 1916, Alonso Adams looked for a buyer for "his" Swan Islands and found a Dr. Will Brooks of Boston. From the U.S. standpoint the islands were claimed under the Guano Islands Act of 1863, and were occupied by a radio broadcast station from 1907 to 1927, and since 1961 by a U.S. radio beacon. The U.S. Central Intelligence Agency was involved. By 1970 the long-standing problem of sovereignty was being resolved in favor of Honduras, providing the U.S. could make arrangement to keep its radio installations on the island. The 1965 constitution of Honduras specifically designated the Swan

Islands as Honduran.
Swan Island Radio figured in the Bay of Pigs invasion of Cuba in April of 1961. It had been broadcasting propaganda to Cuba on a regular basis.
By 1974 the U.S. and Honduras had agreed on Honduran sovereignty for the islands, furthering the 1970 talks, with the proviso that the U.S. could maintain a radio facility.

- T -

TABACALERA HONDUREÑA, S.A. The Honduran Tobacco Company, largest in the country. Most of the tobacco grown is of the leaf type for cigars, but some light cigarette tobaccos are grown. Production is principally by 2,400 farmers in the Department of Copán.

TABOADA, DIEGO DE. Lieutenant governor in the 1747 period, with Fernández de Heredia.

TACA. The well-known and long established Central American airline. See TRANSVIAS AEREAS DE CENTRO AMERICA.

TACOMA, U.S.S. The United States warship aboard which a settlement was made (at Puerto Cortéz) of the Dávila (q.v.) and Bonilla (q.v.) dispute over the Honduran presidency in 1911. Francisco Bertrand (q.v.) was agreed upon as provincial president. This agreement spelled an end to Nicaraguan predominance in the affairs of Honduras, as it coincided with the end of the Zelaya (q.v.) regime in that country. It also represented increasing concern of the U.S. over Central American affairs.

TAGUZGALPA. An alternate spelling for Tegucigalpa, 18th century.

TAITAP. A species of sour orange used to scrub floors and tables, combined with rough leaves as sandpaper, in the Mosquito coastal area. It is also used as a bleach for bark cloth.

TALANGA RIVER. A tributary of the Río del Agua Caliente, in Francisco Morazán Department.

TAMAGAS. A very short, heavy, ill-tempered poisonous snake of the genus Bothrops, found in high mountain areas of Honduras.

TAN see TRANSPORTES AEREOS NACIONALES, S.A.

TANDAS. Drafts of Indians into a virtual slavery for working the placer gold-bearing streams of central Honduras. Each village was given a "tanda" or draft quota for a given period of time. The period of this labor was the middle 1500s.

341 Tansín, Isla de

TANSIN, ISLA DE. A large low island in the Caratasca Lagoon. About 20 miles long, it supports several tiny settlements, among them Tauwanta, Palkaka, Tasba Raya, and Walpata. All are in Gracias a Dios Department near Puerto Lempira.

TANSIN, LAGUNA DE. The large lagoon which with Caratasca lagoon forms the Island of Tansín (q.v.).

TAOO. Lenca Indian word for "house" or hut. Also Tahu.

TAPIA MARTINEZ, ISIDRO see MILITARY ZONE COMMANDS, 1972

TAPIR. The heavy animal used as food in Mosquitia; Elasmognathus Bairdir, a dangerous animal under some conditions; a night forager.

TAS. A term used in Mosquitia for a plot of land fifty meters square; four tas equal one hectare.

TASAJO. Dried meat, rubbed with salt and dried in the sun. Similar to "jerky" in the western United States.

TASBA RAYA. Village on the island of Tansín in Laguna Caratasca.

TATTON, GABRIEL. English geographer who published maps in 1600 showing Honduras in considerable detail considering the period. The Bay of Honduras was somewhat distorted, as were the principal features along the north coast, including the Bay and Swan Islands, Cartago Lagoon, Puerto Caballos, etc. These maps are now part of the Harley Collection in the British Museum.

TAULEBE, LAGO. Alternate and older name for Lake Yojoa (q.v.). This name was most commonly used during colonial days.

TAUWANTA. Village on the island of Tansín in Laguna Caratasca.

TAYLOR, SCHOONER. A vessel used by William Walker (q.v.) in a projected attack on Honduras in 1860. Walker landed on the Bay Island of Roatán, but used the Mexican island of Cozumel as a supply base. Walker cruised off the Honduran Coast in the Taylor, and finally decided to storm and capture the Fort at Trujillo. It was following his unsuccessful attempt to carry out this attack that he was captured and executed by a Honduran firing squad. See FAYSSOUX.

TAX--BANANAS. The Standard Fruit Company in early 1974 deliberately destroyed 145,000 boxes of bananas each week in order to bring pressure on the Honduran government to remove the tax on bananas which had been imposed. Banana prices were at a low ten cents per pound retail while some other fruits had increased 400 to 500 per cent. Honduras imposed the tax as one answer to the world inflationary trend. It followed that in 1974 there was a considerable disturbance over the tax on bananas exported by Honduras, Panama, and Costa Rica, which was set at $1.00 U.S. per 40-pound box shipped from these countries.

In June 1974, the Panamanian ambassador to Costa Rica claimed that American and British mercenaries, including Viet Nam veterans, had been hired by the Standard Fruit to assassinate the strongman, Omar Torrijos of Panama, and to overthrow the Honduran and Panamanian governments. D. I. Kirchoff (q.v.), president of Standard Fruit's parent company, categorically denied the allegation and requested U.S. State Department investigation and a meeting of the Organization of American States, if necessary. Standard Fruit has been foremost in the fight against the banana export tax.

TEACH, EDWARD. Best known as Blackbeard, this villainous pirate, once a privateer, was a frequenter of the Bay of Honduras, where in late 1717 or early 1718 he took Stede Bonnet (q.v.) aboard as partner-prisoner. The Blackbeard vessel Queen Anne's Revenge, teamed with Bonnet's Revenge in a piratical cruise from Honduras to Charleston, South Carolina, where in May 1718 Teach's fleet blockaded the port. Teach was killed in Ocracoke Inlet, North Carolina, in 1718.

TEACHING CATEGORIES. There are six categories or classes of teachers in Honduran schools, and these categories apply to administrative, directive, teaching, and technical personnel in pre-school, primary, special, and adult education. The classifications are based on years of service, educational levels, and other professional achievements. They are:
First class: Teacher with certificate (título docente), 12 years satisfactory service, with completed work in administration and supervision of schools, in upper level institutions.
Second class: Teacher with certificate, with a minimum of nine years satisfactory service, having had studies in administration and supervision in upper-level institutions.
Third class: Teacher with certificate, minimum of seven years, and studies in kindergarten, nuclear schools, and special education, etc.
Fourth class: Teacher with certificate or título docente."
Fifth class: Teacher with diploma or certificate of aptitude, but no título docente.
Temporary class: No título docente.

TEACHING, REGULATION. Under Dr. Juan Lindo (q.v.), who in 1822 had made an effort to establish primary schooling, there was a decree of March 23, 1847 regulating service in primary schools.

TECHNICAL INSTITUTE    see    FRANCISCO MORAZAN TECHNICAL INSTITUTE

**TECPATL.** Eighteenth day of the Aztec month; meaning, "flint."

**TEGUCIGALPA.** The capital city of Honduras, located in the south central portion of the country, is also the cabacera of Francisco Morazán Department. In the highlands of the upper Choluteca River valley, Tegucigalpa is in such a basin of the hills that there is at present no jet airport. Nevertheless Tegucigalpa is the largest population center of the nation, with near 300,000 inhabitants, and is the chief commercial center, as well as the heart of the Central District or seat of government. Only Tegucigalpa and San Pedro Sula among Honduran cities have over 100,000 inhabitants, and these two make up over half of the Honduran urban population. Established in 1578, the city was begun essentially because of the silver strikes in the general area to the southeast. It was undoubtedly an Indian center at an earlier time. Rivalry with Comayagua, the older colonial capital, persisted from the 1570s to 1880, at which time Tegucigalpa was named permanent capital. Not all the ancient feelings of rivalry are dead, however. The population of this central department of Francisco Morazán now exceeds 500,000, which indicates the assured growth, the progress, and the concentration of activity in the capital city.

The silver discoveries of the late 1500s caused the establishment of the Alcaldia Mayor of Tegucigalpa which took in most of eight of the present-day departmental subdivisions; even in the 16th century this was the major portion of the country. Even though the capital was landlocked, it was on an important cross-country transportation route. In 1823 there was an alternation of Honduran capitals from Tegucigalpa to Comayagua and back. Needless to say, this unusual arrangement caused dissension, and was satisfactory to neither.

Tegucigalpa is the center of the social, political, and cultural activity of the country. San Pedro Sula (q.v.) is a serious rival in industrial, commercial, and economic areas of endeavor. "La Primera," "La Sociedad," or "La Capitalista" classes of leadership make the capital their home. They are all "old families" who travel world-wide, and who educate their children abroad. From them stems what is in effect a ruling class. The National Library, National University, National Penitentiary, Armed Forces Headquarters, and the National Palace, seat of the Executive Power, are all here. There is no Capitol building as such, the various functions being dispersed about the city. The city is also the center of secondary and higher education. Many of the 60 or more radio stations in the country broadcast from this area. There is a television station of the Honduran Radio Television Company. There are a number of banks, and the capital is the commercial center for all the southern portion of Honduras. There is no rail service, no jetport, and only one main paved cross-country highway to San Pedro Sula, which was opened in 1970. The same road extends south to

THE DOME

THE FAÇADE

PRESIDENTIAL PALACE: The presidential residence in Tegucigalpa occupies a partially fortified site along the riverbank, and is of late 19th century origin.

TEGUCIGALPA - THE CATHEDRAL: Central among the city's colonial churches, this one is an example of "earthquake baroque." The columns are unique.

---

the cross-Honduran Pan American Highway which traverses the southern part of the country and curls around the Bay of Fonseca.
    Military activities of army and air force are centered in the capital. There are also housing developments of a modern nature. Tegucigalpa is in many respects the most isolated of Central American capitals. There are marked contrasts, from the architecturally excellent colonial cathedral and other old churches to the equally excellent Honduras Maya Hotel. Parks, hospitals, and public buildings are basically good. The setting of the city in its bowl of the mountains is dramatic but not confining.

TEGUSIGALPA. Alternate spelling for Tegucigalpa, early 19th century.

TEHAUNTEPEC, ISTHMUS see SHIP-RAILWAY, TEHAUNTEPEC

TELA. A north coastal town on the Bay of the same name, about 35 miles east of Puerto Cortés. Tela is a banana town, on the Tela Railroad which is a subsidiary of United Fruit Co. The road has 236 miles of track and serves nearby towns, going into the hinterland no more than 75 miles. The guage is different from that of Standard Fruit Co.'s railroad, which makes transshipment awkward. Tela is a municipal <u>cabacera</u> in Atlantida department. It is also a seaport.

TELA RAILROAD COMPANY. A banana railroad from the early 1900s in the Tela area; established by and owned by the United Fruit Company, it reaches a number of different points in the area around Tela, west to the Ulua valley at Guanacastales, and eastward to La Ceiba. It has 236 miles of track, 1,700 freight cars, 32 passenger cars. It has the same guage as the Ferrocarril Nacional (q.v.), but a different one from the Standard Fruit Railway (q.v.).

TELEVISION. There is a Honduran Television Company, Radiotelevisora Hondurena, S.A., operating three channels. There are no relay stations, and the high cost of receivers is a problem. Many receivers are located in public places. They numbered in all about 17,000 in 1970, although numbers have increased rapidly since that time. In general, availability factors limit utilization to the two urban areas of San Pedro Sula and Tegucigalpa, where the Honduran Radio Television Company has two stations; it also operates a repeater in Siguatepeque. By law radio and television broadcast operations must be controlled by Honduras. A Central American telecommunications network is planned, which was begun in 1970, to extend 800 miles from Guatemala to Costa Rica, and to have interconnections with Mexico and Panama. Presumably this net will make more television programming available. It was in limited operation in 1974.

TEMPERATURES, HONDURAN COAST. From observations taken in 1840-41, the following table by months indicates temperature ranges in degrees Fahrenheit at the mouth of Black River:

| January 62-66 | July 82 |
| February 66-70 | August 84-86 |
| March 70-74 | September 84-86 |
| April 74-76 | October 78 |
| May 78 | November 72 |
| June 78-82 | December 62-66 |

Diurnal temperatures (Fahrenheit) taken at Carataska Lagoon in August 1844:

| 6:00 a.m. | 70.5 |
| 11:00 a.m. | 83.1 |
| 3:00 p.m. | 83.4 |
| 7:00 p.m. | 82 |

Note the annual range was from 62-86 degrees F.

TEMPORAL. A rain lasting several days during the rainy season. It is fairly rare, the usual rain conditions consisting of heavy afternoon showers. Essentially unknown in such central Honduran points as Comayagua.

TENAMPUA. A large area of ruins to the southeast of Comayagua near a tiny village called Lo de Flores 100 years ago. Described by Squier (q.v.), the archaeological area was called (in the 1850s) Pueblo Viejo or Old Town. Walls were from six to 15 feet high. Part of the construction seems to have been a fortification. The area covered is nearly a square mile. There were many terraced stone mounds, of as many as four lifts or stages. The main enclosure was sixty by one hundred yards. There is a ball-court in the Maya manner. Squier found pottery fragments, ornamentally painted, as well as obsidian knives. There were a total of 300 to 400 terraced pyramids. Tenampua is known and under investigation, and is one of the sites believed to date from about A.D. 1000. There are two Honduran sites dating between 8000 and 1000 B.C. One is San Marcos in Olancho, the other is Wankybila in Gracias a Dios.

TENCOA. One of several chieftains (caciques) of the Sula Zicaque (q.v.) tribe found by Olid when he landed near present-day Puerto Cortés.

TENTE EN EL AIRE. A cross between a Tornatras (q.v.) male and a Spanish female. See RACIAL MIXTURES.

TEOSINTE. The grass which is considered to be a parent or close relative of maize, the ubiquitous American corn. This is botanically Euchlaena Mexicana, and the various varieties were diffused along fertile river valleys. Corn was developed about 4,500 years ago, fully developed by 3,000 years ago. See YARUMELA.

TEOTIHUACAN. The great ceremonial center near Mexico City, significant to Honduras because from Kaminaljuyu in the Guatemalan highlands cultural influences from Teotihuacán were penetrating in radial fashion to such centers as Copán. The date of these influences is around A.D. 500. Teotihuacán, now famed for its pyramids of the Sun and Moon and many other masterpieces uncovered by archaeology, seems to have been destroyed about 600-650 A.D., and by 900 A.D. it was abandoned. The beginnings of the city and center of Teotihuacán were around 300 B.C., so it flourished for about a millennium. It covered more than eight square miles and had a population of 60,000. Called the "place where the gods reside," its influence was to permeate a 2,000-mile stretch of Mexico and Central America. By the time of the Aztecs in Mexico, the lore of Teotihuacán had so been lost that they knew much less about it than do modern archaeologists.

TEPEYAC, COLONIA. A southeastern suburb of Tegucigalpa.

TEPEZCUINTLE. A rodent, not unlike a small pig, and highly edible.

TERCERO, JULIAN see ALVARADO, CASTO

TERCERO BERTRAND, ALONZO  see  MILITARY ZONE COMMANDS, 1972

TERCIOPELO. "Velvet," usually applied to the dangerous and poisonous snake, the bushmaster; a localized usage in Central America.

TERREROS, PEDRO DE  see  EL GALLEGO

TERRITORIO EN LITIGIO. This disputed territory matter was finally settled between Nicaragua and Honduras in 1963, after a brief armed clash over the territory in 1957, and a rejection of a world court decision by Nicaragua, backed by military forces which entered the Gracias a Dios territory in question in 1961 (north of the Río Coco and near the Caribbean). The Court had supported Honduras' claim in 1960. The 1963 bilateral agreement finally confirmed the decision of the commission appointed by the international court of Justice, and diplomatic relations between the two countries since that time have been normal.

TEXIQUAT RIVER. A major tributary of the Río Choluteca (q.v.), flowing from Valle Department.

TGWA. Radio station in Communist Guatemala involved in the 1954 General strike on the Honduran banana coast. See GENERAL STRIKE, 1954.

THEOCRATIC FORMATIVE. A period of formative cultures in the Americas which is characterized by evidence of organized politico-religious social organization and control such as is shown by mound, pyramid, and temple structures. The time is 1200 B.C. to 400 B.C., thus following Colonial Formative.

THOMPSON, J. ERIC S. Scholar who spent over 25 years in study of the Maya, including ten major field trips as an archaeologist of the Carnegie Institution in Washington, D.C. His 1954 book, The Rise and Fall of Maya Civilization, is one of the definitive works in the field.

THREE GRINGOS IN VENEZUELA AND CENTRAL AMERICA. Book with Honduran passages by Richard Harding Davis (q.v.). Of particular interest because, in spite of the inclusive title, he includes 122 pages about Honduras, out of a total of 282, and because he crossed Honduras, north to south, in a 22-day trip in 1894. The approach was fresh and realistic.

THUACOS. This Indian tribal group (also called Juacos), was found in the lower Río Patuca region in the mid-1800s. Probably related to the Payas and Xicaques near whom they lived, they were in the remote fastnesses of Gracias a Dios Department. They now have no tribal identity.

TIBALALKAN LAGOON. One of the tributary lagoons to the big Laguna de Caratasca (q.v.), on the northwest extremity of that lagoon. There are connections by water all the way from the Caratasca lagoon through the Tibalalkan to the Patuca River and its delta.

TICOS. A nickname for Costa Rican natives, used throughout Central America.

TIERRA CALIENTE. The "hot lands" below 2,500 feet altitude in the Central American area. Honduras has especially large low areas in the east, northeast, and Caribbean coastal portions. The coastal plain is relatively infertile and has excess rainfall.

TIERRA FRIA. Occasional very high portions of the central highlands area have the cool climate which is thus termed. Portions of Central America lying above 5,000 to 6,000 feet were given this appellation by the Spanish conquerors. Most of this part of the isthmian area lies in Guatemala and the Mexican state of Chiapas, but there is some of the type in western Honduras.

TIERRA TEMPLADA. Term in Spanish used for the mild climate to be found in higher elevations of the Central highlands. Such temperate lands lay between 2,500 feet altitude and the tierra fría (q.v.). Much of interior Honduras comes within this temperature zone. Many of these lands are quite fertile.

TIERRAS, MARES, Y CIELOS. Early modernist book of poems by Ramón Molina (q.v.). See also MODERNISMO.

TIGRE ISLAND. A round-conical volcanic island in the Bay of Fonseca, site of the major seaport of the Honduran Pacific side, Amapala. The island is centered in the northern part of the bay, just south of the somewhat similar Zacate Grande (q.v.), and is geologically a dead cone of the 600-mile long line of volcanoes which stretches from Mexico to Panama along the Pacific coast of Central America. The island has an altitude of about 2,700 feet.

TIGUZIGALPA. An alternate spelling for Tegucigalpa, 18th century.

TIJERINO, TORIBIO. Leader of a group of Nicaraguan emigrés living in Honduras during the Sandino (q.v.) war in Nicaragua. Tijerino's group was believed to be shipping arms to Sandino, arms which had been used in the recent Ferrera revolt in Honduras.

TILBALAKAN, LAGUNA. One of the coastal lagoons, farthest northwest of the Caratasca series.

TINGNI. A Miskito word for "stream." In the upper Río Coco Valley the word is used dozens of times in that stream-laced high jungle.

TINOCO DE CONTRERAS, JOSE GREGORIO. The last colonial governor before independence, this one served from 1819 to 1821, the final date being November 12, 1821. He then appointed Juan Lindo to an interim term, and technically speaking, Lindo served until February 11, 1824, although independence had been declared, and the news of independence reached Comayagua on September 28, 1821.

TINTA ANIL. Dye made from indigo.

TINTO RIVER. Known as the Río Negro, Río Sico, Río Román or Río Tinto, this large stream enters the Caribbean near the Ibans Lagoon, at Plaplaya. There are several major tributaries, among them the Río Grande, the Río Paulaya, and the Río Tayaco. During the 16th and 17th centuries the Tinto was the center of a major English "squatter" colony, the "Black River" settlements and plantations, and along with Belize, the Bay Islands, and the Mosquito Shore was a principal element in British claims on the area over a period of two centuries.

TITULO DOCENTE. Teaching credential, degree, or certificate. See STATE CONTROL OF EDUCATION.

TOBACCO. A considerable cash crop in Honduras, especially in the northwest, around Santa Rosa de Copán. In the early 1800s the tobacco of the Copán area had the reputation of being the best in Central America. These were cigar tobaccos. Present-day tobacco farms are of the "flue-cured" type. Some of the tall narrow curing buildings are made of adobe, and present an unmistakable appearance.

TOCHTLI. Eighth day of the Aztec month; meaning, "rabbit."

TONCONTIN AIRPORT. Tegucigalpa's airport, quite near the city. The Honduran Air Force has a large castellated hangar across the field from the commercial terminal. This is not a jet field--the runways are too short. LACSA, SAHSA, and ANHSA (all q.v.) are Honduran lines operating out of Toncontín, much of the short-line work being handled in aging DC-3 Douglas aircraft. The nation's jet port is at San Pedro Sula.

TOQUEGUA. Tribal sub-branch in the Ulua River valley. Probably related to the Jicaque (q.v.).

TORNATRAS. A cross between an Albino (q.v.) male and a Spanish female. See RACIAL MIXTURES.

TORNOS, JOSE ANTONIO DE. Governor of Honduras following Serrano Polo's interim term in 1815.

TORRUPAN. An alternative name for the Jicaque Indians (q.v.).

TORTILLA. A thin flat baked cake of cornmeal and water, usually prepared as a pliable dough called massa, and then slapped into the desired thinness with great skill. A pre- and post-conquest Meso-American staple. Central American tortillas tend to be thicker than Mexican ones.

TOSTA, VICENTE. General Tosta was a Provisional President after the ousting of López Guitérrez (q.v.) and the short rule of a council of ministers. He served from April 30, 1924 to February 1, 1925.

TOTTEN, GABRIEL--MAP. A map of the new world dated 1600 and engraved by Benjamin Wright is especially clear in showing Honduras. The Bay Islands are listed as Utila, Laguaiaba, and Laguanaia, and Santa Anna (Swan Island) is also shown. The easternmost land of Honduras is shown as C. dez Panta, and the name of the country as Fondueras. No interior towns are shown but fifteen coastal names include "P. de Canallos" and "Trugillo."

TOURISM COUNCIL OF THE CENTRAL AMERICAN STATES. An offshoot of the Central American Common Market (q.v.), the joint effort for tourism in all of Central America is coordinated under SITCA. With help from the Central American Bank, an indepth study of area tourism was made by Porter International (Washington, D.C.). A brochure, Discover the Gems, promotes the five countries as a unit.

TRABAJO, DIA DEL. Labor Day for Honduras follows the international pattern, and falls annually on May 1. The decree was dated February 14, 1929.

TRADE, FOREIGN. Honduran trade, both export and import, had the second highest growth rate in Latin America during the 1960-1970 decade. The growth averaged 12 per cent per annum, and reached about $200,000,000 in 1970. Growth since has fallen off because of the political and diplomatic effect of the 1969 war with El Salvador (q.v.).

TRADE, PRE-CONQUEST. The evidences of trade in ceramics and metal items exist for the period 600-800 A.D. in the isthmus area from Mexico to Panama. Early "formative period" (q.v.) evidence is ample if not conclusive. See METALLURGY.

TRADE, SPAIN TO GULF OF HONDURAS, 17th CENTURY. While the northern Honduran coastal ports were closer to Spain than the major Mexican port of Vera Cruz, a series of conditions and events conspired toward neglect of these ports by mid-17th century. Such items of marginal profit as indigo would decline, and the uses of the entry ports of Puerto Caballos and Trujillo would correspondingly shrink. The King of Spain decided in 1649 that the port of Trujillo was to be "defended with care," but that he could not help in the expense. The average Honduran flotilla in those years was two or three small ships. Obviously trade was not very flourishing.

TRADE GOODS. Orlando Roberts (q.v.) has listed the trade goods in most demand toward the end of the Spanish colonial period. Such goods were provided by English traders in small vessels along the Caribbean coast of Mosquitia as well as in other places, and from the standpoint of Spanish authorities were of a contraband nature. However, the demand was so great that the trade flourished. Goods were:

| | |
|---|---|
| Coarse linen | Needles |
| Coarse cotton articles | Pins |
| (showy red colors) | Fishhooks |
| Machetes | Iron pots |
| Large knives | Frying pans |
| Table knives | Rum |
| Felling axes | Gunpowder |
| Saws | Fowling pieces (shotguns) |
| Locks and hinges | Flat iron plates |
| Nails | Other ironware |
| Tin ware--cooking | Glass beads |
| Small Dutch mirrors | Muskets |

Return items were gold, silver, pearl shell, turtle shell, dye woods.

TRADE SCHOOL. The Escuela de Artes y Officios was created in 1890, during the administration of Luis Bográn (q.v.).

TRANS-ISTHMIAN ROUTE, 16th CENTURY. Honduras was picked early as a site for a trans-isthmian crossing. Far longer than the Panama route and more arduous than the Nicaraguan route, the choice was advanced by partisans who had personal gain in mind rather than on any logical basis. See VALVERDE, FRANCISCO DE, and ANTONELLI, JUAN BATISTA.

TRANSPORTES AEREAS NACIONALES, S.A. An established airline in the Mexican and Central American region, flying from Miami to Mexico, Honduras, British Honduras, and El Salvador.

TRANSVIAS AEREAS DE CENTRO AMERICA. This earliest Central American airline (TACA) was once nearly ubiquitous in the field, with sixty different airfields in Honduras alone. The old parrot insignia has given way to something more staid, and the flamboyant early days of jungle and mountain airstrips 30 to 40 years ago have settled down to more routine operations.

TRAPICHE. A primitive "sugar mill," powered by oxen, used in 19th century (and earlier) Honduras for grinding cane.

TRAVIESO, JORGE FEDERICO. Born in San Francisco, Atlántida Department, in 1920, this medical student and poet was in 1949 cultural attaché for the Honduran embassy in Mexico. He died in Rio de Janeiro in 1953. A posthumous book published in Tegucigalpa in 1959 is La espera infinita.

TREASURE, NEW SPAIN. Mexico, Peru, New Granada (Colombia), Honduras and other Central American countries, and part of Venezuela were all part of New Spain. By 1600, $35,000,000 per year of treasure was leaving New Spain. During the more than 300 years of colonization, somewhere between six and fifteen billion dollars worth of treasure were extracted.

TREASURY, MINISTRY OF see CABINET

TREATIES OF MADRID, 1667-1670. The first treaty between Spain and England in 1667 was only a preliminary to the second and definitive one in 1670, the so-called "American Treaty" which was a cornerstone of Britain's Caribbean position and policy for a century following. The usual pledges of peace and friendship were followed by the outlawing of piracy and permitting trade in "accustomed places." To Spain this meant designated Spanish ports, like Porto Bello in Panama. To England, it was more like a hunting license. The British were granted lands then occupied by them, which meant the North American mainland, Jamaica, and other islands. Neither power even thought about the little timber-cutting settlements along the Mosquito coast. Later, England claimed this area, because it was technically "occupied," and Spain denied the claim.

The indefiniteness of these English holdings, and the failure to define contraband, were weaknesses of the treaty, which in 1739-1748 led to the "War of Jenkins' Ear." The effect of the Jamaican occupation and its permanence was to turn a flood of Jamaica-based buccaneers loose on the islands and coasts of Central America. From 1665 to 1685 the raiders dominated the Caribbean. While Nicaragua took the worst beating, no spot on the coast was exempt.

TREATY OF MADRID, 1814. Not related to the Treaties of Madrid in 1667-1670, this 1814 treaty between England and Spain was influenced by confusion in Spanish affairs introduced during the Napoleonic regime. England and Spain were allies in the final campaign, and when the Peninsular War was over, certain matters were left unsettled about the Central American coast. The Treaty of Madrid confirmed all conventions of 1783 and 1786 between the two powers, which interestingly left the Carib Indians occupying the Bay Islands of Honduras (whence they had been transported from the island of St. Vincent), the Mosquitos still in control of the Honduran and Nicaraguan coasts, and the settlers in Belize confirmed in their original seizure. The Mosquito question was finally settled in the late 1800s; the Belize question still exists for Guatemala, and the Caribs have assimilated. The coveted Nicaraguan canal route was left in the hands of Spain, but the old Spanish monopoly was broken forever, and seven years after the treaty, the colonies declared independence. Meanwhile, British possessions ringed the eastern Caribbean.

TREE, NATIONAL. The national tree of Honduras is the pine.

TRELAWNEY, EDWARD. Governor in Jamaica, 1738-1752, this Englishman from Cornwall tried to promote contraband trade between the English Shoremen of the Mosquito Coast and the Spanish of the interior. He believed Spanish and creole colonists were ripe for revolt. It was he who sent Captain Robert Hodgson (q.v.) to Honduras' Black River as Superintendent of the Shore. Hodgson remained for almost half a century following 1740.

TRES GARANTIAS. Under the Plan of Iguala (q.v.) in 1821, the "Guarantees" were an offering to make the establishment of a Mexican empire attractive.

TRIANGULAR STRATEGY. The strategic concept under which Great Britain was operating in the 18th century in relation to the Central American area. By 1762 England was attempting to complete a series of three conquests, beginning with that of Havana in 1761, going on to the San Juan River and Lake Nicaragua trans-isthmian route, and culminating in the capture of Manila in the Philippines on October 5, 1762. This triple play would have given England the treasured geopolitical prize of a sure transit between Atlantic and Pacific oceans, with Havana to control the Caribbean and Manila to control the other end of the Oriental trade routes. The strategy ended when the isthmian expedition failed in Central America at Fort Inmaculada in 1762.

TRIBES, HONDURAN. The various Indian tribes existing at the time of the Spanish Conquest were:

| Copantl | - in the west |
|---|---|
| Cares | - in the southeast |
| Potones | - southeast |
| Xicaques (or Jicaques) | - northeast |
| Payas | - northeast |
| Taguacas | - northeast |
| Albatuinas | - northeast |
| Agaltecas | - center |

These tribal groups exist in vestiges with their own dialects to this day.

TRIBES, MAYA. The Chorti Maya are those found in the Copán area of western Honduras. Other Maya groups are as follows: Pokomam, Tzutuhil, Quiché, Rabinal, Pokonchi, Uspantec, Aguacatec, Mam, Solomec, Ixil, Kanhobal, Chuh, Jacaltec, Toholabal, Tzotzil, Motozintlic, Tzeltal, Chol, Chontal, Lacandón, Kekchi, Potosino, Veracruzano, and Yucatec. Most of the Maya (over 2,000,000) live in Guatemala.

TRISTAN, DIEGO. Captain of La Capitana, one of Columbus' four exploring vessels when Honduras was discovered in 1502.

TRIUNFO DE LA CRUZ. A "city" founded on the north coast of Honduras by Olid (q.v.) in 1524.

TRONCOSO Y MARTINEZ DEL RINCON, BERNARDO. Appointed Captain General of Guatemala, he governed 1789-1794, but as an octogenarian brigadier at the outset and ill much of the time, he represented the decadence of Spanish policy and control as well as of the vigor of the governorship. No further efforts of significance were made to pacify or subdue the Sambo-Miskitos of the Caribbean coast, which was a principal frontier problem of the period in question.

TROPICAL RADIO AND TELEGRAPH. A private communications company connecting the four largest cities and with service to the other Central American countries, the United States, and Mexico.

TROPICAL TRADING AND TRANSPORT CO., LTD. see KEITH, MINER COOPER

TROPICAL ZONES see LIFE ZONES

TRUGILLO. An alternate form of Trujillo as found on Totten's map (q.v.).

TRUJILLO. Founded by Hernán Cortés in 1524, this north coastal town was the metropolis of Spanish Colonial Honduras and the seat of a bishopric by 1539. In the bight of the Bahía de Trujillo (q.v.), the town is an entry port and also the cabacera of Colón Department, with port facilities at nearby Puerto Castilla on the same bay. There is land access by road, but no railroad. The mountains crowd the sea very closely at this point. Trujillo was the site of the execution of William Walker (q.v.), the American filibuster, on September 12, 1860. Other historical events abound in the annals of the old port city, among them the attack of the English fleet in 1789. There was an attack by pirates in 1639, who sacked the city and held prominent citizens for ransom. Henry Morgan, the Jamaican freebooter, was involved in the attacks on Trujillo. There are extensive ruins of old fortifications. The church of Trujillo was declared a cathedral in 1539 by Pope Pius III, and so it remained for more than two decades. Trujillo was also the place where O. Henry (q.v.) gathered the color for some of his Central American writings. It is the major town nearest the landing place of Columbus on the Central American mainland on his fourth voyage in 1502.

TRUJILLO, BASE FOR SPANISH ACTION, 1782. While British troops were pinned down in the rebellion of their North American colonies, and following Spanish re-occupation of Fort Inmaculada in Nicaragua, an extensive fleet and thousands of militia were gathered by the Spanish to mount an attack on the Bay Islands (q.v.) and the Mosquito Coast (q.v.). Following a Bay Island attack was to be one on the Black River English settlements (present Río Tinto on the Honduran coast east of Trujillo). For this second attack a combined militia force of Hondurans, Salvadorans, and Nicaraguans were to advance on Black River from the landward side. This was a joint effort nearly unique in Central American annals; it was later likened to the similar cooperative effort against filibuster Walker (q.v.) in 1856-57. By marching time, in mid-March 1782, there were 1,500 of the combined militia on the Honduran frontier at Juticalpa ready to cross the country for the Black River attack. The march ahead of them was 200 miles over very rugged country. The militia were led by Lieutenant Colonels Urrutia and Arizabalaga. On March 14 Gálvez (q.v.) led a twenty-ship fleet to attack Roatán. He had 600 troops and 40 cannon. Fort George, near New Port Royal on the island, fell on the 17th. Gálvez burned the town and pulled down the fort.

Meanwhile the cross-Honduran army had run into two ambushes, and finally Arizabalaga, having had no news of the seaborne attack on Black River, began the return march, reaching Juticalpa on April 23 with over 300 casualties. These struggles in rain, rivers, mountains, and mud had been monumental.

The attack from Trujillo was a success, and the Black River Shoremen were defeated, although Colonel Lawrie and many of the Shoremen escaped through the complex of lagoons and waterways which lace the northeastern Honduran coast. The Shoremen reached the Sambo settlement at Cabo Gracias a Dios. The fort at Black River was renamed Fort Inmaculada Concepción de Honduras, and the one at Brewer's Lagoon, Fort Quepriva.

It was at Black River that the offensive begun from the Trujillo base ground to a halt. When British Admiral Rodney captured the 22 ships of the French Comte de Grasse, the whole balance of power in the Caribbean was altered. Spain had to go on the defensive. In August the British under Lawrie (q.v.) and Despard (q.v.) mounted an attack on Fort Dalling, and massacred the 33-man garrison except for one man, Manuel Rivas, who escaped to report to Tomás Julia at Fort Inmaculada de Honduras. The Massacre occurred because the British officer could not control his Sambo allies.

The Black River was in a weak position, and Julia was forced to surrender less than five months after assuming command. The Dalling (Quipriva) massacre infuriated Gálvez. He called for "mastiffs" to hunt down the Sambos, but a peace treaty was in the offing, so his vengeance could not be carried out. Galvez' appointment as Lieutenant General and Viceroy of New Spain was deserved for the hero who recovered Omoa, stopped the English at Black River, and held Trujillo.

TRUJILLO RAILROAD COMPANY. With a sea-port outlet and railroad yards at Puerto Castilla (near Trujillo) the railroad has about 150 miles of mainline, and a total of about 230 miles. The principal inland station is at Olanchito.

TRUXILLO. Antique and frequently encountered spelling of Trujillo (q.v.).

TSII. An evil female goddess of the Jicaque (q.v.), who are sun-worshippers.

TUAS, RIO. A minor stream flowing into the western end of the Brus Laguna on the north coast of Honduras.

TUKRUNG. One of the points on the Patuca River where precooperatives have been developed by Diakonia (q.v.).

TUN. Maya year of 360 days (see TZOLKIN) divided into 18 months of 20 days each. The month is called "Uinal." The sacred year always was known by the day which began the year; for example, the "year 13 Kan."

TUNA see GRANA COCHINILLA and NOPAL CACTUS

TUNU. A tree with a flexible bark much used for tapa-like handcraft articles in northeastern Honduras. See DIAKONIA.

TURA. Miskito name for the large reptile known as caiman; similar to the alligator.

TURCIOS, FROYLAN. A Honduran poet who became the official foreign representative of Sandino's (q.v.) "Defending Army of the National Sovereignty of Nicaragua." Couriers rode from Sandino's El Chipote headquarters to Turcios in the Honduran capital. Turcios was described at this time as charming, middle-aged, politician as well as poet.
In 1928, Turcios was seeking a post in the government of Honduras, and finally he broke with Sandino on January 7, 1929. Turcios was then appointed Honduran consul in Paris. The breach with Sandino came because the guerrilla leader considered himself "indo-Hispanic," and objected to Turcios' siding with his own Honduras in a border dispute with Guatemala.

Turcios' achievements as short story writer, novelist, and poet should overshadow his considerable political activity. One of the early modernists, with Darío and Molina (q.v.), Turcios produced <u>Cuentos de amor y de la Muerte</u>, <u>Paginas de ayer</u>, <u>El vampire</u>, and <u>Fantasma blanca</u>, showing even in his titles the familiar Honduran absorption with the supernatural, the nostalgic, and with love, death, and legend.

<u>TWEED</u> (FRIGATE). A British naval vessel involved in occupation of the Honduran Bay Island of Roatán in 1841, and in the incident at San Juan del Norte when a Nicaraguan officer defied the British and their Mosquito "allies."

TWO-PARTY SYSTEM. Honduras has been both remarkable and unique in Latin American annals for the consistency and durability of its two-party system. Reference to the other Central American countries will bear this out with cause for astonishment, for in those countries the parties have been all too frequently personal vehicles, simply a cloak for the "personalismo" of one political figure or another. But in Honduras the Liberal Party came into being at the turn of the last century. At first, it was indeed a personal machine for Céleo Arias, but at his death it reformed under Policarpo Bonilla (q.v.) who created a true political organization, with general policies, and a regularized and pre-determined hierarchy. While platforms do not differ materially from those of the Nationalist Party, the two have remained distinct.

The National Party was also created before the turn of the century, and was at the outset weaker than the liberals. It was organized on a firm base with a planned hierarchy in 1911, and began to have great influence following 1920. In 1919 Carias Andino (q.v.) and Dr. Paulino Valladores drafted a program, and the party was named the Democratic National Party, but in 1923 the program was again revised and has retained the same policies since. It advocates "strict" observance of the constitution, establishment of a Central American Union when feasible, less politics and more administration in government, financial reform, free elections, "protection of capital and labor," and "harmony among the Honduran people."

There is no Conservative group as such; Honduran politics therefore differ greatly from the Central American politics of mid-nineteenth century, and are in a sense unique in the present period.

TZOLKIN. The sacred year of the Maya, of 260 days, having 13 months of 20 days each, and also divided in 20 thirteen-day periods, the latter being the equivalent of a week. See MONTHS, MAYA CALENDAR, and DAYS, MAYA NAMES.

UASH see HUAS

UAYEB. The five-day "Month" which was the last and final one of the Maya year, which was divided in 18 months of 20 days each (see MONTHS, MAYA CALENDAR) and then concluded by this five-day period which was considered very ominous; the total 365 days was the haab (q.v.).

UFCO. The initials for United Fruit Company (q.v.) used verbally as an acronym.

UHLE, MAX. German archaeological investigator during the 1890s in Peru, who held that the Peruvian cultures derived from the Central American Maya. Modern scholarship indicates that there was indeed some Central American influence in the Andes, but not to the extent postulated by Uhle.

UINAL. A month of 20 days (the sacred month) which is multiplied by 18 to make the "tun" (q.v.) or 360-day year.

ULANCHO. Alternate spelling of Olancho (q.v.).

ULASSA. Evil spirits identified as a class by Miskito Indians around 1900.

ULUA MARBLE. Honduras is the seat of an outstanding contribution to New World art, outside the Maya region, from the Ulua Valley, in its lower portion. More recently examples of these characteristic marble cylindrical jars have been found in the Comayagua Valley. There are only a few dozen pieces known to date. The period of the pieces discovered is Post-Classic. Similar to the Classical Vera Cruz style, they are nevertheless far separated in style. These marble pieces are covered with scrolls which usually frame or include a human face. Scrolls also form profiled reptilian heads. The style seems to be a refinement of a well-known pottery type found on the north coast of Honduras. The Ulua jars also resemble Chinese bronzes of the Shang and Chen dynasties, but these periods span 1766-249 B.C., whereas the Post-Classic (Maya) period of the jars is after A.D. 1000, a minimum separation of more than 12 centuries.

ULUA RIVER. A large stream with a fertile lower valley, it empties into the Caribbean a few miles west of the Chamelecón estuary and about 15 miles west of Puerto Cortés. It is an extension of a major tributary of the Río Humuya (q.v.). Banana culture is a conspicuous feature of the great flat valley just east of San Pedro Sula.

UMANZOR, JUAN PABLO. Colonel of Sandino (q.v.) guerrillas initially under Ortez in May 1931. At the death of his chief, this Honduran fighter took over the unit. He had charge of the Eighth Column. Many Hondurans were members of the force.

UNCTAD. These are the initials (and acronym) for the world-wide conference on commerce and development under the auspices of the United Nations, with its first conference in Geneva, Switzerland, in 1964. The organization is of particular meaning to developing countries such as Honduras. The purpose is to present pertinent problems of development and to propose and initiate appropriate measures.

UNION DEMOCRATICA CRISTIANA DE CENTROAMERICANA. The UDCCA is a general movement to establish Christian Democratic Parties throughout Central America, pressing for basic reforms of a social, political, and economic nature.

UNION OF BANANA EXPORTING COMPANIES. The UPEB (Spanish initials) was formed by seven banana-producing nations in 1974 to protect their banana crop as a major export. The tax they projected was expected to provide a revenue of $160,000,000 annually, distributed among Honduras, Colombia, Ecuador, Nicaragua, Guatemala, Costa Rica, and Panama. But the "Banana War" produced some problems. See BANANA WAR, 1974; also TAX--BANANAS; also BANANA PRODUCTION.

UNION UNDER BARRIOS. On February 28, 1885, Justo Rufino Barrios suddenly and dramatically announced a plan for Central American union. With the examples of Cavour and Bismarck before him, Barrios hoped to make an economically strong union. Luis Bográn (q.v.) in Honduras supported the idea, perhaps perforce. But many Central American leaders felt they would only be satellites of the strong Guatemala created by Barrios. Porfirio Díaz of Mexico objected, and when Barrios led troops to the Salvadoran border, he was killed by a sniper's bullet. His instant death stopped another Central American union venture.

UNITED FRUIT COMPANY. Incorporated in New Jersey in 1899 with a capital of $20,000,000, this sprawling and ubiquitous organization became the largest business in the isthmian tropics. Having purchased the Miner Keith (q.v.) banana interests, the company had 38,000 acres of bananas at the outset. At that time the Honduran holdings were only 500 acres. Central American ownership by United Fruit in the 1960s topped 2,000,000 acres. During that decade, the company had 30 to 40 per cent of the world banana market. It controlled 42 per cent of the Honduran foreign exchange earnings. On the Honduran north coast, United Fruit has built schools, clinics, and agricultural experiment stations.

Once having the reputation for making and breaking Central American governments, this huge corporation was formed to produce and ship bananas from the growing belt on the low Caribbean littoral. Banana lands of United Fruit are centered in the San Pedro Sula area of Honduras. The Panama disease and sigatoka decimated crops in the 1920s and '30s, and the operation has been hampered in consequence. Originally a major fiscal force as well as a behind-the-scenes political power, United Fruit has lost much of its picturesque influence along with its bananas. The whitepainted United Fruit steamers used to be a principal form of access to the banana coast, and United Fruit has been the center and subject of much "banana republic" literary effort. See BANANAS.

UNITED PROVINCES OF CENTRAL AMERICA, 1824-38. After the fall of Emperor Agustín Iturbide, Central America convened a constituent assembly in Guatemala City and declared a free and independent United Provinces of Central America, specifically free from "old Spain," Mexico, and every other power. The Honduran representatives ratified the declaration, affirmed the accord, and put signatures to a federal constitution. They did, however, have some disagreement as to whether Honduras would enter as one or two separate states. The decision to enter as one included the rather cumbersome decision to alternate the capital between the two rivals, Tegucigalpa and Comayagua. In 1824 an assembly elected a provisional president, Dionisio de Herrera, to follow Manuel José Arce who was the first president of the federation. Disputes between Conservative and Liberal forces created problems from the beginning. Honduras was a stronghold of Liberal sentiments. Civil War erupted in 1826, lasting till 1829. The Honduran Liberal stand-bearer, Francisco Morazán (q.v.), led forces to the federal capital, resulting in its occupation and the installation of Morazán as President.

A plot in 1831 involved Conservative seizure of Fort Omoa and Trujillo. Morazán moved his capital to San Salvador, but the fragmentation process by this time (1834) was far advanced. By 1837 local revolts were proliferating. Civil War again struck in Guatemala in 1838, and the entire disruption of mail and press services added to the general collpase.

Costa Rica sought a constitutional convention, Nicaragua declared independence, and in October 26, 1838, Honduras declared its independence from the Union, following this act with a constitution and declaration of the Republic of Honduras in January 1839.

UNITED STATES MILITARY MISSION TO HONDURAS see MILITARY SCHOOL FRANCISCO MORAZAN

UNITED STATES OF CENTRAL AMERICA. Name of the Republica Major chosen under a Constitution of November 1, 1898 for the three countries, Honduras, El Salvador, and Nicaragua. This union, while short lived, was the basis for the Partido

Unionista which developed.

**UNIVERSIDAD NACIONAL AUTONOMA DE HONDURAS.** Located in Comayaguela across the Choluteca River from Tegucigalpa, this university is the principal institution of higher learning in the country (see UNIVERSITY OF HONDURAS). Three per cent of net national revenue is devoted to the University by constitutional fiat. The institution became autonomous in 1957. Shortage of funds for libraries and laboratories is a continual problem. Very little applied and pure research has been undertaken. There is little publication beyond Honduran borders. The library of the university had 5,000 volumes in the 1960s, but the available National Library in Tegucigalpa had 55,000.

**UNIVERSITY OF HONDURAS.** Established by Juan Lindo (q.v.) in 1847, the University began with the usual curriculum of the times: civil and canon law, philosophy, and the indispensable Latin. The university had sprung from the Academia Literaria of Tegucigalpa which was founded by José Trinidad Reyes. In 1882, contemporary science was added to the curriculum, and the present faculties of Legal and Social Sciences and of Medical Sciences stem from that period. In 1923, Engineering was added; in 1935, Chemical Sciences and Pharmacy; Economic Sciences and Odontology were further provided.

In the year 1950, however, there were still fewer than 1,600 persons attending the university. In 1950 the enrollment of the University of Honduras was 1,164 men and 146 women. In 1957 the institution was made completely autonomous. It is supported by annual grants from the national government, and by private and international agency grants of a variety of types. The university is governed by faculty and student representatives convening in a general assembly. They elect the presiding officer, or rector, and each school within the university selects its dean by action of a council which includes alumni.

By 1970, the total enrollments were well over 3,000. Programs of studies last from four to six years, with the first year being a general studies program of Spanish, cultural history, philosophy, and science. Most students work part time. Many do not receive degrees because they cannot pass the rigorous comprehensive examinations. Since many government jobs require university part-time attendance, there is a considerable student body which is enrolled but with little reason to continue for a degree. Tending toward isolation from the country at large, the university is showing signs of significant change. The creation of an Extension Department and modernization of programs are recent progressive trends. Most professors were and are part-time, being involved in professions and business for most of their time. Shortage of library and laboratory facilities, antiquated lecture and rote memory methods, and limited funds have all been limiting factors.

The Consejo Superior Universitario Centroamericana (q.v.) has chosen the University of Honduras as its center for regional instruction in Agriculture.

UO. Second month of the Maya Calendar.

UPEB see UNION OF BANANA EXPORTING COUNTRIES

URBAN-RURAL CONTRAST. There is a sharp differentiation between rural and urban cultures and segments of society in Honduras as in the rest of Central America, partly due to wealth and political power centered in the cities, partly due to differing rates of economic and social change. In some ways Honduras resembles the Renaissance city-states of Northern Italy, with, of course, many modern and variant overtones. The fort-palace of the President in Tegucigalpa is reminiscent of Italian antecedents. The "campesino" or countryman often lives in a thatched or wattled hut on a dirt floor.

URRUTIA, NICOLAS. This lieutenant colonel led a portion of the militia who were to cross Honduras for an attack on the English at Black River in 1782. See TRUJILLO, BASE ... 1782.

UTILA. Westernmost of the Bay Islands of Honduras, Utila is about eight miles long, is lower than the other islands, and is populated by white descendants of the early British squatters and colonists.

- V -

VALENCIA, MANUEL. A professor who began to emerge in May of 1954 as leader of the General Strike (q.v.). He called himself Secretary-General. He accused the Progreso Committee of being Communist-filled. It was he who announced formation of the Union Sindical de Trabajadores, with Miguel Ruiz as secretary of organization and Arturo Rivera Santamaría as secretary of relations. Valencia disclaimed the leftist orientation of the Progreso strike committee, and attacked Agusto Coto's (q.v.) role. He was the moving force behind a conference of strike delegates representing all but the Progreso group. This was the prelude to a settlement with the Tela Railroad Company.

VALENZUELA, HECTOR see AGUIRRE, SALVADOR

VALENZUELA, J. EDGARDO. Foreign Minister of Honduras during the critical days of the 1954 general strike (q.v.). He rejected a Guatemalan offer of a non-aggression pact, basing the rejection on the fact that treaties of friendship existed.

VALENZUELA BENEGAS, FRANCISCO DEL. Inspector of the

Tegucigalpa Mines about 1695. He ordered that all Spaniards, Negroes, Mulattos and Mestizos should have a job in the mines or leave. This dictum was aimed at gambling and other vice, increased and promoted by jobless drifters and loiterers.

VALERY. A disease-resistant banana developed following 1961 by United Fruit Co. (q.v.); stronger and more shippable than the Giant Cavendish (q.v.) variety.

VALIENTES. An Indian tribe described by Orlando Roberts in 1827, presumably on the Honduran-Nicaraguan east coast hinterland, in the area of "La Mosquitia" and the highlands backing it up.

VALLADARES, ALEJANDRO. Editor of El Cronista (q.v.) who allegedly advocates a "second Cuba" for Honduras and who in the 1960s visited Fidel Castro in Havana on numerous occasions.

VALLADOLID. Older designation for the Spanish colonial capital of Honduras, Comayagua. From November 20, 1542 to May 16, 1544 it was the seat of colonial government for all Isthmian America from the present Mexican state of Tabasco to Panama. Like so many names in both Spanish and English America, it was derived from the parent country. The full name was Valladolid de Santa María de Comayagua.

VALLE, ANGELA. Born in Comayaguela in 1927, a niece of Rafael Heliodoro Valle (q.v.), at the age of 16 she wrote a book of verse called Miel y acibar and in 1967 won the Juan Ramón Molina prize for poetry with her book Lúnulas. Other poetry was published in 1961 as Iniciales.

VALLE, RAFAEL HELIODORO. Contemporary poet, writer, and diplomat, author of a six-volume work which is a study of the annexation of Central America to Mexico just following independence in 1821-22.

VALLE DE ANGELES. This is essentially a trade school. Venturo Quesada is director of courses in arts and crafts.

VALLE DEPARTMENT. One of the smallest in the country, this department is bounded on the north by La Paz and Francisco Morazán departments; on the west by the Río Goascoran and the El Salvador national border; on the east by Choluteca Department, and on the south by the Bay of Fonseca (or Gulf of Fonseca), of the Pacific Ocean. In the bay are the Offshore Islands (q.v.), Territories of Tigre, Zacate Grande, etc. The departmental cabecera is Nacaome. There are nine municipios. The area is 610 square miles. The population of cabeceras in 1973 was 23,381, of village and rural areas 86,388, for a total of 109,769. Towns are Aremecina,

Alianza, Goascorán, San Francisco de Coráy, San Lorenzo, and Caridad.

VALLEJO, ANTONIO R. Author of a Honduran history published in 1882-83. See HISTORY HONDURAN.

VALLEJO, GONZALES. Captain and second commissioner sent by the Spanish government to Central America in 1785-86. He was in command of the corvette San Pío off the Honduran coast. The Spanish did not venture south of Cabo Gracias a Dios as they took possession of the coast following war with England. This left the Mosquito Kingdom (so-called) to continue its somewhat independent status.

VALLEYS. The mountainous nature of the land in general and the many ranges (see MONTAÑAS and CORDILLERAS) make the existence of great valleys a natural result. Some of the largest are:

| | |
|---|---|
| Sensenti | Quinistán |
| Otoro | Comayagua |
| Sirio | Goascorán |
| Olanchito | Yoro |
| Agalta | Lepaguare |
| Yeguare | Jamastrán |

VALVERDE, FRANCISCO DE. In 1590, Valverde was assigned to report on the feasibility of a trans-isthmian route across Honduras. He traveled from Puerto Caballos to the Bay of Fonseca, also to Realejo in Nicaragua. He studied the economy of the surrounding country, the nature of harbors, and the mountainous route. In spite of that direct experience, he was sanguine about the possibilities, a rather remarkable stance at such an early date, possibly romanticized by the sheer size and majesty of the wild new land.

VALVERDE, GARCIA DE. As governor from 1578 to 1589, he was faced with coastal raids which necessitated defense measures. Tribute policies were reformed during this period. This 11 years was one of the longer terms in this particular colonial office, which seemed prone to frequent change.

VAN HORNE, WILLIAM. Builder of the Canadian Pacific Railway who was brought in by Minor Keith (q.v.) to the purchase of a Guatemalan railway as part of a larger concept of the International Railways of Central America (q.v.). Van Horne was involved with Keith about 1900. Each man was to develop between the two Americas the types of railway link which had crossed the North American continent short decades before.

VANKES see RIO COCO

VANNESEN. Probably a Dutchman, this resident of Hamburg owned a Spanish ship in 1647. He boarded the ship on the way to

Honduras, unloaded it, loaded up indigo, sarsaparilla, and hides, and then seized the ship with the help of foreign sailors. He sailed direct to Holland. Spain was exercised, having lost the customs payment due at Seville, as well as the trade involved. Reparations were paid to the Spanish Crown, but nothing was said of the owners of the cargo. It was doubtless a plot on the part of the Central Americans and the Hamburg owner, and in effect amounted to a partially successful "highjack."

VAQUERO. The familiar Spanish word for cowboy, used in Honduran cattle country, especially on the ranches of Olancho Department.

VARA. A length measure of about 33 inches (2.76 feet), used in square measure as well as in distance. A manzana is 100 varas square, or 10,000 square varas. The vara in colonial days and earlier was a linear measure of thirty-two to thirty-three inches, derived from a rod or staff used as a symbol of office and also for measurement. It was the rough equivalent (in usage) of the English yard.

VASCONCELOS, DOROTEO. A president of El Salvador in 1845-51 who assumed personal command of a joint Honduran-Salvadoran Army, but was beaten at the Battle of La Arada (q.v.) on February 2, 1851.

VASQUEZ, DOMINGO. As minister, Vásquez governed as "President by Law" from April 18, 1893 to September 15 that year, and then became Constitutional President, serving until February 1894. His regime was overthrown by liberals under Policarpo Bonilla, aided by a large body of Nicaraguan troops. Bonilla (q.v.) succeeded as Provisional President.

VASQUEZ, JOSE V. Compiler of the Album curio hondureño in its second edition (1970), Professor Vásquez holds honors and memberships which include the Academy of Geography and History of Honduras and Guatemala, and active membership on the Committee of Instruction of History and Improvement of Texts of the Panamerican Institute of Geography and History.

VASQUEZ, JUSTINIANO. Poet, author of Confesiones de la sangre (1951), Vásquez was born in San Andrés, Lempira, in 1929.

VEGETATION. There is a great variety of tropical growth in Honduras; the whole country turns green following the onset of the rains after mid-May of each year. Among the types are tall, straight broadleaf evergreen (rain)forest trees over 100 feet high, with trunks up to four to six feet in diameter and buttress roots spreading 40-foot spans. Low crooked evergreen forest also abounds. Pine savannahs stretch over the northeast of the country. Evergreen oak and pine forest is prevalent, with some virgin pines still in existence, and very large grassland, which, burned annually, has small spring trees and shrubs. Coconuts abound near the sea; mahogany and other valuable hardwoods dot the high jungle. Honduras mahogany is a major forest product. Mangrove swamps border the coasts. Crops include corn, cotton, beans, rice, tobacco, cassava, sugar cane, bananas (a major export crop), plaintains, melons, gourds (jicaros), etc. Tobacco from Honduras is considered especially fine. Flowers grow profusely --lilies, orchids of myriad varieties, many bromiliads, and so on. There is a wealth of vegetation in both quantity and variety. See BANANAS.

VEHICLES. Due to the relatively slow development of roads in Honduras, there has been a correspondingly lagging accretion of motor vehicles. Paved roads were almost non-existent until the late 1950s, the 90-mile section of Inter-American Highway crossing southern Honduras being unpaved until that time. In 1950 there were 1,300 passenger cars and 1,900 commercial vehicles (including many four-wheel-drive "jeep" types). The cross-Honduras paved road from San Pedro Sula to Tegucigalpa was completed after 1970. By 1970 there were about 25,000 registered motor vehicles, approximately 40 per cent of these being commercial vehicles, and 2,000 of them buses.

VEHICLE-USE TAX. An annual tax which varies with the age of the vehicle.

VELASQUEZ, ANTONIO. Perhaps the best-known of Honduran artists, Velásquez' paintings of his native village of San Antonio de Oriente, a 16th century mining center high in the Sierras southeast of Tegucigalpa have brought him international fame and acclaim. Classed as a primitive, he was self-taught and prolific. Mayor of his village a quarter-century ago, he was also the town barber, and served similarly at El Zamarano (q.v.), the Pan-American agricultural school. Handicapped in speech by a cleft palate, he was somewhat of a philosopher and also a treasury of simple folk lore.

His paintings of San Antonio are characterized by freshness and an every-roof-tile accuracy which is somehow highly representational and yet not at all photographic. His son has carried on the tradition and he has joined such other well-known Central American "Primitive Moderns" as Asilia Guillén, the "Grandma Moses" of Nicaragua. Velásquez' work is on permanent exhibit in Tegucigalpa hotels and galleries, and is prized by collectors, with values continually rising.

VELASQUEZ, DIEGO. Governor of Cuba who in the early 1500s instituted slave raids on the Bay Islands off the Honduran Coast. It was he who launched Cortés.

**VELASQUEZ, JUAN PEREZ DE.** This friar was chaplain to the ill-fated Olid (q.v.) expedition of conquest to Honduras in 1524, and was destined to be indirectly responsible for Olid's death.

**VENEZUELAN OIL** see **OIL AGREEMENTS, VENEZUELA**

**VERA, JUAN DE.** By orders of the Marquis of Ensenada, Somodevilla (q.v.), Colonel Vera was, in 1745, appointed <u>Commandante General de Armas</u> of Honduras. He was given power as governor in Comayagua (following Machado's interim term), authority over the Alcaldía Mayor in Tegucigalpa, and also over the coast from Cabo Gracias a Dios to Yucatán. Vera had previously been governor of the pearl island Margarita, off Venezuela, and of Santa Marta in New Granada (Colombia). His appointment blocked jurisdiction of the captain general in Guatemala over the coastal area. This was a unique subdivision of authority that reversed temporarily the centralizing trend which had begun in the middle 1600s. Vera was to supervise the construction of Fort Omoa, and to prepare offensives and outfit Corsairs. The fact that Díez Navarro (q.v.) was delayed at Fort Inmaculada meant that Vera had no military engineer to assign to the Fort Omoa construction, and therefore that effort was delayed. He died in 1747 before the planned offensive got well under way.

**VERMONT PARTNERS** see **RELIEF EFFORTS, PARTNERS OF THE AMERICAS**

**VERREZANO, GIROLAMO--MAPS.** The brother of Giovanni Verrezano who explored the east coast of North America from Florida northward. Girolamo, with his brother, was the probable author of the undated world chart, first made in about 1529 on vellum, which shows Honduras, the Bay Islands and Yucatán very clearly, but does not show the great Nicaraguan Lakes, a fact which indicates the partiality and selectivity of information during the early colonial period.

**VESPUCCI, AMERIGO.** The man for whom (presumably) America was named went on a voyage of expedition for King Ferdinand, consisting of four ships under the command of Vincente Yánez Pinzón and Juan Díaz de Solís, with the famed Juan de la Cosa as their pilot. According to the letter which Vespucci wrote (as a Florentine) to Pier Soderini, Gonfalonier of the Republic of Florence, and in accord with a geographical summary by his English translator, Vespucci reached the Coast of Honduras on July 4, 1497. If this indeed happened, it would make the Pinzón-Vespucci expedition the first discoverers of mainland middle America, and in nearly the same place credited to Columbus some five years later. Since the latitude determinations of the period were quite accurate, when Vespucci states that the North Pole was 16 degrees above the horizon, this puts the latitude probably within 20-30 miles, and since both Capes Camerón (q.v.) and Honduras (q.v.) are within a mile or two of the 16th parallel, the location is definitive. The translator feels sure it was near Cape Camerón, or in the Bay of Honduras. Vespucci gave detailed description of the people and their customs. The voyage which followed was north-westward, which certainly could have been along the Yucatán Coast.

VESPUCHE, EMERIGO. Spelling of Amerigo Vespucci (Americus Vespucius) used by Alonso de Ojeda in testimony at Santo Domingo in 1512; it is significant as a variant in relation to the naming of America, still a somewhat moot question.

VICEROY. As a direct representative of the Spanish Crown, the "vice-king" represented the king in a direct manner, and was the loftiest of the colonial officials. Honduras, under the Viceroyalty of New Spain and the "Kingdom of Goethemal" (Guatemala) was somewhat remote from the viceregal center in Mexico, yet was also subject to the viceregal prerogatives of appointing officials (even to very minor posts) and of granting encomiendas, the most significant function during the colonial era. At the termination of an incumbency, the viceroy was subject to a review of his acts in office by a residencia, and to some limitations during his office by the advisory group known as audiencia. Conversion of Indians, tax collection, law enforcement, and general administration were the viceregal functions.

VIDES, OSCAR. Dr. Vides is in 1974 the incumbent doctor and medical director of the Clínica Morava in Ahuas, in Mosquitia.

VIGIL, DIEGO. A Honduran native who governed Honduras (as part of the Central American Federation) in 1836-38. He then became vice-president of the Federal Republic.

VIGILANTE. The official magazine of the Cuerpo Especial de Seguridad (q.v.).

VILLA ADELA. A southern suburb of Comayaguela.

VILLALOBOS, PEDRO DE. Governor from 1573 to 1578, soon after which he died (1579). His residency was a time of disruptive earthquakes in 1575 and 1578. In modern times Honduras has been plagued very little by quakes.

VILLALVA Y TOLEDO, FRANCISCO. Spanish commander of an expedition to expel pirates (principally English) from the Bay Islands in March 1650. He had a fleet of four warships, and was sent by the combined efforts of the Viceroy of Guatemala, the President of the Audiencia Real of San Domingo, and the Governor of Havana. Turned away by the fortified harbors on Roatán (q.v.) at his first attempt, Villalva returned and routed the freebooters on the second. The Spanish found the islands ravished, with a few natives who had been made slaves. The natives went to the mainland and the islands remained deserted for nearly a century.

VILLEDA MORALES, RAMON. Chosen as Constitutional President following the constituent assembly set up by the Junta Militar de Gobierno under General Roque J. Rodríguez, Dr. Villeda Morales served from December 21, 1957 until October 3, 1963, when another military coup ousted him just before the end of his legal term of office. At both the beginning and end of his term, the two coups d'état initiated by the military were symptomatic of the essential turbulence of his term of office. There were border conflicts with Nicaragua in 1957, and with Guatemala as well. Communist elements began to make attacks upon the Villeda Morales government. It was he who separated the police from the armed forces and who formed them into an independent "civil guard," not unlike the guardia civil of Spain. This civil guard was changed to "El Ces," the Cuerpo Especial de Seguridad (q.v.), in 1963. This corps has around 3,000 men. Villeda Morales disarmed the guard just before the 1963 elections.

VILLEGAS, JUAN BUSTOS. Assigned as governor to take office in 1569, he died en route and his place continued to be held by Francisco Briceño (q.v.).

VINICULTURE. Soon after the conquest, grapes were raised in northern Honduras for a brief period. But, considered a Spanish monopoly, wine-making soon died out. Peruvian vineyards began to compete by the mid-1600s. Ships of the Honduran flotilla were charged to allot one-third of their cargo space to wine and oil, but the orders were seldom adhered to, and often the flotilla did not sail at all. Between 1673 and 1679 only three official ships reached Honduras from Spain. Wine was in short supply in the struggling colony.

VINO DE COYOL. Wine made from the Coyol palm in the Olancho area of Honduras. Apparently the method derives from the Jicaque Indians who hollowed the palm trunk just under the bud of the palm and drew off the sap. In modern Olancho the trees are cut down. The sap ferments in a box cut in the bud end of the palm trunk, giving in several days a wine not unlike champagne. The chamber in the trunk is shaved with a sharp knife to renew the flow and the wine supply.

VIRGEN DE LA CANDELERIA. A nine-day fiesta held in February each year in Intibuca. This is a town greatly influenced by the Lenca Indian population, and the fiesta has a certain syncretistic character as it blends aboriginal beliefs and practices with the avowed Catholicism. The guancasco or exchange visit of patron saints is a major element in this fiesta. Chicha (q.v.) is drunk and copal (q.v.) is burned as incense. Offerings are made to the sun; there are ceremonial dances.

VIRGIN OF SUYAPA. The patron saint of Honduras. The fiestas in celebration of the saint's days are from February 2nd for the ensuing two weeks. In Tegucigalpa the saint has a special basilica near the city.

VIRREY. An abbreviated form of the word Viceroy (q.v.).

VITERI Y UNGO, JORGE. Bishop of El Salvador who fled into Honduras when he called for the resignation of President Eugenio Aguilar, in July of 1846. This was one of the events which contributed to the frequently strained relations between El Salvador and Honduras for nearly a century and a half.

VOCATIONAL EDUCATION. Most vocational education in Honduras is on an apprenticeship basis or by on-the-job training. There are primary school courses in crafts, agriculture, secretarial skills, and home economics, but the preparation is essentially basic. There are specialized courses at secondary levels, leading directly to jobs or to further apprenticeships. There is a vocational-technical institute in Tegucigalpa.

VOLCANOES. Honduras shows signs of ancient volcanology, but has at present no active volcanoes. In 1887 William T. Brigham listed volcanic peaks in Central America in the following numbers:

|  | Total | Quiescent | Active |
| --- | --- | --- | --- |
| Guatemala | 21 | 4 | 2 |
| San Salvador | 11 | 3 | 5 |
| Nicaragua | 17 | 8 | 4 |
| Costa Rica | 9 | 2 | 1 |
| Honduras | 5 | 1 | 0 |
| Totals | 63 | 18 | 12 |

Since that time one other in Costa Rica has been quite active. It is obvious that the greatest activity has been in Nicaragua, the least in Honduras. Brigham felt that Congrehoy (or Cangrejal) was the "sharpest cone he had ever seen." He also showed three peaks in Colombia (now Panama) which made a total of 66 volcanic peaks along the Central American littoral.

VOLLAMAERE, ANTON. Belgian researcher who in mid-1974 announced he was close to "breaking the code" of the Maya hieroglyphs which have been considered undecipherable (except for numerical values) since their discovery in places like Copán (q.v.), Honduras, and Quiriguá, Guatemala. In both places are numerous stelae and a great variety of glyphs. Vollemaere's degree in Mayan paleology was awarded by the

Sorbonne in Paris. He has deciphered verb conjugations and a system of precise suffixes; he is working on a Maya dictionary.

- W -

WALDSEEMÜLLER, MAP OF 1507. The twelve-sheet World Maps of 1507 by Waldseemüller definitely indicated a coastal area to the west of the Greater Antilles. Whether or not any part of it can be definitely identified as Honduras is problematical. Waldseemüller's 1516 map indicates the Honduran coast and possibly Florida, although it may likely be that this is the Honduran projection toward Cuba. The point of this comparison is that around the second decade of the 16th century Honduras entered the consciousness of Europe as maps began to delineate her shores.

WALKER, WILLIAM, 1824-1860. Famous (or infamous) filibuster of the mid-1800s, especially identified with his Central American adventures in Honduras and Nicaragua. In April 1860 an Englishman representing the British community on the Island of Roatán in the Bay of Honduras sought out Walker to gain his help in throwing off Honduran rule, following the turning over of that island by the British to the Honduran government. Walker agreed to help in this enterprise, for he wished to join a revolt against the existing Honduran government by Trinidad Cabañas, a former president of the country. Walker was internationally known already, as a result of his previous ventures in Mexico and Nicaragua. Born in Nashville, Tennessee, this slightly-built adventurer was a central figure in turbulent events of the isthmian region for several years. His activities were in the spirit of "Manifest Destiny" which was rampant in the United States following the war with Mexico in the late 1840s, which had resulted in the annexation to the U.S. of a great deal of Mexican territory.

Walker graduated from the University of Nashville at the age of 14, a prodigy, and from the University of Pennsylvania's Medical College at age 19. He was one of the youngest qualified physicians on record. After study at the Sorbonne in Paris, he read law in New Orleans, and was admitted to the bar, opening a law office. In 1848 he became an editor of the newspaper Crescent, so that by age 24 he had already had careers in medicine, law, and journalism. By this time he had also earned a reputation as a duellist. The death of his only love Ellen Martin sent him, despondent, to California, where again he became a newsman. In 1853 he led an abortive venture aimed at the creation of a "Republic of Lower California" from Mexican territory, but was chased back into California in 1855.

All this was but a prelude to the main events of his short life, which took place in Central America, principally in Nicaragua. Hired to assist in a revolution, with 58 men (later dubbed "The Immortals"), Walker landed in Nicaragua. His campaigns there won worldwide notice, and when by rigged elections he declared himself President of Nicaragua, all of Central America united (temporarily) long enough to drive him out. In April of 1857 he was chased out after the final Battle of Rivas, surrendering to Commander Davis of a United States naval vessel. He then returned in custody to the United States of America, almost as a conquering hero, and there published a book, The War in Nicaragua, which was later used as an accurate source even by his enemies!

Walker's subsequent Honduran expedition was to prove his downfall. When his forces attempted to hold the old Spanish fort near Trujillo, Honduras, they were decimated and defeated. Walker then surrendered to a British naval Captain, Norvell Salmon (q.v.) of the warship, Icarus, and Salmon, somewhat treacherously (but from the standpoint of British-Honduran relations, quite diplomatically), turned Walker over to Honduran authorities. At 8:00 a.m., September 12, 1860, Walker was shot by a firing squad against a ruined Trujillo wall, and so at the age of 36 his incredible career ended. Speculation ever since has toyed with the alterations of history which might have been made if Walker had succeeded in annexing all or part of Central America and Cuba to the United States, as he hoped to do. Would the U.S. Civil War have been averted, or the outcome changed? (For Walker in his later planning wanted to perform the annexation with Central America as slave territory.) Would Central America have been better off for the "Progress and Democracy" which Walker professed? Or was he just a failure and a villain, which has been the view of him in Central America ever since?

WALLIS RIVER. An alternate name for the Río Coco (q.v.), doubtlessly named for the Wallis who gave his name to Belize (a corrupted form of "Wallis" or "Wallace").

WALPATA. Village on the island of Tansín in Laguna Caratasca.

WAMPUSIRPI. River "port" on the lower Patuca River in Gracias a Dios Department. It is the only designated airfield location other than Ahuas in the lower 250 miles of the stream. Wampusirpi is in the hills nearest to the sea, about fifty miles from the Caribbean coast. They are the Sierras de Warunta.

WANGKI RIVER. The Río Coco (q.v.). Other forms include Wangks, Wanks, and Wanx.

WANKYBILA ARCHEOLOGICAL SITE see TENAMPUA

WAR, EL SALVADOR, 1969. In July of 1969 war broke out between El Salvador and Honduras, and during the five-day conflict there was considerable bloodshed as well as a sharp break in long-standing peaceful relationships between the two neighboring countries. Originating as a Sarajevo-like spark in an international soccer game, the conflict's real reasons lay in social and geographical factors. There had been a great deal of illegal immigration into Honduras, stemming from population pressures in overcrowded El Salvador. A poorly defined border between the countries fostered these incursions. Expulsion of many of the illegal immigrants heightened tensions, and the soccer game spark served to touch off war. An increase of nationalist sentiments in both countries was no small factor.

Action centered around the town of Nueva Ocotepeque. Refugees from the town fled northward into Guatemala, only ten miles or so away. Units of the Salvadoran army invaded as far as 25 miles into Honduras during two thrusts across the border, along the Inter-American Highway. Salvadoran airstrikes by the Honduran Air Force seriously damaged an oil refinery owned by U.S. interests at the Salvadoran port of Acajutla. Since the Rio de Janeiro Treaty of Reciprocal Assistance of 1947 applied to the conflict, the Organization of American States sent an investigative team at ambassadorial levels. After three days a ceasefire was established.

The Organization of American States, having acted quickly, soon established a demilitarized zone extending approximately two miles on each side of the border. By June 1970, the OAS mediation had resulted in an armistice agreement whereby, although relations were not restored, the armed forces of both countries were withdrawn from the demilitarized strip and thirteen-man police patrols were established in the sensitive area to cope with civilian acts of hostility. Civilians in the zone were disarmed.

The most significant results lay in the disruption of the Central American Common Market (q.v.) and the slowing rate of growth of the Honduran economy. There were also political repercussions which extend to the present.

The war casualties amounted to 2,000 dead. Fighting continued in border skirmishes through 1971. By 1972 there was an evident sentiment for developing a lasting peace, however. Diplomatic relations were still ruptured in 1974. Such events as the destruction of the Goascorán River bridge at the Honduran-Salvadoran border aggravated problems of trade. For many months, truck traffic on the Inter-American Highway crossed the Bay of Fonseca on ferries from El Salvador to Nicaragua, thus entirely by-passing Honduras. The bitterness and intense nationalism resulting from the brief conflict have shadowed the whole Central American area for six years.

WAR OF 1839   see   SALVADOR, WAR OF 1839

WAR OF 1850   see   SALVADOR, 1850 WAR

WAR OF 1853   see   GUATEMALA, 1853 WAR

WAR OF 1872 see SALVADOR AND GUATEMALA, WAR OF 1872

WAR OF 1876 see SALVADOR AND HONDURAS VERSUS GUATEMALA, WAR OF 1876

WAR OF 1908. A guerrilla war developed in 1908 soon after the Central American Court of Justice was formed. The soldier of fortune Lee Christmas (q.v.) led an invasion of Honduras, and soon after, all of the Central American countries except Costa Rica were embroiled. The colorful Christmas was the archetype of the "gun-for-hire" soldier of fortune. See CENTRAL AMERICAN COURT OF JUSTICE.

WARI. The white-lipped peccary, considered a very dangerous animal, a pig-like creature of about the size of medium domestic porkers. Often spelled Waree and known as the wild hog of Mosquitia, Dycoliles Torguatus. Dangerous, especially in herds, but nevertheless considered excellent food.

WASPARASNI RIVER. A short tributary of the Río Patuca over 100 miles from the mouth.

WASS see HUAS

WATERBURY, JOHN J. One of two Americans, the other being Joseph L. Hance, who leased the Honduras Inter-Oceanic Railway in 1883. The railroad was in serious disrepair.

WATSON, JOHN see MISSIONARY AVIATION FELLOWSHIP

WEBSTER-CRAMPTON AGREEMENT. An 1852 accord by which Britain tried to retreat gracefully from the Mosquito Protectorate, surrendering sovereignty without giving up dignity. She was not wholly successful.

WEIGHTS AND MEASURES. The following list of weights and measures gives an idea of the blend of old and new in the current usage of Honduras.

| | | |
|---|---|---|
| Cuarta (one-fourth of a vara) | 8.3 | inches |
| Vara | 2.76 | feet |
| Cuadra | 91.9 | yards |
| Legua | 3.0 | miles |
| Manzana | 1.75 | acres |
| Caballería | 27.9 | acres |
| Legua Cuadrada | 9.0 | square miles |
| Fanega | 500.0 | cubic inches |
| Arroba | 25.0 | pounds |
| Libra | 1.014 | English pounds |
| Galón | .888 | English gallons |
| Quintal | 101.44 | English pounds (100 Libras or hundredweight) |

WEITZEL, GEORGE T. American Minister to Nicaragua who negotiated with the Nicaraguan government a treaty which included rights to build naval stations in the Gulf of Fonseca. This became the basis of a bitter controversy, as the Central American republics with seacoast on the Gulf felt it an infringement of their rights; in this case El Salvador and Honduras were the nations affected. When the treaty was ratified by the U.S. Senate in 1916, it stipulated that the rights of Honduras or the other countries would not be affected, but Honduras objected, as did Costa Rica, and Honduras brought suit against Nicaragua in the Central American Court of Justice in Cartago.

WESTERN DESIGN, CROMWELL. Oliver Cromwell's great design in the 1650s was to capture a part of the Spanish Empire in the New World. He did take Jamaica, and managed to hold it. His plan to take Panama or Nicaragua didn't work out, but the fact of a British Jamaica did change things all along the Caribbean western littoral.

WESTERN ZONE. The Western Zone of Honduras is made up of the departments of Cortéz, Santa Bárbara, Copán, Ocotepeque, Lempira, Intibuca, La Paz, and Comayagua. It includes Comayagua, the old capital; Gracias in Lempira, first Central American Colonial capital; and Santa Rosa de Copán, Nueva Ocotepeque, La Paz, La Esperanza, and Santa Bárbara; all are population centers. The urban industrial center of San Pedro Sula is the most important place in this zone from an economic standpoint; from a cultural standpoint, the magnificent Maya site of Copán is preeminent.

WINDWARD SQUADRON. A Caribbean-based Spanish patrol intended to break British, French, and Dutch piracy in the Caribbean around 1635. It was reestablished by Conde Duque Olivares, the Spanish prime minister. The attack of the squadron on Providence Island in 1635 (see PROVIDENCE COMPANY) turned that trading company into a militant striking force. Francisco Díaz de Pimienta was commander of the galleons.

"WINGS FOR HEALTH." This is a spirited and successful civic action program carried out by the Honduran air force. It provides medical services to isolated parts of the republic, and to particularly needy citizens. There is a cooperative arrangement with both foreign and Honduran health and social services. There is a free dispensary at Toncontín Airport, another in Tegucigalpa, and an air ambulance service for quick medical evacuation from all parts of the country. Medical and dental students are also flown to remote areas for free assistance to residents.

WODEHOUSE, P. E., COLONEL. The British officer who, as newly appointed superintendent at Belize, proclaimed and occupied the "Colony of the Bay Islands" (q.v.) in 1852. Wodehouse had previously been attached to the notorious Torrington in Ceylon. The violation of Honduran rights to the island was part of a long succession of acts by the British aimed at a quasi-legal foothold in Central America, particularly in the area of the Bay of Honduras. Wodehouse became Superintendent at Belize in about 1850. He visited Roatán in person, and from his brig of war Persian called a meeting on August 10, 1852 and finally occupied Roatán (q.v.), annexing the offshore islands as the Colony of the Bay Islands. This was characterized as "sublime effrontery." The islands were finally turned over to the Republic of Honduras in 1859.

WON AISA. Miskito designation of a Supreme Being--meaning akin to "Our Father."

WONKS see RIO COCO

WOODHOUSE, DR. S. W. A companion of E. G. Squier (q.v.) in the surveys across Honduras accomplished in 1853. He ran a line of observations from León, Nicaragua to Comayagua, Honduras. Woodhouse had been a member of the Colorado Government Expedition under Sitgreaves, and as such was experienced in this particular type of exploratory survey in wild and rugged country.

WOODSMAN'S DISEASE see AËDES AEGYPTI

WORKERS' BANK see BANCO DE LOS TRABAJADORES

WORLD COUNCIL OF CHURCHES. The Commission in Interchurch Aid, Refugee and World Service (CICARWS) of the World Council of Churches gave $20,000 in immediate relief aid to Honduras just after disastrous Hurricane "Fifi" (q.v.), and the Church World Service, an arm of the United States churches, airlifted clothing and medical supplies to the area.

WORLD GOSPEL MISSION BIBLE INSTITUTE. A ministerial school for Honduran candidates in Protestant denominations. Located in El Hatillo in the hills near Tegucigalpa.

WORLD WAR II, HONDURAN ROLE. Honduras declared war on Japan, December 8, 1941, and on Italy and Germany, December 12, 1941. In November 1942 the regime of President Arías Andino broke off diplomatic relations with Vichy France, and culminating this position with the nations opposing the Axis powers, became a charter member of the United Nations in 1945.

WORMAN, FRED see DIAKONIA

WOULAH. A large snake found in the forests of northern Honduras, bluish-white color, harmless. It is thought to destroy smaller poisonous snakes, as does the king-snake in the southern United States.

WYKE-CRUZ TREATY. Negotiated at Comayagua in 1859, this treaty between Honduras and Great Britain resulted in the British giving up all claims to the Bay Islands, and simultaneously the British gave up all formal claims to the Mosquito coast, although they did not relinquish the Mosquito protectorate until 30 years later. As British influence declined, United States influence increased. The Wyke-Cruz Treaty cleared the Bay Islands (q.v.) as Honduran Territory, which they have remained ever since.

- X -

XATRUCH, FLORENCIO. As leader of a revolution against José María Medina (q.v.), Xatruch was proclaimed president and thus by force served from March 26, 1871 to May 17, 1871. Medina was in and out of the presidency at least eleven times!

XATRUCH, FRANCISCO see PASAQUINA

XEREX DE LA FRONTERA DE CHOLUTECA see CHOLUTECA

XICAQUE. A variant form of "Jicaque" (from the Arabic influence of old Spanish, the "h" pronunciation of "x").

XIQUILITE. A Nahuatl word signifying indigo. The bush is three to six feet high, a tropical perennial.

XOCHITL. Twentieth (and final) day of the Aztec month; meaning, "flower."

XUL. Sixth month of the Maya calendar.

- Y -

YAHURABILA. In Gracias a Dios Department, on the outer beaches of the Caratasca Lagoon, this village is a few miles from the lagoon channel at the Barra de Caratasca. It is a center of fishing activities.

YAMARINGUILA. A town near Intibuca which engages in an exchange of patron saints in a mutual visit during the festival of the Virgen de la Candeleria (q.v.).

YANCUNU. Dances performed by Black Caribs on Christmas and New Year's days; the dancers are men wearing elaborate masks. The dance steps are like those of South American rainforest Indians; the music a reminder of West Africa.

YAÑEZ PINZON, VINCENTE  see  VESPUCCI, AMERIGO

YANQUI. A nickname or "apodo" given to North Americans (specifically, citizens of the United States of America). The word probably originated with the Dutch "Jan Kees," or "John Cheese." It was applied in the English Americas in early colonial days to Hollanders, then to the Dutch pirates of the 16th and 17th centuries, finally to Dutch colonials in New York and, by contiguity, to the English colonials in Connecticut, whence "Yankee Doodle" and the almost universal Latin American application to citizens of the United States.

YARE RIVER  see  RIO COCO

YARRINCE, CARLOS ANTONIO. Chief of the Yarrinces, an Indian tribal family of La Mosquitia in the 1700s, Carlos Antonio once offered 500 warriors to the Spanish governor in order to fight the English. Governor Domingo Cabello gave Yarrince the title of "Captain and Governor of the Caribs." The chief destroyed the Guadelupe mission in 1762. He was, however, essentially loyal to the Spanish.

YARUMELA. Oldest known village culture in Honduras, and one of only eight or ten outside of the Tehuacán Valley. The date of Yarumela, a village farming culture based on corn, is around 1700 to 1600 B.C. It is in Comayagua Department.

YAX. Tenth month of the Maya calendar.

YAXKIN. Seventh month of the Maya calendar.

YBUERAS. Spelling of Honduras as rendered by Herrera in early writings.

YEAR OF THE GREAT DARKNESS. Term still used on the Gulf of Fonseca to describe the explosion of the volcano Coseguina on the Nicaraguan side of the bay in 1838.

YELLOW FEVER  see  AËDIS AEGYPTI

YOJOA (LAKE). A natural lake about ten miles long, in a lovely mountain setting of Santa Bárbara Department, the south shore just touching Comayagua Department for a three-mile segment. The only major freshwater inland body of water in the country, Yojoa is in an area relatively sparsely settled for the center of the country, with the villages of El Sauce, El Jaral, El Eden, and Los Caminos near the shores. (See map p. 52.)

YORO. Departmental cabacera of Yoro Department, in a valley flanked by the Montañas de Yoro, the M. de Pijol, and the Cordillera Nombre de Dios. It is not reached by rail, but there is a good road and an airfield. Timber and ranching are principal activities.

YORO DEPARTMENT. Bounded on the north by Atlántida Department, on the east by Colón Department; on the southeast by Olancho and on the south by Francisco Morazán and Comayagua departments; and on the west by the major Río Ulúa and by Cortés and Santa Bárbara departments, Yoro touches a total of seven other departments, more than does any other of the eighteen except Francisco Morazán. Yoro is also in contact with two major river systems, the Ulúa and the Aguán. There are 11 municipios, and the cabecera is also named Yoro. The area is 3,100 square miles. The population of cabaceras in 1973 was 56,832, and of the villages and rural areas, 127,687, for a total of 184,519. Yoro is in a peculiarly central position, like Francisco Morazán and Comayagua departments. There are the mountain ranges of Mico Quemado, Pijol, and Yoro, which are part of the essentially very rugged terrain in the whole area. Towns are Las Flores, Olanchito, Arenál, Jocón, Yorito, El Negrito, Morazán, Santa Rita, and El Progreso.

YORO MUNICIPIOS. In Yoro Department the municipios and their cabaceras are El Progreso, Santa Rita, Victoria, Yorito, Jocón, Arenal, and Las Flores. While near population centers in airline miles, the department is not very easy of access.

YORO RIVER see RIO COCO

YOUNGBERG, STEPHEN. In the early 1960s this physician from Texas went into the Honduran highlands to give his skill to the people of the region around Lake Yojoa. His interesting contribution is not only through medicine in his own clinic, but through agricultural development, seeking protein-rich foods. He now has a staff of 30 and an $80,000 annual budget. He deals continually with the very basic problems of malnutrition.

YOURA RIVER. An alternate name for the Río Coco (q.v.), another spelling of "Yare."

YUCA. The common Central American word for the important food, manioc or cassava. A number of tropical plants are of the genus Manihot. The Manihot Esculenta or M. Utilíssima is a plant with a large, starchy root, best known to the English-speaking world as the source of tapioca. The word cassava comes from the West Indian word cacabi, from which the Spanish derive cazabe. There is a sweet and a bitter yuca, the latter being poisonous, but this one is rare though not unknown in Honduras. Boiling renders the poison harmless, if the cooking water is discarded. It is the bitter root which provides tapioca. The roots look like sweet potatoes, are often peeled, boiled, and served plain with fish or soup. Pronounced "Yoo-cah" the plant (and the word) is entirely different from the spiky "Spanish Bayonet" or yucca plant so prevalent in the United States' southwest, which is pronounced "yukkah."

YUCATAN. Thought to be an island, the Yucatán Peninsula was first sighted from the Honduran coast in the early 1500s by Pinzón and Solís.

YUGUARE RIVER. The valley of this stream is one of great beauty. El Zamarano (q.v.) is located here. The stream is tributary to the Río Choluteca.

YUM KAX see MAIZE GOD (also illustration p. 308.)

YURE RIVER. Tributary of the Ulua (q.v.) in Comayagua Department.

YUSCARAN. Departmental cabacera of El Paraiso, Yuscarán is in the tumbled topography of the western part of that department, which borders on Nicaragua with the wild and remote Cordillera de Depilto.

- Z -

ZAC. Eleventh month of the Maya calendar.

ZACATE GRANDE, ISLAND. Twin dead volcanic cone on El Tigre Island in the Bay of Fonseca (see map), Zacate Grande has an altitude of over 2,000 feet and like Tigre, is part of the Central American coastal line of dead, quiescent, and live volcanoes. Zacate Grande is connected to the mainland of the north shore of the bay by tidal flats, the nearest mainland settlement being Puerto Soto.

ZAVALA, GUSTAVO ADOLFO. Leader of the developing labor movement in 1954-55, during the disturbed election period which resulted in Lozano (q.v.) taking power as "chief of state."

ZELAYA, ARMANDO. Editor of the weekly El Chilio and founding member of the Honduran Press Association (APH), he was born in 1928 in Comayaguela. For a time he was chief of public relations for the Honduran Armed Forces, during 1956-58. He was alternate delegate for Honduras to the United Nations Assembly in New York, in 1965. See ROSA, RAMON.

ZELAYA, JERONIMO. Lawyers Zelaya, Crescencio Gómez, and Rafael Alvarado Manzano held executive power as a council of ministers from August 30, 1884 to November 17, 1884, between constitutional terms of President Luis Bográn.

ZELAYA, JOSE MARIA. From January 13 to February 3, 1876, Zelaya was the first designate and presided over the Honduran government.

ZELAYA, JOSE SANTOS. Significant to Honduras because of a war with Honduras and also his desire to form a new Central American Union with El Salvador and Honduras, this controversial and energetic President of Nicaragua took over by force of arms in 1893 from the Roberto Sacasa administration and ruled Nicaragua until 1909. A new constitution was promulgated by the Zelaya regime on December 10, 1893, which clearly separated church and state, a moot question for the previous decade which had caused an 1881 rebellion in Matagalpa. Mosquitia was permanently incorporated in Nicaragua during Zelaya's time, after three centuries of British involvement, and there was a war with Honduras. Zelaya suffered continual coup attempts, one in February 1896 which failed. Zelaya was interested in the formation of the Republic of Central America (that perennial dream) with El Salvador and Honduras, but the union was short-lived. Railway service was instituted from Corinto to Granada, Masaya, and Diriamba. In 1904, a more serious garrison revolt erupted, and in 1905 the "Rebellion of the Great Lake" (q.v.). The final anti-Zelaya revolution was led by the President's old friend, Juan José Estrada. Through U.S. intervention, Zelaya was forced to leave the country in 1910. He wrote a short book from exile entitled The Revolution in Nicaragua and the United States, an early commentary on intervention. José Madriz succeeded the tenacious Zelaya, whose name lives on in the huge Atlantic coastal department of Nicaragua, by far the largest in that country. If the union with Honduras and El Salvador had been formed, much of the recent turbulent history might well have been different, and this dreamer-dictator might have been revered as the architect of a permanent peace.

ZELAYA AYES, FRANCISCO. Interim president of Honduras from September 21, 1839 to January 1, 1841.

ZEPEDA RODRIGUEZ, ERNESTO A. see MILITARY ZONE COMMANDS, 1972

ZEPEDA Y ZEPEDA, JUAN FELIX DE JESUS. Bishop of Comayagua in 1881, Fray Juan was born in the little mining village of San Antonio de Oriente (q.v.). He had a reputation for being just, prudent, and virtuous.

ZIP. Third month of the Maya calendar.

ZONES, GEOGRAPHIC.

    Eastern  -  (Departments)
Colón
Gracias a Dios
Olancho

|          |   | (Departments)     |
|----------|---|-------------------|
| Central  | - | Atlántida         |
|          |   | Choluteca         |
|          |   | El Paraíso        |
|          |   | Francisco Morazán |
|          |   | Yoro              |
|          |   |                   |
| Western  | - | Comayagua         |
|          |   | Copán             |
|          |   | Cortés            |
|          |   | Intibuca          |
|          |   | La Paz            |
|          |   | Lempira           |
|          |   | Ocotopeque        |
|          |   | Santa Bárbara     |
|          |   | Valle             |

ZONES--HUMID, ARID, TROPICAL  see  LIFE ZONES

ZORZI, ALLESSANDRO. A sketch map by Zorzi of the coasts of Central and South America, which is curious in that the north coast of Honduras is shown as running due North and South, with the Bay Islands on a north-south axis, well identified by the name Banassa (Guanaja, q.v.). The Zorzi map is based on a map by Bartolomé Columbus, and thereby, in spite of its orientational bias, bears an aura of early authority.

ZOTZ. Fourth month of the Maya calendar.

## BIBLIOGRAPHY AND LIST OF MAPS

One of the problems of bibliographical choice is that in spite of the paucity of relatively accessible material on Honduras, there is such a dispersed variety of what is available that it is difficult to make choices for inclusion.

The listing which follows is by no means exhaustive. With few exceptions all these sources have been used in the compilation. The degree of utilization varies widely. On occasion only one or two obscure yet interestingly pertinent facts are derived.

None of the sources here is primary. Several are secondary sources of a high order of significance, due to such characteristics as currency during the colonial period, such as Juarros' Compendio de la historia de la Ciudad de Guatemala or the facsimile periodical reprints of original proceedings against William Walker in 1860.

Some of the sources are quite recent. The hurricane of 1974 was treated extensively in the press. While not bibliographical in the strict sense, first hand notes and observations of the compiler in travels about Honduras in particular and Central America in general are minor in quantity but qualitatively of high significance.

As Jacques Barzun has reminded scholars in Clio and the Doctors, "quanto-history" in its statistical straitjacket and "psycho-history" with its analytic categories leave out the main streams of motivation by exhibiting the sterility of effect rather than the fecundity of causation.

The effort here, then, from a bibliographical point of view, has been to exhibit the breadth of the potential rather than either a comprehensive or an intensively specific presentation. Here is a variety of published materials, typical of many which deal with Honduras, frequently in a larger matrix than the narrowly historical.

The maps are at best a small sampling, but indicate the long time-span of available materials from the early 16th century on, as well as the growing body of precise and comprehensive topographical materials which have rapidly accrued since the mapping work of the 1950s and 1960s. The settled portion of Honduras (the central and western portions and the northwest and southern coasts) are now well-mapped. The eastern third of the country is as sparsely mapped as it is meagerly settled.

## BIBLIOGRAPHY

Acosta, Oscar (Director). Imágenes de Honduras. No. 1 of a series. Tegucigalpa: Editorial Nuevo Continente, Crecosa Publicitaria, 1974.

───── , and Del Valle, Pompeyo. Exaltación de Honduras. Tegucigalpa: Editorial Nuevo Continente, 1971.

Alden, John D. The American Steel Navy. Annapolis, Maryland: Naval Institute Press, 1972.

Allen, William H. "Bay Islands," Travel Magazine, 1968.

Anderson, Dr. C. L. G. Old Panama and Castilla de Oro. New York: North River Press, 1944.

Arbaiza, Norman D. Mars Moves South; The Future Wars of South America. New York: Exposition Press, 1974.

Arévalo, Juan José. The Shark and the Sardines. (Trans. by June Cobb and Dr. Paul Osegueda.) New York: Lyle Stuart, 1961.

Ashe, Geoffrey. Land to the West. London: Collins, 1962.

Aspinall, Algernon. Pocket Guide to the West Indies. New York: Brentano's, 1927.

Atkins, G. Pope and Larman C. Wilson. The United States and the Trujillo Regime. New Brunswick, New Jersey: Rutgers University Press, 1972.

Austin, Oliver L., Jr. Birds of the World. Illus. by Arthur Singer. New York: Golden Press, 1961.

Bacon, Edward. Vanished Civilizations of the Ancient World. London: McGraw-Hill, 1963.

Bagrow, Leo (Shelton, R. A., Editor). History of Cartography. Cambridge, Mass.: Harvard University Press, 1966.

Bailey, Thomas A. The American Pageant. Boston: D. C. Heath and Co., 1956.

Barron, Louis, ed. The Worldmark Encyclopedia of the Nations.

Bibliography

New York: Worldmark Press, 1960.

Banco Central de Honduras. Honduras en cifras. Tegucigalpa: Departmento de Estudios Económicos, 1971-1973.

Bancroft, Hubert Howe. History of Central America. 2 vols. San Francisco: A. L. Bancroft and Co., 1882-1887.

Bard, Samuel A. (Ephraim G. Squier). Waikna, or Adventures on the Mosquito Shore. (Facsimile of 1855 edition - Latin American Gateway Series.) Gainesville: University of Florida Press, 1965.

Barzun, Jacques. Clio and the Doctors. Chicago: University of Chicago Press, 1974.

Beals, C. "In Quest of Sandino, Imperialism Still Rides," Nation, September 20, 1965.

Belly, F. A travers l'Amérique Centrale. 2 vols. Paris: 1860.

Bendala Lucot, Manuel. Seville. 2nd ed. León, Spain: Editorial Everest, 1970.

Berreman, Gerald (et al. -33 consultants). Anthropology Today. Del Mar, California: Communications Research Machines, Inc., 1971.

Bettex, Albert. The Discovery of the World. New York: Simon and Schuster, 1960.

Blacker, Irwin R. Cortes and the Aztec Conquest. New York: American Heritage Pub. Co., 1965.

Boddam-Whetham, J. W. Across Central America. London: Hurst and Blackett, 1877.

Borhek, Mary Virginia. Watchmen on the Walls. Bethlehem, Pa.: Society for Propagating the Gospel, Kutztown, Pa., 1949.

Brandon, William. The American Heritage Book of Indians. Ed. by Alvin M. Josephy. New York: American Heritage Publ. Co., 1961.

Brigham, William T. Guatemala - The Land of the Quetzal. Gainesville, Florida: University of Florida Press, 1965.

Brun, Geoffrey. The World in the Twentieth Century. 3rd ed. Boston: D. C. Heath and Co., 1957.

Calderón, Héctor M. La ciencia matemática de los Mayas. Mexico: Editora Cuzamil, S.A., 1966.

_____. Clave fonética de los jeroglíficos mayas. Mexico: Editorial Orión, 1962.

Carr, Albert Z. The World and William Walker. New York: Harper and Row, 1963.

Carr, Archie. High Jungles and Low. Gainesville: University of Florida Press, 1953.

Chapelle, Howard I. The Search for Speed Under Sail, 1700-1855. New York: W. W. Norton and Co., Inc., 1967.

Charnock, John, Esq. Biographical Memoirs of Lord Viscount Nelson. Boston: Etheridge and Bliss, 1806.

Cochran, Hamilton. Pirates of the Spanish Main. New York: American Heritage Pub. Co., 1961.

Cottrell, Leonard. Lost Worlds. Ed. by Marshall B. Davidson. New York: American Heritage Pub. Co., 1962.

Crow, John A. and G. D. Crow. Panorama de las Américas. Rev. ed. New York: Henry Holt and Co., 1956.

Crowther, Samuel. The Romance and Rise of the American Tropics. Garden City, N.Y.: Doubleday, Doran and Co., 1929.

Cummins, Lejeune. Quijote on a Burro. Mexico City: La Impresora Azteca, 1958.

Davidson, Marshall B. and Leonard Cottrell, eds. The Horizon Book of Lost Worlds. New York: American Heritage Publishing Co., Inc., 1962.

Davis, Richard Harding. Three Gringos in Venezuela and Central America. New York: Harper and Brothers, 1896.

De Leeuw, Hendrik. Crossroads of the Buccaneers. London: Arco Publishers, 1957.

Díaz Solís, Lucila. La flor caléndrica de los Mayas. Mérida, (Yucatán) Mexico: Díaz Massa, 1966, 1968.

Dockstader, Frederick J. Indian Art in America. Greenwich, Conn.: New York Graphic Society, 1958.

Doubleday, Charles William. Reminiscences of the "Filibuster" War in Nicaragua. New York: G. P. Putnam, 1886.

DuBois, Jules. Operation America. New York: Walker and Co., 1963.

Durant, Will and Ariel. The Lessons of History. New York: Simon and Schuster, 1968.

Durón, Francisco José. Las islas del cisne en la cartográfia de los siglos, xvi al xx. London: Durón, 1962.

Duval, Miles P. Cádiz to Cathay. Palo Alto, Calif.: Stanford University Press, 1940.

Espey, Hilda Cole. Another World: Central America. New York: The Viking Press, Inc., 1970.

Espinosa Estrada, Jorge. Nicaragua, cuna de América. Managua: Editorial Alemana, 1969.

Farb, Peter. Man's Rise to Civilization as Shown by the Indians of North America from Primeval Times to the Coming of the Industrial State. New York: E. P. Dutton, 1968.

Flemion, Philip F. Historical Dictionary of El Salvador. Metuchen, N.J.: Scarecrow Press, 1972.

Floyd, Troy S. The Anglo-Spanish Struggle for Mosquitia. Albuquerque: University of New Mexico Press, 1967.

Ford, James A. A Comparison of Formative Cultures in the Americas. Washington, D.C.: Smithsonian Institution Press, 1969.

Foster, Harry L. A Gringo in Mañana Land. New York: Dodd Mead and Co., 1924.

Gaceta de Honduras. Tomo 3 - Numero 92. Comayagua: Administración Imprenta del Gobierno, August 20, 1860.

_____. Tomo 3 - Numero 93. Comayagua: Administración Imprenta del Gobierno, August 31, 1860.

_____. Tomo 3 - Numero 94. Comayagua: Administración Imprenta del Gobierno, September 10, 1860.

Gage, Thomas. Travels in the New World. Norman: University of Oklahoma Press, 1958.

Gerassi, John. The Great Fear in Latin America. London: The Macmillan Co.; New York: Collier Macmillan Ltd., 1969.

Giardini, Cesare. The Life and Times of Columbus. Trans. by Frances Lanza. New York: Curtis Publishing Co., 1967.

Gohm, Douglas. Antique Maps. London: Crown Publishers and Octopus Books, 1972.

Grau Sanz, Mariano. Segovia. León, Spain: Editorial Everest, 1967.

Greene, Lawrence. The Filibuster (The Career of William Walker). Indianapolis: Bobbs-Merrill, 1937.

Griffin, Paul F. and Ronald L. Chatham. Introductory College Geography. 2nd ed. Belmont, Calif.: Fearon Publishers, 1971.

_____, ed. Geography of Population. Palo Alto, California: Fearon Publishers, 1969.

Grosvenor, Melville Bell, ed. National Geographic Atlas of the World. Washington, D.C.: National Geographic Society, 1963.

Gunther, John. Inside Latin America. 1st ed. New York: Harper and Brothers, 1941.

Hale, John R. Age of Exploration. New York: Time, Inc., 1966.

Hannau, Hans W. Islands of the Caribbean. Munich: Wilhelm Andermann Verlag, 1962.

Hartman, Theodore F. In Honduras - What Does Education Mean...? Bethlehem, Penn.: Board of Foreign Missions of Moravian Church in America, 1971.

Hawkes, Jacquetta, ed. The World of the Past. 2 vols. New York: Alfred A. Knopf, 1963.

Hedrick, Basil Calvin. Historical Dictionary of Panama. Metuchen, N.J.: Scarecrow Press, 1970.

Helms, Mary W. Asang. Gainesville, Florida: University of Florida Press, 1971.

Herring, Hubert. A History of Latin America. 2nd ed., rev. New York: Knopf, 1961.

Hitchcock, H.R., et al. World Architecture--An Illustrated History. New York: McGraw-Hill, 1963.

Howarth, David. The Golden Isthmus. London: Collins, 1966.

Howse, Derek and Michael Sanderson. The Sea Chart. New York: McGraw-Hill Book Co., 1973.

Hoyt, Edwin P. Commodore Vanderbilt. Chicago: Reilly and Lee Co., 1962.

Hydrographic Office, U.S. Navy. Naval Air Pilot, Central America.

Washington, D. C. : Government Printing Office, 1937.

Indicador 1965-66. San Pedro Sula: Oficina de Información y Publicidad de San Pedro Sula Editoria Nacional, 1965.

Innes, Hammond. The Conquistadors. New York: Alfred A. Knopf, 1969.

Instituto Hondureño de Cultura Interamericana. Tegucigalpa as Seen by the Artists. Tegucigalpa, Honduras: 1968.

Jackson, Melvin H. Privateers in Charleston, 1793-1796. Washington, D. C. : U. S. Gov't. Printing Office, Smithsonian Institution Press, 1969.

Jane, Cecil. The Journal of Christopher Columbus. New York: Bramhall House, 1960.

Johnson, Haynes, et al. The Bay of Pigs. New York: W. W. Norton, 1964.

Johnson, Thomas Crawford. Did the Phoenicians Discover America? London: James Nisbet and Co., 1913.

Josephy, Alvin M., Jr. The Indian Heritage of America. New York: Knopf, 1968.

Joyce, Thomas A. Central American and West Indian Archaeology. London: Philip Lee Warner, 1916.

Juarros, D. Domingo. Compendio de la historia de la Ciudad de Guatemala. Guatemala City: Tomos I and II, Tercera Edición. Tipografía Nacional, April, 1937.

Kamman, William. A Search for Stability; United States Diplomacy Toward Nicaragua, 1925-1933. Notre Dame, Ind. : University of Notre Dame Press, 1968.

Kapp, Kit S. The Early Maps of Panama. North Bend, Ohio: K. S. Kapp Publications, 1971.

Keasbey, Lindley Miller. The Nicaragua Canal and the Monroe Doctrine; A Political History of Isthmus Transit, with Special Reference to the Nicaragua Canal Project and the Attitude of the United States Government Thereto. New York: G. P. Putnam, 1896.

Kelemen, Pal. Baroque and Rococo in Latin America. New York: Macmillan, 1951.

_____. Medieval American Art. 2 vols. New York: Macmillan Co., 1946.

Laing, Alexander. Seafaring America. New York: American Heritage Publishing Co., 1974.

Landstrom, Bjorn. Columbus. New York: The Macmillan Co., 1966-67.

Langer, William L., ed. An Encyclopedia of World History. 4th ed. Boston: Houghton Mifflin Co., 1968.

Lanning, John Tate. The University in the Kingdom of Guatemala. Ithaca, N.Y.: Cornell University Press, 1955.

Leonard, Jonathan Norton. Ancient America. New York: Time, Inc., 1967.

Leslie, Robert C. Life Aboard a British Privateer. (The Journal of Capt. Woodes Rogers). London: Conway Maritime Press, 1970.

Lieuwen, Edwin. Arms and Politics in Latin America. New York: Praeger, 1961.

Lothrop, S. K. Treasures of Ancient America. Cleveland: World Pub. Co., 1964.

Macaulay, Rose. Pleasure of Ruins. London: Thames and Hudson, Ltd., 1964.

Macauley, Neill. The Sandino Affair. Chicago: Quadrangle Books, 1967.

MacLeod, Murdo J. Spanish Central America: Socio-Economic History, 1520-1720. Berkeley: University of California Press, 1973.

Marco Dorta, Enrique. Cartagena de Indias puerto y plaza fuerte. Madrid: Gráficas Condor, 1960.

Martínez, Ildefonso Palma. La guerra nacional. (Edición del Centenario, 1856-1956) Managua, Nicaragua: 1965.

Martínez, López E. Biografía del General Francisco Morazán. Comayaguela, Honduras: Editora Nacional, 1966.

Martz, John D. Central America, The Crisis and the Challenge. Chapel Hill: University of North Carolina Press, 1959.

Mata Gavidia, José. Anotaciones de historia patria centroamericana. Guatemala: Editorial Universitaria, 1969.

Mendieta, Pedro Aplicano. The Mayas, a Chosen People. Tegucigalpa: Guia de Honduras, 1972.

# Bibliography

Meyer, Harvey K. Historical Dictionary of Nicaragua. Metuchen, N.J.: Scarecrow Press, Inc., 1972.

Miami Herald, Special Section - CA. "Central America-Story of Progress." Sunday, March 12, 1967.

Michel, Bernard E. "Relief for Honduras," The North American Moravian, Vol. 5, No. 10. Bethlehem, Penn, 1974.

Miller, Hugh Gordon. The Isthmian Highway. New York: Macmillan, 1929.

Miller, Wick R. Uto-Aztecan Cognate Sets. Berkeley, University of California Press, 1967.

Mollett, J. W. An Illustrated Dictionary of Art and Archeology. New York: American Archives of World Art, Inc., 1965.

Mondadori, Arnoldo. The Life and Times of Columbus. New York: Curtis Publishing Co., 1966.

Moore, Richard E. Historical Dictionary of Guatemala. Metuchen, N.J.: Scarecrow Press, 1967.

Moore, W. G. A Dictionary of Geography. 3rd ed. Baltimore: Penguin Books, 1963.

Moravian Missionary Atlas. New ed. London: Moravian Church and Mission Agency, 1908.

Morison, Samuel Eliot. Admiral of the Ocean Sea. 2 vols. Boston: Little Brown and Co., 1942.

_____. The Caribbean as Columbus Saw It. Boston: Little, Brown & Co., 1964.

_____. The European Discovery of America. The Southern Voyages 1492-1616. New York: Oxford University Press, 1974.

_____. The Oxford History of the American People. New York: Oxford University Press, 1965.

Morley, Sylvanus Griswold and George W. Brainerd. The Ancient Maya. Stanford, California: Stanford University Press, 1946-1956.

Mueller, Karl A. Among Creoles, Miskitos and Sumos. Bethlehem, Pa.: Christian Education Board, 1932.

Navarro, Miguel. América - estudios sociales. Tegucigalpa: Publicaciones Navarro, 1971.

_____. Estudios sociales centro américa. Tegucigalpa: Publicaciones Navarro, 1971.

New York Historical Society. Kemble Papers. Vol. II, Vol. XVII, New York: 1885.

Núñez Chinchilla, Jesús. Copán Ruins. Tegucigalpa: 1970.

Palma Martínez, Ildefonso. La guerra nacional. Mexico: Impresa "Aldina," 1956.

Palmer, Mervyn G. Through Unknown Nicaragua. London: Jarrolds Publishers, 1920.

Parker, Franklin D. The Central American Republics. New York: Oxford University Press, 1964.

Parkinson, F. Latin America, the Cold War and the World Powers, 1945-1973. Beverly Hills and London: Sage Publications, 1974.

Parry, J. H. The Spanish Seaborne Empire. New York: Knopf, 1966.

Paz Rivera, Narciso. Boletín del Servicio Geológico Nacional de Nicaragua. No. 6, Reconocimiento geológico en la cuenca hidrográfica de los Ríos Coco y Bocay. Managua: Ministerio de Economia, 1962.

Peace Corps, the How and Why. Brochure. Washington, D.C.: Peace Corps, 1970.

Peterson, Harold L. Forts in America. New York: Scribner, 1964.

Peterson, Mendell. History Under the Sea. Washington, D.C.: Smithsonian Institution Press, 1965-1969.

Pike, Ruth. Enterprise and Adventure. The Genoese in Seville and the Opening of the New World. Ithaca, New York: Cornell University Press, 1966.

Potter, John S., Jr. The Treasure Diver's Guide. Garden City, New York: Doubleday and Co., 1972.

Proceso contra el filibustero William Walker. Comandancia principal del puerto de Trujillo, 1860.

Proskouriakoff, Tatiana. An Album of Maya Architecture. Norman, Oklahoma: University of Oklahoma Press, 1963.

Quijano, José Antonio Calderón. Historia de las fortificaciones en Nueva España. Sevilla: La Escuela de Estudios Hispano-

Americanos, 1953.

Rand McNally. The International Atlas. Chicago: Rand McNally and Co., 1969.

Recinos, Adrián. Populvuh - The Sacred Book of the Ancient Quiché Mayas. Norman: University of Oklahoma Press, 1972.

Revista conservadora de el pensamiento centroamericano. Nicaragua: Publicidad de Nicaragua, Managua, 1971.

Reynold, Clark G. Command of the Sea. New York: William Morrow & Co., Inc., 1974.

Roberts, Orlando W. Narrative of Voyages and Excursions on the East Coast and in the Interior of Central America; Describing a Journey up the River San Juan, and Passage Across the Lake of Nicaragua to the City of León. (Facsim. of 1827 ed.) Gainesville, Fla,: University of Florida Press, 1965.

Robertson, Donald. Pre-Columbian Architecture. New York: George Braziller, 1963.

Rodríguez, Mario. Central America. Englewood Cliffs, N.J.: Prentice Hall, 1965.

Ross, Norman P., ed. Life Pictorial Atlas of the World. New York: Time Inc., 1961.

Rovirosa, José N. Estado de Tabasco. Mexico City: Oficina Tipográfica de la Secretaría de Fomento, 1888.

Ruz, Alberto. Palenque. Mexico City: Talleres de Edimex, 1960.

Schmidt, Hans. The United States Occupation of Haiti, 1915-1934. New Brunswick, N.J.: Rutgers University Press, 1971.

Schmitter, Philip C., ed. Military Rule in Latin America. Beverly Hills, California: Sage Publications, Inc., 1973.

Schott, Joseph L. Rails Across Panama. Indianapolis: Bobbs-Merrill, 1967.

Scroggs, William O. Filibusters and Financiers: The Story of William Walker and His Associates. New York: Macmillan, 1916.

Sears, Stephen W., ed. The Horizon History of the British Empire. 2 vols. New York: American Heritage Pub. Co., Inc., 1973.

Skelton, R. A. Decorative Printed Maps of the 15th to 18th Centuries. London: Staples Press, 1952.

Smith, Bradley. Mexico--A History in Art. New York: Harper and Row, 1968.

Soltera, María. A Lady's Ride Across Honduras. Gainesville: University of Florida Press, 1964. (Reprint of 1884 edition.)

Spaulding, Robert K. How Spanish Grew. Berkeley, California: University of California Press, 1971.

Squier, E. G. Notes on Central America, Particularly the States of Honduras and San Salvador. 2 vols. New York: A. M. S. Press, Inc., 1971. (Reprint of 1855 edition.)

Stephens, John L. Incidents of Travel in Central America, Chiapas, and Yucatan. 2 vols. New Brunswick, N. J.: Rutgers Univ. Press, 1949. (Reprint of 1856 edition.)

──────. Incidents of Travel in Yucatan. 2 vols. New York: Dover Publications, 1963. (Reprint of 1843 work publ. by Harper and Brothers.)

Stokes, William S. Honduras: An Area Study in Government. Madison: The University of Wisconsin Press, 1950.

Stout, Peter F. Nicaragua: Past, Present, and Future. Philadelphia: John E. Potter and Co., 1859.

Stuart, George E. and Gene S. Discovering Man's Past in the Americas. Washington, D. C.: National Geographic Society, 1969.

Sykes, Percy. A History of Exploration. New York: Harper and Brothers, 1961.

Szulc, Tad. The Winds of Revolution. Rev. ed. New York: Praeger, 1965.

Thompson, J. Eric S. The Rise and Fall of Maya Civilization. Norman, Oklahoma: University of Oklahoma Press, 1959.

Trigueros, Roberto. Las defensas estratégicas del Río de San Juan de Nicaragua. Sevilla, Spain: Anuario de Estudios Americanos XI, 1954.

Ugarte, Francisco. Que hace el CREFAL. Mexico City: Editorial Múñoz, 1956.

UNESCO--Educación Fundamental. Espanól - Miskito - Inglés (A Vocabulary). Managua: UNESCO - Río Coco Project, Mimeo., 1955.

U. S. Air Force--U. S. Navy. Flight Information Publication Terminal (Low Alt.) Caribbean and South America. Washington, D. C.; U. S. Armed Forces, 1 February 1964.

Vaillant, G. C. The Aztecs of Mexico. Baltimore: Doubleday Doran, 1944. Penguin Books, 1960.

Van Alstyne, Richard W. The Rising American Empire. Chicago: Quadrangle Books, 1960.

Vásquez, José V. Album civico hondureño. 2nd ed. Tegucigalpa: 1970.

Velásquez de la Cadena, Mariano, Edward Gray and Juan Iribas, eds. Velásquez Spanish and English Dictionary. Chicago: Wilcox and Follett Co., 1954.

Verrill, A. Hyatt. Old Civilizations of the New World. New York: Tudor Pub. Co., 1938.

Vespucci, Amerigo. Letter of Amerigo Vespucci to Pier Soderini, Gonfalonier of the Republic of Florence. Boston: Old South Leaflets, No. 34. Old South Association. (Reprint--first published 1505-6.)

Von Hagen, Victor W. The Aztec, Man and Tribe. New York: New American Library, Inc., 1961.

_____. Maya Explorer. Norman, Oklahoma: University of Oklahoma Press, 1947.

Walker, William. The War in Nicaragua. Mobile and New York: S. H. Goetzal and Co., 1860.

Wallace, Holland. Central American Coinage Since 1821. Weslaco, Texas: Wallace, 1965.

Warner, Oliver. Nelson and the Age of Fighting Sail. New York: American Heritage Publishing Co., 1963.

_____. Victory, the Life of Lord Nelson. Boston: Little, Brown and Company, 1958.

Watkins, T. H., et al. The Grand Colorado. Palo Alto, Calif.: American West Publ. Co., 1969.

Whitaker, Arthur P. The Western Hemisphere Idea, Its Rise and Decline. Ithaca, New York: Cornell University Press, 1954.

Wilgus, A. Curtis. Latin America, 1492-1942. A Guide to Historical and Cultural Development Before World War II. Metuchen, N.J.: Scarecrow Reprint Corp., 1973.

_____, ed. The Caribbean at Mid-Century. Series One, Vol. I. Gainesville: University of Florida Press, 1951.

_____. The Caribbean: The Central American Area. Series One, Vol. XI. Gainesville: University of Florida Press, 1961.

_____. The Caribbean: Contemporary Education. Series One, Vol. X. Gainesville, University of Florida Press, 1960.

_____. The Caribbean: Contemporary International Relations. Series One, Vol. VII. Gainesville: University of Florida Press, 1957.

_____. The Caribbean: Contemporary Trends. Series One, Vol. III. Gainesville: University of Florida Press, 1953.

_____. The Caribbean: Its Culture. Series One, Vol. V. Gainesville: University of Florida Press, 1955.

_____. The Caribbean: Its Economy. Series One, Vol. IV. Gainesville: University of Florida Press, 1954.

_____. The Caribbean: Its Hemispheric Role. Series One, Vol. XVII. Gainesville: University of Florida Press, 1966.

_____. The Caribbean: Its Political Problems. Series One, Vol. VI. Gainesville: University of Florida Press, 1956.

_____. The Caribbean: Natural Resources. Series One, Vol. IX. Gainesville: University of Florida Press, 1959.

_____. The Caribbean: Peoples, Problems, and Prospects. Series One, Vol. II. Gainesville: University of Florida Press, 1952.

_____ and Raul D'Eça. Latin American History. New York: Barnes and Noble, 1969.

Wilson, J. Tuzo. Continents Adrift. San Francisco: Scientific American. W. H. Freeman & Co., 1972.

Ypsilanti de Moldavia, George. Los Israelitas in América pre-columbina. Managua: Talleres Nacionales, 1962.

Zarur, Jorge. Geography and Cartography for Census Purposes in Latin America. Washington, D.C.: Inter-American Statistical Institute, June, 1948.

## MAPS

American Automobile Association. Mexico and Central America. 1972-73 edition. Washington: AAA, 1972.

Central Intelligence Agency (U.S.). Honduras. 1973.

Colton & Co. Central America. New York: J. H. Colton Co., 1856.

Dunn, Samuel. A Complete Map of the West Indies. London: Robert Sayer, 1774.

Editorial Kapelusz. Honduras-colormapa. Scale 1:1,550,000 (Mercator).

Esso Standard Oil S.A. Mar Caribe y Las Islas Bahamas y Bermuda. Scale 1:6,250,000. New York: General Drafting Co., 1951.

Grosvenor, Gilbert, ed. Indians of North America. Supplement. Washington: National Geographic Society, 1972.

_____. Mexico and Central America. (Honduras.) Washington: National Geographic Society, 1961.

_____. North America Before Columbus. Supplement to "Indians of North America." Washington: National Geographic Society, 1972.

_____. West Indies. (Eastern Honduras.) Washington: National Geographic Society, 1962.

Hydrographic Office, U.S. Navy. Bonacca Island, Caribbean Sea, Honduras. H.O. 1633 - Scale 1:36,481. 11th ed. Washington, D.C.

_____. Trujillo Bay, Central America, Honduras. H.O. 5389 - Scale 1:24,000. 3rd ed. Washington, D.C., July 1927, Revised 1967.

Instituto Geográfico Nacional. Guanaja. HOJA 3065 III. Primera Edición - 16 N. Scale 1:50,000. Tegucigalpa: Ministerio de Comunicaciones y Obras Públicas, 1968.

_____. Mapa de Honduras. Tegucigalpa: Honduras Industrial, S.A. June, 1968.

_____. Roatán. HOJA 2864-I. Primera Edición - IGN. Scale 1:50,000. Tegucigalpa: Ministerio de Communicaciones y Obras Públicas, 1968.

———. Roatán - Barbareta. Sheet 2965III. Edition I-TPC. Scale 1:50,000. U. S. Army Topographic Command, 1969.

———. Utila. Hoja 2864-III. Scale 1:50,000. Tegucigalpa: Ministerio de Comunicaciones y Obras Públicas, 1968.

Jeffreys, Thomas. Map of the Bay of Honduras, the Island of Jamaica, and Cape Gracias a Dios. Printed by Robert Sayers, London. 1775. (Now in British Museum, Harley Collection.)

National Geographic Society, Cartographic Division. Archeological Map of Middle America. Washington: National Geographic Society, 1968.

Reinel, Pedro. Map of the New World, 1519.

Sanches. Planisphere. (British Museum, London.) 1623.

Tatton, Gabriel. Maris Pacifici quod vulgo Mar del Zur. (British Museum, Harley Collection) 1600.

———. Nova et rece Terraum et regnorum Californiae nova Hispaniae, Mexicanae, et Peruviae. (British Museum, Harley Collection) 1600.

Texaco, America Central. La Carretera Interamericana. Rand McNally and Co., 1959.

———. Honduras. Rand McNally & Co., 1971.

Visscher, Nicolaum. Insulae Americanae in Oceano Septentrionali ac Regiones Adiacentes. Amsterdam (British Museum) 1690.